M000074464

THE LIFE OF NELSON

VICE-ADMIRAL, LORD NELSON.

From the portrait in the possession of Sir W. Biddulph Parker, Bart., Blackbrook House, Fareham, Hants. On the back of the picture is written, " This head was sketched from the Hero during his short stay at Merton, the beginning of September, 1805, by me, John Whichelo."

THE LIFE OF NELSON

THE EMBODIMENT

of the

SEA POWER OF GREAT BRITAIN

Alfred Thayer Mahan

Naval Institute Press
Annapolis, Maryland

Naval Institute Press
291 Wood Road
Annapolis, MD 21402

Introduction © 2001 by the U.S. Naval Institute, Annapolis, Maryland

All rights reserved. No part of this book may be reproduced or utilized in any form or by any means, electronic or mechanical, including pho-tocopying and recording, or by any information storage and retrieval system, without permission in writing from the publisher.

Library of Congress Cataloging-in-Publication Data
Mahan, A. T. (Alfred Thayer), 1840–1914.
    The life of Nelson : the embodiment of the sea power of Great
    Britain / Alfred Thayer Mahan.
       p.   cm.
    Originally published: Boston : Little, Brown, 1899.
    ISBN 1-55750-484-9 (alk. paper)
    1. Nelson, Horatio Nelson, Viscount, 1758–1805. 2. Great Britain—
History, Naval—18th century. 3. Great Britain—History, Naval—
19th century. 4. Great Britain. Royal Navy—Biography.
    5. Admirals—Great Britain—Biography. I. Title.
DA87.1.N4 M3 2001
359'.0092—dc21
[B]
                                          2001018335

Printed in the United States of America on acid-free paper ♾
08 07 06 05 04 03 02 01   9 8 7 6 5 4 3 2
First printing

INTRODUCTION

ALFRED Thayer Mahan, the son of a U.S. Military
Academy graduate, was born at West Point on 27 September 1840. He entered the Naval Academy at sixteen
years of age, after two years at Columbia College. The early
signs of genius were evident in his academic work, and on
30 September 1856 the Naval Academy admitted him directly
to the second year. George Dewey, the future hero of the battle at Manila Bay, was in the class ahead of Mahan; Winfield
Schley, who commanded the U.S. Navy's Flying Squadron
during the Spanish-American War was one class behind;
and William Sampson, victor at the battle of Santiago, was
two classes behind. Although all four were to play historic
roles as the U.S. Navy became a significant geopolitical
force, Mahan's role was more philosophical and strategic
than the achievements of the other three.

The Naval Academy had not overestimated Mahan's academic potential. He graduated a close second in the class of
1855, standing first in seamanship, physics, and not sur-
prisingly, political science. After his commissioning, his
career generally followed the pattern of the time, alternat-
ing between sea and shore duty. Then in 1885, after he had
become a captain, Mahan was asked to give a series of lectures on naval history and tactics at the new Naval War
College in Newport, Rhode Island. At the time, the assignment did not seem momentous, but history has proved
that Mahan's decision to take an intellectual path would

profoundly influence naval policies worldwide. Continuing on that path, he later served as president of the Naval War College for two separate tours between 1886 and 1893.

In 1890, between his periods of service at the Naval War College, Mahan's *The Influence of Sea Power upon History* was published. During his last tour of sea duty, from 1893 to 1895, he served as commanding officer of the cruiser, USS *Chicago*. When Mahan had requested that this final sea duty assignment be delayed so he could complete his two-volume *The Influence of Sea Power on the French Revolution,* his superior at the old Bureau of Navigation advised him that it was "not the business of a naval officer to write books." During his command of the *Chicago,* Mahan was also working on his Nelson biography, which was first published in 1897. About this effort, he wrote, "If I succeed in bringing the work up to the mark at which I aim, it will stand as the work of my life."

Mahan retired from active duty in 1896 but was recalled in 1898 to serve on the Naval War Board. As a member of that board he was one of a small group of naval officers selected to advise the secretary of the Navy on the increasingly complicated elements of naval power. The board helped shape naval operations during the Spanish-American War, a conflict that redefined the U.S. Navy.

Aside from the war, other sweeping changes during the last two decades of the nineteenth century also changed the U.S. Navy, and Mahan was at the intellectual center of the process. These changes were driven by expanding national perspectives, increasingly powerful news media, the marriage of steam and steel in the precursors of the twentieth-century battleship, and a more offensive, fleet-oriented naval approach. Concurrently, the navy leadership in the United States was beginning to think beyond technical and tactical matters and attempting to clarify the navy's rationale. As a result of that movement, the U.S. Naval Institute was established in 1873 at Annapolis, Maryland, to advance "professional and scientific knowledge in the Navy," and in 1884, the Naval War College was founded at Newport, Rhode Island.

In the midst of this turbulent environment, Mahan used his lectures and writings to explain the increasingly relevant elements of sea power to navalists, politicians, and journalists. Over the next three decades, Mahan wrote more than twenty books—many still in print and many translated into other languages—explaining sea power's geopolitical role; *The Life of Nelson* was among the most important. In a circumstance of fate missed by many, he accelerated the influence of sea power on American history through a fortuitous association with then assistant secretary of the Navy, Theodore Roosevelt. The studious, reserved naval theorist and the quintessential political man of action were brought together in 1888 by then president of the Naval War College, Rear Adm. Stephen Luce. Naval historian Kenneth Hagen nicely captured the importance of this meeting in his book, *This People's Navy,* where he wrote, "The Roosevelt-Mahan axis, around which would pivot so much of the history of the American battleship navy, had been formed." And that axis did much more than influence the American victory in the Spanish-American War; it was also instrumental in generating a far-reaching intellectual change in how America viewed naval power. In 1915, well after the radical change in U.S. naval policy had begun, Roosevelt himself summed up Mahan's special qualities, calling him "the only great naval writer who also possessed the mind of a statesman of the first class."

By the time Mahan emerged as a respected author and proponent of sea power, Admiral Lord Nelson's biographers had been writing about Nelson for nearly one hundred years. Much of that work, although extremely valuable, was colored by hero worship. For example, in their early biography, *The Life of Admiral Lord Nelson,* published in 1809, Clarke and M'Arthur were so eager to embed Nelson as a legend in the British psyche that they felt compelled to "improve" some of Nelson's own written words. British poet laureate Robert Southey was similarly enthralled by the image of Nelson as hero in his beautifully written work, *The Life of Nelson,* published in 1813.

Mahan had a different view; he saw the victor at the battles of the Nile, Copenhagen, and Trafalgar from across a century of time. The century between Nelson's death in 1805 and Mahan's work enabled him to take a detached view, while also allowing him to take advantage of the considerable body of information that had been assembled since Nelson's death, including Nelson's own dispatches and letters. Mahan also saw Nelson from across an ocean; his Nelson was not an object of national veneration, but a singular, professional naval officer who demonstrated on deck Mahan's own broad theories of sea power. For Mahan, Nelson was indeed "the embodiment of the sea power of Great Britain." This emphasis on Nelson's status as a professional naval officer along with the biography's penetrating detail— there are twenty-three chapters—dispels any possibility that hero worship attracted Mahan to his subject. As a result, despite initial and understandable skepticism, ultra-critical British audiences soon saw Mahan's biography of Nelson for what it was, a classic in a crowded field. The one hundred years since its publication has only solidified its position globally.

Republishing Mahan's *The Life of Nelson* at the midpoint of Britain's "Nelson Decade," which commemorates the two hundredth anniversary of his electrifying victory and death at the battle of Trafalgar, is historically appropriate. But beyond marking a bicentennial, is Nelson's career relevant to the twenty-first century? Without question, geopolitical and military circumstances have changed radically since

Nelson's day. The obvious differences notwithstanding, there are some significant parallels between Nelson's world and our own. For example, just as Nelson's navy was tied to a government driven by economic factors and was often stretched thin as a result, so today's U.S. Navy, which many consider the world's most powerful, is shaped by federal budgetary constraints that are seriously taxing personnel and matériel.

The most compelling reason Nelson is relevant today, however, has little to do with economic or political parallels. It has to do with the frequently forgotten truth that both the military and society in general need outstanding leaders. In the face of that constant need, Nelson's implausibly dramatic life demonstrates the unique qualities that make him an exemplary leader.

Joseph F. Callo

PREFACE

TO THE SECOND EDITION.

SINCE the first publication of this book, there have appeared two principal criticisms upon the accuracy of its presentation of Nelson. The first, in order of time, revived the often debated question of his action towards the Neapolitan republicans, in 1799, challenging the author's verdict with much parade of evidence. The second disputed the estimate of Nelson's affection for his wife, basing the argument chiefly upon some recently found letters from him to her, the hiding-place of which had escaped even the diligent search of Sir Harris Nicolas.

Concerning the former of these, the author, after due consideration, has seen no cause to change the opinion first expressed; but he has recognized a necessity to protect the fair fame of the admiral, as well as to fortify his own position, by recasting and amplifying the discussion of the subject. He has therefore embodied in the text such demonstration of Nelson's integrity as may in the future enable a studious reader to rebut the accusations, if renewed.

As regards Nelson's affection for his wife, it is enough to say that the author never thought or said that he did not love her tenderly at marriage, and for years afterwards. But there is love and love. What was noted, and emphasized, was the absence of any tendency to idealize her, as he did other women to whom he became attached from time to time, and as lovers commonly do. The newly found letters, as far as published, — the author has not been permitted to see the others, — afford no reason to modify this remark, and consequently no change of treatment has been made. These letters contain also some small details which have novelty and interest, connected with the separation between Nelson and his wife. These have been incorporated in the text; but, beyond accentuating slightly his hardness to her in the particular instance, they throw no new light upon his character.

As far as they go, these new letters confirm the remark made more than once by the author during his first study of the life of Nelson : that more letters might yet be found; that a trivial detail of fact might here and there receive correction, altering a little the background, or the framing, of the portrait; but that the mass of correspondence published by Nicolas was so extensive, so continuous, and addressed to so many different persons, as to make it highly improbable that any further light, not to be found in those volumes, would be shed upon the admiral's character. So much being known, biographies of Nelson will contrast one with another, not in point of abundance of material, but, as portraits do, according to the ability of the workman to reproduce, from the original before him, an impression of the man which shall be at once true, full, and living.

The work of revision has embraced also the correction or amplification of certain minor details, noted by the author himself or by others. Of these, the most important concerns the reason for withholding the medals for Copenhagen. In the author's judgment, his previous presentment of Nelson's character and conduct is not affected in the slightest degree by these changes. They are part of the frame, not of the picture.

A. T. M.

April, 1899.

PREFACE

TO THE FIRST EDITION

THE Life of Nelson has been written so often, that an explanation — almost an apology — seems due for any renewal of the attempt; but, not to mention the attractiveness of the theme in itself, it is essential to the completeness and rounding off of the author's discussion of the Influence of Sea Power, that he present a study, from his own point of view, of the one man who in himself summed up and embodied the greatness of the possibilities which Sea Power comprehends, — the man for whom genius and opportunity worked together, to make him the personification of the Navy of Great Britain, the dominant factor in the periods hitherto treated. In the century and a half embraced in those periods, the tide of influence and of power has swelled higher and higher, floating upward before the eyes of mankind many a distinguished name; but it is not until their close that one arises in whom all the promises of the past find their finished realization, their perfect fulfilment. Thenceforward the name of Nelson is enrolled among those few presented to us by History, the simple mention of which suggests, not merely a personality or a career, but a great force or a great era concrete in a single man, who is its standard-bearer before the nations.

Yet, in this process of exaltation, the man himself, even when so very human and so very near our own time as Nelson is, suffers from an association which merges his individuality in the splendor of his surroundings; and it is perhaps pardonable to hope that the subject is not so far exhausted but that a new worker, gleaning after the reapers, may contribute something further towards disengaging the figure of the hero from the glory that cloaks it. The aim of the present writer, while not neglecting other sources of knowledge, has been to make Nelson describe himself, — tell the story of his own inner life as well as of his external actions. To realize this object, it has not seemed the best way to insert numerous letters, because, in the career of a man of action, each one commonly deals with a variety of subjects, which bear to one another little relation, except that, at the moment of writing, they all formed part of the multifold life the writer was then leading. It is true, life in general is passed in that way; but it is not by such distraction of interest among minute details that a particular life is best understood. Few letters, therefore, have been inserted entire; and those which have, have been chosen because of their unity of subject, and of their value as characteristic.

The author's method has been to make a careful study of Nelson's voluminous correspondence, analyzing it, in order to detect the leading features of temperament, traits of thought, and motives of action; and thence to conceive within himself, by gradual familiarity even more than by formal effort, the character therein revealed. The impression thus produced he has sought to convey to others, partly in the form of ordinary narrative, — daily living with his hero, — and partly by such grouping of incidents and utterances, not always, nor even nearly, simultaneous, as shall serve by their joint evidence to emphasize particular traits, or particular opinions, more forcibly than when such testimonies are scattered far apart; as they would be, if recounted in a strict order of time.

A like method of treatment has been pursued in regard to that purely external part of Nelson's career in which are embraced his military actions, as well as his public and private life.   The same aim is kept in view of showing clearly, not only what he did, but the principles which dominated his military thought, and guided his military actions, throughout his life; or, it may be, such changes as must inevitably occur in the development of a man who truly lives.   This cannot be done satisfactorily without concentrating the evidence from time to time; and it is therefore a duty a writer owes to his readers, if they wish such acquaintance with his subject as he thinks he has succeeded in acquiring for himself.

The author has received individual assistance from several persons.   To a general expression of thanks he wishes to add his special acknowledgments to the present Earl Nelson, through whose aid he has obtained information of interest which otherwise probably would have escaped him; and to Lords Radstock and De Saumarez, both of whom have been good enough to place in his hands letters contemporary with Nelson, and touching incidentally matters that throw light on his career.   Material of the same kind has also been furnished him by Professor John Knox Laughton, whose knowledge of Nelson and of the Navy of that period is second to none; it is not the least of the writer's advantages that he has had before him, to check possible errors in either fact or conclusions, the admirable, though brief, Life of Nelson published by Mr. Laughton two years since.

Illustrative anecdotes have also been supplied by Admiral Sir William R. Mends, G. C. B., who has shown his continued interest in the work by the trouble he has taken for it; by Mr. Stuart J. Reid, of Blackwell Cliff, East Grinstead; and by Mr. Edgar Goble, of Fareham, Hants.   Mr. B. F. Stevens, of 4 Trafalgar Square, has also kindly exerted himself on several occasions to obtain needed information.   To Mrs. F. H. B. Eccles, of Sherwell House, Plymouth, granddaughter of Josiah Nisbet, Nelson's stepson, the author is indebted for reminiscences of Lady Nelson, and for her portrait here published; and his thanks are also due to Lieutenant-Colonel W. Clement D. Esdaile, of Burley Manor, Ringwood, Hants, through whom he was brought into communication with Mrs. Eccles, and who has in other ways helped him.

Throughout the writing of the book constant assistance has been received from Mr. Robert B. Marston, to whom cordial acknowledgment is made for the untiring pains taken in prosecuting necessary inquiries, which could not have been done without great delay by one not living in England. Suggestions valuable to the completeness of the work have been given also by Mr. Marston.

For the portrait of Mrs. Philip Ward, the "Horatia" whom Nelson called generally his adopted daughter, but at times spoke of as his daughter simply, and whom, on the last morning of his life, he commended to the care of his Country, the author has to thank Mr. and Mrs. Nelson Ward, of 15 Lancaster Road, Belsize Park, London. Mr. Nelson Ward is her son.

To the more usual sources of information already in print, it is not necessary to refer in detail; but it is right to mention especially the collection of Hamilton and Nelson letters, published by Mr. Alfred Morrison, a copy of which by his polite attention was sent the writer, and upon which must necessarily be based such account of Nelson's relations with Lady Hamilton as, unfortunately, cannot be omitted wholly from a life so profoundly affected by them.

A. T. MAHAN.

March, 1897.

CONTENTS

CHAPTER I.

1758–1783.

CHAPTER II.

1784–1793.   AGE, 26–34.

CHAPTER III.

FEBRUARY–DECEMBER, 1793.   AGE, 34.

CHAPTER IV.

JANUARY–DECEMBER, 1794.   AGE, 35.

CHAPTER V.

JANUARY–JULY, 1795.   AGE, 36.

LIST OF ILLUSTRATIONS.

THE LIFE OF NELSON

CHAPTER I.

THE FIRST TWENTY-FIVE YEARS.

1758–1783.

IT is the appointed lot of some of History's chosen few to come upon the scene at the moment when a great tendency is nearing its crisis and culmination. Specially gifted with qualities needed to realize the fulness of its possibilities, they so identify themselves with it by their deeds that they thenceforth personify to the world the movement which brought them forth, and of which their own achievements are at once the climax and the most dazzling illustration. Fewer still, but happiest of all, viewed from the standpoint of fame, are those whose departure is as well timed as their appearance, who do not survive the instant of perfected success, to linger on subjected to the searching tests of common life, but pass from our ken in a blaze of glory which thenceforth forever encircles their names. In that evening light break away and vanish the ominous clouds wherewith human frailties or tyrant passions had threatened to darken their renown; and their sun goes down with a lustre which the lapse of time is powerless to dim. Such was the privilege of the stainless Wolfe; such, beyond all others, that of Nelson. Rarely has a man been more favored in the hour of his appearing; never one so fortunate in the moment of his death.

Yet, however accidental, or providential, this rarely allotted portion, this crowning incident of an heroic career, it is after all but an incident. It the man has not contrived; but to it he has contributed much, without which his passing hour would have faded to memory, undistinguished among those of the myriads, great and small, who have died as nobly and are

1

forever forgotten. A sun has set; but before its setting it has run a course, be it long or short, and has gathered a radiance which fixes upon its parting beams the rapt attention of beholders. The man's self and the man's works, what he was and what he did, the nature which brought forth such fruits, the thoughts which issued in such acts, hopes, fears, desires, quick intuitions, painful struggles, lofty ambitions, happy opportunities, have blended to form that luminous whole, known and seen of all, but not to be understood except by a patient effort to resolve the great result into its several rays, to separate the strands whose twisting has made so strong a cord.

Concerning the man's external acts, it will often happen that their true value and significance can best be learned, not from his own personal recital, but from an analytic study of the deeds themselves. Yet into them, too, often enters, not only the subtile working of their author's natural qualities, but also a certain previous history of well-defined opinions, of settled principles firmly held, of trains of thought and reasoning, of intuitions wrought into rational convictions, all of which betray both temperament and character. Of these intellectual antecedents, the existence and development may be gleaned from his writings, confirming the inference reached somewhat mechanically by the scrutiny of his actions. They play to the latter the part of the soul to the body, and thus contribute to the rather anatomical result of the dissecting process a spiritual element it would otherwise lack. But if this is so even of the outward career, it is far more deeply true of the inner history, of that underlying native character, which masterfully moulds and colors every life, yet evades the last analysis except when the obscure workings of heart and mind have been laid bare by their owner's words, recording the feelings of the fleeting hour with no view to future inspection. In these revelations of self, made without thought of the world outside, is to be found, if anywhere, the clue to that complex and often contradictory mingling of qualities which go to form the oneness of the man's personality. This discordance between essential unity and superficial diversities must be harmonized, if a true conception of his being is to be formed. We know the faces of our friends, but we see each as one. The features can, if we will, be separately considered, catalogued, and valued; but who ever thus thinks habitually of one he knows well? Yet to know well must be the aim of biography, — so to present the traits in their totality, without suppression of any, and in their true relative proportions, as to produce, not the blurred or distorted outlines seen through an imperfect lens, but the vivid apprehension which follows long intimacy with its continual, though unconscious, process of correction.

For such a treatment of Nelson's character, copious, if imperfect, material is afforded in his extensive and varied correspondence. From it the author aims, first, to draw forth a distinct and living image of the man himself, as sketched therein at random and loosely by his own hand. It is sought to reach the result by keeping the reader in constant contact, as by daily acquaintance, with a personality of mingled weakness and strength, of grave faults as well as of great virtues, but one whose charm was felt in life by all who knew it. The second object, far less ambitious, is to present a clear narrative of the military career, of the mighty deeds of arms, of this first of British seamen, whom the gifts of Nature and the course of History have united to make, in his victories and in their results, the representative figure of the greatest sea-power that the world has known.

It will not be thought surprising that we have, of the first thirty years of Nelson's life, no such daily informal record as that which illustrates the comparatively brief but teeming period of his active fighting career, from 1793 to 1805, when he at once, with inevitable directness and singular rapidity, rose to prominence, and established intimate relations with numbers of his contemporaries. A few anecdotes, more or less characteristic, have been preserved concerning his boyhood and youth. In his early manhood we have his own account, both explicit and implied in many casual unpremeditated phrases, of the motives which governed his public conduct in an episode occurring when, scarcely yet more than a youth, he commanded a frigate in the West Indies, — the whole singularly confirmatory, it might better be said prophetic, of the distinguishing qualities afterwards so brilliantly manifested in his maturity. But beyond these, it is only by the closest attention and careful gleaning that can be found, in the defective and discontinuous collection of letters which remains from his first thirty years, the indisputable tokens, in most important particulars, of the man that was to be.

The external details of this generally uneventful period can be rapidly summarized. He was born on the 29th of September, 1758, the fifth son and sixth child of Edmund Nelson, then rector of the parish of Burnham Thorpe, in Norfolk, a county which lies along the eastern coast of England, bordering the North Sea. His mother, whose name before marriage was Catherine Suckling, was grandniece to Sir Robert Walpole, the famous prime minister of Great Britain during twenty years of the reigns of the first two Georges. Sir Robert's second brother was called Horatio; and it was from the latter, or from his son, that the future hero took his baptismal name, which, in a more common form, was also that of Sir Robert's younger son, the celebrated letter and memoir writer, Horace Walpole.

Of the eleven children borne by Nelson's mother in her eighteen wedded years, only two lived to grow old. She herself died at forty-two; and her brother, Captain Maurice Suckling, of the Royal Navy, was also cut off in the prime of his age. As the earlier Nelsons were unusually long-lived, it seems probable that a certain delicacy of constitution was transmitted through the Sucklings to the generation to which the admiral belonged. He was himself, at various periods through life, a great sufferer, and frequently an invalid; allusions to illness, often of a most prostrating type, and to his susceptibility to the influences of climate or weather, occur repeatedly and at brief intervals throughout his correspondence. This is a factor in his career which should not be lost to mind; for on the one hand it explains in part the fretfulness which at times appears, and on the other brings out with increased force the general kindly sweetness of his temper, which breathed with slight abatement through such depressing conditions. It enhances, too, the strength of purpose that trod bodily weakness under foot, almost unconsciously, at the call of duty or of honor. It is notable, in his letters, that the necessity for exertion, even when involving severe exposure, is apt to be followed, though without apparent recognition of a connection between the two, by the remark that he has not for a long time been so well. He probably experienced, as have others, that it is not the greater hardships of the profession, much less the dangers, but its uncertainties and petty vexations, which tell most severely on a high-strung organization like his own.

The immediate occasion of his going to sea was as follows. In 1770 the Falkland Islands, a desolate and then unimportant group, lying in the South Atlantic, to the eastward of Patagonia, were claimed as a possession by both Spain and Great Britain. The latter had upon them a settlement called Port Egmont, before which, in the year named, an overwhelming Spanish squadron suddenly appeared, and compelled the British occupants to lower their flag. The insult aroused public indignation in England to the highest pitch; and, while peremptory demands for reparation were despatched to Spain, a number of ships of war were ordered at once into commission. Among these was the "Raisonnable," of sixty-four guns, to the command of which was appointed Nelson's uncle, Captain Maurice Suckling. The latter had some time before promised to provide for one of his sister's children, the family being very poor; and, the custom of the day permitting naval captains, as a kind of patronage, to take into the King's service on board their own ships a certain number of lads, as midshipmen or otherwise, the opportunity of giving a nephew a start in life was now in his hands. The story is that Horatio, though then but twelve years old, realized the burden of pecuniary care that his father was carrying, and himself volunteered the wish that his uncle would take him to sea. However it happened, the suggestion staggered Suckling, who well knew the lad's puny frame and fragile constitution. "What has poor little Horatio done," cried he, "that he, being so weak, should be sent to rough it at sea? But let him come, and if a cannon-ball takes off his head, he will at least be provided for." Under such gloomy foreboding began the most dazzling career that the sea, the mother of so many heroes, has ever seen.[1]

[1] The precise date of Nelson's entering the Navy, which would be that of his being rated upon the books of the "Raisonnable," is not stated. Accepting the times during which he was borne upon the books of different ships, as given by Sir Harris Nicolas (Letters and Despatches of Lord Nelson, vol. i. p. 4, note), and with them calculating back from October 15, 1773, the day

Spain, after a short hesitation, yielded the British demands, so that war did not come, and the "Raisonnable," with other ships, was again put out of commission. The incident of the Falkland Islands, however, had served the purpose of introducing Nelson to his profession, for which otherwise the opportunity might not have offered. Being so young when thus embarked, he, in common with many of the most successful seamen of that day, got scanty schooling; nor did he, as some others did, by after application remedy the eccentricities of style, and even of grammar, which are apt to result from such early neglect. His letters, vigorous and direct as they are, present neither the polished diction of Collingwood, nor the usual even correctness of St. Vincent and Saumarez, but are, on the contrary, constantly disfigured by awkward expressions and bad English. There was rarely, however, danger of mistaking his meaning, as was sometimes charged against Lord Howe.

Here, before fairly parting with the humble home life, of which the motherless boy had seen, and was throughout his career to see so little, is a fit place to introduce two anecdotes associated with those early days which his biographers have transmitted to us. We of these critical times have learned to look with incredulity, not always unmixed with derision, upon stories relating to the childhood of distinguished men; but it can safely be said that the two now to be given are in entire keeping, not merely with particular traits, but with the great ruling tenor of Nelson's whole life. He and his elder brother were going to school one winter day upon their ponies. Finding the snow so deep as to delay them seriously, they went back, and the elder reported that they could not get on. The

mentioned by Nelson himself as that on which he was paid off from the "Carcass" (Nicolas, p. 5), the date of entry upon the books of the "Raisonnable" would be November 27, 1770; unless, which is unlikely, there were any lost days. The news of the Port Egmont business reached England in October, 1770. Clarke and M'Arthur (Life of Nelson, vol. i. p. 14, note) infer January 1, 1771, for his entry upon the "Raisonnable's" books; but this would not allow the times which Nicolas gives with minute exactness. For his actually joining the "Raisonnable" they give, loosely, the spring of 1771, — March or April. This is very possible, as rating back, for the sake of gaining constructive time needed to qualify for promotion, was tolerated by the practice of the day.

father very judiciously replied: "If that be so, I have of course nothing to say; but I wish you to try again, and I leave it to your honour not to turn back, unless necessary." On the second attempt, the elder was more than once for returning; but Horatio stuck it out, repeating continually, "Remember it was left to our honour," and the difficult journey was accomplished.

The children in this instance seem to have felt that there was danger in going on. The other recorded occurrence shows in the lad that indifference to personal benefit, as distinguished from the sense of conspicuous achievement, which was ever a prominent characteristic of the man. The master of his school had a very fine pear-tree, whose fruit the boys coveted, but upon which none dared hazard an attempt. At last Nelson, who did not share their desires, undertook the risk, climbed the tree by night, and carried off the pears, but refused to eat any of them, — saying that he had taken them only because the others were afraid.

Trivial though these incidents may seem, they are so merely because they belong to the day of small things. To those accustomed to watch children, they will not appear unworthy of note. Taken together, they illustrate, as really as do his greatest deeds, the two forms assumed at different times by the one incentive which always most powerfully determined Nelson's action through life, — the motive to which an appeal was never made in vain. No material considerations, neither danger on the one hand, nor gain on the other, ever affected him as did that idealized conception which presented itself, now as duty, now as honor, according as it bore for the moment upon his relations to the state or to his own personality. "In my mind's eye," said he to his friend Captain Hardy, who afterwards bent over him as his spirit was parting amid the tumult of his last victory, "I ever saw a radiant orb suspended which beckoned me onward to renown." Nelson did not often verge upon the poetical in words, but to the poetry of lofty aspiration his inmost being always answered true.

To the young naval officer of a century ago, especially if without political or social influence, it was a weighty advantage to be attached to some one commanding officer in active employment, who by favorable opportunity or through professional friendships could push the fortunes of those in whom he was interested. Much of the promotion was then in the hands of the admirals on foreign stations; and this local power to reward distinguished service, though liable to abuse in many ways, conduced greatly to stimulate the zeal and efforts of officers who felt themselves immediately under the eye of one who could make or mar their future. Each naval captain, also, could in his degree affect more or less the prospects of those dependent upon him. Thus Suckling, though not going to sea himself, continued with intelligent solicitude his promised care of the young Nelson. When the "Raisonnable" was paid off, he was transferred to the command of the "Triumph," of seventy-four guns, stationed as guard-ship in the river Medway; and to her also he took with him his nephew, who was borne upon her books for the two following years, which were, however, far from being a period of inactive harbor life. Having considerable professional interest, he saw to the lad's being kept afloat, and obtained for him from time to time such service as seemed most desirable to his enterprising spirit.

The distinction between the merchant seaman and the man-of-war's man, or even the naval officer, in those days of sailing ships and simple weapons was much less sharply marked than it has since become. Skill in seamanship, from the use of the marlinespike and the sail-needle up to the full equipping of a ship and the handling of her under canvas, was in either service the prime essential. In both alike, cannon and small arms were carried; and the ship's company, in the peaceful trader as well as in the ship of war, expected to repel force with force, when meeting upon equal terms. With a reduced number of naval vessels in commission, and their quarter-decks consequently over-crowded with young officers, a youth was more likely to find on board them a life of untasked idleness than a call to professional occupation and improvement. Nelson therefore was sent by his careful guardian to a merchant-ship trading to the West Indies, to learn upon her, as a foremast hand, the elements of his profession, under conditions which, from the comparative fewness of the crew and the activity of the life, would tend to develop his powers most rapidly. In this vessel he imbibed, along with nautical knowledge, the prejudice which has usually existed, more or less, in the merchant marine against the naval service, due probably to the more rigorous exactions and longer terms of enlistment in the latter, although the life in other respects is one of less hardship; but in Nelson's day the feeling had been intensified by the practice of impressment, and by the severe, almost brutal discipline that obtained on board some ships of war, through the arbitrary use of their powers by captains, then insufficiently controlled by law. In this cruise he seems to have spent a little over a year; a time, however, that was not lost to him for the accomplishment of the period of service technically required to qualify as a lieutenant, his name continuing throughout on the books of the " Triumph," to which he returned in July, 1772.

Suckling's care next insured for him a continuance of active, semi-detached duty, in the boats of the " Triumph," — an employment very different from, and more responsible than, that in which he had recently been occupied, and particularly calculated to develop in so apt a nature the fearlessness of responsibility, both professional and personal, that was among the most prominent features of Nelson's character. " The test of a man's courage is responsibility," said that great admiral and shrewd judge of men, the Earl of St. Vincent, after a long and varied experience of naval officers; and none ever shone more brightly under this supreme proof than the lad whose career is now opening before us. It may be interesting, too, to note that this condition of more or less detached service, so early begun, in which, though not in chief command, he held an authority temporarily independent, and was immediately answerable for all that happened on the spot, was the singular characteristic of most of his brilliant course, during which, until 1803, two years before Trafalgar, he was only for brief periods commander-in-chief, yet almost always acted apart from his superior. Many a man, gallant, fearless, and capable, within signal distance of his admiral, has, when out of sight of the flag, succumbed with feeble knees to the burden of independent responsible action, though not beyond his professional powers. This strength, like all Nature's best gifts, is inborn; yet, both for the happy possessor and for the merely average man, it is susceptible of high development

only by being early exercised, which was the good fortune
of Nelson.

Of these two years of somewhat irregular service, while
nominally attached to the "Triumph," it will be well to give
the account in his own words ; for, having been written a full
quarter of a century later, they record the deepest and most
lasting impressions made upon him during that susceptible
period when first becoming familiar with the calling he was
to adorn : —

" The business with Spain being accommodated, I was sent in a
West India ship belonging to the house of Hibbert, Purrier, and
Horton, with Mr. John Rathbone, who had formerly been in the
Navy, in the Dreadnought with Captain Suckling. From this voyage
I returned to the triumph at Chatham in July, 1772; and, if I did not
improve in my education, I returned a practical Seaman, with a horror
of the Royal Navy, and with a saying, then constant with the Seamen, '*Aft the most honour, forward the better man !*' It was many
weeks before I got the least reconciled to a Man-of-War, so deep was
the prejudice rooted; and what pains were taken to instil this erroneous principle in a young mind ! However, as my ambition was to
be a Seaman, it was always held out as a reward, that if I attended
well to my navigation, I should go in the cutter and decked long-boat,
which was attached to the Commanding officer's ship at Chatham.
Thus by degrees I became a good pilot, for vessels of that description,
from Chatham to the Tower of London, down the Swin, and the
North Foreland; and confident of myself amongst rocks and sands,
which has many times since been of great comfort to me. In this
way I was trained, till the expedition towards the North Pole was
fitted out; when, although no boys were allowed to go in the Ships,
(as of no use,) yet nothing could prevent my using every interest to
go with Captain Lutwidge in the Carcass; and, as I fancied I was to
fill a man's place, I begged I might be his cockswain ; which, finding
my ardent desire for going with him, Captain Lutwidge complied with,
and has continued the strictest friendship to this moment. Lord
Mulgrave, whom I then first knew, maintained his kindest friendship
and regard to the last moment of his life. When the boats were fitting out to quit the two Ships blocked up in the ice, I exerted myself
to have the command of a four-oared cutter raised upon, which was
given me, with twelve men; and I prided myself in fancying I could
navigate her better than any other boat in the Ship."

It will be recognized from this brief yet suggestive and
characteristic narrative, that, however valuable and even

indispensable may have been his uncle's assistance in forwarding his wishes, it was his own ambition and his own impulse
that even at this early day gave direction to his course, and
obtained opportunities which would scarcely have been offered
spontaneously to one of his physical frailty. In this Arctic
expedition he underwent the experiences common to all who
tempt those icebound seas. During it occurred an incident
illustrative of Nelson's recklessness of personal danger, — a
very different thing from official recklessness, which he never
showed even in his moments of greatest daring and highest
inspiration. The story is so hackneyed by frequent repetition
as to make its relation a weariness to the biographer, the
more so that the trait of extreme rashness in youth is one
by no means so rare as to be specially significant of Nelson's character. It will be given in the words of his first
biographers : —

"There is also an anecdote recollected by Admiral Lutwidge,
which marked the filial attention of his gallant cockswain. Among
the gentlemen on the quarter-deck of the Carcass, who were not
rated midshipmen, there was, besides young Nelson, a daring shipmate of his, to whom he had become attached. One night, during
the mid-watch, it was concerted between them that they should steal
together from the ship and endeavour to obtain a bear's skin. The
clearness of the nights in those high latitudes rendered the accomplishment of this object extremely difficult : they, however, seem to
have taken advantage of the haze of an approaching fog, and thus to
have escaped unnoticed. Nelson in high spirits led the way over the
frightful chasms in the ice, armed with a rusty musket. It was not,
however, long before the adventurers were missed by those on board;
and, as the fog had come on very thick, the anxiety of Captain Lutwidge and his officers was very great. Between three and four in
the morning the mist somewhat dispersed, and the hunters were discovered at a considerable distance, attacking a large bear. The
signal was instantly made for their return ; but it was in vain that
Nelson's companion urged him to obey it. He was at this time
divided by a chasm in the ice from his shaggy antagonist, which
probably saved his life ; for the musket had flashed in the pan, and
their ammunition was expended. 'Never mind,' exclaimed Horatio,
'do but let me get a blow at this devil with the butt-end of my
musket, and we shall have him.' His companion, finding that
entreaty was in vain, regained the ship. The captain, seeing the
young man's danger, ordered a gun to be fired to terrify the enraged

animal. This had the desired effect; but Nelson was obliged to
return without his bear, somewhat agitated with the apprehension of
the consequence of this adventure. Captain Lutwidge, though he
could not but admire so daring a disposition, reprimanded him
rather sternly for such rashness, and for conduct so unworthy of the
situation he occupied; and desired to know what motive he could
have for hunting a bear? Being thought by his captain to have
acted in a manner unworthy of his situation, made a deep impression
on the high-minded cockswain; who, pouting his lip, as he was wont
to do when agitated, replied, ' Sir, I wished to kill the bear, that I
might carry its skin to my father.' "

Upon his return to England from the Arctic Seas, Nelson
again by his own choice determined his immediate future.
Within a fortnight of leaving the " Carcass," he was, through
his uncle's influence, received on board by the captain of the
" Seahorse," of twenty guns, one of the ships composing a
squadron that was just then fitting out for the East Indies.
To quote himself, " Nothing less than such a distant voyage
could in the least satisfy my desire of maritime knowledge."
During an absence of three years he for much of the time, as
formerly in his West India cruise, did the duty of a seaman
aloft, from which he was afterwards rated midshipman, and
placed, this time finally, upon the quarter-deck as an officer.
In the ordinary course of cruising in peace times, he visited
every part of the station from Bengal to Bussorah; but the
climate, trying even to vigorous Europeans, proved too much
for his frail health. After a couple of years he broke down
and was invalided home, reaching England in September, 1776.
His escape from death was attributed by himself to the kind
care of Captain Pigot of the " Dolphin," in which ship he came
back. At this period we are told that, when well, he was of
florid countenance, rather stout and athletic; but, as the result
of his illness, he was reduced to a mere skeleton, and for some
time entirely lost the use of his limbs, — a distressing symptom, that returned upon him a few years later after his Central American expedition in 1780, and confirms the impression
of extreme fragility of constitution, which is frequently indicated in other ways.

During this absence in the East Indies Captain Suckling, in
April, 1775, had been named Comptroller of the Navy, — a

civil position, but one that carried with it power and consequent influence. This probably told for much in obtaining for Nelson, who was but just eighteen, and had not yet passed the examinations for his first promotion, an acting appointment as lieutenant. With this he joined a small ship-of-the-line, the "Worcester," of sixty-four guns, on board which he remained for six months, engaged in convoy duty between the Channel and Gibraltar, seeing from her decks for the first time the waters of the Mediterranean and its approaches, since then indissolubly associated with his name and his glory. He took with him a letter from his uncle to the captain of his new ship; but while such introduction, coming from so influential a quarter, doubtless contributed powerfully to clear from his path the obstacles commonly encountered by young men, Nelson had gained for himself a reputation for professional capacity, which, here as throughout his life, quickly won him the full confidence of his superiors. In later years, when his admiral's flag was flying, he recorded, with evident pride in the recollection, that while on board the "Worcester," notwithstanding his youth, his captain used to say, "He felt as easy when I was upon deck as any officer of the ship." It is doubtful, indeed, whether Nelson ever possessed in a high degree the delicate knack of handling a ship with the utmost dexterity and precision. He certainly had not the reputation for so doing. Codrington — a thorough Nelsonian, to use his own somewhat factious expression — used to say in later years, "Lord Nelson was no seaman; even in the earlier stages of the profession his genius had soared higher, and all his energies were turned to becoming a great commander." His apprenticeship, before reaching command, was probably too short; and, as captain, his generous disposition to trust others to do work for which he knew them fitted, would naturally lead him to throw the manipulation of the vessel upon his subordinates. But although, absorbed by broader and deeper thoughts of the responsibilities and opportunities of a naval commander, to which he was naturally attracted by both his genius and his temperament, he was excelled in technical skill by many who had no touch of his own inspiration, he nevertheless possessed a thoroughly competent knowledge of his profession as a simple seaman; which, joined to his zeal, energy, and intelligence, would more than justify the confidence expressed by his early commander. Of this knowledge he gave full proof a year later, when, before a board of captains, strangers to him, he successfully passed his examinations for a lieutenancy. His uncle Suckling, as Comptroller of the Navy, was indeed on the board; but he concealed the fact of relationship until the other members had expressed themselves satisfied.

His examination was held within a week of his leaving the "Worcester," on the 8th of April, 1777; and Suckling once more, but for the last time in his life, was able to exert his influence in behalf of his relative by promptly securing for him, not only his promotion to lieutenant, which many waited for long, but with it his commission, dated April 10, to the " Lowestoffe," a frigate of thirty-two guns. This class of vessel was in the old days considered particularly desirable for young officers, being more active than ships-of-the-line, while at the same time more comfortable, and a better school for the forming of an officer, than were the smaller cruisers; and his uncle probably felt that Nelson, whose service hitherto had been mainly upon the latter, needed yet to perfect the habits and methods distinctive of a ship of war, for he now wrote him a letter upon the proprieties of naval conduct, excellently conceived, yet embracing particulars that should scarcely have been necessary to one who had served his time on board well-ordered ships. The appointment to the " Lowestoffe " was further fortunate, both for him and for us, as in the commander of the vessel, Captain William Locker, he found, not only an admirable officer and gentleman, but a friend for whom he formed a lasting attachment, ending only with Locker's death in 1800, two years after the Battle of the Nile. To this friendship we owe the fullest record, at his own hands, of his early career; for Locker kept the numerous letters written him by Nelson while still an unknown young man. Of seventy odd which now remain, covering the years from 1777 to 1783, thirty-seven were to this one correspondent.

In another respect the appointment to the " Lowestoffe " was fortunate for Nelson. The ship was destined to the West Indies — or, to speak more precisely, to Jamaica,

which was a command distinct from that of the eastern
Caribbean, or Lesser Antilles, officially styled the Leeward
Islands Station.   Great Britain was then fully embarked
in the war with her North American colonies, which ended
in their independence; and the course of events was has-
tening her to the rupture with France and Spain that followed within a year.   In this protracted contest the chief
scene of naval hostilities was to be the West Indies; but
beyond even the casualties of war, the baneful climate of
that region insured numerous vacancies by prostration and
death, with consequent chances of promotion for those who
escaped the fevers, and found favor in the eyes of their
commander-in-chief.   The brutal levity of the old toast,
"A bloody war and a sickly season," nowhere found surer
fulfilment than on those pestilence-stricken coasts.   Captain
Locker's health soon gave way.   Arriving at Jamaica on the
19th of July, 1777, we find Nelson in the following month
writing to him from the ship during an absence produced by
a serious illness, from which fatal results were feared.   The
letter, like all those to Locker, was marked by that tone of
quick, eager sympathy, of genial inclination always to say
the kindest thing, that characterized his correspondence, and,
generally, his intercourse with others, — traits that through
life made him, beyond most men, acceptable and beloved.
He was, from first to last, not merely one of those whose
services are forced upon others by sheer weight of ability,
because indispensable, — though this, too, he was, — but men
wanted him because, although at times irritable, especially
after the wounds received in later years, he was an easy yoke-
fellow, pleasant to deal with, cordial and ready to support
those above him, a tolerant and appreciative master to subordinates.   It may even be said that, in matters indifferent to him, he too readily reflected the feelings, views, and
wishes of those about him; but when they clashed with
his own fixed convictions, he was immovable.   As he himself
said in such a case, "I feel I am perfectly right, and you
know upon those occasions I am not famous for giving up a
point."

Of his connection with the "Lowestoffe" he himself, in
the short autobiographical sketch before quoted, mentions

two circumstances, which, from the very fact of their remaining so long in his memory, illustrate temperament.
" Even a frigate," he says, " was not sufficiently active for my
mind, and I got into a schooner, tender to the Lowestoffe.
In this vessel I made myself a complete pilot for all the
passages through the [Keys] Islands situated on the north
side Hispaniola." This kind of service, it will be noted, was
in direct sequence, as to training, to his handling of the
" Triumph's " long-boat in the lower waters of the Thames,
and would naturally contribute to increase that " confidence
in himself among rocks and sands," which was afterwards to
be so " great a comfort " to him. In his later career he had
frequent and pressing need of that particular form of professional judgment and self-reliance for which these early experiences stood him in good stead. As he afterwards wrote to
the First Lord of the Admiralty, when pleading the cause of
a daring and skilful officer who had run his ship ashore :
" If I had been censured every time I have run my ship, or
fleets under my command, into great danger, I should long
ago have been *out* of the service, and never *in* the House of
Peers." At the critical instants of the Nile and Copenhagen,
as well as in the less conspicuous but more prolonged anxieties
of the operations off Corsica and along the Riviera of Genoa,
this early habit, grafted upon the singularly steady nerve
wherewith he was endowed by nature, sustained him at a
height of daring and achievement to which very few have
been able to rise.

The other incident recorded by him as happening while on
board the " Lowestoffe," he himself cites as illustrative of
temperament. " Whilst in this frigate, an event happened
which presaged my character ; and, as it conveys no dishonour
to the officer alluded to, I shall insert it. Blowing a gale of
wind, and a very heavy sea, the frigate captured an American
letter-of-marque. The first Lieutenant was ordered to board
her, which he did not do, owing to the very heavy sea. On
his return, the Captain said, ' Have I no officer in the ship
who can board the prize ? ' On which the Master ran to the
gangway, to get into the boat: when I stopped him, saying,
' It is my turn now ; and if I come back, it is yours.' This
little incident," he continues, " has often occurred to my

mind; and I know it is my disposition, that difficulties and dangers do but increase my desire of attempting them." An action of this sort, in its results unimportant, gives keener satisfaction in the remembrance than do greater deeds, because more purely individual, — entirely one's own. It is upon such as this, rather than upon his victories, that Nelson in his narrative dwells caressingly. His personal daring at St. Vincent, and against the gunboats off Cadiz, ministered more directly to his self-esteem, to that consciousness of high desert which was dear to him, than did the Battle of the Nile, whose honors he, though ungrudgingly, shared with his "band of brothers."

When the "Lowestoffe" had been a year upon the station, it became very doubtful whether Locker could continue in her, and finally he did go home ill. It was probably due to this uncertainty that he obtained the transfer of Nelson, in whom he had become most affectionately interested, to the "Bristol," flagship of Sir Peter Parker, the commander-in-chief. Here, under the admiral's own eye, warmly recommended by his last captain, and with a singular faculty for enlisting the love and esteem of all with whom he was brought into contact, the young officer's prospects were of the fairest; nor did the event belie them. Joining the "Bristol" as her third lieutenant, not earlier than July, 1778, he had by the end of September risen "by succession" — to use his own phrase — to be first; a promotion by seniority whose rapidity attests the rate at which vacancies occurred. Both Parker and his wife became very fond of him, cared for him in illness, and in later years she wrote to him upon each of the occasions on which he most brilliantly distinguished himself — after St. Vincent, the Nile, and Copenhagen. "Your mother," said she after the first, "could not have heard of your deeds with more affection; nor could she be more rejoiced at your personal escape from all the dangers of that glorious day;" and again, after the Nile, "Sir Peter and I have ever regarded you as a son." The letter following the victory at Copenhagen has not been published; but Nelson, whose heart was never reluctant to gratitude nor to own obligation, wrote in reply: "Believe me when I say that I am as sensible as ever that I owe my present position in life to your and good Sir

2

Peter's partiality for me, and friendly remembrance of Maurice Suckling."

This last allusion indicates some disinterestedness in Parker's patronage, and its vital importance to Nelson at that time. Captain Suckling had died in July, 1778, and with him departed the only powerful support upon which the young lieutenant could then count, apart from his own merits and the friends obtained by them. There was in those days an immense difference in prospects between the nephew of the Comptroller of the Navy and a man unknown at headquarters. By what leading principles, if any, Sir Peter Parker was guided in the distribution of his favors, can scarcely now be ascertained; but that he brought rapidly forward two men of such great yet widely different merit as Nelson and Collingwood, is a proof that his judgment was sound and the station one where vacancies were frequent. Collingwood, who was then a lieutenant on board a sloop-of-war, went to the "Lowestoffe" in Nelson's place. When the latter, in December, 1778, was made commander into the brig "Badger," the other was transferred to the vacant room in the "Bristol;" and when Nelson, on the 11th of June, 1779, became post-captain in the "Hinchinbrook" frigate, Collingwood again followed him as commander of the "Badger." Finally, when through a death vacancy a better frigate offered for Nelson, Collingwood also was posted into the "Hinchinbrook;" this ship thus having the singular distinction of conferring the highest rank obtainable by selection, and so fixing the final position of the two life-long friends who led the columns at Trafalgar, the crowning achievement of the British Navy as well as of their own illustrious careers. The coincidence at the earlier date may have been partly factitious, due to a fad of the commander-in-chief; but it assumes a different and very impressive aspect viewed in the light of their later close association, especially when it is recalled that Collingwood also succeeded, upon Nelson's death, to the Mediterranean command, and was there worn out, as his predecessor fell, in the discharge of his duty upon that important station, which thus proved fatal to them both. Few historic parallels are so complete. Sir Peter Parker, living until 1811, survived both his illustrious juniors, and at the age of eighty-two followed Nelson's coffin, as chief mourner at the imposing obsequies, where the nation, from the highest to the lowest, mingled the exultation of triumph with weeping for the loss of its best-beloved.

Of Nelson's exterior at this time, his early biographers have secured an account which, besides its value as a portrait, possesses the further interest of mentioning explicitly that charm of manner which was one of his best birth-gifts, reflecting, as it did, the generous and kindly temper of his heart. "The personal appearance of Captain Nelson at this period of his life, owing to his delicate health and diminutive figure, was far from expressing the greatness of his intellectual powers. From his earliest years, like Cleomenes, the hero of Sparta, he had been enamoured of glory, and had possessed a greatness of mind. Nelson preserved, also, a similar temperance and simplicity of manners. Nature, as Plutarch adds of the noble Spartan, had given a spur to his mind which rendered him impetuous in the pursuit of whatever he deemed honourable. The demeanour of this extraordinary young man was entirely the demeanour of a British seaman; when the energies of his mind were not called forth by some object of duty, or professional interest, he seemed to retire within himself, and to care but little for the refined courtesies of polished life." No saving sense of humor seems to have suggested that the profane might here ask, "Is this the British seaman?" "In his dress he had all the cleanliness of an Englishman, though his manner of wearing it gave him an air of negligence; and yet his general address and conversation, when he wished to please, possessed a charm that was irresistible." [1]

In June, 1779, when posted into the "Hinchinbrook," Nelson wanted still three months of being twenty-one. By the custom of the British Navy, then and now, promotions from the grade of Captain to that of Admiral are made by seniority only. Once a captain, therefore, a man's future was assured, so far as concerned the possibility of juniors passing over his head, — neither favor nor merit could procure that; his rank relatively to others was finally fixed. The practical difficulty of getting at a captain of conspicuous ability, to make of him a flag-officer, was met by one of those clumsy yet adequate expedients by which the practical English mind contrives to

[1] Clarke and M'Arthur, vol. i. p. 31.

reconcile respect for precedent with the demands of emergency. There being then no legal limit to the number of
admirals, a promotion was in such case made of all captains
down to and including the one wanted; and Lord St. Vincent,
one of the most thorough-going of naval statesmen, is credited
with the declaration that he would promote a hundred down
the list of captains, if necessary, to reach the one demanded
by the needs of the country. Even with this rough-riding
over obstacles, — for the other officers promoted, however
useful in their former grade, not being wanted as admirals,
remained perforce unemployed, — the advantage of reaching
post-rank betimes is evident enough; and to this chiefly Nelson referred in acknowledging his permanent indebtedness to
Sir Peter Parker. With this early start, every artificial impediment was cleared from his path; his extraordinary ability
was able to assert itself, and could be given due opportunity,
without a too violent straining of service methods. He had,
indeed, to wait eighteen years for his flag-rank; but even so,
he obtained it while still in the very prime of his energies,
before he was thirty-nine, — a good fortune equalled by none
of his most distinguished contemporaries.[1]

A somewhat singular feature of this early promotion of
Nelson is that it was accorded without the claim of service in
actual battle, — a circumstance that seems yet more remarkable when contrasted with the stormy and incessant warfare of
his later career. While he was thus striding ahead, his equals
in years, Saumarez and Pellew, were fighting their way up step
by step, gaining each as the reward of a distinct meritorious
action, only to find themselves outstripped by one who had
scarcely seen a gun fired in anger. The result was mainly due
to the nature of the station, where sickness made vacancies
more rapidly than the deadliest engagement. But while this
is true, and must be taken into the account, it was characteristic of Nelson that his value transpired through the simplest
intercourse, and amid the commonplace incidents of service.
Locker and Parker each in turn felt this. A little later, while
he and Collingwood were still unknown captains, the latter,
usually measured and formal in his language, wrote to him in

[1] Collingwood was nearly fifty when he got his flag. Howe was forty-five,
St. Vincent fifty-three, Saumarez forty-four, Exmouth (Pellew) forty-eight.

these singularly strong words : " My regard for you, my dear Nelson, my respect and veneration for your character, I hope and believe, will never lessen." So, some years afterwards, but before he became renowned or had wrought his more brilliant achievements, an envious brother captain said to him, " You did just as you pleased in Lord Hood's time, the same in Admiral Hotham's, and now again with Sir John Jervis; it makes no difference to you who is Commander-in-chief." This power of winning confidence and inspiring attachment was one of the strongest elements in Nelson's success, alike as a subordinate and when himself in chief command.

With his mind ever fixed upon glory, or rather upon honor, — the word he himself most often used, and which more accurately expresses his desire for fame; honor, which is to glory what character is to reputation, — the same hard fortune persisted in denying to him, during the War of the American Revolution, the opportunities for distinction which he so ardently coveted. In the " Badger " and in the " Hinchinbrook," during the year 1779, his service was confined to routine cruising about Jamaica and along the Mosquito coast of Central America. A gleam of better things for a moment shone upon him in August of that year, when the French fleet, under Count D'Estaing, appeared in Haïti, numbering twenty-two ships-of-the-line, with transports reported to be carrying twenty thousand troops. All Jamaica was in an uproar of apprehension, believing an attack upon the island to be imminent ; for its conquest was known to be one of the great objects of the enemy. Nelson was at the time living on shore, the " Hinchinbrook " seemingly [1] not having returned to the port since his appointment to her, and he eagerly accepted the duty of commanding the land batteries. The odds were great, — " You must not be surprised to hear of my learning to speak French," he wrote, laughingly, to Locker in England, — but if so, the greater the honor attendant, whether upon success or defeat. D'Estaing, however, passed on to America to encounter disaster at Savannah, and Nelson's hopes were again disappointed.

In January, 1780, an opportunity for service offered, which

[1] This appears certain from his letters of July 28 and August 12, which explicitly mention that ship's absence.

ended in no conspicuous or permanent result, but nevertheless conferred distinction upon one who, to use his own expression, was determined to climb to the top of the tree, and to neglect no chance, however slight, that could help him on. War with Spain had then been about seven months declared, and the British governor of Jamaica had sagaciously determined to master Lake Nicaragua, and the course of the river San Juan, its outlet to the Caribbean Sea. The object of the attempt was twofold, both military and commercial. The route was recognized then, as it is now, as one of the most important, if not the most important, of those affording easy transit from the Pacific to the Atlantic by way of the Isthmus. To a nation of the mercantile aptitudes of Great Britain, such a natural highway was necessarily an object of desire. In her hands it would not only draw to itself the wealth of the surrounding regions, but would likewise promote the development of her trade, both north and south, along the eastern and western coasts of the two Americas. But the pecuniary gain was not all. The military tenure of this short and narrow strip, supported at either end, upon the Pacific and the Atlantic, by naval detachments, all the more easily to be maintained there by the use of the belt itself, would effectually sever the northern and southern colonies of Spain, both by actual interposition, and by depriving them of one of their most vital lines of intercommunication. To seek control of so valuable and central a link in a great network of maritime interests was as natural and inevitable to Great Britain a century ago, as it now is to try to dominate the Mediterranean and the Suez Canal, which fulfil a like function to her Eastern possessions and Eastern commerce.

Preoccupied, however, with numerous and more pressing cares in many quarters of the world, and overweighted in a universal struggle with outnumbering foes, Great Britain could spare but scanty forces to her West India Islands, and from them Governor Dalling could muster but five hundred men for his Nicaraguan undertaking. Nelson was directed to convoy these with the " Hinchinbrook " to the mouth of the San Juan del Norte, where was the port now commonly called Greytown, in those days a fine and spacious harbor. There his charge ended; but his mental constitution never allowed

him to look upon a military task as well done while anything
remained to do. In the spirit of his famous saying, fifteen
years later, "Were ten ships out of eleven taken, I would
never call it well done if the eleventh escaped, if able to get
at her," he determined to go with the troops. With his
temperament it was impossible to turn his back upon the
little body of soldiers, whose toilsome advance up the tropical
stream might be aided and hastened by his ready seamen.

The first objective of the expedition was Fort San Juan, a
powerful work controlling the river of the same name, and
thereby the only natural water transit between the sea and
Lake Nicaragua. Upon the possession of this, as a position
of vantage and a safe depot for supplies and reinforcements,
Dalling based his hopes of future advance, both west and
south. Nelson took with him forty-seven seamen and marines from his ship's company; the former, aided by some
Indians, doing most of the labor of forcing the boats against
the current, through shoal and tortuous channels, under his
own constant supervision and encouragement. A small outpost that withstood their progress was by him intrepidly
stormed, sword in hand, by sudden assault; and upon reaching Fort San Juan he urgently recommended the same summary method to the officer commanding the troops. The
latter, however, was not one of the men who recognize the
necessity for exceptional action. Regular approaches, though
the slower, were the surer way of reducing a fortified place,
and entailed less bloodshed. Professional rule commonly
demanded them, and to professional rule he submitted.
Nelson argued that through delays, which, however incurred,
were now past discussion, the expedition had reached its
destination in April, at the end of the healthy, dry season,
instead of shortly after its beginning, in January. Consequently, owing to the fall of the water, much additional
trouble had been experienced in the advance, the men were
proportionately weakened by toil and exposure, and the wet
months, with their dire train of tropical diseases, were at
hand. Therefore, though more might fall by the enemy's
weapons in a direct attack, the ultimate loss would be less
than by the protracted and sickly labors of the spade; while
with San Juan subdued, the force could receive all the care

possible in such a climate, and under the best conditions await
the return of good weather for further progress.

In military enterprises there will frequently arise the question, Is time or life in this case of the greater value? Those
regularly ordered and careful procedures which most econo-
mize the blood of the soldier may, by their inevitable delays,
seriously imperil the objects of the campaign as a whole; or
they may even, while less sanguinary, entail indirectly a
greater loss of men than do prompter measures. In such
doubtful matters Nelson's judgment was usually sound; and
his instinct, which ever inclined to instant and vigorous
action, was commonly by itself alone an accurate guide, in
a profession whose prizes are bestowed upon quick resolve
more often than upon deliberate consultation. The same intuition that in his prime dictated his instant, unhesitating
onslaught at the Nile, depriving the French of all opportunity
for further preparation, — that caused him in the maturity of
his renown, before Copenhagen, to write, "every hour's delay
makes the enemy stronger; we shall never be so good a match
for them as at this moment," — that induced him at Trafalgar
to modify his deliberately prepared plan in favor of one vastly
more hazardous, but which seized and held the otherwise fleeting chance, — led him here also at San Juan, unknown, and
scarcely more than a boy, to press the policy of immediate
attack.

The decision was not in his hands, and he was overruled;
whereupon, with his usual readiness to do his utmost, he
accepted the course he disapproved, and, without nursing a
grievance, became at once active in erecting batteries and
serving the guns. "When unfortunate contentions," says one
dispassionate narrator, "had slackened the ardour for public
service, Captain Nelson did not suffer any narrow spirit to
influence his conduct. He did more than his duty: where
anything was to be done, he saw no difficulties." Great as
his merits were, he was never insensible to them; and, in the
sketch of his career, furnished by him to his chief biographers,
he records his exploits with naïve self-satisfaction, resembling
the sententious tablets of Eastern conquerors: "I boarded, if
I may be allowed the expression, an outpost of the enemy,
situated on an island in the river; I made batteries, and

afterwards fought them, and was a principal cause of our success." But this simple, almost childlike, delight in his own performances, which continually crops out in his correspondence, did not exaggerate their deserts. Major Polson, commanding the land forces, wrote to Governor Dalling: "I want words to express the obligations I owe to Captain Nelson. He was the first on every service, whether by day or night. There was not a gun fired but was pointed by him, or by Captain Despard, Chief Engineer." Dalling, after some delay, wrote in the same sense to the Minister of War in London, warmly recommending Nelson to the notice of the home Government.

While the siege was in progress, Nelson received word of his appointment to a better ship, the "Janus," of forty-four guns, and it became necessary for him to join her. He left Fort San Juan only the day before it surrendered, and returned to Jamaica; but his health now gave way wholly, and his command of the "Janus," for the most part merely nominal, soon came to an end altogether. Dalling had truly said, "Captain Nelson's constitution is rather too delicate for service in this northern ocean." [1] Before starting on the expedition, he had himself written to his friend Locker: "If my health is not much better than it is at present, I shall certainly come home after this trip, as all the doctors are against my staying so long in this country. You know my old complaint in my breast: it is turned out to be the gout got there. I have twice been given over since you left this country with that cursed disorder, the gout." In such weakness he lived and worked through a month of a short campaign, in which, of the "Hinchinbrook's" crew of two hundred, one hundred and forty-five were buried in his time or that of his successor, Collingwood, — a mortality which he justly cites as a further proof of the necessity for expedition in such climates. But, though he survived, he escaped by the skin of his teeth. Worn out by dysentery and fatigue, he was carried ashore in his cot, and soon after taken to Sir Peter Parker's house, where Lady Parker herself nursed him through. Her kind-

[1] The Caribbean was formerly thus styled in contradistinction to the South Sea, the Pacific, which was so called because its first discoverers saw it to the south from the Isthmus.

ness to him and his own debility are touchingly shown by a
note written from the mountains, where he was carried in
his convalescence : " Oh, Mr. Ross, what would I give to be
at Port Royal! Lady Parker not here, and the servants letting me lay as if a log, and take no notice." By September,
1780, it was apparent that perfect restoration, without change
of climate, was impossible, and in the autumn, having been
somewhat over three years on the station, he sailed for home
in the " Lion," of sixty-four guns, Captain Cornwallis,[1] to
whose careful attention, as formerly to that of Captain Pigot,
he gratefully attributed his life. The expedition with which
he had been associated ended in failure, for although a part
of the force pushed on to Lake Nicaragua, sickness compelled
the abandonment of the conquests, which were repossessed by
the Spaniards.

Arriving in England, Nelson went to Bath, and there passed
through a period of extreme suffering and tedious recovery.
" I have been so ill since I have been here," says one of his
letters, " that I was obliged to be carried to and from bed,
with the most excruciating tortures." Exact dates are wanting; but he seems to have been under treatment near three
months, when, on the 28th of January, 1781, he wrote to
Locker, in his often uncouth style : " Although I have not
quite recovered the use of my limbs, yet my inside is a new
man ; " and again, three weeks later, " I have now the perfect
use of all my limbs, except my left arm, which I can hardly tell
what is the matter with it. From the shoulder to my fingers'
ends are as if half dead." He remained in Bath until the
middle of March, latterly more for the mild climate than because feeling the necessity of prosecuting his cure; yet that
his health was far from securely re-established is evident, for
a severe relapse followed his return to London. On the 7th
of May, 1781, he writes to his brother : " You will say, why
does not he come into Norfolk ? I will tell you : I have entirely lost the use of my left arm, and very near of my left
leg and thigh." In estimating Nelson's heroism, the sickly

[1] Cornwallis was an officer of marked gallantry and conduct, who distinguished himself on several occasions, as captain, during the War of 1778, and
as admiral during the wars of the French Revolution. He was brother to
Lord Cornwallis, who surrendered at Yorktown, in 1781.

fragility of his bodily frame must be kept in memory; not to excuse shortcomings of nerve or enterprise, for there were none, but to exalt duly the extraordinary mental energy which rather mocked at difficulties than triumphed over them.

While yet an invalid he had again applied for employment, and, as the war was still raging, was appointed in August, 1781, to the "Albemarle," a small frigate of twenty-eight guns. He was pleased with the ship, the first commissioned by himself at home, with a long cruise in prospect; and, together with his expressions of content with her, there appears that manifestation of complete satisfaction with his officers and crew, with those surrounding him as subordinates, that so singularly characterized his habit of mind. "I have an exceeding good ship's company. Nót a man or officer in her I would wish to change. . . . I am perfectly satisfied with both officers and ship's company." Down to the month before Trafalgar, when, to the bidding of the First Lord of the Admiralty to choose his own officers, he replied, "Choose yourself, my lord; the same spirit actuates the whole profession, you cannot choose wrong," there is rarely, it might almost be said never, anything but praise for those beneath him. With the "Agamemnon," "We are all well; indeed, nobody can be ill with my ship's company, they are so fine a set." At the Nile, "I had the happiness to command a band of brothers; therefore night was to my advantage. Each knew his duty, and I was sure each would feel for a French ship. *My friends* readily conceived my plan." His ships in the Mediterranean, in 1803, "are the best commanded and the very best manned" in the navy. So his frequent praise of others in his despatches and letters has none of the formal, perfunctory ring of an official paper; it springs evidently from the warmest appreciation and admiration, is heartfelt, showing no deceptive exterior, but the true native fibre of the man, full of the charity which is kind and thinketh no evil. It was not always so toward those above him. Under the timid and dilatory action of Hotham and Hyde Parker, under the somewhat commonplace although exact and energetic movements of Lord Keith, he was restive, and freely showed what he felt. On the other hand, around Hood and Jervis, who commanded his professional respect and esteem, he quickly threw the same halo of excellence, arising from his tendency to idealize, that colored the medium through which he invariably saw the men whom he himself commanded. The disposition to invest those near to him with merits, which must in part at least have been imaginary, is a most noteworthy feature of his character, and goes far to explain the attraction he exerted over others, the enthusiasm which ever followed him, the greatness of his success, and also, unhappily, the otherwise almost inexplicable but enduring infatuation which enslaved his later years, and has left the most serious blot upon his memory.

Though thus pleased with his surroundings, his own health continued indifferent. He excuses himself for delay in correspondence, because " so ill as to be scarce kept out of bed." In such a state, and for one whose frame had been racked and weakened by three years spent in the damp heat of the tropics, a winter's trip to the Baltic was hardly the best prescription; but thither the " Albemarle " was sent, — " it would almost be supposed," he wrote, " to try my constitution." He was away on this cruise from October to December, 1781, reaching Yarmouth on the 17th of the latter month, with a large convoy of a hundred and ten sail of merchant-ships, all that then remained of two hundred and sixty that had started from Elsinore on the 8th. " They behaved, as all convoys that ever I saw did, shamefully ill ; parting company every day." After being several days wind-bound in Yarmouth Roads, he arrived in the Downs on the first day of 1782. The bitter cold of the North had pierced him almost as keenly as it did twenty years later in the Copenhagen expedition. " I believe the Doctor has saved my life since I saw you," he wrote to his brother. The ship was then ordered to Portsmouth to take in eight months' provisions, — a sure indication that she was intended for a distant voyage. Nelson himself surmised that she would join the squadron of Sir Richard Bickerton, then fitting out to reinforce the fleet in the East Indies. Had this happened, he would have been on hand to hear much and perchance see something of one of his own professional forerunners, the great French Admiral Suffren, as well as of the latter's doughty antagonist, Sir Edward Hughes ; for Bickerton arrived in time to take part in the last of the five pitched battles between those two hard fighters. Unluckily, a severe accident had befallen the "Albemarle," — a large East Indiaman having dragged down upon her during a heavy gale in the Downs. The injuries received by this collision were so extensive that the ship was under repairs at Portsmouth for six weeks, during which time Bickerton sailed.

While thus detained in one of the principal dockyards and naval stations of the kingdom, another large detachment, belonging to the Channel fleet, assembled before Nelson's eyes. It comprised twelve sail-of-the-line, under Admiral Barrington ; and among these was the " Foudroyant," the most famous ship of her time, then commanded by Captain John Jervis, with whom, as the Earl of St. Vincent, Nelson was afterwards closely associated; but the young frigate captain did not now come in contact with his stately superior, who in later years so highly valued and loved him. It was for him still the day of small things. Though thus thrown in the midst of the din and bustle of extensive naval preparations, he had not the fortune to be directly connected with them ; and consequently no occasion arose for becoming known to admirals who could recognize his worth, and give him the opportunities without which distinction cannot be achieved. It is, however, a significant and instructive fact that, while thus persistently dissociated from the great operations then in progress, and employed wholly in detached service, Nelson's natural genius for war asserted itself, controlling the direction of his thoughts and interests, and fixing them to that broad field of his profession from which he was as yet debarred. "The height of his ambition," an acquaintance of this period tells us, "was to command a line-of-battle ship; as for prize money," for which frigates offered the best chances, " it never entered his thoughts." A few months later, while still in the "Albemarle," it was said of him by Lord Hood, the most original tactician of the day, that he knew as much about naval tactics as any officer in the fleet. When this high encomium was bestowed, Nelson had barely passed his twenty-fourth birthday.

Meanwhile the "Albemarle" was again ordered upon convoy duty, this time to Quebec. This destination also was distasteful on account of the climate. " I want much to get off from this d——d voyage," he wrote. " Mr. Adair," an eminent London surgeon, who the year before had treated him for the paralysis of his limbs, "has told me that if I was sent to a cold damp climate it would make me worse than ever." He himself had scruples about applying for an exchange, and the efforts of some friends who interfered proved useless. The " Albemarle " started with a convoy of thirty-odd vessels on the 10th of April, 1782 ; and after a short stop at Cork, anchored at St. John's, Newfoundland, on May 27, whence she reached Quebec July 1. Three days later she again sailed on a cruise that lasted over two months, spent chiefly about Boston Bay and Cape Cod. During this time several enemy's vessels were taken or destroyed ; but, with the bad luck that so often followed Nelson in the matter of prize-money, none of the captures reached port, and the cruise was pecuniarily unprofitable. It afforded him, however, an opportunity for displaying conduct and gaining deserved reputation, which he valued more highly. On the 14th of August the sudden lifting of a fog showed the "Albemarle" within gunshot of a French squadron, of four ships-of-the-line and a frigate, that had just come out of Boston. A close chase followed, lasting nine or ten hours ; but Nelson threw off the heavy ships by running among the shoals of George's Bank, which he ventured to do, trusting to the cool head and aptitude for pilotage acquired in earlier life. The frigate followed warily, watching for a chance to strike at advantage ; but when the ships-of-the-line had been dropped far enough to be unable to help their consort, the British vessel hove-to [1] in defiance, and the enemy fell back upon his supports.

Shortly after this escape, so many of the ship's company fell ill with scurvy that Nelson decided to go back to Quebec, where he arrived on the 17th of September. " For eight weeks," he wrote, " myself and all the officers lived upon salt beef ; nor had the ship's company had a fresh meal since the 7th of April." The fears for his health that he had expressed before sailing from England had happily proved groundless, and a month's stay in port which now followed, at the most delightful and invigorating of the American seasons, wrought wonders for him. His letters to Locker state that the voyage

[1] That is, stopped.

agreed with him better than he had expected; while from the
St. Lawrence he wrote to his father, " Health, that greatest of
blessings, is what I never truly enjoyed until I saw *Fair*
Canada. The change it has wrought, I am convinced, is truly
wonderful." This happy result had been due, in part at
least, to surroundings that told favorably upon his sensitive
nervous system, and not to the bracing climate alone. He had
been actively occupied afloat, and had fallen desperately in love
with a fair Canadian, around whom his ardent imagination
threw that glamour of exaggerated charm in which he saw all
who were dear to him, except his wife. Her he seems from
the first to have looked upon with affection indeed, but without rapture or illusion. The Canadian affair came near ending
in an imprudent offer, from which he was with difficulty deterred by a cool-headed friend. The story runs that, the ship
being ordered to New York and ready for sea, he had bidden
her good-bye and gone on board, expecting to sail next day;
but that, unable to bear the approaching separation, he returned to the city, and was on his way to the lady's home
when his friend met him.

Tearing himself away from his mistress by a violent effort,
Nelson, on the 20th of October, sailed for New York. Arriving on the 13th of November, he found there a large part of
the West India fleet, under Lord Hood, who had been second
in command to Rodney on the occasion of the latter's celebrated victory over De Grasse in the previous April. Rodney
had since then been recalled to England, while Hood had gone
to Boston to look after a division of the beaten French fleet,
which was there refitting. He was now on his return to the
islands, where the enemy was expected to make a vigorous
aggressive campaign the following spring. Extensive preparations were in fact on foot for the reduction of Jamaica, frustrated six months before by De Grasse's mishap. Nelson
thus found himself again in tantalizing contact with the stirring circumstance that preludes hostilities, in which he himself had little hope to share; for the " Albemarle " belonged
to the North American station, where all active naval operations had ceased with the surrender of Cornwallis the year
before. He went, therefore, to Hood, and begged to be transferred to his squadron. In vain did Admiral Digby, his own

commander-in-chief, tell him that he was on a good station for prize-money. "Yes," he replied, "but the West Indies is the station for honour."

Digby was reluctant to part with a frigate, as all admirals were; but Hood, either from an intuitive faculty for judging men, or from his conversations with Nelson eliciting the latter's singular knowledge of the higher part of his profession, wished to push an officer of so much promise, and succeeded in obtaining the transfer of the "Albemarle" to his squadron. "I am a candidate with Lord Hood for a line-of-battle ship," wrote Nelson to Locker; "he has honoured me highly, by a letter, for wishing to go off this station to a station of service, and has promised me his friendship." A few months later he wrote again: "My situation in Lord Hood's fleet must be in the highest degree flattering to any young man. He treats me as if I were his son, and will, I am convinced, give me anything I can ask of him." This was really the beginning, the outstart, of Nelson's great career; for Hood's interest in him, then aroused, and deepened by experience to the utmost confidence and appreciation, made itself felt the instant the French Revolutionary War began. Nelson then came at once under his orders, went with him to the Mediterranean, and there speedily made his mark, being transferred from admiral to admiral with ever-growing tokens of reliance. Despite the lapse of time, and the long interval of peace, it is no exaggeration to say that there is a direct connection of cause and effect between his transfer to Hood's fleet, in the harbor of New York, and the battle of Cape St. Vincent, in 1797, when he emerged from merely professional distinction to national renown, standing head and shoulders above all competitors. In the four days that followed his arrival in New York, Nelson took the tide at the flood, and was borne on to fortune. Yet in this, as in many other instant and happy decisions, we may not see the mere casting of a die, the chance result of an irreflective impulse. The determination to change into Hood's squadron, with its powerful, far-reaching effect upon his future, was in necessary logical sequence to Nelson's whole habit of thought, and wish, and previous preparation. He was swept into the current that carried him on to fame by the irresistible tendency of his own conscious will and cherished purpose. Opportunity flitted by; he was ready, and grasped it.

At this turning-point the commendable diligence of his principal biographers has again secured for us a striking description of the young captain's personal appearance, and of the impression produced by his manner upon an interested acquaintance, who afterwards became a warm friend and admirer as well as a frequent correspondent. The narrator — then Prince William Henry, afterwards King William IV. — gave the following account, apparently at some period between 1805, when Nelson fell, and 1809, when the first edition of Clarke and M'Arthur's Life appeared. "I was then a midshipman on board the Barfleur," Lord Hood's flagship, "lying in the Narrows off Staten Island, and had the watch on deck, when Captain Nelson, of the Albemarle, came in his barge alongside, who appeared to be the merest boy of a captain I ever beheld; and his dress was worthy of attention. He had on a full-laced uniform; his lank unpowdered hair was tied in a stiff Hessian tail, of an extraordinary length; the old-fashioned flaps of his waistcoat added to the general quaintness of his figure, and produced an appearance which particularly attracted my notice; for I had never seen anything like it before, nor could I imagine who he was, nor what he came about. My doubts were, however, removed when Lord Hood introduced me to him. There was something irresistibly pleasing in his address and conversation; and an enthusiasm, when speaking on professional subjects, that showed he was no common being." The Countess of Minto, in her Life of Lord Minto, speaks of Nelson's "shock head" at the time (1794) when he was a frequent visitor at the house of Minto, then Sir Gilbert Elliott, and Viceroy of Corsica; a trivial detail, but confirmatory, so far, of the picture drawn by the prince. The latter continued: "Nelson, after this, went with us to the West Indies, and served under Lord Hood's flag during his indefatigable cruise off Cape François. . . . I found him warmly attached to my father [King George III.], and singularly humane. He had the honour of the King's service and the independence of the British navy particularly at heart; and his mind glowed with this idea as much when he was simply captain of the Albemarle, and had obtained none of the honours of his Country, as when he was afterwards decorated with so much well-earned distinction."

The war of 1778 was now fast drawing to its close; the preliminaries of peace being signed in January, 1783, though not ratified till the following September. Hood cruised off Cap François, a naval station of the French at the west end of Haïti, to intercept the fleet from Boston, which was understood to be on its way to the Caribbean; but the enemy, learning his whereabouts, went through the Mona Passage, east of the island, thus avoiding a meeting, and was next heard of by the British as being off Curaçao, far to the southward. Nelson, therefore, had no opportunity to show his prowess in battle; and as only three letters remain covering this uneventful period, little is known of his movements, except that he made an abortive attempt to recapture Turk's Island from the French with a small force of ships he was able to gather at short notice. An interesting indication of the spirit which animated him transpires in the first of the three letters mentioned. He had received unexpected orders to wait in New York after Hood's leaving. "I was to have sailed with the fleet this day, but for some private reasons, when my ship was under sail from New York to join Lord Hood, at Sandy Hook, I was sent for on shore, and told I was to be kept forty-eight hours after the sailing of the fleet. It is much to my private advantage," allowing more latitude for picking up prizes, without having to share with the other ships, "but I had much rather have sailed with the fleet." "Money," he continues, "is the great object here," on the North American Station, "nothing else is attended to," — a motive of action which he always rejected with disdain, although by no means insensible to the value of money, nor ever thoroughly at his ease in the matter of income, owing largely to the lavish liberality with which he responded to the calls upon his generosity or benevolence. A year later he wrote in the same strain: "I have closed the war without a fortune; but I trust, and, from the attention that has been paid to me, believe, that there is not a speck in my character. True honour, I hope, predominates in my mind far above riches."

When news of the peace reached the West Indies, Hood was ordered to return with his fleet to England. Nelson went home at the same time, being directed first to accompany Prince William Henry in a visit to Havana. The "Albemarle" reached Spithead on the 25th of June, 1783, and was paid off a week later, her captain going on half-pay until the following April. The cruise of nearly two years' duration closed with this characteristic comment: "Not an officer has been changed, except the second lieutenant, since the Albemarle was commissioned; therefore, it is needless to say, I am happy in my ship's company." And again he writes: "My ship was paid off last week, and in such a manner that must flatter any officer, in particular in these turbulent times. The whole ship's company offered, if I could get a ship, to enter for her immediately." Nelson was keenly alive to the impolicy and injury to the service involved in the frequent changes of officers and men from ship to ship. "The disgust of the seamen to the Navy," he wrote immediately after leaving the "Albemarle," "is all owing to the infernal plan of turning them over from ship to ship, so that men cannot be attached to their officers, or the officers care twopence about them." This element of personal attachment is never left out of calculation safely.

Nelson was now nearly twenty-five. In direct achievement he had accomplished little, and to most he was unknown; but he did not deceive himself in believing that his reputation was established, and his promise, as a capable man of action, understood by those who knew him, and especially by the brilliant admiral under whom he had last served. Within a week of his release from the ship Hood carried him to Court, and presented him to the King, — an evident proof of his approbation; and Nelson notes that the sovereign was exceedingly attentive. The next few months were spent in London, or at his old home in Norfolk, to which and to his family he was always fondly attached. Toward the end of October he obtained a leave of absence, in order to visit France and acquire the French language. His impressions of that country, as far as he went, — from Calais to St. Omer, — are given in lively enough style in a few letters; but they differ little from what might be expected from any very young man deeply tinged with insular prejudice. "I hate their country and their manners," he wrote, soon after his return; and his biographers were quite right in saying that he had been brought up in the old anti-Gallican school, with prejudices not to be eradicated by a flying visit. He duly records his disgust with two British naval captains, one of whom was afterwards among his most valued and valuable friends, for wearing epaulettes, at that time confined to the French service. "I hold them a little *cheap*," he said, "for putting on any part of a Frenchman's uniform."

It is more interesting to notice that his impressionable fancy was again taken by an attractive young Englishwoman, the daughter of a clergyman named Andrews, living at St. Omer. "Two very beautiful young ladies," he writes to Locker and to his brother; "I must take care of my heart, I assure you." "My heart is quite secured against the French beauties; I almost wish I could say as much for an English young lady, the daughter of a clergyman, with whom I am just going to dine, and spend the day. She has such accomplishments that, had I a million of money, I am sure I should at this moment make her an offer of them." "The most accomplished woman my eyes ever beheld," he repeats, a month later. The sentimental raptures of a young man about a handsome girl have in themselves too much of the commonplace to justify mention. What is remarkable, and suggests an explanation of the deplorable vagary of his later years, is that his attachment to his wife, even in the days of courtship, elicited no such extravagance of admiration as that into which he freely lapses in his earlier fancies, and yet more in his last absorbing passion. Respect and tenderness for her he certainly felt and expressed; but there is no indication that she ever enkindled his ardent imagination, or filled for him the place of an ideal, which his mental constitution imperatively demanded as an object of worship. The present attachment went so far with him that he wrote to his uncle William Suckling, asking for an allowance to enable him to marry. "If nothing can be done for me," said he, gloomily, "I know what I have to trust to. Life is not worth preserving without happiness; and I care not where I may linger out a miserable existence. I am prepared to hear your refusal, and have fixed my resolution if that should happen. . . . I pray you may never know the pangs which at this instant tear my heart." If, as is said by the gentleman into whose hands this letter passed, Suckling consented to help him, as he certainly did at the time of his actual marriage, it seems probable that the lady refused him.

CHAPTER II.

1784–1793. AGE, 26–34.

WHATEVER the cause, Nelson's visit to France ended
prematurely and abruptly. Early in January, 1784,
after an absence of two months, he went back to England,
announcing to his friends that his coming was only temporary, partly on business, partly for treatment; for his
delicate health again occasioned him anxiety. "The frost,
thank God, is broke," he wrote; "cold weather is death to
me." But even while speaking confidently of his speedy
return to the Continent, he dropped a hint that he was disposed to resume the active pursuit of his profession, although
on leaving the "Albemarle," six months before, he had said
that he could not afford to live afloat, in peace times, in the
style then prevalent. "My stay in England will be but very
short, without the First Lord in the Admiralty thinks proper
to employ me. I shall offer my services." He did see Lord
Howe, at that time First Lord, asking him for a ship; and
he renewed his cordial relations with Hood, then living in
London. On the 18th of March Howe appointed him to the
command of the frigate "Boreas." Occupation in peace,
with a reduced establishment, was not easy to get, and his
brother, an inveterate wirepuller, must needs know to whose
favor Nelson owed it. "You ask," replied the hero, "by
what interest did I get a ship? I answer, having served
with credit was my recommendation to Lord Howe. Anything in reason that I can ask, I am sure of obtaining from
his justice." The statement was no more than fair to Howe;
but in his knowledge of the merits of Nelson, whose claim

lay rather in evident promise than in conspicuous performance, we can probably trace the friendly intervention of Lord
Hood.

Nelson's wish was that the "Boreas" should go to the East
Indies. To this he inclined, apparently, because the station
was to be under the command of Commodore Cornwallis, in
whose ship he had returned from Jamaica as an invalid in
1780, and to whom on that occasion he was indebted for the
most friendly care. He was not long allowed to indulge this
hope, for five days after receiving his appointment he wrote
that the ship was bound to the Leeward Islands, and that he
had been asked to take as passengers the wife and family of
the commander-in-chief, Sir Richard Hughes, who had already
gone out. In a small vessel, for such the "Boreas" was, the
request, which he could not well refuse, gave Nelson cause of
reasonable discontent, entailing crowding and a large outlay
of money. "I shall be pretty well filled with *lumber*," he
wrote; and later, on the voyage out, "I shall not be sorry to
part with them, although they are very pleasant, good people;
but they are an incredible expense." The incident, annoying
though it was, was not without compensations. After arriving
on the station, he soon became involved in a serious difference
with Sir Richard Hughes; and the latter, though a weak man
and in the wrong, might have acted more peremptorily, had
he not laid himself under such obligations. On the other hand,
Lady Hughes, many years later, shortly after Nelson's death,
committed to writing some recollections of his personal traits
and actions during the passage, so characteristic, even though
trivial, that we could ill have spared them.

"I was too much affected when we met at Bath," wrote she
to Mr. Matcham, Nelson's brother-in-law, "to say every particular in which was always displayed the infinite cleverness
and goodness of heart of our dearly beloved Hero. As a
woman, I can only be a judge of those things that I could
comprehend — such as his attention to the young gentlemen
who had the happiness of being on his quarter-deck. It may
reasonably be supposed that among the number of thirty, there
must be timid as well as bold; the timid he never rebuked,
but always wished to show them he desired nothing of them
that he would not instantly do himself: and I have known him

say, ' Well, Sir, I am going a race to the masthead, and beg I
may meet you there.' No denial could be given to such a wish,
and the poor fellow instantly began his march. His Lordship
never took the least notice with what alacrity it was done, but
when he met in the top, instantly began speaking in the most
cheerful manner, and saying how much a person was to be
pitied that could fancy there was any danger, or even anything
disagreeable, in the attempt. After this excellent example, I
have seen the timid youth lead another, and rehearse his captain's words. In like manner, he every day went into the
school-room, and saw them do their nautical business, and at
twelve o'clock he was the first upon deck with his quadrant.
No one there could be behindhand in their business when their
captain set them so good an example. One other circumstance
I must mention which will close the subject, which was the
day we landed at Barbadoes. We were to dine at the Governor's. Our dear captain said, ' You must permit me, Lady
Hughes, to carry one of my aid-de-camps with me ; ' and when
he presented him to the Governor, he said, ' Your Excellency
must excuse me for bringing one of my midshipmen, as I make
it a rule to introduce them to all the good company I can, as
they have few to look up to besides myself during the time
they are at sea.' This kindness and attention made the young
people adore him ; and even his wishes, could they have been
known, would have been instantly complied with."

The charm and wisdom of such a bearing is patent ; but it
was the natural character of the man that thus shone out, and
no mere result of conscientious care. To the last, through all
his ill-health, anxiety, and sufferings, the same genial sweetness of manner, the outcome of an unaffected, cordial good-will
to all, was shown to those who came in contact with him.
Captain Duff, who met him for the first time three weeks before
Trafalgar, and who fell in the battle, wrote to his wife in almost
the same words as Lady Hughes : " You ask me about Lord
Nelson, and how I like him. I have already answered that
question as every person must do that ever served under him.
He is so good and pleasant a man, that we all wish to do what
he likes, without any kind of orders. I have been myself very
lucky with most of my admirals, but I really think the present
the pleasantest I have met with." There do, it is true, occur

in Nelson's letters occasional, though very rare, expressions of that passing annoyance with individuals which is inseparable from the close and long-continued contact of ship life. Thus, shortly before leaving the "Boreas," he writes: "I begin to be very strict in my Ship. Whenever I may set off in another, I shall be indifferent whether I ever speak to an Officer in her, but upon duty." One wonders what passing and soon forgotten breeze was responsible for this most un-Nelson-like outburst. But to the end it remained true that between the officers and crews under Nelson's command and their chief, there was always that cordial regard which can only spring from the hearty sympathy of the commander with those beneath him.

While thoughtful and considerate, even to gentleness, for the weak and dependent, the singular energy that quickened Nelson's frail and puny frame showed itself on occasion in instant resentment of any official slight to himself or his ship, or injury to the interests of the country. During the "Boreas's" stay at Madeira, the British Consul neglected to return his visit, on the plea that the Government allowed him no boat. Nelson declined any further intercourse with him. While lying in the Downs, he learns that sixteen British seamen are detained by force on board a Dutch Indiaman. He requires their delivery to him; and when their effects were withheld, on the alleged ground of their being in debt to the ship, he stops all intercourse between it and the shore, sending an armed cutter to enforce his order. "The Admiralty," he wrote, "have fortunately approved my conduct in the business," and added grimly, "a thing they are not very guilty of where there is a likelihood of a scrape." When entering the harbor of Fort Royal, Martinique, the principal French island in the Lesser Antilles, the officer at the citadel neglected to hoist the colors, a ceremonial observance customary when a ship of war approached. Nelson at once demanded an explanation and received ample amends; the offending party being placed under arrest. To the governor of some of the British West India islands, he wrote making suggestions for the better discharge of certain duties, in which both of them were interested. He received, it is said, a testy message that "old generals were not in the habit of taking advice from young gentlemen." "I have the honour, Sir," replied Nelson, "of being as old as the

prime minister of England, and think myself as capable of
commanding one of his majesty's ships as that minister is of
governing the state ; " and throughout he held to the stand he
had taken.

The most remarkable instance, however, of this promptness
to assert the dignity and rights of his official position, allowing no man to despise his youth, occurred very soon after his
arrival upon the station, and brought him to a direct issue with
his commander-in-chief, — if not, indeed, with an authoritative
precedent set by so great a man as Lord Rodney. Young
though he still was in years, — only twenty-six, — Nelson was
by date of commission the senior captain in the small squadron,
of some half-dozen vessels, to which the economies of the administration had reduced the Leeward Islands station. Being
thus next in rank to the admiral, the latter, who made his
headquarters at Barbadoes in the southern part of the station,
sent him to the northern division, centring about the island of
Antigua. Having remained in harbor, as was usual, during the
hurricane months, Nelson cruised during the winter and until
February, 1785, when some damage received compelled the
" Boreas " to put into Antigua for repairs. Here he found a
vessel of the squadron, whose own captain was of course junior
to him, flying a Commodore's broad pendant, which asserted
the official presence of a captain superior to himself in rank
and command, and duly qualified to give him orders. He at
once asked the meaning of this from the ship's proper commander, and was informed by him that Captain Moutray, an
old officer, twenty years his senior on the post list, and then
acting as Commissioner of the Navy, a civil office connected
with the dockyard at Antigua, had directed it to be hoisted,
and claimed to exercise control over all men-of-war in the
harbor, during the admiral's absence.

Nelson was not wholly unprepared for this, for Hughes had
notified him and the other captains that Moutray was authorized by himself to take this step. Being then away from the
island, he had replied guardedly that if Commissioner Moutray
was put into commission, he would have great pleasure in
serving under him, — thus reserving his decision to the
moment for action. He now took the ground that an officer
not commissioned afloat, but holding only a civil appointment,

could not exercise naval command, — that an order authorizing him to do so was invalid, — that to entitle him to such command he must be put into military commission by being attached to a ship in commission. He therefore flatly declined to obey Moutray's orders, refusing to admit his claim to be considered a commodore, or entitled to military obedience, unless he produced a commission. This he held to when Moutray gave him a written order to put himself under his command.

On technical points of this kind Nelson was a clear and accurate thinker, and in the admiral he had to do with a muddle-headed, irresolute superior. Hughes had already been badly worried and prodded, on matters concerning his own neglected duties, by his unquiet young subordinate, who was never satisfied to leave bad enough alone, but kept raising knotty points to harass an easy-going old gentleman, who wanted only to be allowed to shut his eyes to what went on under his nose. He was now exasperated by Nelson's contumacy, but he was also a little afraid of him, and supported his own order by no more decisive action than laying the case before the Admiralty, who informed Nelson that he should have referred his doubts to the admiral, instead of deciding for himself in a matter that concerned "the exercise of the functions of his [the admiral's] appointment." This was rather begging the question, for Nelson expressed no doubts, either to Hughes or in his explanatory letter to the Admiralty. The latter in turn shirked thus the decision of the question, — for, if Nelson was right, Hughes's order was illegal and not entitled to obedience; if he was wrong, he had been guilty of flagrant insubordination, and should have been sharply dealt with. The Government probably thought that the admiral had blundered in undertaking to give military authority to a civil official, — a step so generally disastrous in experience that it is now explicitly forbidden by the regulations of most navies. It is worthy of note that twenty years later, when commander-in-chief in the Mediterranean, Nelson directed the captains of ships cruising in the Straits of Gibraltar to consult on all occasions with the Commissioner of the Navy resident in Gibraltar, as well as to receive his advice, if proffered, — adding that the commissioner's opinion of their conduct would have great weight with himself; but he did not put them under his orders.[1]

Reasoning from Nelson's position, as the pendant was flying without proper authority on board a ship under his immediate command, he should, as senior captain afloat, have gone further and hauled it down. Of his authority to do so he felt no doubt, as is evident from his letter to the Admiralty; but his motive for refraining was characteristic. He was unwilling to wound Moutray; just as, before Trafalgar, in direct disregard of the Admiralty's orders, he allowed an admiral going home under charges to take with him his flagship, a vessel of the first force and likely to be sorely needed in the approaching battle, because he was reluctant to add to the distress the officer was undergoing already. "I did not choose to order the Commissioner's pendant to be struck, as Mr. Moutray is an old officer of high military character; and it might hurt his feelings to be supposed wrong by so young an officer." The question solved itself shortly by the Commissioner's returning to England; but the controversy seems to have made no change in the friendly and even affectionate relations existing between him and his wife and Nelson. For Mrs. Moutray the latter had formed one of those strong idealizing attachments which sprang up from time to time along his path. "You may be certain," he writes to his brother at the very period the discussion was pending, "I never passed English Harbour without a call, but alas! I am not to have much comfort. My dear, sweet friend is going home. I am really an April day; happy on her account, but truly grieved were I only to consider myself. Her equal I never saw in any country or in any situation. If my dear Kate [his sister] goes to Bath next winter she will be known to her, for my dear friend promised to make herself known. What an acquisition to any female to be acquainted with, what an example to take pattern from." "My sweet, amiable friend sails the 20th for England. I took my leave of her three days ago with a heavy heart. What a treasure of a woman." Returning to Antigua a few weeks later, he writes again in a sentimental vein very rare in him: "This country appears now intolerable, my dear friend being absent. It is barren indeed. English Harbour I

[1] Nicolas, vol. v. p. 356.

hate the sight of, and Windsor I detest. I went once up the hill to look at the spot where I spent more happy days than in any one spot in the world. E'en the trees drooped their heads, and the tamarind tree died : — all was melancholy : the road is covered with thistles ; let them grow. I shall never pull one of them up." His regard for this attractive woman seems to have lasted through his life ; for she survived him, and to her Collingwood addressed a letter after Trafalgar, giving some particulars of Nelson's death. Her only son also died under the latter's immediate command, ten years later, when serving in Corsica.

The chief interest of the dispute over Moutray's position lies not in the somewhat obscure point involved, but in the illustration it affords of Nelson's singular independence and tenacity in a matter of principle. Under a conviction of right he throughout life feared no responsibility and shrank from no consequences. It is difficult for the non-military mind to realize how great is the moral effort of disobeying a superior, whose order on the one hand covers all responsibility, and on the other entails the most serious personal and professional injury, if violated without due cause ; the burden of proving which rests upon the junior. For the latter it is, justly and necessarily, not enough that his own intentions or convictions were honest : he has to show, not that he meant to do right, but that he actually did right, in disobeying in the particular instance. Under no less rigorous exactions can due military subordination be maintained. The whole bent of advantage and lifelong training, therefore, draws in one direction, and is withstood by nothing, unless either strong personal character supplies a motive, or established professional standing permits a man to presume upon it, and to exercise a certain right to independence of action. At this time Nelson was practically unknown, and in refusing compliance with an order he took a risk that no other captain on the station would have assumed, as was shown by their failure a few months later to support their convictions in an analogous controversy, upon which Nelson had entered even before the Moutray business. In both cases he staked all upon legal points, considered by him vital to the welfare of the navy and the country. The spirit was identically the same that led him to swing his ship out of the line at Cape St. Vincent without waiting for signals. After that day and the Nile he could afford to take liberties, and sometimes took them with less justification than in his early career.

When the Moutray question arose, Nelson was already engaged in a more far-reaching dispute, not only with his commander-in-chief, but with the colonial authorities and the popular sentiment of the West India Islands. Like most men, great and small, he shared the prepossessions of his day and generation; differing, however, from others, in that he held his opinions as principles, from asserting which he was not to be deterred by the ill-will or dislike of those immediately about him. Upon arriving in the West Indies he found flourishing a system of trade extremely beneficial to the islands, but which his education condemned as hurtful to Great Britain, as it certainly was contrary to then existing laws that had for a century previous regulated the commerce of the kingdom. In 1784, a year only had elapsed since the United States had been formally recognized as independent, thereby becoming, in British estimation as well as in their own, a nation foreign to the British flag. By the Navigation Laws, first established by Cromwell, but continued under the restored monarchy without serious modification until 1794, trade with the Colonies was reserved to vessels built in Great Britain or her dependencies, and manned in three-fourths part by British subjects. The chief object and advantage of the law were conceived to be, not merely a monopoly of the trade, — concerning the economical wisdom of which serious doubts began to be felt, — but the fostering of the British merchant service as a nursery of seamen, upon whom, in time of war, the navy could draw. The military strength of the Empire was thought to be involved in the enforcement of the Navigation Act.[1]

Before the United States declared their independence, they, as British colonies, enjoyed the privilege of trading with their

[1] Thus Collingwood, rarely other than sober and restrained in his language, wrote to Hughes : " It is from the idea that the greatness and superiority of the British navy very much depends upon preserving inviolate the Act of Navigation, excluding foreigners from access to the colonies, that I am induced to make this representation to you." Nicolas, vol. i. p. 172.

fellow-colonists under what was then the common flag; and the nearness of the two regions contributed to the advantage of both in this traffic, in which the continental communities were the chief suppliers of many articles essential to the islands, notably provisions and lumber. This mutual intercourse and dependence promoted a sympathy which was scarcely disguised in the West Indies during the War of Independence; indeed, Nelson wrote that many of the inhabitants were as arrant rebels as those who had renounced their allegiance. Under these conditions, when peace was restored, the old relations were readily resumed; and as there had really been considerable inconvenience and loss to the islanders from the deprivation of American products, the renewal was eagerly promoted by popular sentiment. The local authorities, as usual and natural, yielded to the pressure around them, and in entire disregard of the known policy of the home government permitted American vessels to trade openly under their own colors. In Jamaica the governor had even gone so far as to authorize formally a free trade, during pleasure, with the United States, contrary to the explicit orders of his superiors in Great Britain. Where scruples were felt or hesitation was shown, advantage was taken of the exceptions of the law, which allowed vessels in distress to sell so much of their cargoes as would pay for necessary repairs. With the tendency of commerce to evade restrictions by liberal stretching of the conscience, the merchant-captain and the colonial officer found little difficulty in arranging that the damage should be great enough to cover the sale of the whole lading.

After laying up in Antigua during the hurricane season of 1784, Nelson was summoned to Barbadoes in November, with the other captains, to receive orders for the winter's cruising. These, when issued, were found to direct only the examination of anchorages, and the gathering of information about supplies of wood and water. Nelson's attention had been drawn already to the American traffic; and he, with his friend Collingwood, who was again on the station, went to the admiral, and urged that it was the duty of ships of war to enforce the Navigation Laws. The admiral professed ignorance of these; and Nelson himself remarks that British vessels up to that time had been so much cheaper built than others, that they had, without artificial protection, naturally absorbed their own colonial trade, — the question, therefore, had dropped out of sight till it was revived by American competition. A copy of the Act being then produced, Hughes gave an order requiring his vessels to enforce it; making special mention of the changed relations of the United States to Great Britain, whereby they were "to be considered as foreigners, and excluded from all commerce with the islands in these seas."

With these instructions Nelson sailed again for the north, where the Virgin Islands, with those of Montserrat, Nevis, and St. Christopher, were put under his especial charge, — the sloop "Rattler," Captain Wilfred Collingwood, a brother of the well-known admiral, being associated with the "Boreas." At first the two officers confined their action to warning off American vessels, and at times forcing them to leave ports where they had anchored; but they found that either the vessels returned during the absence of the ships of war, or that permissions to land, upon what they thought trivial grounds, were given by the Customs' officials, in virtue of the exceptions to the law above mentioned.

There matters stood until the 11th of January, 1785, Nelson acting by the authority of the commander-in-chief, but exercising his own discretion, and with forbearance, in carrying out his instructions. On the day named he received another order from the admiral, modifying the first upon the grounds of a more mature consideration, and of "the opinion of the King's Attorney-General" in the islands. Nelson was now directed, in case of a foreign merchant-ship coming within the limits of his station, to cause her to anchor near his own vessel and to report her arrival, and situation in all respects, to the governor of the colony where he then was; "and if, after such report shall have been made and received, the governor or his representative shall think proper to admit the said foreigner into the port or harbour of the island where you may be, *you are on no account to hinder or prevent such foreign vessel from going in accordingly, or to interfere any further in her subsequent proceedings.*"

Here the admiral not only raised, but also decided, the

point as to whether the enforcement of the Navigation Act rested with naval officers, or was vested only in the civil authorities of the islands. Nelson was convinced that an essential part of the duty of ships of war, and especially when peace took from them so much of their military function, was to afford to the commerce of the nation proper protection, of which a necessary feature, according to the ideas of the age, was the interdiction of foreign traders. A seaman, he plausibly argued, could decide better than an unprofessional man the questions of injuries and distress upon which the unlawful traffic largely hinged. "In judging of their distress, no person can know better than the sea officers," he wrote to Hughes. "The governors may be imposed upon by false declarations; we, who are on the spot, cannot." He was aware, also, that a petition for relaxing the Act in favor of the American trade with the West Indies had been referred to the home government, by which it had been explicitly rejected. Strengthened by this knowledge, but actuated, after all, chiefly by his invariable resoluteness to assume responsibility where he felt he was right, he replied to the admiral's letter with a clear statement of the facts, concluding with the words : "Whilst I have the honour to command an English man-of-war, I never shall allow myself to be subservient to the will of any Governor, nor co-operate with him in doing *illegal acts.* . . . If I rightly understand your order of the 29th of December, it is founded upon an Opinion of the King's Attorney-General, viz.: 'That it is legal for Governors or their representatives to admit foreigners into the ports of their government, if they think fit.' How the King's Attorney-General conceives he has a right to give an illegal opinion, which I assert the above is, he must answer for. I know the Navigation Laws." As he summed up the matter in a letter to his friend Locker : "Sir Richard Hughes was a delicate business. I must either disobey my orders, or disobey Acts of Parliament, which the admiral was disobeying. I determined upon the former, trusting to the uprightness of my intention. In short, I wrote the Admiral that I should decline obeying his orders, till I had an opportunity of seeing and talking to him, at the same time making him an apology."

Hughes's first impulse was to supersede his recalcitrant

subordinate, and bring him to trial. He learned, however, that many of the other captains, of whom the court must be formed, shared his junior's views, although they shrank, with the submissiveness of military men, from the decisive act of disobedience. The result of a trial must therefore be doubtful. He was, moreover, a fiddler, as Nelson continually styled him, shifting back and forth, from opinion to opinion, and to be relied upon for only one thing, — to dodge responsibility, if possible. Consequently, no official action was taken; the commander-in-chief contented himself with washing his hands of all accountability. He had given orders which would clear himself, in case Nelson's conduct was censured in England. If, on the contrary, it was approved, it would redound to the credit of the station.

The matter was soon brought to a test. The governors and all the officials, particularly of the Custom House, resented the action of the naval officers; but the vigilance of the latter so seriously interrupted the forbidden traffic under American colors, that recourse was had to giving British registers to the vessels concerned, allowing them to trade under British flags. This, however, was equally contrary to the Navigation Act, which forbade British registry to foreign-built ships, except when prizes taken in war; and the disguise was too thin to baffle men like Collingwood and Nelson. The latter reported the practice to the home Government, in order that any measures deemed necessary might be taken. Meanwhile he patiently persisted in turning away all vessels, not British built, which he encountered, confining himself for the time to this merely passive prevention; but finding at last that this was not a sufficient deterrent, he gave notice that after the 1st of May, 1785, he would seize all American vessels trading to the islands, "let them be registered by whom they might." Accordingly, on the 2d of May he arrested an American-built schooner, owned in Philadelphia and manned entirely by Americans, but having a British register issued at the island of St. Christopher.

The Crown lawyer was now called upon to prosecute the suit. He expressed grave doubts as to a naval captain's power to act by virtue simply of his commission, the sole authority alleged by the captor; and, although he proceeded with the case, his manner so betrayed his uncertainty that Nelson felt it necessary to plead for himself. To the confusion of all opponents the judge decided in his favor, saying he had an undoubted right to seize vessels transgressing the Navigation Laws. The principle thus established, Nelson on the 23d of the same month, at the island of Nevis, upon the same grounds, seized four vessels, — one of which had been registered at Dominica by Governor Orde, a naval captain senior in rank to himself, and with whom he came into unpleasant contact upon several occasions in his later life.

There was no serious question as to the condemnation of the four last seizures, the facts being clear and the principle settled ; [1] but the rage of the inhabitants of Nevis led them to seek revenge upon Nelson for the injury they could no longer prevent. He had summoned the masters of the ships on board the "Boreas," and, after satisfying himself that the vessels were not entitled to British registers, had sent marines to hold them, and to prevent essential witnesses from leaving them, until the cases were tried. Upon these circumstances was based an accusation of assault and imprisonment, the masters swearing that they had made their statements under bodily fear. Writs were issued against Nelson, damages being laid at four thousand pounds, a sum which to him meant ruin. Although he asserted that there was absolutely no truth in the charges, which are certainly in entire contradiction to the general, if not invariable, tenor of his life and conduct, he was advised by the Crown lawyers not to subject himself to trial, as in the state of public feeling he could not expect a fair verdict. To avoid arrest, he was forced to confine himself to the ship for seven weeks, during which the marshal made several attempts to serve the writ, but without success. On the day that the case of the seized ships came up, he was able to be present in court only by the safe conduct of the judge.

[1] Nelson's letters are contradictory on this point. In a letter to Locker of March 3, 1786, he says, "Before the first vessel was tried I had seized four others;" whereas in the formal and detailed narrative drawn up — without date, but later than the letter to Locker — he says the first vessel was tried and condemned May 17, the other four seized May 23. (Nicolas, vol. i. pp. 177, 178.) The author has followed the latter, because from the particularity of dates it seems to have been compiled from memoranda, that of Locker written from memory, — both nearly a year after the events.

Two days after the seizure of the four vessels, Sir Richard Hughes, who was making a tour of the station under his command, arrived at Nevis; but he had no support to give his zealous lieutenant. "He did not appear to be pleased with my conduct," wrote Nelson to Locker. "At least he did not approve it, but told me I should get into a scrape. Seven weeks I was kept a close prisoner to my ship; nor did I ever learn that the admiral took any steps for my release. He did not even acquaint the Admiralty Board how cruelly I had been treated; nor of the attempts which had been made to take me out of my ship by force, and that indignity offered under the fly of his flag." "I had the governor, the Customs, all the planters upon me; subscriptions were soon filled to prosecute; and my admiral stood neuter, although his flag was then in the roads." To this lack of countenance on the part of his superior, and direct persecution by those injuriously affected by his action, there was added a general social ostracism, to which he frequently alludes, and which was particularly emphasized by its contrast with the habits of hospitality prevalent among the small and wealthy planter community. One friend, however, stood by him, and offered to become his bail in the sum of ten thousand pounds, — Mr. Herbert, the President of Nevis, and one of the wealthiest men in the island. He had, Nelson said, suffered more than any one else from the interruption of the trade, but he considered that the young captain had done only his duty. Possibly there may have been a warmer feeling underlying this esteem, for he was the uncle of the lady whom Nelson afterwards married, and to whom he seems to have been paying attention already.

Despite his indomitable pluck and resolve, the confinement, uncertainty, and contention told heavily on Nelson's health and spirits. His temper was too kindly and social not to feel the general alienation. It could not affect his purpose; but the sense of right-doing, which sustained him in that, did not make his road otherwise easier. It is, indeed, especially to be noticed that there was not in him that hard, unyielding fibre, upon which care, or neglect, or anxiety makes little impression. He was, on the contrary, extremely sympathetic, even emotional; and although insensible to bodily fear, he

was by no means so to censure, or to risk of other misfortune.
To this susceptibility to worry, strong witness is borne by an
expression of his, used at the very time of which we are now
writing. One of his friends — Captain Pole of the Navy —
had detained and sent in a neutral vessel for breach of belligerent rights. After long legal proceedings, extending over
five years, she was condemned, and proved to be a very valuable prize to the captors. " Our friend Charles Pole," he
writes, " has been fortunate in his trial; but the lottery is so
very much against an officer, that never will I knowingly
involve myself in a doubtful cause. Prize-money is doubtless
very acceptable ; but my mind would have suffered so much,
that no pecuniary compensation, at so late a period, would
have made me amends." Contrasting this utterance with the
resolution shown by him at this time, in fighting what he
considered the cause of his country in the West Indies, it can
be seen how much stronger with him was the influence of
duty than that exercised by any considerations of merely
material advantage. In the one he could find support; in
the other not. But in neither case was he insensible to care,
nor could he escape the physical consequences of anxiety
upon a delicate frame and nervous organization. Of this, his
harassment in the pursuit of the French fleet in 1798, during
Bonaparte's Egyptian expedition, gave a very conspicuous
illustration.

With such a temperament, being now very much in the
position of an individual fighting a corporation, he appealed
to the home Government; addressing, on the 29th of June,
1785, a memorial to the King, setting forth the facts of the
case, as already given, adding that his health was much
impaired, and asking for assistance. He received a reply to
this in the following September, informing him that the King
had directed that he should be defended by the Crown lawyers. This implied approval of his course was succeeded, in
November, by a letter from the Secretary of the Treasury,
through the usual official channels of the Admiralty, acquaint-
ing him that the Government was "of opinion that the
commander-in-chief of the Leeward Islands, and officers under
him, have shown a very commendable zeal, in endeavouring
to put a stop to the very illicit practices which were carrying

on in the islands, in open violation of the law, and to the
great detriment of the navigation and trade of his Majesty's
dominions." Verily, Hughes had his reward. Here he was
commended in express terms for doing that which he had
been too prudent to do, for zeal which he had never shown,
for maintaining a law which he had given orders not to maintain. "I own I was surprised," wrote Nelson, "that the
commander-in-chief should be thanked for an· act which he
did not order, but which, if I understand the meaning of
words, by his order of the 29th December, 1784, he ordered not
to be." " To the end of the station,[1] his order of the 29th of
December was never repealed, so that I always acted with a rod
over me." How heavily the responsibility he assumed was felt
by others, is clearly shown in another statement made by him.
" The Captains Collingwood were the only officers, with myself,
who ever attempted to hinder the illicit trade with America;
and I stood singly with respect to seizing, for the other officers
were fearful of being brought into scrapes."

Backed by the royal approval, and with his legal expenses
guaranteed, Nelson's course was now smooth. He continued
in all parts of the station to suppress the contraband trade,
and his unpopularity, of course, also continued; but excitement necessarily subsided as it became clear that submission
was unavoidable, and as men adapted themselves to the new
conditions. The whole procedure now looks somewhat barbarous and blundering, but in no essential principle differs
from the methods of protection to which the world at present
seems again tending. It is not for us to throw stones at it.
The results, then, were completely successful, judged by the
standards of the time. " At this moment," wrote Nelson
some few months later, " there are nearly fifty sail employed
in the trade between the Islands of St. Kitts, Nevis, and
America, which are truly British built, owned, and navigated.
Had I been an idle spectator, my firm belief is that not a
single vessel would have belonged to those islands in the
foreign trade." His own action was further endorsed by the
ministry, which now gave captains of ships-of-war much more

---

[1] This word is used by Nelson, apparently, as equivalent to "season," —
the cruising period in the West Indies. " The admiral wishes to remain another station," he writes elsewhere.

extensive powers, thereby justifying his contention that it was within their office to enforce the Navigation Act. Nor was this increased activity of the executive branch of the government the only result of Nelson's persistence. His sagacious study of the whole question, under the local conditions of the West Indies, led to his making several suggestions for more surely carrying out the spirit of the Law; and these were embodied the next year in a formal Act of the Legislature.

With so vivid a career as that of Nelson ahead, the delay imposed by this wrangling episode is somewhat dreary ; but it undeniably shows his characteristics in the strongest light. Duty, not ease; honor, not gain; the ideal, not the material, — such, not indeed without frailty and blemish, were ever his motives. And, while he craved his reward in the approval and recognition of those around and above him, he could find consolation for the lack of them in his own sense of right-doing. "That thing called Honour," he writes to a friend soon after the "Boreas" cruise, "is now, alas! thought of no more. My integrity cannot be mended, I hope ; but my fortune, God knows, has grown worse for the service ; so much for serving my country. But I have invariably laid down, and followed close, a plan of what ought to be uppermost in the breast of an officer: that it is much better to serve an ungrateful Country than to give up his own fame. Posterity will do him justice; a uniform conduct of honour and integrity seldom fails of bringing a man to the goal of fame at last."

This struggle with Sir Richard Hughes, in which Nelson took the undesirable, and to a naval officer invidious, step of disobeying orders, showed clearly, not only the loftiness of his motives, but the distinguishing features which constituted the strength of his character, both personal and military. There was an acute perception of the right thing to do, an entire readiness to assume all the responsibility of doing it, and above all an accurate judgment of the best way to do it, — to act with impunity to himself and with most chances of success to his cause. Its analogy to a military situation is striking. There was a wrong condition of things to be righted — a victory to be won. To achieve this a great risk

must be taken, and he was willing to take it; but in so doing
he made such choice of his ground as to be practically unassailable — to attain his end without lasting harm to himself.
That Nelson would have managed better had he been ten
years older is very probable. Likely enough he betrayed
some of the carelessness of sensibilities which the inexperi-
ence of youth is too apt to show towards age; but, upon a
careful review of the whole, it appears to the writer that his
general course of action was distinctly right, judged by the
standards of the time and the well-settled principles of
military obedience, and that he pursued an extremely difficult line of conduct with singular resolution, with sound
judgment, and, in the main, with an unusual amount of tact,
without which he could scarcely have failed, however well
purposing, to lay himself open to serious consequences. Certainly he achieved success.

It was in the midst of this legal warfare, and of the pre-
occupations arising from it, that Nelson first met the lady
who became his wife. She was by birth a Miss Frances
Woolward, her mother being a sister of the Mr. Herbert
already mentioned as President of the Council in Nevis. She
was born in the first half of 1758,[1] and was therefore a few
months older than Nelson. In 1779 she had married Dr.
Josiah Nisbet, of Nevis, and the next year was left a widow
with one son, who bore his father's full name. After her
husband's death, being apparently portionless, she came to
live with Herbert, who looked upon and treated her as his
own child, although he also had an only daughter. When
Nelson first arrived at Nevis, in January, 1785,[2] she was
absent, visiting friends in a neighboring island, so that they
did not then meet, — a circumstance somewhat fortunate for
us, because it led to a description of him being sent to her in
a letter from a lady of Herbert's family, not improbably her

[1] Lady Nelson's tombstone in Littleham Churchyard, Exmouth, reads that
she died May 6, 1831, "aged 73." She would then have been born before
May 6, 1758. The Annual Register for 1831 gives May 4, as the date of her
death, and her age 68.

[2] Prior to May, 1785, the only stops of the "Boreas" at Nevis were January 6–8, February 1–4, and March 11–15. (Boreas's Log in Nicolas's
Letters and Despatches of Lord Nelson, vol. vii. Addenda, pp. viii, ix.)

cousin, Miss Herbert. Nelson had then become a somewhat conspicuous factor in the contracted interests of the island society, owing to the stand he had already publicly assumed with reference to the contraband trade. People were talking about him, although he had not as yet enforced the extreme measures which made him so unpopular. " We have at last," so ran the letter, " seen the little captain of the Boreas of whom so much has been said. He came up just before dinner, much heated, and was very silent; but seemed, according to the old adage, to think the more. He declined drinking any wine; but after dinner, when the president, as usual, gave the three following toasts, ' the King,' 'the Queen and Royal Family,' and 'Lord Hood,' this strange man regularly filled his glass, and observed that those were always bumper toasts with him ; which, having drank, he uniformly passed the bottle, and relapsed into his former taciturnity. It was impossible, during this visit, for any of us to make out his real character ; there was such a reserve and sternness in his behaviour, with occasional sallies, though very transient, of a superior mind. Being placed by him, I endeavoured to rouse his attention by showing him all the civilities in my power; but I drew out little more than 'Yes,' and 'No.' If you, Fanny, had been there, we think you would have made something of him, for you have been in the habit of attending to these odd sort of people."

Mrs. Nisbet very quickly made something of him. Little direct description has been transmitted to us concerning the looks or characteristics of the woman who now, at the time when marriage was possible to him, had the misfortune to appear in the line of succession of Nelson's early fancies, and to attract the too easily aroused admiration and affection of a man whose attachment she had not the inborn power to bind. That Nelson was naturally inconstant, beyond the volatility inherent in youth, is sufficiently disproved by the strength and endurance of his devotion to the one woman, in whom he either found or imagined the qualities that appealed to the heroic side of his character. How completely she mastered all the approaches to his heart, and retained her supremacy, once established, to the end, is evidenced by the whole tenor of his correspondence with her, by his mention of her in letters to others, by the recorded expressions he used in speaking to or about her. Despite all that he certainly knew of her, and much more that it is unreasonable to doubt he must have known of her history, there is no mistaking the profound emotions she stirred in his spirit, which show themselves continually in spontaneous outbreaks of passionate fondness and extravagant admiration, whose ring is too true and strong for doubt concerning their reality to find a place.

Many men are swayed by strong and wayward impulses; but to most the fetters imposed by social conventions, by inherited or implanted standards of seemliness and decorum, suffice to steady them in the path of outward propriety. Of how great and absorbing a passion Lord Nelson was capable is shown by the immensity of the sacrifice that he made to it. Principle apart, — and principle wholly failed him, — all else that most appeals to man's self-respect and regard for the esteem of others was powerless to exert control. Loyalty to friendship, the sanctity which man is naturally fain to see in the woman he loves, and, in Nelson's own case, a peculiar reluctance to wound another, — all these were trampled under foot, and ruthlessly piled on the holocaust which he offered to her whom he worshipped. He could fling to the winds, as others cannot, considerations of interest or expediency, as he flung them over and over in his professional career. My motto, he said once and again, is " All or nothing." The same disregard of consequences that hazarded all for all, in battle or for duty, broke through the barriers within which prudence, reputation, decency, or even weakness and cowardice, confine the actions of lesser men. And it must be remembered that the admitted great stain upon Nelson's fame, which it would be wicked to deny, lies not in a general looseness of life, but in the notoriety of one relation, — a notoriety due chiefly to the reckless singleness of heart which was not ashamed to own its love, but rather gloried in the public exhibition of a faith in the worthiness of its object, and a constancy, which never wavered to the hour of his death.[1] The pitifulness of

[1] The author is satisfied, from casual expressions in Nelson's letters to Lady Hamilton, that his famous two years' confinement to the ship, 1803–1805, and, to a less extent, the similar seclusion practised in the Baltic and the Downs, proceeded, in large part at least, from a romantic and chivalrous

it is to see the incongruity between such faith, such devotion, and the distasteful inadequacy of their object.

To answer the demands of a nature capable of such energetic manifestation — to fulfil the imagination of one who could so cast himself at the feet of an ideal — was beyond the gentle, well-ordered, and somewhat prosaic charms with which alone Mrs. Nisbet was invested by Nelson, even when most loverlike in tone. "My greatest wish," he writes in the first of his letters to her that has been preserved, "is to be united to you; and the foundation of all conjugal happiness, real love and esteem, is, I trust, what you believe I possess in the strongest degree toward you." Fifteen months later, and but a short time before their wedding, he says again : "His Royal Highness often tells me, he believes I am married; for he never saw a lover so easy, or say so little of the object he has a regard for. When I tell him I certainly am not, he says, 'Then he is sure I must have a great esteem for you, and that it is not what is (vulgarly), I do not much like the use of that word, called love.' He is right: my love is founded on esteem, the only foundation that can make the passion last." But general maxims, even when less disputable than this, do not admit of universal application ; and if an affection was to hold its own in a nature enthusiastic and imaginative as that of Nelson, it had need to strike root deeper than that surface soil indicated by mere esteem, at least when the latter rests simply upon an assemblage of upright and amiable qualities, and not upon that force of character which compels dependence as well as appreciation. At their last parting he solemnly avowed that his esteem was not lessened; while he was destined also to afford a conspicuous illustration of how enduring a passion may flourish where no just title to esteem exists.

The progress of his wooing was rapid enough. On the 12th of May he first mentions their meeting ; on the 28th of June he writes to his brother : "*Entre nous.* — Do not be surprised to hear I am a *Benedict*, for if at all, it will be before a month. Do not tell." On the 11th of September is dated his first letter to her, already quoted, in which he addresses her as "My dear Fanny," and alludes to the understanding existing

resolve to leave no room for doubt, in the mind of Lady Hamilton or of the world, that he was entirely faithful to her.

between them. At the expiration of six months he wrote, formally announcing his engagement, to Mr. William Suckling,
his mother's brother.   He anticipates the latter's doubts as to
the permanence of this fancy: "This Horatio, you will say, is
for ever in love;" but he considers that six months without
change settles that question.   "My present attachment is of
pretty long standing; but I was determined to be fixed before
I broke this matter to any person."   He then explains the situation, — that the lady herself has little or nothing; that Mr.
Herbert, though rich, is not likely to help the young couple
much, and he asks his uncle's assistance.   This Suckling consented to give, and for several years continued liberally to
extend. But still, impatient though Nelson always was to
complete whatever he had on hand, various causes delayed the
wedding for another year.   Even with Suckling's help the
question of means was pressing; and while, with pardonable
self-justification, he gloried to his betrothed that "the world
is convinced that I am superior to pecuniary considerations in
my public and private life, as in both instances I might have
been rich," he nevertheless owned to regretting that he "had
not given greater attention to making money."   Besides, as
he wrote to his brother, "What should I do carrying a wife
in a ship, and when I marry I do not mean to part with my
wife."   The cruising duty of the "Boreas" took her from
port to port of the limited area embraced in the Leeward
Islands Station, and Nevis was among the least important of
the points demanding his attention.   He was, therefore, frequently away from his betrothed during this period, and
absence rather fanned than cooled the impetuous ardor which
he carried into all his undertakings.   Whether it were the
pursuit of a love affair, or the chase of an enemy's fleet, delays served only to increase the vehemence with which Nelson
chafed against difficulties.   "Duty," he tells Mrs. Nisbet, "is
the great business of a sea officer, — all private considerations
must give way to it, however painful it is;" but he owns he
wishes "the American vessels at the Devil, and the whole
continent of America to boot," because they detain him from
her side.

  There is no singularity in the experience that obstacles tend
rather to inflame than to check a lover's eagerness.   What is

noteworthy in Nelson's letters at this time is the utter absence
of any illusions, of any tendency to exaggerate and glorify the
qualities of the woman who for the nonce possessed his heart.
There is not a sign of the perturbation of feeling, of the stirring of the soul, that was afterwards so painfully elicited
by another influence. "The dear object," he writes to his
brother, "you must like. Her sense, polite manners, and, to
you I may say, beauty, you will much admire. She possesses
sense far superior to half the people of our acquaintance, and
her manners are Mrs. Moutray's." The same calm, measured
tone pervades all his mention of her to others. His letters to
herself, on the other hand, are often pleasing in the quiet,
simple, and generally unaffected tenderness which inspires
them. In a more ordinary man, destined to more commonplace fortunes, they might well be regarded as promising that
enduring wedded love which strikes root downward and bears
fruit upward, steadily growing in depth and devotion as the
years roll by. But Nelson was not an ordinary man, and
from that more humble happiness a childless marriage further
debarred him. He could rise far higher, and, alas! descend
far lower as he followed the radiant vision, — the image of his
own mind rather than an external reality, — the ideal, which,
whether in fame or in love, beckoned him onward. The calm,
even, and wholly matter-of-fact appreciation of his wife's esti-
mable traits can now be seen in the light of his after career,
and its doubtful augury descried; for to idealize was an essential attribute of his temperament. Her failure, even in the
heyday of courtship, to arouse in him any extravagance of
emotion, any illusive exaltation of her merits, left vacant that
throne in his mind which could be permanently occupied only
by a highly wrought excellence, — even though that were the
purely subjective creation of his own enthusiasm. This hold
Lady Nelson never gained; and the long absence from 1793
to 1797, during the opening period of the war of the French
Revolution, probably did to death an affection which owed
what languid life it retained chiefly to propinquity and custom. Both Saumarez and Codrington, who served under him,
speak passingly of the lightness with which his family ties
sat upon Nelson in the years following his short stay at home
in 1797. The house was empty, swept, and garnished, when

the simple-minded, if lion-hearted, seaman came under the
spell of one whose fascinations had overpowered the resistance
of a cool-headed man of the world, leading him in his old age,
with open eyes, to do what every prepossession and every
reasonable conviction of his life condemned as folly.

In the summer of 1786 Sir Richard Hughes was recalled to
England.   During the later part of his association with
Nelson, the strain which had characterized their earlier relations had not only disappeared, but had been succeeded by
feelings approaching cordiality.   The Government's approval
of his subordinate's action, and of himself as credited with
supporting it, had removed that element of apprehension
which in timid men induces irritation; and Hughes, who,
though irresolute, was naturally kindly, had been still farther
placated by the prize-money falling to him from the vessels
condemned through the zeal of Nelson.   The latter, who never
harbored malice, easily forgave the past, and responded to this
change of tone.   "I have been upon the best terms with the
Admiral," he wrote from Barbadoes to his intended wife in
April, 1786, "and I declare I think I could ever remain so.
He is always remarkably kind and civil to every one;" and
again, a few days earlier, "The admiral is highly pleased with
my conduct here, as you will believe, by sending me such fine
lines with a white hat.   I well know I am not of abilities to
deserve what he has said of me: but I take it as they are
meant, to show his regard for me; and his politeness and
attention to me are great: nor shall I forget it.   I like the
man, although not all his acts."   He then directs that the
lines shall not be shown to any one, "as the compliment is
paid to me at the expense of the officers of the squadron," an
injunction thoroughly characteristic of the man's kindly consideration for others.   It was creditable to Hughes that, after
being so braved, and his instructions set at naught by his
junior, he had candor enough to see and acknowledge his
merit; but the fact still remained that in the hour of trial he
had failed Nelson, nor did the latter, though he forgave, forget it.   As he wrote to Locker in September, 1786, after the
admiral's departure, "Instead of being supported by my
admiral, I was obliged to keep him up, for he was frightened
at this business;" of which business he truly said, emphasiz-

ing, but not at all exaggerating, the gravity of the responsibility he had taken in defiance of his superior: "After loss of
health and risk of fortune, another is thanked for what I did
against his orders. *Either I deserved to be sent out of the
service,*[1] or at least to have had some little notice taken of
me."

Nelson indeed, in the West Indies, as an unknown captain,
had done that which as a junior admiral he did later at Copenhagen, at a moment far more critical to Great Britain. By
his own unusual powers of impulse and resolve he had enforced, as far as was possible against the passive, inert lethargy
— not to say timidity — of his superior, the course of action
which at the moment was essential to the interests of his
country. Truly great in his strength to endure, he knew not
the perturbations nor the vacillations that fret the temper,
and cripple the action, of smaller men ; and, however harassed
and distressed externally, the calmness of a clear insight and
an unshaken purpose guided his footsteps, unwavering, in the
path of duty, through all opposition, to the goal of success.
It is reported that an officer of the "Boreas," speaking to him
of the vexations and odium he had undergone, used the word
"pity." Nelson's reply showed the profound confidence which
throughout had animated him, keenly as he had undoubtedly
felt the temporary anxieties. "Pity, did you say ? I shall
live, Sir, to be envied; and to that point I shall always direct
my course."

By the departure of Sir Richard Hughes Nelson was left
senior officer upon the station until his own return home, a
twelvemonth later. In November he renewed his acquaintance with Prince William Henry, whom he had known as a
midshipman in 1782, and who now came to the Leeward
Islands a post-captain, in command of the frigate "Pegasus."
The two young men were not far apart in age, and an
intimacy between them soon arose, which ended only with the
death of Nelson. The latter had a profound reverence for
royalty, both as an institution and as represented in its mem-

[1] The author has italicized these words because they accurately express the
just penalty that military law would have required of Nelson, had he not
shown adequate grounds for his disobedience. They measure, therefore, the
responsibility he shouldered, and the reward he deserved.

bers; and to this, in the present case, was added a strong personal esteem, based upon the zeal and efficiency in the discharge of official duties, which he recognized in one whose rank would assure him impunity for any mere indifference. The prince, on the other hand, quickly yielded to the charm of Nelson's intercourse, so vividly felt by most who knew him, and to the contagious enthusiasm which animated his conversation when talking of his profession. This, also, his ardent imagination endowed with possibilities and aspirations, not greater, indeed, than its deserts, but which only the intuitions of a genius like his could realize and vivify, imparting to slower temperaments something of his own fire. To this association the prince afterwards attributed the awakening of that strong interest in maritime affairs which he retained to the day of his death. The two friends dined alternately one with the other, and, in their association of some six months at this time, they together fought over all the naval battles that during the recent war had illustrated the waters through which they were then cruising.

The incessant energy displayed by Nelson, and the agitations through which he passed during the three years of this stay upon the West Indian station, again produced distressing symptoms in his general health. To use his own words, the activity of the mind was "too much for my puny constitution." "I am worn to a skeleton," he writes to Mr. Suckling in July, 1786; and three months later to Locker, "I have been since June so very ill that I have only a faint recollection of anything which I did. My complaint was in my breast, such a one as I had going out to Jamaica [in 1777]. The Doctor thought I was in a consumption, and quite gave me up." This fear, however, proved unfounded; nor does there appear at any time to have been any serious trouble with his lungs.

On the 11th[1] of March, 1787, the marriage of Captain Nelson to Mrs. Nisbet took place at Nevis. Prince William Henry, whose rule it was never to visit in any private house, made an exception on this occasion, having exacted from

---

[1] Sir Harris Nicolas (Nelson's Despatches and Letters, vol. i. p. 217) gives March 12 as the day of the wedding, upon the ground of a letter of Lady Nelson's. Her mention of the date is, however, rather casual; and March 11 is given in the parish register of the church in Nevis.

Nelson a promise that the wedding should wait until he could be present; and he gave away the bride. Three months later, on the 7th of June, the "Boreas" sailed for England, and on the 4th of July anchored at Spithead. Whether Mrs. Nelson accompanied him in the ship does not appear certainly; but from several expressions in his letters it seems most probable that she did. Five days after his arrival he sent a message from her to Locker, in terms which indicate that she was with him.

A newly married man, who had just concluded a full cruise of such arduous and unremitting exertions, might reasonably have wished and expected a period of relaxation; but the return of the "Boreas" coincided with a very disturbed state of European politics. In the neighboring republic of Holland two parties were striving for the mastery; one of which was closely attached to France, the other, that of the Stadtholder, to Great Britain. In 1785 the former had gained the upper hand; and, by a treaty signed on Christmas Day of that year, a decided preponderance in the councils of the United Provinces had been given to France. The enfeebled condition of the latter country, however, had allowed little prospect of permanence to this arrangement; and in the summer of 1787, an insult offered by the French party to the wife of the Stadtholder led to a forcible intervention by the King of Prussia, whose sister she was. Louis XVI. prepared to support his partisans, and notified his purpose to Great Britain; whereupon the latter, whose traditional policy for over a century had been to resist the progress of French influence in the Low Countries, replied that she could not remain a quiet spectator, and at once began to arm. "The Dutch business," wrote Nelson, "is becoming every day more serious; and I hardly think we can keep from a war, without giving forever the weight of the Dutch to the French, and allowing the Stadtholdership to be abolished, — things which I should suppose hardly possible." Already his eager spirit was panting for the fray. "If we are to have a bustle, I do not want to come on shore; I begin to think I am fonder of the sea than ever." Only five months married!

The threatening aspect of affairs necessitated the "Boreas" being kept in commission, — the more so because the economies

5

introduced by Mr. Pitt into the administration of the two
military services had reduced the available naval force below
that which France could at once send out. "The Boreas is
kept in readiness to go to sea with the squadron at Spithead,"
wrote Nelson; " but in my poor opinion we shall go no further
at present. The French have eight sail in Brest water ready
for sea: therefore I think we shall not court the French out
of port,"— a singular illustration of the unreadiness of Great
Britain in the years immediately preceding the French Revolution. He looks for war, however, the following summer. As
not only ships, but men also, were urgently needed, the impress
service was hastily organized. His friend Locker was summoned from his long retirement to superintend that work in
Exeter, and the "Boreas" was ordered to the Thames on the
same business, arriving on the 20th of August at the Nore.
There her duty was to board passing vessels, and take from
them as many of their crew as were above the number barely
necessary for the safety of the ship. She herself, besides acting as receiving ship for the men thus pressed, was to be kept
in readiness to sail at a moment's warning. Mrs. Nelson had
therefore to leave her and go to London. " Here we are,"
wrote Nelson on the 23d of September, " laying seven miles
from the land on the Impress service, and I am as much separated from my wife as if I were in the East Indies;" and he
closes the letter with the words, "I am this moment getting
under sail after some ships."

His early biographers say that Nelson keenly felt and resented the kind of service in which he was then engaged; so
much so that, moved also by other causes of irritation, he
decided at one time to quit the Navy. No indication of such
feeling, however, appears in his letters. On the contrary, one
of the surest signs with him of pleasurable, or at least of interested, excitement was now manifested in his improving
health. As he himself said, many years later, "To say the
truth, when I am actively employed I am not so bad."[1]   A
month after reaching England, though then midsummer, he

[1] The same symptom will be noted in the anxious pursuit of Villeneuve to
the West Indies in 1805, where he grew better, although for some months he
had had in his hands the Admiralty's permission to return home on account of
his health.

wrote: "It is not kind in one's native air to treat a poor wanderer as it has me since my arrival. The rain and cold at first gave me a sore throat and its accompaniments; the hot weather has given me a slow fever, not absolutely bad enough to keep my bed, yet enough to hinder me from doing anything;" and again, "I have scarcely been able to hold up my head." In blustering October, on the other hand, while in the midst of the detested Impress work, he says: "My health, thank God, was never better, and I am fit for any quarter of the globe;" although "it rains hard, and we have had very bad weather of late." Whatever momentary vexation he may have vented in a hasty expression, it was entirely inconsistent with his general tone to take amiss an employment whose vital importance he would have been the first to admit. Lack of zeal, or haggling about the duty assigned him, was entirely foreign to his character; that the country needed the men who were to be pressed was reason sufficient for one of his temper. If, indeed, there had been an apparent intention to keep him in such inglorious occupation, and out of the expected war, he might have chafed; but his orders to be constantly ready indicated the intention to send him at once to the front, if hostilities began. Doubtless he was disappointed that the application he made for a ship-of-the-line was not granted; but he knew that, being still a very young captain, what he asked was a favor and its refusal not a grievance, nor does he seem to have looked upon it otherwise.

There were, however, some annoyances, which, joined to the lack of appreciation for his eminent services to the interests of the nation in the West Indies, must have keenly stung him. Without the slightest necessity, except that laid upon him by his own public spirit, he had fought and struggled, and endured three years of hot water to serve the Government. He might have gone easy, as did the admiral and the other captains; but instead of so doing he had destroyed the contraband trade, and re-established the working of laws upon which the prosperity and security of the kingdom were thought to depend. For this he had received a perfunctory, formal acknowledgment, though none apparently from the Admiralty, the head of his own service. But he soon found that, if slow to thank, they were prompt to blame, and that with no light hand nor disposition to make allowances. He had run his head against various regulations of the bureaucracy ; and this let him know, with all the amenities of official censure, that if they could not recognize what he had done well, they were perfectly clear-sighted as to where he had gone wrong.

So far from appreciation, there seems even to have been a prejudice against Nelson in high quarters, due not only to the discomposure felt by the routine official, at the rude irregularities of the man who is more concerned to do his work than nice about the formalities surrounding it, but also to misrepresentation by the powerful interests he had offended through his independent course in the West Indies. After Hughes had gone home, Nelson, as senior officer on the station, began to examine the modes of conducting government business, and especially of making purchases. Conceiving that there were serious irregularities in these, he suggested to the Civil Department of the Navy, under whose cognizance the transactions fell, some alterations in the procedure, by which the senior naval officer would have more control over the purchases than simply to certify that so much money was wanted. The Comptroller of the Navy replied that the old forms were sufficient, — "a circumstance which hurt me," wrote Nelson; while all the civil functionaries resented his interference with their methods, and seem to have received the tacit support, if not the direct sympathy, of the Navy Board, as the Civil Department was then called. His disposition to look into matters, however, had become known, and the long struggle over the contraband trade had given him in the islands a reputation for tenacity and success. It was probably in dependence upon these that two merchants came to him, two months before he left the station, and told him of the existence of very extensive frauds, dating back several years, in which were implicated both civil officials of the Navy and private parties on shore. It is possible that the informants themselves had shared in some of these transactions, and they certainly demanded in payment a part of the sums recovered; but, as Nelson truly said, the question was not as to their character, but how to stop the continuance of embezzlements which had then amounted to over two millions sterling.

The reports made by him upon this subject reached London about a month before the return of the "Boreas;" but the war scare, and the urgent call upon all departments of the Navy to mobilize the available force, prevented any immediate steps being taken. His letters were acknowledged, and the intention expressed to investigate the matter, but nothing more was then done. In October, however, the Prussian troops occupied Amsterdam, reinstating the Stadtholder in all his privileges, and restoring to power the partisans of Great Britain; while France remained passive, her power for external action paralyzed by the dying convulsions of the monarchy. The curtain had just risen upon the opening scene in the great drama of the Revolution, — the first Assembly of Notables. Warlike preparations consequently ceased, and on the 30th of November, 1787, the cruise of the "Boreas" came to an end.

It was during this last month of servitude, and immediately before quitting the ship, that Nelson is said to have used the vehement expressions of discontent with "an ungrateful service," recorded by his biographers, concluding with his resolve to go at once to London and resign his commission. In the absence of the faintest trace, in his letters, of dissatisfaction with the duty to which the ship was assigned, it is reasonable to attribute this exasperation to his soreness under the numerous reprimands he had received, — a feeling which plainly transpires in some of his replies, despite the forms of official respect that he scrupulously observed. Even in much later days, when his distinguished reputation might have enabled him to sustain with indifference this supercilious rudeness, he winced under it with over-sensitiveness. "Do not, my dear lord," he wrote to Earl Spencer a year after the battle of the Nile, "let the Admiralty write harshly to me — my generous soul cannot bear it, being conscious it is entirely unmerited." This freedom of censure, often felt by him to be undeserved, or at least excessive, and its sharp contrast with the scanty recognition of his unwearied efforts, — of whose value he himself was by no means forgetful, — though not unusual in the experience of officers, are quite sufficient to account for the sense of neglect and unjust treatment by which he was then outraged. This feeling was probably accentuated, also, by a renewal of the legal persecution

which had been begun in the West Indies; for towards the
end of the year he received formal notice of suits being instituted against him for the seizure of the American vessels, and
it is likely enough that some intimation of what was coming
reached him before leaving the "Boreas." Scanty thanks,
liberal blame, and the prospect of an expensive lawsuit based
upon his official action, constituted, for a poor man lately
married, causes of disturbance which might well have upset
his equanimity.

Lord Howe, who was then at the head of the Admiralty,
though formal and unbending in outward bearing, was a just
and kind man, and one fully appreciative of professional
worth. A mutual friend acquainted him with Nelson's irritation, and Howe wrote a private letter asking that he would
call upon him as soon as he came to town. Though quick to
resent, Nelson was easily soothed by attention and pleased by
compliment, even when it rose to flattery, — which Howe's
was not likely to do. A short interview gave the First Lord
a clearer idea than he before had of the extent, value, and
wholly voluntary character of the services rendered by the
young captain in the West Indies; and he indicated the completeness of his satisfaction by offering to present him to the
King, which was accordingly done at the next levee. George
III. received him graciously; and the resentment of Nelson,
whose loyalty was of the most extreme type, melted away in
the sunshine of royal favor.

Thus reconciled to the service, and convinced, as in his less
morbid moods he often said, that gratitude and honor, though
long deferred, were sure to follow upon steadfast performance
of duty, he speedily renewed his efforts to bring to light the
frauds practised in the colonies. His letters on the subject to
Mr. Pitt, the Prime Minister, had been turned over to the
Secretary of the Treasury, Mr. George Rose, and upon the
latter Nelson now called. Rose received him at first with
that courteous nonchalance which is the defensive armor of
the beset official, — the name of his visitor, and the business
with which it was connected, had for the moment slipped his
mind. Nelson's mastery of his subject, however, and his
warmth in it, soon roused the attention of his hearer, who,
being then pressed for time, asked to see him again the next

day, stipulating only that the interview should be early, before office hours. "It cannot be too early for me," replied Nelson, whose habit, in his career as admiral, was to get through his correspondence before eight o'clock, — "six o'clock, if you please."

The arrangement was so made, and the consequent meeting lasted from six to nine the next morning. Of its general nature and results we have an authentic outline, given in later years to Nelson's biographers by Rose, who became, and to the last remained, his warm personal friend. The conversation ranged, apparently, over all the chief occurrences in the West Indies during the cruise of the "Boreas," including both the naval frauds and the contraband trade. The breadth and acuteness of Nelson's intellect have been too much overlooked, in the admiration excited by his unusually grand moral endowments of resolution, dash, and fearlessness of responsibility. Though scarcely what could be called an educated man, he was one of close and constant observation, thereby gaining a great deal of information; and to the use of this he brought a practical sagacity, which coped with the civil or political questions placed before it, *for action*, much as it did with military questions — for, after all, good generalship, on its intellectual side, is simply the application, to the solution of a military problem, of a mind naturally gifted therefor, and stored with experience, either personal or of others. As a strategist and tactician, Nelson made full proof of high native endowments, of wisdom garnered through fruitful study and meditation, and of clear insight into the determining conditions of the various military situations with which he had to deal. To Mr. Rose, the young captain of barely thirty years displayed a precise knowledge of several political subjects, connected with the commerce of the country, that would not naturally come under his notice as an officer, and which therefore the mere seaman would probably not have imbibed. Not only so, but his suggestions for dealing practically with the interests at stake were so judicious, that Rose, a valued associate of Pitt and intimately acquainted with the financial measures of that brilliant administrator, complimented him warmly upon the justice and correctness of his views, the result, as they were, of reflection based upon a mastery of the data involved. With Nelson's consent, he undertook to lay them before the prime minister, as the direct testimony of a singularly competent first-hand observer.

It is to be noted, however, of Nelson, that this accuracy of mental perception, this power of penetrating to the root of a matter, disregarding unessential details and fastening solely on decisive features, was largely dependent upon the necessity laid upon him for action; which is probably equivalent to saying that it was usually elicited by a sobering sense of responsibility. In his letters and despatches may be found many wild guesses, inconsistent from week to week, colored by changing moods and humors, — the mere passing comments of a mind off guard, — the records of evanescent impressions as numerous, fickle, and unfounded as those of the most ordinary mortal. It is when urgency presses and danger threatens, when the need for action comes, that his mental energies are aroused, and he begins to speak, as it were, *ex cathedrâ*. Then the unsubstantial haze rolls away, and the solid features of the scene one by one appear, until, amid all the unavoidable uncertainties of imperfect information, it becomes plain that the man has a firm grasp upon the great landmarks by which he must guide his course. Like the blind, who at first saw men as trees walking, and then saw everything clearly, so his mental illumination gradually reduces confusion to order, and from perplexity evolves correct decision. But what shall be said of those flashes of insight, as at Cape St. Vincent, elicited in a moment, as by the stroke of iron on rock, where all the previous processes of ordered thought and labored reasoning are condensed into one vivid inspiration, and transmuted without a pause into instant heroic action? Is that we call "genius" purely a mystery, of which our only account is to give it a name? Or is it true, as Napoleon said, that "on the field of battle the happiest inspiration is often but a recollection"?

From Rose Nelson went to the Comptroller of the Navy, Sir Charles Middleton, who afterwards, as Lord Barham, sent him forth to Trafalgar. Middleton had replied promptly to the first report of the fraudulent transactions, giving assurance of his readiness to act, and urging that all the information possible should be secured, as he feared that the allegations were substantially true. He now showed the instructions of the Navy Board, under which its colonial employees acted, to Nelson, who said that, if honestly followed, they must prevent the unlawful practices; but that he believed they were habitually violated, and that he himself, though senior officer on the station, had never before seen the instructions. This failure to intrust supervision to the one person upon whom all responsibility should ultimately have rested, practically neutralized the otherwise laudable methods prescribed by the Board. It was simply another instance of the jealousy between the civil and military branches of the naval organization, which, as is well known, resulted in constant strained relations between the Admiralty and the Naval Commissioners, until the latter Board was at last abolished.

It is, fortunately, unnecessary to follow farther this dreary record of old-time dishonesty. Nelson continued to interest himself strenuously in the matter for two years after his return to England, both by letter and interview with persons in authority. His own position and influence were too insignificant to effect anything, except by moving the home officials, whose administration was compromised and embarrassed by the malpractices of their representatives. Though up-hill work, it was far from fruitless. "His representations," said Mr. Rose, in a memorandum furnished to his biographers, "were all attended to, and every step which he recommended was adopted. He thus put the investigation into a proper course; which ended in the detection and punishment of some of the parties whose conduct was complained of." The broad result appears to have been that the guilty for the most part escaped punishment, unless, indeed, some of them lost their positions, of which no certain information exists; but the corrupt combination was broken up, and measures were adopted to prevent the recurrence of the same iniquities. Upon Nelson himself the effect was twofold. His energy and intelligence could not fail to impress the powerful men with whom he was in this way brought into contact. The affair increased his reputation, and made him more widely known than as a simple captain in the Navy he

would otherwise have been. As the various public Boards
whose money had been stolen realized the amount of the
thefts, and the extent of the conspiracy to rob the Government, they felt their obligations to him, and expressed them
in formal, but warm, letters of thanks. On the other hand,
the principal culprits had command of both money and influence; and by means of these, as so often happens, they
not only impeded inquiry, but, according to Southey, who
wrote not very long after the events, "succeeded in raising
prejudices against Nelson at the Board of Admiralty which
it was many years before he could subdue." Clarke and
M'Arthur make the same assertion.

That these prejudices did at one time exist is beyond
doubt, and that they should have been fostered by this
means is perfectly in keeping with common experience.
Such intrigues, however, work in the dark and by in-
direction; it is not often easy to trace their course. The
independence and single-mindedness with which Nelson followed his convictions, and the outspoken frankness with
which he expressed his views and feelings, not improbably
gave a handle to malicious misrepresentation. His known
intimacy with Prince William Henry, upon whose favor he
to some extent relied, was also more likely to do him harm
than good; and he entertained for the royal captain prepossessions not far removed from partisanship, at a time
when the prince avowed himself not a friend to the present
minister. "Amidst that variety of business which demanded
his attention on his return to England," say his biographers,
"he failed not, by every means in his power, to fulfil the
promise which he had made to his Royal Highness Prince
William of counteracting whatever had been opposed to the
merited reputation of his illustrious pupil, and to the friendship they had invariably preserved for each other." It was
a difficult task. Opinionated and headstrong as the King,
his father, the young man was an uneasy subordinate to the
Admiralty, and made those above him realize that he was
full as conscious of his personal rank as of his official position as a captain in the Navy. It was, indeed, this self-
assertive temperament that afterwards frustrated his natural
ambition to be the active head of the service. Having such

an ally, there is something ominous for Nelson's own prospects to find him writing in evident sympathy : "The great folks above now see he will not be a cypher, therefore many of the rising people must submit to act subordinate to him, which is not so palatable ; and I think a Lord of the Admiralty is hurt to see him so able, after what he has said about him. He has certainly not taken a leaf out of his book, for he is steady in his command and not violent." Upon this follows, "He has wrote Lord Hood what I cannot but approve," — a sentence unquestionably vague, but which sounds combative. Nelson had already felt it necessary to caution the prince to be careful in the choice of those to whom he told his mind.

In fact, at the time when the letter just quoted was written, the conduct of the prince had been such as necessarily, and not wholly unjustly, to prejudice an officer who displayed marked partisanship for him, such as certainly was indicated by Nelson's expressions. He had brought his ship from Newfoundland to Ireland in flat disobedience of orders, issued by the commander of the station, to go to Quebec. When this action became known to the Admiralty by his arrival at Cork, in December, 1787, it was at once reported to the King, who himself directed that the prince should proceed to Plymouth with his ship, should remain within the limits of the port for as many months as he had been absent from his station, and should then be sent back to Halifax. The Prince of Wales, afterwards George IV., who was already at variance with the King, took advantage of this flagrant breach of discipline to flaunt his opposition before the world. In company with his second brother, the Duke of York, he went down to Plymouth, and paid a ceremonious visit to Prince William on board his ship. The round of festivities necessitated by their presence emphasized the disagreement between the sovereign and the heir to the throne, and drew to it public attention. Immediately after this, in January, 1788, Nelson also visited the prince, having been summoned by him from London. He could, indeed, scarcely decline, nor was he at all the man to turn his back on a friend in difficulty, but, in his fight against corruption, the matter could scarcely fail to be represented by his opponents under the worst light to the King, to whom

corruption was less odious than insubordination. If, in conversation, Nelson uttered such expressions as he wrote to his
friend Locker, he had only himself to blame for the disfavor
which followed; for, to a naval officer, the prince's conduct
should have appeared absolutely indefensible. In the course
of the same year the King became insane, and the famous
struggle about the Regency took place. The prince had meantime returned to America, in accordance with his orders, and
by the time he again reached England the King had recovered.
He could, therefore, have refrained from any indication of his
own sympathies; but instead of this he openly associated
himself with the party of the Prince of Wales, whose course
throughout, when it became known to his father, had bitterly
displeased the latter, and accentuated the breach between them.
At a banquet given by the Spanish ambassador in celebration
of the King's recovery, the three princes sat at a table separate
from the rest of the royal family. A formal reconciliation
took place in September, 1789; but the Duke of Clarence, as
he had then become, continued attached to the Prince of
Wales's clique. Those who know how party considerations
influenced naval appointments at that time, will in these facts
find at least a partial explanation of the cloud which then
hung over Nelson.

Lord Chatham, brother of the minister to whom Prince
William was not a friend, became head of the Admiralty in
July, 1788, and so remained until after the war with France
began in 1793. With him was associated Lord Hood, between
whom and Nelson there arose what the latter called "a difference of opinion," which led to a cessation of "familiar
correspondence." The exact date at which this occurred does
not appear, but it was probably before May, 1790; for Hood
refused to use his influence to get Nelson a ship, in the armament which was then ordered on account of a difficulty with
Spain, whereas eighteen months before he had assured him
that in case of hostilities he need not fear not having a good
ship. This refusal was the more marked, because "almost
the whole service was then called out." On the same occasion,
Nelson wrote, " he made a speech never to be effaced from my
memory, viz.: that the King was impressed with an unfavourable opinion of me." Knowing Nelson's value as an officer as

well as Hood did, there can scarcely remain a doubt that some
serious indiscretion, real or imagined, must have caused this
alienation ; but of what it was there is no trace, unless in his
evident siding with the prince, who was then out of favor with
both the King and the administration.

The five years — from 1788 to 1792 inclusive — intervening
between the cruise of the "Boreas" and the outbreak of war
with the French Republic, were thus marked by a variety of
unpleasant circumstances, of which the most disagreeable, to
a man of Nelson's active temperament, was the apparently
fixed resolve of the authorities to deny him employment. He
was harassed, indeed, by the recurring threats of prosecution
for the West India seizures ; but both the Admiralty and the
Treasury agreed that he should be defended at the expense of
the Crown, — a fact which tends to show that his subsequent
disfavor arose from some other cause than disapproval of his
official action, however some incidents may have been misrepresented. On its private side, his life during this period seems
to have been happy, though uneventful; but in the failure of
children he was deprived, both then and afterwards, of that
sweetest of interests, continuous yet ever new in its gradual
unfolding, which brings to the most monotonous existence its
daily tribute of novelty and incident. The fond, almost rap-
turous, expressions with which he greeted the daughter afterwards born to him out of wedlock, show the blank in his home,
— none the less real because not consciously realized.

The lack of stimulus to his mind from his surroundings at
this time is also manifested by the fewness of his letters. But
thirty remain to show his occupation during the five years, and
seventeen of these are purely official in character. From the
year 1791 no record survives. His wife being with him, one
line of correspondence was thereby closed; but even to his
brother, and to his friend Locker, he finds nothing to write.
For the ordinary country amusements and pursuits of the
English gentry he had scant liking ; and, barring the occasional
worry over his neglect by the Admiralty, there was little else
to engage his attention. The first few months after his release
from the "Boreas" were spent in the West of England, chiefly
at Bath, for the recovery of Mrs. Nelson's health as well as
his own ; but toward the latter part of 1788 the young couple

went to live with his father at the parsonage of Burnham Thorpe, and there made their home until he was again called into active service. "It is extremely interesting," say his biographers, "to contemplate this great man, when thus removed from the busy scenes in which he had borne so distinguished a part to the remote village of Burnham Thorpe;" but the interest seems by their account to be limited to the energy with which he dug in the garden, or, from sheer want of something to do, reverted to the bird-nesting of his boyhood. His favorite amusement, we are told, was coursing, and he once shot a partridge; but his habit of carrying his gun at full cock, and firing as soon as a bird rose, without bringing the piece to his shoulder, made him a dangerous companion in a shooting-party. His own account is somewhat different: "Shoot I cannot, therefore I have not taken out a license; but notwithstanding the neglect I have met with I am happy;" and again, to his brother, he says: "It was not my intention to have gone to the coursing meeting, for, to say the truth, I have rarely escaped a wet jacket and a violent cold; besides, to me, even the ride to the Smee is longer than any pleasure I find in the sport will compensate for." The fact is that Nelson cared for none of these things, and the only deduction of real interest from his letters at this time is the absolute failure of his home life and affections to content his aspirations, — the emptiness both of mind and heart, which caused his passionate eagerness for external employment to fill the void. Earnestness appears only when he is brooding over the slight with which he was treated, and the resultant thwarting of his career. For both mind and heart the future held in store for him the most engrossing emotions, but it did not therefore bring him happiness.

Of his frames of mind during this period of neglect and disfavor, his biographers give a very strongly colored picture, for which, it is to be presumed, they drew upon contemporary witnesses that were to them still accessible. "With a mortified and dejected spirit, he looked forward to a continuance of inactivity and neglect. . . . During this interval of disappointment and mortification, his latent ambition would at times burst forth, and despise all restraint. At others, a sudden melancholy seemed to overshadow his noble faculties, and to affect his temper; at those moments the remonstrances

of his wife and venerable father alone could calm the tempest
of his passions." That Nelson keenly felt the cold indifference he now underwent, is thoroughly in keeping with the
sensitiveness to censure, expressed or implied, which his correspondence frequently betrays, while his frail organization
and uncertain health would naturally entail periods of depression or nervous exasperation; but the general tenor of his
letters, few as they at this time were, shows rather dignified
acceptance of a treatment he had not merited, and a steady
resolve not to waver in his readiness to serve his country, nor
to cease asking an opportunity to do so. Many years later, at
a time of still more sickening suspense, he wrote: "I am in
truth half dead, but what man can do shall be done, — I am
not made to despair; " and now, according to a not improbable
story, he closed an application for employment with the
words, "If your Lordships should be pleased to appoint me
to a cockle boat, I shall feel grateful." Hood, whose pupil he
in a sense was, and who shared his genius, said of himself,
when under a condition of enforced inactivity: "This proves
very strongly the different frames of men's minds; some are
full of anxiety, impatience, and apprehension, while others,
under similar circumstances, are perfectly cool, tranquil, and
indifferent."

The latter half of the year 1792 was marked by the rapid
progress in France of the political distemper, which was so
soon to culminate in the worst excesses of the Revolution.
The quick succession of symptoms, each more alarming than
the other, — the suspension of the royal power at the tumult-
uous bidding of a mob, the September massacres, the abolition
of royalty, the aggressive character of the National Convention
shown by the decrees of November 19 and December 15, —
roused the apprehensions of most thoughtful men throughout
Europe; and their concern was increased by the growing
popular effervescence in other countries than France. The
British cabinet, as was natural, shifted more slowly than did
the irresponsible members of the community; nor could Pitt
lightly surrender his strong instinctive prepossessions in
favor of peace, with the continuance of which was identified
the exercise of his own best powers.

During this stormy and anxious period, Nelson shared the

feelings of his day and class. It is noteworthy, however, that, in regarding the perils of the time, he was no mere panic-monger, but showed the same discriminating carefulness of observation that had distinguished him as captain of the "Boreas," and had elicited the admiration of Mr. Rose. Strenuous and even bigoted royalist as he always was, satisfied of the excellence of the British Constitution, and condemning utterly the proceedings of the more or less seditious societies then forming throughout the kingdom, he yet recognized the substantial grievances of the working-men, as evident in the district immediately under his eye. The sympathetic qualities which made him, fortune's own favorite in his profession, keenly alive to the hardships, neglect, and injustice undergone by the common seaman, now engaged him to set forth the sad lot of the ill-paid rural peasantry. In his letters to the Duke of Clarence, he on the one hand strongly blames the weakness and timidity of the justices and country gentlemen, in their attitude towards the abettors of lawlessness ; but, on the other, he dwells upon the sufferings of the poor, prepares a careful statement of their earnings and unavoidable expenses, and insists upon the necessity of the living wage. The field laborers, he said, "do not want loyalty, many of their superiors, in many instances, might have imitated their conduct to advantage; but hunger is a sharp thorn, and they are not only in want of food sufficient, but of clothes and firing."

Under the threatening outlook, he considers that every individual will soon "be called forth to show himself; " and for his own part, he writes on the 3d of November, he sees no way so proper as asking for a ship. But, even at that late moment, neither Pitt nor his associates had abandoned the hope of peace, and this, as well as other applications of Nelson's, received only a formal acknowledgment without encouragement. Roused, however, by the Convention's decree of November 19, which extended the succor of France to all people who should wish to recover their liberty, and charged the generals of the republic to make good the offer with the forces under their command, the ministry decided to abandon their guarded attitude ; and their new resolution was confirmed by the reception, on the 28th of November, of deputations from British revolutionary societies at the bar of the Convention, on which occasion the president of the latter affected to draw a dividing line between the British government and the British nation. On the 1st of December the militia was called out by proclamation, and Parliament summoned to meet on the 15th of the month. On the latter day the Convention put forth another decree, announcing in the most explicit terms its purpose to overthrow all existing governments in countries where the Republican armies could penetrate. Pitt now changed his front with an instantaneousness and absoluteness which gave the highest proof of his capacity as a leader of men. It was not so much that war was then determined, as that the purpose was formed, once for all, to accept the challenge contained in the French decree, unless France would discontinue her avowed course of aggression. Orders were immediately given to increase largely the number of ships of war in commission.

When danger looms close at hand, the best men, if known, are not left in the cold shade of official disfavor. " Post nubila Phœbus," was the expression of Nelson, astonished for a rarity into Latin by the suddenness with which the sun now burst upon him through the clouds. " The Admiralty so smile upon me, that really I am as much surprised as when they frowned." On the 6th of January, 1793, the First Lord, with many apologies for previous neglect, promised to give him a seventy-four-gun ship as soon as it was in his power to do so, and that meanwhile, if he chose to take a sixty-four, he could have one as soon as she was ready. On the 30th he was appointed to the " Agamemnon," of the latter rate. Within the preceding fortnight Louis XVI. had been beheaded, and the French ambassador ordered to leave England. On February 1, 1793, two days after Nelson's orders were issued, the Republic declared war against Great Britain and Holland.

6

CHAPTER III.

FEBRUARY–DECEMBER, 1793. AGE, 34.

NELSON'S page in history covers a little more than twelve years, from February, 1793, to October, 1805. Its opening coincides with the moment when the wild passions of the French Revolution, still at fiercest heat, and which had hitherto raged like flame uncontrolled, operative only for destruction, were being rapidly mastered, guided, and regulated for efficient work, by the terrors of the Revolutionary Tribunal and the Committee of Public Safety. In the object to which these tremendous forces were now about to be applied lay the threat to the peace of Europe, which aroused Great Britain to action, and sent into the field her yet unknown champion from the Norfolk parsonage. The representatives of the French people had imparted to the original movement of their nation, — which aimed only at internal reforms, however radical, — a new direction, of avowed purposeful aggression upon all political institutions exterior to, and differing from, their own. This became the one characteristic common to the successive forms of government, which culminated in the pure military despotism of Napoleon.

To beat back that spirit of aggression was the mission of Nelson. Therein is found the true significance of his career, which mounts higher and higher in strenuous effort and gigantic achievement, as the blast of the Revolution swells fiercer and stronger under the mighty impulse of the great Corsican. At each of the momentous crises, so far removed in time and place, — at the Nile, at Copenhagen, at Trafalgar, — as the unfolding drama of the age reveals to the onlooker the schemes of the arch-planner about to touch success, over against Napoleon rises ever Nelson; and as the latter in the hour of victory drops upon the stage where he has played so chief a part, his task is seen to be accomplished, his triumph secured. In the very act of dying he has dealt the foe a blow from which recovery is impossible. Moscow and Waterloo are the inevitable consequences of Trafalgar; as the glories of that day were but the fit and assured ending of the illustrious course which was begun upon the quarter-deck of the " Agamemnon."

With the exception of the " Victory," under whose flag he fell after two years of arduous, heartbreaking uncertainties, no ship has such intimate association with the career and name of Nelson as has the "Agamemnon." And this is but natural, for to her he was the captain, solely, simply, and entirely; identified with her alone, glorying in her excellences and in her achievements, one in purpose and in spirit with her officers and seamen; sharing their hopes, their dangers, and their triumphs; quickening them with his own ardor, moulding them into his own image, until vessel and crew, as one living organism, reflected in act the heroic and unyielding energy that inspired his feeble frame. Although, for a brief and teeming period, he while in command of her controlled also a number of smaller vessels on detached service, it was not until after he had removed to another ship that he became the squadron-commander, whose relations to the vessel on which he himself dwelt were no longer immediate, nor differed, save in his bodily presence, from those he bore to others of the same division. A personality such as Nelson's makes itself indeed felt throughout its entire sphere of action, be that large or small; but, withal, diffusion contends in vain with the inevitable law that forever couples it with slackening power, nor was it possible even for him to lavish on the various units of a fleet, and on the diverse conflicting claims of a great theatre of war, the same degree of interest and influence that he concentrated upon the "Agamemnon," and upon the brilliant though contracted services through which he carried her. Bonds such as these are not lightly broken, and to the " Agamemnon " Nelson clave for three long years and more, persistently refusing larger ships, until the exhausted hulk could no longer respond to the demands of her masters, and separation became inevitable. When he quitted her, at the moment of her departure for England, it was simply a question whether he would abandon the Mediterranean, and the prospect of a great future there opening before him, or sever a few weeks earlier a companionship which must in any event end upon her arrival home.

There is yet another point of view from which his command of the "Agamemnon" is seen to hold a peculiar relation to Nelson's story. This was the period in which expectation passed into fulfilment, when development, long arrested by unpropitious circumstances, resumed its outward progress under the benign influence of a favoring environment, and the bud, whose rare promise had long been noted by a few discerning eyes, unfolded into the brilliant flower, destined in the magnificence of its maturity to draw the attention of a world. To the fulness of his glorious course these three years were what the days of early manhood are to ripened age; and they are marked by the same elasticity, hopefulness, and sanguine looking to the future that characterize youth, before illusions vanish and even success is found to disappoint. Happiness was his then, as at no other time before or after; for the surrounding conditions of enterprise, of difficulties to be overcome, and dangers to be met, were in complete correspondence with those native powers that had so long struggled painfully for room to exert themselves. His health revived, and his very being seemed to expand in this congenial atmosphere, which to him was as life from the dead. As with untiring steps he sped onward and upward, — counting naught done while aught remained to do, forgetting what was behind as he pressed on to what was before, — the ardor of pursuit, the delight of achievement, the joy of the giant running his course, sustained in him that glow of animation, that gladness in the mere fact of existence, physical or moral, in which, if anywhere, this earth's content is found. Lack of recognition, even, wrung from him only the undaunted words: "Never mind! some day I will have a gazette of my own." Not till his dreams were realized, till aspiration had issued in the completest and most brilliant triumph ever wrought upon the seas, and he had for his gazette the loud homage of every mouth in Europe, — not till six months after the battle of the

Nile, — did Nelson write : "There is no true happiness in this life, and in my present state I could quit it with a smile. My only wish is to sink with honour into the grave."

The preparation of the Mediterranean fleet, to which the "Agamemnon" was assigned, was singularly protracted, and in the face of a well-ordered enemy the delay must have led to disastrous results. Nelson himself joined his ship at Chatham on the 7th of February, a week after his orders were issued; but not until the 16th of March did she leave the dockyard, and then only for Sheerness, where she remained four weeks longer. By that time it seems probable, from remarks in his letters, that the material equipment of the vessel was complete; but until the 14th of April she remained over a hundred men short of her complement. "Yet, I think," wrote Nelson, "that we shall be far from ill-manned, even if the rest be not so good as they ought to be." Mobilization in those days had not been perfected into a science, even in theory, and the difficulty of raising crews on the outbreak of war was experienced by all nations, but by none more than by Great Britain. Her wants were greatest, and for supply depended upon a merchant service scattered in all quarters of the globe. "Men are very hard to be got," Nelson said to his brother, "and without a press I have no idea that our fleet can be manned." It does not appear that this crude and violent, yet unavoidable, method was employed for the "Agamemnon," except so far as her crew was completed from the guard-ship. Dependence was placed upon the ordinary wiles of the recruiting-sergeant, and upon Nelson's own popularity in the adjacent counties of Suffolk and Norfolk, from which the bulk of his ship's company was actually drawn. "I have sent out a lieutenant and four midshipmen," he writes to Locker, "to get men at every seaport in Norfolk, and to forward them to Lynn and Yarmouth; my friends in Yorkshire and the North tell me they will send what men they can lay hands on;" but at the same time he hopes that Locker, then Commander-in-chief at the Nore, will not turn away any who from other districts may present themselves for the "Agamemnon." Coming mainly from the same neighborhood gave to the crew a certain homogeneousness of character, affording ground for appeal to local pride, a most powerful incentive in moments of difficulty and emulation; and this feeling was enhanced by the thought that their captain too was a Norfolk man. To one possessing the sympathetic qualities of Nelson, who so readily shared the emotions and gained the affections of his associates, it was easy to bind into a living whole the units animated by this common sentiment.

His step-son, Josiah Nisbet, at this time about thirteen years old, now entered the service as a midshipman, and accompanied him on board the "Agamemnon." The oncoming of a great war naturally roused to a yet higher pitch the impulse towards the sea, which in all generations has stirred the blood of English boys. Of these, Nelson, using his captain's privilege, received a number as midshipmen upon his quarter-deck, among them several from the sons of neighbors and friends, and therefore, like the crew, Norfolk lads. It is told that to one, whose father he knew to be a strong Whig, of the party which in the past few years had sympathized with the general current of the French Revolution, he gave the following pithy counsels for his guidance in professional life: "First, you must always implicitly obey orders, without attempting to form any opinion of your own respecting their propriety; secondly, you must consider every man as your enemy who speaks ill of your king; and thirdly, you must hate a Frenchman as you do the devil." On the last two items Nelson's practice was in full accord with his precept; but to the first, his statement of which, sound enough in the general, is open to criticism as being too absolute, he was certainly not obedient. Not to form an opinion is pushing the principle of subordination to an indefensible extreme, even for a junior officer, though the caution not to express it is wise, as well as becoming to the modesty of youth. Lord Howe's advice to Codrington, to watch carefully all that passed and to form his own conclusions, but to keep them to himself, was in every respect more reasonable and profitable. But in fact this dictum of Nelson's was simply another instance of hating the French as he did the devil. The French were pushing independence and private judgment to one extreme, and he instinctively adopted the other.

It was not till near the end of April that the "Agamemnon" finally left the Thames, anchoring at Spithead on the

28th of that month. Still the fleet which Lord Hood was to command was not ready. While awaiting her consorts, the ship made a short cruise in the Channel, and a few days later sailed as one of a division of five ships-of-the-line under Admiral Hotham, to occupy a station fifty to a hundred miles west of the Channel Islands. Nelson's disposition not to form any opinion of his own respecting the propriety of orders was thus evidenced: "What we have been sent out for is best known to the great folks in London: to us, it appears, only to hum the nation and make tools of us, for where we have been stationed no enemy was likely to be met with, or where we could protect our own trade." There can be no doubt that not only was the practical management of the Navy at this time exceedingly bad, but that no sound ideas even prevailed upon the subject. Hotham's squadron gained from neutral vessels two important pieces of information, — that Nantes, Bordeaux, and L'Orient were filled with English vessels, prizes to French cruisers; and that the enemy kept eight sail-of-the-line, with frigates in proportion, constantly moving in detachments about the Bay of Biscay. Under the dispositions adopted by the British Admiralty, these hostile divisions gave, to the commerce destroying of the smaller depredators, a support that sufficiently accounts for the notorious sufferings of British trade during the opening years of the war. Nelson had no mastery of the terminology of warfare, — he never talked about strategy and little about tactics, — but, though without those valuable aids to precision of thought, he had pondered, studied, and reasoned, and he had, besides, what is given to few, — real genius and insight. Accordingly he at once pierced to the root of the trouble, — the enemy's squadrons, rather than the petty cruisers dependent upon them, to which the damage was commonly attributed. "They are always at sea, and England not willing to send a squadron to interrupt them." But, while instancing this intuitive perception of a man gifted with rare penetration, it is necessary to guard against rash conclusions that might be drawn from it, and to remark that it by no means follows that education is unnecessary to the common run of men, because a genius is in advance of his times. It is well also to note that even in him this flash of

insight, though unerring in its indications, lacked the definiteness of conviction which results from ordered thought.
However accurate, it is but a glimmer, — not yet a fixed
light.

Hotham's division joined the main body under Lord Hood,
off the Scilly Islands, on the 23d of May, the total force then
consisting of eleven sail-of-the-line, with the usual smaller
vessels. It remained cruising in that neighborhood until the
6th of June, keeping the approaches of the Channel open for
a homeward-bound convoy of merchantmen, which passed on
that day. The fleet then bore up for the Straits, and on the
14th six ships, the " Agamemnon " among them, parted company for Cadiz, there to fill up with water, in order to avoid
the delays which would arise if the scanty resources of Gibraltar had to supply all the vessels. On the 23d this division
left Cadiz, reaching Gibraltar the same evening ; and on the
27th Hood, having now with him fifteen of the line, sailed
for Toulon.

Nelson's mind was already busy with the prospects of the
campaign, and the various naval factors that went to make
up the military situation. " Time must discover what we are
going after," he writes to his brother; while to Locker he
propounds the problem which always has perplexed the
British mind, and still does, — how to make the French
fight, if they are unwilling. So long as that question remains unsolved, the British government has to bear the
uncertainties, exposure, and expense of a difficult and protracted defensive. " We have done nothing," he says, "and
the same prospect appears before us : the French cannot
come out, and we have no means of getting at them in Toulon." In "cannot come out," he alludes to the presence of
a Spanish fleet of twenty-four ships-of-the-line. This, in
conjunction with Hood's force, would far exceed the French
in Toulon, which the highest estimate then placed at
twenty-one of the line. He had, however, already measured
the capabilities of the Spanish Navy. They have very fine
ships, he admits, but they are shockingly manned, — so much
so that if only the barges' crews of the six British vessels
that entered Cadiz, numbering at the most seventy-five to a
hundred men, but all picked, could have got on board one of

their first-rates, he was certain they could have captured her, although her ship's company numbered nearly a thousand. "If those we are to meet in the Mediterranean are no better manned," he continues, "much service cannot be expected of them." The prediction proved true, for no sooner did Hood find the Spanish admiral than the latter informed him he must go to Cartagena, having nineteen hundred sick in his fleet. The officer who brought this message said it was no wonder they were sickly, for they had been sixty days at sea. This excited Nelson's derision — not unjustly. "From the circumstance of having been longer than that time at sea, do we attribute our getting healthy. It has stamped with me the extent of their nautical abilities: long may they remain in their present state." The last sentence reveals his intuitive appreciation of the fact that the Spain of that day could in no true sense be the ally of Great Britain; for, at the moment he penned the wish, the impotence or defection of their allies would leave the British fleet actually inferior to the enemy in those waters. He never forgot these impressions, nor the bungling efforts of the Spaniards to form a line of battle. Up to the end of his life the prospect of a Spanish war involved no military anxieties, but only the prospect of more prize money.

Among the various rumors of that troubled time, there came one that the French were fitting their ships with forges to bring their shot to a red heat, and so set fire to the enemy's vessel in which they might lodge. Nelson was promptly ready with a counter and quite adequate tactical move. "This, if true," he wrote, "I humbly conceive would have been as well kept secret; but as it is known, we must take care to get so close that their red shots may go *through* both sides, when it will not matter whether they are hot or cold." This sentence is among the most characteristic occurring at this period in Nelson's correspondence; indicative of the continuous mental activity which, throughout his career, sought to anticipate difficulties, and to devise means of meeting them.

On the 14th of July Nelson notes that the fleet had received orders to consider Marseilles and Toulon as invested, and to take all vessels of whatever nation bound into those ports. He at once recognized the importance of this step, and the accurate judgment that dictated it. The British could not, as he said, get at the enemy in his fortified harbor; but they might by this means exercise the pressure that would force him to come out. Undoubtedly, whether on a large or on a small scale, whether it concern the whole plan of a war or of a campaign, or merely the question of a single military position, the best way to compel an unwilling foe to action, and to spoil his waiting game which is so onerous to the would-be assailant, is to attack him elsewhere, to cut short his resources, and make his position untenable by exhaustion. "This has pleased us," Nelson wrote; "if we make these red-hot gentlemen hungry, they may be induced to come out."

The investment by sea of these two harbors, but especially of Toulon, as being an important dockyard, was accordingly the opening move made by the British admiral. On the 16th of July he approached the latter port, and from that time until August 25 a close blockade was maintained, with the exception of a very few days, during which Hood took the fleet off Nice, and thence to Genoa, to remonstrate with that republic upon its supplying the south of France with grain, and bringing back French property under neutral papers. "Our being here is a farce if this trade is allowed," said Nelson, and rightly; for so far as appearances then went, the only influence the British squadrons could exert was by curtailing the supplies of southern France. That district raised only grain enough for three months' consumption; for the remainder of the year's food it depended almost wholly upon Sicily and Barbary, its communications with the interior being so bad that the more abundant fields of distant French provinces could not send their surplus.

In the chaotic state in which France was then plunged, the utmost uncertainty prevailed as to the course events might take, and rumors of all descriptions were current, the wildest scarcely exceeding in improbability the fantastic horrors that actually prevailed throughout the land during these opening days of the Reign of Terror. The expectation that found most favor in the fleet was that Provence would separate from the rest of France, and proclaim itself an independent republic under the protection of Great Britain; but few looked for the amazing result which shortly followed, in the delivery of Toulon by its citizens into the hands of Lord Hood. This Nelson attributed purely to the suffering caused by the strictness of the blockade. "At Marseilles and Toulon," wrote he on the 20th of August, "they are almost starving, yet nothing brings them to their senses. Although the Convention has denounced them as traitors, yet even these people will not declare for anything but Liberty and Equality." Three days later, Commissioners from both cities went on board Hood's flagship to treat for peace, upon the basis of re-establishing the monarchy, and recognizing as king the son of Louis XVI. The admiral accepted the proposal, on condition that the port and arsenal of Toulon should be delivered to him for safe keeping, until the restoration of the young prince was effected. On the 27th of August the city ran up the white flag of the Bourbons, and the British fleet, together with the Spanish, which at this moment arrived on the scene, anchored in the outer port. The allied troops took possession of the forts commanding the harbor, while the dockyards and thirty ships-of-the-line were delivered to the navies.

"The perseverance of our fleet has been great," wrote Nelson, "and to that only can be attributed our unexampled success. Not even a boat could get into Marseilles or Toulon, or on the coast, with provisions; and the old saying, 'that hunger will tame a lion,' was never more strongly exemplified." In this he deceived himself, however natural the illusion. The opposition of Toulon to the Paris Government was part of a general movement of revolt, which spread throughout the provinces in May and June, 1793, upon the violent overthrow of the Girondists in the National Convention. The latter then proclaimed several cities outlawed, Toulon among them; and the bloody severities it exercised were the chief determining cause of the sudden treason, the offspring of fear more than of hunger, — though the latter doubtless contributed, — which precipitated the great southern arsenal into the arms of the Republic's most dangerous foe. Marseilles fell before the Conventional troops, and the resultant panic in the sister city occasioned the hasty step, which in less troubled moments would have been regarded with just horror. But in truth Nelson, despite his acute military perceptions, had not yet developed that keen political sagacity, the fruit of riper judgment grounded on wider information, which he afterwards showed. His ambition was yet limited to the sphere of the " Agamemnon," his horizon bounded by the petty round of the day's events. He rose, as yet, to no apprehension of the mighty crisis hanging over Europe, to no appreciation of the profound meanings of the opening strife. " I hardly think the War can last," he writes to his wife, " for what are we at war about ? " and again, " I think we shall be in England in the winter or spring." Even some months later, in December, before Toulon had reverted to the French, he is completely blind to the importance of the Mediterranean in the great struggle, and expresses a wish to exchange to the West Indies, " for I think our Sea War is over in these seas."

It is probable, indeed, that in his zeal, thoroughness, and fidelity to the least of the duties then falling to him, is to be seen a surer indication of his great future than in any wider speculations about matters as yet too high for his position. The recent coolness between him and Lord Hood had been rapidly disappearing under the admiral's reviving appreciation and his own aptitude to conciliation. " Lord Hood is very civil," he writes on more than one occasion, " I think we may be good friends again ; " and the offer of a seventy-four-gun ship in place of his smaller vessel was further proof of his superior's confidence. Nelson refused the proposal. " I cannot give up my officers," he said, in the spirit that so endeared him to his followers ; but the compliment was felt, and was enhanced by the admiral's approval of his motives. The prospective occupation of Toulon gave occasion for a yet more flattering evidence of the esteem in which he was held. As soon as the agreement with the city was completed, but the day before taking possession, Hood despatched him in haste to Oneglia, a small port on the Riviera of Genoa, and thence to Naples, to seek from the latter court and that of Turin [1] a reinforcement of ten thousand troops to hold the new acquisition. The " Agamemnon " being a fast sailer undoubtedly contributed much to this selection ; but the character of the commanding officer could not but be considered on

[1] Turin was capital of the Kingdom of Sardinia, which embraced the island of that name and the Province of Piedmont.

so important, and in some ways delicate, a mission. " I should have liked to have stayed one day longer with the fleet, when they entered the harbour," he wrote to Mrs. Nelson, " but service could not be neglected for any private gratification," — a sentiment she had to hear pretty often, as betrothed and as wife, but which was no platitude on the lips of one who gave it constant demonstration in his acts. " Duty is the great business of a sea officer," he told his intended bride in early manhood, to comfort her and himself under a prolonged separation. " Thank God ! I have done my duty," was the spoken thought that most solaced his death hour, as his heart yearned towards those at home whom he should see no more.

About this time he must have felt some touch of sympathy for the effeminate Spaniards, who were made ill by a sixty days' cruise. " All we get here," he writes, " is honour and salt beef. My poor fellows have not had a morsel of fresh meat or vegetables for near nineteen weeks; and in that time I have only had my foot twice on shore at Cadiz. We are absolutely getting sick from fatigue." " I am here [Naples] with news of our most glorious and great success, but, alas! the fatigue of getting it has been so great that the fleet generally, and I am sorry to say, my ship most so, are knocked up. Day after day, week after week, month after month, we have not been two gun shots from Toulon." The evident looseness of this statement, for the ship had only been a little over a month off Toulon, shows the impression the service had made upon his mind, for he was not prone to such exaggerations. " It is hardly possible," he says again, " to conceive the state of my ship; I have little less than one hundred sick." This condition of things is an eloquent testimony to the hardships endured; for Nelson was singularly successful, both before and after these days, in maintaining the health of a ship's company. His biographers say that during the term of three years that he commanded the " Boreas " in the West Indies, not a single officer or man died out of her whole complement, — an achievement almost incredible in that sickly climate;[1] and he himself records

[1] This statement, which apparently depends upon a memoir supplied many years later by the first lieutenant of the " Boreas," is not strictly accurate, for Nelson himself, in a letter written shortly after her arrival in the West Indies,

that in his two months' chase of Villeneuve, in 1805, no death
from sickness occurred among the seven or eight thousand
persons in the fleet. He attributed these remarkable results
to his attention, not merely to the physical surroundings of
the crews, but also to the constant mental stimulus and
interest, which he aroused by providing the seamen with occupation, frequent amusements, and change of scene, thus
keeping the various faculties in continual play, and avoiding
the monotony which most saps health, through its deadening
influence on the mind and spirits.

The "Agamemnon" reached Naples on the 12th of September, and remained there four days. Nelson pressed the matter of reinforcements with such diligence, and was so heartily
sustained by the British minister, Sir William Hamilton, that
he obtained the promise of six thousand troops to sail at once
under the convoy of the "Agamemnon." "I have acted for
Lord Hood," he wrote, "with a zeal which no one could
exceed;" and a few weeks later he says: "The Lord is very
much pleased with my conduct about the troops at Naples,
which I undertook without any authority whatever from him;
and they arrived at Toulon before his requisition reached
Naples." It appears, therefore, that his orders were rather
those of a despatch-bearer than of a negotiator; but that he,
with the quick initiative he always displayed, took upon himself diplomatic action, to further the known wishes of his
superior and the common cause of England and Naples. It
was upon this occasion that Nelson first met Lady Hamilton,
who exercised so marked an influence over his later life; but,
though she was still in the prime of her singular loveliness,
being yet under thirty, not a ripple stirred the surface of his
soul, afterward so powerfully perturbed by this fascinating
woman. "Lady Hamilton," he writes to his wife, "has been
wonderfully kind and good to Josiah [his step-son]. She is a
young woman of amiable manners, and who does honour to
the station to which she is raised." His mind was then too
full of what was to be done; not as after the Nile, when, un-
strung by reaction from the exhausting emotions of the past

mentions that several of her ship's company had been carried off by fever
(Nicolas, vol. i. p. 111); but it can doubtless be accepted as evidence of an
unusually healthy condition.

months, it was for the moment empty of aspiration and cloyed with flattery only.

The prospect of sailing with the convoy of troops, as well as of a few days' repose for the wearied ship's company, was cut short by the news that a French ship of war, with some merchant vessels in convoy, had anchored on the Sardinian coast. Although there were at Naples several Neapolitan naval vessels, and one Spaniard, none of them moved; and as the Prime Minister sent the information to Nelson, he felt bound to go, though but four days in port. "Unfit as my ship was, I had nothing left for the honour of our country but to sail, which I did in two hours afterwards. It was necessary to show them what an English man-of-war would do." The expected enemy was not found, and, after stretching along the coast in a vain search, the "Agamemnon" put into Leghorn on the 25th of September, nine days after leaving Naples, — "absolutely to save my poor fellows," wrote her captain to his brother. But even so, he purposed staying at his new anchorage but three days, "for I cannot bear the thought of being absent from the scene of action" at Toulon. In the same letter he mentions that since the 23d of April — five months — the ship had been at anchor only twenty days.

The unwavering resolution and prompt decision of his character thus crop out at every step. In Leghorn he found a large French frigate, which had been on the point of sailing when his ship came in sight. "I am obliged to keep close watch to take care he does not give me the slip, which he is inclined to do. I shall pursue him, and leave the two Courts [Great Britain and Tuscany] to settle the propriety of the measure, which I think will not be strictly regular. Have been up all night watching him — ready to cut the moment he did." The enemy, however, made no movement, and Nelson was not prepared to violate flagrantly the neutrality of the port. On the 30th of September he sailed, and on the 5th of October rejoined Lord Hood off Toulon, where four thousand of the Neapolitan troops, for which he had negotiated, had already arrived.

The high favor in which the admiral had held him ten years before in the West Indies, though slightly overcast by the coolness which arose during the intervening peace, had been rapidly regained in the course of the present campaign ; and the customary report of his proceedings during the six weeks' absence could not but confirm Hood in the assurance that he had now to deal with a very exceptional character, especially fitted for separate and responsible service. Accordingly, from this time forward, such is the distinguishing feature of Nelson's career as a subordinate. He is selected from among many competitors, frequently his seniors, for the performance of duty outside the reach of the commander-in-chief, but requiring the attention of one upon whose activity, intelligence, and readiness, the fullest dependence could be placed. Up to the battle of the Nile, — in which, it must always be remembered, he commanded a squadron detached from the main fleet, and was assigned to it in deliberate preference to two older flag-officers, — Nelson's life presents a series of detached commands, independent as regarded the local scene of operations, and his method of attaining the prescribed end with the force allotted to him, but dependent, technically, upon the distant commanders-in-chief, each of whom in succession, with one accord, recognized his singular fitness. The pithy but characteristic expression said to have been used by Earl St. Vincent, when asked for instructions about the Copenhagen expedition, — " D—n it, Nelson, send them to the devil your own way," — sums up accurately enough the confidence shown him by his superiors. He could not indeed lift them all to the height of his own conceptions, fearlessness, and enterprise ; but when they had made up their minds to any particular course, they were, each and all, perfectly willing to intrust the execution to him. Even at Copenhagen he was but second in command, though conspicuously first in achievement. It was not till the opening of the second war of the French Revolution, in May, 1803, that he himself had supreme charge of a station, — his old familiar Mediterranean.

Being held in such esteem, it was but a short time before Nelson was again sent off from Toulon, to which he did not return during the British occupation. He was now ordered to report to Commodore Linzee, then lying with a detachment of three ships-of-the-line in the harbor of Cagliari, at the south end of Sardinia. On her passage the " Agamemnon " met and engaged a French squadron, of four large frigates and a brig. Though without decisive results, Nelson was satisfied with his own conduct in this affair, as was also Lord Hood when it came to his knowledge ; for, one of the frigates being badly crippled, the whole force, which was on its way to Nice, was compelled to take refuge in Corsica, where it was far from secure. Two days later, on the 24th of October, Cagliari was reached, and the " Agamemnon " accompanied the division to Tunis, arriving there on the 1st of November.

Linzee's mission was to try and detach the Bey from the French interest, and it was hoped he could be induced to allow the seizure of a number of French vessels which had entered the port, under the convoy of a ship-of-the-line and four frigates. When the British entered, the frigates had disappeared, being in fact the same that Nelson had fought ten days before. In accordance with his instructions, Linzee strove to persuade the Bey that the Republican government, because of its revolutionary and bloodthirsty character, should receive no recognition or support from more regular states, not even the protection usually extended by a neutral port, and that in consequence he should be permitted to seize for Great Britain the vessels in Tunis. The Turk may possibly have overlooked the fallacy in this argument, which assumed that the protection extended by neutral governments was rather for the benefit of the belligerent than for the quiet and safety of its own waters ; but he was perfectly clear-sighted as to his personal advantage in the situation, for the French owners, in despair of getting to France, were selling their cargoes to him at one third their value. To the argument that the French had beheaded their king, he drily replied that the English had once done the same; and he decisively refused to allow the ships to be molested. Nelson was disgusted that his consent should have been awaited. " The English seldom get much by negotiation except the being laughed at, which we have been ; and I don't like it. Had we taken, which in my opinion we ought to have done, the men-of-war and convoy, worth at least £300,000, how much better we could have negotiated : — given the Bey £50,000, he would have been glad to have put up with the insult offered to his dignity ;" and he plainly intimates his dissatisfaction with Linzee. This

7

irresponsible and irreflective outburst was, however, only an instance of the impatience his enterprising, energetic spirit always felt when debarred from prompt action, whether by good or bad reasons; for almost on the same day he expresses the sounder judgment: " Had we latterly attempted to take them I am sure the Bey would have declared against us, and done our trade some damage." No advantage could have accrued from the seizure of the French vessels, at all proportioned to the inconvenience of having the hostility of Tunis, flanking as it did the trade routes to the Levant. The British had then quite enough on their hands, without detaching an additional force from the north coast of the Mediterranean, to support a gratuitous quarrel on the south. As a matter of mere policy it would have been ill-judged.

Nelson, however, did not as yet at all realize the wideness of the impending struggle, for it was in these very letters that he expressed a wish to exchange to the West Indies. " You know," he writes to his old friend Locker, " that Pole is gone to the West Indies. I have not seen him since his order, but I know it was a thing he dreaded. Had I been at Toulon I should have been a candidate for that service, for I think our sea war is over in these seas." Perhaps his intrinsic merit would have retrieved even such a mistake as we can now see this would have been, and he would there have come sooner into contact with Sir John Jervis — to whom, if to any one, the name of patron to Nelson may be applied — for Jervis then had the West India command ; but it is difficult to imagine Nelson's career apart from the incidents of his Mediterranean service. The Mediterranean seems inseparable from his name, and he in the end felt himself identified with it beyond all other waters.

His longing for action, which prompted the desire for the West Indies, was quickly gratified, for orders were received from Hood, by Linzee, to detach him from the latter's command. The admiral sent him a very handsome letter upon his single-handed combat with the French frigates, and directed him to go to the north end of Corsica, to take charge of a division of vessels he would there find cruising, and to search for his late enemies along that coast and through the neighboring waters, between the island and the shores of Italy. He was also to warn off neutral vessels bound to Genoa, that port being declared blockaded, and to seize them if they persisted in their voyage thither. "I consider this command as a very high compliment," wrote Nelson to his uncle Suckling, "there being five older captains in the fleet." This it certainly was, — a compliment and a prophecy as well.

In pursuance of these orders Nelson left Tunis on the 30th of November, and on the 8th of December discovered the French squadron, protected by shore batteries, in San Fiorenzo Bay, in Corsica. This island, which during the middle ages, and until some twenty years before the beginning of the French Revolution, was a dependency of Genoa, had then by the latter been ceded to France, against the express wishes of the inhabitants, whose resistance was crushed only after a prolonged struggle. Although it was now in open revolt against the Revolutionary government, the troops of the latter still held three or four of the principal seaports, among them the northern one in which the frigates then lay, as well as Bastia upon the east coast of the island, and Calvi on the west. His force being insufficient to engage the works of any of these places, there was nothing for Nelson to do but to blockade them, in hopes of exhausting their resources and at least preventing the escape of the ships of war. In this he was successful, for the latter either were destroyed or fell into the hands of Great Britain, when the ports were reduced.

Meanwhile affairs at Toulon were approaching the crisis which ended its tenure by the British and their allies. The garrison had never been sufficient to man properly the very extensive lines, which the peculiar configuration of the surrounding country made it necessary to occupy for the security of the town; and the troops themselves were not only of different nations, but of very varying degrees of efficiency. Under these conditions the key of the position, accurately indicated by Napoleon Bonaparte, then a major and in command of the artillery, was held in insufficient force, and was successfully stormed on the night of December 16, 1793. It was immediately recognized that the ships could no longer remain in the harbor, and that with them the land forces also must depart. After two days of hurried preparations, and an attempt, only partially successful, to destroy the dockyard and

French ships of war, the fleets sailed out on the 19th of December, carrying with them, besides the soldiery, as many as possible of the wretched citizens, who were forced to fly in confusion and misery from their homes, in order to escape the sure and fearful vengeance of the Republican government. The "Agamemnon" was in Leghorn, getting provisions, when the fugitives arrived there, and Nelson speaks in vivid terms of the impression made upon him by the tales he heard and the sights he saw. "Fathers are here without families, and families without fathers, the pictures of horror and despair." "In short, all is horror. I cannot write all: my mind is deeply impressed with grief. Each teller makes the scene more horrible." He expressed the opinion that the evacuation was a benefit to England, and it unquestionably was. He had not always thought so ; but it must be allowed that the hopes and exultation with which he greeted the acquisition of the place had sufficient foundation, in the reported attitude of the people of Southern France, to justify the first opinion as well as the last. The attempt was worth making, though it proved unsuccessful. As it was, the occupation had resulted in a degree of destruction to the French ships and arsenal in Toulon, which, though then over-estimated, was a real gain to the allies.

CHAPTER IV.

Reduction of Corsica by the British. — Departure of Lord Hood for England. — The "Agamemnon" Refitted at Leghorn.

January–December, 1794.   Age, 35.

BY the loss of Toulon the British fleet in the Mediterranean was left adrift, without any secure harbor to serve as a depot for supplies and a base for extended operations. Hood took his ships to Hyères Bay, a few miles east of Toulon, a spot where they could lie safely at anchor, but which was unsuitable for a permanent establishment,— the shores not being tenable against French attack. He now turned his eyes upon Corsica, whence the celebrated native chieftain, Paoli, who had led the natives in their former struggle against France, had made overtures to him, looking to the union of the island to the British crown. Nelson in person, or, during his brief absence in Leghorn, his division, had so closely invested the shores, that neither troops nor supplies of any kind had been able to enter since the early part of December, nor had the blockaded vessels been able to get out. The thoroughness with which this work was done brought him, on the 6th of January, 1794, yet further compliments from Hood, who wrote him that "he looked upon these frigates as certain, trusting to my zeal and activity, and knows, if it is in the power of man to have them, I will secure them." At the same time he was instructed to enter into communication with Paoli, and settle plans for the landing of the troops. In attending to this commission his intermediary was Lieutenant George Andrews, brother to the lady to whom he had become attached at St. Omer, and who had afterwards been a midshipman with him on board the "Boreas." "This business going through my hands," he wrote with just pride, "is a proof of Lord Hood's confidence in me, and that I shall pledge myself for nothing but what will be acceptable to him." It was indeed

evident that Hood was more and more reposing in him a
peculiar trust, a feeling which beyond most others tends to
increase by its own action. Nelson repaid him with the most
unbounded admiration. " The Lord is very good friends with
me," he writes ; " he is certainly the best officer I ever saw.
Everything from him is so clear it is impossible to misunder-
stand him." " His zeal, his activity for the honour and benefit
of his country," he says at another time, " are not abated.
Upwards of seventy, he possesses the mind of forty years of
age. He has not a thought separated from honour and glory."
The flattering proofs of his superior's esteem, and the demand
made upon his natural powers to exert themselves freely, had
a very beneficial effect upon his health and spirits. .It was
not effort, however protracted and severe, but the denial of
opportunity to act, whether by being left unemployed or
through want of information, that wore Nelson down. " I
have not been one hour at anchor for pleasure in eight months ;
but I can assure you I never was better in health."

Meanwhile a commission from the fleet arrived in Corsica.
Sir Gilbert Elliot, the representative of the British government in the island, was at its head, and with him were associated two army officers, one of whom afterwards became widely
celebrated as Sir John Moore. A satisfactory agreement
being concluded, Hood sailed from Hyères Bay with the ships
and troops, and operations began against San Fiorenzo, terminating in the evacuation of the place by the French, who upon
the 19th of February retreated by land to Bastia. Nelson was
not immediately connected with this undertaking; but he had
the satisfaction of knowing that two of the four frigates, of
whose detention in the island he was the immediate cause,
were here lost to the enemy. He was during these weeks actively employed harrying the coast — destroying depots of
stores on shore, and small vessels laden with supplies. These
services were mainly, though not entirely, rendered in the
neighborhood of Bastia, a strongly fortified town, which was
to become the next object of the British efforts, and the scene
of his own exertions. There, also, though on a comparatively
small scale, he was to give striking evidence of the characteristics which led him on, step by step, to his great renown.

When Hood himself took command at San Fiorenzo, he

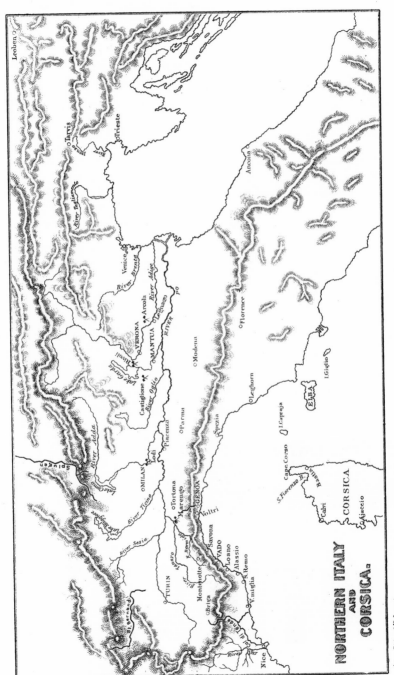

NORTHERN ITALY
AND
CORSICA.

(For Life of Nelson.)

relieved Nelson from that part of his charge, and sent him on the 7th of February to blockade Bastia, — a strictly detached service, and one of the utmost importance, as upon the intercepting of supplies the issue of the siege largely turned. Three weeks later, on the 1st of March, Nelson wrote: " We are still in the busy scene of war, a situation in which I own I feel pleasure, more especially as my actions have given great satisfaction to my commander-in-chief. The blocking up of Corsica he left to me: it has been accomplished in the most complete manner, not a boat got in, nor a soldier landed, although eight thousand men were embarked at Nice ;" and, he might have added, although a vessel was said to sail from Nice every thirty-six hours. Nor was his activity confined to blockading. He continually reconnoitered the town and the works, in doing which on the 23d of February he engaged the batteries at short range, with the " Agamemnon " and two frigates, — the action lasting for nearly two hours. While it was at its height, the heads of the British columns, coming from San Fiorenzo, only twelve miles distant by land, were seen upon the heights overlooking Bastia from the rear. "What a noble sight it must have been " to them! wrote Nelson enthusiastically, in the ardor of his now opening career, — for it must be remembered that this hero of a hundred fights was even then but beginning to taste that rapture of the strife, in which he always breathed most freely, as though in his native element.

Bastia, as he saw it and reported to Lord Hood, was a walled town with central citadel, of some ten thousand inhabitants, on the east coast of Corsica, and twenty miles south of Cape Corso, the northern extremity of the island. The main fortifications were along the sea-front; but there was, besides, a series of detached works on either flank and to the rear. The latter not only guarded the approaches from the interior, but also, being situated on the hills, much above the town, were capable of commanding it, in case of an enemy gaining possession. Nelson, while modestly disclaiming any presumptuous dependence upon his own judgment, expressed a decided opinion, based upon the engagement of the 23d, that the " Agamemnon " and the frigates could silence the fire of the sea-front, batter down the walls, and that then five hundred troops could carry the place by assault. "That the works on the hills would annoy the town afterwards is certain, but the enemy being cut off from all supplies — the provisions in the town being of course in our possession — would think of nothing but making the best terms they could for themselves." To his dismay, however, and to the extreme annoyance of the admiral, General Dundas, commanding the army, refused to move against Bastia, condemning the attempt as visionary and rash. Meantime the French, unmolested except by the desultory efforts of the insurgent Corsicans, were each day strengthening their works, and converting the possibilities Nelson saw into the impossibilities of the cautious general.

Hood on the 25th of February came round from San Fiorenzo to Bastia; but he purposely brought with him no captain senior to Nelson, in order that the latter might remain in charge of the operations he had begun so well. When Dundas retreated again to San Fiorenzo, Hood on the 3d of March followed him there with the flagship, to urge his co-operation; leaving Nelson with six frigates to conduct the blockade and take such other steps as the opportunities might justify. By the middle of March, nearly three months having elapsed since her last hasty visit to Leghorn, the "Agamemnon" was wholly destitute of supplies. "We are really," wrote Nelson to Hood, "without firing, wine, beef, pork, flour, and almost without water: not a rope, canvas, twine, or nail in the ship. The ship is so light she cannot hold her side to the wind. . . . We are certainly in a bad plight at present, not a man has slept dry for many months. Yet," he continues, with that indomitable energy which made light of mere difficulties of material, and conveys so impressive a lesson to our modern days, when slight physical defects appear insurmountable, and ships not wholly up to date are counted obsolete, — "yet, if your Lordship wishes me to remain off Bastia, I can, by going to Porto Ferrajo, get water and stores, and twenty-four hours in Leghorn will give us provisions; and our refitting, which will take some time, can be put off a little. My wish is to be present at the attack of Bastia."

On the 18th of March Hood summoned him to San Fiorenzo. The difference between him and Dundas had become a quarrel, and the latter had quitted his command. Hood wished to strengthen the argument with his successor, by a report of the observations made by Nelson; but the latter records that, after expressing his opinion that eight hundred troops with four hundred seamen could reduce the place, it was found that all the army was united against an attack, declaring the impossibility of taking Bastia, even if all the force were united, — and this, notwithstanding that an engineer and an artillery officer had visited the scene, and agreed with Nelson that there was a probability of success. On the north side both they and he considered the place weak, and at the same time found the ground favorable for establishing the siege guns. Moreover, even during the winter gales, he had succeeded in so closing the sea approaches, while the revolted Corsicans intercepted those by land, that a pound of coarse bread was selling for three francs. The spring equinox was now near at hand, and with better weather the blockade would be yet more efficient. Between actual attack and famine, he argued, the place must fall. "Not attacking it I could not but consider as a national disgrace. If the Army will not take it, we must, by some way or other."

If every particular operation of war is to be considered by itself alone, and as a purely professional question, to be determined by striking a balance between the arguments pro and con, it is probable that the army officers were right in their present contention. In nothing military was scientific accuracy of prediction so possible as in forecasting the result and duration of a regular siege, where the force brought to bear on either side could be approximately known. But, even in this most methodical and least inspired of processes, the elements of chance, of the unforeseen, or even the improbable, will enter, disturbing the most careful calculations. For this reason, no case must be decided purely on its individual merits, without taking into account the other conditions of the campaign at large. For good and sufficient reasons, the British had undertaken, not to conquer a hostile island, but to effect the deliverance of a people who were already in arms, and had themselves redeemed their country with the exception of two or three fortified seaports, for the reduction of which they possessed neither the materials nor the technical skill. To pause in the movement of advance was, with a half-civilized race of unstable temperament, to risk everything. But besides, for the mere purpose of the blockade, it was imperative to force the enemy as far as possible to contract his lines. Speaking of a new work thrown up north of the town, Nelson said with accurate judgment: "It must be destroyed, or the Corsicans will be obliged to give up a post which the enemy would immediately possess; and of course throw us on that side at a greater distance from Bastia." The result would be, not merely so much more time and labor to be expended, nor yet only the moral effect on either party, but also the uncovering of a greater length of seaboard, by which supplies might be run into the town.

The strength of the place, in which, when it fell, were found "seventy-seven pieces of ordnance, with an incredible amount of stores," was far superior to that estimated by the eye of Nelson, untrained as an engineer. Not only so, but the force within the walls was very much larger than he thought, when he spoke with such confidence. "I never yet told Lord Hood," he wrote nearly a year later, "that after everything was fixed for the attack of Bastia, I had information given me of the enormous number of troops we had to oppose us; but my own honour, Lord Hood's honour, and the honour of our Country must have all been sacrificed, had I mentioned what I knew; therefore you will believe what must have been my feelings during the whole siege, when I had often proposals made to me by men, now rewarded, to write to Lord Hood to raise the siege." "Had this been an English town," he said immediately after the surrender, "I am sure it would not have been taken by them. The more we see of this place, the more we are astonished at their giving it up, but the truth is, the different parties were afraid to trust each other." The last assertion, if correct, conveys just one of those incidents which so frequently concur to insure the success of a step rightly taken, as that of Nelson and Hood in this instance certainly was. "Forty-five hundred men," he continues, "have laid down their arms to under twelve hundred troops and seamen. If proofs were wanting to show that perseverance, unanimity, and gallantry, can accomplish almost incredible things, we are an additional instance."

"I always was of opinion," he wrote in the exultation of

reaction from the weight of responsibility he had assumed by his secrecy, — " I always was of opinion, have ever acted up to it, and never have had any reason to repent it, that one Englishman was equal to three Frenchmen." This curious bit of the gasconade into which Nelson from time to time lapsed, can scarcely be accepted as a sound working theory, or as of itself justifying the risk taken; and yet it undoubtedly, under a grossly distorted form, portrays the temperament which enabled him to capture Bastia, and which made him what he was, — a man strong enough to take great chances for adequate ends. " All naval operations undertaken since I have been at the head of the government," said Napoleon, " have always failed, because the admirals see double, and have learned — where I do not know — that war can be made without running risks." It is not material certainty of success, the *ignis fatuus* which is the great snare of the mere engineer, or of the merely accomplished soldier, that points the way to heroic achievements. It is the vivid inspiration that enables its happy possessor, at critical moments, to see and follow the bright clear line, which, like a ray of light at midnight, shining among manifold doubtful indications, guides his steps. Whether it leads him to success or to failure, he may not know ; but that it is the path of wisdom, of duty, and of honor, he knows full well by the persuasion within, — by conviction, the fortifier of the reason, though not by sight, the assurance of demonstration. Only a man capable of incurring a disaster like that at Teneriffe could rise to the level of daring, which, through hidden perils, sought and wrought the superb triumph of Aboukir Bay. Such is genius, that rare but hazardous gift, which separates a man from his fellows by a chasm not to be bridged by human will. Thus endowed, Nelson before the walls of Bastia showed, though in a smaller sphere, and therefore with a lighter hazard, the same keen perception, the same instant decision, the same unfaltering resolve, the same tenacity of purpose, that, far over and beyond the glamour of mere success, have rendered eternally illustrious the days of St. Vincent, of the Nile, and of Copenhagen.

Of the spirit which really actuated him, in his unwavering support of Lord Hood's inclination to try the doubtful issue, many interesting instances are afforded by his correspondence. " I feel for the honour of my Country, and had rather be beat than not make the attack. If we do not try we can never be successful. I own I have no fears for the final issue : it will be conquest, certain we will deserve it. My reputation depends on the opinion I have given ; but I feel an honest consciousness that I have done right. We must, we will have it, or some of our heads will be laid low. I glory in the attempt." " What would the immortal Wolfe have done ? " he says again, refreshing his own constancy in the recollection of an equal heroism, crowned with success against even greater odds. " As he did, beat the enemy, if he perished in the attempt." Again, a fortnight later : "We are in high health and spirits besieging Bastia; the final event, I feel assured, will be conquest." When the siege had already endured for a month, and with such slight actual progress as to compel him to admit to Hood that the town battery had been " put in such a state, that firing away many shot at it is almost useless till we have a force sufficient to get nearer," his confidence remains unabated. "I have no fears about the final issue," he writes to his wife ; " it will be victory, Bastia will be ours; and if so, it must prove an event to which the history of England can hardly boast an equal." Further on in the same letter he makes a prediction, so singularly accurate as to excite curiosity about its source: " I will tell you as a secret, Bastia will be ours between the 20th and 24th of this month " — three weeks after the date of writing — "if succours do not get in." It surrendered actually on the 22d. One is tempted to speculate if there had been any such understanding with the garrison as was afterwards reached with Calvi; but there is no other token of such an arrangement. It is instructive also to compare this high-strung steadfastness of purpose to dare every risk, if success perchance might be won thereby, with his comment upon his own impulses at a somewhat later date. " My disposition cannot bear tame and slow measures. Sure I am, had I commanded our fleet on the 14th, that either the whole French fleet would have graced my triumph, or I should have been in a confounded scrape." Surely the secret of great successes is in these words.

The siege of Bastia was not in its course productive of

striking events. Having reasoned in vain with the two successive generals, Hood demanded that there should be sent back to him a contingent of troops, which had originally been detailed to serve as marines in the fleet, but which he had loaned to the army for the operations against San Fiorenzo. Having received these, he returned to Bastia, and on the 4th of April, 1794, the besieging force, twelve hundred troops and two hundred and fifty seamen, landed to the northward of the town. They at once began to throw up batteries, while the Corsicans harassed the landward approaches to the place. Nelson being with the troops, the "Agamemnon" with some frigates was anchored north of the city, Hood with his ships south of it. During the nights, boats from the fleet rowed guard near to the sea-front, with such diligence that few of the craft that attempted to run in or out succeeded in so doing. When darkness covered the waters, British gunboats crept close to the walls, and by an intermitting but frequent fire added much to the distress of the enemy. On the 11th of April the garrison was formally summoned, and, the expected refusal having been received, the British batteries opened. There was not force enough, however, to bring the place to terms as a consequence of direct attack, and after three weeks Nelson, while betraying no apprehension of failure, practically admitted the fact. "Although I have no doubt but even remaining in our present situation, and by strict guard rowing close to the town, and the Corsicans harassing them on the hills, and the gunboats by night, but that the enemy must surrender before any great length of time, yet, if force can be spared, a successful attack on the heights must much facilitate a speedy capture. I own it will give me the highest pleasure to assist in the attack."

It was by such an attack, or rather by the fear of it, coming upon the long and exhausting endurance of cannonade and hunger, that Bastia finally fell. "We shall in time accomplish the taking of Bastia," wrote Nelson on the 3d of May. "I have no doubt in the way we proposed to attempt it, by bombardment and cannonading, joined to a close blockade of the harbour." "If not," he adds, "our Country will, I believe, sooner forgive an officer for attacking his enemy than for letting it alone." On the 12th a large boat was captured

coming out from the port; and on her were found letters from
the governor, Gentili, confessing the annoyance caused by the
British fire, and saying that if relief did not arrive by the
29th, the place must be looked upon as lost. Three nights
later another boat was caught attempting to enter. On board
her was a brother of the Mayor of Bastia. This man, while
talking with Hood's secretary, expressed his fears for the
result to his relatives, if the town were carried by assault.
The secretary replied that Hood could not prevent those evils,
if the garrison awaited the attack, and gave the Corsican to
understand that it was imminent, troops being expected from
San Fiorenzo. At the urgent request of the prisoner, one of
the seamen taken with him was permitted to land with a letter,
stating the impending danger. By a singular concidence, or
by skilful contrivance, the San Fiorenzo troops appeared on
the heights upon the evening, May 19, following this conversation. Flags of truce had already been hoisted, negotiations
were opened, and on the 22d the French colors were struck
and the British took possession. "When I reflect what we
have achieved," confessed the hitherto outwardly unmoved
Nelson, "I am all astonishment. The most glorious sight
that an Englishman can experience, and which, I believe,
none but an Englishman could bring about, was exhibited, —
4,500 men laying down their arms to less than 1,000 British
soldiers, who were serving as marines." As towards the
French this account is perhaps somewhat less than fair; but
it does no more than justice to the admirable firmness and
enterprise shown by Hood and Nelson. As a question of
Bastia only, their attempt might be charged with rashness;
but having regard to the political and military conditions, to
the instability of the Corsican character, and to the value of
the island as a naval station, it was amply justified, for the
risks run were out of all proportion less than the advantage
to be gained.

Thus the siege of Bastia ended in triumph, despite the
prior pronouncement of the general commanding the troops,
that the attempt was "most visionary and rash." These
epithets, being used to Hood after his own expressions in
favor of the undertaking, had not unnaturally provoked from
him a resentful retort; and, as men are rarely conciliated by

the success of measures which they have ridiculed, there arose a degree of strained relations between army and navy, that continued even after the arrival of a new commander of the land forces, and indeed throughout Hood's association with the operations in Corsica.

During this busy and laborious period, despite his burden of secret anxiety, Nelson's naturally delicate health showed the favorable reaction, which, as has before been noted, was with him the usual result of the call to exertion. His letters steadily reflect, and occasionally mention, the glow of exultation produced by constant action of a worthy and congenial nature. " We are in high health and spirits besieging Bastia," he writes to his wife soon after landing; and shortly before the fall of the place he says again : " As to my health, it was never better, seldom so well." Yet, although from beginning to end the essential stay of the enterprise, the animating soul, without whose positive convictions and ardent support Lord Hood could scarcely have dared so great a hazard, he was throughout the siege left, apparently purposely, in an anomalous position, and was at the end granted a recognition which, though probably not grudging, was certainly scanty. No definition of his duties was ever given by the commander-in-chief. He appears as it were the latter's unacknowledged representative ashore, a plenipotentiary without credentials. " What my situation is," he writes to a relative, " is not to be described. I am everything, yet nothing ostensible; enjoying the confidence of Lord Hood and Colonel Villettes, and the captains landed with the seamen obeying my orders." A fortnight later he writes to Hood : " Your Lordship knows exactly the situation I am in here. With Colonel Villettes I have no reason but to suppose I am respected in the highest degree ; nor have I occasion to complain of want of attention to my wishes from any parties; but yet I am considered as not commanding the seamen landed. My wishes may be, and are, complied with ; my orders would possibly be disregarded. Therefore, if we move from hence, I would wish your Lordship to settle that point. Your Lordship will not, I trust, take this request amiss : I have been struggling with it since the first day I landed."

Hood apparently gave him full satisfaction as regards his

own view of the situation. " I am happy," Nelson wrote, when acknowledging his reply, " that my ideas of the situation I am in here so perfectly agree with your Lordship's ; " but he did not settle the matter by a decisive order. His object, as he seems to have explained, was to bestow a certain amount of prominence upon a young captain, Hunt, who had recently lost his ship, and who, Hood thought, would be sooner provided with another, if he appeared as in command at the guns. Nelson acceded to this arrangement with his usual generosity. " Your kind intention to Captain Hunt," he wrote, " I had the honour of telling your Lordship, should be furthered by every means in my power; and my regard for him, I assure you, is undiminished. He is a most exceeding good young man, nor is any one more zealous for the service. I don't complain of any one, but an idea has entered into the heads of some under him, that his command was absolutely distinct from me; and that I had no authority over him, except as a request." Unfortunately, Hood, in his desire to serve Hunt, not only unduly but absurdly minimized Nelson's relations to the whole affair. His despatch ran: " Captain Nelson, of his Majesty's ship Agamemnon, who had the command and directions of the seamen *in landing the guns, mortars and stores,*[1] and Captain Hunt *who commanded at the batteries,*[1] . . . have an equal claim to my gratitude." To limit Nelson's share in the capture of Bastia to the purely subsidiary though important function of landing the guns, was as unjust as it was unnecessary to the interests of Hunt. The latter, being second in command ashore, and afterwards sent home with the despatches, was sure to receive the reward customarily bestowed upon such services.

The incident singularly and aptly illustrates the difference, which in a military service cannot be too carefully kept in mind, between individual expressions of opinion, which may be biassed, and professional reputation, which, like public sentiment, usually settles at last not far from the truth. Despite this curious inversion of the facts by Lord Hood, there probably was no one among the naval forces, nor among the soldiery, who did not thoroughly, if perchance somewhat vaguely, appreciate that Nelson was the moving spirit of the

[1] The italics are the author's.

whole operation, even beyond Hood himself. As the Greek
commanders after Salamis were said to have voted the award
of merit each to himself first, but all to Themistocles second,
so at Bastia, whatever value individuals might place on their
own services, all probably would have agreed that Nelson
came next.

The latter meantime was happily unconscious of the wrong
done him, so that nothing marred the pleasure with which he
congratulated the commander-in-chief, and received the latter's
brief but hearty general order of thanks, wherein Nelson's
own name stood foremost, as was due both to his seniority
and to his exertions. When the despatch reached him, he
freely expressed his discontent in letters to friends ; but being,
at the time of its reception, actively engaged in the siege of
Calvi, the exhilaration of that congenial employment for the
moment took the edge off the keenness of his resentment.
" Lord Hood and myself were never better friends — *nor,
although his Letter does*,[1] did he wish to put me where I never
was — in the rear. Captain Hunt, who lost his ship, he
wanted to push forward for another, — a young man who never
was on a battery, or ever rendered any service during the
siege; if any person ever says he did, then I submit to the
character of a story-teller. Poor Serocold, who fell here,[2]
was determined to publish an advertisement, as he commanded
a battery under my orders. The whole operations of the siege
were carried on through Lord Hood's letters to me. I was the
mover of it — I was the cause of its success. Sir Gilbert
Elliot will be my evidence, if any is required. I am not a
little vexed, but shall not quarrel." " I am well aware," he
had written to Mrs. Nelson a few days before, " my poor services will not be noticed : I have no interest; but, however
services may be received, it is not right in an officer to slacken
his zeal for his Country."

These noble words only voiced a feeling which in Nelson's
heart had all the strength of a principle ; and this light of the
single eye stood him in good stead in the moments of bitterness
which followed a few months later, when a lull in the storm
of fighting gave the sense of neglect a chance to rankle.

[1] The italics are Nelson's.
[2] Written at the siege of Calvi.

"My heart is full," he writes then to his uncle Suckling, speaking not only of Bastia, but of the entire course of operations in Corsica, "when I think of the treatment I have received: every man who had any considerable share in the reduction has got some place or other — I, only I, am without reward. . . . Nothing but my anxious endeavour to serve my Country makes me bear up against it; but I sometimes am ready to give all up." "Forgive this letter," he adds towards the end: "I have said a great deal too much of myself; but indeed it is all too true." In similar strain he expressed himself to his wife: "It is very true that I have ever served faithfully, and ever has it been my fate to be neglected; but that shall not make me inattentive to my duty. I have pride in doing my duty well, and a self-approbation, which if it is not so lucrative, yet perhaps affords more pleasing sensations." Thus the consciousness of duty done in the past, and the clear recognition of what duty still demanded in the present and future, stood him in full stead, when he failed to receive at the hands of others the honor he felt to be his due, and which, he never wearied in proclaiming, was in his eyes priceless, above all other reward. "Corsica, in respect of prizes," he wrote to Mrs. Nelson, "produces nothing but honour, far above the consideration of wealth: not that I despise riches, quite the contrary, yet I would not sacrifice a good name to obtain them. Had I attended less than I have done to the service of my Country, I might have made some money too: however, I trust my name will stand on record when the money-makers will be forgot," — a hope to be abundantly fulfilled.

At the moment Bastia fell there arrived from England a new commander-in-chief for the land forces, General Stuart, an officer of distinguished ability and enterprise. Cheered by the hope of cordial co-operation, Hood and Nelson resumed without delay their enthusiastic efforts. Within a week, on the 30th of May, the latter wrote that the "Agamemnon" was taking on board ammunition for the siege of Calvi, the last remaining of the hostile strongholds. In the midst of the preparations, at eleven P. M. of June 6, word was received that nine French ships-of-the-line had come out of Toulon, and were believed to be bound for Calvi, with reinforcements for the garrison. At seven the next morning the squadron was under way; the "Agamemnon," which had two hundred tons of ordnance stores to unload, sailing only half an hour after her less encumbered consorts, whom she soon overtook.

Hood shaped his course for Calvi, being constrained thereto, not only by the rumor of the enemy's destination, but also by the military necessity of effecting a junction with the rest of his fleet. Admiral Hotham, who commanded the British division of seven ships in front of Toulon, instead of waiting to verify the report brought to him of the enemy's force, — which was actually the same, numerically, as his own, — bore up hastily for Calvi, intending, so wrote Nelson at the time, to fight them there, rather than that they should throw in succors. Whatever their numbers, thus to surrender touch of them at the beginning was an evident mistake, for which, as for most mistakes, a penalty had in the end to be paid; and in fact, if the relief of Calvi was the object of the sortie, the place to fight was evidently as far from there as possible. Off Toulon, even had Hotham been beaten, his opponents would have been too roughly handled to carry out their mission. As it was, this precipitate retirement lost the British an opportunity for a combat that might have placed their control of the sea beyond peradventure; and a few months later, Nelson, who at first had viewed Hotham's action with the generous sympathy and confident pride which always characterized his attitude towards his brother officers, showed how clearly he was reading in the book of experience the lessons that should afterwards stand himself in good stead. " When 'Victory' is gone," he wrote, "we shall be thirteen sail of the line [to the French fifteen], when the enemy will keep our new Commanding Officer [Hotham] in hot water, who missed, unfortunately, the opportunity of fighting them, last June." Ten years later, in his celebrated chase of Ville-neuve's fleet, he said to his captains : " If we meet the enemy we shall find them not less than eighteen, I rather think twenty, sail of the line, and therefore do not be surprised if I should not fall on them immediately [he had but eleven] — *we won't part* [1] without a battle ; " and he expressed with the utmost decision his clear appreciation that even a lost battle, if

[1] Author's italics.

delivered at the right point or at the right moment, would
frustrate the ulterior objects of the enemy, by crippling the
force upon which they depended. As will be seen in the
sequel, Hotham, throughout his brief command as Hood's
successor, suffered the consequences of permitting so important a fraction of the enemy's fleet to escape his grasp, when
it was in his power to close with it.

The British divisions met off the threatened port two days
after leaving Bastia, and two hours later a lookout frigate
brought word that the French fleet had been seen by her the
evening before, to the northward and westward, some forty
miles off its own coast.   Hood at once made sail in pursuit,
and in the afternoon of the 10th of June caught sight of the
enemy, but so close in with the shore that they succeeded in
towing their ships under the protection of the batteries in
Golfe Jouan, where, for lack of wind, he was unable to follow
them for some days, during which they had time to strengthen
their position beyond his powers of offence.   Hotham's error
was irreparable.   The "Agamemnon" was then sent back to
Bastia, to resume the work of transportation, which Nelson
pushed with the untiring energy that characterized all his
movements.   Arriving on the 12th, fifteen hundred troops
were embarked by eight the next morning, and at four in the
afternoon he sailed, having with him two smaller ships of war
and twenty-two transports.   On the 15th he anchored at San
Fiorenzo.

Here he met General Stuart.   The latter was anxious to
proceed at once with the siege of Calvi, but asked Nelson
whether he thought it proper to take the shipping to that
exposed position; alluding to the French fleet that had left
Toulon, and which Hood was then seeking.   Nelson's reply
is interesting, as reflecting the judgment of a warrior at once
prudent and enterprising, concerning the influence of a hostile
"fleet in being" upon a contemplated detached operation.
"I certainly thought it right," he said, "placing the firmest
reliance that we should be perfectly safe under Lord Hood's
protection, who would take care that the French fleet at Gourjean [1] should not molest us."   To Hood he wrote a week later:
"I believed ourselves safe under your Lordship's wing."   At

[1] Golfe Jouan; on the coast of France between Toulon and Nice.

this moment he thought the French to be nine sail-of-the-line to the British thirteen, — no contemptible inferior force. Yet that he recognized the possible danger from such a detachment is also clear; for, writing two days earlier, under the same belief as to the enemy's strength, and speaking of the expected approach of an important convoy, he says: "I hope they will not venture up till Lord Hood can get off Toulon, or wherever the French fleet are got to." When a particular opinion has received the extreme expression now given to that concerning the "fleet in being," and apparently has undergone equally extreme misconception, it is instructive to recur to the actual effect of such a force, upon the practice of a man with whom moral effect was never in excess of the facts of the case, whose imagination produced to him no paralyzing picture of remote contingencies. Is it probable that, with the great issues of 1690 at stake, Nelson, had he been in Tourville's place, would have deemed the crossing of the Channel by French troops impossible, because of Torrington's "fleet in being"?

Sailing again on June 16, the expedition arrived next day off Calvi. Although it was now summer, the difficulties of the new undertaking were, from the maritime point of view, very great. The town of Calvi, which was walled and had a citadel, lies upon a promontory on the west side of an open gulf of the same name, a semicircular recess, three miles wide by two deep, on the northwest coast of Corsica. The western point of its shore line is Cape Revellata; the eastern, Point Espano. The port being fortified and garrisoned, it was not practicable to take the shipping inside, nor to establish on the inner beach a safe base for disembarking. The "Agamemnon" therefore anchored outside, nearly two miles south of Cape Revellata, and a mile from shore, in the excessive depth of fifty-three fathoms; the transports coming-to off the cape, but farther to seaward. The water being so deep, and the bottom rocky, the position was perilous for sailing-ships, for the prevailing summer wind blows directly on the shore, which is steep-to and affords no shelter. Abreast the "Agamemnon" was a small inlet, Porto Agro, about three miles from Calvi by difficult approaches. Here Nelson landed on the 18th with General Stuart; and, after reconnoitring both the beach and the town, the two officers decided that, though a very bad landing, it was the best available. On the 19th, at 7 A. M., the troops disembarked. That afternoon Nelson himself went ashore to stay, taking with him two hundred and fifty seamen. The next day it came on to blow so hard that most of the ships put to sea, and no intercourse was had from the land with those which remained. The "Agamemnon" did not return till the 24th. Lord Hood was by this time in San Fiorenzo Bay, having abandoned the hope of attacking the French fleet in Golfe Jouan. On the 27th he arrived off Calvi, and thenceforth Nelson was in daily communication with him till the place fell.

As the army in moderate, though not wholly adequate, force conducted the siege of Calvi, under a general officer of vigorous character, the part taken by Nelson and his seamen, though extremely important, and indeed essential to the ultimate success, was necessarily subordinate. It is well to notice that his journal, and correspondence with Lord Hood, clearly recognize this, his true relation to the siege of Calvi; for it makes it probable that, in attributing to himself a much more important part at Bastia, and in saying that Hood's report had put him unfairly in the background, he was not exaggerating his actual though ill-defined position there. That Nelson loved to dwell in thought upon his own achievements, that distinction in the eyes of his fellows was dear to him, that he craved recognition, and was at times perhaps too insistent in requiring it, is true enough; but there is no indication that he ever coveted the laurels of others, or materially misconceived his own share in particular events. Glory, sweet as it was to him, lost its value, if unaccompanied by the consciousness of desert which stamps it as honor. It is, therefore, not so much for personal achievement as for revelation of character that this siege has interest in his life.

Besides the defences of the town proper, Calvi was protected by a series of outworks extending across the neck of land upon which it lay. Of these the outermost was on the left, looking from the place. It flanked the approaches to the others, and commanded the communications with the interior. It was, by Nelson's estimate, about twenty-two hundred yards from the town, and had first to be reduced. By the 3d of July thirteen long guns, besides a number of mortars and howitzers, had been dragged from the beach to the spot by the seamen, who also assisted in placing them in position, and for the most part worked them in battle, an artillerist from the army pointing. Nelson, with Captain Hallowell, already an officer of mark and afterwards one of distinction, took alternate day's duty at the batteries, a third captain, Serocold, having fallen early in the siege. Fearing news might reach his wife that a naval captain had been killed, without the name being mentioned, he wrote to her of this sad event, adding expressively: "I am very busy, yet own I am in all my glory; except with you, I would not be anywhere but where I am, for the world." On July 7th the first outwork fell. The attack upon the others was then steadily and systematically prosecuted, until on the 19th all had been captured, and the besiegers stood face to face with the town walls.

During this time Nelson, as always, was continually at the front and among the most exposed. Out of six guns in the battery which he calls "ours," five were disabled in six days. On the 12th at daylight, a heavy fire opened from the town, which, he says, "seldom missed our battery;" and at seven o'clock a shot, which on the ricochet cleared his head by a hair's breadth, drove sand into his face and right eye with such violence as to incapacitate him. He spoke lightly and cheerfully of the incident to Lord Hood, "I got a little hurt this morning: not much, as you may judge by my writing," and remained absent from duty only the regular twenty-four hours; but, after some fluctuations of hope, the sight of the eye was permanently lost to him. Of General Stuart's conduct in the operations he frequently speaks with cordial admiration. "He is not sparing of himself on any occasion, he every night sleeps with us in the advanced battery. If I may be allowed to judge, he is an extraordinary good judge of ground. No officer ever deserved success more." At the same time he expresses dissatisfaction with some of the subordinate army officers, to whose inefficiency he attributes the necessity for undue personal exertion on the general's part: "The General is not well. He fatigues himself too much, but I can't help seeing he is obliged to do it. He has not a person to forward his views, — the engineer sick, the artillery

captain not fit for active service ; therefore every minute thing
must be done by himself, or it is not done at all."

The work was tedious and exhausting, and the malaria of
the hot Corsican summer told heavily on men's health and
patience. The supply of ammunition, and of material of war
generally, for the army seems to have been inadequate ; and
heavy demands were made upon the fleet, not only for guns,
which could be returned, but for powder and shot, the expenditure of which might prove embarrassing before they could
be renewed. The troops also were not numerous enough,
under the climatic conditions, to do all their own duty. In
such circumstances, when two parties are working together to
the same end, but under no common control, each is prone to
think the other behindhand in his work and exacting in his
demands. "Why don't Lord Hood land 500 men to work ? "
said Colonel Moore, the general's right-hand man. "Our
soldiers are tired." Nelson, on the other hand, thought that
Moore wanted over-much battering done to the breach of a
work, before he led the stormers to it ; and Hood, who was
receiving frequent reports of the preparations of the French
fleet in Toulon, was impatient to have the siege pushed, and
thought the army dilatory. "The rapidity with which the
French are getting on at Toulon," he wrote confidentially to
Nelson, "makes it indispensably necessary for me to put the
whole of the fleet under my command in the best possible
state for service ; and I must soon apply to the general for
those parts of the regiments now on shore, ordered by his
Majesty to serve in lieu of marines, to be held in readiness to
embark at the shortest notice. I shall delay this application
as long as possible."

Nelson, being a seaman, sympathized of course with his
own service, and with Hood, for whom he had most cordial
admiration, both personal and professional. But at the same
time he was on the spot, a constant eye-witness to the difficulties of the siege, a clear-headed observer, with sound military
instincts, and fair-minded when facts were before him. The
army, he wrote to Hood, is harassed to death, and he notices
that it suffers from sickness far more than do the seamen.
He repeats the request for more seamen, and, although he
seems to doubt the reasonableness of the demand, evidently

thinks that they should be furnished, if possible. Hood accordingly sent an additional detachment of three hundred, raising the number on shore to the five hundred suggested by Moore. "I had much rather," he wrote, "that a hundred seamen should be landed unnecessarily, than that one should be kept back that was judged necessary." On the other hand, when the general, after a work bearing on the bay had been destroyed, suggests that the navy might help, by laying the ships against the walls, Nelson takes "the liberty of observing that the business of laying wood before walls was much altered of late," and adds the common-sense remark, that "the quantity of powder and shot which would be fired away on such an attack could be much better directed from a battery on shore." This conversation took place immediately after all the outworks had been reduced. It was conducted "with the greatest politeness," he writes, and "the General thanked me for my assistance, but it was necessary to come to the point whether the siege should be persevered in or given up. If the former, he must be supplied with the means, which were more troops, more seamen to work, and more ammunition." Nelson replied that, if the requisite means could not be had on the spot, they could at least hold on where they were till supplied from elsewhere.

It will be noticed that Nelson was practically the intermediary between the two commanders-in-chief. In fact, there appears to have been between them some constraint, and he was at times asked to transmit a message which he thought had better go direct. In this particularly delicate situation, one cannot but be impressed with the tact he for the most part shows, the diplomatic ability, which was freely attributed to him by his superiors in later and more influential commands. This was greatly helped by his cordial good-will towards others, combined with disinterested zeal for the duty before him; the whole illumined by unusual sagacity and good sense. He sees both sides, and conveys his suggestions to either with a self-restraint and deference which avert resentment; and he preserves both his calmness and candor, although he notices in the camp some jealousy of his confidential communication with his immediate superior, the admiral. Though never backward to demand what he thought the rights of himself or

his associates, Nelson was always naturally disposed to reconcile differences, to minimize causes of trouble, and this native
temperament had not yet undergone the warping which followed his later wounds — especially that on the head received
at the Nile — and the mental conflict into which he was
plunged by his unhappy passion for Lady Hamilton. At this
time, in the flush of earlier enthusiasm, delighting as few men
do in the joy of battle, he strove to promote harmony, to
smooth over difficulties by every exertion possible, either by
doing whatever was asked of him, or by judicious representations to others. Thus, when Hood, impatient at the disturbing news from Toulon, wishes to hasten the conclusion by
summoning the garrison, in the hope that it may yield at
once, the general objected, apparently on the ground that the
statement of their own advantages, upon which such a summons might be based, would be prejudicial, if, as was most
probable, the demand was rejected. Whatever his reason,
Nelson, though indirectly, intimates to Hood that in this
matter he himself agrees, upon the whole, with the general,
and Hood yields the point, — the more so that he learns from
Nelson that the outposts are to be stormed the next night;
and sorely was the captain, in his judicious efforts thus to
keep the peace, tried by the postponement of the promised
assault for twenty-four hours. "*Such things are,*" he wrote
to Hood, using a favorite expression. "I hope to God the
general, who seems a good officer and an amiable man, is not
led away; but Colonel Moore is his great friend."

The feeling between the land and sea services was emphasized in the relations existing between Lord Hood and Colonel
Moore, who afterwards, as Sir John Moore, fell gloriously at
Corunna. To these two eminent officers fortune denied the
occasion to make full proof of their greatness to the world;
but they stand in the first rank of those men of promise
whose failure has been due, not to their own shortcomings,
but to the lack of opportunity. Sir John Moore has been the
happier, in that the enterprise with which his name is chiefly
connected, and upon which his title to fame securely rests,
was completed, and wrought its full results; fortunate, too, in
having received the vindication of that great action at the
hands of the most eloquent of military historians. His coun-

ADMIRAL, LORD HOOD.

From the painting by L. F. Abbott, in the National Portrait Gallery.

try and his profession may well mourn a career of such fair opening so soon cut short. But daring and original in the highest degree as was the march from Salamanca to Sahagun, it did not exceed, either in originality or in daring, the purposes nourished by Lord Hood, which he had no opportunity so to execute as to attract attention. Condemned to subordinate positions until he had reached the age of seventy, his genius is known to us only by his letters, and by the frustrated plans at St. Kitts in 1782, and at Golfe Jouan in 1794, in the former of which, less fortunate than Moore, he failed to realize his well-grounded hope of reversing, by a single blow, the issues of a campaign.

It is to be regretted that two such men could not understand each other cordially. Hood, we know from his letters, was "of that frame and texture that I cannot be indifferent," — "full of anxiety, impatience, and apprehension," — when service seemed to him slothfully done. Moore, we are told by Napier, "maintained the right with vehemence bordering upon fierceness." Had he had the chief command on shore, it is possible that the two, impetuous and self-asserting though they were, might have reached an understanding. But in the most unfortunate disagreement about Bastia, — wherein it is to a naval officer of to-day scarcely possible to do otherwise than blame the sullen lack of enterprise shown by the army, — and afterwards at Calvi, Moore appeared to Hood, and to Nelson also, as the subordinate, the power behind the throne, who was prompting a line of action they both condemned. No position in military life is more provocative of trouble than to feel you are not dealing with the principal, but with an irresponsible inferior; and the situation is worse, because one in which it is almost impossible to come to an issue. Moore's professional talent and force of character naturally made itself felt, even with a man of Stuart's ability. Hood and Nelson recognized this, and they resented, as inspired by a junior, what they might have combated dispassionately, if attributed to the chief. There was friction also between Moore and Elliot, the viceroy of the island. Doubtless, as in all cases where suspicion, not to say jealousy, has been begot, much more and worse was imagined by both parties than actually occurred. The apportionment of blame, or prolonged discussion of the matter, is out of place in a biography of Nelson. To that it is of moment, only because it is proper to state that Nelson, on the spot and in daily contact, — Nelson, upon whose zeal and entire self-devotion at this period no doubt is cast, — agreed in the main with Hood's opinion as to what the latter called the San Fiorenzo leaven, of which Moore was to them the exponent. It is true that Nelson naturally sympathized with his profession and his admiral, whom he heartily admired; but some corrective, at least, to such partiality, was supplied by his soreness about the latter's omission duly to report his services at Bastia, of which he just now became aware. The estrangement between the two commanders-in-chief was doubtless increased by the apparent reluctance, certainly the lack of effort, to see one another frequently.

The principal work, called by Nelson the Mozelle battery, was carried before daylight of July 19, and before dark all the outposts were in the hands of the British. "I could have wished to have had a little part in the storm," wrote Nelson, characteristically covetous of strenuous action, "if it was only to have placed the ladders and pulled away the palisadoes. However, we did the part allotted to us." That day a summons was sent to the garrison, but rejected, and work upon batteries to breach the town walls was then pushed rapidly forward; for it was becoming more and more evident that the siege must be brought to an end, lest the entire force of besiegers should become disabled by sickness. On the 28th the batteries were ready, and General Stuart sent in word that he would not fire upon the hospital positions, where indicated by black flags. The besieged then asked for a truce of twenty-five days, undertaking to lay down their arms, if not by then relieved. The general and admiral refused, but were willing to allow six days. This the garrison in turn rejected; and on the night of the 30th four small vessels succeeded in eluding the blockading frigates and entering supplies, which encouraged the besieged. On the 31st the batteries opened, and after thirty-six hours' heavy cannonade the town held out a flag of truce. An arrangement was made that it should surrender on the 10th of August, if not relieved; the garrison to be transported to France without becoming prisoners of war.

No relief arriving, the place capitulated on the day named. It was high time for the besiegers. "We have upwards of one thousand sick out of two thousand," wrote Nelson, "and the others not much better than so many phantoms. We have lost many men from the season, very few from the enemy." He himself escaped more easily than most. To use his own quaint expression, "All the prevailing disorders have attacked me, but I have not strength enough for them to fasten upon. I am here the reed amongst the oaks: I bow before the storm, while the sturdy oak is laid low." The congenial moral surroundings, in short, — the atmosphere of exertion, of worthy and engrossing occupation, — the consciousness, to him delightful, of distinguished action, of heroic persistence through toil and danger, — prevailed even in his physical frame over discomfort, over the insidious climate, and even over his distressing wound. "This is my ague day," he writes when the batteries opened; "I hope so active a scene will keep off the fit. It has shaken me a good deal; but I have been used to them, and now don't mind them much." "Amongst the wounded, in a slight manner, is myself, my head being a good deal wounded and my right eye cut down; but the surgeons flatter me I shall not entirely lose the sight. It confined me, thank God, only one day, and at a time when nothing particular happened to be doing." "You must not think my hurts confined me," he tells his wife; "no, nothing but the loss of a limb would have kept me from my duty, and I believe my exertions conduced to preserve me in this general mortality." In his cheery letters, now, no trace is perceptible of the fretful, complaining temper, which impaired, though it did not destroy, the self-devotion of his later career. No other mistress at this time contended with honor for the possession of his heart; no other place than the post of duty before Calvi distracted his desires, or appealed to his imagination through his senses. Not even Lord Hood's report of the siege of Bastia, which here came to his knowledge, and by which he thought himself wronged, had bitterness to overcome the joy of action and of self-contentment.

Not many days were required, after the fall of Calvi, to remove the fleet, and the seamen who had been serving on shore, from the pestilential coast. Nelson seems to have been

intrusted with the embarkation of the prisoners in the transports which were to take them to Toulon. He told his wife
that he had been four months landed, and felt almost qualified
to pass his examination as a besieging general, but that he
had no desire to go on with campaigning. On the 11th of
August, the day after the delivery of the place, he was again
on board the " Agamemnon," from whose crew had been drawn
the greatest proportion of the seamen for the batteries. One
hundred and fifty of them were now in their beds. "My
ship's company are all worn out," he wrote, "as is this whole
army, except myself; nothing hurts me, — of two thousand
men I am the most healthy. Every other officer is scarcely
able to crawl." Among the victims of the deadly climate was
Lieutenant Moutray, the son of the lady to whom, ten years
before, he had been so warmly attracted in the West Indies.
Nelson placed a monument to him in the church at San
Fiorenzo.

On the 15th of August the " Agamemnon " sailed from
Calvi, and after a stop at San Fiorenzo, where Hood then was,
reached Leghorn on the 18th. Now that the immediate
danger of the siege was over, Nelson admitted to his wife the
serious character of the injury he had received. The right
eye was nearly deprived of sight, — only so far recovered as
to enable him to distinguish light from darkness. For all
purposes of use it was gone; but the blemish was not to be
perceived, unless attention was drawn to it.

At Leghorn the ship lay for a month, — the first period of
repose since she went into commission, a year and a half
before. While there, the physician to the fleet came on board
and surveyed the crew, finding them in a very weak state, and
unfit to serve. This condition of things gave Nelson hopes
that, upon the approaching departure of Lord Hood for England, the " Agamemnon " might go with him; for he was loath
to separate from an admiral whose high esteem he had won,
and upon whom he looked as the first sea-officer of Great
Britain. Hood was inclined to take her, and to transfer the
ship's company bodily to a seventy-four. This he considered
no more than due to Nelson's distinguished merit and services,
and he had indeed offered him each ship of that rate whose
command fell vacant in the Mediterranean; but the strong

sense of attachment to those who had shared his toils and dangers, of reluctance that they should see him willing to leave them, after their hard work together, — that combination of sympathy and tact which made so much of Nelson's success as a leader of men, — continued to prevent his accepting promotion that would sever his ties to them.

The exigencies of the war in the Mediterranean forbade the departure, even of a sixty-four with a disabled crew. A full month later her sick-list was still seventy-seven, out of a total of less than four hundred. "Though certainly unfit for a long cruise," Nelson said, "we are here making a show," — a military requirement not to be neglected or despised. He accepted the disappointment, as he did all service rubs at this period, with perfect temper and in the best spirit. "We must not repine," he wrote to his wife on the 12th of October, the day after Hood sailed for England. "Lord Hood is very well inclined towards me, but the service must ever supersede all private consideration. I hope you will spend the winter cheerfully. Do not repine at my absence; before spring I hope we shall have peace, when we must look out for some little cottage." She fretted, however, as some women will; and he, to comfort her, wrote more sanguinely about himself than the facts warranted. "Why you should be uneasy about me, so as to make yourself ill, I know not. I feel a confident protection in whatever service I may be employed upon; and as to my health, I don't know that I was ever so truly well. I fancy myself grown quite stout." To his old captain, Locker, he admitted that he could not get the better of the fever.

Corsica being now wholly in the power of its inhabitants, allied with and supported by Great Britain, his attention and interest were engrossed by the French fleet centring upon Toulon, the dominant factor of concern to the British in the Mediterranean, where Vice-Admiral Hotham had succeeded Hood as commander-in-chief. Nelson realizes more and more the mistake that was made, when a fraction of it was allowed to escape battle in the previous June. The various reasons by which he had at first excused the neglect to bring it to action no longer weigh with him. He does not directly blame, but he speaks of the omission as an "opportunity lost," — a phrase than which there are few more ominous, in char-

acterizing the closely balanced, yet weighty, decisions upon
which the issues of war depend. Nothing, he thinks, can
prevent the junction of the two fragments, — then in Golfe
Jouan and Toulon, — one of which, with more resolution and
promptitude on Hotham's part, might have been struck singly
at sea a few months before; and if they join, there must follow a fleet action, between forces too nearly equal to insure to
Great Britain the decisive results that were needed. The
thought he afterwards expressed, "Numbers only can annihilate," was clearly floating in his brain, — inarticulate,
perhaps, as yet, but sure to come to the birth. "If we are
not completely victorious, — I mean, able to remain at sea
whilst the enemy must retire into port, — if we only make a
Lord Howe's victory, take a part, and retire into port, Italy
is lost." Criticism clearly is going on in his mind; and not
mere criticism (there is enough and to spare of that in the
world, and not least in navies), but criticism judicious, well
considered, and above all fruitful. The error of opportunity
lost he had seen; the error of a partial victory — "a Lord
Howe's victory," another opportunity lost — he intuitively
anticipated for the Mediterranean, and was soon to see. He
was already prepared to pass an accurate judgment instantly,
when he saw it. May we not almost hear, thundering back
from the clouds that yet veiled the distant future of the Nile,
the words, of which his thought was already pregnant, "You
may be assured I will bring the French fleet to action the
moment I can lay my hands upon them."

The year closed with the British fleet watching, as best it
could, the French ships, which, according to Nelson's expectation, had given the blockaders the slip, and had made their
junction at Toulon. There was now no great disparity in the
nominal force of the two opponents, the British having fourteen ships-of-the-line, the French fifteen; and it was quite in
the enemy's power to fulfil his other prediction, by keeping
Hotham in hot water during the winter. In the middle of
November the "Agamemnon" had to go to Leghorn for extensive repairs, and remained there, shifting her main and
mizzen masts, until the 21st of December. Nelson, who had
endured with unyielding cheerfulness the dangers, exposure,
and sickliness of Calvi, found himself unable to bear patiently

the comfort of quiet nights in a friendly port, while hot work might chance outside. " Lying in port is misery to me. My heart is almost broke to find the Agamemnon lying here, little better than a wreck. I own my sincere wish that the enemy would rest quiet until we are ready for sea, and a gleam of hope sometimes crosses me that they will." " I am uneasy enough for fear they will fight, and Agamemnon not present, — it will almost break my heart; but I hope the best, — that they are only boasting at present, and will be quiet until I am ready." " It is misery," he repeats, " for me to be laid up dismantled."

It was during this period of comparative inactivity in port, followed by monotonous though arduous winter cruising off Toulon, which was broken only by equally dreary stays at San Fiorenzo, that Nelson found time to brood over the neglect of which he thought himself the victim, in the omission of Lord Hood to notice more markedly his services in Corsica. It is usually disagreeable to the uninterested by-stander to see an excessive desire for praise, even under the guise of just recognition of work done. Words of complaint, whether heard or read, strike a discord to one who himself at the moment is satisfied with his surroundings. We all have an instinctive shrinking from the tones of a grumbler. Nelson's insistence upon his grievances has no exemption from this common experience; yet it must be remembered that these assertions of the importance of his own services, and dissatisfaction with the terms in which they had been mentioned, occur chiefly, if not solely, in letters to closest relations, — to his wife and uncle, — and that they would never have become known but for the after fame, which has caused all his most private correspondence to have interest and to be brought to light. As a revelation of character they have a legitimate interest, and they reveal, or rather they confirm, what is abundantly revealed throughout his life, —that intense longing for distinction, for admiration justly earned, for conspicuous exaltation above the level of his kind, which existed in him to so great a degree, and which is perhaps the most potent — certainly the most universal — factor in military achievement. They reveal this ambition for honor, or glory, on its weak side; on its stronger side of noble emula-

9

tion, of self-devotion, of heroic action, his correspondence
teems with its evidence in words, as does his life in acts.   To
quote the words of Lord Radstock, who at this period, and
until after the battle of Cape St. Vincent, was serving as one
of the junior admirals in the Mediterranean, and retained his
friendship through life, " a perpetual thirst of glory was ever
raging within him." " He has ever showed himself as great
a despiser of riches as he is a lover of glory ; and I am fully
convinced in my own mind that he would sooner defeat the
French fleet than capture fifty galleons."

After all allowance made, however, it cannot be denied that
there is in these complaints a tone which one regrets in such
a man.   The repeated " It was I " jars, by the very sharpness
of its contrast, with the more generous expressions that
abound in his correspondence.   " When I reflect that I was
the cause of re-attacking Bastia, after our *wise* generals gave
it over, from not knowing the force, fancying it 2,000 men ;
that it was I, who landing, joined the Corsicans, and with only
my ship's party of marines, drove the French under the walls
of Bastia; that it was I, who, knowing the force in Bastia to
be upwards of 4,000 men, as I have now only ventured to tell
Lord Hood, landed with only 1,200 men, and kept the secret
till within this week past ; — what I must have felt during
the whole siege may be easily conceived.   Yet I am scarcely
mentioned.   I freely forgive, but cannot forget.   This and
much more ought to have been mentioned.   It is known that,
for two months, I blockaded Bastia with a squadron ; only
fifty sacks of flour got into the town.   At San Fiorenzo and
Calvi, for two months before, nothing got in, and four French
frigates could not get out, and are now ours.   Yet my diligence is not mentioned ; and others, for keeping succours out
of Calvi for a few summer months, are handsomely mentioned.
Such things are.   I have got upon a subject near my heart,
which is full when I think of the treatment I have received.
. . . The taking of Corsica, like the taking of St. Juan's, has
cost me money.   St. Juan's cost near £500 ; Corsica has cost
me £300, an eye, and a cut across my back ; and my money,
I find, cannot be repaid me."

As regards the justice of his complaints, it seems to the
author impossible to read carefully Hood's two reports, after

the fall of Bastia and that of Calvi, and not admit, either that Nelson played a very unimportant part in the general operations connected with the reduction of Corsica, with which he became associated even before it was effectively undertaken, and so remained throughout; or else that no due recognition was accorded to him in the admiral's despatches. Had he not become otherwise celebrated in his after life, he would from these papers be inferred to stand, in achievement, rather below than above the level of the other captains who from time to time were present. That this was unfair seems certain; and notably at Calvi, where, from the distance of the operations from the anchorage, and the strained relations which kept Hood and Stuart apart, he was practically the one naval man upon whose discretion and zeal success depended. It is probable, however, that the failure to do him justice proceeded as much from awkward literary construction, phrases badly turned, as from reluctance to assign due prominence to one subordinate among several others.

How readily, yet how keenly, he derived satisfaction, even from slight tributes of recognition, is shown by the simplicity and pleasure with which he quoted to Mrs. Nelson the following words of Sir Gilbert Elliot, the Viceroy of Corsica, then and always a warm friend and admirer: "I know that you, who have had such an honourable share in this acquisition, will not be indifferent at the prosperity of the Country which you have so much assisted to place under His Majesty's government." "Whether these are words of course and to be forgotten," wrote Nelson, "I know not; they are pleasant, however, for the time." Certainly his demands for praise, if thus measured, were not extreme.

CHAPTER V.

NELSON'S SERVICES WITH THE FLEET IN THE MEDITERRANEAN UNDER
ADMIRAL HOTHAM. — PARTIAL FLEET ACTIONS OF MARCH 13 AND 14,
AND JULY 13.— NELSON ORDERED TO COMMAND A DETACHED SQUAD-
RON CO-OPERATING WITH THE AUSTRIAN ARMY IN THE RIVIERA OF
GENOA.

JANUARY–JULY, 1795. AGE, 36.

FROM the naval point of view, as a strategic measure, the
acquisition of Corsica by the British was a matter of
great importance. It was, however, only one among several
factors, which went to make up the general military and political situation in the Mediterranean at the end of the year
1794. Hitherto the exigencies of the well-nigh universal
hostilities in which France had been engaged, and the anarch-
ical internal state of that country, had prevented any decisive
operations by her on the side of Italy, although she had, since
1792, been formally at war with the Kingdom of Sardinia, of
which Piedmont was a province.

At the close of 1794 the conditions were greatly modified.
In the north, the combined forces of Great Britain, Austria,
and Holland had been driven out of France and Belgium, and
the United Provinces were on the point of submission. On
the east, the Austrians and Prussians had retreated to the
far bank of the Rhine, and Prussia was about to withdraw
from the coalition, which, three years before, she had been
so eager to form. On the south, even greater success had
attended the French armies, which had crossed the Pyrenees
into Spain, driving before them the forces of the enemy, who
also was soon to ask for peace. It was therefore probable
that operations in Italy would assume greatly increased
activity, from the number of French soldiers released elsewhere, as well as from the fact that the Austrians themselves,
though they continued the war in Germany, had abandoned

other portions of the continent which they had hitherto contested.

The political and military conditions in Italy were, briefly, as follows. The region north of the Maritime Alps and in the valley of the Po was, for the most part, in arms against France,— the western province, Piedmont, as part of the Kingdom of Sardinia, whose capital was at Turin, and, to the eastward of it, the duchies of Milan and Mantua, as belonging to Austria. The governments of the numerous small states into which Northern and Central Italy were then divided — Venice, Genoa, Tuscany, the States of the Church, and others — sympathized generally with the opponents of France, but, as far as possible, sought to maintain a formal though difficult neutrality. The position of Genoa was the most embarrassing, because in direct contact with all the principal parties to the war. To the westward, her territory along the Riviera included Vintimiglia, bordering there on the county of Nice, and contained Vado Bay, the best anchorage between Nice and Genoa. To the eastward, it embraced the Gulf of Spezia, continually mentioned by Nelson as Porto Especia.

The occupation of the Riviera was of particular moment to the French, for it offered a road by which to enter Italy, — bad, indeed, but better far than those through the passes of the upper Alps. Skirting the sea, it afforded a double line of communications, by land and by water; for the various detachments of their army, posted along it, could in great degree be supplied by the small coasting-vessels of the Mediterranean. So long, also, as it was in their possession, and they held passes of the Maritime Alps and Apennines, as they did in 1794, there was the possibility of their penetrating through them, to turn the left flank of the Sardinian army in Piedmont, which was, in fact, what Bonaparte accomplished two years later. These inducements had led the French to advance into the county of Nice, then belonging to Sardinia, which in the existing state of war it was perfectly proper for them to do; but, not stopping there, they had pushed on past the Sardinian boundary into the neutral Riviera of Genoa, as far as Vado Bay, which they occupied, and where they still were at the end of 1794.

Genoa submitted under protest to this breach of her neutrality, as she did both before[1] and after to similar insults
from parties to the war. She derived some pecuniary benefit
from the condition of affairs, — her ports, as well as those of
Tuscany, immediately to the southward, becoming depots of a
trade in grain, which supplied both the French army and the
southern provinces of France. These food stuffs, absolutely
essential to the French, were drawn chiefly from Sicily and
the Barbary States, and could not be freely taken into French
ports by the larger class of sea-going vessels, in face of the
British fleet. They were, therefore, commonly transshipped
in Leghorn or Genoa, and carried on by coasters. As so much
Genoese seacoast was occupied by French divisions, it was
practically impossible for British cruisers to distinguish
between vessels carrying corn for the inhabitants and those
laden for the armies, and entirely impossible to know that
what was intended for one object would not be diverted to
another. If, too, a vessel's papers showed her to be destined
for Vintimiglia, near the extreme of the Genoese line, there
could be no certainty that, having got so far, she might not
quietly slip by into a French port, either Nice or beyond. The
tenure of the neutral Riviera of Genoa by the French army
was a threat to the allies of Great Britain in Piedmont and
Lombardy, as well as to the quasi-neutrals in Genoa, Tuscany,
Venice, and the Papal States. Its further advance or successes would imperil the latter, and seriously affect the
attitude of Naples, hostile to the Republic, but weak, timid,
and unstable of purpose. On the other hand, the retention of
its position, and much more any further advance, depended
upon continuing to receive supplies by way of the sea. To
do so by the shore route alone was not possible. Southern
France itself depended upon the sea for grain, and could send
nothing, even if the then miserable Corniche road could have
sufficed, as the sole line of communications for forty thousand
troops.

Thus the transfer of Corsica to Great Britain had a very
important bearing upon the military and political conditions.
At the moment when Italy was about to become the scene of

[1] In the year 1793 the French frigate "Modeste" had been forcibly taken
from the harbor of Genoa by an English squadron.

operations which might, and in the event actually did, exercise a decisive influence upon the course of the general war, the British position was solidified by the acquisition of a naval base, unassailable while the sea remained in their control and the Corsicans attached to their cause, and centrally situated with reference to the probable scenes of hostilities, as well as to the points of political interest, on the mainland of Italy. The fleet resting upon it, no longer dependent upon the reluctant hospitality of Genoese or Tuscan ports, or upon the far distant Kingdom of Naples, was secure to keep in its station, whence it menaced the entire seaboard trade of France and the Riviera, as well as the tenure of the French army in the latter, and exerted a strong influence upon the attitude of both Genoa and Tuscany, who yielded only too easily to the nearest or most urgent pressure. The fleet to which Nelson belonged had spent the greater part of the year 1794 in securing for itself, as a base of operations, this position, by far the most suitable among those that could be considered at all. It remained now to utilize the advantage obtained, to make the situation of the French army in Italy untenable, by establishing an indisputable control of the sea. To this the holding of Corsica also contributed, indirectly; for the loss of the island forced the French fleet to go to sea, in order, if possible, to expedite its re-conquest. In all the operations resulting from these various motives, Nelson bore a part as conspicuous and characteristic as he had done in the reduction of Corsica. Almost always on detached service, in positions approaching independent command, he was continually adding to his reputation, and, what was far more important, maturing the professional character, the seeds of which had been so bountifully bestowed upon him by nature. His reputation, won hard and step by step, obtained for him opportunity; but it was to character, ripened by experience and reflection, that he owed his transcendent successes.

The scheme for the government of the island as a British dependency, stated broadly, was that it should be administered by the Corsicans themselves, under a viceroy appointed by the British crown. Its military security was provided for by the control of the sea, and by British soldiers holding the fortified ports, — a duty for which the Corsicans themselves had not

then the necessary training. Nelson, who did not yet feel
the impossibility of sustaining a successful over-sea invasion,
when control of the sea was not had, was anxious about the
expected attempts of the French against the island, and urged
the viceroy, by private letter, to see that Ajaccio, which he
regarded as the point most favorable to a descent, was garrisoned sufficiently to keep the gates shut for a few days.
This caution did not then proceed from a distrust of the
Corsicans' fidelity, without which neither France nor England
could hold the island, as was shown by the quickness of its
transfer two years later, when the inhabitants again revolted
to France. "With this defence," he wrote, "I am confident
Ajaccio, and I believe I may say the island of Corsica, would
be perfectly safe until our fleet could get to the enemy, when
I have no doubt the event would be what every Briton might
expect."

The repairs of the "Agamemnon" were completed before
Nelson's anxious apprehensions of a battle taking place in his
absence could be fulfilled. On the 21st of December, 1794, he
sailed from Leghorn with the fleet, in company with which
he remained from that time until the following July, when
he was sent to the Riviera of Genoa on special detached service. He thus shared the severe cruising of that winter, as
well as the abortive actions of the spring and early summer,
where the admiral again contrived to lose opportunities of
settling the sea campaign, and with it, not improbably, that
of the land also. There were plain indications in the port of
Toulon that a maritime enterprise of some importance was in
contemplation. In the outer road lay fifteen sail-of-the-line,
the British having then fourteen; but more significant of the
enemy's purpose was the presence at Marseilles of fifty large
transports, said to be ready. "I have no doubt," wrote Nelson, "but Porto Especia is their object." This was a mistake,
interesting as indicating the slight weight that Nelson at that
time attributed to the deterrent effect of the British fleet " in
being" upon such an enterprise, involving an open-sea passage
of over a hundred miles, though he neither expressed nor
entertained any uncertainty as to the result of a meeting, if
the enemy were encountered. The French Government, not
yet appreciating the inefficiency to which its navy had been

reduced by many concurrent circumstances, was ready to dispute the control of the Mediterranean, and it contemplated, among other things, a demonstration at Leghorn, similar to that successfully practised at Naples in 1792, which might compel the Court of Tuscany to renounce the formally hostile attitude it had assumed at the bidding of Great Britain; but it does not appear that there was any serious purpose of exposing a large detachment, in the attempt to hold upon the Continent a position, such as Spezia, with which secure communication by land could not be had.

Though none too careful to proportion its projects to the force at its disposal, the Directory sufficiently understood that a detachment at Spezia could not be self-dependent, nor could, with any certainty, combine its operations with those of the army in the Riviera; and also that, to be properly supported at all, there must be reasonably secure and unbroken communication, either by land or water, neither of which was possible until the British fleet was neutralized. The same consideration dictated to it the necessity of a naval victory, before sending out the expedition, of whose assembling the British were now hearing, and which was actually intended for Corsica; although it was known that in the island there had already begun the revulsion against the British rule, which culminated in open revolt the following year. Owing to the dearth of seamen, the crews of the French ships were largely composed of soldiers, and it was thought that, after beating the enemy, four or five thousand of these might be at once thrown on shore at Ajaccio, and that afterwards the main body could be sent across in safety. First of all, however, control of the sea must be established by a battle, more or less decisive.

On the 24th of February, 1795, the British fleet arrived at Leghorn, after a very severe cruise of over a fortnight. On the 2d of March Nelson mentioned, in a letter to his wife, that the French were said then to have a hundred and twenty-four transports full of troops, from which he naturally argued that they must mean to attempt something. On the evening of the 8th, an express from Genoa brought Hotham word that they were actually at sea, fifteen ships-of-the-line, with half a dozen or more smaller vessels. He sailed in pursuit early

the next morning, having with him thirteen [1] British ships-of-
the-line and one Neapolitan seventy-four. Of the former,
four were three-decked ships, carrying ninety-eight to one
hundred guns, a class of vessel of which the French had but
one, the "Sans Culottes," of one hundred and twenty, which,
under the more dignified name of "L'Orient," afterwards met
so tragic a fate at the Battle of the Nile; but they had, in
compensation, three powerful ships of eighty guns, much
superior to the British seventy-fours. As, however, only
partial engagements followed, the aggregate of force on either
side is a matter of comparatively little importance in a Life
of Nelson.

Standing to the northward and westward, with a fresh
easterly wind, the British fleet through its lookouts discovered the enemy on the evening of the day of sailing, and by
the same means kept touch with them throughout the 10th
and 11th; but the baffling airs, frequent in the Mediterranean,
prevented the main body seeing them until the morning of
the 12th. At daylight, then, they were visible from the
"Agamemnon," in company with which were five British
ships and the Neapolitan; the remainder of the fleet being so
far to the eastward that their hulls were just rising out of the
water. The British lying nearly becalmed, the French, who
were to windward, bore down to within three miles; but
although, in Nelson's judgment, they had a fair opportunity
to separate the advanced British ships, with which he was,
from the main body, they failed to improve it. Nothing
happened that day, and, a fresh breeze from the west springing up at dusk, both fleets stood to the southward with it, the
French being to windward. That night one of the latter, a
seventy-four, having lost a topmast, was permitted to return
to port.

The next morning the wind was still southwest and squally.
Hotham at daylight ordered a general chase, which allowed
each ship a certain freedom of movement in endeavoring to
close with the French. The "Agamemnon" had been well to
the westward, from the start; and being a very handy, quick-
working ship, as well as, originally at least, more than com-

[1] The "Berwick," seventy-four, had been left in San Fiorenzo for repairs.
Putting to sea at this time, she fell in with the French fleet, and was taken.

monly fast, was early in the day in a position where she had
a fair chance for reaching the enemy. A favorable opportunity soon occurred, one of those which so often show that,
if a man only puts himself in the way of good luck, good luck
is apt to offer. At 8 A. M. the eighty-gun ship "Ça Ira," third
from the rear in the French order, ran on board the vessel
next ahead of her, and by the collision lost her fore and main
topmasts. These falling overboard on the lee side — in this
case the port [1] — not only deprived her of by far the greater
part of her motive power, but acted as a drag on her progress,
besides for the time preventing the working of the guns on
that side. The "Ça Ira" dropped astern of her fleet. Although this eighty-gun ship was much bigger than his own,
— "absolutely large enough to take Agamemnon in her hold,"
Nelson said, — the latter saw his chance, and instantly seized
it with the promptitude characteristic of all his actions. The
"Agamemnon," if she was not already on the port tack, opposite to that on which the fleets had been during the night,
must have gone about at this time, and probably for this
reason. She was able thus to fetch into the wake of the
crippled vessel, which a frigate had already gallantly attacked, taking advantage of the uselessness of the Frenchman's lee batteries, encumbered with the wreckage of the
masts.

At 10 A. M., the "Ça Ira" and the "Agamemnon" having
passed on opposite tacks, the latter again went about and
stood in pursuit under all sail, rapidly nearing the enemy,
who at this time was taken in tow by a frigate. But although
in this position the French ship could not train her broadside
guns upon her smaller opponent, she could still work freely
the half-dozen stern guns, and did so with much effect. "So
true did she fire," noted Nelson, "that not a shot missed some
part of the ship, and latterly the masts were struck every
shot, which obliged me to open our fire a few minutes sooner
than I intended, for it was my intention to have touched his
stern before a shot was fired." At quarter before eleven, the
"Agamemnon" was within a hundred yards of the "Ça Ira's"
stern, and this distance she was able to keep until 1 P. M.

[1] The port side, or, as it was called in Nelson's day, the larboard side, is the
left, looking from the stern to the bow of a ship.

Here, by the use of the helm and of the sails, the ship alternately turned her starboard side to the enemy to fire her batteries, and again resumed her course, to regain the distance necessarily lost at each deviation. This raking fire not only killed and wounded many of the " Ça Ira's " crew, and injured the hull, but, what was tactically of yet greater importance, preventing the replacing of the lost spars. Thus was entailed upon the French that night a crippled ship, which they could not in honor abandon, nor yet could save without fighting for her, — a tactical dilemma which was the direct cause of the next day's battle.

Brief and cursory as is the notice of this action of the " Agamemnon " in Hotham's despatches, he mentions no other ship-of-the-line as engaged at this time, and states that she and the frigate were so far detached from the fleet, that they were finally obliged to retire on account of other enemy's vessels approaching. Nelson's journal says that two French ships, one of one hundred and twenty guns and a seventy-four, were at gun-shot distance on the bow of the " Ça Ira " when he began to attack her. These, with several others of their fleet, went about some time before one, at which hour the frigate, towing the disabled ship, tacked herself, and also got the latter around. The " Agamemnon " standing on, she and the " Ça Ira " now crossed within half pistol-range ; but, the French guns being too much elevated, the shot passed over their antagonist, who lost in this day's work only seven men wounded. Nelson then again tacked to follow, but by this time the French admiral had apparently decided that his crippled vessel must be rescued, and his fleet no longer defied by a foe so inferior in strength. Several of the enemy were approaching, when Hotham made a signal of recall, which Nelson on this occasion at least had no hesitation in obeying, and promptly. There was no pursuit, the hostile commander-in-chief being apparently satisfied to save the " Ça Ira " for the moment, without bringing on a general engagement.

In this affair, what is mainly to be noted in Nelson is not the personal courage, nor yet even the professional daring, or the skill which justified the daring. It may be conceded that all these were displayed in a high degree, but they can scarcely be claimed to have exceeded that shown by other

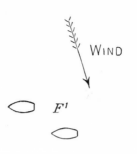

WIND

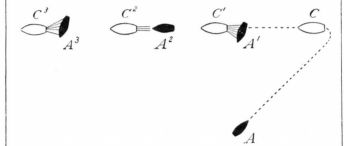

AGAMEMNON & ÇA IRA

March 13, 1795.

A — *Agamemnon*
C — *Ça Ira*
F — *French Ships of Line*
B — *Nearest British do.*

officers, not a few, when equally tried. What is rather striking, account for it how we will, is that Nelson, here as always, was on hand when opportunity offered ; that after three days of chase he, and he only, was so far to the front as to be able to snatch the fleeting moment. " On looking round," he says at ten o'clock, when about to begin the action, " I saw no shipof-the-line within several miles to support me; the Captain was the nearest on our lee-quarter." With the looseness and lack of particularity which characterize most logs and despatches remaining from those days, and make the comprehension of naval engagements, other than the greatest, a matter of painful and uncertain inference, it is impossible accurately to realize the entire situation ; but it seems difficult to imagine that among all the other thirteen captains, " where emulation was common to all and zeal for his Majesty's service the general description of the fleet," to use Hotham's words, none could have been on the spot to support so promising an attempt, had there been " common " that sort of emulation which takes a man ever to the front, not merely in battle but at all times, — the spirit that will not and cannot rest while anything remains to be done, ever pressing onward to the mark. To this unquestionably must be added the rapid comprehension of a situation, and the exceeding promptitude with which Nelson seized his opportunity, as well as the tenacious intrepidity with which he held to his position of advantage, despite the imminent threat to his safety from the uninjured and gigantic " Sans Culottes," barely out of gunshot to windward. It is right also to note the accessibility to advice, a feature of his genial and kindly temperament, to which he admitted much of the success was due. The trait is not rare in mankind in general, but it is exceptional in men of a character so self-reliant and decided as Nelson. " If the conduct of the Agamemnon on the 13th," he generously wrote, " was by any means the cause of our success on the 14th, Lieutenant Andrews has a principal share in the merit, for a more proper opinion was never given by an officer than the one he gave me on the 13th, in a situation of great difficulty."

The same hot spirit, the same unwearying energy, made itself still more manifest the next day, when were to be garnered the results of his own partial, yet, in its degree, decisive action of the 13th. " Sure I am," said he afterwards, "had I commanded our fleet on the 14th, that either the whole French fleet would have graced my triumph, or I should have been in a confounded scrape." A confounded scrape he would have been in on the 13th, and on other days also, great and small, had there been a different issue to the risks he dared, and rightly dared, to take. Of what man eminent in war, indeed, is not the like true ? It is the price of fame, which he who dare not pay must forfeit; and not fame only, but repute.

During the following night the " Sans Culottes " quitted the French fleet. The wind continued southerly, both fleets standing to the westward, the crippled " Ça Ira " being taken in tow by the " Censeur," of seventy-four guns. At daylight of March 14, being about twenty miles southwest from Genoa, these two were found to be much astern and to leeward of their main body, — that is, northeast from it. The British lay in the same direction, and were estimated by Nelson to be three and a half miles from the disabled ship and her consort, five miles from the rest of the French. At 5.30 A. M. a smart breeze sprang up from the northwest, which took the British aback, but enabled them afterwards to head for the two separated French ships. Apparently, from Nelson's log, this wind did not reach the main body of the enemy, a circumstance not uncommon in the Mediterranean. Two British seventy-fours, the " Captain " and the " Bedford," in obedience to signals, stood down to attack the " Censeur " and the " Ça Ira ; " and, having in this to undergo for twenty minutes a fire to which they could not reply, were then and afterwards pretty roughly handled. They were eventually left behind, crippled, as their own fleet advanced. The rest of the British were meantime forming in line and moving down to sustain them. The French main body, keeping the southerly wind, wore in succession to support their separated ships, and headed to pass between them and their enemies. The latter, having formed, stood also towards these two, which now lay between the contestants as the prize to the victor.

Apparently, in these manœuvres, the leading British ships ran again into the belt of southerly wind, — which the French

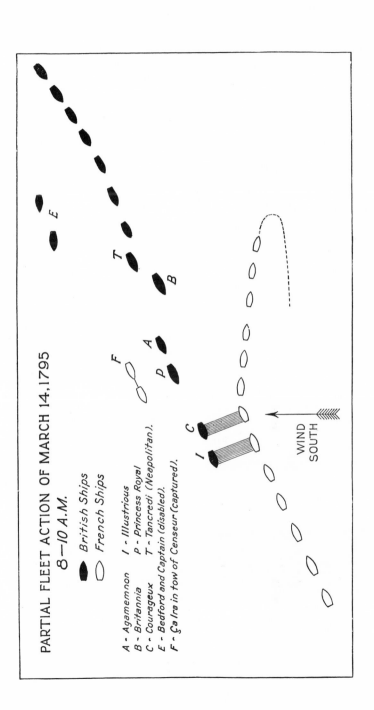

PARTIAL FLEET ACTION OF MARCH 14, 1795
8–10 A.M.

◖ British Ships
◗ French Ships

A - Agamemnon   I - Illustrious
B - Britannia   P - Princess Royal
C - Courageux   T - Tancredi (Neapolitan).
E - Bedford and Captain (disabled).
F - Ça Ira in tow of Censeur (captured).

WIND
SOUTH

kept throughout, — while part of the centre and rear were left becalmed, and had little or no share in the cannonade that followed. Under these conditions the resolution of the French admiral seems to have faltered, for instead of passing to leeward — north — of the enemy's line, which was quite in his power, and so covering his endangered ships, he allowed the latter to be cut off, thus insuring their surrender. His fleet kept to windward of the British, passing fairly near the two leading ships, the "Illustrious" and the "Courageux," who thus underwent a "concentration by defiling," that took the main and mizzen masts out of both, besides killing and wounding many of their people. The "Princess Royal" and "Agamemnon," which came next, could only engage at long range. "The enemy's fleet kept the southerly wind," wrote Nelson in his journal, "which enabled them to keep their distance, which was very great. At 8 A.M. they began to pass our line to windward, and the Ça Ira and Le Censeur were on our lee side; therefore the Illustrious, Courageux, Princess Royal, and Agamemnon were obliged to fight on both sides of the ship." At five minutes past ten A.M. both the French vessels struck, the "Ça Ira" having lost her three masts, and the "Censeur" her mainmast. It was past one P.M. when firing wholly ceased; and the enemy then crowded all possible sail to the westward, the British fleet lying with their heads to the southeast.

When the British line was forming, between seven and eight in the morning, Nelson was directed by Vice-Admiral Goodall, the second in command, to take his station astern of his flagship, the "Princess Royal," of ninety guns. Immediately behind the "Agamemnon" came the "Britannia," carrying Hotham's flag. This position, and the lightness of the wind, serve to explain how Nelson came to take the step he mentions in several letters; going on board the "Britannia," after the two French vessels struck, and urging the commander-in-chief to leave the prizes in charge of the British frigates and crippled ships-of-the-line, and vigorously to pursue the French, who having lost four ships out of their fleet, by casualty or capture, were now reduced to eleven sail. "I went on board Admiral Hotham as soon as our firing grew slack in the van, and the Ça Ira and the Censeur had struck,

to propose to him leaving our two crippled ships, the two
prizes, and four frigates, to themselves, and to pursue the
enemy; but he, much cooler than myself, said, ' We must be
contented, we have done very well.' Now, had we taken ten
sail, and had allowed the eleventh to escape, when it had been
possible to have got at her, I could never have called it well
done. Goodall backed me; I got him to write to the admiral,
but it would not do: we should have had such a day as I believe the annals of England never produced."

Nelson here evidently assumes that it was possible to have
got at the French fleet. After a man's reputation has been
established, there is always the danger of giving undue weight
to his opinions, expressed at an earlier time, somewhat
casually, and not under the sobering sense of responsibility.
Hotham may have questioned the possibility of getting at the
French effectively, having regard to the fickle lightness of
the wind then prevalent, and to the fact that, besides the two
ships partially dismasted and for the moment useless, two
others, the "Captain" and the "Bedford," had suffered
severely in sails and rigging. He would also doubtless consider that the three-decked ships, of which he had four, were
notoriously bad sailers, and sure to drop behind if the chase
lasted long, leaving to eight ships, including the "Neapolitan," the burden of arresting the enemy, who had shown very
fair offensive powers in the morning. Nelson was not blind
to these facts, and not infrequently alludes to them. "Had
we only a breeze, I have no doubt we should have given a
destructive blow to the enemy's fleet." "Sure I am, that
had the breeze continued, so as to have allowed us to close
with the enemy, we should have destroyed their whole fleet."
Whether these remarks apply to the heat of the engagement,
or to the proposed chase, which Hotham declined to permit,
is not perfectly clear; but inasmuch as the second part of
the action of the 14th consisted, actually, in the French filing
by the "Courageux" and the "Illustrious," upon whom their
fire was thus concentrated, while the rest of the British were
becalmed out of gunshot, it is very possible he was thinking
of that incident only, which doubtless would have taken a
very different turn had the main body been able to come
down. His wish to pursue is unquestionable, both from his

assertion and from the whole character of his career before and after; and a casual remark, written ten days after the affair, shows his opinion confirmed by time. "Had our good admiral followed the blow, we should probably have done more, but the risk was thought too great."

The question attracts attention, both impersonally, as of military interest, and also as bearing upon Nelson's correctness of judgment, and professional characteristics, at this time. As regards the amount of wind, it is sufficient to say that the French fleet, having borne away to the westward in the afternoon, was next day out of sight.[1] Most of the British might equally have been out of sight from the position in which they remained. As for the risk — of course there was risk; but the whole idea of a general chase rests upon the fact that, for one reason or another, the extreme speed of the ships in each fleet will vary, and that it is always probable that the fastest of the pursuers can overtake the slowest of the pursued. The resulting combats compel the latter either to abandon his ships, or to incur a general action, which, from the fact of his flight, it is evident he has reason to avoid. In this case many of the retreating French were crippled, — some went off towed by frigates, and some without bowsprits. Unquestionably, the pursuers who thus engage may be overpowered before those following them come up; but the balance of chances is generally in their favor, and in the particular instance would have been markedly so, as was shown by the results of the two days' fighting, which had proved the superior quality of the British ships' companies.

The fact is, neither Hotham nor his opponent, Martin, was willing to hazard a decisive naval action, but wished merely to obtain a temporary advantage, — the moment's safety, no risks. "I have good reason," wrote Hotham in his despatch, "to hope, from the enemy's steering to the westward after having passed our fleet, that whatever might have been their design, *their intentions are for the present frustrated.*" It is scarcely necessary to say that a man who looks no further ahead than this, who fails to realize that the destruction of the enemy's fleet is the one condition of permanent safety to

[1] Nelson to the Duke of Clarence, March 15, 1795. (Nicolas.)

10

his cause, will not rise to the conception presented to him on his quarter-deck by Nelson. The latter, whether by the sheer intuition of genius, which is most probable, or by the result of well-ordered reasoning, which is less likely, realized fully that to destroy the French fleet was the one thing for which the British fleet was there, and the one thing by doing which it could decisively affect the war. As he wrote four years later to St. Vincent, "Not one moment shall be lost in bringing the enemy to battle; for I consider the best defence for his Sicilian Majesty's dominions is to place myself alongside the French."

Yet Nelson was far from unconscious of the difficulties of Hotham's position, or from failing duly to allow for them. "Admiral Hotham has had much to contend with, a fleet half-manned, and in every respect inferior to the enemy; Italy calling him to her defence, our newly acquired kingdom[1] calling might and main, our reinforcements and convoy hourly expected; and all to be done without a force by any means adequate to it." Add to this the protection of British trade, of whose needs Nelson was always duly sensible. Yet, as one scans this list of troubles, with the query how to meet them running in his mind, it is scarcely possible not to see that each and every difficulty would have been solved by a crushing pursuit of the beaten French, preventing their again taking the sea. The British admiral had in his control no means to force them out of port. Therefore, when out, he should by no means have allowed them to get back. It is only just to Hotham, who had been a capable as well as gallant captain, to say that he had objected to take the chief command, on account of his health.

Nelson was delighted with his own share in these affairs, and with the praise he received from others for his conduct, — especially that on the 13th. He was satisfied, and justly, that his sustained and daring grapple with the "Ça Ira," in the teeth of her fleet, had been the effective cause of the next day's action and consequent success. It was so, in truth, and it presented an epitome of what the 14th and 15th ought to have witnessed, — a persistent clinging to the crippled ships, in order to force their consorts again into battle.

[1] Corsica.

"You will participate," he wrote to his uncle, "in the pleasure I must have felt in being the great cause of our success. Could I have been supported, I would have had Ça Ira on the 13th." Elliot, the Viceroy of Corsica, wrote to him: "I certainly consider the business of the 13th of March as a very capital feature in the late successful contest with the French fleet; and the part which the Agamemnon had in it must be felt by every one to be one of the circumstances that gave lustre to this event, and rendered it not only useful, but peculiarly honourable to the British arms." "So far," added Nelson, in quoting this to his wife, "all hands agree in giving me the praises which cannot but be comfortable to me to the last moment of my life." He adds then a reflection, evincing that he was assimilating some of the philosophy of life as well as of fighting. "The time of my being left out here by Lord Hood," which he had so much regretted, "I may call well spent; had I been absent, how mortified should I now be. What has happened may never happen to any one again, that only one ship-of-the-line out of fourteen should get into action with the French fleet for so long a time as two hours and a half, and with such a ship as the Ça Ira." It may be of interest to mention that the French fleet, upon this occasion, was largely composed of the vessels which three years later were destroyed by him at the Battle of the Nile.

In all his interests, ambitions, and gratification with success and praise, he at this period writes fully and intimately to his wife, between whom and himself there evidently still existed, after these two years of absence, a tender and affectionate confidence. "It is with an inexpressible pleasure I have received your letters, with our father's. I rejoice that my conduct gives you pleasure, and I trust I shall never do anything which will bring a blush on your face. Rest assured you are never absent from my thoughts." When looking forward to the action of March 14, he tells her: "Whatever may be my fate, I have no doubt in my own mind but that my conduct will be such as will not bring a blush on the face of my friends; the lives of all are in the hands of Him who knows best whether to preserve mine or not; to His will do I resign myself. My character and good name are in my own keeping. Life with disgrace is dreadful. A glorious death is to be envied;" and he signs himself with unwonted tenderness, "Ever your most faithful and affectionate husband." Save of the solemn hours before Trafalgar, when another image occupied his thoughts, this is the only personal record we have of the feelings with which this man, dauntless above his fellows, went into battle. He refrains thoughtfully from any mention of his health that may cause her anxiety, which she had shown herself over weak and worrying to bear; but he speaks freely of all that passes, confiding that with her he need have no reserves, even in a natural self-praise. "This I can say, that all I have obtained I owe to myself, and to no one else, and *to you* I may add, that my character stands high with almost all Europe. Even the Austrians knew my name perfectly." While silent on the subject of illness, he admits now that his eye had grown worse, and was in almost total darkness, besides being very painful at times; "but never mind," he adds cheeringly, "I can see very well with the other."

It is instructive to note, in view of some modern debated questions, that, despite the recent success, Nelson was by no means sure that the British fleet could defend Corsica. "I am not even now certain Corsica is safe," he wrote on the 25th of March, "if they undertake the expedition with proper spirit." The threat, never absent while the French fleet remained, was emphasized by the arrival of six ships-of-the-line from Brest, which reached Toulon on the 4th of April, materially altering the complexion of affairs in the Mediterranean, and furnishing an instructive instance of the probable punishment for opportunity imperfectly utilized, as on the 14th of March. Great discontent was felt at the apparent failure of the Admiralty to provide against this chance. "Hotham is very much displeased with them," wrote Nelson, "and certainly with reason;" and doubtless it is satisfactory to believe, rightly or wrongly, that our disadvantages are due to the neglect of others, and not to our own shortcomings.

Although the nominal force of the French was thus raised to twenty of the line, the want of seamen, and the absence of discipline, prevented their seizing the opportunity offered by the temporary inferiority of the British, reduced to thirteen besides two Neapolitans, in whose efficiency, whether justly or not, Nelson placed little confidence. At this critical moment, with a large British military convoy expected, and the fleet, to use his impatient expression, "skulking in port," a Jacobin outbreak occurred in Toulon, and the seamen assumed the *opéra-bouffe* rôle of going ashore to assist in deliberations upon the measures necessary to save the country. Before they were again ready to go to sea, the convoy had arrived. On the 7th of June, however, the French again sailed from Toulon, seventeen ships-of-the-line; and the following day Nelson, writing to his brother, thus gave vent to the bitterness of his feelings: "We have been cruising off Minorca for a long month, every moment in expectation of reinforcements from England. Great good fortune has hitherto saved us, what none in this fleet could have expected for so long a time. Near two months we have been skulking from them. Had they not got so much cut up on the 14th of March, Corsica, Rome, and Naples would, at this moment, have been in their possession, and may yet, if these people [the Admiralty] do not make haste to help us. I am out of spirits, although never better in health."

His depression was due less to the inadequacy of the British fleet than to the dismissal of Lord Hood from the command, news of which was at this time received. When about to sail from England, to resume his duty as commander-in-chief, he got into a controversy with the Government about the force necessary in the Mediterranean, and, giving offence by the sharpness of his language, was ordered to haul down his flag. He never again went to sea. Nelson deplored his loss in terms unusually vivacious: "Oh, miserable Board of Admiralty! They have forced the first officer in our service away from his command." In more temperate but well-weighed words, he said: "This fleet must regret the loss of Lord Hood, the best officer, take him altogether, that England has to boast of. Lord Howe is certainly a great officer in the management of a fleet, but that is all. Lord Hood is equally great in all situations which an admiral can be placed in." In the judgment of the present writer, this estimate of Hood is as accurate as it is moderate in expression. It was nothing less than providential for the French that he was not in command on the 14th of March, or in the yet more trivial and discreditable affair of July 13th, when, to use again Nelson's words, "To say how much we wanted Lord Hood at that time, is to say, will you have all the French fleet or no action?"

On the 14th of June the expected reinforcement from England, nine ships-of-the-line, joined the fleet off Minorca; and a few days later a large convoy also arrived, with which the whole body of ships of war put into San Fiorenzo Bay on the 29th. This concluded for Nelson a period of three months, counting from the action of March 14th, of pretty monotonous cruising with the fleet, the last in which he was to take part until his admiral's flag was hoisted, two years later. Though unmarked by any event of importance, the time was passed not unprofitably to himself, for his correspondence bears marks of fruitful reflection, not merely upon the evident inadequacy of his commander-in-chief to the position he unwillingly occupied, but upon the character of the operations and the line of conduct that ought to be followed. If he does criticise the former's want of head for enterprise, he formulates for himself a general principle which showed its vital influence in his future career. "After all my complaints, I have no doubt but, if we can get close to the enemy, we shall defeat any plan of theirs; *but we ought to have our ideas beyond mere defensive measures.*"

Among other matters for reflection, he had at this time a curious cause of anxiety, lest he should be promoted to flag rank, or rather that, being promoted, he should be obliged to return to England at once, as there would be too many admirals in the Mediterranean to permit his retention. A rumor was current, which proved to be correct, that there would be a large promotion on the 1st of June, the first anniversary of the victory celebrated by that name. Being then forty-six on the list of captains, Nelson feared that it might include him; in which case, if not permitted to hoist his flag where he was, not only would he lose his ardently desired opportunities for distinction, — "not an hour this war will I, if possible, be out of active service," — but he would be put to much inconvenience and loss. "If they give me my flag, I shall be half ruined: unless I am immediately employed in this country, I should, by the time I landed in England, be a loser, several hundred pounds out of pocket." To be taken "from actual service would distress me much, more especially as I almost believe these people will be mad enough to come out." He escaped this disappointment, however, for the promotion left him still on the post-captains' list, seven from its head; but he received, what was both complimentary and profitable, the honorary rank of Colonel of Marines, — a sinecure appointment, of which there were then four, given to post-captains of distinguished services, and vacated by them upon promotion. These are now discontinued, and replaced, as a matter of emolument, by Good Service Pensions. Nelson heard later that this reward had been conferred upon him, not merely as a favor, but with a full recognition of all his claims to it. "The Marines have been given to me in the handsomest manner. The answer given to many was, the King knew no officer who had served so much for them as myself."

These promotions came timely to insure for him an employment particularly suited to his active temperament and fearlessness of responsibility, but which, though the fittest man for it, he might, with less seniority, not have received from Hotham, despite the well-known confidence in him shown by Hood. Since the spring opened, the Austrians and their allies, the Sardinians, had been waiting, ostensibly at least, for assistance from the Navy, to begin a forward movement, the first object of which was the possession of Vado Bay as a safe anchorage for the fleet. Until the arrival of Man and the convoy, Hotham had not felt strong enough to spare the required force; but now, after the ships had filled their wants from the transports, he, on the 4th of July, detached Nelson, with the "Agamemnon" and six smaller vessels, to co-operate with the Austrian commander-in-chief. The latter had begun his movement on the 13th of June, passing through Genoese territory despite the remonstrances of the Republic, whose neutrality could claim but slight regard from one belligerent, when she had already permitted the occupation of so much of her shore line by the other. The French had fallen back, when attacked, abandoning Vado Bay to the enemy, whose headquarters were established at that point.

Nelson, having sailed with four of his squadron, fell in with the French fleet of seventeen of the line, off the Riviera, on

the 6th of July. He had, of course, to retreat, which he did
upon San Fiorenzo, to join the body of the fleet. On the
morning of the 7th the "Agamemnon" and her followers,
with the French in close pursuit, were sighted from the anchorage, much to the surprise of the admiral, who knew the
enemy had come out, but, upon the information of the Austrian general, believed them returned to Toulon. Why he
had not more accurate news from lookout frigates is not clear;
but, as Nelson said, he took things easy, and he had persuaded
himself that they had left harbor only to exercise their men.
As it was, the "Agamemnon" was hard pressed, but escaped,
chiefly through the enemy's lack of seamanship. The fleet,
when she arrived, was in the midst of refitting and watering,
but succeeded in getting to sea the following morning in search
of the enemy, who meantime had disappeared.

Precise information of the French whereabouts could not be
obtained until the evening of the 12th, when two of the British lookout ships reported that they had been seen a few hours
before to the southwest, south of the Hyères Islands. The
fleet made sail in that direction. During the night a heavy
gale came on from west-northwest, out of the Gulf of Lyons,
which split the main-topsails of several British ships. At
daybreak the enemy were discovered in the southeast, standing
north to close the land. After some elaborate manœuvring —
to reach one of those formal orders, often most useful, but
which the irregular Mediterranean winds are prone to dis-
arrange as soon as completed — the admiral at 8 A. M. signalled
a general chase. The British being to windward, and the
breeze fresh, the half-dozen leading ships had at noon closed
the enemy's rear within three-quarters of a mile; but, from
their relative positions, as then steering, the guns of neither
could be used effectively. At this time a shift of wind to
north headed off both fleets, which put their bows to the
eastward, throwing the British advanced vessels, to use
Nelson's expression, into line abreast, and bringing to bear
the broadsides of the ships, of both fleets, that were within
range. The action then began, the British fire being directed
mainly upon the French rear ship, the "Alcide," which surrendered at about 2 P. M., and soon afterwards blew up. The
wind had meanwhile changed again to the eastward, giving

the weather-gage to the French, most of whom were considerably nearer the shore than their opponents, and better sailers.

Up to this time Nelson, who in the forenoon had thought
there was every prospect of taking every ship in the French
fleet, still felt almost certain that six would be secured; but,
to use his own words, it was now "impossible to close." In
the space between the ships engaged, and to leeward, the
light air seems to have been killed by the cannonading;
whereas the French, who were now to windward, still received enough to draw slowly away. Hotham, being in one
of the very worst sailers in the fleet, if not in the Navy, had
fallen eight miles astern, and not seeing clearly how things
were going, made at this time a signal of recall, which was
certainly premature. It seems a not improper comment that,
in light and baffling weather, such as that of the Mediterranean, the commander-in-chief should have been in a fast
and handy ship, able at the least to keep him within eyeshot
of the decisive scene. Remaining in the "Britannia" may
have been due to the natural unwillingness of an invalid to
quit his well-ordered surroundings, by which even St. Vincent
was led to take a first-rate ship away with himself at a critical moment; but, if so, it only emphasizes the absolute
necessity of physical vigor to a commander-in-chief.

Nelson had again managed to keep the "Agamemnon" well
to the front, for the other ships that succeeded in getting
into action were almost wholly from among those which had
recently arrived from England with Rear-Admiral Man.
These, being fresh from home, should naturally outsail a ship
now two and a half years in commission, and which, not long
after, had to be wrapped with hawsers to hold her together.
In his comments on the action he says comparatively little of
the signal of recall, which, though ill-timed, he does not seem
to have thought affected the result materially; but he was
utterly dissatisfied with the previous management of the
business, and into the causes of this dissatisfaction it is desirable to look, as bearing at once upon his natural military
characteristics, and the development they received from time
and thought. "The scrambling distant fire was a farce," he
wrote; "but if one fell by such a fire, what might not have
been expected had our whole fleet engaged? Improperly

as the part of the fleet which fired got into action, we took
one ship; but the subject is unpleasant, and I shall have done
with it." The criticism, though far from explicit, evidently
bears upon the manner in which the fleet was handled, from
the moment the enemy was sighted until the firing began.
During the latter, Man was the senior officer on the spot, and
Nelson does not blame him; on the contrary, punning on the
name, says, "He is a good *man* in every sense of the word."

The precise working of his thought can only be inferred.
"The whole fleet" failed to get into action. Why? Because
the signal for a general chase was delayed from 4 to 8 A. M.,
pending certain drill-ground manœuvres, upon whose results,
however well intended, no dependence could be placed in
Mediterranean weather. During these four hours the wind
was fresh, — the heel of a short summer's gale, invaluable to
both sides, — and the enemy were using it to close the shore,
where wind, the sole dependence for motive power, baffles
most. Had the fastest British ships, under a competent flag-
officer, utilized that time and that wind, there was, to put the
case most mildly, the chance that they could repeat, upon the
French rear, the same part the "Agamemnon" alone had
played with the "Ça Ira," — and such a chance, were it no
more, should not have been dawdled with. "Missed the
opportunity," — the fatal words, "it might have been." Is
it far-fetched to see in his reflections upon "this miserable
action," as it is styled independently by James and himself,
the forecast of the opening sentence of his celebrated order
before Trafalgar? — "Thinking it almost impossible to bring
a fleet of forty sail-of-the-line[1] into a line of battle in variable winds, thick weather, and other circumstances which
must occur, *without such a loss of time that the opportunity
would probably be lost of bringing the enemy to battle in such a
manner as to make the business decisive,* I have therefore made
up my mind — " Or, again, as he saw Man dragged off — with
too little remonstrance, it may be — by a superior, who could
by no means see what was the state of the action, is there not
traceable a source of the feeling, partly inborn, partly
reasoned, that found expression in the generous and yet most
wise words of the same immortal order? — "The second in

[1] There were twenty-three present on July 13, 1795.

command will [in fact command his line and],[1] after my intentions are made known to him, have the entire direction of his line to make the attack upon the enemy, and to follow up the blow until they are captured or destroyed." Whether such words be regarded as the labored result of observation and reflection, or whether as the flashes of intuition, with which genius penetrates at once to the root of a matter, without the antecedent processes to which lesser minds are subjected, — in either case they are instructive when linked with the events of his career here under discussion, as corroborative indications of natural temperament and insight, which banish altogether the thought of mere fortuitous valor as the one explanation of Nelson's successes.

With this unsatisfactory affair, Nelson's direct connection with the main body of the fleet came to an end for the remainder of Hotham's command. It is scarcely necessary to add that the prime object of the British fleet at all times, and not least in the Mediterranean in 1795, — the control of the sea, — continued as doubtful as it had been at the beginning of the year. The dead weight of the admiral's having upon his mind the Toulon fleet, undiminished in force despite two occasions for decisive action, was to be clearly seen in the ensuing operations. On this, also, Nelson did much thinking, as passing events threw light upon the consequences of missing opportunities. "The British fleet," he wrote, five years later, and no man better knew the facts, "could have prevented the invasion of Italy ; and, if our friend Hotham had kept his fleet on that coast, I assert, and you will agree with me, no army from France could have been furnished with stores or provisions ; even men could not have marched." But how keep the fleet on the Italian coast, while the French fleet in full vigor remained in Toulon ? What a curb it was appeared again in the next campaign, and even more clearly, because the British were then commanded by Sir John Jervis, a man not to be checked by ordinary obstacles. From the decks of his flagship Nelson, in the following April, watched a convoy passing close in shore. "To get at them was impossible be-

---

[1] The words in brackets were erased in the rough draft, but are here inserted, because they emphasize the underlying thought, that the second was to have real command, not wait nor look for signals, nor yet fear them.

fore they anchored under such batteries as would have crippled our fleet; and, had such an event happened, *in the present state of the enemy's fleet,* Tuscany, Naples, Rome, Sicily, &c., would have fallen as fast as their ships could have sailed along the coast. Our fleet is the only saviour at present for those countries."

CHAPTER VI.

JULY–DECEMBER, 1795. AGE, 37.

AFTER the action of July 13, Nelson was again despatched
upon his mission to co-operate with the Austrians on
the Riviera. His orders, dated July 15, were to confer first
with the British minister at Genoa, and thence to proceed
with his squadron to the Austrian headquarters at Vado Bay.
The seniority he had now attained made his selection for this
detached and responsible service less evidently flattering than
Hood's preferment of him to such positions when he was
junior in rank ; but the duty had the distinction of being not
only arduous from the purely naval standpoint, but delicate
in the diplomatic management and tact required. Although
Great Britain at that period was rarely slack in resorting to
strong and arbitrary measures in dealing with neutrals, when
her interests seemed to demand it, she was always exceedingly
desirous to avoid causes of needless offence. The exigencies
of Southern France, and of both the opposing armies in
the Riviera, had created a busy neutral trade, occupied in
supplying all parties to the war, as well as the inhabitants of
Genoese towns then in military occupation by the French.
Although the latter and the Austrians had both openly disregarded the neutrality of Genoa, it was the policy of Great
Britain now to manifest respect for it as far as possible, and
at the same time not to raise causes of diplomatic contention
over the neutral trade, although this was well known to be
supporting the enemy's army.

When Nelson left the fleet, he had, besides his special
orders for his own mission, a circular letter from the admiral

to all vessels under his command, framed upon instructions received from England a month before, directing special care "not to give any just cause of offence to the foreign powers in amity with his Majesty, and whenever any ships or vessels belonging to the subjects of those powers shall be detained, or brought by you into port, you are to transmit to the Secretary of the Admiralty a complete specification of their cargoes, and not to institute any legal process against such ships or vessels until their lordships' further pleasure shall be known."

To the naval officers on the spot this order was calculated to increase vastly the perplexities, which necessarily arose from the occupation of the Genoese coast by French troops. But, besides questions of trade, the weaker States, Genoa and Tuscany, — the latter of which had recently made peace with France, — were driven to manifold shifts and compromises, in order to maintain in their ports such semblance of impartial neutrality as would save them from reprisals by either party. These measures, while insuring to some extent the end in view, gave rise also to a good deal of friction and recrimination between the neutral and the belligerents. The vessels of the latter were admitted, under certain limitations as to number, into the neutral port, where they lay nearly side by side, jealously watching each other, and taking note of every swerving, real or presumed, from an exact and even balance. Each sailed from the neutral port to carry on war, but it is obvious that the shelter of such a port was far more useful to the belligerent who did not control the water, who moved upon it only by evasion and stealth, and who was therefore tempted, in order to improve such advantages, to stretch to the verge of abuse the privileges permitted to him by the neutral. "The Genoese allow the French," wrote Nelson, "to have some small vessels in the port of Genoa, that I have seen towed out of the port, and board vessels coming in, and afterwards return into the mole ; the conduct of the English is very different." He elsewhere allows, however, that, "in the opinion of the Genoese, my squadron is constantly offending ; so that it almost appears a trial between us, who shall first be tired, they of complaining, or me of answering them."

After the first successes of the Austrians and Sardinians, in the previous June, the French commander-in-chief, Kellerman, feeling his inferiority to be such as compelled him to a defensive attitude, had carefully selected the most advanced line that he thought could be held. His right rested upon the sea, near the village of Borghetto, some fifty or sixty miles east of Nice, extending thence to and across the mountains, to Ormea. The Austrian front was parallel, in a general sense, to that of the enemy, and a couple of leagues to the eastward; thus securing for the British Vado Bay, considered the best anchorage between Genoa and Nice. In rear of Vado, to the eastward, and on the coast road, lay the fortress of Savona, esteemed by Bonaparte of the first importance to an army operating in the Riviera and dependent upon the control of the road. The town was occupied by the Austrians, but they were excluded from the citadel by Genoese troops, — a condition of weakness in case of sudden retreat. It ought, said Bonaparte, to be the object of all the enemy's efforts. In these positions, both armies depended for supplies partly upon the sea, partly upon the land road along the Riviera. Across the mountains, in Piedmont, lay the Sardinian forces, extending perpendicularly to the main front of the French operations, and, so far as position went, threatening their communications by the narrow land road. The character of the ground intervening between the French and Austrians rendered an attack upon either line, once fairly established, very difficult; and it was doubtless a fault in the Austrian commander, De Vins, while superior in force, to allow the enemy to strengthen himself in a position which at the first had its weak points; the more so as the plainly approaching peace between Spain and France foretold that the Army of Italy would soon be reinforced. Having, however, made this mistake, the Austrian settled himself in his works, shrugged the responsibility off his own shoulders, and awaited that either the Sardinians by land, or the British by sea, should, by choking the communications of the French, compel them to abandon their lines.

Such was the situation when Nelson, on the 21st of July, had his first interview with De Vins; on the 22d peace between Spain and France was formally concluded. Within a month, Bonaparte, who then occupied a prominent position in Paris, as military adviser to the Government, was writing: "Peace with Spain makes offensive war in Piedmont certain;

my plan is being discussed; Vado will soon be taken;" and a few days later, on the 25th of August, "Troops from Spain are marching to Italy." It was incumbent upon the French to repossess Vado, for, by affording safe anchorage to small hostile cruisers, it effectually stopped the trade with Genoa. De Vins had there equipped several privateers, under the Austrian flag. Of it Bonaparte said : " By intercepting the coasters from Italy, it has suspended our commerce, stopped the arrival of provisions, and obliged us to supply Toulon from the interior of the Republic. It is recognized that our commerce and subsistence require that communication with Genoa be promptly opened." Having in view Bonaparte's remarkable campaign of the following year, and the fact that Vado was now held in force by the Austrians, the importance of British co-operation by the fleet, at this critical moment, becomes strikingly apparent. The future thus throws back a ray of illuminating significance upon the otherwise paltry and obscure campaign of 1795, dragging out into broad daylight the full meaning of lost opportunities in the early year, and of Nelson's strenuous efforts in his detached command.

Immediately upon his arrival in Genoa, on July 17, the effect of the neutral trade, if unchecked, upon the operations of both armies, was brought before him by the British min- ister. Unless the supplies thus received by the French could be stopped, the Austrian general would not only be unable to advance, but feared he could not hold his present position. If, on the other hand, the forage and grain thus brought to them could be intercepted, they would be forced to retreat, and there were hopes that the Austrians might reach Nice before winter, thus covering the excellent and advanced harbor of Villefranche as an anchorage for their British allies. Nelson readily understood the situation, and admitted the necessity of the service demanded of his squadron, which was simply a blow at the enemy's communications; but he pointed out to the minister that the circular instructions, before quoted, tied his hands. Not only would the ordinary diffi- culties of proving the ownership and destination of a cargo give rise to the usual vexatious disputes, and irritate neutrals, contrary to the spirit of the order; but there was a particular complication in this instance, arising from the occupation of

Genoese towns by French troops, and from the close proximity of the neutral and hostile seaboards. These embarrassments might be met, were it permissible to sell the cargoes, and hold the money value, subject to the decision of an admiralty court upon the propriety of the seizure; but this the circular explicitly forbade, until the case was referred to England. If the decision there was adverse to the captors, the other party would look to the responsible naval officer for pecuniary redress, and as, during the delay, the cargo would be spoiled, costs could come only out of the captor's pocket. Nelson's experiences in the West Indies, ten years before, naturally made him cautious about further legal annoyances.

All this he stated with his usual lucidity; but the case was one in which his course could have been safely predicted by a person familiar with his character. The need for the proposed action was evident. "The whole of the necessity of stopping all the vessels is comprised in a very few words: that, if we will not stop supplies of corn, etc., going to France, the armies will return from whence they came, and the failure of this campaign, from which so much is expected, will be laid to our want of energy; for the only use of the naval co-operation is the keeping out a supply of provisions." He therefore, after a night's reflection, told the minister that if he would tell him, officially, that it was for the benefit of his Majesty's service that he should stop all trade between the neutral towns and France, and places occupied by the armies of France, he would give the proper directions for that purpose. It would have been possible for him, though with some delay, to refer the matter to Hotham, but he knew the latter's temperament, and distrusted it. "Our admiral has no political courage whatever," he wrote to Collingwood, "and is alarmed at the mention of any strong measure; but, in other respects, he is as good a man as can possibly be." With a superior so little decided, it was better, by his own independent initiative, to create a situation, which the former would be as backward to reverse as he would have been to change the previous and wholly different state of things. Like the American frontiersman, whose motto was, "Be sure you're right, then go ahead," Nelson, when convinced, knew no hesitations; but further, he unquestionably derived keen enjoy-

11

ment from the sense that the thing done involved risk to himself, appealed to and brought into play his physical or moral courage, in the conscious exercise of which he delighted. "I am acting, not only without the orders of my commander-in-chief, but in some measure contrary to them. However, I have not only the support of his Majesty's ministers, both at Turin and Genoa, but a consciousness that I am doing what is right and proper for the service of our King and Country. Political courage in an officer abroad is as highly necessary as military courage." "The orders I have given are strong, and I know not how my admiral will approve of them, for they are, in a great measure, contrary to those he gave me; but the service requires strong and vigorous measures to bring the war to a conclusion."

The case bore some resemblance to that in which he had disobeyed Hughes in the West Indies; but the disregard of the superior's orders on the earlier occasion was more direct, and the necessity for it less urgent. In both he disobeyed first, and referred afterwards, and in both his action was practically sustained; for, whatever the technical fault, the course taken was the one demanded by the needs of the situation. It is possible to recognize the sound policy, the moral courage, and the correctness of such a step in the particular instance, without at all sanctioning the idea that an officer may be justified in violating orders, because he thinks it right. The justification rests not upon what he thinks, but upon the attendant circumstances which prove that he *is* right; and, if he is mistaken, if the conditions have not warranted the infraction of the fundamental principle of military efficiency, — obedience, — he must take the full consequences of his error, however honest he may have been. Nor can the justification of disobedience fairly rest upon any happy consequences that follow upon it, though it is a commonplace to say that the result is very apt to determine the question of reward or blame. There is a certain confusion of thought prevalent on this matter, most holding the rule of obedience too absolutely, others tending to the disorganizing view that the integrity of the intention is sufficient; the practical result, and for the average man the better result, being to shun the grave responsibility of departing from the letter of the order.

But all this only shows more clearly the great professional courage and professional sagacity of Nelson, that he so often assumed such a responsibility, and so generally — with, perhaps, but a single exception — was demonstrably correct in his action.

Hotham in this case very heartily approved what had been done, and issued, to the fleet in general, orders similar to those given by Nelson; but he did not like the difficulties that surrounded the question of co-operation, and left the conduct of affairs on the spot wholly to his eager and enterprising subordinate. The latter directed the seizure of all vessels laden with corn for France or the French armies, an order that was construed to apply to the Genoese towns occupied by them. The cargoes appear to have been sold and the money held. The cruisers in his command were stationed along the Riviera, east and west of Genoa itself. Those to the eastward, in the neighborhood of Spezia, where no French were, gave great offence to the Government of the Republic, which claimed that their chief city was blockaded; but Nelson refused to remove them. They are not blockading Genoa, he said, but simply occupying the station best suited to intercept a contraband trade. The various British vessels displayed the full activity that might have been expected from the character of their leader, and the pressure was speedily felt by the enemy, and by the neutrals whose lucrative trade was summarily interrupted. The traffic in vessels of any considerable size, seagoing vessels, soon ceased, and Nelson entertained at first great hopes of decisive results from the course adopted by him. "We have much power here at present to do great things, if we know how to apply it," he wrote, after being ten days on the ground; and at the end of a month, "The strong orders which I judged it proper to give on my first arrival, have had an extraordinary good effect; the French army is now supplied with almost daily bread from Marseilles; not a single boat has passed with corn." The enemy themselves admitted the stringency of their situation. But Nelson had yet to learn how ingenuity and enterprise could find a way of eluding his care. The coasting-trade soon began to take on a large development. The Spaniards, now at peace with France, supplied Marseilles, and from both that port and

Genoa grain was carried by small boats, that could be moved by oar as well as sail, could hug closely the rocky shore, and run readily under the batteries with which the French had covered the small bays of the western Riviera, whither the cruisers could not follow. The operations of the latter, dependent only upon their canvas, could not always be extended to within easy gunshot of the beach, along which the blockade-runners kept, usually under cover of night.

Hence, although seriously inconvenienced, the French did not find their position untenable. There were two ways by which the pressure might be increased. A flotilla of small vessels, similar to the coasters themselves, but armed and heavily manned, might keep close in with the points which the latter had to round, and prevent their passage; but the British had no such vessels at their disposal, and, even if they had, the operations would be exposed to danger from the weather upon a hostile, iron-bound coast, whose shelter was forbidden them by the enemy's guns. The Neapolitans had such a flotilla, and it seems probable that its co-operation was asked, for Nelson speaks of it as a desirable aid on the 23d of August; but it did not actually join him until the 15th of September, when the season for its acting was almost past. "Had I the flotilla," wrote he, "nothing should be on this coast. A few weeks more and they will not stay a night at sea to save an empire." Prior to its arrival the British attempted to harass the traffic with their ships' boats, but these were undecked, and of limited capacity compared to those against which they were to act. They were occasionally successful, but the results were too uncertain and hazardous to warrant perseverance, although Bonaparte had to admit that " The audacity of the English boats and the indolence of the Genoese, who allow their own vessels to be taken in their own roads, make it necessary to erect a battery for hot shot at a proper point, which you will exact shall be done by the governor of San Remo."

Nelson's active mind, clinging with its usual accurate insight to the decisive factor in the situation, now fixed upon the idea of seizing a suitable point upon the Riviera to the westward of the French, upon their line of communication with Nice. A body of troops there, strong enough to hold the position, would stop the passage of supplies by land, and, if they controlled an anchorage, a condition indispensable to their support, — and to their retreat, if necessary to retire, — the small vessels based upon that could better interrupt the coasting business. In pursuance of this plan, he in the first week of September made a cruise with the "Agamemnon" as far to the westward as Nice, reconnoitring carefully all recesses of the shore line that seemed available for the purpose. Upon his return, he wrote to De Vins what he had done, and described San Remo as the only available spot. He mentioned its disadvantages as well as its advantages, but undertook positively to land there five thousand men with field-guns, and provisions for a few days, to maintain their supplies by sea, and to cover their embarkation in case retreat became imperative. In short, he guaranteed to land such a force safely, and to be responsible for its communications; for both which he practically pledged his professional reputation. He added, what was indisputable, that the French army must abandon its present lines for want of supplies, if San Remo were held for some time.

De Vins replied on the 14th of September, expressing his interest in the matter thus broached to him, but carefully evading the issue. He addressed his remarks to the comparative merits of Vado and San Remo as anchorages, upon which Nelson had touched barely, and only incidentally, for the gist of his proposal was simply to intercept the enemy's communications; if this were feasible, all other considerations were subsidiary and matters of detail. San Remo was admitted to be the poorer anchorage, unfit for the fleet, but open to small vessels, which could carry the supplies to the Austrian detachment, and stop those of the enemy. The move proposed was intended to effect by sea, substantially, the object which De Vins himself had told Nelson, three weeks before, that he was trying to secure through the co-operation of the Sardinian land forces. "He has been long expecting," wrote Nelson on the 13th of August, "an attack by General Colli with the Piedmontese, near Ormea, directly back from Vintimiglia. This is the great point to be carried, as the Piedmontese army would then get Vintimiglia, and . . . probably, unless the enemy are very active, their retreat to Nice will be cut off. De Vins says he has flattered and abused the Piedmontese and Neapolitans, but nothing will induce them to act." Colli was a good soldier, but his relations with the Austrian were very strained, and coalitions rarely act cordially. This plan, however, becoming known to the French, was commended by Bonaparte as well conceived. " We have examined attentively the project attributed to the enemy in the enclosed note. We have found it conformable to his real interests, and to the present distribution of his troops. The heights of Briga are in truth the key to the Department of the Maritime Alps, since from there the high-road may be intercepted and we be obliged to evacuate Tende. We charge you to pay serious attention to this matter." [1] Disappointed in Sardinian support, Nelson and De Vins had then discussed a plan, of which the former's present proposal was the very clear and practical outcome. Some risk must be run, he said; but De Vins, when it came to the point, saw the dangers too plainly. He did not distinctly refuse, but talked only, and instead of San Remo proposed to land west of Nice, between it and the Var. Nothing, however, was done, or even attempted, and Hotham refused co-operation.

Having regard to the decisive effect exercised upon any strategic position, or movement, by a valid threat against the communications, — considering, for example, the vital influence which the French occupation of Genoa in 1800 had upon the campaign which terminated at Marengo, — it is impossible to speak otherwise than with respect of this proposal of Nelson's. Nevertheless, serious reflection can scarcely fail to affirm that it was not really practicable. There is an immeasurable difference between the holding of a strongly fortified city with an army corps, and the mere seizure of a comparatively open position by a detachment, which, if it means to remain, must have time to fortify itself, in order to withstand the overwhelming numbers that the enemy must at once throw upon it. The time element, too, is of the utmost importance. It is one thing to grasp a strong position with a few men, expecting to hold it for some hours, to delay an advance or a retreat until other forces can come into play,

[1] Correspondance de Napoléon, August 30, 1795. The letter was from Bonaparte's hand, though signed by the Committee of Public Safety.

and quite another to attempt to remain permanently and unsupported in such a situation. In the case before us, De Vins would have landed five thousand men in a comparatively exposed position; for, although the town of San Remo was in possession of the French, who might be driven out for the moment, the only strong point, the citadel, was occupied — as in the case of Savona, to the eastward of the Austrians — by the Genoese, who would doubtless have refused admission. Before his main body would still lie the works which the French had been diligently strengthening for more than two months, and which, with his whole force in hand, he did not care to assail. The enemy, knowing him thus weakened, could well afford to spare a number greatly superior to the detachment he had adventured, certain that, while they were dislodging it, he could make no serious impression upon their lines. As for retreat and embarkation under cover of the guns of a squadron, when pressed by an enemy, the operation is too critical to be hazarded for less than the greatest ends, and with at least a fair possibility of success for the undertaking whose failure would entail it.

Nelson's confidence in himself and in his profession, and his accurate instinct that war cannot be made without running risks, combined with his lack of experience in the difficulties of land operations to mislead his judgment in the particular instance. In a converse sense, there may be applied to him the remark of the French naval critic, that Napoleon lacked " le sentiment exact des difficultés de la marine." It was not only to British seamen, and to the assured control of the sea, that Nelson thought such an attempt offered reasonable prospect of success. He feared a like thing might be effected by the French, — by evasion. " If the enemy's squadron comes on this coast, and lands from three to four thousand men between Genoa and Savona, I am confident that either the whole Austrian army will be defeated, or must inevitably retreat into Piedmont, and abandon their artillery and stores." These words, the substance of which he frequently repeats, though written immediately before the disastrous Battle of Loano, do not apply to the purpose entertained by the French on that occasion, of endeavoring, by a small detachment at Voltri, to check the Austrian retreat till their pursuers came up. He is contemplating a much more considerable and sustained effort, strategic in character, and identical in aim with his own proposal to De Vins about San Remo. It is clear that Nelson, in his day, did not attach absolute deterrent effect to a fleet in being, even to such an one as the British then had in the Mediterranean. Important a factor as it was, it might conceivably be disregarded, by a leader who recognized that the end in view justified the risk.

There was yet another motive actuating Nelson in his present proposals. Justly impatient of the delays and colorless policy of both De Vins and the British leaders, he foresaw that the latter would be made to take the blame, if the campaign proved abortive or disastrous. The Austrians had at least something to show. They had advanced, and they had seized Vado Bay, cutting off the intercourse between Genoa and France, which Bonaparte deemed so important, and at the same time securing an anchorage for the fleet. The latter had done nothing, although its co-operation had been promised; except Nelson's little squadron, in which was but one small ship-of-the-line out of the twenty-three under Hotham's command, it had not been seen.[1] Nelson was determined, as far as in him lay, to remove all grounds for reproach. He urged the admiral to send him more ships, and abounded in willingness towards De Vins. For the latter he had at first felt the esteem and confidence which he almost invariably showed, even to the point of weakness, towards those associated with him; but he now became distrustful, and devoted himself to stopping every loophole of excuse which might afterwards be converted into reproaches to the navy.

The cause for the inadequacy of the force left under his command, of which he often complains, is not apparent. The question was put direct to the admiral whether he would co-operate with the fleet in the proposed descent of the Austrians. He said that he could not, owing to the nature of his instructions from home; but that he would answer for

---

[1] The fleet passed once, August 14, in sight of Vado Bay. Nelson went on board, and tried to induce Hotham to go in and meet De Vins. He refused, saying he must go to Leghorn, but would return, and water the fleet in Vado; but he never came.

it that the French navy should not interfere. Six weeks later the question was repeated; but the admiral replied that, after a consultation with the flag-officers under his command, he refused co-operation in what he considered a wild scheme. In this opinion he was probably right, though Nelson possibly was reminded of Dundas's objections to besieging Bastia. Nelson then went in person to Leghorn, and saw Hotham. He asked to be given two seventy-fours and the transports, to make the attempt himself. Hotham again refused a single ship; but not only so, reduced Nelson's squadron, and ordered him, in addition to his present duties, to reconnoitre Toulon continually, "whilst he," said Nelson, scornfully, "lies quiet in Leghorn Roads." It would almost seem as if the admiral thought that the time had come for a little judicious snubbing, and repression of ardor in the uncomfortable subordinate, whose restless energy conflicted so much with his repose of mind. The fleet spent its time chiefly in San Fiorenzo Bay or in Leghorn, making occasional cruises off Toulon to observe the French navy in that port. The latter was undoubtedly its principal care; but, being distinctly inferior to the British, it is impossible to say why Nelson should not have been reinforced. If it was due to the wish to continue so largely superior in numbers, it certainly illustrates with singular appositeness the deterrent effect of an inferior "fleet in being," and that that effect lies less in the nature of things than in the character of the officer upon whom it is produced. Moreover, the employment of adequate force upon the Riviera, in active aggressive work under Nelson during the summer, when it was practicable to do so, would have compelled the French fleet to come out and fight, or the French army to fall back.

On the 1st of November Hotham struck his flag in Genoa, and departed, bequeathing to his successors a military estate encumbered by the old mortgage of the French fleet, still in being, which he might have cleared off, and by a new one in the numerous and powerful batteries of the Riviera, built and controlled by troops whose presence to erect them might have been prevented by a timely action on his part. The harm, being done, was thenceforth irreparable. As time passed, the situation became more and more favorable to the French. The reinforcements from Spain arrived, and gunboats and flatboats,

fitted out at Toulon, began to come upon the scene. Their
appearance revived in Nelson the apprehension, so consonant
to his military ideas at this time, of an attempt upon the coast
road in rear of the Austrians. He even feared for Genoa itself,
and for the " Agamemnon," while she lay there, as the result
of such a dash. The recurrence of this prepossession is illustrative of his view of possibilities. The true and primary
object of the French was to consolidate their communications;
nor, with Bonaparte in the influential position he then occupied, was any such ex-centric movement likely. For useful
purposes, Genoa was already at his disposal; the French subsistence department was, by his plans, to collect there rations
of corn for sixty thousand men for three months, preparatory
to an advance. For the same object the coasting activity
redoubled along the Riviera, from Toulon to the French front.
By November 1st a hundred sail — transports and small ships
of war — had assembled fifteen miles behind Borghetto, in
Alassio Bay, whither Nelson had chased them. Depots and
supplies were collecting there for the prospective movement.
Nelson offered to enter the bay with three ships-of-the-line, specified by name, and to destroy them; but this was declined by
Sir Hyde Parker, who had temporarily succeeded Hotham in
command, and who at a later day, in the Baltic, was to check
some of Nelson's finest inspirations. "I pretend not to say,"
wrote the latter, a month afterwards, when the Austrians had
been driven from their lines, " that the Austrians would not
have been beat had not the gunboats harassed them, for, on
my conscience, I believe they would; but I believe the French
would not have attacked had we destroyed all the vessels of
war, transports, etc." As to the practicability of destroying
them, Nelson's judgment can safely be accepted, subject only
to the chances which are inseparable from war.

So far from reinforcing the squadron on the Riviera, Sir
Hyde Parker first reduced it, and then took away the frigates
at this critical moment, when the indications of the French
moving were becoming apparent in an increase of boldness.
Their gunboats, no longer confining themselves to the convoy
of coasters, crept forward at times to molest the Austrians,
where they rested on the sea. Nelson had no similar force to
oppose to them, except the Neapolitans, whom he ordered to

act, but with what result is not clear. At the same time the French partisans in Genoa became very threatening. On the 10th of November a party of three hundred, drawn from the ships in the port, landed at Voltri, about nine miles from Genoa, seized a magazine of corn, and an Austrian commissary with £10,000 in his charge. The place was quickly retaken, but the effrontery of the attempt from a neutral port showed the insecurity of the conditions. At the same time a rumor spread that a force of between one and two thousand men, partly carried from Genoa in the French ships of war then lying there, partly stealing along shore in coasters from Borghetto, was to seize a post near Voltri, and hold it. Nelson was informed that men were absolutely being recruited on the Exchange of Genoa for this expedition. When the attack at Voltri was made, the "Agamemnon" was lying in Vado Bay. Leaving a frigate there, Nelson started immediately for Genoa, in order, by the presence of a superior naval force and the fear of retaliation, both to compel the Republic to have its neutrality observed, and to check similar undertakings in the future. The "Agamemnon" was laid across the harbor's mouth, and no French vessel was allowed to sail. Urgent representations were made to Nelson by the Austrian minister and commander-in-chief, that if, the ship were withdrawn, the consequences to the army would be most serious. Contrary, therefore, to his personal inclinations, which were always to be at the front, he remained, although the demonstrations of the gunboats continued, and it was evident that they would at least annoy the Austrian flank in case of an assault. The latter evil, however, was much less disquieting than a descent on the army's line of retreat, at the same moment that it was assailed in front in force; and it was evident that the Austrian general was feeling an uneasiness, the full extent of which he did not betray. De Vins had by this time quitted his command, ill, and had been succeeded by General Wallis.

In this condition of affairs, a general attack upon the Austrian positions was made by the French on the morning of November 24. As had been feared, the gunboats took part, in the absence of any British ships, — the frigate having been removed, Nelson asserts, without his knowledge; but the matter was of very secondary importance, for the weight of the enemy's attack fell upon the positions in the mountains, the centre and right, which were routed and driven back. Swinging round to their own right, towards the sea, the victorious French pushed after the disordered enemy, seeking to intercept their retreat by the coast. Had there then been established, in a well-chosen point of that narrow road, a resolute body of men, even though small, they might well have delayed the fliers until the main body of the pursuers came up; but the presence of the "Agamemnon" controlled the departure of the intended expedition from Genoa, upon which alone, as an organized effort, the projected obstruction depended. Thus she was the efficient cause, as Nelson claimed, that many thousands of Austrians escaped capture. As it was, they lost in this affair, known as the Battle of Loano, seven thousand men, killed, wounded, or prisoners. The entire Riviera was abandoned, and they retreated across the Apennines into Piedmont.

When things go wrong, there is always a disposition on the part of each one concerned to shift the blame. The Austrians had complained before the action, and still more afterwards, of the failure of the fleet to aid them. Nelson thought their complaint well founded. " They say, and true, they were brought on the coast at the express desire of the English, to co-operate with the fleet, which fleet nor admiral they never saw." On his own part he said : " Our admirals will have, I believe, much to answer for in not giving me that force which I so repeatedly called for, and for at last leaving me with Agamemnon alone. Admiral Hotham kept my squadron too small for its duty ; and the moment Sir Hyde took the command of the fleet he reduced it to nothing, — only one frigate and a brig; whereas I demanded two seventy-four-gun ships and eight or ten frigates and sloops to insure safety to the army."

It is unnecessary to inquire into the motives of the two admirals for the distribution of their force. Unquestionably, the first thing for them to do was to destroy or neutralize the French fleet; and next to destroy, or at least impede, the communications of the French army. That it was possible to do this almost wholly may be rested upon the authority of Nelson, whose matured opinion, given five years later, has already been quoted. Two opportunities to cripple the Toulon

fleet were lost; but even so, after the junction of Man, in
June, the superiority over it was so great that much might
have been spared to the Riviera squadron. The coast was
not at this time so extensively fortified that coasting could
not, in Nelson's active hands, have been made a very insufficient means of supply. As an illustration of the operations
then possible, on the 26th of August, six weeks after the
naval battle of July 13, the "Agamemnon," with her little
squadron, anchored in the Bay of Alassio, three cables' length
from the fort in the centre of the town, and with her boats
took possession of all the French vessels in the harbor. Two
months later, so much had the place been strengthened, he
could not vouch for success with less than three ships-of-the-
line; but had the pressure been consistently applied during
those months, the French position would long before have
become untenable. That a shore line, by great and systematic
effort, could be rendered secure throughout for coasters, was
proved by Napoleon's measures to cover the concentration of
the Boulogne flotilla in 1803–5; but such conditions did not
obtain between Nice and Vado in 1795.

Despite the abortive and ignominious ending to the campaign, Nelson's own reputation issued from it not only un-
scathed, but heightened; and this is saying much, for,
although due public recognition of his services had scarcely
been extended, — except in conferring the Marines upon him,
— he had already, before its beginning, made upon all who
were brought into contact with him that impression of unusual efficiency, zeal, and sound judgment, to which subsequent employment and opportunity apply a sure and searching
test. As he entered upon his detached duties, the Viceroy of
Corsica, who had necessarily seen and known much of his past
conduct, wrote to him thus : "Give me leave, my dear Sir, to
congratulate you on the Agamemnon's supporting uniformly,
on all occasions, the same reputation which has always distinguished that ship since I have been in the Mediterranean.
It gives me great pleasure also to see you employed in your
present important service, which requires zeal, activity, and
a spirit of accommodation and co-operation, qualities which
will not be wanting in the Commodore of your squadron. I
consider the business you are about, I mean the expulsion of

the enemy from the Genoese and Piedmontese territories, as the most important feature in the southern campaign." These anticipations of worthy service and exceptional merit were confirmed, after all the misfortunes and disappointments of the campaign, by the singularly competent judgment of the new commander-in-chief, Sir John Jervis. The latter at his first interview with Nelson, nearly two months after his arrival on the station, so that time enough had elapsed to mature his opinion, asked him to remain under his command, as a junior admiral, when he received his promotion. Having regard to Jervis's own high endowments, it was not then in the power of the British Navy to pay an officer of Nelson's rank a higher compliment.

During these months of service upon the Riviera, there occurred an incident, which, from the reflection made upon Nelson's integrity, drew from him a letter, struck off at such white heat, and so transparently characteristic of his temperament, aspirations, and habit of thought, as to merit quotation. A report had been spread that the commanders of the British ships of war connived at the entry of supply-vessels into the ports held by the French, and a statement to that effect was forwarded to the Secretary of State for Foreign Affairs. The latter sent the paper, for investigation, to the Minister to Genoa, who mentioned its tenor to Nelson. The latter, justly stigmatizing the conduct imputed to him and his officers as "scandalous and infamous," requested a copy of the accusation, in order that by his refutation he might convince the King, that he was "an officer who had ever pursued the road of honour, very different from that to wealth." Having received the copy, he wrote to the Secretary as follows : —

AGAMEMNON, GENOA ROAD, 23d November, 1795.

MY LORD, — Having received, from Mr. Drake, a copy of your Lordship's letter to him of October, enclosing a paper highly reflecting on the honour of myself and other of His Majesty's Officers employed on this Coast under my Orders, it well becomes me, as far as in my power lies, to wipe away this ignominious stain on our characters. I do, therefore, in behalf of myself, and much injured Brethren, demand, that the person, whoever he may be, that wrote, or gave that paper to your Lordship, do fully, and expressly bring home his charge; which, as he states that this agreement is made by numbers of people on both sides, there can be no difficulty in doing. We dare him, my Lord, to the proof. If he cannot, I do most humbly implore, that His Majesty will be most graciously pleased to direct his Attorney-General to prosecute this infamous libeller in His Courts of Law; and I likewise feel, that, without impropriety, I may on behalf of my brother Officers, demand the support of His Majesty's Ministers: for as, if true, no punishment can be too great for the traitors; so, if false, none can be too heavy for the villain, who has dared to allow his pen to write such a paper. Perhaps I ought to stop my letter here; but I feel too much to rest easy for a moment, when the honour of the Navy, and our Country, is struck at through us; for if nine [ten] Captains, whom chance has thrown together, can instantly join in such a traitorous measure, it is fair to conclude we are all bad.

As this traitorous agreement could not be carried on but by concert of all the Captains, if they were on the Stations allotted them, and as they could only be drawn from those Stations by orders from me, I do most fully acquit all my brother Captains from such a combination, and have to request, that I may be considered as the only responsible person for what is done under my command, if I approve of the conduct of those under my orders, which in this most public manner I beg leave to do: for Officers more alert, and more anxious for the good, and honour, of their King and Country, can scarcely ever fall to the lot of any Commanding Officer: their Names I place at the bottom of this letter.

For myself, from my earliest youth I have been in the Naval Service; and in two Wars, have been in more than one hundred and forty Skirmishes and Battles, at Sea and on shore; have lost an eye, and otherwise blood, in fighting the Enemies of my King and Country; and, God knows, instead of riches, my little fortune has been diminished in the Service: but I shall not trouble your Lordship further at present, than just to say — that at the close of this Campaign, where I have had the pleasure to receive the approbation of the Generals of the Allied Powers; of his Excellency Mr. Drake, who has always been on the spot; of Mr. Trevor, who has been at a distance; when I expected and hoped, from the representation of His Majesty's Ministers, that His Majesty would have most graciously condescended to have favourably noticed my earnest desire to serve Him, and when, instead of all my fancied approbation, to receive an accusation of a most traitorous nature — it has almost been too much for me to bear. Conscious innocence, I hope, will support me.

I have the honour to be,
My Lord,
Your Lordship's most obedient, humble servant,
HORATIO NELSON.

Except this vexatious but passing cloud, his service upon the Riviera, despite the procrastinations and final failure of his associates in the campaign, was pleasant both personally and officially. He earned the warm esteem of all with whom he acted, notably the British ministers at Turin and Genoa; and though necessarily in constant collision with the Genoese authorities upon international questions, he upheld the interests and policy of his own government, without entailing upon it serious cause of future reclamations and disputes.[1] Hotham's very indifference and lethargy, while crippling his enterprise, increased his independence. "I cannot get Hotham on the coast," he said, "for he hates this co-operation;" but he owns to the fear that the admiral, if he came, might overrule his projects. The necessity for exertion delighted him. "My command here is so far pleasant," he wrote to his friend Collingwood, "as it relieves me from the inactivity of our fleet, which is great indeed, as you will soon see." "At present," he tells his wife, "I do not write less than from ten to twenty letters every day; which, with the Austrian general, and aide-de-camps, and my own little squadron, fully employ my time: this I like; active service or none." As usual, when given room for the exercise of his powers, he was, for him, well. He had a severe attack of illness very soon after assuming the duty — "a complaint in the breast" — the precursor perhaps of the similar trouble from which he suffered so much in later years; but it wore off after an acute attack of a fortnight, and he wrote later that, except being at home, he knew no country so pleasant to serve in, nor where his health was so good. This well-grounded preference for

---

[1] A year later, when all his transactions with Genoa as an independent republic were concluded, Nelson received from the British Minister of Foreign Affairs, through the Admiralty, the following strong and comprehensive endorsement of his political conduct: —

"I esteem it an act of justice due to that officer, to inform your lordships that His Majesty has been graciously pleased entirely to approve of the conduct of Commodore Nelson in all his transactions with the Republic of Genoa. I have the honour to be, &c., &c.   GRENVILLE."

The First Lord of the Admiralty about the same time expressed "the great satisfaction derived here from the very spirited, and at the same time dignified and temperate manner, in which your conduct has been marked both at Leghorn and Genoa."

the Mediterranean, as best suited to his naturally frail constitution, remained with him to the end.

Besides his official correspondence, he wrote freely and fully to those at home, unburdening to them the thoughts, cares, and disappointments of his career, as well as the commendations he received, so dear to himself as well as to them. Mrs. Nelson and his father lived together, and to her most of his home letters were addressed. " I have been very negligent," he admits to her, " in writing to my father, but I rest assured he knows I would have done it long ago, had you not been under the same roof. . . . Pray draw on me," he continues, " for £200, my father and myself can settle our accounts when we meet ; at present, I believe I am the richer man, therefore I desire you will give my dear father that money." One wonders whether, in the slightly peremptory tone of the last sentence, is to be seen a trace of the feeling she is said, by one biographer, to have shown, that he was too liberal to his relatives ; an indication of that lack of sympathy, which, manifested towards other traits of his, no less marked than openhandedness, struck a jarring note within him, and possibly paved the way to an indifference which ended so unfortunately for both. An absent husband, however, very possibly failed to realize what his extreme generosity might mean, to one who had to meet household expenses with narrow means.

The political surmises with which his correspondence at this period abounds were often crude, though not infrequently also characterized by the native sagacity of his intellect, as yet undisciplined, and to some extent deficient in data for accurate forecasts. The erroneous military conception which colored much of his thought, the propositions for ex-centric movements in an enemy's rear, by bodies comparatively small, out of supporting distance from the rest of the army, and resting upon no impregnable base, contributed greatly to the faulty anticipations entertained and expressed by him from time to time. When applied to operations directed by the consummate and highly trained genius of Bonaparte, speculations so swayed naturally flew wide of the mark. His sanguine disposition to think the best of all persons and all things — except Frenchmen — made him also

12

a ready prey to the flattering rumors of which war is ever
fertile. These immaturities will be found to disappear, as
his sphere widens and his responsibilities increase.

After the close of the campaign, Nelson made a short
cruise from Genoa to the westward, seeing the French on
November 29 in full possession of Vado Bay. He then went
to Leghorn, where he arrived on the 6th of December and
remained till the middle of January, repairing, to make the
"Agamemnon" "as fit for sea as a rotten ship can be." The
longing for rest and for home, after nearly three years' absence, was again strong upon him in this moment of relaxation. " I fear our new admiral is willing to keep me with
him," he wrote to his brother. " He has wrote me, I am
sorry to say, a most flattering letter, and I hear I am to be
offered St. George or Zealous [much larger ships], but, in my
present mind, I shall take neither. My wish is to see England once more, and I want a few weeks' rest." But here
again, having regard to that fame which was to him most
dear, he was mistaken, as he now owned he had been in the
wish, a year before, to accompany Lord Hood on his return.
In Sir John Jervis he was to meet, not only one of the most
accomplished and resolute officers of the British Navy, closely
akin to himself in enterprise and fearlessness, though without
his exceptional genius, but also a man capable of appreciating
perfectly the extraordinary powers of his subordinate, and of
disregarding every obstacle and all clamor, in the determination to utilize his qualities to the full, for the good of the
nation.

CHAPTER VII.

January–December, 1796. Age, 38.

WHILE the " Agamemnon " was refitting in Leghorn, the sensitive mind of her captain, no longer preoccupied with the cares of campaigning and negotiations, dwelt with restless anxiety upon the reflections to which the British Navy was liable, for its alleged failure to support the Austrians throughout the operations, and especially at the critical moment of the Battle of Loano, when the left flank of their army was harassed with impunity by the French gunboats. Nelson felt rightly that, with the British superiority at sea, this should have been impossible ; and he feared that his own name might be unpleasantly involved, from the fact that the " Agamemnon " had remained throughout at Genoa, instead of being where the fighting was. He was by nature, and at all times, over-forward to self-vindication, — an infirmity springing from the innate nobility of his temperament, which was impatient of the faintest suspicion of backwardness or negligence, and at the same time resolved that for any shortcoming or blunder, occurring by his order or sanction, no other than himself should bear blame, directly or indirectly.

After the first unsuccessful pursuit of Bonaparte's expedition to Egypt, in 1798, in the keenness of his emotions over a failure that might by some be charged to a precipitate error of judgment, he drew up for Lord St. Vincent a clear and able statement of all the reasons which had determined his action, arraigning himself, as it were, at the bar of his Lordship's opinion and that of the nation, and assuming entire responsibility for the apparent mistake, while at the same time justifying the step by a review of the various considerations which at the time had occasioned it. His judicious friend and subordinate, Captain Ball, whom he consulted, strongly advised him not to send the paper. "I was particularly struck," he wrote, "with the clear and accurate style, as well as with the candour of the statement in your letter, but I should recommend a friend never to begin a defence of his conduct before he is accused of error." Nevertheless, in February, 1805, when he once more went to Alexandria in search of Villeneuve, this time really misled by the elaborate mystifications of Napoleon, he again brought himself before the Admiralty. "I am entirely responsible to my King and Country for the whole of my conduct. . . . I have consulted no man, therefore the whole blame of ignorance in forming my judgment must rest with me. I would allow no man to take from me an atom of my glory, had I fallen in with the French fleet, nor do I desire any man to partake any of the responsibility — all is mine, right or wrong."

In 1795, being a much younger man, of less experience of the world, and with a reputation, already brilliant indeed, but still awaiting the stamp of solidity which the lapse of time alone can give, Nelson felt strongly, and not improperly, that it was necessary to be vigilant against any possible imputations upon his action. This was the more true, because blame certainly did attach to the service of which he was the representative on the spot, and the course he had been obliged to follow kept him to the rear instead of at the front. There would have been no greater personal danger to a man on board the "Agamemnon" in one place than in the other; but current rumor, seeking a victim, does not pause to analyze conditions. Not only, therefore, did he draw up for Sir John Jervis a succinct synopsis of occurrences subsequent to his taking command of the operations along the Riviera, in which he combined a justification of his own conduct with the general information necessary for a new commander-in-chief, but to all his principal correspondents he carefully imparted the facts necessary to clear him from blame, and to show just what the Navy had effected, and where it had fallen short through inadequate force.

To the British minister to Genoa, who was constantly at the Austrian headquarters, he wrote with clear emphasis, as to one cognizant of all the truth, and so a witness most important to himself. Having first asked certain certificates, essential to be presented in the Admiralty Courts when Genoese prizes came to be adjudicated, he continued characteristically: "The next request much more concerns my honour, than the other does my interest — it is to prove to the world, to my own admiral, or to whoever may have a right to ask the question, why I remained at Genoa. I have therefore to desire that you will have the goodness to express, in writing, what you told me, .that the Imperial minister and yourself were assured, if I left the port of Genoa unguarded, not only the Imperial troops at St. Pierre d'Arena and Voltri would be lost, but that the French plan for taking post between Voltri and Savona would certainly succeed; and also, that if the Austrians should be worsted in the advanced posts, the retreat by the Bocchetta would be cut off: to which you added, that if this happened, the loss of the Army would be laid to my leaving Genoa, and recommended me most strongly not to think of it. I am anxious, as you will believe, to have proofs in my possession, that I employed to the last the Agamemnon as was judged most beneficial to the common cause."

A week later he wrote again, having heard that the Austrian commander-in-chief, General Wallis, had declared that the defeat was due to the failure of the British to co-operate. Nelson thought that they had a strong hold on Wallis, and he therefore enclosed a letter to him, which he asked might be forwarded by the minister. The experience and training of the latter, however, here interposed to prevent his sensitive uneasiness leading to a false step, and one that might involve him farther than he foresaw. While bearing the clearest and strongest witness to the facts which Nelson had asked him to establish, he hinted to him, tactfully and with deference, that it was scarcely becoming a public servant to justify his conduct to a foreign official, he being accountable only to his own government. Nelson accepted the suggestion, and in so doing characterized aptly enough the temperament which then and at other times carried him farther than discretion warranted. "My feelings ever alive, perhaps, to too nice a sense of honour, are a little cooled."

Along with this care for the stainless record of the past,

there went on in his mind a continual reasoning upon the probable course of the next year's operations. In his forecasts it is singular to notice how, starting from the accurate premise that it is necessary for the French to get into the plains of Italy, — "the gold mine," — he is continually misled by his old prepossession in favor of landing in rear of the enemy a body of troops, supported neither by sure communication with their main army, nor by a position in itself of great strength. The mistake, if mistake it was, illustrates aptly the errors into which a man of great genius for war, of quick insight, such as Nelson indisputably had, can fall, from want of antecedent study, of familiarity with those leading principles, deduced from the experience of the past, which are perhaps even more serviceable in warning against error than in prompting to right. Everything assures him that the French will carry some twenty thousand men to Italy by sea. "If they mean to carry on the war, they must penetrate into Italy. I am convinced in my own mind, that I know their very landing-place." This, it appears afterwards, he believed would be between Spezia and Leghorn, in the districts of Massa and Carrara, whence also they would doubtless turn upon Leghorn, though neutral, as a valuable and fortified seaport. "The prevention," he continues, "requires great foresight; for, if once landed, our fleet is of no use."

The importance of Vado Bay, so discreditably lost the year before, strikes him from this point of view, as it did also Bonaparte from his more closely coherent plan of operations. Nelson reasoned that, if Vado were possessed by the allies, the French, in their attempt to reach the Tuscan coast, would be compelled to put to sea, where they would be exposed to the British fleet, while such an anchorage would enable the latter, when necessary, to keep the coast close aboard, or would provide a refuge to a small squadron, if threatened by the sudden appearance of a superior force. Bonaparte thought Vado important, because, on the one hand, essential to uninterrupted coasting-trade with Genoa, and on the other as advancing his water line of communications — that by land being impassable for heavy articles, such as siege-guns and carriages — to Savona, from which point the mountains could be crossed at their lowest elevation, and by their most practicable passes.

Nelson's analysis of the conditions, in other respects than the one mentioned, was not unworthy of his great natural aptitudes. There are three things to be guarded against, he says. One is that pet scheme of his imagination, the transport of a corps by sea to Tuscany; the other two are an invasion of Piedmont, and the entrance into Italy by the pass of the Bocchetta, behind Genoa. "If three are to be attended to, depend upon it one will fall, and the Emperor, very possibly, may be more attentive to the Milanese than to Piedmont." Upon this divergence of interests in a coalition Bonaparte also explicitly counted; and his plan, in its first inception, as laid before the Directory in the summer of 1795, looked primarily to the subjugation of Piedmont, by separating it from the support of the Austrian Army. The bearing of Vado Bay upon this project is not definitely recognized by Nelson. He sees in the possession of it only the frustration of both the enemy's supposed alternatives, — invasion of Italy by the Bocchetta, and of Tuscany by sea.

With these views Nelson arrived, at San Fiorenzo, on the 19th of January, and had his first interview with Jervis. His reception by the latter, whom he never before had met, was not only cordial but flattering. He was at once offered the choice of two larger ships, which were declined, "but with that respect and sense of obligation on my part which such handsome conduct demanded of me." The admiral then asked him if he would have any objection to remain on the station, when promoted, as he soon must be. Nelson's longing to go home had worn off with his disgust, occasioned by the impotent conclusions of last year's work. Then he was experiencing the feeling voiced by the great Frenchman, Suffren, some dozen years before: "It was clear that, though we had the means to impose the law, all would be lost. I heartily pray you may permit me to leave. War alone can make bearable the weariness of certain things." Now his keen enjoyment of active service revived as the hour of opening hostilities drew near. With these dispositions, the graciousness of his reception easily turned the scale, and before long he was not only willing to remain, but fearful lest he should be disappointed, despite the application for his retention which the admiral hastened to make.

"The credit I derive from all these compliments," he wrote to his wife, "must be satisfactory to you; and, should I remain until peace, which cannot be very long, you will, I sincerely hope, make your mind easy." But more grateful than open flattery, to one so interested in, and proud of, his military activities, was the respect paid by Jervis to his views and suggestions relative to the approaching operations. "He was so well satisfied with my opinion of what is likely to happen, and the means of prevention to be taken, that he had no reserve with me respecting his information and ideas of what is likely to be done;" or, as he wrote a month later, "he seems at present to consider me more as an associate than a subordinate officer; for I am acting without any orders. This may have its difficulties at a future day; but I make none, knowing the uprightness of my intentions. 'You must have a larger ship,' continued the admiral, 'for we cannot spare you, either as captain or admiral.'" Such were the opening relations between these two distinguished officers, who were in the future to exert great influence upon each other's career.

It is far from improbable that the ready coincidence of Jervis's views with those of Nelson, as to future possibilities, arose, partly indeed from professional bias and prepossession as to the potency of navies, but still more from the false reports, of which Bonaparte was an apt promoter, and which a commission of the allies in Genoa greedily swallowed and transmitted. The deterrent effect of their own fleet, "in being," seems not to have prevented either of them from believing that the attempt upon Tuscany by sea was seriously intended. True, Nelson does at times speak of the French as being so unreasonable that one may expect anything from them; but this scheme, which probably had not even a paper existence in France, was accepted by him as imminent, because he thought it suitable. As he cogently remarked to Beaulieu, it is likely that your enemy will not do the thing which you wish him to do; and conversely, in this case, what to him appeared most threatening to his own cause was just what he expected to occur. Jervis, sharing his views, and already knowing his man, despatched him again to the Gulf of Genoa, within forty-eight hours of his arrival in San Fiorenzo, some-

ADMIRAL, SIR JOHN JERVIS, EARL OF
ST. VINCENT.

*From an engraving by H. Robinson, after the painting by John
Hoppner, in St. James's Palace.*

what to the disgust of the other captains, weary of being ever
under the eye of an observant and exacting admiral. "You
did as you pleased in Lord Hood's time," said one grumbler,
"the same in Admiral Hotham's, and now again with Sir
John Jervis; it makes no difference to you who is commander-
in-chief." The tone of these words, which in the reading are
almost flattering, is evident from Nelson's comment: " I returned a pretty strong answer to this speech."

The object of his present mission was to ascertain what preparations for the expected descent were being made along the
Riviera, and to frustrate them as far as lay in the power of
his squadron. He soon reported to Jervis that there was as
yet no collection of vessels between Nice and Genoa. He
then went on to reconnoitre Toulon, where he saw thirteen
sail-of-the-line and five frigates lying in the outer roads, ready
for sea, while five more of the line he learned were fitting at
the arsenal. During the six days he remained off the port he
noted that continual progress was being made in the enemy's
preparations. At the end of this time, on the 23d of Feb-
uruary, 1796, the admiral joined with the fleet, and the same
afternoon the "Agamemnon" again parted company for
Genoa, where she anchored on the 2d of March.

The bustle on board the French ships confirmed Nelson's
belief in the descent upon Tuscany; and it is interesting here
to quote his words upon the possibilities of the operation, regarded from the naval point of view by one of the ablest of
sea-generals. His opinion throws light upon the vexed question of the chances for and against Napoleon's projected
invasion of England in 1805, — so far, that is, as the purely
naval part of the latter project is concerned. He imagines as
perfectly feasible ("I firmly believe," are his words) a combination at Toulon, of the fleet already there with divisions
arriving from Cadiz and Brest, giving a total much superior
to that actually with Jervis. This anticipates Napoleon's
projected concentration under Villeneuve in the Channel.
Nelson then continues: "One week's very superior fleet will
effect a landing between Port Especia and Leghorn, I mean on
that coast of Italy. . . . We may fight their fleet, but unless
we can destroy them [i. e. the transports], their transports
will push on and effect their landing. What will the French

care for the loss of a few men-of-war ?   It is nothing if they
can get into Italy."   " Make us masters of the channel for
three days, and we are masters of the world," wrote Napoleon
to his admirals, with preparations far more complete than
those Nelson was considering in 1796, and the distance across
the Channel is less than from Vado to Spezia.[1]

With these convictions, Nelson immediately began to urge
the necessity of again occupying Vado upon the Austrian commander-in-chief, through the medium of the British ministers
to Genoa and Turin, with whom he was in frequent correspondence.   If this were not done, he assured them, the
enemy's fleet could with ease convoy a body of troops in
transports to Italy, which they could not do with their present
force unless they held Vado.   It was also the only means, he
added, by which the French could be prevented from receiving plenty of provisions from Genoa.   " Unless the Austrians
get possession of a point of land, we cannot stop the coasting-
trade."   The latter argument, at any rate, was incontestable ;
and it was also true that only by an advance to Vado could
communication between the army and the British fleet be restored and maintained.   Beaulieu, who had lately acquired a
high reputation on the battle-fields of Belgium, had now succeeded De Vins in the command.   He was averse to opening
the campaign by an advance to the sea, a feeling shared by
the Austrians generally.   He wished rather to await the
enemy in the plains of Lombardy, and to follow up by a decisive
blow the victory which he confidently expected there.   It was
in this connection that Nelson warned him, that he must not
reckon upon the French following the line of action which he
himself would prefer.

The time for hostilities had now arrived ; from February to
August being the period that Bonaparte, who knew the wars

---

[1] This indicates no opinion as to the fortune of the military operations in
England, a landing once effected.   It has, however, seemed to the author
singular that men fail to consider that Napoleon would not have hesitated to
abandon an army in England, as he did in Egypt and in Russia.   A few
hours' fog or calm, and a quick-pulling boat, would have landed himself again
in France ; while the loss of 150,000 men, if it came to that, would have
been cheaply bought with the damage such an organized force could have done
London and the dock yards, not to speak of the moral effect.

of Italy historically, considered the most proper for operations in the field, because the least sickly. But for the backwardness of the spring, — for snow that year lay upon the mountains late into March, — the campaign doubtless would have been begun before. At the same time came fresh reports, probably set afloat by the French, of large reinforcements of seamen for the fleet and transports, in Toulon and Marseilles; and Nelson furthermore received precise information that the enemy's movement would be in three columns, — one upon Ceva, which was Bonaparte's original scheme, one by the Bocchetta, and the third either to march through Genoese territory to Spezia, or to be carried thither by sea. Nelson felt no doubt that the last was the real plan, aiming at the occupation of Leghorn and entrance into the plains of Italy. The others he considered to be feints. There will in this opinion be recognized the persistency of his old ideas. In fact, he a month later revived his proposal of the previous year, to occupy San Remo, — this time with British troops.

The urgency of the British, aided, perhaps, by the reports of the French designs, prevailed at last upon Beaulieu to advance as requested; nor can it be denied that the taking of Vado was in itself a most proper and desirable accessory object of the campaign. Unfortunately, the Austrian general, as is well known, fastening his eyes too exclusively upon the ulterior object of his movement, neglected to provide for the immediate close combination and mutual support of the organized forces, — his own and the Piedmontese, — upon which final success would turn. Manœuvring chiefly by his own left, towards the Riviera, and drawing in that direction the efforts of the centre and right, he weakened the allied line at the point where the Austrian right touched the Sardinian left. Through this thin curtain Bonaparte broke, dividing the one from the other, and, after a series of combats which extended over several days, rendering final that division, both political and military, for the remainder of the war.

To one who has accustomed himself to see in Nelson the exponent of the chief obstacle Napoleon had to meet, — who has recognized in the Nile, in Copenhagen, and in Trafalgar, the most significant and characteristic incident attending the failure of each of three great and widely separated schemes, —

there is something impressive in noting the fact, generally disregarded, that Nelson was also present and assisting at the very opening scene of the famous campaign in Italy. This was not, certainly, the beginning of Napoleon's career any more than it was of Nelson's, who at the same moment hoisted for the first time his broad pendant as commodore ; but it was now that, upon the horizon of the future, toward which the world was fast turning, began to shoot upward the rays of the great captain's coming glory, and the sky to redden with the glare from the watchfires of the unseen armies which, at his command, were to revolutionize the face of Europe, causing old things to pass away, never to be restored.

The Austrians had asked for a clear assurance that their movement to the seashore should receive the support of the fleet, whether on the Riviera or at Spezia; Nelson having laid stress upon the possession of the latter, as a precaution against the invasion of Tuscany. These engagements he readily made. He would support any movement, and provide for the safety of any convoys by water. He told the aid-de-camp whom Beaulieu sent to him that, whenever the general came down to the sea-coast, he would be sure to find the ships; and to the question whether his squadron would not be risked thereby, he replied that it would be risked at all times to assist their allies, and, if lost, the admiral would find another. "If I find the French convoy in any place where there is a probability of attacking them," he wrote about this time, "you may depend they shall either be taken or destroyed at the risk of my squadron, . . . which is built to be risked on proper occasions." Here was indeed a spirit from which much might be expected. The fleet, doubtless, must be husbanded in coastwise work so long as the French fleet remained, the legacy of past errors, — this Nelson clearly maintained; but such vessels as it could spare for co-operation were not to be deterred from doing their work by fear of harm befalling them. Warned by the recriminations of the last campaign, he had minutes taken of his interview with the Austrian officer, of the questions he himself put, as well as of the undertakings to which he pledged himself; and these he caused to be witnessed by the British consul at Genoa, who was present.

On the 8th of April the "Agamemnon," having shortly before left the fleet in San Fiorenzo Bay, anchored at Genoa; and the following morning the port saluted the broad pendant of the new commodore. The next day, April 10, Beaulieu attacked the French at Voltri. The "Agamemnon," with another sixty-four-gun ship, the "Diadem," and two frigates, sailed in the evening, and stood along the shore, by preconcerted arrangement, to cover the advance and harass the enemy. At 11 P. M. the ships anchored abreast the positions of the Austrians, whose lights were visible from their decks — the sails hanging in the clewlines, ready for instant movement. They again got under way the following day, and continued to the westward, seeing the French troops in retreat upon Savona. The attack, Nelson said, anticipated the hour fixed for it, which was daylight; so that, although the ships had again started at 4 A. M. of the 11th, and reached betimes a point from which they commanded every foot of the road, the enemy had already passed. "Yesterday afternoon I received, at five o'clock, a note from the Baron de Malcamp [an aid-de-camp], to tell me that the general had resolved to attack the French at daylight this morning, and on the right of Voltri. Yet by the Austrians getting too forward in the afternoon, a slight action took place; and, in the night, the French retreated. They were aware of their perilous situation, and passed our ships in the night. Had the Austrians kept back, very few of the French could have escaped." Whether this opinion was wholly accurate may be doubted; certain it is, however, that the corps which then passed reinforced betimes the positions in the mountains, which steadfastly, yet barely, checked the Austrian attack there the following day. Beaulieu wrote that the well-timed co-operation of the squadron had saved a number of fine troops, which must have been lost in the attack. This was so far satisfactory; but the economizing of one's own force was not in Nelson's eyes any consolation for the escape of the enemy, whose number he estimated at four thousand. "I beg you will endeavour to impress on those about the general," he wrote to the British minister, "the necessity of punctuality in a joint operation, for its success to be complete."

There was, however, to be no more co-operation that year

on the Riviera.   For a few days Nelson remained in suspense,
hoping for good news, and still very far from imagining the
hail-storm of ruinous blows which a master hand, as yet
unrecognized, was even then dealing to the allied cause.   On
the 15th only he heard from Beaulieu, through the minister,
that the Austrians had been repulsed at Montenotte; and on
the 16th he wrote to Collingwood that this reverse had been
inflicted by the aid of those who slipped by his ships.   On the
18th news had reached him of the affairs at Millesimo and
Dego, as well as of further disasters; for on that day he wrote
to the Duke of Clarence that the Austrians had taken position between Novi and Alessandria, with headquarters at
Acqui.   Their loss he gave as ten thousand.   "Had the
general's concerted time and plan been attended to," he repeats, "I again assert, none of the enemy could have escaped
on the night of the 10th.   By what has followed, the disasters
commenced from the retreat of those troops."

There now remained, not the stirring employment of accompanying and supporting a victorious advance, but only the
subordinate, though most essential, duty of impeding the communications of the enemy, upon which to a great extent must
depend the issues on unseen and distant fields of war.   To
this Nelson's attention had already been turned, as one of the
most important functions intrusted to him, even were the allies
successful, and its difficulties had been impressed upon him by
the experience of the previous year.   But since then the conditions had become far more onerous.   The defeat of the
Austrians not only left Vado Bay definitively in the power of
the French, but enabled the latter to push their control up to
the very walls of Genoa, where they shortly established a
battery and depot on the shore, at St. Pierre d'Arena, within
three hundred yards of the mole.   Thus the whole western
Riviera, from the French border, was in possession of the
enemy, who had also throughout the previous year so multiplied and strengthened the local defences, that, to use
Nelson's own words, "they have batteries from one end of
the coast to the other, within shot of each other."   Such were
the means, also, by which Napoleon, the true originator
of this scheme for securing these communications, insured
the concentration of the flotilla at Boulogne, eight or ten

years later, without serious molestation from the British
Navy.

It may not unnaturally cause some surprise that, with the
urgent need Nelson had felt the year before for small armed
vessels, to control the coastwise movements of the enemy,
upon which so much then depended, no serious effort had been
made to attach a flotilla of that kind to the fleet. The reply,
however, to this very obvious criticism is, that the British
could not supply the crews for them without crippling the
efficiency of the cruising fleet; and it was justly felt then, as
it was some years later at the time of the Boulogne flotilla,
that the prime duty of Great Britain was to secure the sea
against the heavy fleets of the enemy. If, indeed, the Italian
States, whose immediate interests were at stake, had supplied
seamen, as they might have done, these could quickly have
been formed to the comparatively easy standard of discipline
and training needed for such guerilla warfare, and, supported
by the cruising fleet, might have rendered invaluable service,
so long as the system of coast defence was defective. How
far the rulers of those States, trained heretofore to the narrowest considerations of personal policy, could have been induced
to extend this assistance, is doubtful. They did nothing, or
little.

Nelson measured the odds against him accurately, and saw
that the situation was well-nigh hopeless. Nevertheless, there
was a chance that by vigorous and sustained action the enemy
might be not only impeded, but intimidated. He sought
earnestly to obtain the co-operation of the Sardinians and
Neapolitans in manning a flotilla, with which to grapple the
convoys as they passed in shore. By this means, and the
close securing of the coast by the vessels of his squadron,
something might be effected. He contemplated also using the
crews of the British vessels themselves in gunboats and light-
armed feluccas; but he said frankly that, important as was
the duty of intercepting communications, the efficiency of
the fleet was more important still, and that to divert their
crews overmuch to such objects would hazard the vessels
themselves, and neutralize their proper work. The resort,
therefore, could only be occasional. The general political complexion of affairs in the Mediterranean depended greatly upon

the presence and readiness of the British fleet, and its efficiency therefore could not be risked, to any serious extent, except for the object of destroying the enemy's naval forces, to which it was then the counterpoise.

Acting, however, on his determination to co-operate effectively, at whatever risk to his own squadron, — to the detachment, that is, which the commander-in-chief thought could safely be spared from his main force for the secondary object, — Nelson applied all his intelligence and all his resolution to the task before him. In words of admirable force and clearness, he manifests that exclusiveness of purpose, which Napoleon justly characterized as the secret of great operations and of great successes. "I have not a thought," he writes to the minister at Genoa, "on any subject separated from the immediate object of my command, nor a wish to be employed on any other service. So far the allies," he continues, with no unbecoming self-assertion, "are fortunate, if I may be allowed the expression, in having an officer of this character." He felt this singleness of mind, which is so rare a gift, to be the more important, from his very consciousness that the difficulty of his task approached the border of impossibility. "I cannot command winds and weather. A sea-officer cannot, like a land-officer, form plans; his object is to embrace the happy moment which now and then offers, — it may be this day, not for a month, and perhaps never." Nothing can be more suggestive of his greatest characteristics than this remark, which is perhaps less applicable to naval officers to-day than it was then. In it we may fairly see one of those clearly held principles which serve a man so well in moments of doubt and perplexity. At the Nile and at Trafalgar, and scarcely less at St. Vincent and Copenhagen, the seizure of opportunity, the unfaltering resolve "to embrace the happy moment," is perhaps even more notable and decisive than the sagacity which so accurately chose the proper method of action.

Nelson's deeds did not belie his words. Immediately after definite news of Beaulieu's retreat to the Po was received, Sir John Jervis appeared off Genoa with the fleet. The "Agamemnon" joined him, and remained in company until the 23d of April, when by Nelson's request she sailed on a cruise to the westward. From that time until the 4th of June she was actively employed between Nice and Genoa, engaging the batteries, and from time to time cutting out vessels from the anchorages. His attempts were more or less successful; on one occasion he captured a considerable portion of the French siege-train going forward for the siege of Mantua; but upon the whole the futility of the attempt became apparent. "Although I will do my utmost, I do not believe it is in my power to prevent troops or stores from passing along shore. Heavy swells, light breezes, and the near approach to the shore which these vessels go are our obstacles. . . . You may perceive I am distressed. Do you really think we are of any use here? If not, we may serve our country much more by being in other places. The Levant and coast of Spain call aloud for ships, and they are, I fancy, employed to no purpose here." The position was almost hopelessly complicated by the Genoese coasters, which plied their trade close to the beach, between the mother city and the little towns occupied by the French, and which Nelson felt unable to touch. "There are no vessels of any consequence in any bay from Monaco to Vado," he wrote to Jervis; "but not less than a hundred Genoese are every day passing, which may or may not have stores for the French." "The French have no occasion to send provisions from France. The coasts are covered with Genoese vessels with corn, wine, hay, &c., for places on the coast; and they know I have no power to stop the trade with the towns. I saw this day not less than forty-five Genoese vessels, all laden, passing along the coast. What can I do?"

Although not definitely so stated, it is shown, by an allusion, that Nelson at this time entertained, among other ideas, the project of keeping afloat in transports a body of three thousand troops, which should hover upon the coast, and by frequent descents impose a constant insecurity upon the long line of communications from Nice to Genoa. The same plan was advocated by him against the Spanish peninsula in later years.[1] Of this conception it may be said that it is sound in principle, but in practice depends largely upon the distance from the centre of the enemy's power at which its execution is attempted. Upon the Spanish coast, in 1808, in the hands of Lord Cochrane, it was undoubtedly a most effective second-

[1] Naval Chronicle, vol. xxi. p. 60.

ary operation; but when that distinguished officer proposed
to apply a like method, even though on a much greater scale,
to the western coast of France, against the high-road south of
Bordeaux, it can scarcely be doubted that he would have met
a severe disappointment, such as attended similar actions
upon the Channel in the Seven Years' War. On the Riviera, in
1795, this means might have been decisive; in 1796, in the
face of Bonaparte's fortified coast, it could scarcely have been
more than an annoyance. At all events, the advocacy of it
testifies to the acuteness and energy with which Nelson threw
himself into the operations especially intrusted to him.

His letters during this period reflect the varying phases
of hope and of discouragement; but, upon the whole, the
latter prevails. There is no longer the feeling of neglect by
his superior, of opportunity slipping away through the inadequate force which timid counsels and apathetic indolence allowed him. He sees that the chance which was permitted to
pass unimproved has now gone forever. "As the French cannot want supplies to be brought into the Gulf of Genoa, for
their grand army," he writes to the admiral, "I am still of
opinion that if our frigates are wanted for other services, they
may very well be spared from the Gulf." And again, "As
the service for which my distinguishing pendant was intended
to be useful, is nearly if not quite at an end, I assure you I
shall have no regret in striking it." Sir John Jervis, he
asserts with pride, has cruised with the fleet in the Gulf of
Genoa, close to shore, "where I will venture to say no fleet
ever cruised before — no officer can be more zealous or able to
render any service in our profession to England;" yet from
the decks of the flagship he and Nelson had helplessly watched
a convoy passing close in shore, and directly to windward, but
wholly out of reach of their powers of offence. At times, indeed, somewhat can be accomplished. For several days the
"Agamemnon" "has kept close to shore, and harassed the
enemy's troops very much. Field pieces are drawn out on
our standing in shore. You must defend me if any Genoese
towns are knocked down by firing at enemy's batteries. I
will not fire first." Six weeks later he writes again: "Our
conduct has so completely alarmed the French that all their
coasting trade is at an end; even the corvette, gunboats, &c.,

which were moored under the fortress of Vado, have not thought themselves in security, but are all gone into Savona Mole, and unbent their sails."

This movement, however, which he notes under the date of June 23, proceeded probably less from fear than from the growing indifference of the French concerning their communications by water, now that their occupation of the line of the Adige River had solidified their control over the ample resources of Piedmont and Lombardy. At the very hour when Nelson was thus writing, he learned also the critical condition of Leghorn through the approach of a French division, the mere sending of which showed Bonaparte's sense of his present security of tenure.

Nelson had severed by this time his long and affectionate connection with the battered "Agamemnon." On the 4th of June the old ship anchored at San Fiorenzo, having a few days before, with the assistance of the squadron, cut out from under the French batteries the vessels carrying Bonaparte's siege-train, as well as the gunboats which convoyed them. There was then in the bay the "Egmont," seventy-four, whose commander had expressed to the admiral his wish to return to England. Jervis, therefore, had ordered Nelson to the spot, to make the exchange, and the latter thought the matter settled; but to his surprise he found the captain did not wish to leave the station unless the ship went also. This did away with the vacancy he looked to fill; and, as the "Agamemnon," from her condition, must be the first of the fleet to go home, it seemed for the moment likely that he would have to go in her with a convoy then expected in the bay. "I remained in a state of uncertainty for a week," he wrote to his wife; "and had the corn ships, which were momentarily expected from Naples, arrived, I should have sailed for England." The dilemma caused him great anxiety; for the longing for home, which he had felt in the early part of the winter, had given way entirely before the pride and confidence he felt in the new admiral, and the keen delight in active service he was now enjoying. "I feel full of gratitude for your good wishes towards me," he wrote to Jervis in the first moment of disappointment, "and highly flattered by your desire to have me continue to serve under your command, which I own would afford me infinite satisfaction." The following day he is still more restless. "I am not less anxious than yesterday for having slept since my last letter. Indeed, Sir, I cannot bear the thoughts of leaving your command." He then proposed several ways out of the difficulty, which reduced themselves, in short, to a readiness to hoist his pendant in anything, if only he could remain.

No violent solution was needed, as several applicants came forward when Nelson's wish was known. On the 11th of June, 1796, he shifted his broad pendant to the "Captain," of seventy-four guns, taking with him most of his officers. Soon afterwards the "Agamemnon" sailed for England. Up to the last day of his stay on board, Nelson, although a commodore, was also her captain; it was not until two months after joining his new ship that another captain was appointed to her, leaving to himself the duties of commodore only. In later years the "Agamemnon" more than once bore a share in his career. She was present at Copenhagen and at Trafalgar, being in this final scene under the command of an officer who had served in her as his first lieutenant, and was afterwards his flag-captain at the Nile. In 1809 she was totally lost in the river La Plata, having run aground, and then settled on one of her anchors, which, upon the sudden shoaling of the water, had been let go to bring her up.[1] It is said that there were then on board several seamen who had been with her during Nelson's command.

On the 13th of June the "Captain" sailed from San Fiorenzo Bay, and on the 17th joined the fleet off Cape Sicie, near Toulon, where Jervis, six weeks before, had established the first of those continuous close blockades which afterwards, off Brest, became associated with his name, and proved so potent a factor in the embarrassments that drove Napoleon to his ruin. There were then twelve British ships off the port, while inside the enemy had eleven ready for sea, and four or five more fitting. The following day Nelson again left the fleet, and on the 21st of June arrived at Genoa, where very serious news was to be received.

The triumphant and hitherto unchecked advance of Bona-

[1] An account of this disaster, said to be that of an eye-witness, is to be found in Colburn's United Service Journal, 1846, part i.

parte had greatly encouraged the French party in Corsica, which had been increased by a number of malcontents, dissatisfied with their foreign rulers. Owing to the disturbed condition of the interior, the British troops had been drawn down to the seacoast. Bonaparte, from the beginning of his successes, had kept in view the deliverance of his native island, which he expected to effect by the exertions of her own people, stimulated and supported by the arrival upon the spot of Corsican officers and soldiers from the French armies. These refugees, proceeding in parties of from ten to twenty each, in small boats, movable by sail or oars, and under cover of night, could seldom be stopped, or even detected, by the British cruisers, while making the short trip, of little more than a hundred miles, from Genoa, Nice, and Leghorn. The latter port, from its nearness, was particularly favorable to these enterprises; but, although neutral, and freely permitting the ingress and egress of vessels belonging to both belligerents, its facilities for supporting a Corsican uprising were not so great as they would be if the place were held for the French. For this reason, partly, Bonaparte had decided to seize it; and he was still more moved to do so by the fact that it was a centre of British trade, that it contributed much to the supply and repair of the British fleet, and that the presence of vessels from the latter enabled an eye to be kept upon the movements of the Corsicans, and measures to be taken for impeding them.

"The enemy possessing themselves of Leghorn," Nelson had written in the middle of March, when expecting them to do so by a coastwise expedition, "cuts off all our supplies, such as fresh meat, fuel, and various other most essential necessaries; and, of course, our fleet cannot always [in that case] be looked for on the northern coast of Italy." Bonaparte had not, indeed, at that time, contemplated any such ex-centric movement, which, as things then were, would have risked so large a part of his army out of his own control and his own support; but in the middle of June, having driven the Austrians for the moment into the Tyrol, consolidated his position upon the Adige, established the siege of Mantua, and enforced order and submission throughout the fertile valley of the Po, which lay in rear of his army and amply supplied it with the

necessaries of subsistence, he felt not only able to spare the
force required, but that for the security of the right flank and
rear of his army it had become essential to do so. The Papacy
and Naples, although they had contributed little to the active
campaigning of the allies, were still nominally at war with
France, and might possibly display more energy now that operations were approaching their own frontiers. Should the British
take possession of Leghorn with a body of troops, — their own
or Neapolitan, — the port would remain a constant menace to the
operations and communications of the French, and especially
at the critical moments when the Austrians advanced to the
relief of Mantua, as they must be expected to do, and actually
did on four several occasions during the succeeding six months.

Bonaparte, as he was ever wont, diligently improved the
opportunity permitted to him by the need of the Austrians to
reorganize and reinforce Beaulieu's beaten army before again
taking the field. Threatened, as often again in later years,
by enemies in divergent directions, he with the utmost promptitude and by the most summary measures struck down the
foe on one side, before the other could stir. Occupying
Verona in the first days of June, he immediately afterwards
detached to the southward a corps under Augereau to enter
the Papal States ; and at the same time another small division,
commanded by General Vaubois, started from the upper valley
of the Po, ostensibly destined to proceed against Rome by
passing through Tuscany. The effect of Augereau's movement, which was closely followed by the commander-in-chief
in person, was to bring both Naples and the Pope speedily to
terms. An armistice was signed by the former on the 5th,
and by the latter on the 24th of June. Vaubois, on the other
hand, after passing the Arno below Florence, instead of continuing on to Siena, as the Grand Duke had been assured that
he would, turned sharp to the westward, and on the 28th of
June entered Leghorn, which was thenceforth held by the
French. Thus within a brief month were the British deprived
of two allies, lethargic, it is true, in actual performance, but
possessed of a degree of potential strength that could not but
enter largely into Bonaparte's anxieties; while at the same
time they lost the use of a seaport that had heretofore been
considered essential to their support.

Rumors of Vaubois' movement reached Nelson in Genoa at noon of June 23, but somewhat vaguely. "Reports are all we have here," he wrote to Jervis the same day, "nothing official from the armies;" but he thought the situation critical, and started without delay for Leghorn. Arriving there on the morning of June 27, after a passage rendered tedious by light airs and calms, he found the British merchant vessels that had been in the harbor, to the number of nearly forty sail, already under way, laden with British merchants and their property, and standing out under convoy of several ships of war; while in pursuit of them — a singular indication of the neutrality possible to small States like Tuscany and Genoa at that time — were a dozen French privateers, which had been lying beside them within the mole. One or two of the departing vessels were thus taken.

The first impression upon Nelson's mind was that the occupation of Leghorn was only the prelude to an invasion of Corsica in force. "I have no doubt," he wrote to the Viceroy, "but the destination of the French army was Corsica, and it is natural to suppose their fleet was to amuse ours whilst they cross from Leghorn." Thus reasoning, he announced his purpose of rejoining the admiral as soon as possible, so as not to lose his share in the expected battle. "My heart would break," he says to Jervis, "to be absent at such a glorious time;" but it is difficult to understand why he imagined that the French would transfer their army into the destitution of the Corsican mountains from the fertile plains of Lombardy, abandoning the latter to their enemy, and exchanging their assured communications with France for the uncertainties and irregularities of a water transit over seas commanded by the British fleet. The tenure of the island, as he well knew, depended upon the willing support of the Corsicans themselves; in the equal balance of the existing war, neither belligerent could maintain its control against the opposition of the natives.

This anticipation, in its disregard of the perfectly obvious conditions, was scarcely worthy of Nelson's real native sagacity, and shows clearly how much a man, even of genius, is hampered in the conclusions of actual life by the lack of that systematic ordering and training of the ideas which it is the part of education to supply. Genius is one thing, the acquirements of an accomplished — instructed — officer are another, yet there is between the two nothing incompatible, rather the reverse; and when to the former, which nature alone can give, — and to Nelson did give, — is added the conscious recognition of principles, the practised habit of viewing, under their clear light, all the circumstances of a situation, assigning to each its due weight and relative importance, then, and then only, is the highest plane of military greatness attained. Whether in natural insight Nelson fell short of Napoleon's measure need not here be considered ; that he was at this time far inferior, in the powers of a trained intellect, to his younger competitor in the race for fame, is manifest by the readiness with which he accepted such widely ex-centric conjectures as that of an attempt by sea upon Leghorn at the opening of the campaign, and now upon Corsica by a great part, if not the whole, of the army of Italy.

"On the side of the French," says Jomini, speaking of Bonaparte at this very period, "was to be seen a young warrior, trained in the best schools, endowed with an ardent imagination, brought up upon the examples of antiquity, greedy of glory and of power, knowing thoroughly the Apennines, in which he had distinguished himself in 1794, and already measuring with a practised eye the distances he must overpass before becoming master of Italy. To these advantages for a war of invasion, Bonaparte united an inborn genius, and clearly established principles, the fruits of an enlightened theory."

Jomini doubtless may be considered somewhat too absolute and pedantic in his insistence upon definite formulation of principles ; but in these words is nevertheless to be recognized the fundamental difference between these two great warriors, a difference by which the seaman was heavily handicapped in the opening of his career. As time passed on, responsibility, the best of educators, took under her firm and steady guidance the training of his yet undeveloped genius, gleams of which from time to time, but fitfully and erratically, illumine his earlier correspondence. The material was there from the first, but inchoate, ill-ordered, confused, and therefore not readily available to correct passing impressions, wild rumors, or even to prevent the radically false conceptions of an enemy's possible movements, such as we have had before us. Bonaparte, furthermore, whose career began amid the troubled scenes of a revolution which had shattered all the fetters of established custom, — so strong in England to impede a man's natural progress, — had enjoyed already for some time the singular advantage of being military adviser to the Directory, a duty which compelled him to take a broad view of all current conditions, to consider them in their mutual relations, and not narrowly to look to one sphere of operations, without due reference to its effects upon others.

As to the invasion of Corsica after the manner he had imagined, Nelson was soon undeceived. Bonaparte himself, after a hurried visit to Leghorn, again departed to press the siege of Mantua, having assured himself that for a measurable time he had nothing to apprehend from movements on his flank and rear. Orders were received from Jervis on the 2d of July to institute a commercial blockade of Leghorn, permitting no vessels to enter or depart. The conduct of this business, as well as the protection of British trade in that district, and the support of the Viceroy in securing Corsica against the attempts of French partisans, were especially intrusted to Nelson, whose movements during the following months, until the first of October, were consequently confined to the waters between Corsica and Tuscany, while the Riviera west of Genoa saw him no more. Leghorn became the chief centre of his activities. These redoubled with the demands made upon him ; his energy rose equal to every call. A few weeks before, he had made a conditional application to the admiral, though with evident reluctance, for a short leave of absence on account of his health. "I don't much like what I have written," he confessed at the end of his diffident request, and some days later he again alludes to the subject. "My complaint is as if a girth was buckled taut over my breast, and my endeavours, in the night, is to get it loose. To say the truth, when I am actively employed, I am not so bad. If the Service will admit of it, perhaps I shall at a future day take your leave." The service now scarcely admitted it, and the active duty apparently restored his health ; at all events we now hear no more of it. Everything yielded to the requirements of the war. "The Captain has wants, but I intend she shall last till the autumn: for I know, when once we begin, our wants are innumerable."

In his still limited sphere, and on all matters directly connected with it and his professional duties, his judgment was sound and acute, as his activity, energy, and zeal were untiring. The menace to Corsica from the fall of Leghorn was accurately weighed and considered. Midway between the two lay the since famous island of Elba, a dependence of Tuscany, so small as to be held readily by a few good troops, and having a port large enough, in Nelson's judgment, to harbor the British fleet with a little management. "The way to Corsica," he wrote to the viceroy, "if our fleet is at hand, is through Elba; for if they once set foot on that island, it is not all our fleet can stop their passage to Corsica." The Viceroy took upon himself to direct that the island be occupied by the British. Nelson complied without waiting for Jervis's orders, and on the 10th of July a detachment of troops, convoyed by his squadron, were landed in the island, and took charge, without serious opposition, of the town of Porto Ferrajo and the works for the defence of the harbor. The measure was justified upon the ground that the seizure of Leghorn by the French showed that Tuscany was unable to assure Elba against a similar step, prejudicial to the British tenure in Corsica. The administration remained in the hands of the Tuscan officials, the British occupation being purely military, and confined to the places necessary for that purpose.

The blockade of Leghorn was enforced with the utmost rigor and great effectiveness. For a long time no vessels were allowed to go either out or in. Afterwards the rule was gradually relaxed, so far as to permit neutrals to leave the port in ballast; but none entered. The trade of the place was destroyed. Nelson hoped, and for a time expected, that the populace, accustomed to a thriving commerce, and drawing their livelihood from its employments, would rise against the feeble garrison, whose presence entailed upon them such calamities; but herein, of course, he underestimated the coercive power of a few resolute men, organized for mutual support, over a mob of individuals, incapable of combined action and each uncertain of the constancy of his fellows.

The Austrian preparations in the Tyrol gradually matured as the month of July wore on. Towards its end Marshal Wurmser, the successor of Beaulieu, advanced for the relief of Mantua and the discomfiture of Bonaparte, whose numbers were much inferior to his opponents. The projected movement was of course known to the British, and its first results in raising the siege of Mantua, and throwing reinforcements into the place, gave them great hopes. Amid the conflicting rumors of the succeeding days, the wonderful skill and success of Bonaparte, who overthrew in detail forces greatly superior in the aggregate to his own, escaped notice for the time ; the superficial incidents of his abandoning his previous positions alone received attention, and nothing less than his retreat in confusion was confidently expected. Nelson, justly estimating the importance of Leghorn, and over-sanguine of the support he might hope from the inhabitants, projected a sudden assault upon the town, by troops to be drawn from the garrisons in Corsica, supported by seamen of the squadron. Speaking of the steady intercourse between that island and the mainland by way of Leghorn, he says : "The only way is to cut at the root, for whilst Leghorn is open, this communication must constantly be going on. This moment brings to my eyes a body of about 200 men, with the Corsican flag carrying before them ; they are partly from Nice, and joined by Genoese, &c., on the road. The time approaches," he rightly forecasts, " when we shall either have to fight them in Corsica or Leghorn." The imminence of the danger was evident. " Our affairs in Corsica are gloomy," he had already written to the Duke of Clarence. " There is a very strong republican party in that island, and they are well supported from France ; the first favourable moment, they will certainly act against us."

The details of the intended assault upon Leghorn do not appear, and it is probable that they never passed beyond the stage of discussion to that of acceptance, although he alludes to the plans as "laid." Clear-sighted for the key of a situation, and ardent to strike "at the root," as five years later in the Baltic he was eager to cut away the Russian root of the Armed Neutrality, instead of hewing off the Danish branch, Nelson urged the speedy adoption of the measure,

and pressed his own fitness to harmonize the land and sea
forces under one command, in virtue of his rank as Colonel
of Marines. "Leghorn is in such a state," he writes to Elliot
on the 5th of August, "that a respectable force landed, would,
I have every reason to suppose, insure the immediate possession of the town. Not less than a thousand troops should be
sent, to which I will add every soldier in my squadron, and
a party of seamen to make a show. In every way, pray consider this as private, and excuse my opinions. I well know
the difficulty of getting a proper person to command this
party. Firmness, and that the people of Leghorn should
know the person commanding, will most assuredly have a
great effect. A cordial co-operation with me (for vanity
apart, no one is so much feared or respected in Leghorn as
myself) is absolutely necessary. I am going further: we
know the jealousy of the army against the navy, but I am by
the King's commission a Colonel in the army from June 1st,
1795." After discussing this difficult question of professional
susceptibilities, he concludes: "You will consider, Sir, all
these points, and form a much better judgment than I can,
only give me credit that the nearest wish of my heart is to
serve my King and my Country, at every personal risk and
consideration. It has ever pleased God to prosper all my
undertakings, and I feel confident of His blessing on this
occasion. I ever consider my motto, *Fides et Opera*." [1]

Having, with true strategic insight, chosen the place where
the blow ought to be struck for the preservation of Corsica,
he pressed, with characteristic fervor, the necessity of taking
risks. He discusses details indeed; he proposes no mere adventure, real as was his personal enjoyment of danger and
action. What man can do, shall be done; but being done,
still "something must be left to chance. Our only consideration, is the honour and benefit to our Country worth the risk ?
If it is (and I think so), in God's name let us get to work,
and hope for His blessing on our endeavours to liberate a
people who have been our sincere friends." Hearing at the
same time that an army officer of general rank will have the
command instead of himself, he adds: "Pray assure him

---

[1] This motto was subsequently adopted by Nelson, when arms were assigned to him as a Knight of the Bath, in May, 1797.

there is nothing I feel greater pleasure in than hearing he is to command. Assure him of my most sincere wishes for his speedy success, and that he shall have every support and assistance from me." Truly, in generosity as in ardor, Nelson was, to use the fine old phrase, "all for the service."

The project upon Leghorn had the approval of the Viceroy and of Jervis; but the latter, while expressing perfect reliance upon "the promptitude of Commodore Nelson," was clear that the attempt must depend upon the continued advance of the Austrians. This was also Nelson's own view. "All will be well, I am satisfied, provided Wurmser is victorious; upon this ground only have I adopted the measure." This qualification redeems the plan from the reproach of rashness, which otherwise might have been applied to the somewhat desperate undertaking of carrying a fortified town by such a feat of hardihood. It loses thus the color of recklessness, and falls into place as one part of a great common action, to harass the retreat of a beaten enemy, and to insure the security of one's own positions.

On the 15th of August, when the above words were written, Nelson was still ignorant of the Austrian defeats at Lonato and Castiglione, nearly two weeks before, and of their subsequent retreat to the Tyrol. A rumor of the reverse had reached him through Florence, but he gave it little attention, as the French in Leghorn were not claiming a victory. On the 19th he knew it definitely, and had to abandon the expectation, confided to his brother, that the next letter seen from him would be in the "Public Gazette." "An expedition is thought of, and of course I shall be there, for most of these services fall to my lot." "One day or other," he had written to his wife, apparently with this very enterprise in mind, "I will have a long Gazette to myself; I feel that such an opportunity will be given me. I cannot," he continued with prophetic self-reliance, "if I am in the field of glory, be kept out of sight."

During the remainder of the month he continued to be amused with those unfounded reports of victories, which are among the invariable concomitants of all wars, and which his sanguine temperament and peculiar readiness to trust others made him especially ready to accept. He was not wholly unaware of this tendency in himself, though he continued to repeat with apparent belief reports of the most startling and erroneous character, and never seems to have appreciated, up to the time of his leaving the Mediterranean, the astonishing quickness and sagacity with which Bonaparte frustrated the overwhelming combinations against him. "We hear what we wish," he says on one occasion. "The Toulon information is, as I always thought it, pleasant to know but never to be depended upon; all is guess. I have long had reason to suspect great part is fabricated in Genoa;" but he was continually deceived by it.

Throughout the discomfitures of the Austrians on shore, the purely naval part of the war continued to be successfully maintained. Jervis, with unrelaxing grip, kept his position before Toulon, effectually checking every attempt of the French fleet to escape unobserved into the open, while Nelson shut up Leghorn so rigorously that the enemy lost even the partial advantage, as a port of supply, which they had before drawn from its neutrality. But, during this pregnant summer, grave causes for anxiety were rolling up in the western basin of the Mediterranean. The attitude of Spain had long been doubtful, so much so that before Sir John Jervis left England, in the previous autumn, the ministry had deliberated upon the contingency of her declaring war, and a conditional decision had been reached to evacuate Corsica, if that event occurred. During the spring of 1796 reports of coming hostilities were current in the fleet. Nelson's first opinion was that, if they ensued, there was no object in remaining in the Mediterranean, except to preserve Corsica from the French. This, he thought, was not a sufficient motive, nor had the conduct of the natives entitled them to protection. With all the powers making peace with France, he hoped Great Britain would leave the Mediterranean. This, however, was but a passing expression of discouragement, whence he soon rallied, and, with a spirit worthy of his race, which was soon to face all Europe undismayed, his courage mounted continually as the storm drew nearer.

The summer of 1796 was in truth the period of transition, when the victories of Bonaparte, by bringing near a cessation of warfare upon the land, were sweeping from the scene the

accessories that confused the view of the future, removing
conditions and details which perplexed men's attention, and
bringing into clear relief the one field upon which the contest
was finally to be fought out, and the one foe, the British sea-
power, upon whose strength and constancy would hinge the
issues of the struggle.   The British Navy, in the slight
person of its indomitable champion, was gradually rising to
the appreciation of its own might, and gathering together its
energies to endure single-handed the gigantic strife, with a
spirit unequalled in its past history, glorious as that had often
been.   From 1796 began the rapid ascent to that short noon-
tide of unparalleled brilliancy, in which Nelson's fame out-
shone all others, and which may be said to have begun with
the Spanish declaration of war, succeeded though that was by
the retreat in apparent discomfiture from the Mediterranean,
now at hand.

The approach of this extraordinary outburst of maritime
vigor is aptly foretokened in the complete change, gradual
yet rapid, that passed over Nelson's opinions, from the time
when rumors of a Spanish war first assumed probability, up
to the moment when the fact became tangible by the appearance of the Spanish fleet in the waters of Corsica.   Accentuated thus in a man of singular perceptions and heroic
instincts, it further affords an interesting illustration of the
manner in which a combative race — for Nelson was through
and through a child of his people — however at first averse
to war, from motives of well-understood interest, gradually
warms to the idea, and finally grows even to welcome the
fierce joy which warriors feel, as the clash of arms draws
near.   " If all the states of Italy make peace," he writes on
the 20th of May, "we have nothing to look to but Corsica;
which, in the present state of the inhabitants, is not, in my
opinion, an object to keep us in the Mediterranean : we shall,
I hope, quit it, and employ our fleet more to our advantage."
"Reports here," on the 20th of June, "are full of a Spanish
war.   If that should be the case, we shall probably draw
towards Gibraltar and receive large reinforcements."

On the 15th of August, however, he writes to Jervis, betraying the incipient revulsion, as yet not realized, against
abandoning the Mediterranean, which was already affecting

the current of his thoughts. "I hope we shall have settled
Leghorn before the Dons, if they intend it, arrive. I have
still my doubts as to a Spanish war; and if there should be
one, with your management I have no fears. Should the
Dons come, I shall then hope I may be spared,[1] in my own
person, to help to make you at least a Viscount." A few
days later, having meantime heard of Wurmser's disasters at
Castiglione: "Austria, I suppose, must make peace, and we
shall, as usual, be left to fight it out: however, at the worst,
we only give up Corsica, an acquisition which I believe we
cannot keep, and our fleet will draw down the Mediterranean;" but at the same time, August 19, he writes to the
Duke of Clarence with glowing hopes and rising pride: "I
hope Government will not be alarmed for our safety — I mean
more than is proper. Under such a commander-in-chief as
Sir John Jervis nobody has any fears. We are now twenty-
two sail of the line; the combined fleet will not be above
thirty-five sail of the line. I will venture my life Sir John
Jervis defeats them. This country is the most favourable
possible for skill with an inferior fleet; for the winds are so
variable, that some one time in twenty-four hours you must
be able to attack a part of a large fleet, and the other will be
becalmed, or have a contrary wind." That the Duke trembled
and demurred to such odds is not wonderful; but the words
have singular interest, both as showing the clear tactical apprehensions that held sway in Nelson's mind, and still more,
at the moment then present, as marking unmistakably his
gradual conversion to the policy of remaining in the
Mediterranean, and pursuing the most vigorous aggressive
measures.

A fortnight after this letter was written, Genoa, under
pressure from Bonaparte, closed her ports against British
ships, interdicting even the embarkation of a drove of cattle,
already purchased, and ready for shipment to the fleet off
Toulon. Nelson immediately went there to make inquiries,
and induce a revocation of the orders. While the "Captain"
lay at anchor in the roads, three of the crew deserted, and
when her boats were sent to search for them they were fired

[1] That is, apparently, from detached service, and ordered to the main
fleet.

upon by a French battery, established near the town. Nelson, in retaliation, seized a French supply ship from under the guns of the battery, whereupon the Genoese forts opened against the "Captain," which had meantime got under way and was lying-to off the city. Nelson did not return the fire of the latter, which was kept up for two hours, but threw three shot into the French battery, " to mark," as he said, the power of the English to bombard the town, and their humanity in not destroying the houses and innocent Genoese inhabitants. In the communications which followed under a flag of truce, Nelson was informed, verbally, that all the ports of the Republic were closed against Great Britain. This stand, and the firing on the ship, being considered acts of hostility, the little island of Capraia, between Corsica and Genoa, and belonging to the latter, was seized by Nelson, acting under the counsel of the Viceroy of Corsica. This was done both as a retaliatory measure, and to put a stop to the use which French privateers and parties of Corsicans had hitherto made of it, under cover of Genoese neutrality.

As Jervis was already under apprehension of an outbreak of scurvy in the fleet, consequent upon the failure of supplies of live cattle following the French occupation of Leghorn, the closure of the Genoese ports was a severe blow. It was, however, but one among several incidents, occurring nearly simultaneously, which increased his embarrassments, and indicated the close approach of the long-muttering storm. To use his own words, " The lowering aspect of Spain, with the advanced state of the equipment of the French fleet in Toulon," impelled him to concentrate his force. Rear-Admiral Man, who had been blockading Cadiz since his detachment there by Hotham, in October, 1795, was ordered up to the main fleet. Swayed by fears very unlike to Nelson's proud confidence in his admiral and his service, he acted with such precipitation as to leave Gibraltar without filling with provisions, and arrived so destitute that Jervis had to send him back at once, with orders to replenish with stores and then to rejoin without delay. Under the influence of the panic which prevailed at Gibraltar, Man had also sent such advices to the coast of Portugal as caused the commander-in-chief to fear that expected supplies might be arrested. " Oh, our convoy ! " cried

14

Nelson; "Admiral Man, how could you quit Gibraltar?" Yet, as he wrote to Jervis, he had expected some such step, from what he had already seen "under his hand to you."

Thus, for the time at least, there were lost to the British seven of the ships-of-the-line upon which Nelson had reckoned in his letter to the Duke of Clarence. It was possibly on this account that Jervis wrote him to shift his commodore's pendant to a frigate, and send the " Captain" to the fleet. Nelson obeyed, of course, and at once; but taking advantage of the fact that no captain had yet joined his ship, he thought it "advisable to go in her myself." In this he doubtless was influenced chiefly by his unwillingness to miss a battle, especially against such great numerical odds. " I take for granted," he admitted to the Viceroy, " that the admiral will send me back in a cutter, but I shall give him a good ordered seventy-four, and take my chance of helping to thrash Don Langara, than which few things, I assure you, would give me more real pleasure." The particular emergency seems, however, soon to have passed; for after two days with the fleet he returned off Leghorn in the " Captain," somewhat comforted as to the apprehensions of the British Cabinet. " Whatever fears we may have for Corsica, it is certain Government at home have none, by taking so very respectable a part of your force away." A regiment had been transferred to Gibraltar with Man's squadron, when the latter returned there.

These rising hopes and stirring expectations of brilliant service were speedily dashed. On the 25th of September Jervis received orders from the Admiralty to abandon Corsica, to retreat from the Mediterranean, and to proceed with the fleet to England. In pursuance of these instructions Nelson was directed to superintend the evacuation of Bastia, the " most secret " letter to that effect reaching him at that port on the 29th of September, — his birthday. The purpose of the ministry filled him with shame and indignation. Confronted abruptly with the course which four months before had seemed to him natural and proper, the shock brought out the fulness of the change through which he had passed meantime. He has no illusions about Corsica. The inhabitants had disappointed all the expectations of the British, — " At a peace I should rejoice at having given up the island."

But the days passing over his head had brought wider and maturer views of the general policy of Great Britain, as well as increasing faith in the powers of the fleet, vigorously used in aggressive warfare. "Whilst we can keep the combined fleet in the Mediterranean [by our own presence], so much the more advantageous to us; and the moment we retire, the whole of Italy is given to the French. If the Dons detach their fleet out of the Mediterranean, we can do the same — however, that is distant. Be the successes of the Austrians on the other hand what they may, their whole supply of stores and provisions comes from Trieste, across the Adriatic to the Po, and when this is cut off [as by our uncovering the sea it must be], they must retire." Above all he grieves for Naples. If a weak and vacillating ally, there was no doubt her heart was with them. "I feel more than all for Naples. The King of Naples is a greater sacrifice than Corsica. If he has been induced to keep off the peace, and perhaps engaged in the war again by the expectation of the continuance of the fleet in the Mediterranean, hard indeed is his fate; his kingdom must inevitably be ruined." In the impression now made upon him, may perhaps be seen one cause of Nelson's somewhat extravagant affection in after days for the royal family of Naples, independent of any influence exerted upon him by Lady Hamilton.

With these broad views of the general strategic situation, which are unquestionably far in advance of the comparatively narrow and vague conceptions of a year, or even six months before, and doubtless indicate the results of independent command and responsibility, acting upon powers of a high order, he at the same time shows his keen appreciation of the value of the organized force, whose movements, properly handled, should dominate the other conditions. "When Man arrives, who is ordered to come up, we shall be twenty-two sail of such ships as England hardly ever produced, and commanded by an admiral who will not fail to look the enemy in the face, be their force what it may: I suppose it will not be more than thirty-four of the line. There is not a seaman in the fleet who does not feel confident of success." "The fleets of England," he says again, "are equal to meet the world in arms; and of all fleets I ever saw, I never beheld one in point of officers and men equal to Sir John Jervis's, who is a commander-in-chief able to lead them to glory."

Reasoning so clearly and accurately upon the importance to Great Britain's interests and honor, at that time, of maintaining her position in the Mediterranean, and upon the power of her fleet in battle, it is not strange that Nelson, writing in intimate confidence to his wife, summed up in bitter words his feelings upon the occasion; unconscious, apparently, of the great change they indicated, not merely in his opinions, but in his power of grasping, in well-ordered and rational sequence, the great outlines of the conditions amid which he, as an officer, was acting. "We are all preparing to leave the Mediterranean, a measure which I cannot approve. They at home do not know what this fleet is capable of performing; anything, and everything. Much as I shall rejoice to see England, I lament our present orders in sackcloth and ashes, so dishonourable to the dignity of England." To the British minister at Naples his words were even stronger: "Till this time it has been usual for the allies of England to fall from her, but till now she never was known to desert her friends whilst she had the power of supporting them. I yet hope the Cabinet may, on more information, change their opinion; it is not all we gain elsewhere which can compensate for our loss of honour. The whole face of affairs is totally different to what it was when the Cabinet formed their opinion."

Nevertheless, although Nelson's perceptions and reasoning were accurate as far as they went, they erred in leaving out of the calculation a most important consideration, — the maintenance of the communications with England, which had assumed vital importance since the general defection of the Italian States, caused by Bonaparte's successes and his imperious demands. It would be more true to say that he underestimated this factor than that he overlooked it; for he had himself observed, six weeks earlier, when the approach of a Spanish war first became certain: "I really think they would do us more damage by getting off Cape Finisterre;[1] it is there I fear them," and the reason for that fear is shown

---

[1] On the northwest coast of Spain, at the entrance of the Bay of Biscay, and therefore right in the track of vessels from the Channel to the Straits of Gibraltar.

by his reproach against Man, already quoted, for his neglect of the convoy. The position of the Spanish Navy in its home ports was in fact intermediate — interior — as regarded the British fleet and the source of its most essential supplies. So long as its future direction remained uncertain, it lay upon the flank of the principal British line of communications. Nelson did not use, perhaps did not know, the now familiar terms of the military art; and, with all his insight and comprehensive sagacity, he suffered from the want of proper tools with which to transmute his acute intuitions into precise thought, as well as of clearly enunciated principles, which serve to guide a man's conclusions, and would assuredly have qualified his in the present instance. Upon the supposition that the Spanish Navy, practically in its entirety, entered the Mediterranean and appeared off Corsica, — as it did, — Nelson's reasoning was correct, and his chagrin at a retreat justified ; but, as he himself had wisely remarked to Beaulieu, it is not safe to count upon your enemy pursuing the course you wish. Had the Spanish Government chosen the other alternative open to it, and struck at the communications, such a blow, or even such a threat, must have compelled the withdrawal of the fleet, unless some other base of supplies could be found. The straitness of the situation is shown by the fact that Jervis, after he had held on to the last moment in San Fiorenzo Bay, sailed for Gibraltar with such scanty provisions that the crews' daily rations were reduced to one-third the ordinary amount ; in fact, as early as the first of October they had been cut down to two-thirds. Whether, therefore, the Government was right in ordering the withdrawal, or Nelson in his condemnation of it, may be left to the decision of those fortunate persons who can be cock-sure of the true solution of other people's perplexities.

In evacuating the Mediterranean, Jervis determined, upon his own responsibility, to retain Elba, if the troops, which were not under his command, would remain there. This was accordingly done ; a strong garrison, adequately provisioned, thus keeping for Great Britain a foothold within the sea, at a time when she had lost Minorca and did not yet possess Malta. Nelson hoped that this step would encourage the Two Sicilies to stand firm against the French ; but, however valu-

able Elba would be to the fleet as a base, if held until its
return, it was useless to protect Naples in the absence of the
fleet, and upon the news of the latter's proposed retirement
that Kingdom at once made peace.

After the receipt of his orders for the evacuation of Bastia,
and pending the assembling of the transports, Nelson was
despatched by the admiral to Genoa, to present reclamations
for injuries alleged to have been done to Great Britain, and to
propose terms of accommodation. The little Republic, however, under the coercive influence of Bonaparte's continued
success, was no longer in doubt as to the side which policy
dictated her to take, between the two belligerents who vexed
her borders. During this visit of Nelson's, on the 9th of
October, she signed a treaty with France, stipulating, besides
the closure of the ports against Great Britain, the payment of
a sum of money, and free passage to troops and supplies for
the army of Italy. Thus was Genoa converted formally, as
she for some time had been actually, into a French base of
operations. Returning from this fruitless mission, Nelson
rejoined the commander-in-chief on the 13th of October, at
San Fiorenzo, and the same afternoon left again for Bastia,
where he arrived the following day.

During the fortnight intervening since he left the place, the
fact that the Spanish fleet was on its way to Corsica had become known, and the French partisans in the island were proportionately active. It was impossible for the British to go
into the interior; their friends, if not in a minority, were
effectually awed by the preponderance of their enemies, on
land and sea. Nelson, wishing to cross overland to San
Fiorenzo to visit Jervis, was assured he could not do so with
safety. In Bastia itself the municipality had wrested the
authority from the Viceroy, and consigned the administration
to a Committee of Thirty. The ships of war and transports
being blown to sea, the inhabitants became still more aggressive; for, foreseeing the return of the French, they were
naturally eager to propitiate their future masters by a display
of zeal. British property was sequestered, and shipping not
permitted to leave the mole.

Nelson was persuaded that only the arrival of the ships
accompanying him saved the place. Except a guard at the

Viceroy's house, the British troops had been withdrawn to the citadel. Even there, at the gates of the citadel, and within it, Corsican guards were present in numbers equal to the British, while the posts in the towns were all held by them. Arriving at early dawn of the 14th, Nelson at once visited the general and the Viceroy. The former saw no hope, under the conditions, of saving either stores, cannon, or provisions. "The Army," said Nelson in a private letter to Jervis, with something of the prejudiced chaff of a seaman of that day, "is, as usual, well dressed and powdered. I hope the general will join me cordially, but, as you well know, great exertions belong exclusively to the Navy." After the evacuation, however, he admitted handsomely that it was impossible to "do justice to the good dispositions of the general."

Between the heads of the two services such arrangements were perfected as enabled almost everything in the way of British property — public and private — to be brought away. By midday the ships, of which three were of the line, were anchored close to the mole-head, abreast the town, and the municipality was notified that any opposition to the removal of the vessels and stores would be followed by instant bombardment. Everything yielded to the threat, made by a man whose determined character left no doubt that it would be carried into execution. "Nothing shall be left undone that ought to be done," he wrote to Jervis, "even should it be necessary to knock down Bastia." From time to time interference was attempted, but the demand for immediate desistence, made, watch in hand, by the naval officer on the spot, enforced submission. "The firm tone held by Commodore Nelson," wrote Jervis to the Admiralty, "soon reduced these gentlemen to order, and quiet submission to the embarkation." Owing to the anarchy prevailing, the Viceroy was persuaded to go on board before nightfall, he being too valuable as a hostage to be exposed to possible kidnappers.

On the 18th of October a large number of armed French landed at Cape Corso, and approached the town. On the 19th they sent to the municipality a demand that the British should not be permitted to embark. Under these circumstances even Nelson felt that nothing more could be saved. The work of removal was continued actively until sunset, by which time two hundred thousand pounds worth of cannon, stores, and provisions had been taken on board. At midnight the troops evacuated the citadel, and marched to the north end of the town, where they embarked — twenty-four hours ahead of the time upon which Nelson had reckoned four days before. It was then blowing a strong gale of wind. Last of all, about six o'clock on the morning of the 20th, Nelson and the general entered a barge, every other man being by that time afloat, and were pulled off to the ships, taking with them two field-guns, until then kept ashore to repel a possible attack at the last moment. The French, who "were in one end of Bastia before we quitted the other," had occupied the citadel since one in the morning, and the Spanish fleet, of over twenty sail-of-the-line, which had already arrived, was even then off Cape Corso, about sixty miles distant; but the little British squadron, sailing promptly with a fair wind, in a few hours reached Elba, where every vessel was safely at anchor before night. On the 24th Nelson joined the commander-in-chief in Martello Bay, the outer anchorage of San Fiorenzo. Everything was then afloat, and ready for a start as soon as the transports, still at Elba, should arrive. The evacuation of Corsica was complete, though the ships remained another week in its waters.

The Spanish fleet continued cruising to the northward of the island, and was every day sighted by the British lookout frigates. Jervis held grimly on, expecting the appearance of the seven ships of Admiral Man, who had been ordered to rejoin him. That officer, however, acting on his own responsibility, weakly buttressed by the opinion of a council of his captains, had returned to England contrary to his instructions. The commander-in-chief, ignorant of this step, was left in the sorely perplexing situation of having his fleet divided into two parts, each distinctly inferior to the Spanish force alone, of twenty-six ships, not to speak of the French in Toulon. Under the conditions, the only thing that could be done was to await his subordinate, in the appointed spot, until the last moment. By the 2d of November further delay had become impossible, from the approaching failure of provisions. On that day, therefore, the fleet weighed, and after a tedious passage anchored on the first of December at Gibraltar.

There Nelson remained until the 10th of the month, when he temporarily quitted the "Captain," hoisted his broad pendant on board the frigate "Minerve," and, taking with him one frigate besides, returned into the Mediterranean upon a detached mission of importance.

Nelson's last services in Corsica were associated with the momentary general collapse of the British operations and influence in the Mediterranean; and his final duty, by a curious coincidence, was to abandon the position which he more than any other man had been instrumental in securing. Yet, amid these discouraging circumstances, his renown had been steadily growing throughout the year 1796, which may justly be looked upon as closing the first stage in the history of British Sea Power during the wars of the French Revolution, and as clearing the way for his own great career, which in the re-possession of the Mediterranean reached its highest plane, and there continued in unabated glory till the hour of his death. It was not merely the exceptional brilliancy of his deeds at Cape St. Vincent, now soon to follow, great and dis-tinguished as those were, which designated him to men in power as beyond dispute the coming chief of the British Navy; it was the long antecedent period of unswerving con-tinuance in strenuous action, allowing no flagging of earnest-ness for a moment to appear, no chance for service, however small or distant, to pass unimproved. It was the same unre-mitting pressing forward, which had brought him so vividly to the front in the abortive fleet actions of the previous year, — an impulse born, partly, of native eagerness for fame, partly of zeal for the interests of his country and his profession. " Mine is all honour; so much for the Navy ! " as he wrote, somewhat incoherently, to his brother, alluding to a disap-pointment about prize money.

Nelson himself had an abundant, but not an exaggerated, consciousness of this increase of reputation; and he knew, too, that he was but reaping as he had diligently sowed. " If credit and honour in the service are desirable," he tells his brother, " I have my full share. I have never lost an oppor-tunity of distinguishing myself, not only as a gallant man, but as having a head; for, of the numerous plans I have laid, not one has failed." " You will be informed from my late letters," he writes to his wife, "that Sir John Jervis has such an opinion of my conduct, that he is using every influence, both public and private, with Lord Spencer, for my continuance on this station; and I am certain you must feel the superior pleasure of knowing, that my integrity and plainness of conduct are the cause of my being kept from you, to the receiving me as a person whom no commander-in-chief would wish to keep under his flag. Sir John was a perfect stranger to me, therefore I feel the more flattered; and when I reflect that I have had the unbounded confidence of three commanders-in-chief, I cannot but feel a conscious pride, and that I possess abilities." "If my character is known," he writes to the Genoese Government, which knew it well, "it will be credited that this blockade [of Leghorn] will be attended to with a degree of rigour unexampled in the present war." "It has pleased God this war," he tells the Duke of Clarence, "not only to give me frequent opportunities of showing myself an officer worthy of trust, but also to prosper all my undertakings in the highest degree. I have had the extreme good fortune, not only to be noticed in my immediate line of duty, but also to obtain the repeated approbation of His Majesty's Ministers at Turin, Genoa, and Naples, as well as of the Viceroy of Corsica, for my conduct in the various opinions I have been called upon to give; and my judgment being formed from common sense, I have never yet been mistaken."

Already at times his consciousness of distinction among men betrays something of that childlike, delighted vanity, half unwitting, which was afterward forced into exuberant growth and distasteful prominence, by the tawdry flatteries of Lady Hamilton and the Court of Naples. Now, expressed to one who had a right to all his confidence and to share all his honors, it challenges rather the sympathy than the criticism of the reader. "I will relate another anecdote, all vanity to myself, but you will partake of it: A person sent me a letter, and directed as follows, 'Horatio Nelson, Genoa.' On being asked how he could direct in such a manner, his answer, in a large party, was, 'Sir, there is but one Horatio Nelson in the world.' I am known throughout Italy," he continues; "not a Kingdom, or State, where my name will be forgotten. This is my Gazette. Probably my services may be forgotten by the great, by the time I get home; but my mind will not forget, nor cease to feel, a degree of consolation and of applause superior to undeserved rewards. Wherever there is anything to be done, there Providence is sure to direct my steps. Credit must be given me in spite of envy. Had all my actions been gazetted, not one fortnight would have passed during the whole war without a letter from me. Even the French respect me." After the conclusion of the campaign, when on the way to Gibraltar, he tells her again: "Do not flatter yourself that I shall be rewarded; I expect nothing, and therefore shall not be disappointed: the pleasure of my own mind will be my reward. I am more interested, and feel a greater satisfaction, in obtaining yours and my father's applause than that of all the world besides." The wholesome balance between self-respect and a laudable desire for the esteem of men was plainly unimpaired.

Though devoid of conspicuous events, the year 1796, from the opening of the campaign, early in April, up to the evacuation of the Mediterranean, had been to Nelson one of constant and engrossing occupation. There is therefore little mention by him of his private affairs and feelings. In the home correspondence there is no diminution in the calm tenderness of affection always shown by him towards his wife and father, who continued to live together; rather, perhaps, the expressions to Mrs. Nelson are more demonstrative than before, possibly because letters were less frequent. But there is nothing thrilling in the "assurance of my unabated and steady affection, which, if possible, is increasing by that propriety of conduct which you pursue." He is clearly satisfied to remain away; the path of honor has no rival in his heart; there is no suggestion of an inward struggle between two masters, no feeling of aloneness, no petulant discontent with uneasy surroundings, or longing for the presence of an absent mistress. The quiet English home, the "little but neat cottage," attracts, indeed, with its sense of repose, — "I shall not be very sorry to see England again. I am grown old and battered to pieces, and require some repairs" — but the magnet fails to deflect the needle; not even a perceptible vibration of the will is produced.

Yet, while thus engrossed in the war, eager for personal distinction and for the military honor of his country, he apparently sees in it little object beyond a mere struggle for superiority, and has no conception of the broader and deeper issues at stake, the recognition of which intensified and sustained the resolution of the peace-loving minister, who then directed the policy of Great Britain. Of this he himself gives the proof in a curious anecdote. An Algerine official visiting the " Captain " off Leghorn, Nelson asked him why the Dey would not make peace with the Genoese and Neapolitans, for they would pay well for immunity, as the Americans at that period always did. His answer was : " If we make peace with every one, what is the Dey to do with his ships ? " " What a reason for carrying on a naval war ! " said Nelson, when writing the story to Jervis ; " but has our minister a better one for the present ? " Jervis, a traditional Whig, and opposed in Parliament to the war, probably sympathized with this view, and in any case the incident shows the close confidence existing between the two officers ; but it also indicates how narrowly Nelson's genius and unquestionable acuteness of intellect confined themselves, at that time, to the sphere in which he was visibly acting. In this he presents a marked contrast to Bonaparte, whose restless intelligence and impetuous imagination reached out in many directions, and surveyed from a lofty height the bearing of all things, far and near, upon the destinies of France.

CHAPTER VIII.

THE EVACUATION OF ELBA. — NIGHT COMBAT WITH TWO SPANISH FRIG-
ATES. — BATTLE OF CAPE ST. VINCENT. — NELSON PROMOTED TO
REAR-ADMIRAL. — SERVICES BEFORE CADIZ.

DECEMBER, 1796–JUNE, 1797.   AGE, 38.

"WHEN we quitted Toulon," wrote Nelson to his old captain, Locker, while on the passage to Gibraltar, "I remember we endeavoured to reconcile ourselves to Corsica; now we are content with Elba — such things are." Even this small foothold was next to be resigned. Upon reaching Gibraltar, Jervis received orders from the Admiralty to evacuate the island.

This was the duty upon which Nelson was so soon despatched again to the Mediterranean. Though "most important," wrote he to his wife, "it is not a fighting mission, therefore be not uneasy." The assurance was doubtless honestly given, but scarcely to be implicitly accepted in view of his past career. Leaving the admiral on the evening of December 14, with the frigates "Blanche" and "Minerve," his commodore's pendant lying in the latter, the two vessels, about 11 P. M. of the 19th, encountered two Spanish frigates close to Cartagena. The enemies pairing off, a double action ensued, which, in the case of the "Minerve," ended in the surrender of her opponent, "La Sabina," at half-past one in the morning. Throwing a prize-crew on board, the British ship took her late antagonist in tow and stood away to the southeast. At half-past three another Spanish frigate came up, and, in order to meet this fresh enemy on fairly equal terms, the "Minerve" had to drop her prize. The second fight began at 4.30, and lasted half an hour, when the Spaniard hauled off. With daylight appeared also two hostile ships-of-the-line, which had been chasing towards the sound of the guns. These had already been seen by the "Blanche," which was by them prevented from taking possession of her antagonist, after the latter struck. The pursuit lasted through the day, the "Minerve" being hard pressed in consequence of the injuries received by all her masts during the engagement; but both British frigates succeeded in shaking off their pursuers. "La Sabina" was recaptured; she had already lost one mast, and the remaining two were seen to go over the side as she was bringing-to, when the enemy overtook her. It is interesting to note that her captain, Don Jacobo Stuart, was descended from the British royal house of Stuart. He, with many of his crew, had been transferred to the "Minerve," and remained prisoners.

Nelson reached Porto Ferrajo a week later, on the 26th of December. "On my arrival here," wrote he to his brother, "it was a ball night, and being attended by the captains, I was received in due form by the General, and one particular tune was played:[1] the second was 'Rule Britannia.' From Italy I am loaded with compliments." Having regard to comparative strength, the action was in all respects most creditable, but it received additional lustre from being fought close to the enemy's coast, and in full view of a force so superior as that from which escape had been handsomely made, under conditions requiring both steadiness and skill. Though on a small scale, no such fair stand-up fight had been won in the Mediterranean during the war, and the resultant exultation was heightened by its contrast with the general depression then weighing upon the British cause. Especially keen and warmly expressed was the satisfaction of the veteran commander-in-chief at Lisbon, who first learned the success of his valued subordinate through Spanish sources. "I cannot express to you, and Captain Cockburn, the feelings I underwent on the receipt of the enclosed bulletin, the truth of which I cannot doubt, as far as relates to your glorious achievement in the capture of the Sabina, and dignified retreat from the line-of-battle ship, which deprived you of your well-earned trophy; your laurels were not then within their grasp, and can never fade."

General De Burgh, who commanded the troops in Elba, had

[1] It is evident that this must have involved a compliment personal to Nelson.

received no instructions to quit the island, and felt uncertain about his course, in view of the navy's approaching departure. Nelson's orders were perfectly clear, but applied only to the naval establishment. He recognized the general's difficulty, though he seems to have thought that, under all the circumstances, he might very well have acted upon his own expressed opinion, that "the signing of a Neapolitan peace with France ought to be our signal for departure." "The army," wrote Nelson to the First Lord of the Admiralty, "are not so often called upon to exercise their judgment in political measures as we are; therefore the general feels a certain diffidence." He told De Burgh that, the King of Naples having made peace, Jervis considered his business with the courts of Italy as terminated; that the Admiralty's orders were to concentrate the effort of the fleet upon preventing the allied fleets from quitting the Mediterranean, and upon the defence of Portugal, invaluable to the British as a base of naval operations. For these reasons, even if he had to leave the land forces in Elba, he should have no hesitation in following his instructions, which were to withdraw all naval belongings. "I have sent to collect my squadron, and as soon as they arrive, I shall offer myself for embarking the troops, stores, &c.; and should you decline quitting this post, I shall proceed down the Mediterranean with such ships of war as are not absolutely wanted for keeping open the communication of Elba with the Continent."

The necessary preparations went on apace. Vessels were sent out to summon the scattered cruisers to the port. A frigate was despatched to Naples to bring back Sir Gilbert Elliot, the late Viceroy of Corsica, who, since the abandonment of the latter island, had been on a diplomatic visit to Rome and Naples. It is to this incident that we owe the fullest account transmitted of the Battle of Cape St. Vincent; the narrator, Colonel Drinkwater, being then a member of the Viceroy's suite, and attending him upon his return with Nelson's squadron. The Spanish prisoners were sent to Cartagena in a cartel, Nelson restoring to the captain of the "Sabina" the sword which he had surrendered. "I felt this consonant to the dignity of my Country, and I always act as I feel right, without regard to custom." By the 16th of January all the naval establishment was embarked, ready for departure, though some of the ships of war had not yet returned, nor had the Viceroy arrived. The delay allowed the "Minerve" to be completely refitted, two of her masts and most of her rigging having to be renewed.

When Elliot came, it was decided in a consultation between him, Nelson, and De Burgh, that the troops should remain. The transports had been completely victualled, and so prepared that every soldier could be embarked in three days. With them were left two frigates and a few smaller ships of war. On the 29th of January, Nelson sailed with the rest of his force and the convoy, divided into three sections, which proceeded for the Straits by different routes, to diminish the chances of total loss by capture. Nelson himself, with another frigate, the "Romulus," in company, intended to make a round of the enemy's ports, in order to bring the admiral the latest information of the number of ships in each, and their state of preparation. "I hope to arrive safe in Lisbon with my charge," he wrote to his wife on the eve of sailing, "but in war much is left to Providence : however, as I have hitherto been most successful, confidence tells me I shall not fail : and as nothing will be left undone by me, should I not always succeed, my mind will not suffer; nor will the world, I trust, be willing to attach blame, where my heart tells me none would be due." The habit of taking risks had wrought its beneficial influence upon mind and temper, when he thus calmly and simply reasoned from the experience of the past to the prospective fortnight, to be passed in sight of a hostile coast, and in waters where he could meet no friendly sail. "It has ever pleased Almighty God to give his blessing to my endeavours," was his New Year greeting to his father at this time.

During this month in Elba a slight political reference shows how his views and purpose were changing with the rapidly shifting political scene. In this hour of deepening adversity he no longer looks for peace, nor seeks the reason for the current war, which a few months before he had failed to find. "As to peace, I do not expect it; Lord Malmesbury will come back as he went. But the people of England will, I trust, be more vigorous for the prosecution of the war, which can alone insure an honourable peace."

The "Minerve" and the "Romulus" looked first into the old British anchorage in San Fiorenzo Bay, which was found deserted. Standing thence to Toulon, they remained forty-eight hours off that port, in which were to be seen no ships in condition for sailing. From there they passed off Barcelona, showing French colors, but without succeeding in drawing out any vessel there lying. The wind not being fair for Minorca, where Nelson had purposed to reconnoitre Port Mahon, the frigates next went to Cartagena, and ascertained that the great Spanish fleet was certainly not there. As Toulon also had been found empty, it seemed clear that it had gone to the westward, the more so as the most probable information indicated that the naval enterprises of the French and their allies at that time were to be outside of the Mediterranean. Nelson therefore pushed ahead, and on the 9th of February the "Minerve" and "Romulus" anchored in Gibraltar. All three divisions from Elba passed the Straits within the same forty-eight hours.

The Spanish grand fleet had been seen from the Rock, four days before, standing to the westward into the Atlantic. Two ships-of-the-line and a frigate had been detached from it, with supplies for the Spanish lines before Gibraltar, and had anchored at the head of the bay, where they still were when Nelson arrived. On board them had also been sent the two British lieutenants and the seamen, who became prisoners when the "Sabina" was recaptured. Their exchange was effected, for which alone Nelson was willing to wait. The fact that the Spanish fleet had gone towards Jervis's rendezvous, and the continuance of easterly winds, which would tend to drive them still farther in the same direction, gave him uneasy premonitions of that coming battle which it would "break his heart" to miss. It was, besides, part of his ingrained military philosophy, never absent from his careful mind, that a fair wind may fall or shift. "The object of a sea-officer is to embrace the happy moment which now and then offers, — it may be to-day, it may be never." Regretting at this moment the loss even of a tide, entailed by the engagements of the Viceroy, whom he had to carry to Jervis, and therefore could not leave, he wrote, "I fear a *westerly* wind." The Providence in which he so often expresses his reliance,

now as on many other occasions, did not forsake the favored
son, who never by sluggishness or presumption lost his opportunities.   The wind held fair until the 13th of February, when
Nelson rejoined the commander-in-chief.   That night it shifted
to the westward, and the following day was fought the Battle
of Cape St. Vincent.

Taken in its entirety, the episode of this nearly forgotten
mission to Elba is singularly characteristic, not only of Nelson's own qualities, but also of those concurrences which,
whatever the origin attributed to them by this or that person,
impress upon a man's career the stamp of "fortunate."   An
errand purely of evasion, not in itself of prime importance,
but for an object essentially secondary, it results in a night
combat of unusual brilliancy, which would probably not have
been fought at all could the British have seen the overwhelming force ready to descend upon conqueror and conquered
alike.   With every spar wounded, and a hostile fleet in sight,
the "Minerve" nevertheless makes good her retreat.   Solitary, in an enemy's sea, she roams it with premeditated
deliberateness, escaping molestation, and, except in the first
instance, even detection.   She carries the fortunes of a Cæsar
yet unknown, who is ready to stake them at any moment for
adequate cause; but everything works together, not merely
for his preservation, but to bring him up just in time for the
exceptional action, which showed there was more to him than
even his untiring energy and fearlessness had so far demonstrated.   As when, in later years, burning anxiety pressed
him to hasten after Villeneuve, yet failed so to discompose
him as to cause the neglect of any preparation essential to
due provision for the abandoned Mediterranean ; so now, with
every power at highest tension to rejoin the admiral, eager
not to waste a moment, he mars his diligence by no precipitancy, he grudges no hour necessary to the rounded completion of the present task, — to see, and know, and do, all
that can be seen and done.   He might almost have used
again, literally, the expression before quoted: " I have not
a thought on any subject separated from the immediate object
of my command."

Leaving the " Romulus " in Gibraltar, the " Minerve " sailed
again on the 11th.   The Spanish ships-of-the-line followed

her at once. The east wind blows in wild and irregular puffs upon the anchorages immediately under the lofty Rock, where the frigate lay. Farther up, where the Spaniards were, it crosses the low neck joining the peninsula to the mainland, and is there more equable and more constant. The " Minerve " was consequently at a disadvantage until she got fairly from under its lee, and the chase through the Straits became close enough to draw the idlers of the town and garrison in crowds to the hillsides. It soon became evident that the leading ship-of-the-line was gaining upon the frigate, and the latter cleared for action. Nelson had but a poor opinion of the Spanish navy of his day, and doubtless chose, before surrendering, to take his chance of one of those risks which in war often give strange results. He said to Drinkwater that he thought an engagement probable, but added, "Before the Dons get hold of that bit of bunting I will have a struggle with them, and sooner than give up the frigate, I 'll run her ashore."

About this time the officers' dinner was announced. Drinkwater went below, and was just congratulating Lieutenant Hardy, who had been captured in the " Sabina," upon his exchange, when the cry " Man overboard ! " was heard. The party dispersed hurriedly, in sympathy with the impulse which invariably causes a rush under such circumstances ; and Drinkwater, running to the stern windows, saw a boat already lowering with Hardy in it, to recover the man, who, however, could not be found. The boat therefore, making signal to that effect, soon turned to pull to the ship. The situation was extremely embarrassing, not to say critical ; on the one hand, the natural reluctance to abandon any one or anything to the enemy, on the other, the imminent risk of sacrificing the ship and all concerned by any delay, — for the leading Spaniard, by himself far superior in force, was nearly within gunshot. Temperament and habit decide, in questions where reason has little time and less certainty upon which to act ; by nature and experience Nelson was inclined to take risks. It was evident the boat could not overtake the frigate unless the latter's way was lessened, and each moment that passed made this step more perilous, as the pursuer was already overhauling the " Minerve." " By God, I 'll not lose Hardy ! " he exclaimed : " back the mizzen-topsail." The ship's speed being thus checked, the boat came alongside, and the party scrambled on board. Singularly enough, the enemy, disconcerted by Nelson's action, stopped also, to allow his consort to come up, — a measure wholly inexcusable, and only to be accounted for by that singular moral effect produced in many men by a sudden and unexpected occurrence. The daring deed had therefore the happiest results of a stratagem, and the frigate was troubled no further.

Steering that night to the southward, to throw off her pursuers, the " Minerve " found herself unexpectedly in the midst of a fleet, which, from the signals made, was evidently not that of Jervis, and therefore must be hostile. The hazy atmosphere veiled the British frigate from close observation, and, by conforming her movements to those of the strangers, she escaped suspicion. Nelson was uncertain whether it was the Spanish grand fleet, or, possibly, a detached body proceeding to the West Indies. He had heard a rumor of such an expedition, and the impression was probably confirmed by these ships being met when steering southerly from the Straits ; Cadiz, the known destination of the grand fleet, being north. As the British commercial interests in the Caribbean were of the first importance, and would be much endangered, he told Drinkwater, who lay awake in his cot, that, if he became convinced the ships in sight were bound there, he should give up the attempt to join the commander-in-chief, and should start at once for the Islands, to forewarn them of the approaching danger. The colonel was naturally startled at the prospect of an involuntary trip across the Atlantic, and represented the equally urgent necessity — as he thought — of Jervis and the British Cabinet getting the information, which Elliot was bringing, of the views and intentions of the Italian governments. This Nelson admitted, but replied that he thought the other consideration greater, and that — the condition arising — he must do as he had said. The incident illustrates the activity of his mind, in comprehending instantly the singular opportunity thrust unexpectedly upon him, as well as the readiness to accept responsibility and to follow his own judgment, which he showed on so many other occasions, both before and after this.

Later in the night the hostile ships went about, evidencing

thereby a desire to keep to windward, which pointed much more toward Cadiz than to any western destination. The "Minerve" imitated them, but altered her course so as to edge away gradually from her dangerous neighbors. Nelson, some time after, again entered the cabin, and told Drinkwater and Elliot, the latter having also waked, that he had got clear of the enemy, but that at daylight the course would be altered so as to sight them once more, if they were really going west. Should it prove to be so, they must make up their minds to visit the West Indies. Nothing, however, being seen during the 12th, the commodore, satisfied at last that he had been in the midst of the grand fleet, hastened on, and towards noon of the 13th joined the admiral. Before doing so, some of the Spaniards were again sighted. They had been seen also by the regular British lookouts, one at least of which had kept touch with them through the preceding days of hazy weather. Nelson, after an interview with Jervis, went on board the "Captain," where his broad pendant was again hoisted at 6 P. M.

At daybreak, the position of the two fleets was twenty-five miles west of Cape St. Vincent, a headland on the Portuguese coast, a hundred and fifty miles northwest of Cadiz. During the night the wind had shifted from the eastward to west by south, and, being now fair, the Spaniards were running for their port, heading about east-southeast; but they were in disorder, and were divided into two principal fragments, of which the headmost, and therefore leewardmost, numbered six ships. It was separated from the other division of twenty-one by a space of six or eight miles. In the whole force, of twenty-seven ships, there were seven of three decks, the least of which carried one hundred and twelve guns; the remainder were principally seventy-fours, there being, however, one of eighty-four guns. Jervis's fleet consisted of fifteen ships-of-the-line, — two of one hundred guns, four of ninety-eight or ninety, eight seventy-fours, and one sixty-four. From the intelligence received the previous day of the enemy's proximity, the admiral kept the command throughout the night in two columns, in close order, a formation suited by its compactness to a hazy night, and at the same time manageable in case of encountering an enemy suddenly. The course was

south by west, almost perpendicular to that of the Spaniards.
The two fleets were thus running, one from the westward, and
the other from the northward, to a common crossing.[1]

At daylight the enemy's fleet was partly visible to the
leading ships of the British columns. As the morning advanced, and the situation developed, it was seen that the
Spanish line was long and straggling, and the gap began to
show. As the British were heading directly towards it,
Jervis ordered a half-dozen of his ships, which were all still
under moderate canvas, to press on and interpose between
the enemy's divisions. An hour or so later he made the
signal to form the single column, which was the usual fighting order of those days. The fleet being already properly
disposed for manœuvres, this change of order was effected,
to use his own words, "with the utmost celerity." Nelson's
ship was thirteenth in the new order, therefore nearly the
last. Next after him came the sixty-four, the "Diadem,"
while Collingwood, in the "Excellent," brought up the rear.
Immediately ahead of Nelson was the "Barfleur," carrying
the flag of one of the junior admirals, to whom naturally fell
the command in that part of the line.

Three of the larger Spanish body succeeded in crossing
ahead of the British column and joining the lee group, thus
raised to nine ships. No others were able to effect this, the
headmost British ships anticipating them in the gap. Jervis's plan was to pass between their two divisions with his
one column, protracting this separation, then to go about in
succession and attack the eighteen to windward, because their
comrades to leeward could not help them in any short time.
This was done. The lee ships did attempt to join those to
windward by breaking through the British order, but were
so roughly handled that they gave it up and continued to
the south-southwest, hoping to gain a better opportunity.
The weather ships, on the other hand, finding they could not
pass, steered to the northward, — nearly parallel, but opposite, to the course which both the British and their own lee
group were then following.

A heavy cannonade now ensued, each British ship engaging as its batteries came to bear, through the advance of the

[1] See Plate, Figure 1.

BATTLE OF CAPE ST. VINCENT

FEBRUARY 14, 1797.

◼▶ BRITISH, 15 SHIPS
◻▶ SPANISH, 27 ,,

WIND ↑ W. BY S.

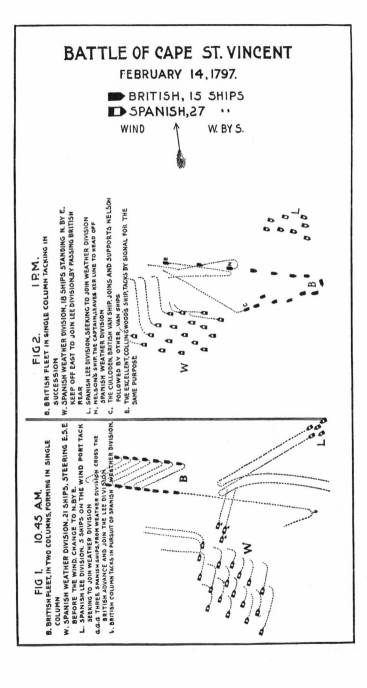

FIG 2. 1 P.M.

B. BRITISH FLEET IN SINGLE COLUMN TACKING IN SUCCESSION
W. SPANISH WEATHER DIVISION, 18 SHIPS STANDING N. BY E. KEEP OFF EAST TO JOIN LEE DIVISION BY PASSING BRITISH REAR
L. SPANISH LEE DIVISION, SEEKING TO JOIN WEATHER DIVISION
N. NELSON'S SHIP, THE CAPTAIN, LEAVES HER LINE TO HEAD OFF SPANISH WEATHER DIVISION
C. THE CULLODEN, BRITISH VAN SHIP, JOINS AND SUPPORTS NELSON FOLLOWED BY OTHER, VAN SHIPS
E. THE EXCELLENT COLLINGWOOD'S SHIP, TACKS BY SIGNAL FOR THE SAME PURPOSE

FIG I. 10.45 A.M.

B. BRITISH FLEET, IN TWO COLUMNS, FORMING IN SINGLE COLUMN
W. SPANISH WEATHER DIVISION, 21 SHIPS, STEERING E.S.E. BEFORE THE WIND, CHANGE TO N.BYE.
L. SPANISH LEE DIVISION, 5 SHIPS ON THE WIND PORT TACK SEEKING TO JOIN WEATHER DIVISION
a.a.a. THREE SPANISH SHIPS, FROM WEATHER DIVISION CROSS THE BRITISH ADVANCE AND JOIN THE LEE DIVISION.
v. BRITISH COLUMN TACKS IN PURSUIT OF SPANISH WEATHER DIVISION.

column to the south-southwest. After an hour of this, the admiral made the signal to tack in succession. This was instantly obeyed by the leader, the "Culloden," which was expecting it, and each following ship tacked also as it reached the same point. But as the Spaniards were continually receding from this point, which the British rear was approaching, it was evident that in time the latter would leave uncovered the ground that had so far separated the two hostile divisions. This the Spanish admiral expected to be his opportunity; it proved to be Nelson's.

At 1 P. M.,[1] by Nelson's journal, the "Captain," standing south by west, had come abreast the rearmost of the eighteen weather ships, having passed the others. He then noticed that the leaders of that body were bearing up before the wind, to the eastward, to cross behind the British column. If this were carried out unmolested, they could join the lee ships, which heretofore had been separated from them by the centre and rear of the British line, and at this moment were not very far distant, being still engaged with the British centre; or else, so Nelson thought, they might fly before the wind, making ineffective all that had been done so far. "To prevent either of their schemes from taking effect, I ordered the ship to be wore, and passing between the Diadem and Excellent, at a quarter past one o'clock, was engaged with the headmost, and of course leewardmost of the Spanish division. The ships which I know were, the Santissima Trinidad, 126; San Josef, 112;[2] Salvador del Mundo, 112;[2] San Nicolas, 80;[2] another first-rate, and seventy-four, names not known. I was immediately joined and most nobly supported by the Culloden, Captain Troubridge. The Spanish fleet,[3] from not wishing (I suppose) to have a decisive battle, hauled to the wind [again] on the larboard tack, which brought the ships afore-mentioned to be the leewardmost and sternmost ships in their fleet."

By this spontaneous and sudden act, for which he had no authority, by signal or otherwise, except his own judgment and quick perceptions, Nelson entirely defeated the Spanish movement. Devoting his own ship to a most unequal con-

---

[1] See Plate, Figure 2. [2] Captured.
[3] That is, the weather division, — the eighteen ships.

test, he gained time for the approaching British van to come up, and carry on the work they had already begun when first passing these ships — before the moment of tacking. The British column being then in a V shape, — part on one tack, part on the other, the point of the V being that of tacking, — he hastened across, by a short cut, from the rear of one arm of the V to a position on the other side, toward which the van was advancing, but which it, being more distant, could not reach as soon as he, and therefore not to as good effect. To quote Jervis's words concerning this incident, "Commodore Nelson, who was in the rear on the starboard tack, *took the lead* on the larboard, and contributed very much to the fortune of the day." On the intellectual side, the side of skill, this is what he did; on the side of valor, it is to be said that he did it for the moment single-handed. The "Culloden," the actual leader, came up shortly, followed afterwards by the "Blenheim;" and the "Excellent" was ordered by Jervis to imitate Nelson's movement, and strengthen the operation which he had initiated. It was the concentration of these ships at the point which Nelson seized, and for a moment held alone, that decided the day; and it was there that the fruits of victory were chiefly reaped.

It must not be understood, of course, that all the honors of the day are to be claimed for Nelson, even conjointly with those present with him at the crucial moment. Much was done, both before and after, which contributed materially to the aggregate results, some of which were missed by the very reluctance of men of solid military qualities to desist from seeking enemies still valid, in order to enjoy what Nelson called the "parade of taking possession of beaten enemies." It seems probable that more Spanish ships might have been secured, had it not been for the eagerness of some British vessels to push on to new combats. But, while fully allowing the merits of many others, from the commander-in-chief down, it is true of St. Vincent, as of most battles, that there was a particular moment on which success or failure hinged, and that upon the action then taken depended the chief outcome, — a decisive moment, in short. That moment was when the enemy attempted, with good prospect, to effect the junction which Nelson foiled. As

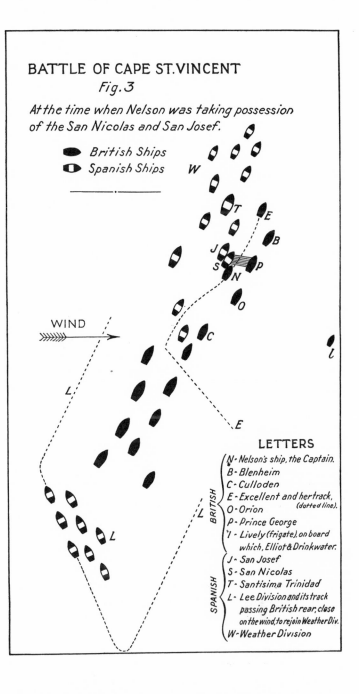

BATTLE OF CAPE ST.VINCENT
Fig.3

At the time when Nelson was taking possession of the San Nicolas and San Josef.

🛢 *British Ships*
🛢 *Spanish Ships*

W

T
E
B
J
S P
N
O
l
WIND
C
L
E
L
L

LETTERS

<table>
<tr><td colspan="2">N - Nelson's ship, the Captain.</td></tr>
<tr><td rowspan="6">BRITISH</td><td>B - Blenheim</td></tr>
<tr><td>C - Culloden</td></tr>
<tr><td>E - Excellent and her track, (dotted line).</td></tr>
<tr><td>O - Orion</td></tr>
<tr><td>P - Prince George</td></tr>
<tr><td>l - Lively (frigate), on board which, Elliot & Drinkwater.</td></tr>
<tr><td rowspan="4">SPANISH</td><td>J - San Josef</td></tr>
<tr><td>S - San Nicolas</td></tr>
<tr><td>T - Santisima Trinidad</td></tr>
<tr><td>L - Lee Division and its track passing British rear, close on the wind, to rejoin Weather Div.</td></tr>
<tr><td colspan="2">W - Weather Division</td></tr>
</table>

Collingwood afterwards summed up the matter: "The highest rewards are due to you and Culloden; you formed the plan of attack, — we were only accessories to the Dons' ruin; for had they got on the other tack, they would have been sooner joined, and the business would have been less complete."

When Collingwood came up with the "Excellent," the "Captain" was practically disabled for further movement, had lost heavily in men, and was without immediate support. The "Culloden" had dropped astern, crippled, as had two of the Spanish vessels; the "Blenheim," after passing the "Culloden" and the "Captain," between them and the enemy, had drawn ahead. The "Excellent," steering between the two Spanish ships that had fallen behind, fired into both of them, and Nelson thought both then struck; but Collingwood did not stop to secure them. "Captain Collingwood," says Nelson in his account, "disdaining the parade of taking possession of beaten enemies, most gallantly pushed up, with every sail set, to save his old friend and messmate, who was to appearance in a critical state. The Excellent ranged up within ten feet of the San Nicolas, giving a most tremendous fire. The San Nicolas luffing up, the San Josef fell on board her, and the Excellent passing on for the Santissima Trinidad, the Captain resumed [1] her situation abreast of them, and close alongside. At this time the Captain having lost her foretopmast, not a sail, shroud,[2] or rope left, her wheel shot away, and incapable of further service in the line, or in chase, I directed Captain Miller to put the helm a-starboard, and calling for the boarders, ordered them to board." [3]

The "Captain" fetched alongside of the "San Nicolas," her bow touching the lee (starboard) quarter of the Spanish vessel, her spritsail yard hooking in the other's mizzen shrouds. Commander Berry, a very young man, who had lately been first lieutenant of the "Captain," leaped actively into the mizzen chains, the first on board the enemy; he was quickly supported by others, who passed over by the spritsail yard. The captain of the ship was in the act of following, at the

[1] That is, was left in.
[2] Shrouds are large ropes which support the masts.
[3] See Plate, Figure 3.

head of his men, when Nelson stopped him. "No, Miller," he said, "*I* must have that honour;" and he directed him to remain. One of the soldiers of the Sixty-ninth Regiment, who were serving on board as marines, broke open the upper quarter-gallery window of the "San Nicolas," and through this Nelson entered, with a crowd of followers, to find himself in the cabin of the enemy's ship. The doors being fastened, they were held there a few moments, while Spanish officers from the quarter-deck discharged their pistols at them; but the doors were soon broken down, and the party, after firing a volley, sallied on the spar deck, which the enemy yielded to them, — a Spanish commodore falling by the wheel as he retreated. Berry had by this time reached the poop, where he hauled down the colors, while Nelson passed to the forward part of the ship, meeting on his way several Spanish officers, who, being by this time in the hands of British seamen, gave up to him their swords. The Spanish guns on the lower decks still continued firing for some moments, apparently at the "Prince George," which had passed to leeward of the "Captain," and now kept her batteries playing upon the hull of the "San Nicolas" forward of the part where the "Captain" touched her.

At this moment a small-arm fire was opened from the stern galleries of the "San Josef" upon the British party in the "San Nicolas." Nelson caused the soldiers to reply to it, and ordered reinforcements sent to him from the "Captain." Parties were stationed at the hatchways of the "San Nicolas" to control the enemy and keep them below decks, and then the boarders charged again for the Spanish three-decker. Nelson was helped by Berry into her main chains; but he had got no farther before a Spanish officer put his head over the rail and said they surrendered. "From this most welcome information," continues Nelson, in his narrative, "it was not long before I was on the quarter-deck, when the Spanish captain, with a bow, presented me his sword, and said the admiral was dying of his wounds below. I asked him, on his honour, if the ship were surrendered? he declared she was; on which I gave him my hand, and desired him to call to his officers and ship's company, and tell them of it — which he did; and on the quarter-deck of a Spanish First-rate, extravagant as the story may seem, did I receive the swords of vanquished Spaniards ; which, as I received, I gave to William Fearney, one of my bargemen, who put them with the greatest sangfroid under his arm. I was surrounded by Captain Berry, Lieutenant Pierson, 69th Regiment, John Sykes, John Thomson, Francis Cook, all old Agamemnons, and several other brave men, seamen and soldiers : thus fell these ships." The firing from the lower deck of the " San Nicolas " was by this time stopped, and the " Prince George " was hailed that both the enemy's vessels were in possession of the British. The " Victory," Jervis's flagship, passed a few moments later and cheered, as did every ship in the fleet.

The dramatic and picturesque surroundings which colored the seizure of these two Spanish ships have doubtless given an exaggerated idea of the danger and difficulty attending the exploit. The impression made upon a sympathetic and enthusiastic eye-witness, Sir Gilbert Elliot, who saw the affair from the decks of the frigate " Lively," has been transmitted to posterity with little diminution. " Nothing in the world was ever more noble than the transaction of the Captain from beginning to end, and the glorious group of your ship and her two prizes, fast in your gripe, was never surpassed, and I dare say never will." Yet it may better be looked upon as another of those " fortunate " occurrences which attend — and in Nelson's career repeatedly attended — the happy meeting of opportunity and readiness. Doubtless they were beaten ships, but other beaten ships have escaped in general actions — did at St. Vincent. " I pretend not to say," wrote Nelson a week later, " that these ships might not have fell, had I not boarded them ; but truly it was far from impossible but they might have forged into the Spanish fleet as the other two ships did." He was there, he could do nothing else, he saw with his rapid glance that he might do this, and he did it. And, after all, it was a big thing, — this boarding a first-rate ship over the decks of another hostile ship, not inaptly characterized in the fleet as " Nelson's patent bridge." We must mark, too, or we shall miss significant indications of character, that the same qualities which led him to the quarter-deck of the " San Josef " had led him but an hour before from the rear of the fleet to the van to save the fight, — the same quickness to see opportunity, the same promptness to seize it, the same audacity to control it. The brilliant crowning of the day may be but an ornament, but it sits well and fitly upon the knightly deed that rolled back the tide of battle in the hour of need.

Those Spanish ships of the weather division which were first encountered by Nelson, after he wore out of the line, bore the brunt of the fighting. As the whole division continued to stand on close to the wind, these ships, becoming crippled, dropped astern of their consorts, and so first received the broadsides of the British van as that arrived. Being also the leaders in the movement frustrated by Nelson, they became the most leewardly; and, as the British van on coming up passed to leeward, this contributed further to concentrate fire upon the same vessels. Among them was the "Santísima Trinidad," of four decks and one hundred and thirty guns, then the largest ship of war in the world. When Collingwood passed ahead of Nelson, he engaged her, but not as near as he wished, and could have done, had not the "Excellent's" rigging been so cut as to prevent her hauling close to the wind. She was also brought to action by Sir James Saumarez, in the "Orion," and towards the close of her contest with the latter ship showed a British Union Jack, — a token of submission possibly unauthorized, as it was almost immediately hauled in again. Besides those boarded by Nelson, two other enemy's ships had already struck.

It was now after four o'clock, and the other Spanish division, of eight ships, was heading for the scene and near at hand. Although effectually blocked in their first attempt to pierce the British line, these had not received such injury as to detract seriously from their efficiency. Continuing to stand south-southwest, after the British began tacking, they at last gained ground sufficiently to come up to windward, the side on which their other division was. In view of the now inevitable junction of a great number of comparatively fresh ships, and of the casualties in his own vessels, Jervis decided to discontinue the action. He ordered his fleet to form on the starboard tack, covering the four prizes and the "Captain;" and with this done the firing soon ceased. The Spanish divisions united, and carried off their other disabled ships.

Nelson's account of the proceedings of the " Captain " on the 14th of February, having been published not long afterwards, apparently by his authority, was challenged as incorrect by Vice-Admiral William Parker, commanding the van, whose flag was on board the third British ship, the "Prince George." Parker claimed that the latter, with the "Blenheim" and " Orion," had been much closer to the " Captain " and " Culloden " than was implied in Nelson's narrative by the words, " For near an hour, I believe, (but do not pretend to be correct as to time,) did the Culloden and Captain support this apparently, but not really, unequal contest; when the Blenheim, passing between us and the enemy, gave us a respite." Parker labored under the misfortune of a singularly involved and obscure style, while in two separate papers he contradicted himself more than once on points of detail; but the tone of his letter to Nelson was temperate and dignified, and he asserted that, "so different to your statement, very soon after you commenced your fire, you had four ships pressing on [Culloden, Blenheim, Prince George, and Orion], almost on board of each other, close in your rear; but " — and the admission following must be noted as well as the charge — " the ships thus pressing upon each other, and the *two latter not far enough ahead to fire with proper effect*,[1] besides having none of the enemy's ships left in the rear for our succeeding ships, at forty-three[2] minutes past one I made the signal to fill and stand on." Parker had also stated, in his log of the action, that the brunt fell upon the " Captain," the " Culloden," and the " Blenheim," but more particularly the two former, " from their being more in the van."

It appears to the writer probable that Nelson overestimated the period that he and Troubridge remained unsupported; time would seem long to the bravest man, when opposed to such heavy odds. Parker seems to have reckoned it to be about fifteen minutes, and he admits that it was impossible for him to open fire with proper effect for some time, although close on the heels of the " Captain " and the " Culloden," because he could not get abreast of the enemy. All the ships —

[1] The italics are the author's.

[2] In his letter to Nelson this is thirteen, but evidently a slip. His log of the action says forty-three.

Spanish and British — were moving ahead, probably at not very different rates of speed. The "Prince George" certainly became in the end actively and closely engaged, much of the time with the "San Josef," a ship of force superior to her own.

Nelson's account is a simple, if somewhat exultant, narrative of the facts as they passed under his observation; and, except in the statement to which Parker objected, they do not even inferentially carry an imputation upon any one else. There was a reflection, though scarcely intended, upon the van ships, which should have been, and Parker says were, close behind the "Culloden;" but the attack was upon the extreme rear of the enemy, and Nelson probably forgot that readers might not understand, as he did, that the ships behind him must need some time to get up, and that his own position, abreast the enemy's rear, was in itself an obstacle to their reaching a place whence their batteries could bear, with the limited train of broadside guns in those days.

Another and interesting illustration of the injustice a man may thus unintentionally do, through inadvertence, is afforded by Nelson's accounts of St. Vincent. There were two drawn up on board the "Captain," — one by himself in his own hand; the second simply signed by him, Miller, and Berry. It is quite evident that the latter is based upon the former, much of the phraseology being identical; but the whole is toned down in many points. The instance of unintentional injustice is this. In his autograph account, Nelson, thinking only of himself,[1] speaks of his going with the boarders, and makes no mention of the captain of the ship, Miller, whose proper business it would be rather than his. In the revision, Miller would naturally feel that his failure to board should be accounted for, and it contains accordingly the statement, "Captain Miller was in the very act of going also, but I directed him to remain." Berry's hand also appears; for whereas Nelson's own account of boarding the "San Josef" simply says, "I got into her main-chains," the published

[1] Both papers are headed: " A few remarks relative to myself in the Captain," etc. It is unfortunate that Nicolas, in giving these two papers, puts first the one which, from internal indications, is (in the author's judgment) the later in date.

copy reads, "Captain Berry assisting me into the main-chains."

So too with reference to Parker's controversy. In the first draft there occurs the unqualified statement: "For an hour the Culloden and Captain supported this apparently unequal contest." The revision reads: "For near an hour, I believe, (*but do not pretend to be correct as to time,*)[1] did Culloden and Captain," etc. Parker quotes from the revision, which was therefore the one published, but does not quote the words italicized. Probably, if the "Blenheim" and the "St. George" had had a hand in this revision, there would have been more modification; but Nelson did not realize where he was hurting them, any more than he did in Miller's case.

The love of glory, the ardent desire for honorable distinction by honorable deeds, is among the most potent and elevating of military motives, which in no breast has burned with a purer flame than in that of Nelson; but it is better that officers leave the public telling of their own exploits to others, and it is evident that Nelson, when taken to task, realized uncomfortably that he had not exercised due thoughtfulness. Parker refrained from addressing him till he had received the printed account. This was not till July, and his remonstrance reached Nelson shortly after the loss of his arm at Teneriffe, when on his way home for what proved to be a tedious and painful recovery. He was then suffering, not only from pain and weakness, but also from discouragement about his professional future, which he thought threatened by disability, and for these conditions allowance must be made; but for all this his reply did not compare favorably with Parker's letter, which had been explicit in its complaint as well as moderate in expression. He wrote curtly: "I must acknowledge the receipt of your letter of the 25th of July; and, after declaring that I know nothing of the Prince George till she was hailed from the forecastle of the San Nicolas,[2] it is impossible I can enter into the subject of your letter."

This course was the more ungenerous, because no explanation, or even admission of involuntary wrong done, could have detracted in the least from the abounding credit due and ac-

[1] Author's italics.
[2] Hailed to stop firing, because the "San Nicolas" had surrendered.

corded to Nelson for his conduct at St. Vincent, which indeed
did not depend upon the length of time he remained unsupported, but upon the rapidity and fearlessness with which he
had acted aright at a very critical juncture. This had been
done so openly, under the eyes of all men, that it could by no
means be hid. Collingwood had borne witness to it, in words
which have been quoted. Drinkwater and Elliot had watched
the whole from the deck of their frigate. The latter had
written to him: "To have had any share in yesterday's glory
is honour enough for one man's life, but to have been foremost on such a day could fall to your share alone." The
commander-in-chief had come out to greet him upon the
quarter-deck of the flagship, — a compliment naval officers
can appreciate, — had there embraced him, saying he could
not sufficiently thank him, and "used every kind expression
which could not fail to make me happy." Jervis had also
insisted upon his keeping the sword of the Spanish rear-
admiral who fell on board the "San Josef."

Before dropping this subject, which has the unpleasantness
that attends all contentions between individuals about their
personal deserts, it is right to say that Nelson had held from
the first that Collingwood, Troubridge, and himself were
the only ones "who made great exertions on that glorious
day: the others did their duty, and some not exactly to my
satisfaction." "Sir John Jervis," he continued, "is not
quite contented, but says nothing publicly." He then quotes
an anecdote which, if he had it from Jervis, confirms his own
opinion about the support given. "Calder [the Chief of
Staff] said, 'Sir, the Captain and Culloden are separated from
the fleet, and unsupported: shall we recall them?' 'I will
not have them recalled. I put my faith in those ships: it is a
disgrace that they are not supported and [are] separated.'"

In his public letter Jervis refrained alike from praise and
from blame. He mentions but one name, that of Calder, as
bearer of despatches, and only incidentally says that he has
been useful to him at all times. In a private letter to the
First Lord he was more explicit, yet scarcely adequately so.
Whatever momentary expression of impatience escaped him,
when anxious about the "Culloden" and "Captain," he knew
that his own flagship could not get to them in time for effi-

cient support, and he gives as the reason for reticence in his public letter that all had behaved well, and that he was "confident that had those who were least in action been in the situation of the fortunate few, their conduct would not have been less meritorious." He then mentions by name Troubridge, — who led the fleet, — Nelson, and Collingwood, and five ships (without the names of the captains, "Blenheim," "Prince George," "Orion," "Irresistible," and "Colossus," which "gallantly supported" Troubridge, though just where or when is not specified. "The ships' returns of killed and wounded," he says explicitly, "although not always the criterion of their being more or less in action, is, in this instance, correctly so." This would include the "Blenheim," whose casualties were in excess of any except the "Captain," and Parker's ship, the "Prince George," which lost not many less than Collingwood. The "Captain's" loss in killed, twenty-four, was double that of any other ship, and in killed and wounded nearly one-third that of the whole fleet.

An interesting anecdote of Jervis shows the importance conceded by him to Nelson's action. It rests on good authority, and is eminently characteristic of one who valued beyond most traits in an officer the power to assume responsibility. "The test of a man's courage," he used to say, "is responsibility." In the evening, while talking over the events of the day, Calder spoke of Nelson's wearing out of the line as an unauthorized departure from the method of attack prescribed by the admiral. "It certainly was so," replied Jervis, "and if ever you commit such a breach of your orders, I will forgive you also." Success covers many faults, yet it is difficult to believe that had Nelson been overwhelmed, the soundness of his judgment and his resolution would not equally have had the applause of a man, who had just fought twenty-seven ships with fifteen, because "a victory was essential to England at that moment." The justification of departure from orders lies not in success, but in the conditions of the case; and Jervis was not one to overlook these, nor hereafter to forget that only one man in his fleet had both seen the thing to do and dared the responsibility of doing it.

A victory so signal entailed, as a matter of course, a number of those rewards and titles with which Great Britain judiciously

16

fostered the spirit of emulation in her Navy. These were to a considerable extent affairs of routine and precedent, and Nelson, knowing that junior flag-officers had on several previous occasions been made baronets, wished to avoid this hereditary dignity because inconsistent with his means. His love of distinction also prompted him to desire one of those Orders which carry with them the outward token of merit. Meeting Drinkwater the day after the battle, he expressed his reluctance to the baronetage, and upon the other's asking him whether he would prefer to be a Knight of the Bath, he replied, "Yes; if my services have been of any value, let them be noticed in a way that the public may know them." To Elliot, who was about to return at once to England, he wrote, asking him to make known his wishes to the Admiralty. "If you can be instrumental in keeping back what I expect will happen, it will be an additional obligation. I conceive to take hereditary honours without a fortune to support the dignity, is to lower that honour it would be my pride to support in proper splendour. There are other honours which die with the possessor, and I should be proud to accept, if my efforts are thought worthy of the favour of my King."

Elliot started for England a few days afterwards, and reached London at a time when the whole country was ringing with the news of the victory. Arriving at such a propitious moment, there could have been for Nelson no better advocate than this man, placed high in political councils, and having to give to the Ministry a long account of his career in the Mediterranean, throughout the whole of which the two had been in intimate contact and constant correspondence. Himself an eye-witness, and filled with enthusiasm for Nelson's latest exploit, Elliot knew better than any one that it was no sporadic outburst, but only a signal manifestation of the intuitive sagacity, the flashing promptness, and the sustained energy, whose steady fires he had known to burn, without slackening of force or change of motive, through two years of close personal association in public action to a common end. The government thus learned more of him than can easily transpire under ordinary service conditions, or be shown even by an incident like that at St. Vincent; and Elliot's admiration, free from all bias of professional partiality or professional jealousy, doubtless was more useful to Nelson than any narrative of his own could have been. Even the royal favor was conciliated, despite the obstinate temper which yielded prejudices with difficulty. "I must rejoice," wrote Nelson to the Duke of Clarence, who had mentioned to him the King's approval, "in having gained the good opinion of my Sovereign, which I once was given to understand I had no likelihood of enjoying."[1] It was to the honor of the monarch that he was thus as pliant to admit merit in an officer as yet only rising to distinction, as he was firm at a later day to stamp with the marks of his displeasure the flagrant moral aberration of the then world-renowned admiral.

The coveted Knighthood of the Bath was accorded on the 17th of March, "in order," wrote the First Lord, "to mark the Royal approbation of your successful and gallant exertions on several occasions during the course of the present war in the Mediterranean, and more particularly of your very distinguished conduct in the glorious and brilliant victory obtained over the fleet of Spain by His Majesty's fleet, on the 14th of February last." Nelson's delight was great and characteristic. Material rewards were not in his eyes the most real or the richest. "Chains and Medals," he wrote to his brother, "are what no fortune or connexion in England can obtain; and I shall feel prouder of those than all the titles in the King's power to bestow." To his wife he said: "Though we can afford no more than a cottage — yet, with a contented mind, my chains, medals, and ribbons are all sufficient." To receive honor was second to no possession, except that of knowing he had deserved it.

On the evening of the Battle of St. Vincent, soon after the firing ceased, Nelson shifted his commodore's pendant to the " Irresistible," of seventy-four guns, the " Captain " being unmanageable from the damage done to her spars and rigging. Her hull also had been so battered, that he wrote a few days later she would never be able to receive him again, which proved to be true; for although, after she had been patched up, he returned to her temporarily, a newly fitted ship, the " Theseus," seventy-four, was assigned to his flag, as soon as a reinforcement arrived from England.

[1] See *ante,* page 89.

After a vain effort to reach the Tagus against contrary winds, with disabled ships, Jervis decided to take his fleet into Lagos Bay, an open roadstead on the southern coast of Portugal, and there to refit sufficiently to make the passage to Lisbon. While lying at Lagos Nelson became a Rear-Admiral of the Blue, by a flag-promotion dated on the 20th of February, although his flag was not hoisted until the first of April, when the official notification of his advancement was received by him. He was then thirty-eight and a half years of age. In this rank he remained until after the Battle of the Nile was fought, but it mattered comparatively little where he stood on the list of flag-officers, while Jervis commanded; that he was an admiral at all made it possible to commit to him undertakings for which he was pre-eminently qualified, but which could scarcely have been intrusted to a simple captain by any stretching of service methods, always — and not improperly — conservative.

On the 23d of February the fleet sailed again, and on the 28th anchored in the Tagus. The same day Nelson wrote to his wife that he was to go to sea on the 2d of March, with three ships-of-the-line, to look out for the Viceroy of Mexico, who was reported to be on his way to Cadiz, also with three ships-of-the-line, laden with treasure. "Two are first-rates," said he, " but the larger the ships the better the mark, and who will not fight for dollars ? " Foul winds prevented his getting away until the 5th. From that date until the 12th of April he remained cruising between Cape St. Vincent and the coast of Africa, covering the approaches to Cadiz; frigates and smaller vessels being spread out to the westward, to gain timely notice of the approach of the specie ships, upon whose safe arrival Spain depended both for her commercial affairs and her naval preparations.

But while thus actively employed, and not insensible to the charm of dollars, the immediate business on board was not in itself so engrossing, nor to him so attractive, as to obtain that exclusiveness of attention which he prided himself upon giving to matters more military in character, and more critical in importance. "The Spaniards threaten us they will come out, and take their revenge," he writes to an occasional correspondent. "The sooner the better; but I will not believe it till I see it; and if they do, what will the mines of Mexico and Peru signify, compared with the honour I doubt not we shall gain by fighting an angry Don ? They will have thirty sail of the line, we twenty or twenty-two ; but fear we shall have a peace before they are ready to come out. What a sad thing that will be ! " His mind reverts to the troops in Elba, which had been left in a most exposed position, and were now about to withdraw under the protection of some frigates, passing through a thousand miles of hostile sea open to the line-of-battle ships at Toulon. He is more concerned about them than about his possible prize-money in the rich ships from Vera Cruz and Havana, whose danger from his own squadron was agitating all Spain. " Respecting myself," he writes to Jervis, "I wish to stay at sea, and I beg, if line-of-battle ships are left out,[1] either on this side the Gut, or to the eastward of Gibraltar, that I may be the man. This brings forward a subject which I own is uppermost in my mind, — that of the safety of our troops, should they embark from Elba. The French have a number of ships at Toulon. They may get two, three, or four ready, with a number of frigates, and make a push for our convoy. I am ready, you know, to go eastward to cover them, even to Porto Ferrajo, or off Toulon, or Minorca, as you may judge proper."

This exposed detachment continued to occupy his thoughts. A month later, on the 11th of April, he again writes : " I own, Sir, my feelings are alive for the safety of our army from Elba. If the French get out two sail of the line, which I am confident they may do, our troops are lost, and what a triumph that would be to them ! I know you have many difficulties to contend with, but I am anxious that nothing should miscarry under your orders. If you think a detachment can be spared, I am ready to go and do my best for their protection." In both letters he apologizes for this freedom of urgency with his superior : " I have said much, but you have spoiled me by allowing me to speak and write freely. I trust you will not imagine that my taking the great liberty of thus mentioning my thoughts, arises from any other motive than affection towards you."

Jervis had already joined him on the 1st of April, before

[1] That is, at sea, the main fleet being still in the Tagus.

the second letter was written. His hesitation about sending the detachment suggested by Nelson had arisen, not from doubt as to the danger of the troops, but from the imminent expectation of the Spanish fleet coming out. The British force was already too inferior, numerically, to risk any diminution, in view of such a contingency. Confronted with divergent objects, Jervis would not be drawn into the snare of dividing his force ; but after reconnoitring the port, he was satisfied that the Spaniards could not sail before Nelson had time to fulfil the proposed mission, and on the 12th of April he gave him the necessary orders. The latter transferred his own squadron to the command of Sir James Saumarez, and started at once. He had now returned to the " Captain," which had doubtless come down with Jervis. " She is little better than a wreck," he wrote to a friend ; but the cripples had to be kept to the front, pending the arrival of fresh ships. Besides her, he had the " Colossus," seventy-four, and " Leander," fifty, with a suitable number of smaller cruisers. Passing within gunshot of Port Mahon in Minorca, he heard from several passing vessels that a French squadron of four ships-of-the-line was at sea, as he had anticipated ; and these, he afterwards learned, were seen off Minorca only twenty-two hours before he passed. Fortunately a fresh northwest gale had carried them to the southward, and on the 21st of April, sixty miles west of Corsica, he joined the convoy, which carried over three thousand soldiers. He reached Gibraltar with it in safety in the early days of May, without adventures of any kind. " I observed a man-of-war brig evidently looking at us ; but my charge was too important to separate one ship in chase of her, especially as three frigates had parted company ; for until this garrison is safe down, I do not think our business is well finished." Its arrival completed the evacuation of the Mediterranean.

At Gibraltar several days were spent, evidently crowded with administrative details concerning the coming and going of convoys, for there is here an almost total cessation of Nelson's usually copious letter-writing. An interesting and instructive incident is, however, made known to us by one of the three letters dated during these ten days. The Consul of the United States of America had to apply to him for the protection of twelve American merchant ships, then at Malaga, against the probable depredations of French privateers lying in that port, which, under the edicts of the government of the French Republic, with whom the United States was at peace, were expected to overhaul and capture them when they sailed. Nelson at once complied, ordering a British frigate to go to Malaga and escort the vessels to the Barbary coast, and even out of the Straits, if necessary. In doing this, he wrote courteously to the Consul: "I am sure of fulfilling the wishes of my Sovereign, and I hope of strengthening the harmony which at present so happily subsists between the two nations."

On the 24th of May Nelson rejoined the admiral off Cadiz, and on the 27th shifted his own flag into the "Theseus." The day before he left the fleet, April 11th, Jervis had decided to institute a strict commercial blockade of Cadiz, with the object of distressing Spanish trade, preventing the entrance of supplies, upon which depended the operations of Spain against Portugal, as well as her naval preparations, and so forcing the Spanish fleet out to fight, in order to rid itself of such embarrassment. Nelson, as commander of the inshore squadron, had then issued the necessary notices to neutrals in the port, and to this charge he now returned. Under Jervis's intelligent partiality, he, the junior flag-officer, was thus intrusted with a command, which in the conduct of details, great and small, and in emergencies, was practically independent. Jervis, knowing his man, was content to have it so, reserving of course to himself the decision of the broad outlines of military exertion. The inshore squadron was gradually increased till it numbered ten sail-of-the-line. The boats of the fleet, which had been rowing guard off the harbor's mouth under the general supervision of the two senior flag-officers, were ordered, shortly after Nelson's arrival, to report to him; and upon him, indeed, devolved pretty nearly all the active enterprises of the fleet. It was his practice to visit the line of boats every night in his barge, to see by personal inspection of these outposts that his instructions were fully observed. "Our inferiority," he wrote about this time, "is greater than before. I am barely out of shot of a Spanish rear-admiral. The Dons hope for peace, but must soon fight us, if the war goes on."

Another motive, perhaps even more imperative than the

wish to force the Dons out, now compelled Jervis to seek by
all means to increase the activity of his fleet, and to intrust
the management of such activities to his most zealous and
capable subordinate. These were the months of the great
mutinies of the British Navy, in which the seamen of the
Channel fleet, and of the North Sea fleet, at the Nore, had
taken the ships out of the hands of their officers. The details
of Jervis's management, which was distinguished as much by
keen judgment and foresight as by iron-handed severity, that
knew neither fear nor ruth when it struck, belong to his
biography, not to Nelson's; but it is necessary to note the
attitude of the latter, a man more sympathetic, and in common
life gentler, than his stern superior. Always solicitous for
everything that increased the well-being and happiness of his
crew, — as indeed was eminently the case with Jervis also, —
he did not withhold his candid sympathy from the grievances
alleged by the Channel fleet; grievances which, when temper-
ately presented to the authorities, had been ignored. "I am
entirely with the seamen in their first complaint. We are a
neglected set, and, when peace comes, are shamefully treated ;
but for the Nore scoundrels," passing on to those who had
rebelled after substantial redress had been given, and had
made unreasonable demands when the nation was in deadly
peril, "I should be happy to command a ship against them."
Jervis's measures received full support from him, clear-headed
as ever to see the essentials of a situation. The senior vice-
admiral, for instance, went so far as to criticise the commander-in-chief for hanging a convicted mutineer on Sunday.
"Had it been Christmas Day instead of Sunday," wrote Nelson, "I would have executed them. We know not what
might have been hatched by a Sunday's grog: *now* your discipline is safe." His glorious reputation and his known
kindly character, supported by that of his captain, made
mutiny impossible under his flag. It had not been up a
month on board the "Theseus," which was lately from the
Channel and infected with the prevalent insubordination,
when a paper was dropped on the quarter-deck, expressing
the devotion of the ship's company to their commander, and
pledging that the name of the "Theseus" should yet be as
renowned as that of the "Captain."

The stringent blockade, and the fears for the specie ships, weighed heavily on the Spaniards, who were not as a nation hearty in support of a war into which they had been coerced by France. Their authorities were petitioned to compel the fleet to go out. Whatever the event, the British would at least have to retire for repairs; while if the Lima and Havana ships — to look for which the Cadiz people every morning flocked to the walls, fearing they might be already in the enemy's hands — should be captured, the merchants of Spain would be ruined. Better lose ten ships-of-the-line, if need be, than this convoy. With rumors of this sort daily reaching him, Nelson's faculties were in a constant state of pleasing tension. He was in his very element of joyous excitement and expectation. "We are in the advance day and night, prepared for battle; bulkheads down, ready to weigh, cut, or slip,[1] as the occasion may require. I have given out a line of battle — myself to lead; and you may rest assured that I will make a vigorous attack upon them, the moment their noses are outside the Diamond. Pray do not send me another ship," he implores ; "if you send any more, they may believe we are prepared, and know of their intention." "If they come out," he writes later to a naval friend, when he had ten sail under him, "there will be no fighting beyond my squadron."

To increase yet further the pressure upon the Spanish fleet to come out, a bombardment was planned against the town and the shipping, the superintendence of which also was intrusted to the commander of the inshore squadron. Only one bomb-vessel was provided, so that very extensive results could scarcely have been anticipated, but Nelson saw, with evident glee, that the enemy's gunboats had taken advanced positions, and intended to have a hand in the night's work. "So much the better," wrote he to Jervis ; "I wish to make it a warm night in Cadiz. If they venture from their walls, I shall give Johnny [2] his full scope for fighting. It will serve to talk of better than mischief." "It is good," he writes to another, " at these times to keep the devil out of their heads.

---

[1] Cut, or let go, the cables, — leaving the anchor in haste, instead of raising it from the bottom.

[2] The British seamen.

I had rather see fifty shot by the enemy, than one hanged by us."

The bombardment, which was continued upon two successive nights, did little direct harm; but it led to a sharp hand-to-hand contest between the British and Spanish boats, in which Nelson personally bore a part, and upon which he seems afterwards to have dwelt with even greater pride and self-satisfaction than upon the magnificent victories with which his name is associated. "It was during this period that perhaps my personal courage was more conspicuous than at any other part of my life." On the first night the Spaniards sent out a great number of mortar gunboats and armed launches. Upon these he directed a vigorous attack to be made, which resulted in their being driven back under the walls of Cadiz; the British, who pursued them, capturing two boats and a launch. In the affray, he says, "I was boarded in my barge with its common crew of ten men, coxswain, Captain Freemantle, and myself, by the commander of the gunboats; the Spanish barge rowed twenty-six oars, besides officers, — thirty men in the whole. This was a service hand-to-hand with swords, in which my coxswain, John Sykes, now no more, twice saved my life. Eighteen of the Spaniards being killed and several wounded, we succeeded in taking their commander." In his report he complimented this Spanish officer, Don Miguel Tyrason, upon his gallantry. Near a hundred Spaniards were made prisoners in this sharp skirmish.

Not even the insult of bombardment was sufficient to attain the designed end of forcing the enemy's fleet out to fight. The Spaniards confined themselves to a passive defence by their shore batteries, which proved indeed sufficient to protect the town and shipping, for on the second night they got the range of the bomb-vessel so accurately that the British were forced to withdraw her; but this did not relieve the vital pressure of the blockade, which could only be removed by the mobile naval force coming out and fighting. So far from doing this, the Spanish ships of war shifted their berth inside to get out of the range of bombs. Nelson cast longing eyes upon the smaller vessels which lay near the harbor's mouth, forming a barricade against boat attack, and threatening the offensive measures to which they rarely resorted.

"At present the brigs lie too close to each other to hope for a dash at them, but soon I expect to find one off her guard, and then — " For the rest, his sanguine resolve to persist in annoyance until it becomes unbearable, and insures the desired object, finds vent in the words: " if Mazaredo will not come out, down comes Cadiz; and not only Cadiz, but their fleet."

This close succession of varied and exciting active service, unbroken between the day of his leaving Lisbon, March 5th, and the date of the last bombardment, July 5th, had its usual effect upon his spirits. His correspondence is all animation, full of vitality and energy, betraying throughout the happiness of an existence absorbed in congenial work, at peace with itself, conscious of power adequate to the highest demands upon it, and rejoicing in the strong admiration and confidence felt and expressed towards him on all sides, especially by those whose esteem he most valued. He complains of his health, indeed, from time to time; he cannot last another winter; he is suffering for the want of a few months' rest, which he must ask for in the coming October, and trusts that, " after four years and nine months' service, without one moment's repose for body or mind, credit will be given me that I do not sham."

Bodily suffering was his constant attendant, to which he always remained subject, but at this time it was powerless to depress the moral energies which, under less stimulating conditions, at times lost something of their elastic force. They never, indeed, failed to rise equal to imminent emergency, however obscured in hours of gloom, or perplexity, or mental conflict; but now, supported by the concurrence of every favoring influence, they carried him along in the full flow of prosperity and exhilaration. Thanking Earl Spencer, the First Lord of the Admiralty, for a complimentary letter, he says: " The unbounded praises Sir John Jervis has ever heaped, and continues to heap on me, are a noble reward for any services which an officer under his command could perform. Nor is your Lordship less profuse in them." To his wife he writes: " I assure you I never was better, and rich in the praises of every man, from the highest to the lowest in the fleet." " The imperious call of honour to serve my country, is the only thing that keeps me a moment from you, and a hope, that by staying a little longer, it may enable you to enjoy those little luxuries which you so highly merit." "My late affair here [1] will not, I believe, lower me in the opinion of the world. I have had flattery enough to make me vain, and success enough to make me confident."

NOTE. In Naval Biography and History, distinguished ships have a personality only less vivid than that of the men who fought them. The fate of the "Captain," Nelson's flagship at St. Vincent, can therefore scarcely fail to interest readers. The author is indebted to Lieutenant Henry Chamberlain, R. N., for calling his attention to the following paragraph in the Naval Chronicle, for 1813, vol. xxix. p. 245 : —

"On the night of Friday, March 22d, the Captain, of 74 guns (Lord Nelson's ship when he took the San Josef), which had recently been converted into a hulk at Plymouth, took fire, and was totally destroyed. The San Josef, which lay alongside, was with difficulty preserved."

[1] The night conflict with the Spanish launches.

CHAPTER IX.

THE UNSUCCESSFUL ATTEMPT AGAINST TENERIFFE. — NELSON LOSES HIS RIGHT ARM. — RETURN TO ENGLAND — REJOINS ST. VINCENT'S FLEET, AND SENT INTO THE MEDITERRANEAN TO WATCH THE TOULON ARMAMENT.

JULY, 1797–APRIL, 1798. AGE, 39.

TOO much success is not wholly desirable; an occasional beating is good for men — and nations. When Nelson wrote the words with which the preceding chapter ends, he was on the eve of a sharp reverse, met in attempting an enterprise that had occupied his thoughts for more than three months. While cruising for the Viceroy of Mexico, before Jervis left Lisbon with the fleet, he had considered the possibility of the enemy's treasure-ships, warned of their danger, taking refuge in the Canary Islands, which belong to Spain. Meditating upon the contingency, he had formed a project of seizing them there, and probably had already suggested the matter to Jervis, taking advantage of the freedom permitted him by the latter in advancing opinions. However that be, immediately before he started to meet the Elba convoy, the commander-in-chief asked for his plan, which he submitted in writing, after talking it over with Troubridge, his intimate friend, upon whose judgment Jervis also greatly relied. Regarded as a purely naval expedition, Nelson pointed out that it was subject to great uncertainties, because, the land being very high, the wind could not be depended on. It might blow in from the sea, but if so it would be by daylight, which would deprive the attack of the benefits of a surprise; while at night the land wind was too fitful and unreliable to assure the ships reaching their anchorage before the enemy could discover them, and have time for adequate preparation against assault.

For these reasons, certainty of success would depend upon co-operation by the army, and for that Nelson suggested that

the Elba troops, over three thousand strong, already in transports and on their way, would provide a force at once available
and sufficient. Save a naval dash by Blake, more than a
century before, Teneriffe had never been seriously attacked.
Probably, therefore, the heights commanding the · town of
Santa Cruz had not been fortified, and could be easily seized
by the detachment designated; besides which, the water supply
was exposed to interruption by an outside enemy. If only
General De Burgh could be persuaded, Nelson· was sure of
success, and offered himself to command the naval contingent.
Failing the consent of De Burgh, whom he and Jervis both
thought deficient in moral courage to undertake responsibility,
could not the admiral get assistance from O'Hara, the governor
of Gibraltar, who would have at his disposal one thousand to
fifteen hundred men ? More would be better, but still with
that number success would be probable. "Soldiers," regretted
Nelson characteristically, "have not the same boldness in undertaking a political measure that we have; we look to the
benefit of our Country and risk our own fame [not life merely]
every day to serve her: a soldier obeys his orders and no
more." But he thought O'Hara an exception, and then —
could not the substantial advantages move him ? The public
treasure of Spain that might be seized would be six or seven
millions sterling. Think what that sum would be, "thrown
into circulation in England!" where specie payments had just
been suspended. It was nearly a year's value of the subsidies
which Great Britain was lavishing on the general war.
Whatever the merits of Nelson's judgment upon the soldiers
of his day, this avowal of readiness, for the nation's sake, to
risk fame — reputation — which was in his eyes the dearest
of possessions, should not be overlooked. It was the best he
had to give; to hazard life was but a vulgar thing compared to
it. His career, both before and after, fully bore out the boast.

While on the return with the Elba troops, in a despatch
sent ahead of the convoy, he jogs Jervis's memory about
O'Hara, having doubtless ascertained that De Burgh, as they
expected, would not deviate from his orders to proceed to
Lisbon. "I hope you will press General O'Hara about
Teneriffe. What a strike it would be!" In a copy of this
letter forwarded to the Admiralty, presumably by Jervis for

its general information, these words were omitted.   Possibly
he had already sounded O'Hara, and found him unwilling, for
he was not optimistic ; possibly Jervis himself thought that the
fitting conditions had not yet obtained, and did not care to let
the idea get abroad before the hour for execution arrived.   For
the time, the commander-in-chief preferred to keep his fleet
concentrated before Cadiz, and to try to worry the enemy out
to battle ; for which object, indisputably the most advantageous to be pursued, he also naturally wished to use his

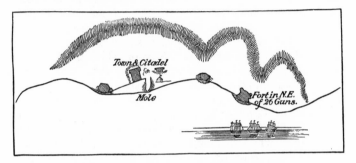

SKETCH OF SANTA CRUZ AND SURROUNDINGS.
(*From Nelson's Journal.*)

most active and efficient subordinate.   Both blockade and
bombardment having failed to provoke the enemy to action,
and intelligence having been received that a treasure-ship
from Manila had put into Teneriffe, it was decided in July to
make the attempt, which had only been postponed — never
abandoned.   In words written by Nelson on the 18th of June,
the conditions determining Jervis's course are clearly indicated.
" I wish these fellows would come out, and then, with the good
ships we have left [after a general engagement], we might
be a little at liberty to make dashes.   I hope your design
about Teneriffe will not get wind, by making inquiries at the
present moment.   Whenever I see it," he added characteristically, " ten hours shall decide its fate."   Although unable
to obtain the troops upon which he considered certainty to
depend, he felt little fear for the result.   Two hundred
additional marines must be given, and certain specified artillery

and ammunition in excess of what he had. With these, " I have no doubt of doing the job as it ought to be, the moment the ships come in sight." "Under General Troubridge ashore, and myself afloat, I am confident of success."

On the 14th of July he received his orders, which were to seize Santa Cruz, the chief town, and hold the island to ransom, unless all public treasure were surrendered to his squadron, in which case the contribution on the inhabitants should not be levied. " God bless and prosper you," wrote Jervis, who, although he considered the enterprise promising, was less sanguine than his junior. " I am sure you will deserve success. To mortals is not given the power of commanding it." On the 15th Nelson sailed, having under his command three seventy-fours, a fifty-gun ship, three frigates, and a cutter. Towards sundown of the 20th the Peak of Teneriffe was sighted, distant fifty or sixty miles. The following morning the landing-party, a thousand strong, under the command of Captain Troubridge, was transferred to the frigates. The intention was to keep the line-of-battle-ships out of sight, while the frigates, whose apparent force would carry no impression of menace, approached near enough to make a dash during the night. It was hoped that thus the assault might be so far a surprise as to enable the British to storm from the rear a fort on the heights, to the northeast of the town, and commanding it. Santa Cruz was then to be summoned. In the meantime the ships-of-the-line would be coming in from the sea, and upon arrival would support the shore movement by bringing their broadsides to bear upon the walls.

By midnight the frigates were within three miles of the landing-place; but there strong wind and contrary current delayed them, and before they could get within a mile the day dawned. Thus discovered, the hope of surprise was lost. At 6 A. M., when the squadron approached, Troubridge went on board the "Theseus" and told Nelson that he thought, if the heights over the fort, in its rear, could be seized, he could yet compel it to surrender. The landing-party was therefore put on shore at nine, but could not dispossess the enemy, who had recognized the importance of the position indicated by Troubridge, and had occupied it in force. The ships-of-the-line endeavored to get within range of the fort, to batter it, but could not come nearer than three miles. They were unable even to reach anchoring-ground, and, as it was blowing very fresh, they struck their topgallantmasts and stood off and on. At night Troubridge re-embarked his men on board the frigates, which had remained where they were. The following morning, July 23d, Nelson abandoned the attempt upon the fort, recalling the frigates ; and, as the wind did not yet serve to approach the shore, he continued under sail during that day and the next. The members of the landing-party rejoined their proper ships.

Troubridge's failure to act at once upon his own judgment, and seize the heights above the fort, instead of waiting until he could communicate with the admiral, whereby were lost more than three invaluable hours, excites surprise, in view of the extremely high value set upon him as an officer by St. Vincent and Nelson; and is the more singular because the latter, in certain " Recommendations," dated July 17, had indicated the heights, as well as the fort, among the objects to be secured. It is, of course, possible that these Recommendations were not given out; but even so, the formal orders issued gave ample discretion. This hesitation was wholly contrary to Nelson's own readiness to assume responsibility, and probably accounts for his subsequent remark, in a private letter, that had he himself been present this first attempt would not have failed. Occurring in an officer of Troubridge's high standing, and contrasted with Nelson's action at St. Vincent, as well as on many other occasions, the incident serves to bring out forcibly the characteristic eminence of the latter, — the distinction between a really great captain and the best type of a simply accomplished and gallant officer. It may safely be said that had Nelson been in the frigates that morning, and thought as Troubridge thought, he would either have had the heights without waiting for orders, or, to use his own words on a former occasion, would have " been in a confounded scrape."

His first plan having miscarried, Nelson was nevertheless unwilling to forsake the enterprise wholly, without attempting a direct assault upon the town itself. Meantime the enemy was not idle, but employed the delay caused by the wind to

17

collect a greater force, and to develop further the preparations to repel attack.   At half-past five in the evening of July 24 the squadron reached an anchorage two or three miles north of Santa Cruz, and all boats were ordered prepared for a night expedition.   Captain Fremantle, of the frigate " Seahorse," had with him his wife, whom he had lately married; and with them Nelson, who intended to lead the attack in person, supped that evening.   He was conscious of the imminent danger to which he was about to expose himself and his followers; it is indeed scarcely possible that he could, in undertaking the adventure, have expected to succeed, except through some happy accident skilfully improved, — the deserved good fortune which had so often attended him.   It was not so much the hope of victory that moved him, as the feeling that to retreat baffled, without a further effort, would be worse than defeat.   This in fact was the reason which he afterwards gave. " Although I felt the second attack a forlorn hope, yet the honour of our Country called for the attack, and that I should command it.   I never expected to return."   " Your partiality will give me credit," he wrote to Jervis, "that all has hitherto been done which was possible, but without effect: this night I, humble as I am, command the whole, destined to land under the batteries of the town, and to-morrow my head will probably be crowned with either laurel or cypress.   I have only to recommend Josiah Nisbet [his stepson] to you and my Country."   He urged Nisbet not to go in the boats, on the ground that his mother should not run the risk of losing both husband and son in one night, and that in the absence of Captain Miller, who was going in charge of a division of men, Nisbet's duties with the ship demanded his remaining.   Nisbet steadily refused, and his presence was the immediate means of saving the admiral's life.

At eleven P. M. the boats shoved off, carrying a thousand men.   The orders were for all to land at the mole, the intention being to storm it, and the batteries covering it, in a body, and to fight their way, thus massed, to the great square, which was designated as the place for rallying.   A considerable sea was running and the night dark, so that the Spaniards did not discover the assailants till they were within half gunshot. The bells of the place then began to ring, and a heavy fire opened, amid which the British pushed vigorously forward. Many, however, missed the mole. Nelson's own boat reached it with four or five besides, and the parties from these succeeded in carrying the mole itself, advancing to its head and spiking the guns; but there they were met with such a sustained fire of musketry and grape from the citadel and the neighboring houses, that they could get no farther. Many were killed and wounded, and the rest after a struggle had to retreat.

Troubridge, with a number of others who missed the mole, landed amid a heavy surf, which stove the boats on a rocky beach and tumbled the men into the water, whereby most of the ammunition was spoiled. In the midst of the turmoil the cutter "Fox" was struck by a shot under water, and went down, taking with her her commander and ninety-seven men. Although the scaling-ladders had all been lost in the general upset, those who here got on shore succeeded in climbing over the walls, and forced their way to the place of rendezvous in the great square. There Troubridge, having assembled between three and four hundred men, held his ground, awaiting Nelson and the party that might have entered by way of the mole.

It was in vain. Nelson had been struck by a grapeshot in the right elbow, as, with sword drawn, he was stepping from the boat to the landing. Bleeding profusely and faint, but clinging with his left hand to the sword, which had belonged to his uncle Maurice Suckling, he fell back into the arms of Josiah Nisbet, who managed with considerable presence of mind to bind up the shattered limb and stop the flowing of the blood. A few men being got together, the boat pushed off to take the admiral back to the ship. At this moment occurred the sinking of the "Fox;" upon which much delay ensued, because Nelson refused to abandon the men struggling in the water, and insisted upon looking personally to their being saved. At last the "Seahorse" was reached; but here again he would not go on board, saying that he would not have Mrs. Fremantle alarmed by seeing him in such a condition and without any news of her husband, who had accompanied the landing. When he got to the "Theseus," he declined assistance to climb to the deck. "At two in the morning,"

wrote Hoste, one of her midshipmen, who had been with him
continuously since the " Agamemnon " left England, " Admiral
Nelson returned on board, being dreadfully wounded in the
right arm. I leave you to judge of my situation, when I beheld our boat approach with him, who I may say has been a
second father to me, his right arm dangling by his side, while
with the other he helped himself to jump up the ship's side,
and with a spirit that astonished every one, told the surgeon
to get his instruments ready, for he knew he must lose his
arm, and that the sooner it was off the better."

At daylight Troubridge, who had collected some ammunition
from Spanish prisoners, started from the square to try what
could be done without ladders against the citadel; but, finding every approach blocked by overwhelming force, he had to
retreat. Having neither powder nor provisions, and no boats
with which to return to the ship, he sent a flag of truce to the
governor to say that he was prepared to burn the place down
with means at his disposal, but, being most reluctant to do so,
was willing to treat, upon condition of the whole party being
permitted to return to the ships, free and with their arms.
One scarcely knows which most to admire, Troubridge's cool
audacity in making such a demand, or the chivalrous readiness with which these honorable terms were at once granted
to a man whose gallant bearing compelled the esteem of his
enemies. Don Juan Gutierrez had repulsed the various attempts with such steadiness and watchfulness, had managed
his business so well, that he could afford to be liberal. He
agreed that Troubridge's men should withdraw, carrying off
with them all British equipments, even to such boats as had
been taken by the Spaniards, but could still swim. On the
other hand, it was stipulated that no further attempt upon
the town should be made by Nelson's squadron. Prisoners on
both sides were to be given up. This arrangement having
been concluded, the governor directed that the British wounded
should be at once received into the hospitals, while the rest of
the party, with their colors flying, marched to the mole, and
there embarked.

Troubridge dwelt with evident pride upon his part in this
night's work, — a pride that was shared then by his superiors,
and will be justified in the eyes of military men now. " The

SIR THOMAS TROUBRIDGE.

From the Painting by Sir William Beechey.

Spanish officers assure me they expected us, and were perfectly prepared with all the batteries, and the number of men I have before mentioned [8,000], under arms : with the great disadvantage of a rocky coast, high surf, and in the face of forty pieces of cannon, though we were not successful, will show what an Englishman is equal to." His conduct affords for all time an example of superb courage in the face of extraordinary and unexpected difficulty and danger, and especially of single-minded energy in carrying through one's own share of an enterprise, without misplaced concern about consequences, or worry as to whether the other parties were prospering or not. Had Nelson reached the square he would have found Troubridge there, and that was the one thing about which the latter needed to care. Nelson's own words recur to mind : " I have not a thought on any subject separated from the immediate object of my command," — a maxim eminently suited to the field and to the subordinate, though not necessarily so to the council chamber or to the general officer. Troubridge that night proved himself invaluable as a subordinate, though the conduct of the previous attempt seems to show a lack of that capacity to seize a favorable moment, although in the presence of a superior, of which Nelson himself had given so brilliant an example at Cape St. Vincent.

The squadron remained off Teneriffe for three days after the assault, intercourse with the shore for the purpose of obtaining fresh provisions being permitted by the governor, between whom and the admiral were exchanged complimentary letters and presents of courtesy. On the 27th Nelson sailed for Cadiz, and on the 16th of August rejoined the commander-in-chief, now become Earl St. Vincent. The latter received him with generous sympathy and appreciation, which leave little doubt as to what his verdict would have been, had the gallant initiative taken by his junior at St. Vincent ended in disaster, instead of in brilliant success. Nelson's letters, sent ahead of the squadron by a frigate, had shown the despondency produced by suffering and failure, which had reversed so sharply the good fortune upon which he had begun to pride himself. " I am become a burthen to my friends and useless to my Country. When I leave your command, I become dead to the world ; I go hence and am no more seen." " Mortals cannot command success," replied St. Vincent. "You and your companions have certainly deserved it, by the greatest degree of heroism and perseverance that ever was exhibited." Nelson had asked for his stepson's promotion, implying that he himself would not hereafter be in a position of influence to help the boy — for he was little more. "He is under obligations to me, but he repaid me by bringing me from the mole of Santa Cruz." "He saved my life," he said more than once afterwards. St. Vincent immediately made him a commander into the vacancy caused by the death of Captain Bowen, who had fallen in the assault. "Pretty quick promotion," wrote his messmate Hoste, who probably knew, from close association, that Nisbet had not the promising qualities with which he was then credited by his stepfather, from whom in later years he became wholly estranged.

On the 20th Nelson received formal leave to return to England in the "Seahorse," and on the 3d of September his flag was hauled down at Spithead. On the way home he suffered much. After amputation the ligature had been awkwardly applied to the humeral artery. As he would not allow the surgeon to examine the stump during the passage, this was not then discovered, but the intense spasms of pain kept him irritable and depressed. It is likely, too, that his discouragement was increased by brooding over the failure of his enterprise; believing, as he did, that had he been with the landing-party, the first attempt would have succeeded. He could scarcely fail now to see that, although it was strictly in accordance with service methods for the senior to remain with the ships, the decisive point in the plan, as first formed, was the seizure of the heights, and that there, consequently, was the true place for the one in chief command. Any captain, Troubridge especially, could have placed the ships as well as Nelson. It is self-accusation, and not fault-finding merely, that breathes in the words: "Had I been with the first party, I have reason to believe complete success would have crowned our efforts. *My pride suffered.*"

Whatever his mental distress, however, he always, from the time of receiving the wound, wrote to his wife with careful cheerfulness. "As to my health, it never was better; and now I hope soon to return to you; and my Country, I trust,

LADY NELSON.

*From a photograph by Mr. E. Kelly, of Plymouth, of a minia-
ture in the possession of Mrs. F. H. B. Eccles, of Sherwell House,
Plymouth, a great-granddaughter of Lady Nelson. Believed to
have been painted about the time of the Battle of the Nile.*

will not allow me any longer to linger in want of that pecuniary assistance which I have been fighting the whole war to
preserve to her. But I shall not be surprised to be neglected
and forgot, as probably I shall no longer be considered as
useful. However, I shall feel rich if I continue to enjoy
your affection. I am fortunate in having a good surgeon on
board; in short, I am much more recovered than I could have
expected. I beg neither you or my father will think much
of this mishap: my mind has long been made up to such an
event."

Immediately after quitting the "Seahorse" he joined his
wife and father at Bath. For a time the wound seemed to
be progressing favorably, but the unlucky complication of the
ligature threw him back. "Much pain and some fever," he
wrote to a friend soon after his arrival; and while he kept up
fairly before his wife, who spoke of his spirits as very good,
he confessed to St. Vincent, on the 18th of September, that he
was then not the least better than when he left the fleet. "I
have suffered great misery." This letter was dated in London,
whither he had gone a few days before to be invested with
the Order of the Bath, which was formally done by George
III. in person on the 27th of September. He was graciously
received by the King, who conversed with him after the
ceremony, and by his manner throughout made a lasting impression upon the mind of Nelson, whose loyalty was intense.
The Order of the Bath remained the most highly prized among
his many decorations. At the same time was awarded him a
pension of £1,000 a year.

He remained in London till near Christmas. Sir Gilbert
Elliot, the late Viceroy of Corsica, who about this time became
Lord Minto, saw him not long after his arrival there, as did
also Colonel Drinkwater. Elliot found him looking better and
fresher than he ever remembered him, although the continued
pain prevented sleep, except by use of opium. He was already
impatient to go to sea again, and chafed under the delay of
healing, concerning the duration of which the surgeons could
give him no assurance. The ligature must be left to slough
away, for it was two inches up the wound, and if, in attempting to cut it, the artery should be cut, another amputation
would be necessary higher up, which would not be easy, for

the stump was already very short. There was consequently
nothing for it but endurance. To his suffering at this time
an accomplished surgeon, who sailed with him shortly before
Trafalgar, attributed a neuralgic predisposition under which
he then labored, and which produced serious effects upon his
general health.

A singular exhibition of his characteristic animation and
temperament was elicited by Drinkwater's visit. The colonel
saw him shortly before the naval battle of Camperdown,
fought on the 11th of October. "One of the first questions
which Nelson put to me was whether I had been at the Admiralty. I told him there was a rumour that the British fleet
had been seen engaged with that of Holland. He started
up in his peculiar energetic manner, notwithstanding Lady
Nelson's attempts to quiet him, and stretching out his unwounded arm, — 'Drinkwater,' said he, 'I would give this
other arm to be with Duncan [1] at this moment;' so unconquerable was the spirit of the man, and so intense his eagerness to
give every instant of his life to the service."

Until the 4th of December his agony continued. On that
day the ligature came away, giving instant and entire relief.
In a letter to a friend, apologizing for delay in replying, he
said: "Truly, till last Monday, I have suffered so much, I
hope for your forgiveness. I am now perfectly recovered,
and on the eve of being employed." On Friday, the 8th, he
wrote to Captain Berry, who had led the boarders to the "San
Nicolas" at Cape St. Vincent, and was designated to command
the ship in which the admiral's flag should next be hoisted,
saying that he was well; and the same day, with that profound recognition of a personal Providence which was with
him as instinctive as his courage, he sent to a London clergyman the following request: "An officer desires to return
thanks to Almighty God for his perfect recovery from a severe
wound, and also for the many mercies bestowed upon him.
(For next Sunday.)"

As the close attention of the skilled surgeons in whose
hands he had been was now no longer needed, he returned to
Bath to await the time when his flagship should be completely

[1] The British admiral in command of the fleet which fought at Camperdown.

equipped. St. Vincent had asked that the "Foudroyant," of eighty guns, should be prepared for him; but, after his sudden recovery, as she was not yet ready, there was substituted for her the "Vanguard," seventy-four, which was commissioned by Berry at Chatham on the 19th of December. In March she had reached Portsmouth, and Nelson then went up to London, where he attended a levee on the 14th of the month and took leave of the King. On the 29th his flag was hoisted, and on the 10th of April, after a week's detention at St. Helen's by head winds, he sailed for Lisbon. There he remained for four days, and on the 30th of the month, off Cadiz, rejoined St. Vincent, by whom he was received with open arms. The veteran seaman, stern and resolved as was his bearing in the face of danger, was unhopeful about the results of the war, which from the first he had not favored, and for whose ending he was eager. Now, at sixty-four, his health was failing, and the difficulties and dangers of the British cause in the Mediterranean weighed upon him, with a discouragement very alien from the sanguine joy with which his ardent junior looked forward to coming battles. His request to be relieved from command, on the score of ill-health, was already on file at the Admiralty. "I do assure your Lordship," he wrote to Earl Spencer, "that the arrival of Admiral Nelson has given me new life; you could not have gratified me more than in sending him; his presence in the Mediterranean is so very essential, that I mean to put the "Orion" and "Alexander" under his command, with the addition of three or four frigates, and send him away, to endeavour to ascertain the real object of the preparations making by the French." These preparations for a maritime expedition were being made at Toulon and the neighboring ports, on a scale which justly aroused the anxiety of the British Cabinet, as no certain information about their object had been obtained.

Nelson's departure from England on this occasion closes the first of the two periods into which his career naturally divides. From his youth until now, wherever situated, the development has been consecutive and homogeneous, external influences and internal characteristics have worked harmoniously together, nature and ambition have responded gladly to

opportunity, and the course upon which they have combined
to urge him has conformed to his inherited and acquired
standards of right and wrong. Doubt, uncertainty, inward
friction, double motives, have been unknown to him; he has
moved freely in accordance with the laws of his being, and,
despite the anxieties of his profession and the frailty of his
health, there is no mistaking the tone of happiness and contentment which sounds without a jarring note throughout his
correspondence. A change was now at hand. As the sails of
the "Vanguard" dip below the horizon of England, a brief
interlude begins, and when the curtain rises again, the scene
is shifted, — surroundings have changed. We see again the
same man, but standing at the opening of a new career, whose
greatness exceeds by far even the high anticipations that had
been formed for him. Before leaving England he is a man of
distinction only; prominent, possibly, among the many distinguished men of his own profession, but the steady upward
course has as yet been gradual, the shining of the light, if it
has latterly shot forth flashes suggestive of hidden fires, is still
characterized by sustained growth in intensity rather than by
rapid increase. No present sign so far foretells the sudden
ascent to fame, the burst of meridian splendor with which the
sun of his renown was soon to rise upon men's eyes, and in
which it ran its course to the cloudless finish of his day.

Not that there is in that course — in its achievements —
any disproportion with the previous promise. The magni-
tude of the development we are about to witness is due, not to
a change in him, but to the increased greatness of the opportunities. A man of like record in the past, but less gifted,
might, it is true, have failed to fill the new sphere which the
future was to present. Nelson proved fully equal to it, because he possessed genius for war, intellectual faculties,
which, though not unsuspected, had not hitherto been allowed
scope for their full exercise. Before him was now about to
open a field of possibilities hitherto unexampled in naval warfare; and for the appreciation of them was needed just those
perceptions, intuitive in origin, yet resting firmly on well-
ordered rational processes, which, on the intellectual side,
distinguished him above all other British seamen. He had
already, in casual comment upon the military conditions sur-

rounding the former Mediterranean campaigns, given indications of these perceptions, which it has been the aim of
previous chapters to elicit from his correspondence, and to
marshal in such order as may illustrate his mental characteristics. But, for success in war, the indispensable complement
of intellectual grasp and insight is a moral power, which
enables a man to trust the inner light, — to have faith, — a
power which dominates hesitation, and sustains action, in the
most tremendous emergencies, and which, from the formidable
character of the difficulties it is called to confront, is in no men
so conspicuously prominent as in those who are entitled to
rank among great captains. The two elements — mental and
moral power — are often found separately, rarely in due combination. In Nelson they met, and their coincidence with the
exceptional opportunities afforded him constituted his good
fortune and his greatness.

The intellectual endowment of genius was Nelson's from
the first; but from the circumstances of his life it was denied
the privilege of early manifestation, such as was permitted to
Napoleon. It is, consequently, not so much this as the constant exhibition of moral power, force of character, which
gives continuity to his professional career, and brings the
successive stages of his advance, in achievement and reputation, from first to last, into the close relation of steady development, subject to no variation save that of healthy and
vigorous growth, till he stood unique — above all competition.
This it was — not, doubtless, to the exclusion of that reputation for having a head, upon which he justly prided himself
— which had already fixed the eyes of his superiors upon him
as the one officer, not yet indeed fully tested, most likely to
cope with the difficulties of any emergency. In the display
of this, in its many self-revelations, — in concentration of purpose, untiring energy, fearlessness of responsibility, judgment
sound and instant, boundless audacity, promptness, intrepidity,
and endurance beyond all proof, — the restricted field of Corsica and the Riviera, the subordinate position at Cape St.
Vincent, the failure of Teneriffe, had in their measure been as
fruitful as the Nile was soon to be, and fell naught behind the
bloody harvests of Copenhagen and Trafalgar. Men have
been disposed, therefore, to reckon this moral energy — call it

courage, dash, resolution, what you will — as Nelson's one
and only great quality. It was the greatest, as it is in all
successful men of action; but to ignore that this mighty
motive force was guided by singularly clear and accurate perceptions, upon which also it consciously rested with a firmness
of faith that constituted much of its power, is to rob him of a
great part of his due renown.

But it was not only in the greatness of the opportunities
offered to Nelson that external conditions now changed. The
glory of the hero brought a temptation which wrecked the
happiness of the man. The loss of serenity, the dark evidences
of inward conflict, of yielding against conviction, of consequent dissatisfaction with self and gradual deterioration, make
between his past and future a break as clear, and far sharper
than, the startling increase of radiancy that attends the Battle
of the Nile, and thenceforth shines with undiminished intensity to the end. The lustre of his well-deserved and worldwide renown, the consistency and ever-rising merit of his
professional conduct, contrast painfully with the shadows of
reprobation, the swerving, and the declension, which begin to
attend a life heretofore conformed, in the general, to healthy
normal standards of right and wrong, but now allowed to
violate, not merely ideal Christian rectitude, but the simple,
natural dictates of upright dealing between man and man.
It had been the proud boast of early years: "There is no
action in my whole life but what is honourable." The attainment of glory exceeding even his own great aspirations
coincides with dereliction from the plain rules of honor
between friends, and with public humiliation to his wife,
which he allowed himself to inflict, notwithstanding that he
admitted her claims to his deferential consideration to be unbroken. In this contrast, of the exaltation of the hero and
the patriot with the degradation of the man, lie the tragedy
and the misery of Nelson's story. And this, too, was incurred
on behalf of a woman whose reputation and conduct were
such that no shred of dignity could attach to an infatuation
as doting as it was blamable. The pitiful inadequacy of the
temptation to the ruin it caused invests with a kind of prophecy
the words he had written to his betrothed in the heyday of
courtship: "These I trust will ever be my sentiments; if

they are not, I do verily believe it will be my *folly* that occasions it."

The inward struggle, though severe, was short and decisive. Once determined on his course, he choked down scruples and hesitations, and cast them from him with the same single-minded resolution that distinguished his public acts. "Fixed as fate," were the remorseless words with which he characterized his firm purpose to trample conscience under foot, and to reject his wife in favor of his mistress. But although ease may be obtained by silencing self-reproach, safety scarcely can. One cannot get the salt out of his life, and not be the worse for it. Much that made Nelson so lovable remained to the end ; but into his heart, as betrayed by his correspondence, and into his life, from the occasional glimpses afforded by letters or journals of associates, there thenceforth entered much that is unlovely, and which to no appreciable extent was seen before. The simple *bonhomie*, the absence of conventional reticence, the superficial lack of polish, noted by his early biographers, and which he had had no opportunity to acquire, the childlike vanity that transpires so innocently in his confidential home letters, and was only the weak side of his noble longing for heroic action, degenerated rapidly into loss of dignity of life, into an unseemly susceptibility to extravagant adulation, as he succumbed to surroundings, the corruptness of which none at first realized more clearly, and where one woman was the sole detaining fascination. And withal, as the poison worked, discontent with self bred discontent with others, and with his own conditions. Petulance and querulousness too often supplanted the mental elasticity, which had counted for naught the roughnesses on the road to fame. The mind not worthily occupied, and therefore ill at ease, became embittered, prone to censure and to resent, suspicious at times and harsh in judgment, gradually tending towards alienation, not from his wife only, but from his best and earliest friends.

During the short stay of seven months in England, which ended with the sailing of the "Vanguard," the record of his correspondence is necessarily very imperfect, both from the loss of his arm, and from the fact of his being with his family. Such indications as there are point to unbroken relations of tenderness with his wife. "I found my domestic happiness perfect," he wrote to Lord St. Vincent, shortly after his arrival home; and some months later, in a letter from Bath to a friend, he says jestingly: "Tell —— that I possess his place in Mr. Palmer's box; but he did not tell me all its charms, that generally some of the handsomest ladies in Bath are partakers in the box, and was I a bachelor I would not answer for being tempted; but as I am possessed of everything which is valuable in a wife, I have no occasion to think beyond a pretty face." Lady Nelson attended personally to the dressing of his arm; she accompanied him in his journeys between Bath and London, and they separated only when he left town to hoist his flag at Portsmouth. The letters of Lady Saumarez, the wife of one of his brother captains then serving with Lord St. Vincent, mention frequent meetings with the two together in the streets of Bath; and upon the 1st of May, the day before leaving the fleet off Cadiz for the Mediterranean, on the expedition which was to result in the Nile, and all the consequences so fatal to the happiness of both, he concludes his letter, "with every kind wish that a fond heart can frame, believe me, as ever, your most affectionate husband."

On the 2d of May the "Vanguard" quitted the fleet for Gibraltar, where she arrived on the 4th. On the 7th Nelson issued orders to Sir James Saumarez, commanding the "Orion," and to Captain Alexander Ball, commanding the "Alexander," both seventy-fours, to place themselves under his command; and the following day the "Vanguard" sailed, in company with these ships and five smaller vessels, to begin the memorable campaign, of which the Battle of the Nile was the most conspicuous incident.

CHAPTER X.

MAY–SEPTEMBER, 1798. AGE, 39.

BETWEEN the time that Nelson was wounded at Teneriffe, July 24, 1797, and his return to active service in April, 1798, important and ominous changes had been occurring in the political conditions of Europe. These must be taken briefly into account, because the greatness of the issues thence arising, as understood by the British Government, measures the importance in its eyes of the enterprise which it was about to intrust, by deliberate selection, to one of the youngest flag-officers upon the list. The fact of the choice shows the estimation to which Nelson had already attained in the eyes of the Admiralty.

In July, 1797, Great Britain alone was at war with France, and so continued for over a year longer. Portugal, though nominally an ally, contributed to the common cause nothing but the use of the Tagus by the British Navy. Austria, it is true, had not yet finally made peace with France, but preliminaries had been signed in April, and the definitive treaty of Campo Formio was concluded in October. By it Belgium became incorporated in the territory of France, to which was conceded also the frontier of the Rhine. The base of her power was thus advanced to the river, over which the possession of the fortified city of Mayence gave her an easy passage, constituting a permanent threat of invasion to Germany. Venice, as a separate power, disappeared. Part of her former domains upon the mainland, with the city itself, went to Austria, but part was taken to constitute the Cisalpine Republic, — a new state in Northern Italy, nominally independent, but really under the control of France, to whom it owed its existence. Corfu, and the neighboring islands at the mouth of the Adriatic, till then belonging to Venice, were transferred to France. The choice of these distant and isolated maritime positions, coupled with the retention of a large army in the valley of the Po, showed, if any evidence were needed, a determination to assure control over the Italian peninsula and the Mediterranean Sea.

The formal acquisitions by treaty, even, did not measure the full menace of the conditions. The Revolutionary ferment, which had partially subsided, received fresh impetus from the victories of Bonaparte and the cessation of Continental war; and the diplomacy of France continued as active and as aggressive as the movement of her armies had previously been. By constant interference, overt and secret, not always stopping short of violence, French influence and French ideas were propagated among the weaker adjoining states. Holland, Switzerland, and the Italian Republics became outposts of France, occupied by French troops, and upon them were forced governments conformed to the existing French pattern. In short, the aggrandizement of France, not merely in moral influence but in physical control, was being pushed forward as decisively in peace as in war, and by means which threatened the political equilibrium of Europe. But, while all states were threatened, Great Britain remained the one chief enemy against which ultimately the efforts of France must be, and were, concentrated. "Either our government must destroy the English monarchy," wrote Bonaparte at this time, "or must expect itself to be destroyed by the corruption and intrigue of those active islanders." The British ministry on its part also realized that the sea-power of their country was the one force from which, because so manifold in its activities, and so readily exerted in many quarters by virtue of its mobility, France had most reason to fear the arrest of its revolutionary advance and the renewal of the Continental war. It was, therefore, the one opponent against which the efforts of the French must necessarily be directed. For the same reason it was the one centre around whose action, wisely guided, the elements of discontent, already stirring, might gather, upon the occurrence of a favorable moment, and constitute a body of resistance capable of stopping aggressions which threatened the general well-being.

REAR ADMIRAL, SIR HORATIO NELSON
IN 1798.

From the painting by L. F. Abbott in the National Portrait Gallery.

When the British Government found that the overtures for peace which it had made in the summer of 1797 could have no result, except on terms too humiliating to be considered, it at once turned its attention to the question of waging a distinctively offensive war, for effect in which co-operation was needed. The North of Europe was hopeless. Prussia persisted in the policy of isolation, adopted in 1795 by herself and a number of the northern German states. Russia was quietly hostile to France, but the interference contemplated by the Empress Catherine had been averted by her death in 1796, and her successor, Paul, had shown no intention of undertaking it. There remained, therefore, the Mediterranean. In Italy, France stood face to face with Austria and Naples, and both these were dissatisfied with the action taken by her in the Peninsula itself and in Switzerland, besides sharing the apprehension of most other governments from the disquiet attending her political course. An advance into the Mediterranean was therefore resolved by the British Cabinet.

This purpose disconcerted St. Vincent, who, besides his aversion from the war in general, was distinguished rather by tenacity and resolution in meeting difficulties and dangers, when forced upon him, than by the sanguine and enterprising initiative in offensive measures which characterized Nelson. Writing to the latter on the 8th of January, 1798, he says: "I am much at a loss to reconcile the plans in contemplation to augment this fleet and extend its operations, with the peace which Portugal seems determined to make with France, upon any terms the latter may please to impose; because Gibraltar is an unsafe depot for either stores or provisions, which the Spaniards have always in their power to destroy, and the French keep such an army in Italy, that Tuscany and Naples would fall a sacrifice to any the smallest assistance rendered to our fleet." In other words, the old question of supplies still dominated the situation, in the apprehension of this experienced officer. Yet, in view of the serious condition of things, and the probable defection of Portugal under the threats of France and Spain, to which he alludes, it seems probable that the ministry were better advised, in their determination to abandon a passive defence against an enemy unrelentingly bent upon their destruction. As Nelson said

18

of a contingency not more serious : "Desperate affairs require desperate remedies."

However determined the British Government might be to act in the Mediterranean, some temporary perplexity must at first have been felt as to where to strike, until a movement of the enemy solved the doubt. In the early months of 1798 the Directory decided upon the Egyptian expedition under General Bonaparte, and, although its destination was guarded with admirable secrecy until long after the armament sailed, the fact necessarily transpired that preparations were being made on a most extensive scale for a maritime enterprise. The news soon reached England, as it did also Jervis at his station off Cadiz. Troops and transports were assembling in large numbers at the southern ports of France, in Genoa, Civita Vecchia, and Corsica, while a fleet of at least a dozen ships-of-the-line was fitting out at Toulon. Various surmises were afloat as to the object, but all at this time were wide of the mark.

On the 29th of April, less than three weeks after Nelson left England, but before he joined the fleet, the Cabinet issued orders to St. Vincent to take such measures as he deemed necessary to thwart the projects of the Toulon squadron. It was left to his judgment whether to go in person with his whole fleet, or to send a detachment of not less than nine or ten ships-of-the-line under a competent flag-officer. If possible, the government wished him to maintain the blockade of Cadiz as it had been established since the Battle of St. Vincent; but everything was to yield to the necessity of checking the sailing of the Toulon expedition, or of defeating it, if it had already started. A speedy reinforcement was promised, to supply the places of the ships that might be detached.

Accompanying the public letter was a private one from the First Lord of the Admiralty, reflecting the views and anxieties of the Government. "The circumstances in which we now find ourselves oblige us to take a measure of a more decided and hazardous complexion than we should otherwise have thought ourselves justified in taking; but when you are apprized that the appearance of a British squadron in the Mediterranean is a condition on which the fate of Europe may at this moment be stated to depend, you will not be surprised that we are disposed to strain every nerve, and incur considerable hazard in effecting it." This impressive, almost solemn, statement of the weighty and anxious character of the intended step, emphasizes the significance of the choice, which the First Lord indicates as that of the Government, of the officer upon whom such a charge is to devolve. "If you determine to send a detachment into the Mediterranean [instead of going in person with the fleet], I think it almost unnecessary to suggest to you the propriety of putting it under the command of Sir H. Nelson, whose acquaintance with that part of the world, as well as his activity and disposition, seem to qualify him in a peculiar manner for that service."

In concluding his letter, Earl Spencer summed up the reasons of the Government, and his own sense of the great risk attending the undertaking, for the conduct of which he designated Nelson. "I am as strongly impressed, as I have no doubt your Lordship will be, with the hazardous nature of the measure which we now have in contemplation; but I cannot at the same time help feeling how much depends upon its success, and how absolutely necessary it is at this time to run some risk, in order, if possible, to bring about a new system of affairs in Europe, which shall save us all from being overrun by the exorbitant power of France. In this view of the subject, it is impossible not to perceive how much depends on the exertions of the great Continental powers; and, without entering further into what relates more particularly to them, I can venture to assure you that no good will be obtained from them if some such measure as that now in contemplation is not immediately adopted. On the other hand, if, by our appearance in the Mediterranean, we can encourage Austria to come forward again, it is in the highest degree probable that the other powers will seize the opportunity of acting at the same time, and such a general concert be established as shall soon bring this great contest to a termination, on grounds less unfavorable by many degrees to the parties concerned than appeared likely a short time since." It may be added here, by way of comment, that the ups and downs of Nelson's pursuit, the brilliant victory at the Nile, and the important consequences flowing from it, not only fully justified this forecast, but illustrated aptly that in war, when a line of action has been rightly chosen, the following it up despite great risks, and with resolute perseverance through many disappointments, will more often than not give great success, — a result which may probably be attributed to the moral force which necessarily underlies determined daring and sustained energy.

As has appeared, the Government's recommendation had been ratified beforehand by St. Vincent, in sending Nelson with three ships to watch Toulon.   Upon receiving the despatches, on the 10th of May, the admiral's first step was to order Nelson to return at once to the fleet, to take charge of the detachment from the beginning. " You, and you only, can command the important service in contemplation; there-fore, make the best of your way down to me."   More urgent letters arriving from England, with news that a heavy rein-forcement had left there, he, on the 19th, hurried off a brig, " La Mutine," commanded by Hardy, Nelson's former lieu-tenant, to notify the rear-admiral that a squadron of ten ships would be sent to him shortly from before Cadiz; and on the 21st this detachment sailed, under the command of Captain Troubridge.

The " Mutine " joined Nelson on the 5th of June.   His little division had so far had more bad fortune than good. Leaving Gibraltar on the 8th of May, late in the evening, so that the easterly course taken should not be visible to either friend or enemy, he had gone to the Gulf of Lyons. There a small French corvette, just out of Toulon, was captured on the 17th, but, except in unimportant details, yielded no information additional to that already possessed. On the 19th Bonaparte sailed with all the vessels gathered in Toulon, directing his course to the eastward, to pass near Genoa, and afterwards between Corsica and the mainland of Italy.   On the night of the 20th, in a violent gale of wind, the " Vanguard " rolled overboard her main and mizzen top-masts, and later on the foremast went, close to the deck. The succession of these mishaps points rather to spars badly secured and cared for than to unavoidable accident.   Fortu-nately, the " Orion " and " Alexander " escaped injury, and

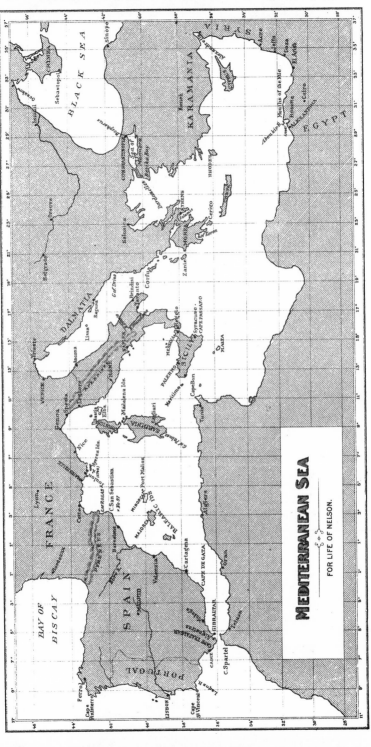

MEDITERRANEAN SEA

FOR LIFE OF NELSON.

(For Life of Nelson.)

the latter, on the following morning, took the "Vanguard" in tow, to go to Oristan Bay, in Sardinia. The situation became extremely dangerous on the evening of the 22d, for, the wind falling light, the sail-power of the "Alexander" was scarcely sufficient to drag both ships against a heavy westerly swell which was setting them bodily upon the Sardinian coast, then not far distant. Thinking the case hopeless, Nelson ordered the "Alexander" to let go the hawser; but Captain Ball begged permission to hold on, and finally succeeded in saving the flagship, which, on the 23d, anchored with her consorts under the Islands of San Pietro, at the southern extremity of Sardinia. The governor of the place sent word that they must not remain, Sardinia being allied to France, but added that, as he had no power to force them out, they would doubtless do as they pleased; and he supplied them with fresh provisions, — a line of conduct which illustrates at once the restrictions imposed upon British operations in the Mediterranean by French insistence, and at the same time the readiness of the weaker states to connive at the evasion of them, other instances of which occurred during this period. By the united efforts of the division, four days sufficed to refit the "Vanguard" with jury-masts, and the three ships again sailed, on the 27th, for an appointed rendezvous, to seek the frigates, which had separated during and after the gale.

This severe check, occurring at so critical a moment, — more critical even than Nelson knew, for he remained ignorant of the French sailing for some days longer, — was in itself disheartening, and fell upon one whose native eagerness chafed painfully against enforced inaction and delay. His manner of bearing it illustrated both the religious characteristics, which the experience of grave emergencies tends to develop and strengthen in men of action, and the firmness of a really great man, never more signally displayed than under the pressure of calamity and suspense, such as he continually had to undergo. The exceptional brilliancy and decisiveness of his greater battles — the Nile, Copenhagen, and Trafalgar — obscure the fact that each of them was preceded by a weary period of strenuous uphill work, a steady hewing of his way through a tanglewood of obstacles, a patient endurance of disappointments, a display of sustained, undaunted resolution under discouragements, nobler far than even the moments of triumphant action, into which at last he joyfully emerges and freely exerts his extraordinary powers. " I trust," he wrote to St. Vincent, " my friends will think I bore my chastisement like a man. I hope it has made me a better officer, as I believe it has made me a better man. On the Sunday evening I thought myself in every respect one of the most fortunate men, to command such a squadron in such a place, and my pride was too great for man." To his wife he wrote in the same strain : "I ought not to call what has happened to the Vanguard by the cold name of accident ; I believe firmly that it was the Almighty's goodness, to check my consummate vanity."

Vanity was rather a hard name to call the natural elation of a young admiral, intrusted with an unusually important service, and proud of his command ; but the providential interposition worked directly to his advantage. The delays caused by the repairs to the "Vanguard," and by the subsequent necessity of seeking the separated frigates at the rendezvous appointed for such a case, made possible the junction of Troubridge, of whose approach Nelson was totally ignorant. On the 2d of June Sir James Saumarez mentions speaking a ship, which a few days before had seen eleven sail-of-the-line, supposed to be English. " We are at a loss what conjectures to put on this intelligence." Five days before this, May 28, a vessel out of Marseilles had informed them of Bonaparte's sailing with all his transports. Nelson would doubtless have pursued them at once, in conformity with his instructions to ascertain the enemy's objects ; but for such operations, essentially those of a scouting expedition, the frigates were too necessary to be left behind. On the 4th of June he reached the rendezvous, and, not finding the frigates, waited. The next morning, by the arrival of the "Mutine," he learned that he was to expect the reinforcement, which converted his division into a fleet, and enlarged his mission from one of mere reconnoissance to the duty of overtaking and destroying a great maritime expedition.

Besides this good news, the " Mutine " brought word of another misfortune, more irretrievable than the loss of spars.

She had fallen in with the frigates three days before, and the senior captain had told Hardy that he was going with them to Gibraltar, persuaded that the condition of the flagship, which he had seen, would necessitate her return to an arsenal for repairs. " I thought Hope would have known me better," commented Nelson, when he became aware of a step which materially affected, in fact probably entirely changed, the course of events, and most seriously embarrassed all his subsequent movements. This untimely and precipitate action, and his remark, illustrate conspicuously the differences between men, and exemplify the peculiar energy and unrelaxing forward impulse which eminently fitted Nelson for his present high charge.

The inconvenience and danger arising from the frigates' departure was instantly felt. "Nothing," wrote Saumarez, "can equal our anxiety to fall in with the reinforcement. Our squadron has been, these two days, detached in all directions, without falling in with them ; and there is strong reason to fear they think us returned to Gibraltar " — from Hope's reports. Such were the risks springing from misplaced caution, more ruinous than the most daring venture, and which from beginning to end well-nigh wrecked the great attempt upon which the Admiralty, St. Vincent, and Nelson had staked so much. In further consequence, the line-of-battle ships became separated by stretching too far apart in their anxious care to find Troubridge, and when he joined the "Vanguard," on the 7th, the "Orion " and " Alexander " were not in sight. The French having so long a start, and there being now with him eleven seventy-fours, Nelson with characteristic promptness would not delay an instant. The fifty-gun ship "Leander," which had come with Troubridge, was directed to wait forty-eight hours for the two absentees, with a memorandum of the course about to be followed. Confident that single ships would be able to overtake a squadron whose route they knew, the admiral at once pushed on for Cape Corso, the north point of Corsica, intending to pass between the island and Italy, seeking information as he went. The "Mutine " was all he had to replace the missing frigates.

June 7th thus marks the beginning of a chase, which

ended only upon the 1st of August in the Battle of the Nile. During this miserable period of suspense and embarrassment, occasioned and prolonged beyond all reason or necessity by the want of lookout ships, the connecting and illuminating thread is the purpose of Nelson, at once clear and firm, to find the French fleet and to fight it the instant found. No other consideration draws his mind aside, except so far as it may facilitate the attainment and fulfilment of this one object. In this one light he sees all things. At the start he writes to St. Vincent: "You may be assured I will fight them the moment I can reach, be they at anchor or under sail." Three days later, he tells Sir William Hamilton: "If their fleet is not moored in as strong a port as Toulon, nothing shall hinder me from attacking them." "Be they bound to the Antipodes," he says to Earl Spencer, "your Lordship may rely that I will not lose a moment in bringing them to action, and endeavour to destroy their transports." Such expressions are repeated with a frequency which proves the absolute hold the resolution had upon his mind. When obstacles occur to him, or are mentioned, they do not make room for the thought of not fighting to be entertained; only Toulon suggests the idea of impossibility. He raises difficulties diligently enough, but it is only that they may be the better overcome, not that they may deter. All possible conditions are considered and discussed, but simply in order that the best fighting solution may be reached. The constant mental attitude is such that the man is unprepared to recede before any opposition; he fortifies his mind beforehand with the best means of meeting and vanquishing it, but the attempt at least shall be made. "Thank God," he wrote at this moment, "I do not feel difficulties;" yet the avowal itself accompanies so plain a statement of his embarrassments as to show that his meaning is that they do not discourage. This characteristic appeared most strongly at Copenhagen, partly because the difficulties there were greatest, partly from the close contrast with a man of very different temper.

Being entirely without intelligence as to the real object of the French, there was nothing to do but to follow upon their track, with eyes open for indications. They were known to have gone southerly, towards Naples and Sicily; and these two points, parts of the Kingdom of the Two Sicilies, had been mentioned by Jervis as probable destinations. The "Orion" and "Alexander" rejoined in two or three days, and on the 14th of June information, second-hand but probable, was obtained that on the 4th the French armament had been seen off the west end of Sicily, steering to the eastward. "If they pass Sicily," said Nelson in his letter to Spencer written the next day, "I shall believe they are going on their scheme of possessing Alexandria, and getting troops to India — a plan concerted with Tippoo Saib, by no means so difficult as might at first view be imagined." Troubridge was now sent ahead in the "Mutine" to communicate with Sir William Hamilton, the British minister at Naples, and with Acton, the prime minister of that Kingdom. He took with him letters from the admiral, who wished to know what co-operation he might hope from the Court of Naples, in the matters of supplies, of frigates to act as lookouts, and of pilots for Sicilian waters.

On the 17th the squadron hove-to ten miles off Naples, and Troubridge rejoined. The Neapolitan Government sent assurances of good wishes, and of hatred to the French; supplies would be given under the rose, and Acton sent a written order to that effect, addressed to the governors of ports in the name of the King. Naples being at peace with France, assistance with ships could not be given, nor, to use the words of Nelson, "the smallest information of what was, or was likely to be, the future destination of the French armament. With this comfortable account I pushed for the Faro of Messina." Troubridge brought word, however, that the French fleet was off Malta, about to attack it, which served to give direction for the squadron's next move.

After leaving Naples Nelson wrote strong and clear letters to Sir William Hamilton upon the existing conditions. Why should Naples stand in shivering hesitation about taking a decided step in support of Great Britain? She had looked and prayed for the arrival of the fleet, as the one force competent to check the designs of the French. Sicily could be approached only by water, and the distance of Naples from Northern Italy rendered the control of the sea most advantageous, if not absolutely essential, to a French army attempting to hold the

boot of the peninsula. Now the British fleet had come, in
force adequate to neutralize the French Navy, and, in Nelson's
belief, to defeat and destroy it, if properly supported. Did
Naples expect to escape by a timid adherence to half measures,
when by her notorious preference for the British she had already gained the ill-will of the French ? " The French know
as well as you and I do, that their Sicilian Majesties called
for our help to save them — even this is crime enough with
the French." Safety — true safety — could be had only by
strenuous and decisive action in support of Nelson's squadron.
Did not the attack on Malta indicate a design upon Sicily ?
" Were I commanding a fleet attending an army which is to
invade Sicily, I should say to the general, 'If you can take
Malta, it secures the safety of your fleet, transports, stores,
&c., and insures your safe retreat [from Sicily] should that
be necessary ; for if even a superior fleet of the enemy should
arrive, before one week passes, they will be blown to leeward
and you may pass with safety.' This would be my opinion. . . .
I repeat it, *Malta is the direct road to Sicily.*" If the French
are overtaken, he continues, and found in some anchorage, it
can scarcely be so strong but that I can get at them, but there
will be needed things which I have not, fire-ships, bomb-
vessels, and gunboats, when one hour would either destroy or
drive them out. Without such aid, the British may be
crippled in their attempt, and forced to leave the Mediterranean. In case of blockade — or necessity to remain for any
reason — the fleet must have supplies, which only Naples can
furnish. Failing these it must retire, and then Sicily and
Naples are lost. Since, then, so much assistance must be
given in time, why postpone now, when one strong blow
would give instant safety ? Why should not his own motto,
" I will not lose a moment in attacking them," apply as well
to the policy of an endangered kingdom as of a British
admiral ?

If this reasoning and advice took more account of the exigencies of the British arms than of the difficulties of a weak
state of the second order, dependent for action upon the support of other nations, they were at least perfectly consonant
to the principles and practice of the writer, wherever he himself had to act. But Nelson could not expect his own spirit

in the King of the Two Sicilies. Even if the course suggested were the best for Naples under the conditions, it is the property of ordinary men, in times of danger, to see difficulties more clearly than advantages, and to shrink from steps which involve risk, however promising of success. The Neapolitan Government, though cheered by the appearance of the British fleet, had to consider danger also on the land side, where it relied upon the protection of Austria, instead of trusting manfully to its own arms and the advantages of its position, remote from the centre of French power. Austria had pledged herself to support Naples, if invaded without just cause; but it was not certain that she would interfere if the cause of attack was the premature admission of British ships into the ports of the kingdom, beyond the number specified in the still recent treaties with France. The Emperor was meditating war, in which he expected to assist Naples and to be assisted by her; but he did not choose to be hurried, and might refuse aid if an outbreak were precipitated.

Actually, what Naples did mattered little. Under some contingencies, such as Nelson was contemplating when he wrote his letter, it might have mattered much whether he received the abundant support of small armed vessels which he indicated; but in the end supplies only were required, and those he had orders from Jervis to exact at the mouth of his cannon from all powers, — friends or neutrals, — Sardinia only excepted. The fleet passed the Straits of Messina on the 20th of June, and continued south, keeping close to the Sicilian shore in hope of information, until the 22d, when it was off Cape Passaro, the southeastern extremity of the island. There a Genoese brig was spoken, which had left Malta the previous day. From her Nelson learned that Malta had surrendered to the French on the 15th, a week before, which was correct; but the information further stated, that, after landing a garrison, the expedition had sailed again on the 16th — it was thought for Sicily. This last news was untrue, whether by intention or not, for Bonaparte remained in Malta till the 19th; but upon it Nelson had to act. Had he seen the captain of the stranger himself, he might have found out more, for he was a shrewd questioner, and his intellect was sharpened by anxiety, and by constant dwelling upon the

elements of the intricate problem before him ; but the vessel
had been boarded by the "Mutine," three hours before, and
was now beyond recall.

At this season the winds in the Mediterranean prevail from
the westward; therefore, with the six days' start the enemy
was believed now to have, no time could be lost. Six days
sufficed to carry the British squadron from its present position
to Alexandria, which Nelson was already inclined to think the
destination of the French. Yet, being dependent upon a wind
then practically constant in direction, it would not do to yield
a mile of ground, except upon a mature, if rapid, deliberation.
Nelson's own mind was, by constant preoccupation, familiar
beforehand with the bearings of the different conditions of
any situation likely to occur, and with the probable inferences
to be drawn ; his opinions were, so to say, in a constant state
of formation and development, ready for instantaneous application to any emergency as it arose. But he had, besides, exercised the same habit in the captains of the ships, by the
practice of summoning them on board the flagship, singly or
in groups ; the slow movement of sailing vessels, particularly
in the light summer weather of the Mediterranean, permitting
such intercourse without materially affecting the progress of
the fleet. Invitations or commands so to visit the flagship
were common. "I have passed the day on board the Vanguard," notes Saumarez on one occasion, "having breakfasted
and stayed to dinner with the admiral." "It was his practice
during the whole of his cruise," wrote Berry, the flag-captain,
"whenever the weather and circumstances would permit, to
have his captains on board the Vanguard, where he would
fully develop to them his own ideas of the different and best
modes of attack, in all possible positions." That such conversations were not confined to tactical questions, but extended
to what would now be called the strategy of the situation, is
evident from allusions by Saumarez to the various surmises
concerning the probable movements of the enemy. Nelson
never yielded a particle of his responsibility, nor of his credit,
but it is clear that such discussion would not only broaden his
own outlook, but prepare his subordinates to give readier and
sounder views upon any new conjuncture that might arise.

He now summoned on board four captains " in whom I place

great confidence," Saumarez, Troubridge, — the two seniors, — Ball and Darby, stated the case, and received their opinions. These seem to have been given in writing,[1] and from his letter to St. Vincent the results of the conference, as shown by his decision, may be summarized as follows. With the existing winds, it would be impossible for such a fleet as the enemy's to get to the westward. Had they aimed at Sicily, an object concerning which explicit disclaimers had been given by the French to the Neapolitan Government, some indication of their approach must have been known at Syracuse, the day before, when the British were off that city. Consequently, the expedition must have gone to the eastward. The size and nature of the armament must also be considered, — forty thousand troops, a dozen ships-of-the-line, besides a staff of scientific men, — all pointed to a great, distant, and permanent occupation. The object might be Corfu, or to overthrow the existing government of Turkey, or to settle a colony in Egypt. As between these, all equally possible, the last was the most direct and greatest menace to present British interests, and should determine his course. "If they have concerted a plan with Tippoo Saib, to have vessels at Suez, three weeks, at this season, is a common passage to the Malabar coast, where our India possessions would be in great danger."

Such was the conclusion — how momentous at the moment can only be realized by those who will be at the pains to consider a man still young, with reputation brilliant indeed, but not established; intrusted with a great chance, it is true, but also with a great responsibility, upon which rested all his future. On slight, though decisive, preponderance of evidence, he was about to risk throwing away an advantage a

[1] The author is indebted to the present Lord De Saumarez for a copy of the opinion of Sir James Saumarez, written on board the "Vanguard" at this meeting: —

"The French fleet having left Malta six days ago, had their destination been the Island of Sicily there is reason to presume we should have obtained information of it yesterday off Syracuse, or the day before in coming through the Pharo of Messina — under all circumstances I think it most conducive to the good of His Majesty's service to make the best of our way for Alexandria, as the only means of saving our possessions in India, should the French armament be destined for that country.

"Vanguard, at sea, 22d June 1798.   JAMES SAUMAREZ."

seaman must appreciate, that of being to windward of his enemy, — able to get at him, — the strategist's position of command. The tongues of envy and censure might well be — we now know that they were — busy in inquiring why so young an admiral had so high charge, and in sneering at his failure to find the enemy. "Knowing my attachment to you," wrote his old friend, Admiral Goodall, alongside whom he had fought under Hotham, "how often have I been questioned: 'What is your favourite hero about? The French fleet has passed under his nose,' &c., &c." Nelson was saved from fatal hesitation, primarily, by his singleness of purpose, which looked first to his country's service, to the thorough doing of the work given him to do, and only afterwards to the consequences of failure to his own fame and fortunes. At that moment the choice before him was either to follow out an indication, slight, but as far as it went clear, which, though confessedly precarious, promised to lead to a great and decisive result, such as he had lately urged upon the King of Naples; or to remain where he was, in an inglorious security, perfectly content, to use words of his own, that "each day passed without loss to our side." To the latter conclusion might very well have contributed the knowledge, that the interests which the Cabinet thought threatened were certainly for the present safe. Broadly as his instructions were drawn, no word of Egypt or the East was specifically in them. Naples, Sicily, Portugal, or Ireland, such were the dangers intimated by Spencer and St. Vincent in their letters, and he was distinctly cautioned against letting the enemy get to the westward of him. He might have consoled himself for indecisive action, which procrastinated disaster and covered failure with the veil of nullity, as did a former commander of his in a gazetted letter, by the reflection that, so far as the anticipations of the ministry went, the designs of the enemy were for the time frustrated, by the presence of his squadron between them and the points indicated to him.

But the single eye of principle gained keener insight in this case by the practised habit of reflection, which came prepared, to the full extent of an acute intellect, to detect every glimmer of light, and to follow them to the point where they converged upon the true solution; and both principle and

reflection were powerfully supported in their final action by
a native temperament, impatient of hesitations, of half measures, certain that the annihilation of the French fleet, and
nothing short of its annihilation, fulfilled that security of his
country's interests in which consisted the spirit of his instructions. His own words in self-defence, when for a moment it
seemed as if, after all, he had blundered in the great risk he
took, though rough in form, rise to the eloquence that speaks
out of the abundance of the heart. "The only objection I
can fancy to be started is, 'you should not have gone such
a long voyage without more certain information of the
enemy's destination:' my answer is ready — who was I to
get it from? The governments of Naples and Sicily either
knew not, or chose to keep me in ignorance. Was I to
wait patiently till I heard certain accounts? If Egypt was
their object, before I could hear of them they would have
been in India. To do nothing, I felt, was disgraceful; therefore I made use of my understanding, and by it I ought to
stand or fall."

The destination of the enemy had been rightly divined,
following out a course of reasoning outlined by Nelson a week
before in his letter to Spencer; but successful pursuit was
baffled for the moment by the wiliness of Bonaparte, who
directed his vast armament to be steered for the south shore
of Candia, instead of straight for Alexandria. Even this
would scarcely have saved him, had Nelson's frigates been
with the fleet. Immediately after the council, the admiral
with his customary promptitude kept away for Egypt under
all sail. "I am just returned from on board the Admiral,"
writes Saumarez, "and we are crowding sail for Alexandria;
but the contrast to what we experienced yesterday is great
indeed, having made sure of attacking them this morning.
At present it is very doubtful whether we shall fall in with
them at all, as we are proceeding upon the merest conjecture
only, and not on any positive information. Some days must
now elapse before we can be relieved from our cruel suspense;
and if, at the end of our journey, we find we are upon a wrong
scent, our embarrassment will be great indeed. Fortunately, I
only act here *en second;* but did the chief responsibility rest
with me, I fear it would be more than my too irritable nerves

would bear." Such was the contemporary estimate of an eye-witness, an officer of tried and singular gallantry and ability, who shared the admiral's perplexities and ambitions, though not his responsibility. His words portray justly the immensity of the burden Nelson bore. That, indeed, is the inevitable penalty of command; but it must be conceded that, when adequately borne, it should convey also an equal measure of renown.

In the morning, before the consultation with the captains, three French frigates had been seen; but Nelson, warned by the parting of the "Orion" and "Alexander" a fortnight before, would not run the risk of scattering the squadron by chasing them. No time could now be lost, waiting for a separated ship to catch up. The circumstance of the fleet being seen by these frigates was quoted in a letter from Louis Bonaparte, who was with the expedition, to his brother Joseph, and was made the ground for comment upon the stupidity of the British admiral, who with this opportunity failed to find the armament. The criticism is unjust; had the frigates taken to flight, as of course they would, the British fleet, if not divided, would certainly not be led towards the main body of the enemy. Concentration of purpose, singleness of aim, was more than ever necessary, now that time pressed and a decision had been reached; but the sneer of the French officer reproduces the idle chatter of the day in London streets and drawing-rooms. These, in turn, but echoed and swelled the murmurs of insubordination and envy in the navy itself, at the departure from the routine methods of officialism, by passing over the claims of undistinguished seniors, in favor of one who as yet had nothing but brilliant achievement, and yet more brilliant promise, to justify committing to him the most momentous charge that in this war had devolved on a British admiral. A letter from one of the puisne lords of the Admiralty was read publicly on board the "Prince George," flagship of Sir William Parker, — the same who had the controversy with Nelson about the Battle of St. Vincent, — denouncing Lord St. Vincent in no very gentle terms for having sent so young a flag-officer.[1] "Sir William Parker and Sir John Orde have written strong remonstrances against

[1] Clarke and M'Arthur's Life of Nelson, vol. ii. p. 100.

your commanding the detached squadron instead of them," wrote St. Vincent to Nelson. " I did all I could to prevent it, consistently with my situation, but there is a faction, fraught with all manner of ill-will to you, that, unfortunately for the two Baronets, domined over any argument or influence I could use : they will both be ordered home the moment their letters arrive." It will be seen how much was at stake for Nelson personally in the issue of these weeks. Happy the man who, like him, has in such a case the clear light of duty to keep his steps from wavering!

The night after Nelson made sail for Alexandria the two hostile bodies crossed the same tract of sea, on divergent courses; but a haze covered the face of the deep, and hid them from each other. When the day dawned, they were no longer within range of sight; but had the horizon of the British fleet been enlarged by flanking frigates, chasing on either side, the immunity of the French from detection could scarcely have continued. For some days not a hundred miles intervened between these two foes, proceeding for the same port. On the 26th, being two hundred and fifty miles from Alexandria, Nelson sent the " Mutine " ahead to communicate with the place and get information ; a single vessel being able to outstrip the progress of a body of ships, which is bound to the speed of its slowest member. On the 28th the squadron itself was off the town, when the admiral to his dismay found that not only the French had not appeared, but that no certain news of their destination was to be had.

Preoccupied as his mind had been with the fear that the enemy had so far the start that their army would be out of the transports before he overtook them, the idea that he might outstrip them does not seem to have entered his head. Only three vessels had been spoken since Sicily was left behind, — two from Alexandria and one from the Archipelago ; but these knew nothing of the French, being doubtless, when met, ahead of the latter's advance. That Nelson again consulted with his captains seems probable — indeed almost certain, from casual mention ; but if so, their opinion as to the future course does not appear. The unremitting eagerness of his temperament, the singleness of his purpose, which saw the whole situation concentrated in the French fleet, had worked

19

together up to the present to bring him to the true strategic point just ahead of time; although, by no fault of his own, he had started near three weeks late.[1] These two high qualities now conspired to mislead him by their own excess. "His active and anxious mind," wrote Captain Berry, "would not permit him to rest a moment in the same place; he therefore shaped his course to the northward, for the coast of Caramania [in Asia Minor], to reach as quickly as possible some quarter where information could probably be obtained."

To say that this was a mistake is perhaps to be wise only after the event. Had Nelson known that the French, when leaving Malta, had but three days' start of him, instead of six, as the Genoese had reported, he might have suspected the truth; it is not wonderful that he failed to believe that he could have gained six days. The actual gain *was* but three; for, departing practically at the same time from points equidistant from Alexandria, Bonaparte's armament appeared before that place on the third day after Nelson arrived. The troops were landed immediately, and the transports entered the port, thus making secure their escape from the British pursuit. The ships of war remained outside.

Meanwhile Nelson, "distressed for the Kingdom of the Two Sicilies," was beating back to the westward against the wind which had carried him rapidly to the coast of Egypt. Rightly or wrongly, he had not chosen to wait at the point which mature reflection had indicated to him as the enemy's goal, and the best course that now occurred to him was to do with his fleet the exploring duty that frigates should have done. "*No frigates*," he wrote to Sir William Hamilton; "to which has been, and may again be, attributed the loss of the French fleet." On his return he kept along the northern shore of the Mediterranean, passing near Candia; but, though several vessels were spoken, he only gathered from them that the French were not west of Sicily, nor at Corfu. On the 19th of July, he anchored the fleet at Syracuse, having, to use his own words, "gone a round of six hundred leagues with an expedition incredible," and yet "as ignorant of the situation of the enemy as I was twenty-seven days ago."

[1] That is, counting from May 19, when Bonaparte left Toulon, to June 7, when Troubridge's squadron joined, and pursuit began.

At Syracuse fresh disappointments awaited him, which only the indomitable single-mindedness and perseverance of the man prevented from becoming discouragements. The minister at Naples had sent despatches to await him at Cape Passaro; when he sent for these, thirsty for news about the French, they had been returned to Naples. The governor of the port, despite Acton's assurances to Troubridge, made difficulties about the admission of so many ships, and about supplying water, which they absolutely required. This Nelson resented, with angry contempt for the halting policy of the weak kingdom. "I have had so much said about the King of Naples' orders only to admit three or four of the ships of our fleet into his ports, that I am astonished. I understood that private orders, at least, would have been given for our free admission. If we are to be refused supplies, pray send me by many vessels an account, that I may in good time take the King's fleet to Gibraltar. Our treatment is scandalous for a great nation to put up with, and the King's flag is insulted at every friendly port we look at." "I wish to know your and Sir William's plans for going down the Mediterranean," he wrote to Lady Hamilton, "for, if we are to be kicked in every port of the Sicilian dominions, the sooner we are gone the better. Good God! how sensibly I feel our treatment. I have only to pray I may find the French and throw all my vengeance on them."

These words show the nervous exasperation superinduced by the tremendous strain of official anxiety and mortified ambition; for the governor's objections were purely formal and perfunctory, as was the Court's submission to the French. "Our present wants," he admitted at the same writing, "have been most amply supplied, and every attention has been paid us." Years afterwards Nelson spoke feelingly of the bitter mental anguish of that protracted and oft-thwarted pursuit. "Do not fret at anything," he told his friend Troubridge; "I wish I never had, but my return to Syracuse in 1798, broke my heart, which on any extraordinary anxiety now shows itself, be that feeling pain or pleasure." "On the 18th I had near died, with the swelling of some of the vessels of the heart. More people, perhaps, die of broken hearts than we are aware of." But the firmness of his purpose, the clearness of his convictions, remained unslackened and unclouded.

" What a situation am I placed in!" he writes, when he finds
Hamilton's despatches returned. " As yet I can learn nothing
of the enemy. You will, I am sure, and so will our country,
easily conceive what has passed in my anxious mind; but I
have this comfort, that I have no fault to accuse myself of.
This bears me up, and this only." " Every moment I have to
regret the frigates having left me," he tells St. Vincent.
" Your lordship deprived yourself of frigates to make mine
certainly the first squadron in the world, and I feel that I
have zeal and activity to do credit to your appointment, and
yet to be unsuccessful hurts me most sensibly. But if they
are above water, I will find them out, and if possible bring
them to battle. You have done your part in giving me so fine
a fleet, and I hope to do mine in making use of them."

In five days the squadron had filled with water and again
sailed. Satisfied that the enemy were somewhere in the
Levant, Nelson now intended a deliberate search for them —
or rather for their fleet, the destruction of which was the
crucial object of all his movements. "It has been said," he
wrote to Hamilton, "that to leeward of the two frigates I saw
off Cape Passaro was a line-of-battle ship, with the riches of
Malta on board, but it was the destruction of the enemy, not
riches for myself, that I was seeking. These would have
fallen to me if I had had frigates, but except the ship-of-the-
line, I regard not all the riches in this world." A plaintive
remonstrance against his second departure was penned by the
Neapolitan prime minister, which depicts so plainly the commonplace view of a military situation, — the apprehensions
of one to whom immediate security is the great object in war,
— that it justifies quotation, and comparison with the clear
intuitions, and firmly grasped principle, which placed Nelson
always, in desire, alongside the enemy's fleet, and twice
carried him, at every risk, to the end of the Mediterranean to
seek it. " We are now in danger of a war, directly on Admiral
Nelson's account; you see fairly our position; will Admiral
Nelson run to the Levant again *without knowing for certain*
the position of the French, and leave the Two Sicilies exposed
in these moments? Buonaparte has absconded himself, but
in any port he has taken securitys not to be forced. God
knows where he is, and whether we shall not see him again in

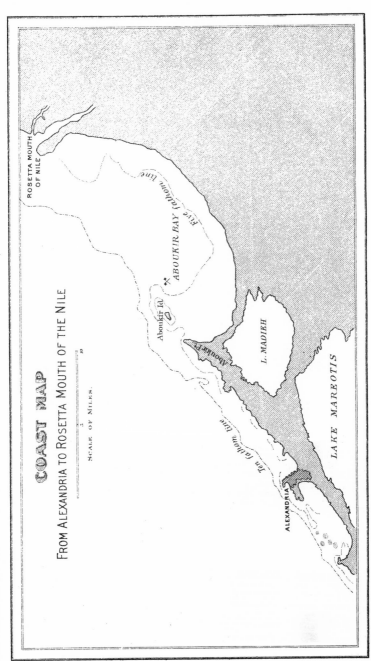

COAST MAP

From Alexandria to Rosetta Mouth of the Nile

SCALE OF MILES.

ROSETTA MOUTH
OF NILE

ABOUKIR BAY (Fathom line)

Aboukir Id.

Aboukir Pt.

L. MADIEH

LAKE MAREOTIS

ALEXANDRIA

Ten fathom line

(*For Life of Nelson.*)

a few days, if we do not hear of what a course he has taken. I present all this to your consideration." To this letter, which oddly enough was written on the very day the Battle of the Nile was fought, Nelson might well have replied then, as he did in terms a year afterwards, "The best defence for His Sicilian Majesty's dominions is to place myself alongside the French fleet."

The fleet left Syracuse on the 25th of July, just one week before the discovery of the enemy in Aboukir Bay put an end to Nelson's long suspense. The course was first shaped for the southern capes of the Morea, and on the 28th Troubridge was sent into the Gulf of Koron for information. He returned within three hours, with the news that the French had been seen four weeks before from the coast of Candia, and were then steering southeast. This intelligence was corroborated by a vessel spoken the same day. Southeast, being nearly dead before the prevailing wind, was an almost certain clue to the destination of an unwieldy body which could never regain ground lost to leeward; so, although Nelson now learned that some of his missing frigates had also been seen recently off Candia, he would waste no time looking for them. It may be mentioned that these frigates had appeared off the anchorage of the French fleet, and had been recognized by it as enemies; but, so far from taking warning from the incident, the French admiral was only confirmed by it in a blind belief that the British feared to attack. Immediately after Troubridge's return, the fleet bore up under all sail, and at 2.45 in the afternoon of the 1st of August, 1798, the masthead lookout of the "Zealous" discovered the long-sought-for enemy, lying in Aboukir Bay, on the coast of Egypt, fifteen miles east of Alexandria.

Suspense was ended, but Nelson's weightiest responsibility had yet to be met. The enemy was still so far distant that he could not be reached till near nightfall, and it was possible that not only would the battle be fought in the dark, but that some at least of the ships would not have daylight to take their positions. The consequent difficulty and risk was in any event great; but in this case the more so, because the ground was unknown to every officer in the fleet. The only chart of it in possession of the British was a rude sketch lately taken out of a prize. There was no time now for calling captains together, nor for forming plans of action. Then appeared conspicuously the value of that preparedness of mind, as well as of purpose, which at bottom was the greatest of Nelson's claims to credit. Much had been received by him from Nature, — gifts which, if she bestows them not, man struggles in vain to acquire by his own efforts; but the care which he took in fitting himself to use those gifts to their utmost capacity is his own glory. The author of the first full narrative of these eventful weeks, Captain Berry, than whom no man had larger occasion to observe Nelson's moods, used his capitals well when he wrote, "The admiral viewed the obstacles with the eye of a seaman DETERMINED ON ATTACK." It was not for him, face to face with opportunity, to hesitate and debate whether he would be justified in using it at once. But this preparation of purpose might have led only to a great disaster, had it not received guidance from a richly stored intellect, which had pondered probable conditions so exhaustively that proper direction could be at once imparted and at once understood. The French admiral, indeed, by his mistaken dispositions had delivered himself into the hands of his enemy; but that might not have availed had that enemy hesitated and given time, or had he not instantly comprehended the possibilities of the situation with a trained glance which had contemplated them long before. "By attacking the enemy's van and centre, the wind blowing directly along their line, I was enabled to throw what force I pleased on a few ships. This plan my friends readily conceived by the signals." [1]

It was, therefore, no fortuitous coincidence that the battle was fought on a plan preconcerted in general outline, though necessarily subject to particular variations in detail. Not only had many situations been discussed, as Berry tells us, but new signals had been inserted in the signal-book to enable the admiral's intentions to be quickly understood. To provide for the case of the enemy being met at sea, the force had been organized into three squadrons, — a subdivision of command which, while surrendering nothing of the admiral's initiative, much facilitated the application of his plans, by

[1] Nelson to Lord Howe.

committing the execution of major details to the two senior captains, Saumarez and Troubridge, each wielding a group of four ships. Among the provisions for specific contingencies was one that evidently sprang from the report that the enemy's fleet numbered sixteen or seventeen of the line, — an impression which arose from there being in it four Venetian ships so rated, which were not, however, fit for a place in the line. In that case Nelson proposed to attack, ship for ship, the rear thirteen of the enemy. That he preferred, when possible, to throw two ships on one is evident enough — the approaching battle proves it ; but when confronted with a force stronger, numerically, than his own, and under way, he provides what was certainly the better alternative. He engages at once the attention of as many ships as possible, confident that he brings against each a force superior to it, owing to the general greater efficiency of British ships over French of that date, and especially of those in his own squadron, called by St. Vincent the *élite* of the Navy.

The position of the French fleet, and the arrangements made by its commander, Admiral Brueys, must now be given, for they constitute the particular situation against which Nelson's general plan of attack was to be directed. Considering it impracticable for the ships-of-the-line to enter the port of Alexandria, Brueys had taken the fleet on the 8th of July to their present anchorage. Aboukir Bay begins at a promontory of the same name, and, after curving boldly south, extends eastward eighteen miles, terminating at the Rosetta mouth of the Nile. From the shore the depth increases very gradually, so that water enough for ships-of-the-line was not found till three miles from the coast. Two miles northeast of the promontory of Aboukir is Aboukir Island, since called Nelson's, linked with the point by a chain of rocks. Outside the island, similar rocks, with shoals, prolong this foul ground under water to seaward, constituting a reef dangerous to a stranger approaching the bay. This barrier, however, broke the waves from the northwest, and so made the western part of the bay a fairly convenient summer roadstead. The French fleet was anchored there, under the shelter of the island and rocks, in an order such that "the wind blew nearly along the line." Its situation offered no local protection against an enemy's approach, except that due to ignorance of the ground.

It was therefore Brueys's business to meet this defect of protection by adequate dispositions; and this he failed to do. Numerically his force was the same as Nelson's; but, while the latter had only seventy-fours, there were in the French fleet one ship of one hundred and twenty guns, and three eighties. In a military sense, every line divides naturally into three parts, — the centre, and the two ends, or flanks; and it is essential that these should so far support one another that an enemy cannot attack any two in superior force, while the third is unable to assist. Shallow water, such as was found in Aboukir Bay, if properly utilized, will prevent a flank being turned, so that an enemy can get on both sides of the ships there, or otherwise concentrate upon them, as by enfilading; and if, in addition, the ships are anchored close to each other, it becomes impossible for two of the attacking force to direct their fire upon one of the defence, without being exposed to reprisals from those next astern and ahead. These evident precautions received no illustration in the arrangements of Admiral Brueys. The general direction of his line was that of the wind, from northwest to southeast, with a very slight bend, as shown in the diagram. The leading — northwestern — ship was brought close to the shoal in thirty feet of water, but not so close as to prevent the British passing round her, turning that flank; and there were between the successive ships intervals of five hundred feet, through any one of which an enemy could readily pass. Brueys had very properly accumulated his most powerful vessels at the centre. The flagship "Orient," of one hundred and twenty guns, was seventh in the order; next ahead and astern of her were, respectively, the "Franklin" and the "Tonnant," each of eighty. By a singular misconception, however, he had thought that any attack would fall upon the rear — the lee flank; and to this utter misapprehension of the exposed points it was owing that he there placed his next heaviest ships. Nelson's fore-determined onslaught upon the van accordingly fell on the weakest of the French vessels.

Such was the French order of battle. The proceedings of the British fleet, under its leader, show an instructive combi-

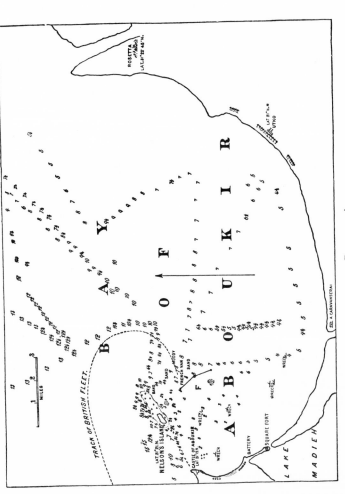

CHART OF THE BAY OF ABOUKIR.

FROM A SURVEY MADE BY THOMAS ATKINSON, MASTER OF H. M. S. THESEUS, 74, IN 1799.

(THE FIGURES REPRESENT SOUNDINGS IN FATHOMS.)

F. POSITION OF THE FRENCH FLEET (DRAWN TO SCALE), AS GIVEN IN THE TEXT.

nation of rapidity and caution, of quick comprehension of the situation, with an absence of all precipitation; no haste incompatible with perfect carefulness, no time lost, either by hesitation or by preparations postponed. When the enemy were first discovered, two ships, the " Alexander " and " Swiftsure," were a dozen miles to leeward, having been sent ahead on frigates' duty to reconnoitre Alexandria. This circumstance prevented their joining till after the battle began and night had fallen. At the same moment the " Culloden " was seven miles to windward. She was signalled to drop the prize she was towing, and to join the fleet. To this separation was due that she went aground. The remaining ten ships, which had been steering about east, hauled sharp on the wind to enable them to weather with ample allowance the shoal off Aboukir Island. It was blowing a whole-sail breeze, too fresh for the lighter canvas; the royals were furled as soon as close-hauled. As the French situation and dispositions developed to the view, signals were made to prepare for battle, to get ready to anchor by the stern, and that it was the admiral's intention to attack the van and centre of the enemy. The captains had long been forewarned of each of these possibilities, and nothing more was needed to convey to them his general plan, which was intrusted to them individually to carry out as they successively came into action.

At about half-past five signal was given to form line of battle. This, for the ships of the day, was a single column, in which they were ranged ahead and astern of each other, leaving the broadside clear. As they came abreast the shoal, Nelson hailed Captain Hood, of the " Zealous," and asked if he thought they were yet far enough to the eastward to clear it, if they then headed for the enemy. Hood replied that he did not know the ground, but was in eleven fathoms, and would, if the admiral allowed, bear up and sound with the lead, and would not bring the fleet into danger. This was done, Hood leading all the fleet except the " Goliath," Captain Foley, which kept ahead, on the lee bow of the " Zealous." No close shaving was done, however, at this critical turn; and it is that steady deliberation, combined with such parsimony of time in other moments, which is most impressive in Nelson. So few realize that five minutes are at once the most

important and the least important of considerations. Thus
the British passed so much beyond the island and the shoal,
before keeping away, that, as the long column swept round to
head for the French van, the ships turned their port broadsides to the enemy, and were steering southwesterly when
they finally ran down. "The English admiral," wrote the
French second in command, "without doubt had experienced
pilots on board; he hauled well round all dangers."

The "Goliath" still leading the fleet, followed closely by
the "Zealous," the flagship was dropped to sixth in the order,
—Nelson thus placing himself so that he could see what the
first five ships accomplished, while retaining in his own hands
the power to impart a new direction to the remaining five of
those then with him, should he think it necessary. Captain
Foley had formed the idea that the French would be less
ready to fight on the inshore side, and had expressed his intention to get inside them, if practicable. Sounding as he
went, he passed round the bows of the leading vessel, the
"Guerrier," on the inner bow of which he intended to place
himself; but the anchor hung, and the "Goliath" brought up
on the inner quarter of the "Conquérant," the second ship.
The "Zealous," following, anchored where Foley had purposed, on the bow of the "Guerrier;" and the next three
ships, the "Orion," "Theseus," and "Audacious," also placed
themselves on the inner side of the French line.

The two leading French vessels were at once crushed. All
the masts of the "Guerrier," although no sail was on them,
went overboard within ten minutes after she was first attacked,
while the "Conquérant" was receiving the united broadsides
of the "Goliath" and the "Audacious," —the latter raking.
Nelson therefore placed the "Vanguard" on the outer side,
and within pistol-shot, of the third French ship, the "Spartiate,"
which was already engaged on the other side by the "Theseus,"
but at much longer range. His example was of course followed
by those succeeding him—the seventh and eighth of the
British engaging the fourth and fifth of the French, which were
already receiving part of the fire of the "Orion" and "Theseus"
on the inner side —the latter having ceased to play upon the
"Spartiate" for fear of hitting the "Vanguard." Thus five
French ships were within half an hour in desperate conflict

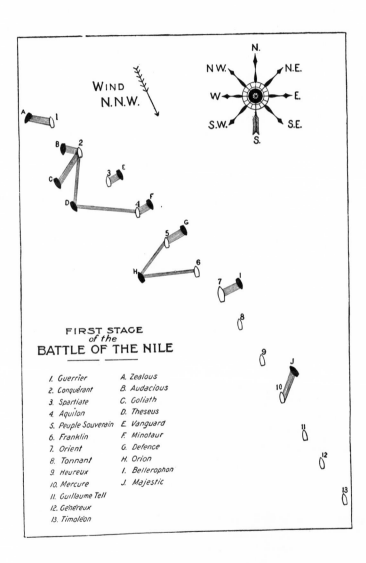

WIND
N.N.W.

FIRST STAGE
of the
BATTLE OF THE NILE

1. Guerrier
2. Conquérant
3. Spartiate
4. Aquilon
5. Peuple Souverain
6. Franklin
7. Orient
8. Tonnant
9. Heureux
10. Mercure
11. Guillaume Tell
12. Généreux
13. Timoléon

A. Zealous
B. Audacious
C. Goliath
D. Theseus
E. Vanguard
F. Minotaur
G. Defence
H. Orion
I. Bellerophon
J. Majestic

with eight British, while their consorts to leeward looked helplessly on.

The ninth and tenth of Nelson's fleet were less fortunate, owing to the envelope of smoke and the growing darkness, which now obscured the scene. The "Bellerophon," missing the sixth French vessel, the "Franklin," brought up abreast the "Orient," whose force was double her own, and which had no other antagonist. The "Majestic," groping her way, ran into the ninth French, the "Heureux," where for some moments she hung in a position of disadvantage and had her captain killed. Then swinging clear, she anchored on the bow of the next astern, the "Mercure," and there continued a deadly and solitary action. Owing to the circumstances mentioned, the loss of each of these ships was greater, by fifty per cent, than that of any other of the British fleet. The movements so far described, and the resultant fighting, may be styled the first stage of the battle. Concerning it may be remarked the unswerving steadiness, rapidity, and yet sound judgment, with which all the movements were executed; and further, that not only was the first direction of the attack that prescribed by Nelson's signal, but that the second, initiated by his own ship, was also imparted by him. The incident of passing round the "Guerrier," and inside of the line, is a detail only, although one which cannot be too highly praised. "The van ship of the enemy being in five fathom," wrote Captain Hood, "I expected the Goliath and Zealous to stick fast on the shoal every moment, and did not imagine we should attempt to pass within her." It is difficult to exaggerate the coolness, intrepidity, and seamanlike care of Captain Foley, to whom is to be attributed, perhaps, the whole conception, and certainly the entire merit of the execution; but they no more detract from Nelson's honors than does the distinguished conduct of the other captains.

The battle had begun a little after half-past six, the "Guerrier's" masts falling at sundown, which was quarter before seven. It continued under the conditions already given until past eight o'clock — none of the ships engaged shifting her position for some time after that hour. It was, apparently, just before the second act of the drama opened with the arrival of the remaining ships — the "Alexander," "Swift-

sure," and "Leander" — that Nelson was severely wounded;
but the precise moment has not been recorded. He was struck
upon the upper part of the forehead by a flying piece of iron,
the skin, which was cut at right angles, hanging down over
his face, covering the one good eye, and, with the profuse flow
of blood, blinding him completely. He exclaimed, "I am
killed! Remember me to my wife!" and was falling, but
Captain Berry, who stood near, caught him in his arms.
When carried below to the cockpit, the surgeon went immediately to him, but he refused to be attended before his turn
arrived, in due succession to the injured lying around him.

The pain was intense, and Nelson felt convinced that his
hurt was mortal; nor could he for some time accept the surgeon's assurances to the contrary. Thus looking for his end,
he renewed his farewell messages to Lady Nelson, and
directed also that Captain Louis of the "Minotaur," which lay
immediately ahead of the "Vanguard," should be hailed to
come on board, that before dying he might express to him his
sense of the admirable support given by her to the flagship.
"Your support," said he, "has prevented me from being
obliged to haul out of the line." [1] From the remark it may
be inferred that the French "Aquilon," their fourth ship,
which became the "Minotaur's" antagonist, had for a measurable time been able to combine her batteries with those of the
"Spartiate" upon the "Vanguard," and to this was probably
due that the loss of the latter was next in severity to that of
the "Majestic" and of the "Bellerophon." The inference is
further supported by the fact that the worst slaughter in the
"Vanguard" was at the forward guns, those nearest the
"Aquilon."

After his wound was bound up, Nelson was requested by
the surgeon to lie quiet; but his preoccupation with the events
of the evening was too great, and his responsibility too immediate, to find relief in inactivity, — the physician's panacea.
He remained below for a while, probably too much jarred for
physical exertion; but his restlessness sought vent by beginning a despatch to the Admiralty. The secretary being too
agitated to write, Nelson tried to do so himself, and it was
characteristic that the few lines he was then able to trace,

[1] G. Lathom Browne's Life of Nelson, p. 198.

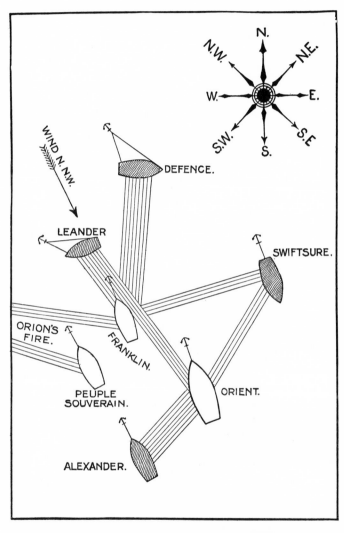

N.

N.W.   N.E.

W.   E.

S.W.   S.E.

S.

WIND N.N.W.

DEFENCE.

LEANDER

SWIFTSURE.

ORION'S FIRE.

FRANKLIN.

PEUPLE SOUVERAIN.

ORIENT.

ALEXANDER.

SECOND STAGE OF THE BATTLE OF THE NILE.
CONCENTRATION OF BRITISH RESERVE ON THE FRENCH CENTRE.

blinded, suffering, and confused, expressed that dependence upon the Almighty, habitual with him, which illustrated a temperament of so much native energy and self-reliance, and is more common, probably, among great warriors than in any other class of men of action. This first outburst of emotion, excited in him by the tremendous event wrought by his hands, was identical in spirit, and not improbably was clothed in the same words, as those with which began the despatch actually sent: "Almighty God has blessed His Majesty's arms."

While Nelson lay thus momentarily disabled, important events were transpiring, over which, however, he could have exerted no control. It has been mentioned that the "Culloden" was seven miles to the northward and westward of the fleet, when the French were first discovered. Doing her best, it was impossible to reach the main body before it stood down into action, and the day had closed when the ship neared the shoal. Keeping the lead going, and proceeding with caution, though not with the extreme care which led Hood and Nelson to make so wide a sweep, Troubridge had the mishap to strike on the tail of the shoal, and there the ship stuck fast, pounding heavily until the next morning. The fifty-gun ship "Leander" went to her assistance, as did the brig "Mutine," but all efforts to float her proved vain. Meanwhile the "Alexander" and "Swiftsure" were coming up from the southwest, the wind being so scant that they could barely pass to windward of the reef, along whose northwestern edge they were standing. The "Alexander," in fact, was warned by the lead that she was running into danger, and had to tack. As they approached, Troubridge, by lantern and signal, warned them off the spot of his disaster, thus contributing to save these ships, and, by removing doubt, accelerating their entrance into action. As they rounded the stranded "Culloden," the "Leander" was also dismissed from a hopeless task, and followed them to the scene of battle.

The delay of the two seventy-fours, though purely fortuitous, worked in furtherance of Nelson's plan, and resulted, practically, in constituting them a reserve, which was brought into play at a most auspicious moment. The "Bellerophon," crushed by the preponderating weight of the "Orient's"

battery, had just cut her cable and worn out of action, with
the loss of forty-nine killed and one hundred and forty-eight
wounded, out of a total of five hundred and ninety men. Her
foremast alone was then standing, and it fell immediately
after. The firing, which had been animated from the French
left ‚towards the centre, now slackened around the latter, at
the point where the "Orient" and her next ahead, the
"Franklin," were lying. For this spot, therefore, the captains of the two fresh British ships steered. The "Swiftsure,"
Captain Hallowell, anchored outside the enemy's line, abreast
the interval separating the "Orient" and the "Franklin,"
between which he divided his fire. The "Alexander," Captain Ball, passed through the line, astern of the "Orient,"
and anchored close on her inner quarter. Just at this time
a shot cut the cable of the "Peuple Souverain," next ahead
of the "Franklin," and she drifted out of her place to abreast
the latter ship, ahead of which a wide gap of a thousand feet
was thus left. Into this the "Leander" glided, fixing herself
with great skill to rake at once the "Franklin" and the
"Orient."

These two French ships had already been much battered,
and the "Franklin" was still receiving part of the fire of the
"Orion," Sir James Saumarez, on her inner bow, as well as
that of the "Defence," hitherto engaged by the "Peuple
Souverain." This accumulation upon them of three fresh
ships would doubtless have proved irresistible, even if a yet
more dire calamity had not supervened. The new-comers
took their positions soon after eight, and a little before nine
a fire was observed on the poop of the "Orient." The British captains, seeing the flames fighting on their behalf, redoubled their efforts, directing their aim especially upon the
scene of the conflagration, and thereby thwarting all attempt
to extinguish it. The blaze spread rapidly, upward through
the tarred rigging and the masts, downward to the lower
decks, where her heroic crew, still ignorant of the approaching doom, labored incessantly at their guns. As the sublime
sight forced itself upon the eyes of all about, friends and
enemies alike busied themselves with precautions for their
own safety in the coming catastrophe. The ships to windward held on; those to leeward for the most part veered or

slipped their cables, the "Alexander" fiercely refusing to do so till assured that the "Orient's" destruction was inevitable. Captain Berry went below to report to the admiral this appalling climax to the night's work, and to his own long-sustained efforts in chase and battle. Nelson demanded to be led on deck, where he gave orders that the only boat still in condition for use should be sent with the "Vanguard's" first lieutenant, to help save the unhappy crew. He then remained watching the progress of the fire. At quarter before ten the "Orient" blew up. At this time the moon rose, and from her tranquil path looked down, through the clear Egyptian air, upon the scene of devastation.

Nelson was now persuaded to go to bed, but he neither got nor sought repose of mind. Throughout the night, and in the early morning, messages went from him to various ships to take this or that step, to garner in the fruits of the victory yet unculled. The fleet responded somewhat spasmodically, if not inadequately, to these calls. Men in truth were worn out with labor and excitement. "My people were so extremely jaded," wrote Captain Miller of the "Theseus," who obeyed a summons to move, "that as soon as they had hove our sheet anchor up they dropped under the capstan bars, and were asleep in a moment in every sort of posture, having been then working at their fullest exertion, or fighting, for near twelve hours." Nelson, in common with other great leaders, could not be satisfied with any but the utmost results. To quote again his words of years gone by: "Had ten ships been taken and the eleventh escaped, we being able to get at her, I should never consider it well done." His idea, Captain Berry tells us, was first to secure the victory, and then to make the most of it, as circumstances might permit. The expression is so luminous that it can scarcely be doubted that the words are substantially those of the admiral himself.[1]

[1] An interesting example of the illuminating effect of a sound maxim upon different phases of a man's life and actions, and one illustrative of the many-sidedness of this motto of Nelson's, occurs later in his career, and not long before his death. When the frigates "Phœbe" and "Amazon" were ordered to cruise before Toulon in October, 1804, "Lord Nelson gave Captains Capel and Parker several injunctions, in case they should get an opportunity of attacking two of the French frigates, which now got under way more frequently. The principal one was, that they should not each single out and

First, the great combination, which necessarily for the moment neglects a part of the enemy in order to disconcert and overwhelm the rest; afterwards, the unremitting pursuit, which completes the triumph.

It was therefore perfectly characteristic of Nelson's habit of thought, and not merely an egotistic expression of baseless discontent with others, that he avowed his dissatisfaction with the results of the night's work, stupendous and wholly unparalleled as they were. But his own condition, prostrated and with disabled head, was doubly typical of the state of his fleet after the "Orient" blew up. Not only were men overcome with fatigue, — from weariness as great men have been aroused by the inspiring call of a trusted chief, — but the guiding head of the body was dazed and incapacitated; that was gone which alone could sustain energy and give unity to movement. Although Nelson indulged in no metaphorical allusions, he had this figure of the head clearly enough in his mind, when he wrote four weeks later to Lord Minto: "I regret that one escaped, and I think, if it had pleased God that I had not been wounded, not a boat would have escaped to have told the tale; but do not believe that any individual in the fleet is to blame. In my conscience, I believe greater exertions could not have been, and I only mean to say, that if my experience could in person have *directed* [1] those exertions of individuals, there was every appearance that Almighty God would have continued to bless my endeavours." This opinion he reiterated to Lord Howe, even more positively, after four months' longer reflection, in a letter dated January 8, 1799; and, whether the result would or would not have equalled his belief, the traces are clear that what was wanted, during the remainder of that eventful night, was just that concord of action which the head imparts to the members. Messages went from ship to ship, captains consulted together and proposed to move to-

attack an opponent, but 'that both should endeavour together to take one frigate; if successful, chase the other; but if you do not take the second, still you have won a victory, and your country will gain a frigate.'" (Phillimore's Last of Nelson's Captains, p. 122.) When summarized, this again is — Victory first; afterwards the results, as circumstances may permit.

[1] Author's italics.

gether, and did move separately; there was no lack of good-will, nor, as Nelson says, of exertion; but men were not quite sure of what the other man would do, and felt no authority to command him; and there was hesitation over risks, and cautious delays about soundings and shaky spars, which, the author is persuaded, would not have deterred Nelson in such conditions, where victory was decisive, though not yet complete. Illustrations would perhaps be invidious, as seeming to imply a blame upon individuals which Nelson expressly disavowed; blame that officers of exceptional professional capacity, concerning whom the measured professional opinion of Lord Howe affirmed that the Battle of the Nile "was unparalleled in this respect, that *every captain* distinguished himself," fell short of the peculiar excellence attained by Nelson only among the men of his day. Moreover, this work does not aim at a discussion of battles, except so far as they touch Nelson personally. It may, however, be permissible to remark, that the incident here under discussion suggests a doubt about the opinion, too easily current, that an admiral's powers of control cease when the battle joins. Under the circumstances, it is probable that Nelson, being so far incapacitated as he thought himself, should have transferred the direction of affairs, formally, to the next senior officer, with general orders to secure the best results attainable.

The following morning it was found that the leading six ships of the French had already struck their colors. The "Orient" having blown up, there were six survivors. Of these, one, the "Tonnant," next astern of the "Orient," though dismasted, was still afloat, a mile behind her former position, having dropped there to avoid the explosion. The "Heureux" and "Mercure," which had slipped their cables for the same reason, were ashore and helpless. The spars of the three rear ships, the "Guillaume Tell," "Généreux," and "Timoléon," were still standing, and they had received little injury. At about noon, these vessels, commanded by Rear Admiral Villeneuve, got under way to go to sea; but the "Timoléon" cast with her head inshore, and, after an ineffectual attempt to wear, ran aground, bows on, her foremast going over the side as she struck. The crew escaped to the beach, and she was then set on fire by her captain, her colors flying as she burned. The two other ships escaped, with two frigates which accompanied them. Only one British ship, the "Zealous," was in condition to follow, and she did so; but Nelson, seeing that she could not be supported, recalled her from the unequal contest.

It is upon the chance that these sole survivors of the great catastrophe might have been secured, by action during the night, that the validity of Nelson's regrets turns. Concerning this, it is impossible to affirm positively one way or the other; therefore his regrets were well grounded. It is not certainties, but chances, that determine the propriety of military action. Had Villeneuve, conscious that he had done nothing as yet, and not fully aware how the fight had gone, hesitated about running away, and had several British ships dropped to leeward together, which was all they had to do, and what the dismasted French had done, it was quite within the bound of possibilities that the "Généreux" and the "Guillaume Tell" would have been crippled at their anchors. "If" and "but," it may be objected. Quite so; it is on if and but, not on yea and nay, that military criticism justly dwells. A flash of lightning and a crash of thunder may be seen and heard; it is the still small voice that leads the hero to success. As regards Villeneuve, indecision was his distinguishing trait; and Bonaparte wrote that if any error could be imputed to him, it was that he had not got under way as soon as the "Orient" blew up, for by that time the battle was lost beyond redemption.

The extent of the victory was decided by this retreat, and Nelson, before devoting himself to the new duties entailed by his successes, paused an instant that he might first acknowledge his debt of gratitude to God and man. A memorandum was issued at once to the captains of the Squadron: —

Vanguard off the mouth of the Nile, 2d August, 1798.

Almighty God having blessed His Majesty's arms with victory, the Admiral intends returning Public Thanksgiving for the same at two o'clock this day; and he recommends every ship doing the same as soon as convenient.

HORATIO NELSON.

To those under his command he at the same time issued a general order, congratulating, by explicit mention of each class, the captains, officers, seamen, and marines, upon the event of the conflict. "The Admiral desires they will accept his most sincere and cordial thanks for their very gallant behaviour in this glorious battle." It was this habit of associating to himself, in full recognition and grateful remembrance, those who followed and fought with him, that enthroned Nelson in the affections of his men; nor will it escape observation that the warmth, though so genuine, breathes through words whose quietness might be thought studied, were they not so transparently spontaneous. There is in them no appeal to egotism, to the gratified passion for glory, although to that he was far from insensible; it is the simple speech of man to man, between those who have stood by one another in the hour of danger, and done their duty — the acknowledgment after the event, which is the complement of the famous signal before Trafalgar.

The order closed with further words of commendation, which will not have the immortal response of the human heart to the other phrases; but which, uttered at such a moment, conveyed a salutary warning, justified as much by recent unhappy events in the British navy, as by the well-known disorganization and anarchy that had disgraced that of France. "It must strike forcibly every British seaman, how superior their conduct is, *when in discipline and good order,* to the riotous behaviour of lawless Frenchmen."[1] Captain Berry states that the assembling of the "Vanguard's" ship's company for the thanksgiving service strongly impressed the prisoners on board, — not from the religious point of view, which was alien from the then prevalent French temper, — but as evidence of an order and discipline which could render such a proceeding acceptable, after a victory so great, and at a moment of such seeming confusion. No small amount of self-possession, indeed, was needed thus to direct the attention of six hundred men, in the confined space of a ship, whose shattered sides and blood-stained decks bore witness to the hundred dead and wounded snatched from their number within the few hours before; yet, on the other hand, nothing

---

[1] Author's italics.

could have been better calculated to compose the thoughts, or
to facilitate the transition from the excitement of battle to
the resumption of daily life.

If, by the escape of two ships-of-the-line, the British triumph
lacked something in technical completeness, the disaster to the
French was no less absolute. Victory, said Nelson truly, is
not the name for such a scene as I have witnessed. There
remained now to gather up the spoils of the field, and to
realize the consequences of the battle, great and small, near
and remote. The first was speedily done; battered as they
were, " only two masts standing out of nine sail-of-the-line,"
within a fortnight six of the nine prizes were ready to start
for Gibraltar. Little by little, yet with the rapidity of his
now highly trained intuitions, Nelson saw the greatness of
what he had effected, and with his full native energy struggled
on, amid mental confusion and bodily suffering, and in the
heat of an Egyptian August, to secure all the fruits of success.
With splitting head and constantly sick, a significant indication of the rattling shock his brain had received, he was
wonderfully helped, so far as the direction of his efforts was
concerned, by the previous familiarity of his mind with the
various elements of the problem. First of all, the home government must be informed of an event that would so profoundly affect the future. Berry's orders, as bearer of despatches to St. Vincent off Cadiz, were issued on the 2d of
August; but there were no frigates, and the "Leander,"
appointed to carry him, could not sail till the 6th. For the
same reason it was not until the 14th that the "Mutine"
could be sent off with duplicates, to go direct to the Admiralty by way of Naples, — a wise precaution in all events, but
doubly justified in this case; for the brig reached port,
whereas the fifty-gun ship was captured by the " Généreux."
The "Mutine's" account, though hastened forward without
delay, reached London only on the 2d of October, two months
after the action.

The news was received at the first with an applause and a
popular commotion commensurate to its greatness, and promised for the moment to overflow even the barriers of routine in
one of the most conservative of nations. "Mr. Pitt told me the
day after Captain Capel arrived," wrote his old admiral, Hood,

to Nelson, "that you would certainly be a Viscount, which I made known to Lady Nelson. But it was objected to in a certain quarter, because your Lordship was not a commander-in-chief. In my humble opinion a more flimsy reason never was given." Official circles regained, or rather perhaps again lost, their senses, and the victory, unquestionably the most nearly complete and the most decisive ever gained by a British fleet, was rewarded, in the person of the commanding officer, with honors less than those bestowed for St. Vincent and Camperdown. Nelson was advanced to the lowest rank of the peerage, as Baron Nelson of the Nile. "In congratulating your Lordship on this high distinction," wrote the First Lord, " I have particular pleasure in remarking, that it is the highest honour that has ever been conferred on an officer of your standing,[1] in the Service, and who was not a commander-in-chief ; and the addition [of the Nile] to the Title is meant more especially to mark the occasion on which it was granted, which, however, without any such precaution, is certainly of a nature never to be forgotten." His Lordship's sense of humor must a little have failed him, when he penned the platitude of the last few words.

To the sharp criticism passed in the House of Commons on the smallness of the recognition, the Prime Minister replied that Nelson's glory did not depend upon the rank to which he might be raised in the peerage ; a truism too palpable and inapplicable for serious utterance, the question before the House being, not the measure of Nelson's glory, but that of the national acknowledgment. As Hood justly said, " All remunerations should be proportionate to the service done to the public ; " and if that cannot always be attained absolutely, without exhausting the powers of the State,[2] there should at least be some proportion between the rewards themselves, extended to individuals, and the particular services. But even were the defence of the Ministers technically perfect, it would have been pleasanter to see them a little blinded by such an achievement. Once in a way, under some provocations, it is refreshing to see men able even to make fools of themselves.

[1] " Rank " doubtless is meant by this singularly ill-chosen word.

[2] As General Sherman justly asked, " What reward adequate to the service, could the United States have given Grant for the Vicksburg campaign ? "

Nelson made to the First Lord's letter a reply that was dignified and yet measured, to a degree unusual to him, contrasting singularly with his vehement reclamations for others after Copenhagen. Without semblance of complaint, he allowed plainly to appear between the lines his own sense that the reward was not proportionate to the service done. "I have received your Lordship's letter communicating to me the Title his Majesty has been graciously pleased to confer upon me — an Honour, your Lordship is pleased to say, the highest that has ever been conferred on an officer of my standing who was not a Commander-in-Chief. I receive as I ought what the goodness of our Sovereign, and not my deserts, is pleased to bestow; but great and unexampled as this honour may be to one of my standing, yet I own I feel a higher one in the unbounded confidence of the King, your Lordship, and the whole World, in my exertions. Even at the bitter moment of my return to Syracuse, your Lordship is not insensible of the great difficulties I had to encounter in not being a Commander-in-Chief. The only happy moment I felt was in the view of the French; then I knew that all my sufferings would soon be at an end." To Berry he wrote: "As to both our Honours, it is a proof how much a battle fought near England is prized to one fought at a great distance."

Whatever was defective in the formal recognition of his own government was abundantly supplied by the tributes which flowed from other quarters, so various, that his own phrase, "the whole world," is scarcely an exaggeration to apply to them. The Czar, the Sultan, the Kings of Sardinia and of the Two Sicilies, sent messages of congratulation and rich presents; the Czar accompanying his with an autograph letter. The Houses of Parliament voted their thanks and a pension of £2,000 a year. The East India Company acknowledged the security gained for their Indian possessions by a gift of £10,000, £2,000 of which he, with his wonted generosity, divided at once among his father and family, most of whom were not in prosperous circumstances. Other corporations took appropriate notice of the great event; instances so far apart as the cities of London and Palermo, and the Island of Zante, showing how wide-spread was the sense of relief. Not least gratifying to him, with his sensitive appreciation of friendship and susceptibility to flattery, must have been the numerous letters of congratulation he received from friends in and out of the service. The three great admirals, — Lords Howe, Hood, and St. Vincent, — the leaders of the Navy in rank and distinguished service, wrote to him in the strongest terms of admiration. The two last styled the battle the greatest achievement that History could produce; while Howe's language, if more measured, was so only because, like himself, it was more precise in characterizing the special merits of the action, and was therefore acknowledged by Nelson with particular expressions of pleasure.

Besides the honors bestowed upon the commander of the squadron, and the comprehensive vote of thanks usual on such occasions, a gold medal commemorative of the battle was given to the admiral and to each of the captains present. The First Lord also wrote that the first-lieutenants of the ships engaged would be promoted at once. The word " engaged " caught Nelson's attention, as apparently intended to exclude the lieutenant of the " Culloden," Troubridge's unlucky ship. " For Heaven's sake, for my sake," he wrote to St. Vincent, " if this is so, get it altered. Our dear friend Troubridge has suffered enough. His sufferings were in every respect more than any of us. He deserves every reward which a grateful Country can bestow on the most meritorious sea-officer of his standing in the service. I have felt his worth every hour of my command." " I well know, he is my superior," he said on another occasion; "and I so often want his advice and assistance. I have experienced the ability and activity of his mind and body : it was Troubridge that equipped the squadron so soon at Syracuse — it was he that exerted himself for me after the action — it was Troubridge who saved the Culloden, when none that I know in the service would have attempted it — it was Troubridge whom I left as myself at Naples to watch movements — he is, as a friend and an officer, a *nonpareil !* " His entreaties prevailed so far that the officer in question received his promotion, not with the others, but immediately after them ; a distinction which Troubridge bewailed bitterly, as a reflection upon himself and his ship.

On the 9th of August Nelson sent a lieutenant to Alexandretta, on the northern coast of Syria, to make his way overland, by way of Aleppo, to India, with despatches to the Governor of Bombay. Resuming briefly the events of the past months, and the numbers and character of the French army in Egypt, he expresses the hope that special care will be exercised against the departure of ships from India, to convey this huge force thither by the Red Sea. On the side of the Mediterranean, their fate is settled by the recent victory. They can receive nothing from France; they cannot advance freely into Syria, as water transport is essential for much of their equipment; even in Egypt itself they are hampered by the difficulties of communication — on land by the guerilla hostility of the natives, and now on the water through his own presence and control. The Nile, through its Rosetta mouth, had been heretofore the easiest communication between Cairo and Alexandria. The garrison of the latter depended largely for daily bread upon this route, now closed by the fleet in Aboukir Bay. By land, nothing short of a regiment could pass over ground where, even before the battle, the French watering-parties from the ships had to be protected by heavy armed bodies. He intended, therefore, to remain where he was as long as possible. "If my letter is not so correct as might be expected," he concludes, "I trust for your excuse, when I tell you that my brain is so shook with the wounds in my head, that I am sensible I am not always so clear as could be wished; but whilst a ray of reason remains, my heart and my head shall ever be exerted for the benefit of our King and Country."

It may be added here, that the scar left by this wound seems to have been the cause of Nelson's hair being trained down upon his forehead, during the later years of his life. Prior to that it was brushed well off and up, as may be seen in the portrait by Abbott, painted during his stay in England, while recovering from the loss of his arm. After his death, a young officer of the "Victory," who had cut off some locks for those who wished such a remembrance of their friend, speaks of "the hair that used to hang over his forehead, near the wound that he received at the Battle of the Nile."

The perception of his control over the communications from Rosetta to Alexandria dawned rather late upon Nelson, for on the 5th of August he had announced his purpose of starting down the Mediterranean on the 19th. This he postponed afterwards to the first part of September, and again for as long as possible. While in this intention, most secret and urgent orders came on the 15th from St. Vincent, to return to the westward with his command, and to co-operate with an expedition planned against Minorca. Six prizes, with seven of the British ships-of-the-line, had started on the 14th for Gibraltar, under the command of Sir James Saumarez. The three remaining prizes were burned, and hasty temporary repairs, adequate only for a summer voyage, were put upon the "Vanguard," "Culloden," and "Alexander," the three most defective ships of his fleet. On the 19th he sailed with these three for Naples, which he had from the first intended to visit, in order to give them the complete overhauling they imperatively needed. On and after the 13th of August several frigates had joined him. Three of these, with three ships-of-the-line, were left with Captain Hood, to conduct the blockade of Alexandria, and to suppress the enemy's communications by water along the coasts of Egypt and Syria.

CHAPTER XI.

SEPTEMBER–DECEMBER, 1798. AGE, 40.

THE voyage of Nelson's small division from Aboukir Bay to Naples occupied between four and five weeks, owing partly to light and contrary winds, and partly to the dull sailing of the "Culloden," which had a sail secured under her bottom to lessen the dangerous leak caused by her grounding on the night of the battle. This otherwise unwelcome delay procured for Nelson a period of salutary, though enforced, repose, which the nature of his injuries made especially desirable. His mind, indeed, did not cease to work, but it was free from harassment; and the obvious impossibility of doing anything, save accept the present easy-going situation, contributed strongly to the quietness upon which restoration depended. Nor were there wanting matters of daily interest to prevent an excess of monotony. Now that frigates were no longer so vitally necessary, they and other light cruisers turned up with amusing frequency, bringing information, and being again despatched hither and yonder with letters from the admiral, which reflected instinctively his personal moods, and his active concern in the future military operations.

The distress from his head continued for some time with little abatement, and naturally much affected his tone of mind. At the first he spoke of his speedy return to England as inevitable, nor did the prospect occasion the discouragement which he had experienced after the loss of his arm; a symptom which had shown the moral effect of failure upon a sensitive and ambitious temperament. "My head is ready to split," he had written to St. Vincent before starting, "and I am always so sick; in short, if there be no fracture, my head is severely shaken." A fortnight after leaving the bay, he writes him again: "I know I ought to give up for a little while; my head is splitting at this moment;" and Nicolas remarks that the letter bears evident marks of suffering, three attempts being made to spell the word "splitting." Yet by this time the pain had become at least intermittent, for Saumarez, whose squadron fell in with the admiral's division several times, notes that on the 26th of August he spent half an hour on board the flagship, and found him in perfect health; and on the 7th of September Nelson himself writes to the British minister at Florence that he felt so much recovered, it was probable he would not go home for the present. A few days later he wrote to Hood, off Alexandria, that he relied upon the thoroughness of the blockade to complete the destruction of the French army. "I shall not go home," he added, "until this is effected, and the islands of Malta, Corfu, &c., retaken."

It is to the furtherance of these objects, all closely allied, and in his apprehension mutually dependent, that his occasional letters are directed. His sphere of operations he plainly conceives to be from Malta, eastward, to Syria inclusive. "I detest this voyage to Naples," he wrote to St. Vincent, two days before reaching the port. "Nothing but absolute necessity could force me to the measure. Syracuse in future, whilst my operations lie on the eastern side of Sicily, is my port, where every refreshment may be had for a fleet." The present necessity was that of refit and repair, to which Syracuse was inadequate. "For myself," he sent word to Sir William Hamilton, "I hope not to be more than four or five days at Naples, for these times are not for idleness." He is urgent that Naples should now actively support the operations against Malta, and shell the transports in Alexandria. "Naples has evidently broken her treaty with France, and yet is afraid to assist in finishing the vast armament of the French. Four hours with bomb-vessels would set all in a blaze, and we know what an army is without stores." To the British minister in Turkey he is similarly insistent. If the Sultan will but send a few ships-of-the-line, and some bombs, he can destroy all the transports in Alexandria; and an army of ten thousand men may retake the place immediately, for the French have in it only four thousand. The need to do this is urgent, for, by the information of French prisoners, Bonaparte only wanted " communication opened by sea to march into Syria, that the transports," — which Nelson proposes to burn, — " with stores for the army, may go alongshore with him."

The same tendency was shown upon the appearance of a Portuguese squadron of four ships-of-the-line, which entered the Mediterranean in July with orders to place themselves under his command. He first learned the fact upon this passage, and at once sent a frigate to Alexandria to beg the Portuguese admiral, the Marquis de Niza, to assume the blockade, as the most important service to be rendered the common cause. When the frigate reached its destination, Niza had come and gone, and Nelson then headed him off at the Strait of Messina, on his way to Naples, and sent him to blockade Malta. It may be added that this squadron remained under his command until December, 1799, and was of substantial utility in the various operations. Nelson professed no great confidence in its efficiency, which was not subjected to the severest tests; but he made a handsome acknowledgment to its commander when it was recalled to Lisbon.

Three weeks after reaching Naples his decision as to the direction of his personal oversight underwent a change, due to a series of events for the initiation of which, by plunging Naples prematurely into war with France, he was himself largely responsible. From the time that ill-considered movement began, under the combined impetus of the Queen and of Lady Hamilton, for both whom he expressed at this time unbounded chivalrous devotion, Nelson felt tied, not merely to the Kingdom of the Two Sicilies, but to the personal protection of its Sovereigns as well. It is true, certainly, that orders from the Admiralty, dated October 3d, immediately after receiving news of the Battle of the Nile, named first among his duties "the protection of the coasts of Sicily, Naples, and the Adriatic, and, in the event of the war being renewed in Italy, an active co-operation with the Austrian and Neapolitan armies;" but long before receiving these, acknowledged by him on the 18th of November, he had induced the hesitating King to precipitate war by advancing against the French army in the Roman States, and had abandoned his purpose of going to Egypt. On October 22d he wrote St. Vincent, "The King having desired my return to Naples in the first week in November, I shall, after having arranged the blockade of Malta, return to Naples, and endeavour to be useful in the movements of their army. In thus acquiescing in the desire of the King of Naples, I give up my plan, which was to have gone to Egypt and attended to the destruction of the French shipping in that quarter." "I do not like going back from the Eastward," he writes two days later, " but I give up my own opinion for this time, as it is impossible to foresee how this new war may turn out." These expressions, repeated to others, show the anxiety of his mind acting against his judgment. " I feel my duty at present is in the East," he tells Lady Hamilton herself ; but devotion to the Court gains upon him until, from the expression " who could resist such a Queen ? " written in Naples in November, he in February, at Palermo, commits himself unreservedly to personal attention to the safety of the sovereigns. "I have promised my flag shall not go out of the mole at Palermo without the approbation of the Court, and that I never expect to get."

On the 22d of September the flagship anchored at Naples. On the 15th her foremast had been carried away in a squall, and the " poor wretched Vanguard," as Nelson called her, having to be towed by a frigate, her two crippled consorts preceded her arrival by six days. The news of the victory had been brought three weeks before by the " Mutine," on the 1st of September. The Court party had gone wild with joy, in which the populace, naturally hostile to the French, had joined with southern vivacity of expression. Captain Capel, who commanded the brig, with Lieutenant Hoste, who was to succeed him when he departed with the despatches for England, had been at once taken to Court and presented. When they left the palace they were met by Lady Hamilton, who made them get into her carriage, and with characteristic bad taste and love of notoriety paraded them until dark through the streets of this neutral capital, she wearing a bandeau round her forehead with the words, " Nelson and Victory." " The populace saw and understood what it meant,"

wrote Hoste, "and 'Viva Nelson!' resounded through the
streets. You can have no idea of the rejoicings that were
made throughout Naples. Bonfires and illuminations all over
the town; indeed, it would require an abler pen than I am
master of to give you any account but what will fall infinitely
short of what was the case."

By Nelson's orders the "Mutine" sailed in a few days to
meet him with despatches, and on the 14th of September
joined the division off Stromboli. With more important information, and letters from persons of greater consequence,
she had brought also one from Lady Hamilton, giving a vivid
picture of the general joy, and in particular an account of the
Queen's state of mind, so highly colored that Nelson hoped he
might not witness a renewal of it. When the "Vanguard"
approached the town, crowds of boats went out to meet her.
The King himself came on board when she was still a league
from the anchorage. He had been preceded by Sir William
and Lady Hamilton. The latter, greatly overcome, dropped
her lovely face and by no means slender figure into the arms
of the admiral, who, on his part, could scarcely fail to be
struck with the pose of one whose attitudes compelled the
admiration of the most exacting critics. The emotion stirred
by the warmth of his welcomes, on this and the following
days, showed itself in phrases of unusual tenderness to his
wife. "If so affecting to those who were only united to me
by bonds of friendship, what must it be to my dearest wife,
my friend, my everything which is most dear to me in this
world?" "The scene in the boat was terribly affecting. Up
flew her ladyship, and exclaiming, 'O God, is it possible?'
she fell into my arm more dead than alive. Tears, however,
soon set matters to rights."

This was the beginning of an intimacy destined, in the end,
to affect profoundly and unhappily the future of Nelson.
Although Sir William Hamilton, in his own congratulatory
letter by the "Mutine," called him "our bosom friend," they
do not seem to have met since the summer of 1793, when the
young captain carried Hood's despatches from Toulon to
Naples; and Nelson, while acknowledging on the present
occasion the kindness of an invitation to take up his quarters
at the embassy, had expressed a preference for rooms at a

EMMA, LADY HAMILTON.

After a painting by G. Romney.

hotel, on account of the business to be transacted. This reluctance, however, was easily and properly overruled, and immediately after anchoring he went to live at the ambassador's house, which, under the management of the celebrated woman who presided there, became the social centre of the welcomes lavished not only upon himself, but upon all the officers of the ships.

Emma, Lady Hamilton, the second wife of Sir William, was at this time thirty-three years old, her husband being sixty-eight. Her name, when first entering the world, was Amy Lyon. Born in Cheshire of extremely poor parents, in the humblest walk of life, she had found her way up to London, while yet little more than a child, and there, having a beautiful face, much natural charm of manner and disposition, utterly inexperienced, and with scarcely any moral standards, — of which her life throughout shows but little trace, — she was speedily ruined, fell so far, in fact, that even with all her attractions it seemed doubtful whether any man would own himself responsible for her condition, or befriend her. In these circumstances, when not yet seventeen, she was taken up by a nephew of Sir William Hamilton, Mr. Charles Greville, who recognized not merely her superficial loveliness, but something of the mental and moral traits underlying it, which promised a capacity for development into an interesting and affectionate household companion. Upon her promises of amendment, in the matter of future relations with men, and of submission to his guidance and wishes in the general conduct of her life, he took her in charge, and the two lived together for nearly four years.

Greville bestowed a good deal of pains upon her training, and was rewarded, not only by gratitude and careful compliance with his directions, but by her sincere and devoted affection. The girl became heartily and fondly in love with him, finding both contentment and happiness in the simply ordered home provided for her. Her education, which hitherto was of the smallest, received attention, — her letters showing a very great improvement both in spelling and mode of expression by the end of their association. On the moral side, of course, there was not much development to be expected from one whose standards, with less excuse, were in no way better than

her own. On this side Greville's teaching was purely utili-
tarian. Her position was considered as a calling, — success in
which demanded certain proprieties and accomplishments,
only to be attained by the practice of habitual self-control,
alike in doing and in not doing.

The future Lady Hamilton was affectionate and impulsive,
good-humored, with generous instincts and a quick temper;
but she was also ambitious and exceptionally clever. She
loved Greville warmly; but she took to heart the hard truths
of his teachings, and they sank deep in a congenial soil.
Under the influence of the two motives, she applied herself to
gain, and did gain, a certain degree of external niceness and
self-control. Her affection for Greville made her willing, for
his sake, because he was not rich, to live quietly, to accept
modest surroundings, and to discard whatever was coarse in
associates, or unbecoming in her own person or conduct. He,
while relaxing none of his requirements, repaid her with
courtesy and increasing admiration, than which nothing was
dearer to her; for, if not appreciative of the satisfaction of
self-respect, she was keenly alive to the delights of homage
from others, though extorted by purely adventitious qualities.
Glory was to her more than honor. This love of admiration,
fostered, yet pruned, by Greville's shrewd precepts, was her
dominant trait.   To its gratification her singular personal
advantages contributed, and they were powerfully supported
by an unusual faculty for assuming a part, for entering into
a character and representing its external traits. Thus gifted
by nature, and swayed by vanity, her development was for the
time regulated and chastened by the disinterestedness of her
passion for her lover. Her worst qualities were momentarily
kept in abeyance. Naturally lovable, not only in exterior but
in temperament, she became more and more attractive.
"Consider," wrote Greville, referring to her surroundings
before she passed into his hands, " what a charming creature
she would have been, if she had been blessed with the advantages of an early education, and had not been spoilt by the
indulgence of every caprice."

Unfortunately the restraining influence, probably ephemeral
in any event, was about to be rudely removed, permitting to
flourish in unrestrained vigor the natural tendency to compel

admiration and secure advantage by the spell of physical beauty, and by the exertion of natural aptitudes for pleasing in the only path to success open to her. In 1782 Hamilton's first wife died, and in 1784 he came to England on leave. There he met Amy Lyon, now known as Emma Hart, in the house provided for her by Greville. His admiration of her was extreme, and its tendency was not misunderstood by her. He returned to his post at Naples at the end of the year. In the course of 1785 Greville, who was now in his thirty-sixth year, decided that the condition of his fortune made it imperative for him to marry, and that as a first step thereto he must break with Emma Hart. Hamilton's inclination for her provided a ready means for so doing, so far as the two men were concerned; but her concurrence was not sure. After some correspondence, it was arranged that she should go to Naples in the spring of 1786, to live there under Hamilton's care, with the expectation on her part that Greville would join her a few months later. Placed as she then would be, it was probable that she would eventually accept the offers made her; though it would be less than just to either Greville or Hamilton, to allow the impression that they did not intend to provide sufficiently for her needs, whatever her decision.

In this way she left England in the spring of 1786, reaching Naples on the 26th of April. When the poor girl, after many of her letters to her lover remained unanswered, fully realized that the separation was final, her grief was extreme, and found utterance in words of tenderness and desolation, which, however undisciplined in expression, are marked by genuine pathos. But anger struggled with sorrow for the mastery in her soul. She was too keen-witted not to have had an inkling of the possible outcome of her departure from England, and of the doubtful position she was occupying at Naples; but her wishes had made her willingly deaf to any false ring in the assurances given her by Greville, and she resented not only the abandonment, but the deceit which she, justly or unjustly, conceived to have been practised, while her womanliness revolted from the cold-blooded advice given by him to accept the situation. The conflict was so sharp that for a time both he and Hamilton expected she would return to England; but Greville had not labored in vain at what he was pleased to consider her education. By the end of the year she was addressing Hamilton in words of very fairly assumed affection, but not until she had written to Greville, with a certain haughty desperation, "If you affront me, I will make him marry me." The threat was two-edged, for Hamilton intended Greville to be his heir; but the latter probably gave little heed to a contingency he must have thought very unlikely for a man of fifty-six, who had passed his life in the world, and held Hamilton's public position.

To effect this, however, Emma Hart now bent her personal charms, strong purpose, and the worldly wisdom with which Greville had taught her to assure her hold upon a man. Love, in its unselfishness, passed out of her life with Greville. Other men might find her pliant, pleasing, seductive ; he alone knew her as disinterested. She followed out her design with a patience, astuteness, and consistency which attest the strength of her resolution, and her acute intellectual perception of the advantages at her disposal. Ambition, a natural trait with her, had been trained to self-control, in order to compass a lowly, colorless success. Unlooked-for opportunity now held before her eyes, distant and difficult of attainment, but not impossible, a position of assured safety, luxury, and prominence, which appealed powerfully to the love of pleasure, still dormant, and to the love of conspicuousness, which became the two most noticeable features of her character.

With all her natural advantages, however, the way was hard and long. She had to become indispensable to Hamilton, and at the same time, and by the same methods, an object the more desirable to him because of her evident attractiveness to others. Above all, she had to contend with her own temper, naturally lively and prone to bursts of anger, which the prolonged suspense of the struggle, acting upon a woman's nerves, tended peculiarly to exasperate. Hamilton was of an age when he might be enslaved by fondness, but not constrained by strength of passion to endure indefinitely household tempests, much less to perpetuate them upon himself by lasting bonds. In all this Emma Hart showed herself fully equal to the task. Tenderly affectionate to him, except when carried away by the fits of irritability which both he and Greville had occasion to observe, she complied readily with all his wishes, and followed out with extraordinary assiduity his plans for her improvement in education and in accomplishments. The society which gathered round them was, of course, almost wholly of men, who one and all prostrated themselves before her beauty and cleverness, with the same unanimity of submission as did the officers of Nelson's division after the Battle of the Nile. But, while giving free rein to coquetry, and revelling in admiration, she afforded no ground for scandal to the world, or dissatisfaction to Hamilton. In the attitude of outsiders towards her, he had reason to see only the general testimony to her charms and to his own good fortune. At the end of 1787 he wrote to Greville : " I can assure you her behaviour is such as has acquired her many sensible admirers, and we have a good man society, and all the female nobility, with the queen at their head, show her every distant civility."

Thus she persisted, keeping her beauty, and growing in mental acquirements and accomplishments, but making little apparent headway towards the great object of her ambition. "I fear," wrote Hamilton towards the middle of 1789, when she had been three years with him, "her views are beyond what I can bring myself to execute ; and that when her hopes on that point are over, she will make herself and me unhappy. Hitherto her behaviour is irreproachable, but her temper, as you must know, unequal." He underrated her perseverance, and exaggerated his own strength of reluctance, innate and acquired. Impossible as it would seem, with his antecedents and with hers, his friends and acquaintances became alarmed for the result, and not without cause. "Her influence over him exceeds all belief," wrote a mutual friend to Greville in March, 1791. "His attachment exceeds admiration, it is perfect dotage." Shortly after this letter was written the two went to England, and there they were married on the 6th of September, 1791. By the end of the year they were back in Naples, and did not again leave Italy up to the time of Nelson's arrival in 1798.

Lady Hamilton did not abuse the security of the place she had won with so much pains, nor on the other hand did her ambition and love of prominence permit her to settle down to inert enjoyment of it. The careful self-restraint with which she had observed the proprieties of her former false position facilitated the disappearance of prejudices naturally arising from it. Many English ladies of rank, passing through Naples, visited her, and those who refused to ignore the past of the woman, in the position of the British minister's wife, were by some sharply criticised. "She has had a difficult part to act," wrote Hamilton, six months after their return, "and has succeeded wonderfully, having gained, by having no pretensions, the thorough approbation of all the English ladies. The Queen of Naples was very kind to her on our return, and treats her like any other travelling lady of distinction; in short, we are very comfortably situated here." "We dined yesterday with Sir William and Lady Hamilton," wrote Lady Malmesbury, whose husband was among the most distinguished diplomatists of the day. "She really behaves as well as possible, and quite wonderfully, considering her origin and education."

This last phrase, used at the culmination of Lady Hamilton's good fortune and personal advance, was wholly good-natured; but it sums up the best of the not very good that can be said of her during the height of her prosperity, and in later years. Although, as has been remarked, she did not at this time abuse the security which as a wife she had attained, — for policy too clearly dictated the continuance of her previous circumspection, — the necessity for strenuous watchfulness, exertion, and self-restraint, in order to reach a distant goal, no longer existed; and, although a woman of many amiable and generous impulses, she had not a shred of principle to take the place of the motive of self-interest, which hitherto had been so peremptory in its exactions. What she was in delicacy in 1791, that she remained in 1796, — five years after the disappearance of her social disabilities; a pretty fair proof that what she possessed of it was but skin-deep, the result of a diligent observance of Greville's proprieties, for her personal advantage, not the token of a noble inner spirit struggling from excusable defilement to the light. "She does the honours of the house with great attention and desire to please," wrote Greville's correspondent of 1791, before quoted, "but wants a little refinement of manners, in which, in the course of six years, I wonder she has not made

greater progress." "She is all Nature and yet all Art," said
Sir Gilbert Elliot, in 1796; "that is to say, her manners are
perfectly unpolished, of course very easy, though not with
the ease of good breeding, but of a barmaid; excessively good
humoured, and wishing to please and be admired by all ages
and sorts of persons that come in her way; but besides considerable natural understanding, she has acquired, since her
marriage, some knowledge of history and of the arts, and one
wonders at the application and pains she has taken to make
herself what she is. With men her language and conversation are exaggerations of anything I ever heard anywhere;
and I was wonderfully struck with these inveterate remains
of her origin, though the impression was very much weakened
by seeing the other ladies of Naples." " I thought her a very
handsome, vulgar woman," curtly commented the lieutenant
of a frigate which visited Naples in the summer of 1798,
while hunting for Nelson in the game of cross-purposes that
preceded the Nile.[1] Allowing for difference of observers, it
is plain that the Lady Hamilton whom Nelson now met, had
not improved in essentials over the Emma Hart of a half-
dozen years before.

Two years afterwards, the verdict of these men was confirmed by Mrs. St. George,[2] a lady in London society, who
viewed her possibly with something of the repugnant prejudice of a refined and cultivated woman, yet evidently measured
her words calmly, even in her private journal. " I think her
bold, daring, vain even to folly, and stamped with the manners of her first situation much more strongly than one would
suppose, after having represented Majesty, and lived in good
company fifteen years. Her dress is frightful. Her waist is
absolutely between her shoulders." Nelson measured her by
a different standard. " In every point of view," he tells herself, " from Ambassatrice to the duties of domestic life, I
never saw your equal. That elegance of manners, accomplishments, and, above all, your goodness of heart, is unparalleled."
The same lady describes her personal appearance, at the time
when his devotion had reached the height from which it never
declined. " Her figure is colossal, but, excepting her feet,

[1] Colburn's United Service Magazine, 1847, part ii. p. 52.
[2] Afterwards Mrs. Trench, the mother of Archbishop Trench.

which are hideous, well shaped. Her bones are large, and she is exceedingly *embonpoint*. The shape of all her features is fine, as is the form of her head, and particularly her ears; her teeth are a little irregular, but tolerably white; her eyes light blue, with a brown spot in one, which, though a defect, takes nothing away from her beauty or expression. Her eyebrows and hair (which, by the bye, is never clean) are dark, and her complexion coarse. Her expression is strongly marked, variable, and interesting; her movements in common life ungraceful; her voice loud, yet not disagreeable." Elliot's briefer mention of her appearance is at once confirmatory and complementary of that of Mrs. St. George: " Her person is nothing short of monstrous for its enormity, and is growing every day. Her face is beautiful."

To these opinions it may be not uninteresting to add the critical estimate of William Beckford, uttered many years later. Beckford was not an admirable character, far from it; but he had known good society, and he had cultivated tastes. Nelson accepted his hospitality, and, with the Hamiltons, spent several days under his roof, about Christmas time, 1800. In reply to the question, " Was the second Lady Hamilton a fascinating woman ? " he said, " I never thought her so. She was somewhat masculine, but symmetrical in figure, so that Sir William called her his Grecian. She was full in person, not fat, but *embonpoint*. Her carriage often majestic, rather than feminine. Not at all delicate, ill-bred, often very affected, a devil in temper when set on edge. She had beautiful hair and displayed it. Her countenance was agreeable, — fine, hardly beautiful, but the outline excellent. She affected sensibility, but felt none — was artful; and no wonder, she had been trained in the Court of Naples — a fine school for an English woman of any stamp. Nelson was infatuated. She could make him believe anything, that the profligate queen was a Madonna. He was her dupe. She never had a child in her life." [1] As to this last assertion, Beckford was not in a position to have personal knowledge.

But along with this native coarseness, which, if not ineradicable, was never eradicated, she possessed an intuitive and perfect sense, amounting to genius, for what propriety and

[1] Beckford's Memoirs, London, 1859, vol. ii. p. 326.

good taste demanded in the presentation of an ideal part, — the gift of the born actress. Of her powers in this way the celebrated " Attitudes " were the chief example, and there is no disagreement among the witnesses, either as to their charm or as to the entire disappearance of the every-day woman in the assumed character. " We had the attitudes a night or two ago by candle light," wrote Sir Gilbert Elliot in 1796. " They come up to my expectations fully, which is saying everything. They set Lady Hamilton in a very different light from any I had seen her in before ; nothing about her, neither her conversation, her manners, nor figure, announce the very refined taste which she discovers in this performance, besides the extraordinary talent which is needed for the execution." " You never saw anything so charming as Lady Hamilton's attitudes," wrote Lady Malmesbury in 1791. " The most graceful statues or pictures do not give you an idea of them." " It is a beautiful performance," wrote Mrs. St. George, who saw her in 1800, when the Hamiltons and Nelson were travelling on the Continent, " amusing to the most ignorant, and highly interesting to the lovers of art. It is remarkable that although coarse and ungraceful in common life, she becomes highly graceful, and even beautiful, during this performance. It is also singular that, in spite of the accuracy of her imitation of the finest ancient draperies, her usual dress is tasteless, vulgar, loaded and unbecoming."

The stormy period of the French Revolution, which was about to burst into universal war at the time she was married, gave Lady Hamilton another opportunity to come yet more conspicuously before men's eyes than she had hitherto done. It is not easy to say what degree of influence she really attained, or what particular results she may have effected ; but she certainly managed to give herself so much the air of a person of importance, in the political intrigues of the day in Naples, as at the least to impose successfully upon a great many, and to be accepted very much at her own valuation. The French ambassador, writing to Bonaparte in 1798, says : " If the preponderance which the French Republic ought to take here, removed hence Acton and the wife of Hamilton, this country, without other changes, would be extremely useful for the execution of all your projects in the Mediterranean;" and Sir William himself, who should have known, speaks of her activity and utility, — "for several years the real and only confidential friend of the Queen of Naples." Nelson, writing to the Queen of Naples in 1804, after Hamilton's death, said : " Your Majesty well knows that it was her capacity and conduct which sustained his diplomatic character during the last years in which he was at Naples." [1] Certainly, Nelson believed, with all the blindness of love, whatever his mistress chose to tell him, but he was not without close personal knowledge of the inside history of at least two of those last years ; for, in 1801, addressing Mr. Addington, then Prime Minister, he used these words : " Having for a length of time seen the correspondence both public and private, from all the Neapolitan ministers to their Government and to the Queen of Naples, I am perfectly acquainted with the views of the several Powers." For her success Lady Hamilton was indebted, partly to her personal advantages, and partly to her position as wife of the British minister and chosen friend to the Queen.   Great Britain played a leading part everywhere in the gigantic struggle throughout the Continent, but to a remote peninsular kingdom like Naples, protected by its distance from the centres of strife, yet not wholly inaccessible by land, the chief maritime state was the one and only sufficient ally.   A rude reminder of his exposure to naval attack had been given to the King of the Two Sicilies, in 1792, by the appearance of a French fleet, which extorted satisfaction for an alleged insult, by threatening instant bombardment of his capital.

Sir William Hamilton, who had been minister since 1765, thus found himself suddenly converted from a dilettante and sportsman, lounging through life, into a busy diplomat, at the centre of affairs of critical moment.   At sixty-two the change could scarcely have been welcome to him, but to his beautiful and ambitious wife the access of importance was sweet, for it led to a close friendship with the Queen, already disposed to affect her, even in the notorious position she had held before her marriage ; and the Queen, a daughter of Maria Theresa and sister to Marie Antoinette, was much more of a man than

[1] Compare an equally strong assertion, Nicolas's Despatches, vol. vi. p. 99.

the King. The intimacy became the talk of Naples, and the report spread, easily believed, because in the nature of things very likely, that the personal relations between the two women cloaked a great deal of underhand work, such as often accompanies diplomatic difficulties. Nor did Lady Hamilton lack natural qualifications for the position into which she undoubtedly wished to thrust herself. She was a brave, capable, full-blooded, efficient woman, not to be daunted by fears or scruples; a woman who, if only nerve and intelligence were required, and if distinction for herself was at stake, could be fairly depended upon. There was in her make-up a good deal of pagan virtue. She could appreciate and admire heroism, and, under the stimulus of excitement, of self-conscious magnanimity, for the glitter of effective performance and the applause of onlookers, she was quite capable of heroic action. It was this daring spirit, coarsely akin to much that was best in himself, and of which she made proof under his own eyes, that Nelson recognized; and this, in the thought of the writer, was the body of truth, from which his enthusiasm, enkindled by her charms and by her tenderness towards himself, projected such a singular phantasm of romantic perfections.

Such was the woman, and such the position in the public eye that she had gained for herself, when to Naples, first in the European continent, came the news which made Nelson for the moment the most conspicuous man of the day. He had achieved a triumph the most startlingly dazzling that had yet been gained, and over one who up to that time had excelled all other warriors in the brilliancy and extent of his victories. Bonaparte was not yet the Napoleon whom history knows, but thus far he had been the most distinguished child of the Revolution. That Lady Hamilton then and there formed the purpose of attaching Nelson to her, by the bonds which have sullied his memory, is most improbable; but it is in entire keeping with the career and the self-revelations of the woman that she should, instinctively, if not with deliberation, have resolved to parade herself in the glare of his renown, and appear in the foreground upon the stage of his triumph, the chief dispenser of his praises, the patroness and proprietor of the hero. The great occasion should shed a glamour round her, together with him. "Emma's passion is admiration," Greville had written soon after they parted, "and it is capable of aspiring to any line which would be celebrated, and it would be indifferent, when on that key, whether she was Lucretia or Sappho, or Scævola or Regulus; anything grand, masculine or feminine, she could take up."

Unhappily, Nelson was not able to stand the heady dose of flattery administered by a woman of such conspicuous beauty and consummate art; nor was his taste discriminating enough to experience any wholesome revolt against the rankness of the draught she offered him. The quick appreciation of the born actress, which enabled her when on the stage to clothe herself with a grace and refinement that dropped away when she left it, conspired with his simplicity of confidence in others, and his strong tendency to idealize, to invest her with a character very different from the true. Not that the Lady Hamilton of reality was utterly different from the Lady Hamilton of his imagination. That she ever loved him is doubtful; but there were in her spirit impulses capable of sympathetic response to his own in his bravest acts, though not in his noblest motives. It is inconceivable that duty ever appealed to her as it did to him, nor could a woman of innate nobility of character have dragged a man of Nelson's masculine renown about England and the Continent, till he was the mock of all beholders; but on the other hand it never could have occurred to the energetic, courageous, brilliant Lady Hamilton, after the lofty deeds and stirring dramatic scenes of St. Vincent, to beg him, as Lady Nelson did, "to leave boarding to captains." Sympathy, not good taste, would have withheld her. In Lady Nelson's letters there is evidence enough of a somewhat colorless womanly affection, but not a thrill of response to the greatness of her husband's daring, even when surrounded herself by the acclamations it called forth.

What Nelson had never yet found in woman Lady Hamilton gave him, — admiration and appreciation, undisguised and unmeasured, yet bestowed by one who had the power, by the admission of even unfriendly critics, of giving a reality and grace to the part she was performing. He was soon at her feet. The playful gallantry with which Ball, Elliot, and even old St. Vincent[1] himself, paid court to a handsome woman, greedy of homage, became in Nelson a serious matter. Romantic in temperament, he was all day in flattering contact with her. Worn out and ill from that "fever of anxiety," to use his own words, which he had endured since the middle of June, she attended and nursed him. " Lady Hamilton," he exclaimed to Lady Nelson, with enthusiasm undiscriminating in more ways than one, " is one of the very best women in this world; she is an honour to her sex." A week later he tells her, with an odd collocation of persons: " My pride is being your husband, the son of my dear father, and in having Sir William and Lady Hamilton for my friends. While these approve my conduct, I shall not feel or regard the envy of thousands." The matter was passing rapidly into the platonic stage, in which Sir William was also erelong assigned an appropriate, if not wholly flattering, position. " What can I say of hers and Sir William's attention to me ? They are in fact, with the exception of you and my good father, the dearest friends I have in this world. I live as Sir William's son in the house, and my glory is as dear to them as their own; in short, I am under such obligations as I can never repay but with my eternal gratitude." " Naples is a dangerous place," he sagely tells Lord St. Vincent, " and we must keep clear of it. I am writing opposite Lady Hamilton, therefore you will not be surprised at the glorious jumble of this letter. Were your Lordship in my place, I much doubt if you could write so well ; our hearts and our hands must be all in a flutter." Matters progressed ; within ten days the veteran seaman learned, among other concerns of more or less official importance, that " Lady Hamilton is an Angel. She has honoured me by being my ambassadress to the queen : therefore she has my implicit confidence and is worthy of it."

That such intimacy and such relations resulted in no influence upon the admiral's public action is not to be believed. That he consciously perverted his views is improbable, but that he saw duty under other than normal lights is not only probable, but evident. His whole emotional nature was stirred

[1] St. Vincent at this time had not met her, at least as Lady Hamilton, but they exchanged occasional letters.

as it never had been. Incipient love and universal admiration
had created in him a tone of mind, and brought to birth feelings, which he had, seemingly, scarcely known. "I cannot
write a stiff formal public letter," he tells St. Vincent effu-
sively. "You must make one or both so. I feel you are my
friend, and my heart yearns to you." Such extravagance of
expression and relaxation of official tone has no pertinent
cause, and is at least noteworthy. The Court, or rather the
Queen through Lady Hamilton, took possession of him. He
became immediately one of the little coterie centring round
Her Majesty, and he reflected its tone and partisanship, which,
fostered probably in the intimate conversations of the two
women, were readily transmitted to the minister by the wife
whom he adored. The Queen, impetuous, enterprising, and
headstrong, like her mother and sister, moved more by feminine feelings of hatred and revenge against the French than
by well-balanced considerations of policy, not only favored war,
but wished to precipitate the action of the Emperor by immediately attacking the French in the Roman territory. The
decision and daring of such a course was so consonant to Nelson's own temperament that he readily sympathized; but it is
impossible to admit its wisdom, from either a political or military standpoint. It was an excessively bad combination, sub-
stituting isolated attacks for co-operation, and risking results
upon the chance of prompt support, by a state which would
be offended and embarrassed by the step taken.

Under ordinary conditions Nelson might have seen this, but
he was well handled. Within three days he had been persuaded that upon his personal presence depended the salva-
tion of Italy. "My head is quite healed, and, if it were
necessary, I could not at present leave Italy, who looks up
to me as, under God, its Protector." He continually, by devout recollection of his indebtedness to God, seeks to keep
himself in hand. "I am placed by Providence in that situation, that all my caution will be necessary to prevent vanity
from showing itself superior to my gratitude and thankfulness," — but the current was too strong for him. and was
swollen to a torrent by the streams of adulation, which from
all quarters flowed in upon a temperament only too disposed
to accept them. "Could I, my dearest Fanny," he writes to

Lady Nelson, "tell you half the honours which are shown me here, not a ream of paper would hold it." A grand ball was given on his birthday, September 29; and a rostral column was "erected under a magnificent canopy, never, Lady Hamilton says, to come down while they remain at Naples." Within a week the conviction of his own importance led him to write to Lady Hamilton, evidently for transmission to the Queen, an opinion, or rather an urgent expression of advice, that Naples should at once begin war. It is only conjectural to say that this opinion, which rested on no adequate knowledge of the strength of the Neapolitan Kingdom, was elicited by the Queen through Lady Hamilton; but the inference derives support from the words, "I have read with admiration the queen's dignified and incomparable letter of September, 1796," — two years before. That his views were not the simple outcome of his own unbiassed study of the situation is evident enough. "This country, by its system of procrastination, will ruin itself," he writes to St. Vincent, the very day after drawing up the letter in question; "the queen sees it and thinks" — not as I do, but — " as *we* do." That Lady Hamilton was one of the " we " is plain, for in the postscript to the letter he says: " Your Ladyship will, I beg, receive this letter as a *preparative for Sir William Hamilton*, to whom I am writing, with all respect, the firm and unalterable opinion of a British admiral," etc. Certainly these words — taken with those already quoted, and written just a week afterwards, " Lady Hamilton has been my ambassadress to the queen " — indicate that she was the intermediary between Nelson and the Court, as well as between him and her husband.

There is no record of any official request for this unofficial and irregular communication of the opinion of a British admiral; and, of course, when a man has allowed himself, unasked, though not unprompted, to press such a line of action, he has bound himself personally, and embarrassed himself officially, in case it turns out badly. Nelson very soon, within a fortnight, had to realize this, in the urgent entreaties of the Court not to forsake them; and to see reason for thinking " that a strong wish for our squadron's being on the Coast of Naples is, that in case of any mishap, that their

Majesties think their persons much safer under the protection
of the British flag than under any other; " that is — than
under their own. They could not trust their own people;
they could not, as the event proved, trust their army in the
field ; and the veteran Neapolitan naval officer, Caracciolo,
whether he deserved confidence or not, was stung to the quick
when, in the event, they sought refuge with a foreign admiral
instead of with himself. That Nelson should not have known
all this, ten days after reaching Naples, was pardonable enough,
and, if formally asked for advice without such facts being
placed before him, he could not be responsible for an error
thus arising ; but the case is very different when advice is
volunteered. He is more peremptory than the minister himself. " You will not believe I have said or done anything,
without the approbation of Sir William Hamilton. His
Excellency is too good to them, and the strong language of
an English Admiral telling them plain truths of their miserable system may do good."

The particular position of Naples relatively to France was
this. French troops had for a year past occupied the Roman
Republic, which had been established by them upon the overthrow of the Papal Government. Their presence there was
regarded by Nelson as a constant threat to the Two Sicilies,
and this to an extent was true ; but rather because of the
contagion of revolutionary ideas than from the military point
of view. From the latter, it should have been obvious to a
man like Nelson that the French must be deterred, under existing conditions, from entering Naples unprovoked ; because
the farther they advanced the more exposed was their army,
in case war, which was darkly threatening, should be renewed
in Upper Italy. They dared not, unless by folly, or because
first attacked, prolong their already too extended ex-centric
movement into Lower Italy. This was true, taking account
of Austria only ; but now that the British fleet was released
by the entire destruction of the French at the Nile, and could
operate anywhere on the coast, it would be doubly imprudent;
and when the news that it had been done reached Egypt,
Bonaparte, who had himself felt the weight of Naples as a
possible enemy, remote and feeble as she was, exclaimed,
" Italy is lost !" That Naples should co-operate in the

general movement against France was right, although, as Nelson well knew, she had never dared do so under much more favorable conditions, — a fact which by itself should have suggested to him caution; but that she should act alone, with the idea of precipitating war, refusing to await the moment fixed by the principal states, was folly. This, however, was the course determined, under the combined impulse of the Queen, Lady Hamilton, and Nelson; and it was arranged that, after visiting the blockade off Malta, he should return to Naples to co-operate in the intended movement.

On the 15th of October Nelson sailed from Naples for Malta in the "Vanguard," with three ships-of-the-line which had lately joined him. He still felt, with accurate instinct, that Egypt and the Ionian Islands, with Malta, constituted the more purely maritime interests, in dealing with which the fleet would most further the general cause, and he alludes frequently to his wish to attend to them; but he promised the King that he would be back in Naples in the first week of November, to support the projected movement against the French. He remained off Malta, therefore, only one week, during which adequate arrangements were made for the blockade of the island, which had been formally proclaimed on the 12th of October, and was conducted for most of the following year by the Portuguese squadron; the senior British officer, Captain Ball, acting ashore with the insurgent Maltese. These had risen against the French during the summer, and now held them shut up in La Valetta. The adjacent island of Gozo surrendered to the British on the 28th. Hood continued in charge off Alexandria with three ships-of-the-line; while the Ionian Islands were left to themselves, until a combined Russian and Turkish squadron entered the Mediterranean a few weeks later.

On the 5th of November Nelson returned to Naples. "I am, I fear, drawn into a promise that Naples Bay shall never be left without an English man-of-war. I never intended leaving the coast of Naples without one; but if I had, who could resist the request of such a queen?" He could ground much upon the Admiralty's orders, given when he was first sent into the Mediterranean, to protect the Kingdom of the Two Sicilies, and he had understood that the Emperor also would give his aid, if Naples attacked. This impression received strength from an Austrian general, Mack, — then of high reputation, but afterwards better known by his surrender to Napoleon at Ulm, in 1805, — being sent to command the Neapolitan army. Sir William Hamilton, however, writing on the 26th of October, was more accurate in saying that the Emperor only advised the King " to act openly against the French *at Malta*, as he would certainly support him ; " for, Naples having a feudal claim upon the island, action there could be represented as merely resistance to aggression. In consequence of this misunderstanding, great confusion ensued in the royal councils when a courier from Vienna brought word, on the 13th of November, that that Court wished it left to the French to begin hostilities ; otherwise, it would give no assurance of help. Nelson was now formally one of the Council which deliberated upon military operations. In virtue of this position he spoke out, roughly enough. " I ventured to tell their Majesties that one of the following things must happen to the King, and he had his choice, — ' Either to advance, trusting to God for his blessing on a just cause, to die with *l'épée à la main*, or remain quiet and be kicked out of your Kingdoms.' " Thus rudely adjured, the King decided to be a hero after the pattern of Nelson.

On the 22d of November a summons was sent to the French to evacuate the Papal States and Malta, and a Neapolitan army marched upon Rome, commanded by Mack in person. At the same time Nelson took on board his squadron a corps of five thousand, to seize Leghorn, the possession of which, with control of the sea, was not unjustly considered threatening to the communications between the centre of French power, in Northern Italy, and the exposed corps at the foot of the peninsula. After landing this body, Nelson again went to Naples, leaving Troubridge in charge at Leghorn, with several ships ; directing him also to keep vessels cruising along the Riviera, and before Genoa, to break up the coastwise traffic, which had resumed great proportions since the absence of the British from the Mediterranean, and upon which the French army in Piedmont and Lombardy now greatly depended.

On the 5th of December the " Vanguard " once more anchored at Naples. Nelson's estimate of affairs as he now found them, is best told in his own words. "The state of this Country is briefly this : The army is at Rome, Civita Vecchia taken, but in the Castle of St. Angelo are five hundred French troops. The French have thirteen thousand troops at a strong post in the Roman State, called Castellana. General Mack is gone against them with twenty thousand: the event in my opinion is doubtful, and on it hangs the immediate fate of Naples. If Mack is defeated, this country, in fourteen days, is lost; for the Emperor has not yet moved his army, and if the Emperor will not march, this country has not the power of resisting the French. But it was not a case of choice, but necessity, which forced the King of Naples to march out of his country, and not to wait till the French had collected a force sufficient to drive him, in a week, out of his kingdom." It is by no means so sure that no other course of action had been open, though Nelson naturally clung to his first opinion. By advancing, the King gave the French occasion, if they were seeking one; and the Neapolitan army, which might well have deterred them, as it had embarrassed even Bonaparte in his time, had its rottenness revealed as only trial can reveal. When reviewed, it had appeared to Mack and Nelson a well-equipped force of thirty thousand of the "finest troops in Europe." Brought face to face with fifteen thousand French, in a month it ceased to exist.

Upon Mack's advance, the French general Championnet had evacuated Rome, into which the King made a vainglorious triumphal entry. The French retired to Castellana, followed by the Neapolitans; but in the campaign that ensued the latter behaved with disgraceful cowardice. Flying in every direction, with scarcely any loss in killed, and preceded in their flight by the King, the whole force retreated in confusion upon the capital. There revolutionary ideas had spread widely among the upper classes ; and, although the populace both in city and country remained fanatically loyal, and hostile to the French, the King and Queen feared to trust their persons to the issue of events. Powerless through suspicions of those around them, apparently well founded, and through lack of any instrument with which to act, now that their army was destroyed, their one wish was to escape to Palermo.

To do this involved some difficulty, as the mob, like that of Paris, was bitterly opposed to their sovereign leaving the capital; but by the management and determination of Nelson, who was greatly helped by the courage and presence of mind of Lady Hamilton, the royal family was embarked on board the "Vanguard" on the evening of December 21st. During several previous days treasure to the amount of two and a half millions sterling was being conveyed secretly to the ship. "The whole correspondence relative to this important business," wrote Nelson to St. Vincent, "was carried on with the greatest address by Lady Hamilton and the Queen, who being constantly in the habits of correspondence, no one could suspect." On the evening of the 23d the "Vanguard" sailed, and after a most tempestuous passage reached Palermo on the 26th. The youngest of the princes, six years old, taken suddenly with convulsions, died on the way in the arms of Lady Hamilton, whose womanly helpfulness, as well as her courage, came out strongly in this trying time. Nelson wrote to St. Vincent: "It is my duty to tell your Lordship the obligations which the whole royal family as well as myself are under on this trying occasion to her Ladyship." These scenes inevitably deepened the impression she had already made upon him, which was not to be lessened by her lapse into feminine weakness when the strain was over. To use her own words, in a letter to her old lover, Greville, "My dear, adorable queen and I *weep together*, and now that is our onely comfort." "Our dear Lady Hamilton," Nelson wrote again a few days later, "whom to see is to admire, but, to know, are to be added honour and respect; her head and heart surpass her beauty, which cannot be equalled by anything I have seen." Upon himself the brief emergency and its sharp call to action had had the usual reviving effect. "Thank God," he wrote to Spencer, "my health is better, my mind never firmer, and my heart in the right trim to comfort, relieve, and protect those who it is my duty to afford assistance to."

In Palermo Nelson again lived in the minister's house, bearing a large, if not a disproportionate, share of the expenses. When they returned to England in 1800, Hamilton was £2,000 in his debt. The intimacy and the manner of life, in the midst of the Neapolitan court, whose corruptness of manners both Nelson and Troubridge openly condemned, was already causing scandal, rumors of which were not long in reaching home. "I am quite concerned," wrote Captain Ball to Saumarez, when Nelson was about to quit the station, "at the many severe paragraphs which have been put in the newspapers respecting him and Lady Hamilton. I am convinced that there has not been anything improper between them — his Lordship could not fail being delighted with her accomplishments and manners, which are very fascinating." Lady Nelson, uneasy as a wife could not fail to be at reports affecting her husband's honor, and threatening her own happiness, quickly formed, and for a time entertained, the thought of joining him on the station;[1] but, if she broached the idea to Nelson, he certainly discouraged it. Writing to her on the 10th of April, 1799, he said: "You would by February have seen how unpleasant it would have been had you followed *any* advice, which carried you from England to a wandering sailor. I could, if you had come, *only* have struck my flag, and carried you back again, for it would have been impossible to have set up an establishment at either Naples or Palermo."[2]

The scandal increased apace after his headquarters were fixed at Palermo. Lady Minto, writing from Vienna to her sister, in July, 1800, says: "Mr. Rushout and Colonel Rooke,[3] whom I knew in Italy, are here. Mr. Rushout is at last going home. He escaped from Naples at the same time as the King did in Nelson's ship, and remained six months at Palermo; so I had a great deal of intelligence concerning the Hero and his Lady. . . . Nelson and the Hamiltons all lived together in a house of which he bore the expense, which was enormous, and every sort of gaming went on half the night. Nelson used to sit with large parcels of gold before him, and generally go to sleep, Lady Hamilton taking from the heap without counting, and playing with his money to the amount of £500 a night. Her rage is play, and Sir William says when he is dead she will be a beggar. However, she has

[1] Nicolas, vol. iii. p. 138, note.   [2] Pettigrew, vol. i. p. 220.
[3] Lord Minto was at this time ambassador to Vienna. Rushout and Rooke were men well known on the Continent. Both are mentioned with some particularity in the Memoirs of Pryse Lockhart Gordon, another continental rambler.

about £30,000 worth of diamonds from the royal family in presents. She sits at the Councils, and rules everything and everybody." Some of these statements are probably beyond the personal knowledge of the narrator, and can only be accepted as current talk; but others are within the obser- vation of an eye-witness, evidently thought credible by Lady Minto, who was a friend to Nelson. Mr. Paget, who succeeded Hamilton as British minister, mentions the same reports, in his private letter to Lord Grenville, the Secretary of State for Foreign Affairs. Hamilton had asked to see his instructions. " I decided at once not to do so, for he would certainly have been obliged to show them to Lady Hamilton, who would have conveyed them next moment to the queen. . . . Lord Nelson's health is, I fear, sadly impaired, and I am assured that his fortune is fallen into the same state, in consequence of great losses which both his Lordship and Lady Hamilton have sustained at Faro and other games of hazard." [1]

The impressions made upon Lord Elgin, who touched at Palermo on his way to the embassy at Constantinople, are worth quoting; for there has been much assertion and denial as to what did go on in that out-of-the-way corner of the world, Lady Hamilton ascribing the falsehoods, as she claimed they were, to the Jacobinical tendencies of those who spread them. "During a week's stay at Palermo, on my passage here," wrote Elgin, " the necessity of a change in our repre- sentative, and in our conduct there, appeared to me most urgent. You may perhaps know from Lord Grenville how strong my impression on that subject was." [2] Troubridge, a pattern of that most faithful friendship which dares to risk alienation, if it may but save, wrote urgently to his chief: "Pardon me, my Lord, it is my sincere esteem for you that makes me mention it. I know you can have no pleasure sit- ting up all night at cards; why, then, sacrifice your health, comfort, purse, ease, everything, to the customs of a country, where your stay cannot be long? . . . Your Lordship is a stranger to half that happens, or the talk it occasions; if you knew what your friends feel for you, I am sure you would cut all the nocturnal parties. The gambling of the people at Palermo is publicly talked of everywhere. I beseech your

[1] The Paget Papers, London, 1896, p. 185.　　[2] Ibid. p. 219.

Lordship leave off. I wish my pen could tell you my feelings, I am sure you would oblige me. Lady H——'s character will suffer, nothing can prevent people from talking. A gambling woman, in the eye of an Englishman, is lost. . . . You will be surprised when I tell you I hear in all companies the sums won and lost on a card in Sir William's house. It furnishes matter for a letter constantly, both to Minorca, Naples, Messina, etc., etc., and finally in England. I trust your Lordship will pardon me; it is the sincere esteem I have for you that makes me risk your displeasure." To this manly appeal Nelson seems to have made no reply; none at least is quoted. In the same letter Troubridge tells him plainly that great discontent had arisen from "the known interference of Lady Hamilton," some months before, in the case of a marine condemned to death for mutiny. "These things get home, and are talked of in a different manner to what your Lordship can have any idea of." [1]

[1] Troubridge to Nelson, Dec. 15 and 28, 1799.

CHAPTER XII.

Nelson's Career, and General Events in the Mediterranean and
Italy, from the Overthrow of the Royal Government in
Naples to the Incursion of the French Fleet under Admiral
Bruix.

January–May, 1799. Age, 40.

THE four and a half months of unbroken residence in
Palermo, which followed the flight of the Court from
Naples, were full of annoyance and distress to Nelson, independent of, and additional to, the disquieting struggle between
his passion and his conscience, which had not yet been silenced. The disasters in Naples continued. The Neapolitan
Navy had been left in charge of one of the Portuguese officers,
who soon found himself compelled to burn the ships-of-the-
line, to prevent their falling into the hands of the revolution-
ists, — a step for which he was severely, but apparently
unjustly, censured by Nelson. The peasantry and the lower
orders of the city took up arms, under the guidance of their
priests, and for some time sought, with rude but undisciplined
fury, to oppose the advance of the enemy; but such untrained
resistance was futile before the veterans of France, and on the
23d of January, 1799, Championnet's troops entered the city.
This was followed by the establishment of the Parthenopeian
Republic, a name which reflected the prevailing French affec-
tation of antiquity. For all this Nelson blamed the Emperor,
and formed gloomy forebodings. "Had the war commenced
in September or October," he had written amid the December
disasters, "all Italy would at this moment have been liberated.
Six months hence, when the Neapolitan Republic will be organized, armed, and with its numerous resources called forth,
I will suffer to have my head cut off, if the Emperor is not
only defeated in Italy, but that he totters on his throne in
Vienna." To this text he stuck. Three months later, when
the preparations of Austria and Russia were complete, he

wrote: " The French have made war upon the Emperor, and have surprised some of his troops. Serve him right ! why did he not go to war before ? " But the rapid, continuous, and overwhelming successes of the Coalition, between April and August, showed how untimely had been the step he had urged upon the King of the Sicilies, disregardful of the needed preparations and of the most favorable season — February to August — for operations in Italy. Naples never recovered such political equilibrium as she had possessed before that ill-advised advance. In Nelson's career it, and its reverses, were to the Battle of the Nile what Teneriffe was to St. Vincent; and it illustrates the inadequacy to success of merely " going ahead," unless both time and method are dictated by that martial intelligence which Nelson so abundantly possessed, but in this case failed to use.

Not in Naples only did fortune now administer to him rebuffs, which seemed singularly to rebuke the change of direction and of base which he had been persuaded to give to his personal efforts. Immediately upon his arrival in Palermo, he heard from St. Vincent that a comparatively junior captain, Sir Sidney Smith, had been sent out by the Cabinet, bearing, besides his naval commission from the Admiralty, one from the Foreign Office as envoy to Turkey, conjointly with his brother, Spencer Smith. This unusual and somewhat cumbrous arrangement was adopted with the design that Smith should be senior naval officer in the Levant, where it was thought his hands would be strengthened by the diplomatic functions ; but the Government's explanation of its intentions was so obscure, that St. Vincent understood the new-comer was to be independent of both himself and Nelson. This impression was confirmed by a letter from Smith to Hamilton, in which occurred the words, " Hood naturally falls under my orders when we meet, as being my junior," while the general tone was that of one who had a right, by virtue of his commission alone, to take charge of such vessels, and to direct such operations, as he found in the Levant. This impression was fairly deducible from a letter of the Secretary of State for Foreign Affairs, that Smith forwarded to Nelson ; after which, without seeking an interview, he at once went on for Constantinople.

Nelson immediately asked to be relieved. "*I do feel, for I am a man,*" he wrote to St. Vincent, "that it is impossible for me to serve in these seas, with the squadron under a junior officer. Never, never was I so astonished." With this private letter he sent an official application for leave. "The great anxiety I have undergone during the whole time I have been honoured with this important command, has much impaired a weak constitution. And now, finding that much abler officers are arrived within the district which I had thought under my command, . . . and, I flatter myself, having made the British nation and our gracious Sovereign more beloved and respected than heretofore ; under these cir- cumstances I entreat, that if my health and uneasiness of mind should not be mended, that I may have your Lordship's permission to leave this command to my gallant and most excellent second in command, Captain Troubridge." In simi- lar terms, though more guarded, he wrote to Earl Spencer. At the same time he took proper steps to prevent the official impropriety, not to say rudeness, which Smith was about to commit by taking from Hood his charge, without either the latter or Nelson receiving personal instructions to surrender it. He sent Troubridge hastily to Alexandria to take com- mand there, with orders that, upon Smith's arrival, he should deliver up the blockade to him, and return to the westward. " I should hope," he wrote to Spencer, "that Sir Sidney Smith will not take any ship from under my command, without my orders ; " but he evidently expected that he would, and was determined to forestall the possibility of such an affront.

Nelson's services had been so eminent, and were at this time so indispensable, and his exceptions to the manner in which Smith had been intruded into his command were so well founded, that the matter was rectified as rapidly as the slow round of communications in that day would permit. The Admiralty disclaimed any intention of circumscribing his con- trol in the Mediterranean, and Smith received peremptory orders from St. Vincent to report himself to Nelson by letter for orders. The latter of course carried out the Admiralty's wishes, by intrusting to Smith the immediate direction of operations in the Levant, while retaining in his own hands the general outlines of naval policy. He kept a very tight rein on Smith, however, and introduced into the situation some dry humor, unusual with him. The two brothers, envoys, he addressed jointly, in his official letters, by the collective term "Your Excellency." "I beg of your Excellency," he says in such a letter, "to forward my letter to Sir Sidney Smith, Captain of the Tigre. I have this day received letters from Sir Sidney Smith, in his Ministerial capacity, I believe. I *wish* that all Ministerial letters should be written in your joint names; for it may be difficult for me to distinguish the Captain of the man-of-war from the Joint Minister, and the propriety of language in one might be very proper to what it is in the other." To the naval captain he writes : "I must *direct* you, whenever you have Ministerial affairs to communicate, that it is done jointly with your respectable brother, and not mix naval business with the other. I have sent you my orders, which your abilities as a sea-officer will lead you to punctually execute."

Nelson resented to the end this giving to a junior naval officer, by a side-wind, an authoritative position in diplomatic affairs, which, on the naval side, properly belonged to him. "Sir Sidney should recollect," he told Earl Spencer, meaning doubtless that the latter also should recollect, "how I must feel in seeing him placed in the situation which I thought naturally would fall to me." It was a singular step on the part of the Government, justified neither by general practice, nor by particular ability on the part of the person chosen; and all Nelson's care and decision were insufficient to prevent the consequent evil, although he was perfectly clear in his intimation to "Your Excellency," the joint ministers, that they should, "upon all occasions, arrange plans of operations with me," and not with Captain Sir Sidney Smith. Smith was active and fought well ; but, as far as he dared, he did as he pleased in virtue of his diplomatic commission, looked only to the interests of his own small part of the field, and, as will appear later, flatly disobeyed both the spirit and the letter of Nelson's orders, as well as the Government's purpose, concerning the French army in Egypt. The general sound judgment and diplomatic ability of Nelson, who was thus superseded, had on the other hand been fully recognized — formally by the Government, explicitly by St. Vincent and

Minto, both of whom had personal experience of his conduct in such matters. " What relates to co-operation with the armies of the allied powers cannot be in better hands than yours," wrote the former. " You are as great in the cabinet as on the ocean, and your whole conduct fills me with admiration and confidence." " There is one other point of excellence," said Minto in the House of Peers, " to which I must say a single word, because I am, perhaps, the man in the world who has had the best opportunity of being acquainted with it. The world knows that Lord Nelson can fight the battles of his country : but a constant and confidential correspondence with this great man, for a considerable portion of time, has taught me, that he is not less capable of providing for its political interests and honour, on occasions of great delicacy and embarrassment. In that new capacity I have witnessed a degree of ability, judgment, temper, and conciliation, not always allied to the sort of spirit which without an instant's hesitation can attack the whole Spanish line with his single ship." Of Nelson's superior fitness in this respect, the unfortunate choice of Sidney Smith for his anomalous position was to furnish the Government an additional proof.

It was not in this matter only that maritime affairs in the East took a turn contrary to Nelson's wishes. The Admiralty's orders to him had prescribed — next after the protection of Naples and Sicily — the blockades of Egypt and Malta, and co-operation with the Russian and Turkish fleets, which were to enter the Mediterranean from the Black Sea. Nelson, although never slow to express want of confidence in foreign navies, wished their efforts to be directed against the French army in Egypt, a factor in the general situation most decisive by its numbers, by its efficiency, and by the genius of its leader. He was urgent, both with the joint ministers and with the representatives of Russia and Turkey, that the fleets of these two powers should relieve Hood off Alexandria, in order to strengthen his own hands on the coast of Italy and off Malta. Neither Russia nor Turkey was easily to be convinced. Egypt was no affair of the former's, except as it concerned the general cause ; and from that point of view it was as much the business of Great Britain, already on the spot, as it was hers. With twenty thousand troops about to enter

into a campaign in Northern Italy, as allies of Austria, Russia
had undeniable interests there, as well as in the Ionian
Islands, which commanded the entrance to the Adriatic, a sea
important to communications between Austria and Lombardy.
The islands also were, in the hands of France, a threat to the
Turkish mainland. It was against these, therefore, that the
Russo-Turkish forces directed their efforts, greatly to Nelson's
disgust, and there they remained, chained by the obstinate
resistance of Corfu, until the 1st of March, 1799, when it surrendered. The fifty-gun ship "Leander," which had been
taken by the French seventy-four "Généreux," when carrying
Nelson's despatches after the Nile, was here recaptured and
restored to Great Britain.

Nelson viewed the progress and policy of Russia with a
mind fully imbued with the distrust, which, for the last
quarter of a century, had been supplanting gradually the
previous friendly feeling of Great Britain toward that country.
As soon as he heard of the intention to attack the islands,
in November, 1798, he hurried off Troubridge to anticipate a
seizure which he expected to be more easy than it proved.
"You will proceed to sea without a moment's loss of time,"
his instructions ran, "and make the best of your way to the
Island of Zante ; and if the Russians have not taken possession of that island and Cephalonia, you will send on shore by
the Priest I shall desire to accompany you, my Declaration.
If you can get possession of the islands before named, you
will send my Declaration into the Island of Corfu, and use
your utmost endeavours to get possession of it. . . . Should
the Russians have taken possession of these Islands and be
cruizing near with the Turkish fleet, you will pay a visit to
the Turkish admiral, and by saluting him (if he consents to
return gun for gun) and every other mark of respect and
attention, gain his confidence. You will judge whether he
is of a sufficient rank to hold a confidential conversation
with." It is evident that Nelson's action was precipitated
by the news of the Russian movement, and its tenor dictated
by a wish to sow distrust between Turkey and Russia. The
omission of any mention of a Russian admiral is most significant. "Captain Troubridge was absolutely under sail,"
he wrote to Spencer Smith, "when I heard with sorrow that

the Russians were there." His eagerness in the matter is the more evident, in that he thus detached Troubridge at the moment when he was about to start for Leghorn, where his trusted subordinate and his ship would be greatly needed.

"I was in hopes that a part of the united Turkish and Russian squadron would have gone to Egypt — the first object of the Ottoman arms," he tells the Turkish admiral. "Corfu is a secondary consideration." To Spencer Smith he writes: "I have had a long and friendly conference with Kelim Effendi on the conduct likely to be pursued by the Russian Court towards the unsuspicious (I fear) and upright Turk. The Porte ought to be aware of the very great danger at a future day of allowing the Russians to get footing at Corfu, and I hope they will keep them in the East. Our ideas have exactly been the same about Russia. . . . Surely I had a right to expect that the united fleets would have taken care of the things east of Candia. I never wished to have them west of it." "The Russians seem to me to be more intent on taking ports in the Mediterranean than destroying Bonaparte in Egypt."

It was well known at this time that the Czar was looking towards Malta and the restoration of the Order of the Knights, of which he had been elected Grand Master the previous October, immediately after Bonaparte's seizure of the island became known. Nelson held that the King of Naples was the legitimate sovereign, and he directed Captain Ball, his own representative there, to have all the Maltese posts and forces fly the Neapolitan flag; but he, with Hamilton, got a note from the King, promising that Malta should never be transferred to any other Power without the consent of England. "Should any Russian ships, or admiral, arrive off Malta," he instructed Ball, "you will convince him of the very unhandsome manner of treating the legitimate sovereign of Malta, by wishing to see the Russian flag fly in Malta, and also of me, who command the forces of a Power in such close alliance with the Russian Emperor, which have been blockading and attacking Malta for near six months. The Russians shall never take the lead."

Three weeks later he authorized Ball, with the consent of the King, to preside over the meetings of the Maltese chiefs, and, by the desire of his Sicilian Majesty, the British flag was to be hoisted alongside the Sicilian in every place where the latter was flown, "side by side, that of England being on the right hand," to show that the island was under the special protection of Great Britain during the war. On the 23d of March he cordially congratulates the Russian admiral upon the fall of Corfu, news of which he has just received, and he mentions, meaningly, "The flag of his Sicilian Majesty, with that of Great Britain, is flying on all parts of Malta, except the town of Valetta, the inhabitants of which have, with his Sicilian Majesty's consent, put themselves under the protection of Great Britain." "I attach no value to it for us," he said explicitly to the First Lord, meaning, no doubt, for the purposes of the existing war. This opinion was perfectly consonant to the secondary importance he had latterly attributed to the presence of the British in the Levant, as compared to their duties towards Naples, but though he reiterated it in the later war, it was with the express qualification that, for the security of communication with India, not then in question, the value of the island was indisputable.

But if, positively, Malta was of little use to England, — "a useless and enormous expense," to use his own words, — yet, negatively, the consequences of its passing into the hands of a powerful rival were too serious to be permitted. "Any expense should be incurred rather than let it remain in the hands of the French." The same distrust of the Russians was suggested by his keen political insight. "You will observe what is said in the despatches of the Consul at Corfu," he writes to St. Vincent, "respecting the Russians being ordered to Malta. I know this is a favourite object of the Emperor's, and is a prelude to a future war with the good Turk, when Constantinople will change masters. This is so clear, that a man must be blind not to see it." "I have just received the Emperor of Russia's picture in a box magnificently set with diamonds; it has done him honour and me a pleasure to have my conduct approved;" "but," he tells Ball, significantly, "this shall not prevent my keeping a sharp look-out on his movements against the good Turk."

As regards Paul I., ferocious and half crazy as he was, this imputation of merely interested foresight scarcely did justice

to the quixotic passions which often impelled him to the most
unselfish acts, but the general tendency was undeniable; and
Nelson's watchful attitude exemplifies the numerous diplomatic, as well as military, responsibilities that weighed upon
him.   He was, practically, commander-in-chief in the Mediterranean, even if Government refused to recognize the fact
by reward, or by proper staff appointments; for St. Vincent,
autocratic as he was towards others, could roll off upon Nelson
all his responsibilities there, — "the uncontrolled direction
of the naval part," were his own words, — and sleep quietly.
Despite his objections to the island itself, and his enthusiastic
fidelity to the Neapolitan royal house, Nelson had evidently
the presentiment that Malta must come to Great Britain, a
solution which Ball and the Maltese themselves were urging
upon him.   "A Neapolitan garrison would betray it to the
first man who would bribe him," he wrote; which, if true,
left to Great Britain no other alternative than to take it herself.   Neither he, Troubridge, nor the sovereigns, had confidence in the fidelity of Neapolitan officers.

The blockade of Malta was maintained with great tenacity,
and, coupled with the maritime prostration of France in the
Mediterranean, resulted in a complete isolation of the French
garrison in La Valetta by sea, the Maltese people hemming it
in by land.   By the 1st of May Ball had erected a battery at
the head of the harbor, sweeping it to the entrance, so that
the French ships, one of which was the "Guillaume Tell,"
eighty, that had escaped from Aboukir, had to be kept in the
coves.   These affairs of Malta brought Nelson into difficult
diplomatic relations with the Barbary States, Tunis and
Tripoli.   The island not affording sufficient food, strenuous
efforts had to be made by him and Ball to get grain from
Sicily and elsewhere, a matter very difficult of accomplishment even were the transit unmolested; but these petty
Mussulman states, for the purposes of piracy, kept themselves
in formal war with Naples and Portugal, and frequently
captured vessels under the Sicilian flag carrying corn to
Malta.   The British had too much on hand now to spare
readily the force necessary to put down these depredators, at
whose misdeeds they had winked in quieter days; and it
required all Nelson's tact, combining threats with compli-

ments, and with appeals to the prejudices of believers in God against those who denied Him, to keep the marauding within bounds. The irrepressible activity of Bonaparte's emissaries also stirred the Beys up to measures friendly to France. "The infamous conduct of the French during the whole war, has at last called down the vengeance of all true Mussulmen," he writes to the Bey of Tunis; "and your Highness, I am sure, will agree with me that Divine Providence will never permit these infidels to God to go unpunished. The conduct of your Highness reflects upon you the very highest honour. Although I have a squadron of Portuguese ships under my orders, I have prevented their cruizing against the vessels of war of your Highness. For at this moment all wars should cease, and all the world should join in endeavouring to extirpate from off the face of the earth this race of murderers, oppressors, and unbelievers."

After these preliminary compliments, Nelson presents his grievances. He has given the passports of a British admiral to Sicilian vessels *bonâ fide* employed in carrying grain to the besiegers of the French, and to such only ; and he must insist upon those passports being respected, as the vessels bearing them are serving the great common cause. He demands, also, that aid be not given to the common enemy. " I was rejoiced," he writes the Bashaw of Tripoli, " to find that you had renounced the treaty you had so imprudently entered into with some emissaries of General Bonaparte — that man of blood, that despoiler of the weak, that enemy of all true Musselmen ; for, like Satan, he only flatters that he may the more easily destroy; and it is true, that since the year 1789, all Frenchmen are exactly of the same disposition." His Highness, however, has relapsed into his former errors. " It is now my duty to speak out, and not to be misunderstood. That Nelson who has hitherto kept your powerful enemies from destroying you, can, and will, let them loose upon you, unless the following terms are, in two hours, complied with. . . . If these proper terms are not complied with, I can no longer prevent the Portuguese ships from acting with vigour against your Highness. Your Highness will, without difficulty, write me a letter, the substance of which will be dictated by the British consul."

The vehemence with which the French are here denounced, though pitched in a key deemed harmonious to the ears for which it was immediately intended, was entirely consonant to the feelings which had lately taken possession of Nelson. They were the result, probably, in part, of the anxious rancor bred by the uncertainties and worry of the pursuit of Bonaparte; in part, also, of more direct contact than before with the unbridled license which the French Government and its generals, impelled by dire necessity and by an unquestionable lack of principle, had given to the system of making war support war. The feebleness and corruption of the Directory had relaxed the reins of discipline from top to bottom, and a practice which finds its justification only when executed with the strictest method and accountability, had degenerated into little better than disorganized pillage. " 'Down, down with the French!' is my constant prayer." " '*Down, down* with the French!' ought to be placed in the council-room of every country in the world." "To serve my King, and to destroy the French, I consider as the great order of all, from which little ones spring; and if one of these little ones militate against it, I go back to obey the great order and object, to *down, down* with the damned French villains. Excuse my warmth; but my blood boils at the name of a Frenchman. I hate them all — Royalists and Republicans." Infidels, robbers, and murderers are the characteristic terms. This detestation of the legitimate enemy spread, intensified, to those who supported them in Naples, — the Jacobins, as they were called. "Send me word some proper heads are taken off," he wrote to Troubridge, "this alone will comfort me." " Our friend Troubridge had a present made him the other day, of the head of a Jacobin," he tells St. Vincent, "and makes an apology to me, the weather being very hot, for not sending it here!" Upon the copy of the letter accompanying this ghastly gift to him, Troubridge had written, " A jolly fellow. T. Troubridge." The exasperation to which political animosities had given rise may be gauged by the brutal levity shown in this incident, by men of the masculine and generous characters of Troubridge and Nelson, and should not be forgotten in estimating the actions that in due consequence followed.

Court was rather political than military [1] in its utility, dependent upon the fears of their own subjects felt by the sovereigns. While these measures were being taken he endeavoured, though fruitlessly, to bring matters to a conclusion at Alexandria and Malta, in order to release the ships there employed and fetch them to the coast of Naples. "The moment the Emperor moves," he wrote to St. Vincent, "I shall go with all the ships I can collect into the Bay of Naples, to create a diversion." Nothing certain can be said as yet, "whether all is lost or may yet be saved; that must depend upon the movements of the Emperor." Yet it was the hand of the emperor which he had advised the King of Naples to force, by his ill-timed advance.

Troubridge rejoined the Flag at Palermo on the 17th of March, having turned over the command in the Levant to Sir Sidney Smith, after an ineffectual attempt to destroy the French shipping in Alexandria. By this time matters had begun to mend. Calabria had returned to its loyalty, and the insurrection of the peasantry against the French was general throughout the country, and in the Roman State. The Directory, taking umbrage at the advance of Russian troops to the frontiers of Austria, demanded explanations from the latter, and when these proved unsatisfactory directed its armies to take the offensive. The French advanced into Germany on the first of March, and in Italy towards the end of the month. But the action of the French Government, though audacious and imposing, rested upon no solid foundation of efficiency in the armies, or skill in the plan of campaign. Serious reverses soon followed, and the fatally excentric position of the corps in Naples was then immediately apparent.

Before this news could reach Palermo, however, Nelson had

[1] Palermo possessed a strategic advantage over Syracuse, in that, with westerly winds, it was to windward, especially as regards Naples; and it was also nearer the narrowest part of the passage between Sicily and Africa, the highway to the Levant and Egypt. With easterly winds, the enemy of course could not proceed thither; and at this time there was no enemy's force in the Mediterranean, so that westward movements had not to be apprehended. All dangers must come from the westward. These considerations were doubtless present to Nelson; but the author has not found any mention of them by him at this period.

sent Troubridge with four ships-of-the-line and some smaller vessels to the Bay of Naples, to blockade it, and to enter into communication, if possible, with the loyalists in the city. As the extreme reluctance of the King and Queen prevented his going in person, — a reason the sufficiency of which it is difficult to admit, — Nelson hoisted his flag on board a transport in the bay, and sent the flagship, in order not to diminish the force detailed for such important duties. Within a week the islands in the immediate neighborhood of Naples — Procida, Ischia, Capri, and the Ponzas — had again hoisted the royal ensign. On the 22d of April the French evacuated the city, with the exception of the Castle of St. Elmo, in which they left a garrison of five hundred men. In Upper Italy their armies were in full retreat, having been forced back from the Adige to the Adda, whence an urgent message was sent to Macdonald, Championnet's successor at Naples, to fall back to the northward and effect a junction with the main body, soon to be sorely pressed by an overwhelming force of the Austro-Russians, at whose head was the famous Suwarrow. On the 29th the Allies entered Milan, and on the 7th of May the Northern French, now under the command of Moreau, had retired as far as Alessandria, in Piedmont. On this same day, Macdonald, having thrown garrisons into Capua and Gaeta, evacuated the kingdom of Naples, and hastened northward to join Moreau. With the exception of these fortified posts and the city of Naples, the country was now overrun by the Christian army, the name applied to the numerous but utterly undisciplined bands of rude peasantry, attached to the royal cause, and led by Cardinal Ruffo. The Jacobins in the city still held out, and had in the bay a small naval force under the command of Commodore Caracciolo.

Troubridge's successes continued. A week later Salerno had been taken, and the royal colors were flying at Castella-mare, on the opposite side of the Bay from Naples, and distant from it only twelve miles by land. Nelson questioned Troubridge about the return of the King, whose most evident political conviction was that the success of the royal cause was vitally connected with the safety of the royal person. "What are your ideas of the King's going into the Bay of Naples, without foreign troops? If it should cause insurrection [of the royalists] in Naples which did not succeed, would it not be worse ? The King, if a rising of loyal people took place, ought to be amongst them ; and that he will never consent to." " The King, God bless him ! is a philosopher," he had said, repeating an expression of Lady Hamilton's, referring to the disasters which caused the headlong flight from Rome, through Naples, to Palermo; " but the great Queen feels sensibly all that has happened." The Queen also was extremely fearful, and Nelson intimated to St. Vincent that a request would be made for British troops to protect the sovereigns. " Their Majesties are ready to cross the water whenever Naples is entirely cleansed. When that happy event arrives, and not till then, a desire will be expressed for the British troops to be removed from Messina into Naples to guard the persons of their Majesties." That Nelson should have considered it essential to maintain in power, by any means, sovereigns devoted to Great Britain, is perfectly comprehensible. What is difficult to understand is the esteem he continued to profess for those whose unheroic bearing so belied the words he had written six months before : " His Majesty is determined to conquer or die at the head of his army." Under other conditions and influences, none would have been more forward to express dissatisfaction and contempt.

Withal, despite the favorable outlook of affairs and the most joyous season of the year, his depression of spirits continued. " I am far from well," he writes on the 3d of May, " and the good news of the success of the Austrian arms in Italy does not even cheer me." But in the midst of the full current of success, and of his own gloom, an incident suddenly occurred which threw everything again into confusion and doubt, and roused him for the time from his apathy. On the 12th of May a brig arrived at Palermo, with news that a French fleet of nineteen ships-of-the-line had escaped from Brest, and had been seen less than a fortnight before off Oporto, steering for the Mediterranean.

CHAPTER XIII.

MAY–JULY, 1799. AGE 40.

THE intention of the French to send a fleet into the Mediterranean had transpired some time before, and the
motive — to retrieve the destruction of their naval power in
that sea by the Battle of the Nile — was so obvious that the
attempt was regarded as probable. As far back as the 7th
of January, Nelson had written to Commodore Duckworth,
commanding the detachment of four ships-of-the-line at Minorca, that he had received notification of the force expected
from Brest. If they got into the Mediterranean, he was confident they would go first to Toulon, and he wished to concert beforehand with Duckworth, who was not under his
orders, the steps necessary to be taken at once, if the case
arose. He did not think, so he wrote to Ball, that they
would venture a squadron to Malta or Alexandria, in view
of the certain destruction which in the end must befall it,
even if successful in reaching the port.

Both remarks show that he did not look for the number
of ships that were sent — nineteen, as the first news said,
twenty-five, as was actually the case. An emergency so great
and so imminent drew out all his latent strength, acute judgment, and promptitude. The brig that brought the news was
sent off the same night to Naples, with orders to proceed from
there to Minorca and Gibraltar, and to notify Duckworth and
St. Vincent what Nelson intended to do. A cutter sailed at
the same time for Malta. Troubridge and Ball were both
directed to send or bring all their ships-of-the-line, save one
each, to Minorca, there to unite with Duckworth. Troubridge's ships were to call off Palermo for further instruc-

tions, but not to lose time by coming to anchor there. Expresses were sent to the different ports of Sicily, in case any Russian or Turkish ships had arrived, to put them on their guard, and to request co-operation by joining the force assembling off Minorca, where Nelson reasoned Lord St. Vincent also would repair. To the latter he wrote: "Eight, nine, or ten sail of the line shall, in a few days, be off Mahon, ready to obey your orders (not in the port);" for his intention was that they should remain outside under sail. "You may depend upon my exertion, and I am only sorry that I cannot move [1] to your help, but this island appears to hang on my stay. Nothing could console the Queen this night, but my promise not to leave them unless the battle was to be fought off Sardinia."

The next day he wrote again in similar terms, seeking to reconcile his promise to the Queen with his impulses, and, it may be said safely, with his duty. "Should you come upwards without a battle, I hope in that case you will afford me an opportunity of joining you; for my heart would break to be near my commander-in-chief, and not assisting him at such a time. What a state I am in! If I go, I risk, and more than risk, Sicily, and what is now safe on the Continent; for we know, from experience, that more depends on *opinion* than on acts themselves. As I stay, my heart is breaking; and, to mend the matter, I am seriously unwell."

That evening, the 13th, at nine o'clock, a lieutenant arrived, who had been landed to the westward of Palermo by a sloop-of-war, the "Peterel," she not being able to beat up to the city against the east wind prevailing. From him Nelson learned that the French fleet had passed the Straits, and had been seen off Minorca. The next day, the "Peterel" having come off the port, he went alongside, and sent her on at once to Malta, with orders to Ball to abandon the blockade, bringing with him all his ships, and to proceed off Maritimo, a small island twenty miles west of Sicily, where he now proposed to concentrate his squadron and to go himself. Troubridge, having already orders to come to Palermo, needed no further instructions, except to bring all his ships, instead of leaving one at Naples. Every ship-of-the-line in the squadron,

[1] That is, in person.

including the Portuguese, was thus summoned to join the
Flag, in a position to cover Palermo and the approaches to
the eastern Mediterranean. To these necessary dispositions
was owing that the senior officer left at Naples was Captain
Foote, who afterwards signed the articles of capitulation with
the insurgents, which gave such offence to Nelson, and have
occasioned much controversy in connection with his subsequent action.

Troubridge, having sailed at once on receipt of his first
orders, arrived on the 17th with three British ships and one
Portuguese. A heavy gale prevented Nelson getting to sea
till the 20th, when he sailed, and was joined the next morning
by the fourth ship from Naples. The same day came a Portuguese corvette from Gibraltar and Mahon, with letters from
St. Vincent and Duckworth. The former announced that
the French had passed the Straits, and that he was about to
start in pursuit. Duckworth, who also was asked to join off
Maritimo, declined to do so, saying that he must await the
commander-in-chief. Nelson had of course immediately communicated to the latter his change of plan. He hoped to
collect ten sail-of-the-line, which, "if Duckworth reinforce me,
will enable me to look the enemy in the face"—fourteen
ships to nineteen; "but should any of the Russians or Turks
be off Malta, I hope to get a force of different nations equal
to the enemy, when not a moment shall be lost in bringing
them to battle."

On the 23d of May he was off Maritimo with seven ships,
Ball not having joined yet. His spirits were fast rising, as in
thought he drew near the enemy. "Duckworth means to leave
me to my fate," he wrote to Lady Hamilton. "Never mind;
if I can get eleven sail together, they shall not hurt me."
"I am under no apprehension for the safety of his Majesty's
squadron," he said in a circular letter to his scattered vessels,
designed to heighten their ardor; "on the contrary, from the
very high state of discipline of the ships, I am confident,
should the enemy force us to battle, that we shall cut a very
respectable figure; and if Admiral Duckworth joins, not one
moment shall be lost in my attacking the enemy." It must
be mentioned that St. Vincent had expressed his opinion that
the French were bound for Malta and Alexandria, and Nelson,

when he wrote these words, was hourly expecting to see their sails appear on the horizon. He did not know yet, however, that they were twenty-five, instead of nineteen, of the line. To St. Vincent he expressed himself with the sober, dauntless resolution of a consummate warrior, who recognized that opportunities must be seized, and detachments, if need be, sacrificed, for the furtherance of a great common object. " Your Lordship may depend that the squadron under my command shall never fall into the hands of the enemy; and before we are destroyed, I have little doubt but the enemy will have their wings so completely clipped that they may be easily overtaken " — by you. In this temper he waited. It is this clear perception of the utility of his contemplated grapple with superior numbers, and not the headlong valor and instinct for fighting that unquestionably distinguished him, which constitutes the excellence of Nelson's genius. This it was which guided him in the great Trafalgar campaign, and the lack of which betrayed Villeneuve at the same period to his wretched shortcomings. Yet, as has before been remarked, mere insight, however accurate and penetrating, ends only in itself, or at best falls far short of the mark, unless accompanied by Nelson's great power of disregarding contingencies — an inspired blindness, which at the moment of decisive action sees, not the risks, but the one only road to possible victory.

Whilst thus expecting an engagement which, from the disparity of numbers, could be nothing short of desperate, he drew up a codicil to his will, making to Lady Hamilton a bequest, in terms that show how complete were the infatuation and idealization now in possession of his mind: " I give and bequeath to my dear friend, Emma Hamilton, wife of the Right Hon. Sir William Hamilton, a nearly round box set with diamonds, said to have been sent me by the mother of the Grand Signor, which I request she will accept (and never part from) as token of regard and respect for her very eminent virtues (for she, the said Emma Hamilton, possesses them all to such a degree that it would be doing her injustice was any particular one to be mentioned) from her faithful and affectionate friend." During this short cruise he wrote her almost daily, and at some length, in addition to the more official communications addressed to Hamilton. At this same

period he was excusing himself to his wife for the shortness
and infrequency of his letters: "Pray attribute it to the true
cause — viz., that in truth my poor hand cannot execute what
my head tells me I ought to do."

On the 28th of May Nelson received letters from St. Vincent, dated the 21st, off Minorca, which put him in possession
of the movements of the enemy up to that date. The French
fleet, under the command of Admiral Bruix, had appeared on
the 4th of the month off Cadiz. It was then blowing a half-
gale of wind, and the French admiral did not care, under that
condition, to engage the fifteen British ships-of-the-line which
were cruising off the harbor, under Lord Keith, who had come
out from England the previous autumn to be St. Vincent's
second in command. The intended junction with the Spanish
squadron in Cadiz being thus thwarted, Bruix passed the
Straits on the 5th, and Lord St. Vincent, having recalled
Keith, followed on the 12th with sixteen ships. On the 20th
he joined Duckworth, and learned that the enemy, when last
seen, were heading for Toulon. Keith's removal had uncovered Cadiz, and St. Vincent fully expected that the Spanish
fleet would leave there for the Mediterranean, which it did,
and on the 20th entered Cartagena, to the number of seventeen of the line, but much crippled from a stormy passage.
This Nelson did not yet know, nor that Bruix had reached
Toulon on the 14th of May, and sailed again on the 26th for
the eastward.

Satisfied that the enemy would not at once come his way,
and knowing that a vessel had passed up the Mediterranean
from St. Vincent to put Sidney Smith on his guard, Nelson
ordered Ball to resume the blockade of Malta with two ships-
of-the-line. The rest of his squadron he kept massed, and took
to Palermo, where he arrived May 29th. Lookout ships were
stationed off the north end of Corsica and west of Sardinia.
"My reason for remaining in Sicily," he wrote St. Vincent,
"is the covering the blockade of Naples, and the certainty of
preserving Sicily in case of an attack, for if we were to withdraw our ships, it would throw such a damp on the people
that I am sure there would be no resistance."

On the 6th of June Duckworth arrived at Palermo from the
main fleet, with four ships-of-the-line, among them the "Fou-

droyant," eighty. This ship had been designated originally for Nelson's flag, and he shifted to her from the "Vanguard" on the 8th. Duckworth brought a report that St. Vincent was about to give up the command and go home, on account of ill-health. This at once aroused Nelson's anxiety, for he had long felt that few superiors would have the greatness of mind to trust him as implicitly, and humor him as tenderly, as the great admiral had done. It is not every one that can handle an instrument of such trenchant power, yet delicate temper, as Nelson's sensitive genius. The combination in St. Vincent of perfect professional capacity with masterful strength of character, had made the tactful respect he showed to Nelson's ability peculiarly grateful to the latter; and had won from him a subordination of the will, and an affection, which no subsequent commander-in-chief could elicit. He wrote to him: —

My dear Lord, — We have a report that you are going home. This distresses us most exceedingly, and myself in particular; so much so, that I have serious thoughts of returning, if that event should take place. But for the sake of our Country, do not quit us at this serious moment. I wish not to detract from the merit of whoever may be your successor; but it must take a length of time, which I hope the war will not give, to be in any manner a St. Vincent. We look up to you, as we have always found you, as to our Father, under whose fostering care we have been led to fame. . . . Give not up a particle of your authority to any one; be again our St. Vincent, and we shall be happy.

Your affectionate   Nelson.

This letter did not reach St. Vincent before he carried his purpose into effect; but Nelson never quite forgave the abandonment of the command at such a moment. In after years he spoke bitterly of it, as a thing he himself could not have done; failing, perhaps, to realize the difference in staying power between forty-five and sixty-five.

On the 2d of June, being then seventy miles southwest of Toulon, St. Vincent turned over to Keith the command of the twenty ships-of-the-line then with him, and went to Port Mahon. For the moment he retained in his own hands the charge of the station, — continued Commander-in-chief, — with

headquarters at Minorca, and two divisions cruising: one of
twenty ships, with Keith, between Toulon and Minorca, and
one of sixteen, including three Portuguese, under Nelson in
the waters of Sicily. Friction between these two began at
once. Lord Keith was an accomplished and gallant officer,
methodical, attentive, and correct; but otherwise he rose little
above the commonplace, and, while he could not ignore Nelson's great achievements, he does not seem to have had the
insight which could appreciate the rare merit underlying
them, nor the sympathetic temperament which could allow
for his foibles. Nelson, exasperated at the mere fact of
the other's succession to the command, speedily conceived
for him an antipathy which Keith would have been more
than mortal not to return; but it is to the honor of the
latter's self-command that, while insisting upon obedience from
his brilliant junior, he bore his refractoriness with dignified
patience.

After St. Vincent left him, Keith continued to stand to the
northward and eastward. On the 5th of June he received
certain information that the French fleet, now twenty-two
ships-of-the-line, was in Vado Bay. This word he at once sent
on to Nelson. Next day his division was so close in with the
Riviera, off Antibes, that it was fired upon by the shore batteries; but the wind coming to the eastward, when off Monaco,
did not permit it to pass east of Corsica, and, fearing that the
French would take that route and fall upon Nelson, Keith
detached to him two seventy-fours, which joined him on the
13th of June.

At the moment of their arrival Nelson had just quitted
Palermo for Naples, taking with him the whole squadron.
The King of Naples had formally requested him to afford to
the royal cause at the capital the assistance of the fleet, because the successes of the royalists elsewhere in the kingdom
rendered imminent an insurrection in the city against the
republican party and the French, which held the castles; and
such insurrection, unless adequately supported, might either
fail or lead to deplorable excesses. Lady Hamilton, whose
irregular interference in State concerns receives here singular
illustration, strongly urged this measure in a letter, written to
the admiral after an interview with the Queen. Nelson con-

sented, took on board seventeen hundred troops, with the Hereditary Prince, who was to represent the King, — the latter not wishing to go, — and was already clear of Palermo Bay when the two ships from Keith appeared. Gathering from their information that the French were bound for Naples or Sicily, in which his own judgment coincided, he returned at once into port, landed the Prince and the troops, and then took the squadron again off Maritimo, where he expected Ball and the two ships off Malta to join him without delay. "The French force being twenty-two sail of the line," he wrote in suppressed reproach to Keith, "four of which are first rates, the force with me being only sixteen of the line, not one of which was of three decks, three being Portuguese, and one of the English being a sixty-four, very short of men, I had no choice left but to return to Palermo."

With this incident of the insufficient reinforcement sent, began the friction with Keith which appears more openly in his correspondence with others. To St. Vincent, still commander-in-chief, he wrote: "I send a copy of my letter to Lord Keith, and I have only stated my regret that his Lordship could not have sent me a force fit to face the enemy: but, as we are, I shall not get out of their way; although, as I am, I cannot think myself justified in exposing the world (I may almost say) to be plundered by these miscreants. I trust your Lordship will not think me wrong in the painful determination I conceived myself forced to make," that is, to go back to Palermo, "for agonized indeed was the mind of your Lordship's faithful and affectionate servant."

Nelson appears to have felt that the return to Palermo, though imperative, in view of the relative forces of himself and the French, would not only postpone and imperil the restoration of the royal family, but would bring discredit upon himself for not seeking and fighting the enemy's fleet. "I shall wait off Maritimo," he wrote Keith, "anxiously expecting such a reinforcement as may enable me to go in search of the enemy's fleet, when not one moment shall be lost in bringing them to battle; for," he continues, with one of those flashes of genius which from time to time, unconsciously to himself, illuminate his writings, "I consider the best defence for his Sicilian Majesty's dominions is to place myself along-

side the French." " My situation is a cruel one," he wrote to
Hamilton, "and I am sure Lord Keith has lowered me in the
eyes of Europe, for they will only know of 18 sail [Ball having joined], and not of the description of them; it has truly
made me ill." But, although not justified in seeking them,
he had off Maritimo taken a strategic position which would
enable him to intercept their approach to either Naples or
Sicily, "and I was firmly resolved," he wrote with another of
his clear intuitions, "they should not pass me without a
battle, which would so cripple them that they might be unable
to proceed on any distant service." " On this you may depend," he had written to Lady Hamilton, on the first cruise
off Maritimo, three weeks before, "that if my little squadron
obeys my signal, not a ship shall fall into the hands of the
enemy; and I will so cut them up, that they will not be fit
even for a summer's cruise."

On the 20th of June, off Maritimo, he received a despatch
from St. Vincent that a reinforcement of twelve ships-of-the-
line from the Channel was then approaching Port Mahon, and
that Keith, having returned thither, had left again in search
of Bruix, whose whereabouts remained unknown. He was
also notified that St. Vincent had resigned all his command,
leaving Keith commander-in-chief. Nelson was convinced —
"I knew," was his expression — that the French intended
going to Naples. He determined now to resume his enterprise
against the republicans in the city; a decision which caused
him unusual mental conflict. " I am agitated," he wrote Hamilton the same day, in a note headed " Most Secret," " but my
resolution is fixed. For Heaven's sake suffer not any one to
oppose it. I shall not be gone eight days. No harm can
come to Sicily. I send my Lady and you Lord St. Vincent's
letter. I am full of grief and anxiety. I must go. It will
finish the war. It will give a sprig of laurel to your affectionate friend, Nelson." The military dilemma of divergent interests confronting him is plain enough, being the same that
had " agonized " his mind in abandoning the first expedition
to Naples on the 14th. Off Maritimo, with winds prevailing
from the westward, he covered both Naples and Sicily, and
could hurry to either at a moment's notice. By going to Naples
he surrendered this advantage as regarded Sicily and the

Court, in order to undertake a strictly offensive movement; and to this he dreaded opposition, which would be the more painful, because the fears that prompted it would rest on arguments, the strength of which he could not but admit. On the 21st he was at Palermo, and after two hours' consultation with their Majesties and Acton, the Prime Minister, he sailed again, accompanied in the "Foudroyant" on this occasion by Sir William and Lady Hamilton, but not by the Hereditary Prince, nor the Sicilian troops. On the 24th, at 9 P. M., the flagship anchored in the Bay of Naples, the rest of the squadron remaining outside for the night. Flags of truce were at that moment flying on the castles of Uovo and Nuovo, which were in the hands of the Neapolitan republicans, and upon the frigate "Seahorse," whose commander, Captain E. J. Foote, had been the senior British officer present, before Nelson's own appearance. The following morning the "Foudroyant" shifted farther in, near the mole, the remainder of the ships taking position from her, in close line of battle, about noon.

The occurrences at Naples during the remaining days of June, 1799, have been the occasion of the most serious imputations ever made against Nelson's character. These imputations are not limited to a breach of faith in disallowing a capitulation, asserted by accusers to have been irrevocably completed by authorities of final action. Nelson openly disallowed and suspended the capitulation on the ground that it had not been executed, and that it was also an improper transaction, entered into contrary to the orders given by the King to Cardinal Ruffo, his representative. Nelson claimed that he had powers direct from the King, to overrule Ruffo; in virtue of which he did openly overrule him in this particular instance, because, although the treaty had been signed, it had advanced no further. "Never executed, and therefore no capitulation," was his own expression. In this he may have done wrong. The present writer does not think so; but the question is one of military public law, as it stood at that date. Whatever the merit of the action otherwise, it was open, positive, aboveboard, and Ruffo was requested to convey the knowledge of it to the enemy. This he refused at first to do. Subsequently, he did communicate to them the substance of Nelson's opinion. The latter asserted that the final surrender was com-

pleted under full knowledge of the attitude assumed by
him.

The serious charges made are : first, that Nelson was not
invested with legal authority to override Ruffo; second, and
chiefly, that not only did he break a treaty, and, as is claimed,
deprive the enemy of rights acquired by lawful compact, but
that he permitted, if he did not induce, them to leave their
fortifications, and to place themselves in his power, under the
supposition that he acquiesced in a treaty of capitulation.
This view was summarized by Captain Foote, writing in
1807: "I believe it is but too true that the garrisons of Uovo
and Nuovo were taken out of these castles under the *pretence*
of putting the capitulation I had signed into execution." [1]
This charge having very recently been repeated, the author
has recast his treatment of the subject from that pursued in
the first editions. This paragraph, and the one preceding it,
convey in brief outline the two contentions to be tested, — that
of Nelson, and that of his accusers.

It is, first, necessary to tell the transactions about Naples
up to the date of Nelson's arrival, on the evening of June 24.
The French having evacuated the kingdom, leaving garrisons
only in Capua, in Gaeta, and in Fort St. Elmo, overlooking
Naples, the Neapolitan republicans were left to their own
defence. Against them were advancing the so-called Christian
Army, composed chiefly of Calabrian peasants and brigands,
under the command of Cardinal Ruffo, the King's Vicar-
General, and a body of some five hundred Russians and Turks
from the Adriatic. The assistance of the latter had been obtained by the Chevalier Micheroux, sent to Corfu for that
purpose by the King. His style and title was, "Minister
plenipotentiary of the King of the Two Sicilies near the
Russo-Ottoman Fleet." Micheroux played a considerable part
in the subsequent treaty, but both Foote and Nelson declined
to recognize any authority save in Ruffo.

On June 13 the British squadron began to co-operate
with Ruffo and his allies, who then reached the Bay ; and on
the 16th Foote reported to Nelson that the city was in Ruffo's
power, except Fort St. Elmo, held by the French, and the two

---

[1] Captain Foote's Vindication, London, 1810, p. 39. The italics are
Foote's.

lower castles, Uovo and Nuovo, into which the Neapolitan insurgents had retired. On the 17th Ruffo notified Foote that Nuovo was admitted to an armistice, from which Uovo stood aloof; but that night a sortie was made by some of the French and republicans, who spiked the guns of a battery and killed a number of the besiegers. Ruffo then resumed operations, informing Foote that negotiations were useless, but on the morning of the 19th, he sent word that an armistice had been again granted, and negotiations begun with good promise of success; he therefore requested Foote to desist from all hostilities. The latter acceded, though unwillingly; saying that so prolonged a cessation of arms was injurious to the common cause. Not hearing anything by the evening of the 20th, he again wrote urgently to the same effect; but about midnight there was brought to him the first draft of a capitulation, which he signed. This then went back to the shore, was put into final shape, and so approved by the French commandant of St. Elmo, as the terms required. It then received the signatures of Ruffo, of Micheroux, of the Russian and Turkish commanders, and finally of Foote himself; the latter being given on the early morning of June 23.

The document may be considered then to have been formally complete; the only question being whether it was susceptible of ratification or disallowance by superior authority. Ruffo, Foote, and the others held that it was not. Nelson maintained that it was, provided it had not received execution. This it had not, for the second article provided that the garrisons should keep possession of the forts until the vessels that were to take them to Toulon were ready to sail, which was not the case when Nelson arrived. The latter also said that the treaty was "infamous." The term was too strong. The treaty, in the author's judgment, was weak and culpable, — weak, because, as Fort St. Elmo dominated the lower castles, terms so very favorable should not have been granted unless St. Elmo was included in the surrender; [1] and culpable, because Ruffo's orders were disobeyed in granting such liberal terms to

---

[1] For Foote's opinion of the terms, see Vindication, pp. 154, 155, 190, 191; and of the commanding position of St. Elmo, pp. 137, 141. The unfavorable opinion of Count Thurn, the senior Neapolitan naval officer present, is given by Maresca (Archivio Storico per le Provincie Napoletane, vol. xix. p. 508).

men of the political and military antecedents of many of those
shut up in the castles.[1] These considerations do not, however,
affect the character of Nelson's act in nullifying the treaty.
That depends upon the questions, whether Ruffo's act was
from the first absolutely final, and, if it were not, whether the
method of revoking it were fair and honorable.

Before proceeding to the consideration of these questions,
it is necessary to draw attention to the fact that there were
before Nelson two principal conditions, which have been confounded one with another.   There was an Armistice, which
had lasted since the morning of the 19th ; and there was the
Treaty of Capitulation, signed on the morning of the 23d.
The Armistice began for the purpose of negotiation, and continued after the signature, awaiting the execution of the terms,
which was to take place when the vessels were ready to embark the garrisons.   This seems so clear as to be unnecessary
to mention, had it not been affirmed in a serious historical
magazine that Nelson persisted in styling the Treaty an
Armistice;[2] upon which an elaborate argument is founded.
Nelson's own words are, " I used every argument in my power
to convince the Cardinal that the Treaty *and* Armistice was at
an end by the coming of the fleet." [3]   If it be thought that the
singular verb " was " shows confusion in Nelson's mind, the
reply is, not only was his grammar notoriously careless,[4] but
that a treaty and an armistice are very different things.
Thus Foote, Nelson's chief English accuser, says, " A treaty
may be infamous ; an armistice, or cessation from hostilities,
cannot deserve this term.   It is only a step towards an accommodation."   Without accepting Foote's dictum as to the
infamy of either, the distinction is obvious, and the undeniable
truth is that there was an armistice and there was a treaty.

The confusion, introduced and asserted by others, but which
did not exist in Nelson's mind, is due probably to the fact that

[1] See the King's letter of May 1, to Ruffo (Dumas, I Borboni di Napoli,
vol. v. p. 240); and of June 17 (p. 253).

[2] English Historical Review, April, 1898, p. 273, and p. 275, note 1.

[3] Nicolas, vol. iii. p. 393. (Author's italics.)

[4] Thus, in the same letter, Nelson writes: " Under this opinion the
Rebels came out of the Castles, which *was* instantly occupied by the Marines
of the squadron." (Ibid.)

before he saw Foote he had received word — erroneous — that an Armistice had been granted, by the terms of which there was to be no fighting for twenty-one days;[1] at the end of which, if not relieved, the garrisons were to march out with the honors of war. Such an Armistice — by no means unprecedented [2] — though so called, is more than an armistice, for it agrees to more than a stoppage of hostilities. To it Nelson applied the term "infamous." *After* seeing Foote, and learning the actual state of affairs, he speaks (in the same letter) of the infamous "terms" entered into with the Rebels. These terms were much the same, though not exactly, as in the supposed Armistice, but they were embodied in a Capitulation, in which no mention of an armistice occurs from first to last. Hamilton, writing for Nelson to Ruffo of the same, calls it the "capitulation," [3] not the armistice; and that the distinction was understood both by Hamilton and by Nelson is clear from the fact that the latter formally disapproved and prevented the *capitulation*, sending Ruffo the information, together with papers to the same effect to be sent in to the enemy. This was positive action, taken independent of Ruffo, and so finished; after which — not before — the question was put to Ruffo, "If Lord Nelson breaks the Armistice, will your Eminence assist him?" The manner and the order in which the events are told by Nelson, and his own course described, in his letter of June 27 to Keith,[4] show that he disapproved and suspended the Capitulation, by his own powers, without consulting Ruffo; but that concerning the Armistice, though he held it to be at an end by the mere arrival of the fleet, he would not take the step of actively breaking it — though he at first fully intended to do so — without previous consultation. This separation in treatment of the two things shows conclusively the distinction between them in his own mind.[5]

---

[1] Nicolas, vol. iii. p. 384.

[2] As at Calvi, in 1794. See *ante*, p. 124.

[3] George Rose's Diaries, vol. i. p. 236.

[4] Nicolas, vol. iii. p. 392.

[5] That the Treaty and the Armistice had separate and independent existences, is an historical fact, beyond doubt. That Nelson so understood them requires to be deduced; that is, to those who doubt his clear-headedness or his honesty. Like men generally, when things are clear in their own minds, he

The treaty, as finally signed, — and afterwards suspended
by him, — read as follows : —

LIBERTY.					EQUALITY.

NEAPOLITAN REPUBLIC.

CASTEL NUOVO, 2d Messidor,[1] Year 7 of Liberty.

Citizen Massa, General of Artillery, and Commandant of Castel
Nuovo, the surrender of Castel Uovo having been demanded by
Commandant Foote of the English Navy; and afterwards that of
Castel Nuovo by Cardinal Ruffo, Vicar General of the Kingdom of
Naples, by Chevalier Micheroux, Minister Plenipotentiary of H. M.
the King of the Two Sicilies near the Russo-Ottoman fleet, and by
the commandant in chief of the Ottoman troops; the Council of War
of Castel Nuovo assembled, and having deliberated upon the said
summons, resolved that the two forts shall be delivered to the
commanders of the troops of the above named by means of an honorable capitulation, and after having communicated to the commandant
of Fort St. Elmo the motives for the said surrender, in consequence
the said Council has drawn up the articles of the following capitulation without the acceptance of which the surrender of the forts
cannot take place.

Article 1. The Forts Nuovo and Uovo shall be delivered to the
Commanders of the Troops of H. M. the King of the Two Sicilies,
and of those of his Allies, the King of England, the Emperor of all
the Russias, and the Ottoman Porte, with all warlike stores, provisions, artillery, and effects of every kind now in the magazines, of
which an inventory shall be made by Commissaries on both sides,
after the present capitulation is signed.

Article 2. The Troops composing the Garrisons shall keep possession of their Forts, until the Vessels which shall be spoken of
hereafter, destined to convey such as are desirous of going to Toulon,
are ready to sail.[2]

did not suspect misunderstanding in others; consequently, intent only on
the business before him, he did not provide for posterity a categorical declaration that he was conscious of a very obvious difference.

[1] June 20.

[2] The first draft here contained these additional words : "The evacuation
shall not take place until the moment of embarcation" (Vindication, p. 195).
These do not appear in the final terms. This might have been important,
because Article 2 fixes the time when, by evacuation, the treaty should receive actual execution, as distinguished from completeness of form. As it
was, Nelson arrived before the transports were ready, and consequently found

Article 3. The Garrisons shall march out with the honors of war, with arms, and baggage, drums beating, colors flying, matches lighted, and each with two pieces of artillery; they shall lay down their arms on the beach.

Article 4. Persons and Property, both movable and immovable, of every individual of the two Garrisons, shall be respected and guaranteed.

Article 5. All the said individuals shall have their choice of embarking on board the cartels, which shall be furnished to carry them to Toulon, or of remaining at Naples without being molested, either in their persons or families.

Article 6. The conditions contained in the present Capitulation are common to every person of both sexes now in the Forts.

Article 7. The same conditions shall hold with respect to all the prisoners which the Troops of His Majesty the King of the Two Sicilies, and those of his Allies, may have made from the Republican troops, in the different engagements which have taken place before the blockade of the Forts.

Article 8. Messieurs, the Archbishop of Salerno, Micheroux, Dillon, and the Bishop of Avellino, detained in the Forts, shall be delivered to the Commandant of Fort St. Elmo, where they shall remain as hostages, until the arrival of the individuals, sent to Toulon, shall be ascertained.

Article 9. All the other hostages and State prisoners, confined in the two Forts, shall be set at liberty, immediately after the present Capitulation is signed.

Article 10. None of the Articles of the said Capitulation can be put into execution until after they shall have been fully approved by the Commandant of Fort St. Elmo.

Thirty-six hours after Foote signed, Nelson arrived, and as soon as he saw the flag of truce flying from the forts and from the "Seahorse," he made a signal annulling the truce.[1] This was before he saw Foote,[2] who, by the log of the "Seahorse," came on board outside of the harbor at 4 P. M., having got the ship under way to meet the admiral.[3] Shortly after his interview with Foote, who brought with him a copy of the capitulation, Nelson sent ahead of the flagship, in a pulling boat,

the Republicans still in possession of the forts. He therefore claimed, and undoubtedly believed, that the treaty could rightfully be suspended, because not executed.

[1] Nicolas, vol. iii. p. 392.   [2] Vindication, p. 71.
[3] Nicolas, vol. iii. p. 494.

Troubridge and Ball — two of his most trusted captains —
to visit Ruffo. These officers carried with them a letter to
the Cardinal,[1] written in the name of Nelson by Sir William
Hamilton, who seems throughout to have accepted a ministerial position between Nelson, as his principal, and the other
parties to these transactions. In this letter it was stated
that Nelson, having seen the treaty, entirely disapproved of
it; that he would not remain neuter with the fleet; and that
the two captains were fully informed of his sentiments and
would explain them to his Eminence. He added that he
hoped the Cardinal would agree with him, and that to-morrow
(the 25th), at break of day, they would be able to act in concert. Besides the letter the captains carried with them two
papers.[2] Of these, one, addressed to the French in St. Elmo,
demanded their surrender within two hours.[3] The other, to
the Republicans in Uovo and Nuovo, informed them that they
would not be permitted "to embark or to quit those places.
They must surrender themselves to His Majesty's Royal
mercy."[4]

Together with the letter and the papers already mentioned,
the captains probably took with them another paper,[5] in which
Nelson, taking for his text the supposed armistice for twenty-
one days, reported to him before his arrival, had developed
his argument to prove that such a compact, which was of the
nature of a treaty rather than of an armistice, could be an-
nulled by a superior power appearing on the scene. This paper
Ruffo had, either from the captains, or from Nelson himself
the next day; for on it is noted, in Nelson's hand, "Read
and explained, and rejected by the Cardinal."[6]

Ruffo absolutely refused to send into the castles the papers
brought by the captains, and upon Troubridge asking him
whether he would co-operate with Nelson, if the latter broke
the armistice, he said he would not. After much communication, he decided to see Nelson personally, and went on board

---

[1] Rose's Diaries, etc. vol. i. p. 236. In a facsimile given by Sacchinelli
the hour of writing appears to have been 5 P. M.

[2] Nicolas, vol. iii. p. 392. [3] Ibid. p. 386.
[4] Ibid. [5] Ibid. p. 384.
[6] Ibid. p. 386.

the flagship [1] the afternoon of the 25th.[2] A long and stormy interview followed, in which neither party yielded his ground, and which ended in Nelson defining his status in the following written opinion, given to the Cardinal: —

FOUDROYANT, 26th [3] June, 1799.

Rear Admiral Lord Nelson arrived with the British fleet the 24th June in the Bay of Naples, and found a treaty entered into with the Rebels, which, in his opinion, cannot be carried into execution, without the approbation of his Sicilian Majesty.[4]

Ruffo then went on shore, and that evening, the 25th, he sent into Castel Nuovo a letter addressed to the commandant, Massa, as follows :

"Although he himself and the representatives of the allies held as sacred and inviolable the treaty of capitulation of the castles, nevertheless the rear-admiral of the English squadron was not willing to recognize it, and therefore the garrisons were at liberty to avail themselves of the 5th article of the capitulation, as the patriots of St. Martin's Hill had done, who had all departed by land; so he made to them this communication, in order that, considering that the English commanded the sea, the garrisons might take the resolution which best pleased them." [5]

At the same time he had proclamation made throughout the city, and notices posted, announcing the surrender of the castles, and forbidding any molestation of the members of the garrison, in goods or person, under penalty of death.[6]

As the garrisons had not yet embarked, although many of their number had been stealing away, even before the *projet* of capitulation was framed,[7] and throughout the succeeding

---

[1] Nelson to Keith, Nicolas, vol. iii. p. 392.

[2] The time of the interview is fixed by the following entry in the log of the flagship, regard being had to the sea-day, which began twelve hours before the civil day : " Wednesday, 26th, Saluted a Cardinal who came on board with 13 guns. A. M. Employed occasionally." (Nicolas, vol. iii. p. 508.)

[3] Sea-time.

[4] From Nelson's Order Book, Nicolas, vol. iii. p. 388.

[5] Maresca, Arch. Stor. Prov. Nap., vol. xix. p. 521.

[6] Ibid. ; quoted from the Diario Napol., of June 25, 1799.

[7] " Ever since this morning (June 19), from the moment they began to *treat* about a capitulation, a great many began to desert from the two castles," etc. Ruffo to Foote, Vindication, p. 185. (Author's italics.)

days, it cannot be said, in view of the above, that they had no warning of Nelson's attitude. Doubtless, in saying thus much, and yet omitting — if he adhered to his first refusal — to send in the papers bearing Nelson's own words, Ruffo did not deal candidly with them; so much so, indeed, that it is fairly open to belief that he may similarly have equivocated to the admiral, who stated positively, and immediately after the transactions,[1] that the rebels came out of the castles "under this opinion "[2] and "with this knowledge," [3] both which were passed to Ruffo to be communicated, and could by him have been transmitted, if he chose.

Massa replied for the garrison:

" We have given to your letter the interpretation which it deserved. Firm, however, in our duties, we shall religiously observe the articles of the treaty, convinced that an equal obligation should be maintained by all the contracting parties who have therein solemnly taken part. For the rest we cannot be either surprised or intimidated, and we shall resume a hostile attitude whenever it may happen that you constrain us thereto." [4]

He then requested an escort for a messenger to communicate with St. Elmo on the matter.

"From these two letters," remarks Maresca,[5] " it appears that we must deduce, even admitting that Nelson did not directly send in his Declaration, that the patriots of the castles were made acquainted with his intentions by means of Ruffo's letter."

The author has had the good fortune to find evidence, hitherto unquoted, strongly corroborative of this deduction. The same evening, June 25, Ruffo wrote to Nelson also, informing him that "the letter " had then gone forward to the castles, that it was to be hoped they would surrender at discretion, but, as they might decide to attack, he wished a reinforcement

---

[1] To Keith, on June 27 (Nicolas, vol. iii. p. 393 ; and to Earl Spencer, on July 13 (Ibid.; p. 406).

[2] Nelson's Opinion (Ibid., pp. 388, 393).

[3] Of Nelson's Opinion, and of his Declaration to the Rebels, Ibid., pp. 386, 388.

[4] Sacchinelli, Memorie sulla Vita del Cardinale Ruffo, Rome, 1895, pp. 233, 234 (Maresca, 522).

[5] Archivio Storico per le Prov. Nap., vol. xix. p. 522.

of 1,200 men might be landed.[1] The contents of "the letter"
are not specified, which indicates that Nelson knew them, while
the results expected tell us what its nature was, and that, in the
matter of the Treaty, Ruffo, as Acton afterwards wrote,[2] had
yielded to Nelson so far as to send the latter's Declaration to
the garrisons, in substance, if not in its exact words. This
step towards a compromise, by which the two chiefs might act
in accord, was met by a corresponding concession, concerning
the Armistice, on the part of Nelson. He apparently did not
receive Ruffo's letter of the evening of the 25th until the 26th
was well advanced, — "I am *just* honoured with your Excellency's letter," — but at an earlier hour Hamilton had written
in his name to the Cardinal, as follows : —

"Lord Nelson begs me to assure your Eminence that he is resolved
to do nothing which can break the armistice which your Eminence
has accorded to the castles of Naples."[3]

This promise referred explicitly to the Armistice, and
gave no assurances concerning his future action upon the
Capitulation. This, Nelson had said in writing, "cannot be
carried into effect without the approval of the King ; " and
that opinion had not been recalled — could not be recalled,
effectively, except by a written paper, the existence of which
has never been even suggested. The Treaty, so far as Nelson
was concerned, remained suspended, but the Armistice was to
continue.

The wording of this letter not only expresses the decisive
conclusion reached by Nelson after a night's reflection, but
appears also to confirm an arrangement already conditionally
reached. In short, as Hamilton wrote to Acton, "If one cannot do exactly as one wishes, one must do the best one can,
and that is what Lord Nelson has done."[4] It was inexpe-
dient, having in view Ruffo's attitude, to proceed to hostilities,
as at first intended. If the Cardinal would acquiesce in the
annulling of the treaty, in submission to the Admiral's powers,

---

[1] British Museum, Nelson MSS., $\frac{34944}{238}$.

[2] Nicolas, vol. vii. p. clxxxvi.

[3] Sacchinelli, p. 236.

[4] Dumas, I Borboni di Napoli, vol. iv. p. 89.

and would send in the latter's declaration to that effect, —
though refusing to join in it, — Nelson would continue the
armistice. This concession met Ruffo's leading idea, which
was to save the city from further injury, not only by stopping fighting, but also by releasing the regular troops available, to suppress the outrages increasingly committed by
Ruffo's undisciplined forces, by the lazzaroni, and by the
Turkish auxiliaries. Such seem to be conclusions fairly
deducible from Ruffo's letter of the 25th, and from the
following reply by Nelson on the 26th. The latter is
undated, but the date is fixed by the reference to that
written by Hamilton.

"I am just honoured with Your Eminency's letter; and as His
Excellency Sir William Hamilton has wrote you this morning, that
I will not on any consideration break the Armistice entered into by
you, I hope Your Eminency will be satisfied that I am supporting
your ideas. I send once more Captains Troubridge and Ball, to
arrange with your Eminency everything relative to an attack on St.
Elmo ; whenever your army and cannon are ready to proceed against
it, I will land 1200 men to go with them, under the present Armistice. I have only to rejoice that His Britannic Majesty's fleet is
here, to secure the city of Naples from all attacks by sea, — I
am, &c.   NELSON." [1]

It will be noticed that the purpose of the present mission
of Troubridge and Ball is strictly defined, and, because defined,
limited. They were to make arrangements for an attack upon
St. Elmo. During the interview Ruffo, according to Sacchinelli, was by them assured that Nelson " does not oppose the
execution of the Capitulation." Sacchinelli states further that
Troubridge drew up the following paper, based on this alleged
assurance : —

"Captains Troubridge and Ball have authority, on the part of
Lord Nelson, to declare to his Eminence that his Lordship will not
oppose the embarkation of the Rebels and of the people who compose
the garrison of the castles Uovo and Nuovo."

It is to be remarked that the one statement, "does not oppose the execution of the Capitulation," is not identical with

---

[1] From Nelson's Letter Book, Nicolas, vol. iii. p. 394.

that of the alleged consequent paper, " will not oppose the embarkation." This effort to confuse two distinct things resembles closely the attempt to confound Armistice and Capitulation. Further, Sacchinelli does not give at all Nelson's own letter, last quoted, but attributes the captains' visit to bearing Hamilton's preceding letter of the same day. " This declaration," he states, "Troubridge wrote *with his own hand,* but was not willing to sign it, saying that they had been charged and accredited with the letter of June 24 to confer verbally concerning military operations, and not at all, in writing, concerning affairs belonging to diplomacy." [1] It is clear from this that Sacchinelli, though Ruffo's secretary, was imperfectly informed as to the details of what happened. Not only is he ignorant of Nelson's letter, which certainly was brought by the captains, but he attributes to Hamilton's of June 24th a scope which pertains only to Nelson's of the 26th. Both these were certainly carried by the captains, while it is not certain that they took Hamilton's of the 26th. In the letter of the 24th, the mission of the captains was clearly diplomatic. They were to convey to the Cardinal Nelson's disapproval of the Capitulation, and his intention not to remain neuter. This agrees with Nelson's statement in his letter of the 27th to Keith, " I sent Captains Troubridge and Ball instantly to the Cardinal Vicar-General, to represent my opinion of the infamous terms entered into with the Rebels, and also two papers which I enclose." These papers were the Summons to the French and the Declaration to the Rebels; both part of the diplomacy of war. By this letter of the 24th they were accredited as "fully informed of Lord Nelson's sentiments and will have the honour to explain them " — verbally, of course — " to your Eminence." These functions are all diplomatic — negotiatory — in character, and that letter goes no further than to hope for agreement with the Cardinal, so that military operations may proceed. There is in it no mention of military arrangements as part of the captains' then mission, although there is in that of the 26th ; and at the very least it is clear that their function on the 24th was not limited, as Sacchinelli states that they said, to military operations. Finally, the declaration which it is

[1] Sacchinelli, p. 236, and Appendix, Facsimile *c.* (Author's italics.)

said the captains refused to sign is not in Troubridge's hand,
as alleged. The author has a letter of Troubridge's, written
in January, 1799, which differs distinctly from the facsimile
of the declaration given by Sacchinelli.

The attempt to implicate Nelson as partner in a disreputable
trick, upon evidence as faulty as this, is mere futile prevarica-
tion. It may be that the captains were asked to sign such a
paper; although Sacchinelli, by stating that Troubridge wrote
it, invalidates his own testimony, — showing that he is willing
to make a statement of infamous import, when he was not
eye-witness, nor had adequate proof. The captains, however,
had neither authority nor power, direct nor indirect, so to
pledge Nelson, by word or script, as was perfectly known to
Ruffo; for he had in his hands the letter they brought him
from Nelson, defining their present mission, viz. to arrange
for the attack on St. Elmo. To say, as some have, that, because accredited, two days before, "as fully informed of Lord
Nelson's sentiments," upon one subject, of a specific character,
they were equally accredited with knowledge of his views, and
with authority to express them, on another subject, when sent
upon a second mission, having no relation to the former, but
clearly defined and limited, would be to introduce anarchy into
negotiation. The verbal assurance of an envoy, sent as Troubridge and Ball then were, is of no weight against two written
declarations of their principal, close at hand, viz.: that the
capitulation could not be carried into effect without the King's
approval, and that they were sent to arrange for an attack
on St. Elmo. Both these Ruffo had in his hands; and only
a written revocation of the former could justify him in assuming it to be withdrawn. There is not the slightest proof, nor
even indication, that Nelson by letter or by word receded from
his attitude towards the Capitulation. He regarded it as beyond his powers. An armistice — a cessation of hostilities —
was within his powers; and this he undertook to observe.

After stating that the captains refused to sign, Sacchinelli
continues: "The Cardinal, although he suspected that there
might here be bad faith, not wishing to dispute with those two
captains, concerned himself no farther than to charge Minister
Micheroux to accompany them to the castles, to concert with
the republican commanders the execution of the stipulated

articles." The insinuation of the last few words, that the execution of the treaty, which Nelson had unwaveringly refused, was now arranged by his representatives with the other party, becomes an explicit affirmation, a few lines on. "At the end of some hours Micheroux reported to the Cardinal that, thanks to God, all had been arranged by common accord." These words end a paragraph, and may be assumed therefore to be all that Micheroux reported. Common accord is stated, but what was arranged is left to inference. What follows is Sacchinelli's inference, which, in view of the looseness of his other statements, must go for what it is worth. "The English themselves executed that treaty, which at first they were unwilling to recognize. They disembarked some hundreds of marines, and, the republicans having embarked, took possession of Castel Nuovo," etc. It is clear in this last quotation that Sacchinelli assumes, in face of the Cardinal's distrust, that the embarkation of the republicans and the taking possession of the castles prove Nelson's acceptance of the Treaty. It is equally clear to a careful reader that the inference is far from inevitable, and that the two acts may equally indicate the submission of the rebels to Nelson's terms. This Nelson explicitly affirmed to be the case in two letters written within three weeks of the transaction to the men to whom he was chiefly responsible — his Commander-in-Chief and the First Lord. "The Rebels came out of the Castles under this opinion," [1] "with this knowledge." [2]

High as Nelson's own reputation is, it is nevertheless fortunate that the stigma of Sacchinelli is rebutted not by that alone, nor yet by Sacchinelli's own carelessness of statement, but by the share borne in these transactions by Ball and Troubridge. Of the latter especially, who, as the senior of the two, stood for their joint action, St. Vincent said, "his honour and his courage are as bright as his sword." Is it to be believed that such a man gave assurances to which he refused to sign his name, and deceived even rebels — much as he hated them — when they were trusting to his honor, with their lives on the stake? Further, Clarke, the biographer of Nelson, writing to Captain Foote, Nelson's bitterest English assailant, quotes two other captains of the fleet as cognizant

[1] To Keith, Nicolas, vol. iii. p. 393.   [2] To Spencer, Ibid. p. 406.

of Nelson's action. "From the conversation I had with Admiral Foley and with Hardy, and from seeing the King of Sicily's private letter in his own hand to Ruffo, I was inclined to think more favourably of Lord Nelson's conduct." [1] This conversation was after Nelson's death, and, though somewhat vague in allusion, it is clear that the opinion of these two honorable men, present throughout, could not have been that the garrisons on surrendering were deceived by Nelson or his representatives. Such also is the deliberate judgment of the Italian Maresca, writing in these present days (1894), when passionate prepossession has given place to historical research and deliberate judgment, and who has devoted especial attention to these transactions. He is far from approving the subsequent treatment of the prisoners, but concerning these facts he says: "It is allowable to believe that Micheroux with the two Englishmen arranged with the commandants of the forts that the capitulation should be executed upon lines subordinated to Nelson's declarations. That it should receive unconditional effect after the declarations of the admiral, and after the enforced adhesion of Ruffo,[2] was no longer to be thought of. Only an unconditional surrender could at that moment be entertained; and, if conditions were offered, they could only have been briefly these: that the patriots should give up the castles, purely and simply, that those who had declared their wish to go to Toulon should embark and remain in the roads, that the others should stay in the forts, until the determination of the King, in the case of each, should be known." [3]

That afternoon the garrisons quitted Uovo and Nuovo, those who so elected embarking in the vessels which were now ready; and in them they remained undisturbed, at the mole, during the 27th. The surrendered castles were occupied on the evening of the 26th by British marines. On the 27th Nelson requested of Ruffo that these should be relieved by two or three hundred Neapolitan soldiers, in order that the

[1] Vindication, p. 56.

[2] Maresca agrees with the German Hüffer in thinking, contrary to Sacchinelli, that Ruffo ended by submitting to Nelson's decision. He thus accepts Acton's words in his letter of August 1, 1799, to Nelson: "The Cardinal yielded to your wise and steady declaration." (Nicolas, vol vii. p. clxxxvi.)

[3] Archivio Storico, 1894, pp. 523–526.

British and Russian troops might proceed with the attack on St. Elmo.[1] On the 28th, early, a despatch, dated the 25th,[2] was received from Palermo, from the contents of which Nelson inferred, correctly, that the terms of the Capitulation could not be approved by the King. He then wrote to the Cardinal, announcing the fact, and that he was about to seize and make sure of those who had embarked.[3] Before noon of the same day,[4] the vessels were brought out from the mole and anchored under the guns of the fleet; some of the ringleaders being transferred to British ships for safer keeping. The transaction, as far as Nelson was concerned in it, was completed by holding them until the King's arrival, on the 10th of July.

So far the author's effort has been confined to stating clearly and fully just what Nelson did, in order to demonstrate that his conduct throughout was open and consistent. This it was, whatever judgment may be passed upon the correctness of the opinion which he avowed, and upon which he acted, viz. that he not only had a right to suspend the Capitulation, because, though signed, it had not been executed, but that it was his bounden duty so to do; having both legal power and adequate force to prevent its execution.

It remains to consider what was the obligation under which he conceived himself to lie, and what was the authority in law by which he assumed to act. The reply, which it is purposed to substantiate, is that he regarded himself as, and for the time being actually was, the representative of the King of the Two Sicilies, as well as the admiral of the British fleet. As representative, he was charged with the interests and honor of the Sovereign and had authority over all Neapolitan officials; as admiral, he wielded power to enforce obedience, if refused.

[1] Diaries, etc. of Geo. Rose, vol. i. p. 237.

[2] On June 25 Acton wrote to Hamilton three letters (Egerton MSS. Br. Museum 2640; Nos. 267, 269, 271). The first of these, sent by a Neapolitan felucca "with the utmost speed," was in reply to Hamilton's of the 23d, which had transmitted the erroneous intelligence of a twenty-one days' armistice, after which the republicans were to march out, if not before relieved. From the tenor of all these, it was clear that the terms, when known, would not be approved.

[3] Diaries, etc. of Geo. Rose, vol. i. p. 238.

[4] Foudroyant's Log, Nicolas, vol. iii. p. 508.

Considering the terms of the Capitulation to be contrary to
the interests and the honor of the Kingdom, he was under
an obligation to prevent their going into effect, until the
King's decision, becoming known, should supersede his own
discretion.

The proof of Nelson's commission to act for the King goes
back of June 21, the day of his second departure from Palermo.
It is admitted that no written instructions have been found
bearing that date, or specifically issued for that occasion. It
must be remembered that the mission which he then undertook, and carried through to the results which we have been
considering, was only the resumption of a similar task, begun
upon the 13th of June. Though then interrupted, the transaction was in effect continuous ; postponed, not abandoned.
The only modification introduced on the second occasion was
in the nature of verbal instructions, consequent upon later
intelligence, which in no wise affected his powers ; for these
had been amply defined on the first occasion, and were indeed
so extensive as scarcely to admit of enlargement.

Looking to Nelson's arranged departure on the first occasion, the King had on the 10th of June addressed him a letter,
in which, after defining the causes which then made it expedient that the fleet should go to Naples, taking with it Neapolitan troops (as before mentioned),[1] he proceeds thus: "This
measure, without your valuable assistance and direction, cannot produce the necessary result. I have recourse, therefore,
to you, my Lord, to obtain both the one and the other, so that,
this Kingdom being speedily delivered from the scourge which
it has experienced, I may henceforward be in a condition to
perform the engagements contracted, which duty and reason
prescribe. *I send, therefore, a copy of the instructions I give
to the superior generals, and which I forward to those on the
Continent,*" i. e. to Ruffo in principal, as Vicar-General, and
to others ; among whom doubtless Micheroux. "At the head
of these [generals] I have placed my son, whom I trust to
your friendly assistance, so that his first steps in the present
critical career which he will have to run, may be guided by
your wise advice, requesting you *not only to help him* with
your powerful aid, *but that you will always act principally,*

[1] *Ante,* p. 364.

as your forces are the true means and support on which I rest my future hopes, as they have hitherto been my safety." [1]

The Instructions to the generals, only alluded to here, are clearly for Nelson's information, as to his own authority, in them set forth, and for his guidance in his relations with the Neapolitan officers. They indicate their duties towards himself, towards the Prince, and towards Ruffo, whose position would be radically affected by the arrival of the newcomers and by the instructions they carried. The articles of the Instructions which are decisive as to Nelson's powers will alone be quoted; but readers who wish to scrutinize closely the regularity of his procedure, as distinguished from the rightfulness of his action, can study the entire document. [2]

" Article 4. All the *military and political* operations shall be agreed upon by the Prince Royal and Admiral Lord Nelson. The opinion of this latter always to have a preponderance, on account of the respect due to his experience, as well as to the forces under his command, which will determine the operations; and also because we are so deeply indebted to him for the zeal and attachment of which he has given so many proofs. Therefore, should the attack take place, the employment of the royal [Neapolitan] forces, and *all other means* tending to obtain the surrender of Naples, shall be thus decided.

" 7. When Naples shall be entirely surrendered and subdued, the Vicar-General [Ruffo] shall at once take possession of the entire government of the Kingdom; and to this intent will receive from the Prince Royal the King's *new* ratification of this his commission and charge, with all the particular determination that the circumstance requires, and any rules that the importance of the time and special considerations indispensably demand.

" 10. The acts of clemency concerning the noted offenders, and the pardoning of the same, *are reserved for the King*, excepting those stipulated in the articles of Capitulation."

It will be observed that these Instructions concerning Capitulation are for the Crown Prince and Nelson; not for Ruffo,

[1] Nicolas, vol. iii. p. 492. The author quotes from the translation. The original is also given, p. 522. There is more that precedes, and also following; but nothing which in the author's judgment impairs — but rather confirms — the force of the words quoted.

[2] George Rose's Diaries, etc., vol. i. pp. 231–236. Both the Italian original and the translation are there given. The italics are the author's.

whose orders at that time were not to approach Naples until the squadron appeared, and who had special directions, less discretional than those in these Instructions, as to terms to be offered to prisoners.

The extent of the powers intrusted to Nelson — who himself received a copy of this paper for his information — are clear from the 4th Article. All *military* operations, and all *political*, were to be agreed upon by him and the Prince ; but in case of a difference arising, it was known to the generals, and to Nelson, and to Ruffo (who also had, or was to have, his copy) — known to each and to all — that the opinion of Nelson was to preponderate — overweigh the others. As this was to be in political as well as in military matters, it is difficult to see what more is wanted to constitute the full powers which Nelson claimed to possess.

Further, it has been questioned whether he held power to supersede Ruffo; but from Article 7 it is clear that Ruffo was already superseded as Vicar-General, *ipso facto*, by the mere coming of the Crown Prince and Nelson. For, after a certain further time should have elapsed, — " when Naples shall be entirely subdued," — " the Vicar-General shall take possession of the entire government of the kingdom, and to this intent will receive from the Prince Royal the King's *new* ratification," etc. The ample vice-regal powers conferred upon the Cardinal by the King's instructions to him of January 25th were superseded by those to the Crown Prince and Nelson, of whose coming and its object, it is stated in Article 2, advices were despatched to him ; for his commission was to be ratified anew when the object of Nelson's coming was accomplished by the subjugation of the city or kingdom — to whichever of these the name Naples is meant to apply. This view of the matter is confirmed by the King's subsequent full approval of Nelson's action. Sacchinelli states that Ruffo received at Avellino, by June 10,[1] an autograph letter from the King, notifying him of the intended expedition, and forbidding

---

[1] Either this date is a mistake, or the King wrote to Ruffo some days before the instructions to the Crown Prince were issued, which is possible. Nelson, on the evening of June 6, wrote to St. Vincent, " It is not yet decided, but it is probable that in forty-eight hours we may sail for the Bay of Naples, in order to replace His Sicilian Majesty on his throne." (Nicolas, vii. clxxxiv.)

him to advance on Naples before the arrival of the fleet. This order Ruffo disobeyed; he claimed, necessarily.

When Nelson came to Palermo on June 21st, and remained two or three hours, it was not needful to invest him with new or ampler powers. The absence of any new credentials at that time is more than overborne by the absence of any revocation of the former instrument. The preponderance he had over all others, even to the Crown Prince, was not lessened by the absence of the latter, to whatever due. But, though nothing formal and written is on record, we have, concerning his powers over Ruffo, incidental confirmation of a kind usually accepted as authoritative. Sir William Hamilton, in an official despatch of July 14 to the British Secretary for Foreign Affairs, says: "Their Sicilian Majesties having received alarming accounts from Naples, that the Calabrese Army upon their entry into Naples was plundering the houses of that city, and setting them on fire under the pretence of their belonging to Jacobins, and that Cardinal Ruffo, elated with his unexpected successes, was taking upon himself a power far beyond the positive instructions of his Sovereign, and actually treating with His Sicilian Majesty's subjects in arms, and in open rebellion against him, earnestly entreated Lord Nelson that he would go immediately with his Majesty's whole squadron to Naples, *and prevent if possible the Cardinal from taking any steps, or coming to any terms with the Rebels,* that might be dishonourable to their Sicilian Majesties, and hurtful to their future government," etc. As towards Ruffo, such were clearly full powers; and although Hamilton's despatch certainly contains errors of fact, in important details, a *general* statement such as the above is entitled to credence, unless his *general* credibility is successfully impeached. The probability of the statement being substantially correct is increased by the fact that, in writing privately to his nephew, Charles Greville, the same day (July 14), he summarizes the conditions by saying shortly, "We had full powers." [1] These four words have been called an inaccurate summary; but are they so, of the words above italicized?

Hamilton's words are here offered simply as corroborative — if no greater weight of proof be assigned to them — that the

[1] The Nelson-Hamilton Letters, Alfred Morrison Collection, No. 405.

force of the Instructions given to the Neapolitan generals, and communicated to Ruffo and Nelson, was not diminished, but rather confirmed, in the interview of the 21st. Although formal record of the latter has not been preserved, its character may be inferred from letters of the King and Queen to Ruffo in the same week. The Queen, writing on the 21st itself, says: "I realise how much all the horrors, which Your Eminence mentions at large in your letter of the 17th to the King, must afflict you. It seems to me that we have done all we can in the matter of clemency to such rebels, and that to treat with them further would be useless, and would lower us. Negotiations might be had with St. Elmo, which is in the hands of the French; but the other two, if they do not surrender immediately and without conditions, to the summons of Admiral Nelson " (whose coming she had already mentioned), "are to be taken by main force and treated as they deserve." [1] The King, writing on the 17th, tells the Cardinal he is sure it is needless to repeat what has already been said with reference to the treatment of the Jacobin rebels, especially the chiefs. "Nevertheless, I recommend you strongly to do nothing unbecoming to that dignity, which it is so necessary to sustain, or to your, and my, honor and reputation. As a Christian, I forgive all; but in the station in which God has placed me, I must be the rigorous avenger of offences done to Him, and of the injury occasioned to the state and to so many poor unfortunates." [2] The views of the Government as to the course which Nelson was expected and requested to pursue are clear from these extracts and references, though his powers were not thereby created. This cumulative evidence is very strong; to the present writer it is demonstra-

[1] Arch. Stor. per le Prov. Nap., 1880, p. 576.   Dumas, I Borboni di Napoli, vol. iv. p. 77.

[2] Dumas, I Borboni di Napoli, vol. v. p. 253.   The King, on May 1, 1799 (Dumas, vol. v. p. 239), had written Ruffo a letter, classifying the Rebels who were *excepted* from a policy of amnesty, then decided. Nelson (Nicolas, vol. iii. p. 341) alludes to this, as published. Ruffo, in his dispute with Nelson, on board the " Foudroyant," alleged in defence of the Capitulation an order from the King, to do the best he could for his Majesty's service. To this Acton replied that such a verbal order, if given, was countermanded by the special written orders, above mentioned (Egerton MSS. Br. Mus. $\frac{2640}{280}$). There were very many of the excepted in the Castles.

tive. To its positive weight, also, is opposed only the negative argument that nothing more precise — more like a formal commission — has been preserved.

To these various written evidences, which remain on record, by persons entirely foreign to Nelson's particular interest in the transactions — which have been so colored as to touch his reputation and his integrity — is to be added his own statement, written less than a year later to his friend Davison, for the purpose of being shown to members of the British Government, or even to be published in the papers, if advisable :[1] "As the whole affairs of the Kingdom of Naples were at the time alluded to absolutely placed in my hands, it is *I* who am called upon to explain my conduct, and therefore send you my observations on the infamous Armistice entered into by the Cardinal," etc. Concerning the substantial exactness of this statement, opinion will be formed upon the corroborative evidence before adduced, and upon Nelson's own claim to be believed, as affected by his record for truthfulness, by his age and intelligence, and generally by his competency to remember and to report correctly a transaction then less than a year old.

It was in virtue of the same unlimited powers as representative of the King, that Nelson, three days after the surrender of the castles, proceeded to take peremptory action in the case of Caracciolo. In the mean time, in pursuance of the agreements with Ruffo, additional marines were landed from the fleet under the command of Troubridge, to besiege St. Elmo, an undertaking in which the five hundred Russians and some royalists also took part.

On the 29th of June, Commodore Francesco Caracciolo, lately head of the Republican Navy, was brought on board the "Foudroyant," having been captured in the country, in disguise. This man had accompanied the royal family in their flight to Palermo; but after arrival there had obtained leave to return to Naples, in order to avert the confiscation of his property by the Republican government. He subsequently joined the Republicans, or Jacobins, as they were

[1] (P. S.) "Show these papers to Mr. Rose, or some other, and, if thought right, you will put them in the papers." Nelson to Davison, May, 1800. Nicolas, vol. iv. p. 232.

called by Nelson and the Court. His reasons for so doing
are immaterial; they were doubtless perfectly sound from
the point of view of apparent self-interest; the substantial
fact remains that he commanded the insurgent vessels in
action with the British and Royal Neapolitan navies, firing
impartially upon both. In one of these engagements the Neapolitan frigate " Minerva " was struck several times, losing
two men killed and four wounded. Caracciolo, therefore,
had fully committed himself to armed insurrection, in company with foreign invaders, against what had hitherto been,
and still claimed to be, the lawful government of the country.
He had afterwards, as the Republican cause declined, taken
refuge with the other insurgents in the castles. When he
left them is uncertain, but on the 23d of June he is known to
have been outside of Naples, and so remained till captured.

It is not easy to understand in what respect his case differed from that of other rebels who surrendered uncondi-
tionally, and whom Nelson did not try himself, but simply
placed in safe keeping until the King's instructions should
be received, except that, as a naval officer, he was liable to
trial by court-martial, even though martial law had not been
proclaimed. It was to such a tribunal that Nelson decided
instantly to bring him. A court-martial of Neapolitan officers
was immediately ordered to convene on board the " Foudroyant," the precept for the Court being sent to Count
Thurn, captain of the " Minerva," who, because senior officer
in the bay, was indicated by custom as the proper president.
The charges, as worded by Nelson, were two in number,
tersely and clearly stated. " Francisco Caracciolo, a commodore in the service of His Sicilian Majesty, stands accused
of rebellion against his lawful sovereign, and for firing at his
colours hoisted on board his Frigate, the Minerva." The
court assembled at once, sitting from 10 A. M. to noon. The
charges being found proved, sentence of death was pronounced; and Caracciolo, who had been brought on board at
9 A. M., was at 5 P. M., by Nelson's orders, hanged at the fore-
yard-arm of the " Minerva." He was forty-seven years old
at the time of his death.

The proceedings of the court-martial were open, but the
record, if any was drawn up, has not been preserved. It is

impossible, therefore, now to say whether the evidence sustained the charges; but the acts alleged were so simple and so notorious, that there can be little doubt Caracciolo had fairly incurred his fate. Even in our milder age, no officer of an army or navy would expect to escape the like punishment for the same offence; if he did, it would be because mercy prevailed over justice. As regards the technicalities of the procedure, it would seem probable that Nelson's full powers, especially when committed to a military man, included by fair inference, if not expressly, the right of ordering courts-martial; whereas he had not at hand the machinery of judges and civil courts, for proceeding against the civilians who had joined in the insurrection. Despite his fearlessness of responsibility, he was always careful not to overpass the legal limits of his authority, except when able to justify his action by what at least appeared to himself adequate reasons. The Portuguese squadron, for instance, was absolutely under his orders, so far as its movements went; but, when a case of flagrant misconduct occurred, he confined himself to regretting that he had not power to order a court. Anomalous as his position was in the Bay of Naples, before the arrival of the King, and regrettably uncertain as is the commission under which he acted, there is no ground for doubting that he had authority to order a court-martial, and to carry its sentence into execution, nor that Caracciolo came within the jurisdiction of a court-martial properly constituted. Having regard, therefore, to the unsettled conditions of things prevailing, no fatal irregularity can be shown either in the trial or execution of this prisoner.

But, while all this is true, the instinctive aversion with which this act of Nelson's has been regarded generally is well founded. It was not decent, for it was not necessary, that capture should be followed so rapidly by trial, and condemnation by execution. Neither time nor circumstances pressed. The insurrection was over. Except the siege of St. Elmo, hostilities near Naples were at an end. That Caracciolo's judges were naval officers who had recently been in action with him would be, with average military men, rather in the prisoner's favor than otherwise; but it was very far from being in his favor that they were men in whom the angry passions engendered by civil warfare, and licentious spoliation, had not yet had time to cool. Neither the judges nor the revising power allowed themselves space for reflection. Nelson himself failed to sustain the dispassionate and magnanimous attitude that befitted the admiral of a great squadron, so placed as to have the happy chance to moderate the excesses which commonly follow the triumph of parties in intestine strife. But, however he then or afterwards may have justified his course to his own conscience, his great offence was against his own people. To his secondary and factitious position of delegate from the King of Naples, he virtually sacrificed the consideration due to his inalienable character of representative of the King and State of Great Britain. He should have remembered that the act would appear to the world, not as that of the Neapolitan plenipotentiary, but of the British officer, and that his nation, while liable like others to bursts of unreasoning savagery, in its normal moods delights to see justice clothed in orderly forms, unstained by precipitation or suspicion of perversion, advancing to its ends with the majesty of law, without unseemly haste, providing things honest in the sight of all men. That he did not do so, when he could have done so, has been intuitively felt; and to the instinctive resentment thus aroused among his countrymen has been due the facility with which the worst has been too easily believed.

Commander Jeaffreson Miles of the British Navy, writing in 1843, was one of the first, if not the very first, to clear effectually Nelson's reputation from the stigma of treachery, and of submission to unworthy influences, at this time. He has sought also to vindicate his hasty action in Caracciolo's case, by citing the swift execution of two seamen by Lord St. Vincent, at a time when mutiny was threatening. It cannot be denied that, for deterrent effect, punishment at times must be sudden as well as sharp; but the justification in each case rests upon attendant circumstances. In the instances here compared, we have in the one a fleet in which many ships were seething with mutiny, and the preservation of order rested solely upon the firmness of one man, — the commander-in-chief, — and upon the awe inspired by him. In the other, we see rebellion subdued, the chief rebels in confinement, the foreign enemy, except three small isolated garrisons, expelled beyond the borders of the kingdom six weeks before, and a great British fleet in possession of the anchorage. Punishment in such case, however just, is not deterrent, but avenging. True, Nelson was expecting the appearance of Bruix's fleet; but he himself characterized as "infamous" the capitulation granted by Ruffo and Foote, to which they were largely moved by the same expectation, when wielding a much smaller force than he did. The possible approach of the French fleet did not necessitate the hasty execution of a prisoner.

That Nelson yielded his convictions of right and wrong, and consciously abused his power, at the solicitation of Lady Hamilton, as has been so freely alleged, is not probably true, — there is no proof of it; on the contrary, as though to guard against such suspicion, he was careful to see none but his own officers during Caracciolo's confinement. But it is true that he was saturated with the prevalent Court feeling against the insurgents and the French, which found frequent expression in his letters. After living in the Hamiltons' house for four months, during which, to use his own expression, "I have never but three times put my foot to the ground, since December, 1798," in daily close contact with the woman who had won his passionate love, who was the ardent personal friend of the Queen, sharing her antipathies, and expressing her hatred of enemies in terms which showed the coarseness of her fibre,[1] Nelson was steeped in the atmosphere of the

---

[1] Mr. Pryse Lockhart Gordon, who was in Palermo in January, 1799, tells the following anecdote of Lady Hamilton. He had been dining at the ambassador's, and after dinner a Turkish officer was introduced. In the course of the evening he boasted that he had put to death with his own sword a number of French prisoners. "'Look, there is their blood remaining on it!' The speech being translated, her Ladyship's eye beamed with delight, and she said, 'Oh, let me see the sword that did the glorious deed!' It was presented to her; she took it into her fair hands, covered with rings, and, looking at the encrusted Jacobin blood, kissed it, and handed it to the hero of the Nile. Had I not been an eye-witness to this disgraceful act, I would not have ventured to relate it." (Gordon's Memoirs, vol. i. p. 210.) The author, also, would not have ventured to adduce it, without first satisfying himself, by inquiry, as to the probable credibility of Mr. Gordon, and likewise testing his narrative. It bears marks of the inaccuracy in details to which memory is subject, but the indications of general correctness are satisfactory.

Court of Naples, and separated from that of the British fleet, none of whose strongest captains were long with him during that period. The attitude more natural to men of his blood is shown in a letter signed by the officers of the "Leviathan," Duckworth's flagship. Coming from Minorca, they were out of touch with Neapolitan fury, and they addressed Lady Hamilton, interceding for a family engaged in the rebellion; a fact which shows the prevailing impression — whether well founded or not — of the influence in her power to exert. "We all feel ourselves deeply impressed with the horrid crime of disaffection to one's lawful sovereign, . . . but when we consider the frailty of human nature," &c. "Advise those Neapolitans not to be too sanguinary," wrote Keith to Nelson, apparently immediately after receiving the news of Caracciolo's hanging.

The abrupt execution of Caracciolo was an explosion of fierce animosity long cherished, pardonable perhaps in a Neapolitan royalist, but not in a foreign officer only indirectly interested in the issues at stake; and hence it is that the fate of that one sufferer has roused more attention and more sympathy than that of the numerous other victims, put to death by the King's command after ordinary processes of law. It stands conspicuous as the act of an English officer imbued with the spirit of a Neapolitan Bourbon official. "Could it ever happen," he wrote to Acton, some months after this, "that any English minister wanted to make me an instrument of hurting the feelings of His Sicilian Majesty, I would give up my commission sooner than do it. . . . I am placed in such a situation — a subject of one King by birth, and, as far as is consistent with my allegiance to that King, a voluntary subject of His Sicilian Majesty — that if any man attempted to separate my two Kings, by all that is sacred, I should consider even putting that man to death as a meritorious act." [1] On the other hand, it must be considered that Nelson, though humane, tended even in his calmest moments to severity towards military offenders. Writing with reference to a captain convicted of misbehavior before the enemy, he said, "If a man does not do his utmost in time of action, I think but one punishment ought to be inflicted;" and it

[1] Nelson to Acton, November 18, 1799. (Nicolas.)

may be inferred that he would have approved Byng's execution, where cowardice was not proved, but grave military dereliction was.

On the 10th of July the King of the Two Sicilies arrived from Palermo in the Bay of Naples, and went on board the "Foudroyant," which, for the whole time he remained, — about four weeks, — became practically his seat of government. There the royal standard was hoisted, there the King held his levees, and there business of State was transacted. In and through all moved the figures of Sir William and Lady Hamilton, the latter considering herself, and not without cause, the representative of the Queen. The latter had remained in Palermo, being out of favor with the Neapolitans, and with her husband, who attributed to her precipitancy the disasters of the previous December. The two women corresponded daily; and, if the minister's wife deceived herself as to the amount and importance of what she effected, there is no doubt that she was very busy, that she was commonly believed to exert much influence, and that great admiration for one another was expressed by herself, Hamilton, and Nelson, the "*Tria juncta in uno*," as the latter was pleased to style them. "I never saw such zeal and activity in any one as in this wonderful man [Nelson]," wrote she to Greville. "My dearest Sir William, thank God! is well, and of the greatest use now to the King." "Emma has been of infinite use in our late very critical business," said Hamilton to the same correspondent. "Ld. Nelson and I cou'd not have done without her. It will be a heart-breaking to the Queen of N. when we go " — back to England, as was then expected. "Sir William and Lady Hamilton are, to my great comfort, with me," wrote Nelson to Spencer; "for without them it would have been impossible I could have rendered half the service to his Majesty which I have now done: their heads and their hearts are equally great and good."

The execution of Caracciolo was shortly followed by another very singular incident, which showed how biassed Nelson had become towards the interests of the Neapolitan Court, and how exclusively he identified them — confused them, would scarcely be too strong a word — with the essential interests of the Allied cause and the duties of the British

Navy. On the 13th of July the castle of St. Elmo was surrendered by the French, the whole city of Naples thus returning under the royal authority. On the same day, or the
next, Troubridge, with a thousand of the best men that could
be sent from the squadron, marched against Capua, accompanied by four thousand troops. A letter had already been
received from the commander-in-chief, Keith, to Nelson, intimating that it might be necessary to draw down his vessels
from Naples to the defence of Minorca. "Should such an
order come at this moment," wrote Nelson to the First Lord,
forecasting his probable disobedience, "it would be a cause
for some consideration whether Minorca is to be risked, or the
two Kingdoms of Naples and Sicily? I rather think my decision would be to risk the former;" and he started Troubridge
off with a detachment that seriously crippled the squadron.
Capua is fifteen to twenty miles inland from Naples.

On the 13th — it is to be presumed after closing his letter
to Spencer just quoted — an order reached him from Keith,
in these words: "Events which have recently occurred render
it necessary that as great a force as can be collected should be
assembled near the island of Minorca; therefore, if your Lordship has no detachment of the French squadron in the neigh-
bourhood of Sicily, nor information of their having sent any
force towards Egypt or Syria, you are hereby required and
directed to send such ships as you can possibly spare off the
island of Minorca to wait my orders." The wording was so
elastic, as regards the numbers to be sent, as to leave much to
Nelson's judgment, and he replied guardedly the same day:
"As soon as the safety of His Sicilian Majesty's Kingdoms
is secured, I shall not lose one moment in making the detachment you are pleased to order. At present, under God's
Providence, the safety of His Sicilian Majesty, and his speedy
restoration to his kingdom, depends on this fleet, and the confidence inspired even by the appearance of our ships before
the city is beyond all belief; and I have no scruple in declaring my opinion that should any event draw us from the kingdom, that if the French remain in any part of it, disturbances
will again arise, for all order having been completely over-
turned, it must take a thorough cleansing, and some little
time, to restore tranquillity."

When Keith wrote this first order, June 27, he was at sea somewhere between Minorca and Toulon, trying to find Bruix's fleet, of which he had lost touch three weeks before, at the time he sent to Nelson the two seventy-fours, whose arrival caused the latter's second cruise of Maritimo. He had lost touch through a false step, the discussion of which has no place in a life of Nelson, beyond the remark that it was Keith's own error, not that of Lord St. Vincent, as Nelson afterwards mistakenly alleged; querulously justifying his own disobedience on the ground that Keith, by obeying against his judgment, had lost the French fleet. What is to be specially noted in the order is that Keith gave no account of his reasons, nor of the events which dictated them, nor of his own intended action. No room is afforded by his words for any discretion, except as to the number of ships to be sent by Nelson, and, though the language of the latter was evasive, the failure to move even a single vessel was an act of unjustifiable disobedience. To Keith he wrote privately, and in a conciliatory spirit, but nothing that made his act less flagrant. " To all your wishes, depend on it, I shall pay the very strictest attention."

Conscious of the dangerous step he was taking, Nelson wrote on the same day, by private letter,[1] to the First Lord of the Admiralty. " You will easily conceive my feelings," he said, " but my mind, your Lordship will know, was perfectly prepared for this order; and more than ever is my mind made

---

[1] Much confusion has been introduced into the times, when Keith's several orders were received by Nelson, by the fact that the original of this private letter to Earl Spencer is dated the 19th (Nicolas, vol. vii. p. clxxxv) ; while the secretary, copying it into the letter-book, wrote July 13th. (Nicolas, vol. iii. p. 408.) Nicolas considered the former correct, probably because it came last into his hands. The author considers the 13th correct, because the official letter to Keith bears that date, and reads, " I have to acknowledge the receipt of your Lordship's letter of June 27." (Nicolas, vol. iii. p. 408.)

The date of Troubridge's marching against Capua is similarly brought into doubt by these letters. The author believes it to have been July 13 or 14, from another official letter to Keith of the 13th. (Nicolas, vol. iii. p. 404.) " Captains Troubridge and Hallowell . . . march against Capua to-morrow morning." The odd Sea-Time of that day, by which July 13 began at noon, July 12, of Civil Time, also causes confusion ; writers using them indiscriminatingly. The capitulation of St. Elmo was certainly signed on July 12. (Clarke and M'Arthur, vol. ii. p. 294.)

up, that, at this moment, I will not part with a single ship, as I cannot do that without drawing a hundred and twenty men from each ship now at the siege of Capua, where an army is gone this day. I am fully aware of the act I have committed; but, sensible of my loyal intentions, I am prepared for any fate which may await my disobedience. Do not think that my opinion is formed from the arrangements of any one," an expression which shows that he was aware how talk was running. "*No;* be it good, or be it bad, it is all my own. It is natural I should wish the decision of the Admiralty and my Commander-in-chief as speedily as possible. To obtain the former, I beg your Lordship's interest with the Board. You know me enough, my dear Lord, to be convinced I want no screen to my conduct."

On the 9th of July, Keith wrote again, from Port Mahon, a letter which Nelson received on the 19th. He said that he was satisfied that the enemy's intentions were directed neither against the Two Sicilies, nor to the reinforcement of their army in Egypt; that, on the contrary, there was reason to believe they were bound out of the Straits. "I judge it necessary that all, or the greatest part of the force under your Lordship's orders, should quit the Island of Sicily, and repair to Minorca, for the purpose of protecting that Island during the necessary absence of His Majesty's squadron under my command, or for the purpose of co-operating with me against the combined force of the enemy, wherever it may be necessary." The commander-in-chief, in short, wished to mass his forces, for the necessities of the general campaign, as he considered them. Nelson now flatly refused obedience, on the ground of the local requirements in his part of the field. "Your Lordship, at the time of sending me the order, was not informed of the change of affairs in the Kingdom of Naples, and that all our marines and a body of seamen are landed, in order to drive the French scoundrels out of the Kingdom, which, with God's blessing will very soon be effected, when a part of this squadron shall be immediately sent to Minorca; but unless the French are at least drove from Capua, I think it right not to obey your Lordship's order for sending down any part of the squadron under my orders. I am perfectly aware of the consequences of disobeying the orders of my commander-in-chief." It cannot be said that the offensiveness of the act of disobedience is tempered by any very conciliatory tone in the words used. The reason for disobedience makes matters rather worse. " As I believe the safety of the Kingdom of Naples depends at the present moment on my detaining the squadron, I have no scruple in deciding that it is better to save the Kingdom of Naples and risk Minorca, than to risk the Kingdom of Naples to save Minorca." When he thus wrote, Nelson knew that Bruix had joined the Spanish fleet in Cartagena, making a combined force of forty ships, to which Keith, after stripping Minorca, could oppose thirty-one.

None of Nelson's letters reached Keith until long after he had left the Mediterranean, which probably prevented the matter being brought to a direct issue between the two, such as would have compelled the Admiralty to take some decisive action. On the 10th of July the commander-in-chief sailed from Port Mahon for Cartagena, following on the tracks of the allied fleets, which he pursued into the Atlantic and to Brest, where they succeeded in entering on the 13th of August, just twenty-four hours before the British came up. The narrow margin of this escape inevitably suggests the thought, of how much consequence might have been the co-operation of the dozen ships Nelson could have brought. It is true, certainly, as matters turned out, that even had he obeyed, they could not have accompanied Keith, nor in the event did any harm come to Minorca; but there was no knowledge in Nelson's possession that made an encounter between the two great fleets impossible, nor was it till three days after his former refusal to obey, that he knew certainly that Keith had given up all expectation of a junction with himself. Then, on the 22d of July, he received two letters dated the 14th, and couched in tones so peremptory as to suggest a suspicion that no milder words would enforce obedience — that his commander-in-chief feared that nothing short of cast-iron orders would drag him away from the Neapolitan Court. " Your Lordship is hereby required and directed to repair to Minorca, with the whole, or the greater part, of the force under your Lordship's command, for the protection of that island, as I shall, in all probability, have left the Mediter-

ranean before your Lordship will receive this. Keith." The
second letter of the same date ended with the words: " I
therefore trust the defence of Minorca to your Lordship, and
repeat my directions that the ships be sent for its protection."
On the receipt of these, though Capua had not yet surrendered, Nelson at once sent Duckworth with four ships-of-the-
line to Minorca, detaining only their marines for the land
operations.

It seems scarcely necessary to say that, while an officer in
subordinate command should have the moral courage to tran-
scend or override his orders in particular instances — each of
which rests upon its own merits, and not upon any general
rule that can be formulated — it would be impossible for military operations to be carried on at all, if the commander-in-
chief were liable to be deliberately defied and thwarted in his
combinations, as Keith was in this case. It does not appear
that Nelson *knew* the circumstances which Keith was considering; he only *knew* what the conditions were about Naples,
and he thought that the settlement of the kingdom might be
prevented by the departure of several of his ships. In this
opinion, in the author's judgment, his views were exaggerated,
and colored by the absorbing interest he had come to take in
the royal family and their fortunes, linked as these were with
the affections of a particular woman ; but, even granting that
his apprehensions were well founded, he was taking upon himself to determine, not merely what was best for the Kingdom of
the Two Sicilies, but what was best for the whole Mediterranean
command. It was not within his province to decide whether
Minorca or Naples was the more important. That was the
function of the commander-in-chief. Had the latter, while
leaving Nelson's force unchanged, directed him to follow a
particular line of operations in the district committed to him,
it is conceivable that circumstances, unknown to his superior,
might have justified him in choosing another; but there was
nothing in the conditions that authorized his assumption that
he could decide for the whole command. And this is not the
less true, because Nelson was in the general a man of far
sounder judgment and keener insight than Keith, or because
his intuitions in the particular instance were more accurate,
as they possibly were. He defended his course on the ground,

so frequently and so erroneously taken, that his intentions were right. "I am so confident," he wrote to the Admiralty, "of the uprightness of my intentions for his Majesty's service, and for that of his Sicilian Majesty, which I consider as the same, that, with all respect, I submit myself to the judgment of my superiors." Four years later, in 1803, he used the following singular expressions concerning his conduct at this period: "I paid more attention to another sovereign than my own; therefore the King of Naples' gift of Bronté to me, if it is not now settled to my advantage, and to be permanent, has cost me a fortune, and a great deal of favour which I might have enjoyed, and jealousy which I should have avoided. I repine not on those accounts. I did my duty, to the Sicilifying my own conscience, and I am easy."[1] "As I have often before risked my life for the good cause," he told his old friend the Duke of Clarence, "so I with cheerfulness did my commission: for although a military tribunal may think me criminal, the world will approve my conduct." With such convictions, he might, if condemned, as he almost inevitably must have been, have met his fate with the cheerfulness of a clear conscience; but no military tribunal can possibly accept a man's conscience as the test of obedience.

The Admiralty, who had sent Keith out knowing that St. Vincent, after three arduous years, meant soon to retire, could not of course acquiesce in Nelson's thus overriding the man they had chosen to be his commander-in-chief. "Their Lordships do not, from any information now before them, see sufficient reason to justify your having disobeyed the orders you had received from your Commanding Officer, or having left Minorca exposed to the risk of being attacked, without having any naval force to protect it." To this measured rebuke was added some common-sense counsel upon the pernicious practice of jeopardizing the *personnel* of a fleet, the peculiar trained force so vitally necessary, and so hard to replace, in petty operations on shore. "Although in operations on the seacoast, it may frequently be highly expedient to land a part of the seamen of the squadron, to co-operate with and to assist the army, when the situation will admit of their being immediately re-embarked, if the squadron should be called away to

[1] Nicolas, vol. v. p. 160.

act elsewhere [as Keith had called it], or if information of the approach of an enemy's fleet should be received, — yet their Lordships by no means approve of the seamen being landed to form a part of an army to be employed in operations at a distance from the coast, where, if they should have the misfortune to be defeated, they might be prevented from returning to the ships, and the squadron be thereby rendered so defective, as to be no longer capable of performing the services required of it; and I have their Lordships' commands to signify their directions to your Lordship not to employ the seamen in like manner in future."

It was evident that the Admiralty did not fully share Nelson's attachment to the royal house of Naples, nor consider the service of the King of the Two Sicilies the same as that of the King of Great Britain. Earl Spencer's private letter, while careful of Nelson's feelings, left no room to doubt that he was entirely at one with his colleagues in their official opinion. Nelson winced and chafed under the double rebuke, but he was not in a condition to see clearly any beams in his own eye. "I observe with great pain that their Lordships see no cause which could justify my disobeying the orders of my commanding officer, Lord Keith;" but the motives he again alleges are but the repetition of those already quoted. He fails wholly to realize that convictions which would justify a man in going to a martyr's fate may be wholly inadequate to sap the fundamental military obligation of obedience. "My conduct is measured by the Admiralty, by the narrow rule of law, when I think it should have been done by that of common sense. I restored a faithful ally by breach of orders; Lord Keith lost a fleet by obedience against his own sense. Yet as one is censured the other must be approved. Such things are." As a matter of fact, as before said, it was by departing from St. Vincent's orders that Keith lost the French fleet. Nor did Nelson's mind work clearly on the subject. Thwarted and fretted as he continually was by the too common, almost universal, weakness, which deters men from a bold initiative, from assuming responsibility, from embracing opportunity, he could not draw the line between that and an independence of action which would convert unity of command into anarchy. "Much as I approve of strict obedience to orders, yet to say that an officer is never, for any object, to alter his orders, is what I cannot comprehend." But what rational man ever said such a thing? "I find few think as I do, — but to obey orders is all perfection! What would my superiors direct, did they know what is passing under my nose? To serve my King and to destroy the French I consider as the great order of all, from which little ones spring, and if one of these little ones militate against it, I go back to obey the great order." There is so much that is sound in these words, and yet so much confusion might arise in applying them, that scarcely any stronger evidence could be given that each case must rest on its own merits; and that no general rule can supplant the one general principle of obedience, by which alone unity and concentration of effort, the great goal of all military movement, can be obtained.

During this period of agitation and excitement, Nelson's health did not show the favorable symptoms that usually attended a call to exertion. Much may be attributed to a Mediterranean summer, especially after the many seasons he had passed in that sea; but it can readily be believed that such exceptional responsibilities as he had just assumed could not but tell, even upon his resolute and fearless temper. "I am really sorry," wrote Troubridge to him, from the siege of St. Elmo, "to see your Lordship so low-spirited, all will go well;" and a few days later, "Your Lordship must endeavour to fret as little as possible — we shall succeed. His Majesty's arrival will relieve your Lordship; and if he punishes the guilty, the people will be happy." The day after he had refused to obey Keith's order, he wrote to him, "I am truly so very unwell that I have not the power of writing so much as I could wish;" and the next day, to the Admiralty, he makes the same excuse, adding, "I am writing in a fever, and barely possible to keep out of bed." "My dear friend," he tells Locker, "I am so ill that I can scarcely sit up; yet I will not let the courier go off without assuring you that all your kindnesses to me are fresh in my memory. . . . May God Almighty grant you, my revered friend, that health and happiness which has never yet been attained by your affectionate, grateful friend, Nelson." It cannot but be surmised that he did not feel that profound conviction of right, which had sustained him on previous occasions. The disquiet indicated resembles rather that attending the uncertainties of the Nile campaign. As Colonel Stewart noticed, two years later, "With him mind and health invariably sympathized."

CHAPTER XIV.

August, 1799–June, 1800. Age, 41.

UPON Keith's departure, the command in the Mediterranean devolved upon Nelson, who for some time remained in doubt of the fact, but with his usual promptitude acted as if all depended upon himself. "I am venturing certainly out of my line of duty, but as the commander-in-chief may not even be on the station, I must do the best which my judgment points out during his temporary absence." Six sail-of-the-line, under Admiral Duckworth, were sufficient for service at Gibraltar and Cadiz, if the latter port was deserted. Four of the line were about Minorca, constantly, though inefficiently, threatened from the adjacent coasts of Spain. Three were blockading Malta, conjointly with the Portuguese vessels. Sidney Smith with his division remained in the Levant. Troubridge was operating with a few ships on the coast of Italy, against Civita Vecchia, still in the hands of the French. A small squadron was maintained on the Riviera of Genoa, disturbing the communications of the French, and keeping touch with the advance of the Austro-Russians; but it was expected that the Russian fleet, as was natural and proper, would soon assume the duty of co-operating with their general, Suwarrow. The smaller British cruisers were distributed among these various duties. The flagship "Foudroyant" was at Palermo, whither the King returned from Naples on the 8th of August, and there the headquarters of the squadron remained during Nelson's command. Soon after this arrival in Palermo the King conferred upon him the title of Duke of Bronté, with an estate of the same name in Sicily, valued at £3,000 per

annum. After this the admiral for a time signed his papers
as Bronté Nelson,[1] changed subsequently to Bronté Nelson
of the Nile, and finally settled down to Nelson and Bronté,
which was his form of signature for the last four years of
his life. He placed upon his new estate an annual charge of
£500 in favor of his father for the term of the latter's life.
"Receive this small tribute, my honoured father," he wrote,
"as a mark of gratitude to the best of parents from his most
dutiful son."

On the 20th of September he received letters from the
Admiralty, investing him with the chief command, "till the
return of Lord Keith or some other your superior officer."
He was not, however, allowed the appointments of a commander-in-chief, and often complained of the inadequacy
of his staff to the extent of his duties. Nelson naturally
hoped that his long and eminent services in that particular
field, and the conspicuous ability he had shown on so many
occasions, would lead to the station remaining permanently
in his hands, and that Lord Keith, who was now in England,
would succeed in due course to the Channel Fleet, whose
commander, Lord Bridport, soon after retired. The Mediterranean was naturally attributed to a vice-admiral, and one of
some seniority; but Nelson was now a rear-admiral of the
Red, the highest color, not far, therefore, from promotion,
and it would not be an unreasonable conclusion that the same
ministry which had been fortunate enough to choose him for
the campaign of the Nile, might now prefer to entrust to
such able and enterprising hands the great interests of the
Mediterranean at large.

It was not, however, to be so. Whether moved only by
routine considerations of rank, as afterwards at Copenhagen,
or whether his relations with the Sicilian Court, his conduct
of affairs at Naples, and his collisions with Keith, had excited
doubt of the normal balance of his mind, the Admiralty decided to send Keith back, and Nelson, greatly to his mortification, was kept in charge only till the end of the year. As St.
Vincent had always left him practically independent, he had
known no superior since he entered the Straits, except during

[1] The title of Bronté was assumed in Sicily only, until he received the
consent of George III. to accept it.

Keith's brief period of succession, when leagues of sheltering distance left him free, as has been seen, to defy orders when not in accordance with his views; and he found it impossible now to bow his will to the second place on the very field of his glory. To this feeling, natural in any man, and doubly so to one of Nelson's quick susceptibilities, at once stimulated and soothed by the lavish adulation of the past year, was added personal dislike to his new superior, aggravated, if not originated, by the clash of judgment over the relative importance of Naples and Minorca. "I have serious thoughts of giving up active service," he wrote to Minto; "Greenwich Hospital seems a fit retreat for me after being *evidently* thought unfit to command in the Mediterranean." Complaints of Keith's lack of consideration then abound, nor does he seem to be conscious that there was anything in his mode of life, in current rumor, or in his past relations with his new commander-in-chief, which might make the latter unwilling to give him the loose rein St. Vincent had done.

From the time that Keith left the Mediterranean in July, 1799, to Nelson's own departure a year later, there was little to be done in the naval way except to maintain and press existing advantages, and wait until the fruit was ready to drop. The absolute supremacy of the British squadrons, challenged for a moment by the incursion of Admiral Bruix, had reverted, in even greater degree than before, by the absence of the Spanish ships which had accompanied him to Brest. Impeded by their own numbers, and paralyzed by the insufficiency of the resources of the port, they remained there a huge, inert mass, whose impotence was only partially understood by the British; a fact which conduced to prolong Keith's presence in the Channel. The year under consideration was therefore devoid of stirring events at sea.

In the Mediterranean, it is true, Nelson's unwearying mental energy, and keen sense of the necessity of seizing opportunity, did not allow things to lapse into indolence. Whether or not he was well advised to settle himself at Palermo, aware as he must have been of the actual temptation, and of the serious injury that scandal was doing to his reputation, both professional and personal, may admit of doubt. With numerous detached and minor services carrying on at the same moment, there was much to be said for the commander-in-chief remaining in a fixed position, near the centre of affairs; and in his apprehension everything then revolved about the Kingdom of Naples. There can be no question, however, that all his faculties were constantly on the alert; and that his administration of the station until Keith's return was characterized by the same zeal, sagacity, and politic tact that he had shown in earlier days. It is admirable to note the patience, courtesy, and adroit compliment, he brings into play, to kindle, in those over whom he has no direct control, the ardor for the general good, and the fearlessness of responsibility, which actuate himself; and at the same time to observe how severe the strain was upon his nervous and irritable temper, as betrayed in comments upon these very persons, made in private letters which he never expected would see the light.

The points of principal importance were the consolidation of the royal power in the continental territory of the Two Sicilies, the reduction of Malta, and the retention of the French army in Egypt in entire isolation from France. For the first, Nelson entirely failed in his efforts to induce the King to trust himself again in Naples, as the Hamiltons and he had expected when they came back to Palermo. " My situation here is indeed an uncomfortable one," he said to Earl Spencer; " for plain common sense points out that the King should return to Naples, but nothing can move him." " Our joint exertions have been used to get the King to go to Naples," he wrote to Troubridge, " but of no avail; the Austrians will be there before him." Although the French had been expelled from all the Neapolitan dominions, the presence of fifteen hundred in Rome and Civita Vecchia served then as an excuse. Nelson implored the commander of the British troops at Minorca to spare twelve hundred of his men, to aid Troubridge on the Roman coast. " Sir Charles Stuart," he tells him flatteringly, " by his timely exertion saved this Kingdom [Sicily] from anarchy and confusion, and perhaps from rebellion. So it is now, my dear Sir, I trust, in your power (and I have assured the good King and Queen of your readiness to serve them and the good cause as much as Sir Charles) to send for the taking possession of Civita Vecchia and Rome; this done, and with my life, I will answer for the success of the expedition. All would be quiet and happy; and their Sicilian Majesties might return to their throne without any alarm from mobs. . . . I am sure I need not venture to say more on the subject. Your Excellency's judgment and heart will point out the necessity of the measure if it can be accomplished." "Our King would be much gratified that *Britain* not *Austria* should reinstate the Pope."

Sir James Erskine, thus importuned, did not see his way to sending the troops. Naturally, as a soldier, he did not rely as much upon the navy preventing a landing in his island, as upon his own powers of resistance after it was effected, and was therefore unwilling to spare from the latter. The point of view of a seaman was, and is, different. He complained, too, that Duckworth had taken a great many ships to Gibraltar. Nelson admits the mistake, and expresses his regret, but no word of dissatisfaction with Erskine transpires through his evident disappointment. He only says, "Pardon what I am going to repeat, that either in Malta or on the Continent, a field of glory is open." "Minorca," he wrote to Spencer, "I have never yet considered in the smallest danger, but it has been a misfortune that others have thought differently from me on that point." Towards the end of September, Troubridge, without the aid of British troops, but supported by the arrival of a division sent by Suwarrow, reported the evacuation of Rome and Civita Vecchia. "How happy you have made us!" wrote Nelson to him. "My pen will not say what I feel." The King, however, would not return to Naples, now that this obstacle was withdrawn. "The Queen has a noble, generous disposition," said Nelson two months later. "Unfortunately the King and her Majesty do not at this moment draw exactly the same way; therefore, his Majesty will not go at this moment to Naples, where his presence is much wanted." "We do but waste our breath," he avowed afterwards.

In the beginning of October, a visit which he had intended making to Minorca was hastened by a report that thirteen hostile ships-of-the-line had been seen off Cape Finisterre, and it was thought they might be destined for the Mediterranean. Nelson hoped to assemble ten to meet them; but the news

proved to be false. He left Palermo for this trip on the 5th
of October, and returned again on the 22d, having remained
five days in Port Mahon. The arrangements for the naval
force, depending entirely upon himself, were soon settled;
but he was disappointed in obtaining, as he had hoped to do
from a personal interview with Erskine, a detachment of two
thousand troops for Malta. About that island he was, to use
his own words, almost in despair. For over a year La Valetta
had been blockaded by land and sea. For the latter he could
with difficulty find ships; for the former he could obtain no
men to aid the islanders, who, half starving, dependent for
food chiefly upon Sicily, were sustained in their resistance
mainly by hatred of the invaders, and by the tactful appeals
and encouragement of Captain Ball, who lived ashore among
them. The Barbary pirates, by virtue of their war with
Naples, captured many of the vessels laden with supplies,
despite Nelson's passports; while the Sicilian Court, though
well disposed, lacked the energy and the propelling force
necessary to compel the collection and despatch of the needed
grain. On one occasion Troubridge or Ball, desperate at the
sight of the famine around them, sent a ship of war into
Girgenti, a Sicilian port, seized, and brought away two corn-
laden vessels. "The measure was strong," said Nelson, but
he refrained from censuring; and, while apologizing to the
Government, added he hoped it "would not again force officers
to so unpleasant an alternative." He feared that in their
misery the Maltese would abandon the struggle, particularly
if they got wind of the purpose of Great Britain to restore
the hated Order of Knights, in deference to the wishes of the
Czar. "The moment the French flag is struck," he had been
obliged to write to Ball, "the colours of the Order must be
hoisted and no other; when it was settled otherwise, the
orders from England were not so strong."

About this time came information that several ships were
fitting out at Toulon, with supplies for the besieged. This
increased Nelson's anxieties, and at the same time emphasized
the necessity which he had always urged of using speedier
and surer means to reduce the place, while the undisputed
mastery of the sea gave the opportunity. "What might not
Bruix have done, had he done his duty?" was his own com-

ment upon that recent incursion; and who could tell how
soon as great a force might appear again under an abler man?
He turned in every direction, and was instant in his appeals
for aid. He wrote to Acton that he had positive information
that seven ships were loaded in Toulon. "I therefore beg
leave to propose to your Excellency, whether under our present circumstances, it would not be right for his Sicilian Majesty to desire that the English garrison at Messina should
instantly go to Malta, for I am clear, that if Malta is relieved,
that our forces got together could not take it, and the commencement of a new blockade would be useless. All the
Barbary cruisers would there have their rendezvous, and not
a vessel of his Sicilian Majesty's could put to sea." He ex-
horts the minister also to apply to the Russians for immediate
help at Malta.

At the same time, to augment his embarrassments, orders
came from Lisbon recalling the Portuguese squadron, which
formed the larger part of the sea blockade. Nelson forgot
how often he had abused them as useless, and grappled with
that part of the difficulty with characteristic boldness. He
peremptorily forbade the admiral to obey his orders. "As
the reduction of the Island of Malta is of the greatest consequence to the interests of the allied Powers at war with
France, and the withdrawing of the squadron under your
command, at this time, from the blockade of that island, will
be of the most ruinous consequences to their interests . . .
you are hereby required and directed, in consideration of the
above circumstances, and notwithstanding the orders you may
have received from your Court to return to Lisbon, not on
any consideration whatsoever to withdraw one man from that
island, which may have been landed from the squadron under
your Excellency's command, or detach one ship down the
Mediterranean, until further orders from me for that purpose." Your orders, he tells Niza in a private letter, were
founded upon the belief that your presence was no longer
necessary; "but the contrary is the fact — for your services
were never more wanted than at this moment, when every
exertion is wanting to get more troops of English and Russians
to Malta." He is evidently thinking of his difference with
Keith; but now he is within the limits of his commission as

Commander-in-chief. Doubting, however, whether his official authority will prevail with Niza to disobey his recall, he plies him skilfully with appeals to those sentiments of honor which had received such illustration in his own noble career. "If you quit your most important station till I can get" reliefs for you, "depend upon it, your illustrious Prince will disapprove of (in this instance) your punctilious execution of orders." " We shall soon get more troops from Messina and Minorca; and I am not a little anxious for the honour of Portugal and your Excellency, that you should be present at the surrender. I hold myself responsible." " You was the first at the blockade. Your Excellency's conduct has gained you the love and esteem of Governor Ball, all the British officers and men, and the whole Maltese people; and give me leave to add the name of Nelson, as one of your warmest admirers, as an officer and a friend."

As he dealt with the Portuguese admiral, so, in due measure, he conducted his intercourse with all others who came within the scope of his widely ranging activities. Already more Neapolitan than the King, to the Russian he became as a Russian, to the Turk as a Turk, all things to all men, if he could by any means promote the interest of the Allied cause and save Malta. Amid the diverse and conflicting motives of a coalition, Nelson played a steady hand, his attention unified, and his sight cleared, by an unwavering regard to the single object which he compressed into the words, " Down, down, with the French! " In that sense, he asserts truthfully enough to each and all of his correspondents that the advantage of their country and their monarch is as dear to him as that of Great Britain. He touches with artful skill upon the evident interests of each nation, appeals to the officer's sense of the cherished desires of his sovereign, and, while frankly setting forth the truths necessary to be spoken, as to the comparative claims upon himself of the various portions of the field, he insinuates, rather than suggests, what the person immediately addressed ought to be doing in furtherance of the one great aim. Withal, despite the uneasiness to which he is constantly a prey on account of the failures of others, no lack of confidence in the one to whom he is writing is suffered to appear. Each is not only exhorted and cheered, but patted on the back with an implied approbation, which in his own service constituted much of his well-deserved influence. He is as hearty and generous in his praises to Sir Sidney Smith, whom he never fully trusted, for his services at Acre, as he is to the valued friend, and pattern of all naval efficiency, Troubridge. To the Emperor of Russia he paid the politic attention of sending a detailed report of all that had been done about Malta, made to him as Grand Master of the Order, — a delicate and adroit flattery at the moment, for the Czar then valued himself more as the restorer of an ancient order of chivalry than as the inheritor of a great Sovereignty; and his position was further recognized by asking of him the insignia of the Order for Captain Ball and Lady Hamilton.

This immense load of correspondence and anxiety was additional to the numerous unrecorded cares and interviews, relating to the routine work and maintenance of a great squadron, often left bare of resources from home, and to the support of the destitute population of Malta, — sixty thousand souls; and all was carried on amid the constant going and coming of the ambassador's house, kept open to naval officers and others. This public sort of life and excitement involved considerable expense, and was little to the taste of either Nelson or Hamilton, the latter of whom was now approaching his seventieth year; but in it Lady Hamilton was in all her glory, overwhelmed with compliments, the victor of the Nile at her feet, and "making a great figure in our political line," to use her husband's words. "Except to the Court," wrote Nelson, replying to a censure from the Admiralty for failing to send a letter by a certain channel, when he had sent duplicates by two other conveyances, — "except to the Court, till after eight o'clock at night I never relax from business. I have had hitherto, the Board knows, no one emolument — no one advantage of a Commander-in-chief." It was in reference to this captious rebuff, received when immersed in cares, that he wrote to Spencer: "Do not, my dear Lord, let the Admiralty write harshly to me — my generous soul cannot bear it, being conscious it is entirely unmerited."

While he was striving to gain assistance for the Maltese, he does not forget to sustain them with hopes, not always too

well founded. He tells Ball he trusts the Messina troops will
soon be with him. " You may depend, in October, I will get
2,000 men on shore at Malta. Niza is ordered to Lisbon, but
I have directed his stay off Malta." He appeals personally to
the British commander at Messina, and to the Russian minister at Palermo, reminding the latter how dear Malta and its
Order were to his sovereign. " Malta, my dear Sir, is in my
thoughts sleeping or waking." The Portuguese, he tells him,
are ordered home ; but, wishing Russian assistance, he does
not say that he has stopped them, — as to which, indeed, he
could not feel sure.

The same object pressed upon him while in Port Mahon,
and he succeeded, by his personal enthusiasm, in arousing
Erskine's interest in the matter; but the latter was loaded to
the muzzle with objections. " Sir James," said Nelson to
Troubridge, with the amusing professional prejudice they
both entertained, " enters upon the difficulty of the undertaking in a true soldier way." " I am just come from Sir James,"
he wrote to Hamilton on the 13th of October. " He sees all
the difficulty of taking Malta in the clearest point of views,
and therefore it became an arduous task to make him think
that with God's blessing the thing was possible." He has,
however, consented to prepare fifteen hundred men with stores
and equipments, but only on condition that the Russians will
also give a thousand, — a further draft on Nelson's diplomacy,
— and a thousand be landed from the squadron, etc. Besides,
there is the further difficulty that a superior officer is expected
from England, and what will he say ? And will Erskine be
justified in sending men before his entirely uncertain arrival ?
It may be imagined what such proceedings were to Nelson's
nervous, ardent, unhesitating temperament, and they elicited
the characteristic comment, " This has been my first conference. It has cost me four hours hard labour, and may be upset by a fool." " My heart is, I assure you, almost broke with
this and other things," he wrote to Spencer. " If the enemy
gets supplies in, we may bid adieu to Malta. This would
complete my misery ; for I am afraid I take all services too
much to heart. The accomplishing of them is my study,
night and day."

" My dear Sir James," he writes to Erskine after returning

to Palermo, "I am in desperation about Malta — we shall lose it, I am afraid, past redemption. I send you copies of Niza's and Ball's letters, also General Acton's, so you will see I have not been idle." As it is, Ball can hardly keep the inhabitants in hope of relief; what then will it be if the Portuguese withdraw? "If the islanders are forced again to join the French, we may not find even landing a very easy task, much less to get again our present advantageous position. I therefore entreat for the honour of our King, that whether General Fox is arrived or not, at least the garrison of Messina may be ordered to hold post in Malta until a sufficient force can be collected to attack it. . . . I know well enough of what officers in your situation can do; the delicacy of your feelings on the near approach of General Fox I can readily conceive; but the time you know nothing about; this is a great and important moment, and the only thing to be considered, *is his Majesty's service to stand still for an instant?* . . . Was the call for these troops known at home, would they not order them to proceed when the service near at hand loudly calls for them? *this is the only thing in my opinion for consideration.* If we lose this opportunity it will be impossible to recall it." From this desperate appeal he turns to Ball, with words of encouragement for his islanders. "We shall soon hear to a certainty of at least 5,000 Russian troops for the service of Malta. Within a month I hope to see 10,000 men in arms against La Valetta. I have sent for Troubridge and Martin, that I may get a force to relieve Niza. I trust he will not go till I can get not only a proper force to relieve his ships, but those of his people who are on shore." "The great order of all," he writes Erskine three weeks later, "is to destroy the power of the French. Two regiments for two months would probably, with the assistance of the Russians, give us Malta, liberate us from an enemy close to our doors, gratify the Emperor of Russia, protect our Levant trade, relieve a large squadron of ships from this service, and enable me the better to afford naval protection to the island of Minorca, and assist our allies on the northern coast of Italy, and to annoy the enemy on the coast of France."

Nelson's entreaties and efforts met with success, sufficient at least to stay the ebbing tide. General Fox arrived in Minorca,

gave permission for the garrison of Messina to go to Malta,
and on the 25th of November Troubridge, bringing this news,
arrived off Palermo. Nelson's haste did not permit the
"Culloden" to anchor. Shifting his flag to a transport, he
sent out the "Foudroyant" to meet her, with orders for both
to go to Messina, embark the garrison, and get off Malta as
soon as possible. The "Northumberland," seventy-four, was
also to join off Malta, forming a division to replace the Portuguese squadron. The latter quitted the blockade in December,
Nelson notifying Niza on the 18th of the month that he no
longer considered him under his command. The Messina
troops landed at Malta on the 10th. The British then had
fifteen hundred men on the island, supported by two thousand
Maltese, well disciplined and armed, besides a number of
native irregulars upon whom only partial dependence could
be placed. The Russians never came to take part. They got
as far as Messina, but there received orders to go to Corfu,
both ships and men. This was in pursuance of a change of
policy in the Czar, who, being enraged at the conduct of his
allies, particularly of the Austrians, in the late campaign,
intended withdrawing from the Coalition, and was concentrating troops at Corfu. This revived Nelson's fears for
Malta. "I trust Graham will not think of giving the island
to the French by withdrawing, till he receives orders from
General Fox." The troops remained, but in numbers too
small to admit active operations. The result was left perforce
to the slow pressure of blockade; and final success, insured
mainly by Nelson's untiring efforts, was not attained until
after he had left the Mediterranean.

The six months of his independent command, though unmarked by striking incidents at sea, were crowded with events,
important in themselves, but far more important as pregnant
of great and portentous changes in the political and military
conditions of Europe. When Keith passed the Straits in pursuit of the Franco-Spanish fleet, on the 30th of July, the
forces of the Coalition in Upper Italy were in the full tide of
repeated victories and unchecked success. On that same day
the fortress of Mantua, the siege of which in 1796 had stayed
for nine months the triumphal progress of Bonaparte, was
surrendered by the French, whose armies in the field, driven

far to the westward, were maintaining a difficult position on the crests of the Apennines. Seeking to descend from there into the fields of Piedmont, they were met by Suwarrow, and on the 15th of August, at Novi, received once more a ruinous defeat, in which their commander-in-chief was slain.

At this moment of success, instead of pressing onward to drive the enemy out of Italy, and possibly to pursue him into France, it was decided that the Russians should be sent across the Alps into Switzerland, to take the place of a number of Austrians. The latter, in turn, were to move farther north, on the lower Rhine, to favor by a diversion an intended invasion of Holland by a combined force of Russians and British. This gigantic flank movement and change of plan resulted most disastrously. In the midst of it the French general Masséna, commanding in Switzerland, the centre of the great hostile front which extended from the Mediterranean to the North Sea, made a vehement and sustained attack upon the Austro-Russians at Zurich, on the 25th of September. Gaining a complete victory, he drove the enemy back beyond the point where Suwarrow expected to make his junction. The veteran marshal, who had left Italy on the 11th of September, arrived two days after the Battle of Zurich was fought. Isolated in insufficient numbers from the friends he expected to meet, it was only after severe hardships and superhuman efforts, extending over ten days, that he at length, on the 9th of October, reached a place of safety at Ilanz. Declining further co-operation with the Austrians, and alleging the need of rest for his troops after their frightful exposure in the mountains, he withdrew into winter quarters in Bavaria at the end of the month. Thus Switzerland remained in possession of the French, inactivity continued in Italy, and the Czar, furious at the turn events had taken, was rapidly passing into hatred of both Austria and Great Britain.

On the 9th of October, also, Bonaparte landed in France, after a six weeks' voyage from Alexandria. The immense consequences involved in this single event could not then be foreseen; but it none the less caused mortification and regret to Nelson. It was a cardinal principle with him, vehemently and frequently uttered, that not a single Frenchman should be allowed to return from Egypt; and here their commander-in-chief had passed successfully from end to end of the station, unseen by any British cruiser. He did not, however, consider himself at fault, and his judgment may be allowed, although in his own case. " If I could have had any cruisers, as was my plan, off Cape Bon, in Africa, and between Corsica and Toulon, Mr. Buonaparte could not probably have got to France." This he said to Earl Spencer. Elsewhere he wrote: "I have regretted sincerely the escape of Buonaparte; but those ships which were destined by me for the two places where he would certainly have been intercepted, were, from the Admiralty thinking, doubtless, that the Russians would do something at sea, obliged to be at Malta, and other services which I thought the Russian Admiral would have assisted me in — therefore, no blame lies at my door." He took some comfort in contrasting the stealthy return of the French general, with the great armada that accompanied his departure. "No Crusader ever returned with more humility — contrast his going in L'Orient, &c. &c."

A report that Bonaparte had passed Corsica reached Nelson on October 24th. The same day came despatches from Sir Sidney Smith, narrating a disastrous defeat sustained by the Turks on the shores of Aboukir Bay. Smith's period of command in the Levant had been chiefly, and brilliantly, distinguished by the successful defence of Acre against Bonaparte. The latter, threatened by simultaneous attacks by the Turks from Syria and from the sea, had determined to anticipate such a combination by going himself against the enemy on the land side, before the weather conditions made it possible to disembark any formidable body of men on the shores of Egypt. Starting with this purpose in February, he had proceeded with slight resistance until the 18th of March, when his army appeared before Acre. Smith was then lying in the roads with two ships-of-the-line. The siege which ensued lasted for sixty-two days, so great was Bonaparte's pertinacity, and anxiety to possess the place; and in its course Smith displayed, not only courage and activity, which had never been doubted, but a degree of conduct and sound judgment that few expected of him. His division was fortunate enough to capture the French siege train, which had to be

sent by water, and he very much disturbed the enemy's coastwise communications, besides contributing materially to the
direction of the defence, to which the Turks, though brave
enough, were not adequate. After several desperate assaults
the siege was raised on the 20th of May, and Bonaparte
retreated to Egypt, regaining Cairo on the 14th of June.

Following up the success at Acre, a Turkish fleet of thirteen
ships-of-the-line anchored in Aboukir Bay on the 11th of July,
attended by a body of transports carrying troops, variously
estimated at from ten to thirty thousand. Smith with his
ships accompanied the expedition. The Turks landed, and
stormed the castle of Aboukir; but on the 25th Bonaparte,
having concentrated his forces rapidly, fell upon them and
totally defeated them. All who had landed were either
killed, driven into the sea and drowned, or taken prisoners;
the commander-in-chief being among the latter. Four weeks
later, as is already known, Bonaparte embarked for France.

It was thus conclusively demonstrated that for the present
at least, and until the French numbers were further diminished
by the inevitable losses of disease and battle, the Turks could
not regain control of Egypt. On the other hand, it was
equally evident, and was admitted by both Bonaparte and
his able successor, Kleber, that without reinforcements, which
could not be sent while the British controlled the sea, the
end of the French occupation was only a question of time.
After Bonaparte's departure, Kleber wrote home strongly to
this effect. His letters, being addressed to the Government,
fell upon arrival into Bonaparte's hands; but, with these
convictions, he was ready to enter into an arrangement for
the evacuation of the country, upon condition of being allowed
to return freely to Europe.

Such also appears to have been the disposition of the
British representatives in the East. Immediately after taking over the command in the Levant from Troubridge, Smith
gave him, among other papers, a form of passport which he
intended to use, permitting individual Frenchmen to go to
Europe by sea. This Troubridge handed to Nelson, telling
him also that it was Smith's intention to send word into
Alexandria, that all French ships might pass to France.
This passport, adopted after Smith had been to Constanti-

nople, had doubtless the sanction of the joint minister, his
brother, and was signed by himself both as plenipotentiary
and naval officer. Nelson had by this time been instructed
that Smith was under his command, and he at once sent him
an order, couched in the most explicit, positive, and peremptory terms, which merit especial attention because Smith disobeyed them. *" As this is in direct opposition to my opinion,*
which is, *never to suffer any one individual Frenchman to quit
Egypt* — I must therefore *strictly charge and command you,*[1]
never to give any French ship or man leave to quit Egypt.
And I must also desire that *you will oppose by every means in
your power, any permission which may be attempted to be given
by any foreigner,* Admiral, General, or other person; and you
will acquaint those persons, that I shall not pay the smallest
attention to any such passport after your notification; and
*you are to put my orders in force, not on any pretence to permit
a single Frenchman to leave Egypt."* It seems clear from
these expressions that Nelson had gathered, through Troubridge, that it was the policy of the Sultan and of the British
representatives to get the French out of Egypt at any cost, —
to look, in short, to local interests rather than to the general
policy of the Allies. This he was determined to prevent by
instructions so comprehensive, yet so precise, as to leave no
loophole for evasion.

Here matters seem to have rested for a time. Smith
could scarcely dare to disregard such orders at once, and
Bonaparte was not yet disposed openly to confess failure by
seeking terms. In the autumn of 1799, however, the Earl of
Elgin went to Constantinople as ambassador, Spencer Smith
dropping to secretary of embassy, and his brother remaining
on the Egyptian coast. Elgin was far from being in accord
with Smith's general line of conduct, which was marked with
presumption and self-sufficiency, and in the end he greatly
deplored the terms " granted to the French, so far beyond our
expectation;" but he shared the belief that to rid Egypt of
the French was an end for which considerable sacrifices should
be made, and his correspondence with Smith expressed this
conviction. When prepossessions such as this exist among a
number of men associated with one another, they are apt, as

[1] The italics to this point are Nelson's; afterwards the author's.

in the case of Admiral Man consulting with his captains, to result in some ill-advised step, bearing commonly the stamp of concern for local interests, and forgetfulness of general considerations. The upshot in this particular instance was the conclusion of a Convention, known as that of El Arish, between the Turks and the French, signed on board Smith's ship on the 24th of January, 1800, by which this army of veterans was to be permitted to return to France unmolested, and free at once to take the field against the allies of Turkey and Great Britain, at the moment when Bonaparte's unrivalled powers of administration were straining every nerve, to restore the French forces from the disorganization into which they had fallen, and to prepare for the spring campaign.

Smith, though present, did not sign this precious paper, which, in a letter to Hamilton, he called "the gratifying termination of his labours;" but he had in his hand the orders of his immediate superior, and temporary commander-in-chief, to notify any "foreigner, general, or admiral," that the execution of such an agreement would not be permitted by the British Navy, and it would have been his own duty to stop any ships attempting to carry it out, until other orders were received. His powers as joint plenipotentiary having ceased, he was now simply the naval officer. As it happened, Keith, who by this time had relieved Nelson, brought out from England clear directions from the Government not to allow any transaction of this kind; and although he personally favored the policy of evacuation, feeling perhaps the inconvenience of detaching ships so far from his centre of operations, he was not a man to trifle with orders. Rumors of what was going on had evidently reached him, for on the 8th of January, a fortnight before the convention was signed, he wrote to Kleber a letter, which he directed Smith to deliver, thus placing it out of the power of that very independent officer to leave any mistake as to actual conditions in the mind of the French general. To the latter he said: "I have positive orders not to consent to any capitulation with the French troops, at least unless they lay down their arms, surrender themselves prisoners of war, and deliver up all the ships and stores of the port of Alexandria to the Allied Powers." Even in such case they would not be allowed to leave Egypt until

exchanged. Any persons that attempted to return, pursuant
to an arrangement with one of the Allies, exclusive of the
others, as the El-Arish Convention was, would be made
prisoners of war.

Nelson's opinions in this matter had never wavered. As
rumors of what was brewing got about, he wrote to the Earl
of Elgin, on the 21st of December, 1800: "I own my hope yet
is, that the Sublime Porte will never permit a single Frenchman to quit Egypt; and I own myself wicked enough to wish
them all to die in that country they chose to invade. We
have scoundrels of French enough in Europe without them."
"I never would consent to one of them returning to the Continent of Europe during the war," he tells Spencer Smith.
"I wish them to *perish* in Egypt, and give a great lesson to
the world of the justice of the Almighty." When Elgin, thinking him still commander-in-chief, sent him the Convention, he
replied formally: "I shall forward the papers to Lord Keith,
who will answer your Excellency. But I cannot help most
sincerely regretting that ever any countenance was given to
the Turks to enter into such a treaty with the French; for I
ever held it to be impossible to permit that army to return to
Europe, but as prisoners of war, and in that case, not to
France. And was I commander-in-chief, even when the thing
was done, I should have refused to ratify any consent or
approbation of Sir Sidney Smith, and have wrote to both the
Grand Vizir and the French General, the impossibility of permitting a vanquished army to be placed by one Ally in a position to attack another Ally." The last phrase put the facts
in a nut-shell, and illustrates well Nelson's power of going
straight to the root of a matter, disregardful of confusing side-
issues, of policy or timidity. To Hamilton he wrote passion-
ately concerning the manifold difficulties caused to all, except
the Turks and the Smiths. "If all the wise heads had left
them to God Almighty, after the bridge was broke, all would
have ended well. For I differ entirely with my commander-in-
chief, in wishing they were permitted to return to France;
and, likewise, with Lord Elgin on the great importance of
removing them from Egypt."

"I have wrote to Lord Keith, and home," said Nelson to
Sir Sidney Smith on the 15th of January, "that I did not

give credit that it was possible for you to give any passport for a single Frenchman, much less the Army, after my positive order of March 18th, 1799." The words show what reports had already got about of the general trend of policy, on the part of the Porte and the British representatives; but the irony of the matter as regards Nelson is, that Smith disobeyed his orders, as he himself, six months before, had disobeyed Keith's; and for the same reason, that he on the spot was a better judge of local conditions and recent developments than one at a distance. To one, Naples was more important than Minorca, more important than a half-dozen ships in a possible fleet action; to the other, Egypt was more important than the presence of sixteen thousand veterans, more or less, on a European battle-field. It is impossible and bootless, to weigh the comparative degree of culpability involved in breaches of orders which cannot be justified.

On the 16th of January, 1800, Nelson, who some days before had been notified by Keith of his approach, and directed to place himself under his command, left Palermo for Leghorn, arriving on the 20th. The commander-in-chief was already there in the "Queen Charlotte." On the 25th they sailed together for Palermo, and after nine days' stay in that port went on again for Malta, which they reached on the 15th of February. No incident of particular interest occurred during these three weeks, but Nelson's letters to the Hamiltons show that he was chafing under any act in his superior which could be construed into a slight. "I feel all, and notwithstanding my desire to be as humble as the lowest midshipman, perhaps, I cannot submit to be much lower, I am used to have attention paid me from his superiors." "To say how I miss your house and company would be saying little; but in truth you and Sir William have so spoiled me, that I am not happy anywhere else but with you, nor have I an idea that I ever can be." Keith's comment — the other point of view — is worth quoting. "Anything absurd coming from the quarter you mention does not surprise me," he wrote to Paget, who succeeded Hamilton as minister. "The whole was a scene of fulsome vanity and absurdity all the *long* eight days I was at Palermo." [1]

When Keith returned, the capture of Malta, and of the two

1 The Paget Papers, London, 1896, vol. i. p. 200.

ships-of-the-line which had escaped from the Battle of the
Nile, were, by common consent, all that remained to do, in
order to round off and bring to a triumphant conclusion Nelson's
Mediterranean career. Fortune strove hard against his own
weakness to add all these jewels to his crown, but she strove
in vain. "We may truly call him a *heaven*-born Admiral,
upon whom fortune smiles wherever he goes." So wrote Ball
to Lady Hamilton, alluding to the first of the favors flung at
his head. "We have been carrying on the blockade of Malta
sixteen months, during which time the enemy never attempted
to throw in great succours. His Lordship arrived off here
the day they were within a few leagues of the island, captured
the principal ships, and dispersed the rest, so that not one has
reached the port." It was indeed a marvellous piece of what
men call luck. Nelson had never gone near Malta since
October, 1798, till Keith took him there on the 15th of February, 1800. The division had no sooner arrived at the island,
than a frigate brought word of a French squadron having been
seen off the west end of Sicily. It was then blowing strong
from southeast, and raining. Keith took his own station off
the mouth of the harbor, placed other ships where he thought
best, and signalled Nelson to chase to windward with three
ships-of-the-line, which were afterwards joined by a fourth,
then cruising on the southeast of the island. The next day
the wind shifted to northwest, but it was not until the morning of the 18th that the enemy were discovered. Guns were
then heard to the northward, by those on board the "Foudroyant," which made all sail in pursuit, and soon sighted the
"Alexander" chasing four French sail. "Pray God we may
get alongside of them," wrote Nelson in his journal; "the
event I leave to Providence. I think if I can take one 74 by
myself, I would retire, and give the staff to more able hands."
"I feel anxious to get up with these ships," he wrote to Lady
Hamilton, "and shall be unhappy not to take them myself,
for first my greatest happiness is to serve my gracious King
and Country, and I am envious only of glory; for if it be a
sin to covet glory, I am the most offending soul alive. *But
here I am* in a heavy sea and thick fog — Oh, God! the wind
subsided — but I trust to Providence I shall have them. 18th
in the evening, I have got her — Le Généreux — thank God!

12 out of 13, onely the Guillaume Telle remaining; I am after the others." The enemy's division had consisted of this seventy-four, a large transport, also captured, and three corvettes which escaped.

An account of Nelson on the quarter-deck on this occasion has been transmitted by an eye-witness, whose recollections, committed to paper nearly forty years later, are in many points evidently faulty, but in the present instance reflect a frame of mind in the great admiral in perfect keeping with the words last quoted from his own letter. The writer was then a midshipman of the "Foudroyant;" and the scene as described opens with a hail from a lieutenant at the masthead, with his telescope on the chase.

"'Deck there! the stranger is evidently a man of war — she is a line-of-battle-ship, my lord, and going large on the starboard tack.'

"'Ah! an enemy, Mr. Stains. I pray God it may be Le Généreux. The signal for a general chase, Sir Ed'ard, (the Nelsonian pronunciation of Edward,) make the Foudroyant fly!'

"Thus spoke the heroic Nelson; and every exertion that emulation could inspire was used to crowd the squadron with canvas, the Northumberland taking the lead, with the flagship close on her quarter.

"'This will not do, Sir Ed'ard; it is certainly Le Généreux, and to my flag-ship she can alone surrender. Sir Ed'ard, we must and shall beat the Northumberland.'

"'I will do the utmost, my lord; get the engine to work on the sails — hang butts of water to the stays — pipe the hammocks down, and each man place shot in them — slack the stays, knock up the wedges, and give the masts play — start off the water, Mr. James, and pump the ship.' The Foudroyant is drawing a-head, and at last takes the lead in the chase. 'The admiral is working his fin, (the stump of his right arm,) do not cross his hawse, I advise you.'

"The advice was good, for at that moment Nelson opened furiously on the quarter-master at the conn. 'I'll knock you off your perch, you rascal, if you are so inattentive. — Sir Ed'ard, send your best quarter-master to the weather-wheel.'

" ' A strange sail a-head of the chase! ' called the look-out man.

" ' Youngster, to the mast-head. What! going without your glass, and be d——d to you? Let me know what she is immediately.'

" ' A sloop of war, or frigate, my lord,' shouted the young signal-midshipman.

" ' Demand her number.'

" ' The Success, my lord.'

" ' Captain Peard ; signal to cut off the flying enemy — great odds, though — thirty-two small guns to eighty large ones.'

" ' The Success has hove-to athwart-hawse of the Généreux, and is firing her larboard broadside. The Frenchman has hoisted his tri-colour, with a rear-admiral's flag.'

" ' Bravo — Success, at her again! '

" ' She has wore round, my lord, and firing her starboard broadside. It has winged her, my lord — her flying kites are flying away all together.' The enemy is close on the Success, who must receive her tremendous broadside. The Généreux opens her fire on her little enemy, and every person stands aghast, afraid of the consequences. The smoke clears away, and there is the Success, crippled, it is true, but, bull-dog like, bearing up after the enemy.

" ' The signal for the Success to discontinue the action, and come under my stern,' said Lord Nelson; ' she has done well, for her size. Try a shot from the lower-deck at her, Sir Ed'ard.'

" ' It goes over her.'

" ' Beat to quarters, and fire coolly and deliberately at her masts and yards.'

" Le Généreux at this moment opened her fire on us; and, as a shot passed through the mizen stay-sail, Lord Nelson, patting one of the youngsters on the head, asked him jocularly how he relished the music ; and observing something like alarm depicted on his countenance, consoled him with the information, that Charles XII. ran away from the first shot he heard, though afterwards he was called ' The Great,' and deservedly, from his bravery. ' I, therefore,' said Lord Nelson, ' hope much from you in future.'

"Here the Northumberland opened her fire, and down came the tri-colored ensign, amidst the thunder of our united cannon." [1]

According to Keith, Nelson "on this occasion, as on all others, conducted himself with skill, and great address, in comprehending my signals, which the state of the weather led me greatly to suspect." Nelson's account to Hamilton was, "By leaving my admiral without signal, for which *I may be broke*, I took these French villains." "I have wrote to Lord Spencer," he tells his eldest brother, "and have sent him my journal, to show that the Généreux was taken by me, and my plan — that my quitting Lord Keith was at my own risk, and for which, if I had not succeeded, I might have been broke. The way he went, the Généreux never could have been taken." In a letter to Lord Minto he attributed his success to his knowledge of all the local conditions, acquired by seven years' experience. In his anxiety to make this instance prove his case, in the previous disobedience to Keith, for which the Admiralty had censured him, Nelson overreached himself and certainly fell into an ungenerous action. His vaunt of success by the road of disobedience rested only on the fact that he had failed to see Keith's signal. This the latter did not know, and evidently considered he had complied with its spirit. The signal to chase to windward was not strained to disobedience in being construed to search a fairly wide area for the enemy, keeping the rendezvous, which was also the enemy's destination, to leeward, so as to be readily regained. The "Queen Charlotte," Keith's flagship, covered the inner line, and, being a first-rate, was competent to handle any force that could come out of Toulon. There is a good deal of human nature in this captious unofficial attack on a superior, whose chief fault, as towards himself, was that he had been the victim of disobedience; but it is not pleasant to see in a man so truly great.

The "Généreux" carried the flag of a rear-admiral, who was

[1] Nelsonian Reminiscences, by Lieutenant G. S. Parsons. The author has been able to test Parsons' stories sufficiently to assure himself that they cannot be quoted to establish historical fact; but such scenes as here given, or how many glasses of wine Nelson drank at dinner, or that the writer himself was out of clean shirts, when asked to dine at the admiral's table, are trivialities which memory retains.

killed in the action.   Nelson seized the opportunity of further conciliating the Czar, by sending the sword of this officer to him, as Grand Master of the Order of Malta.   Upon rejoining Keith, he reported in person, as custom demands.   "Lord Keith received my account and myself like a philosopher (but very unlike you)," he wrote to Hamilton; "it did not, that I could perceive, cause a pleasing muscle in his face."   "Had you seen the Peer receive me," he wrote to Lady Hamilton the same day, "I know not what you would have done; but I can guess.   But never mind.   I told him that I had made a vow, if I took the Généreux by myself, it was my intention to strike my flag.   To which he made no answer."   What could he very well say, if a man chose to throw away his chances, especially when that man was a subordinate who a short time before had flatly refused to obey his orders.   Soreness and testiness had full swing in Nelson at this time; at some fancied neglect, he wrote Troubridge a letter which reduced that gallant officer to tears.

Between Palermo and Malta Keith had received letters from General Mélas, commanding the Austrian army in Piedmont, giving the plan of the approaching campaign, in which, as the Austrians were to besiege Genoa, and advance to the Riviera, much depended upon naval co-operation. Rightly judging that to be the quarter calling for the naval commander-in-chief, he was anxious to get away.   On the 24th of February he ordered Nelson to take charge of the blockade, and "to adopt and prosecute the necessary measures for contributing to the complete reduction of Malta."   Short of the chief command, which he coveted and grudged, Nelson himself could not have contrived a position better fitted to crown his work in the Mediterranean.   Within the harbor of La Valetta, concentrating there the two objects yet to be attained, — Valetta itself being one, — was the "Guillaume Tell," the thirteenth ship, which alone was lacking now to complete the tale of the trophies of the Nile.   Yet the fair prospect of success, inevitable since the capture of the "Généreux" had destroyed the French hopes of relief, brought to Nelson nothing but dismay.   "My Lord," he replied the same day, "my state of health is such, that it is impossible I can much longer remain here.   Without some rest, I am gone.   I must therefore, whenever I find the service will admit of it, request your permission to go to my friends, at Palermo, for a few weeks, and leave the command here to Commodore Troubridge. Nothing but absolute necessity obliges me to write this letter." "I could no more stay fourteen days longer here, than fourteen years," he said in a private letter to Keith of the same date.

By the next day he had recognized that even he could not leave at once the task appointed him, without discredit. "My situation," he then wrote to Hamilton, "is to me very irksome, but how at this moment to get rid of it is a great difficulty. The French ships here ["Guillaume Tell" and others] are preparing for sea; the Brest fleet, Lord Keith says, may be daily expected, and with all this I am very unwell. . . . The first moment which offers with credit to myself I shall assuredly give you my company. . . . Lord Keith is commander-in-chief, and I have not been kindly treated." His tried friends, Troubridge and Ball, realized the false step he was about to take, but they could not change his purpose. " Remember, my Lord," wrote the former, "the prospects are rather good at present of reducing this place, and that William Tell, Diane,[1] and Justice,[1] are the only three ships left from the Nile fleet. I beseech you hear the entreaties of a sincere friend, and do not go to Sicily for the present. Cruizing may be unpleasant. Leave the Foudroyant outside, and hoist your flag in the Culloden, to carry on operations with the General. Everything shall be done to make it comfortable and pleasing to you: a month will do all. If you comply with my request, I shall be happy, as I shall then be convinced I have not forfeited your friendship." Ten days later, March 5th, he wrote again: "One part of your Lordship's letter distresses me much, your determination to quit us, and of course the service, for I can draw no line between the one and the other. There is nothing I would not do to prevent it. . . . I beseech your Lordship hear the entreaties of a sincere friend, and stay until the fall of this place." " I dined with his Lordship yesterday, who is apparently in good health," wrote Ball to Lady Hamilton, "but he complains of indisposition and the necessity of repose. I do

[1] Frigates.

not think a short stay here will hurt his health, particularly
as his ship is at anchor, and his mind not harassed. Troubridge and I are extremely anxious that the French ships,
and the French garrison of La Valetta, shall surrender to him.
I would not urge it if I were not convinced that it will ultimately add both to his honour and happiness."

The fear of his friends that he would lose honor, by not
resisting inclination, is evident — undisguised; but they could
not prevail. On the 4th of March he wrote to Lady Hamilton: "My health is in such a state, and to say the truth, an
uneasy mind at being taught my lesson like a school boy,
that my DETERMINATION is made to leave Malta on the 15th
morning of this month, on the first moment after the wind
comes favourable; unless I am SURE that I shall get hold of
the French ships." Keith's directions had been full and explicit on details, and this Nelson seems to have resented.
Among the particular orders was one that Palermo, being so
distant from Malta, should be discontinued as the rendezvous,
and Syracuse substituted for it; Nelson was, however, at
liberty to use Messina or Augusta, both also on the east coast
of Sicily, if he preferred. It will be remembered that Nelson
himself, before he fell under the influence of Naples, had expressed his intention to make Syracuse the base of his operations. Coming as this change did, as one of the first acts of
a new commander-in-chief, coinciding with his own former
judgment, it readily took the color of an implied censure upon
his prolonged stay at Palermo — an echo of the increasing
scandal that attended it.

On the 10th of March he left Malta for Palermo in the
"Foudroyant," sending the ship back, however, to take her
place in the blockade, and hoisting his own flag on board a
transport. His mind was now rapidly turning towards a final
retirement from the station, a decision accelerated by the capture of the "Guillaume Tell." This eighty-gun ship started
on the night of March 29th to run out from La Valetta, to
relieve the famished garrison from feeding the twelve hundred
men she carried. It was a singular illustration of the good
fortune of the "heaven-born" admiral, to repeat Ball's expression, that the "Foudroyant" arrived barely in time, only a
few hours before the event, her absence from which might

have resulted in the escape of the enemy, and a just censure upon Nelson. "If the Foudroyant had not arrived," wrote Troubridge to him, "nothing we have could have looked at her." The French ship was sighted first by a frigate, the "Penelope," Captain Blackwood, which hung gallantly upon her quarters, as Nelson in former days had dogged the "Ça Ira" with the "Agamemnon," until the heavier ships could gather round the quarry. The "Guillaume Tell," necessarily intent only on escape from overpowering numbers, could not turn aside to crush the small antagonist, which one of her broadsides might have swept out of existence; yet even so, the frigate decided the issue, for she shot away the main and mizzen topmasts of the French vessel, permitting the remainder of the British to come up. No ship was ever more gallantly fought than the "Guillaume Tell;" the scene would have been well worthy even of Nelson's presence. More could not be said, but Nelson was not there. She had shaken off the "Penelope" and the "Lion," sixty-four, when the "Foudroyant" drew up at six in the morning. "At half-past six," says the latter's log, "shot away the [French] main and mizen-masts: saw a man nail the French ensign to the stump of the mizen-mast. Five minutes past eight, shot away the enemy's foremast. Ten minutes past eight, all her masts being gone by the board, the enemy struck his colours, and ceased firing." The last of the fleet in Aboukir Bay had surrendered to Nelson's ship, but not to Nelson's flag.

Troubridge took this occasion again to entreat his presence at Malta. "I would have given one thousand guineas your health had permitted your being in the Foudroyant;" and on the same day, April 1st, in a letter marked "private," he repeats, "Will your Lordship come and hoist your flag in the Culloden? Rely on everything I can do to make it pleasant." On the 13th he is yet more pressing: "Your friends absolutely, as far as they dare, insist on your staying to sign the capitulation. Be on your guard, I see a change in language since Lord Keith was here." Himself suffering from frequent severe illness, and harassed by officers of his own grade disregarding his orders, Troubridge still stuck to Malta, and he clearly believed Nelson could do the same under the conditions suggested. If so, the efficiency of the service, as well as his

own reputation, demanded of the admiral to be there instead
of at Palermo.

"I am sensible," wrote Nelson to Sir Edward Berry, the
captain of the "Foudroyant," "of your kindness in wishing
my presence at the finish of the Egyptian fleet, but I have
no cause for sorrow. The thing could not be better done,
and I would not for all the world rob you of one particle of
your well-earned laurels." In the matter of glory Nelson
might well yield much to another, nor miss what he gave; but
there is a fitness in things, and it was not fitting that the commander of the division should have been absent when such
an event was likely to happen. "My task is done, my health
is lost, and the orders of the great Earl St. Vincent are completely fulfilled." "I have wrote to Lord Keith," he tells
Spencer, "for permission to return to England, when you
will see a broken-hearted man. My spirit cannot submit patiently." But by this time, if the First Lord's forbearance
was not exhausted, his patience very nearly was, and already
a letter had been sent, which, while couched in terms of
delicate consideration, nevertheless betrayed the deep disappointment that had succeeded to admiration for services
so eminent, and for a spirit once so indomitable: "To your
letter of the 20th of March, all I shall say is, to express my
extreme regret that your health should be such as to oblige
you to quit your station off Malta, at a time when I should
suppose there must be the finest prospect of its reduction. I
should be very sorry that you did not accomplish that business
in person, as the Guillaume Tell is your due, and that ship
ought not to strike to any other. If the enemy should come
into the Mediterranean, and whenever they do, it will be suddenly, I should be much concerned to hear that you learnt of
their arrival in that sea, either on shore or in a transport at
Palermo."

A nearer approach to censure soon followed. On the 9th
of May, orders were sent to Keith, that if Nelson's health
rendered him unfit for duty, he was to be permitted to return
home by sea when opportunity offered, or by land if he preferred. Earl Spencer wrote him at the same time a private
letter, in which disapprobation was too thinly masked by carefully chosen words to escape attention: "It is by no means

my wish or intention to call you away from service, but having observed that you have been under the necessity of quitting your station off Malta, on account of your health, which I am persuaded you could not have thought of doing without such necessity, it appeared to me much more advisable for you to come home at once, than to be obliged to remain inactive at Palermo, while active service was going on in other parts of the station. I should still much prefer your remaining to complete the reduction of Malta, which I flatter myself cannot be very far distant, and I still look with anxious expectation to the Guillaume Tell striking to your flag. But if, unfortunately, these agreeable events are to be prevented, by your having too much exhausted yourself in the service to be equal to follow them up, I am quite clear, and I believe I am joined in opinion by all your friends here, that you will be more likely to recover your health and strength in England than in an inactive situation at a Foreign Court, however pleasing the respect and gratitude shown to you for your services may be, and no testimonies of respect and gratitude from that Court to you can be, I am convinced, too great for the very essential services you have rendered it. I trust that you will take in good part what I have taken the liberty to write to you as a friend."

Both these letters reached Nelson in June, at Leghorn, on his way home. The underlying censure did not escape him, — "your two letters gave me much pain," he replied, — but he showed no traces of self-condemnation, or of regret for the past. Lord Minto, who was now ambassador at Vienna, wrote thence in March of this year, before the question of going home was decided: "I have letters from Nelson and Lady Hamilton. It does not seem clear whether he will go home. I hope he will not for his own sake, and he will at least, I hope, take Malta first. He does not seem at all conscious of the sort of discredit he has fallen into, or the cause of it, for he still writes, not wisely, about Lady H. and all that. But it is hard to condemn and use ill a hero, as he is in his own element, for being foolish about a woman who has art enough to make fools of many wiser than an admiral." Many years later, immediately after the parting which he did not then know was the last, Minto said of him, "He is in many points

28

a really great man, in others a baby." Nelson himself, conscious of the diligence which he had used in the administration of his wide command and its varied interests, put out of court all other considerations of propriety. "I trust you and all my friends will believe," he told Spencer, "that mine cannot be an inactive life, although it may not carry all the outward parade of *much ado about nothing*."

Had the Hamiltons remained in Palermo, Nelson would have been forced to a choice between leaving her and the Mediterranean, or yielding a submission to orders which to the last he never gave, when fairly out of signal distance. But the Foreign Office had decided that Sir William should not return after the leave for which he had applied; and in the beginning of March it was known at Palermo that his successor had been appointed. This Nelson also learned, at the latest, when he came back there on the 16th. To one correspondent he wrote, on the 28th, "Most probably my health will force me to retire in April, for I am worn out with fatigue of body and mind," and his application was sent in on the 6th of the latter month, after news of the "Guillaume Tell's" capture. On the 22d Hamilton presented his letters of recall, and on the 24th he and Lady Hamilton, with a party, embarked with Nelson on board the "Foudroyant" for a trip to Syracuse and Malta, from which they all returned to Palermo on the first of June.

CHAPTER XV.

NELSON LEAVES THE MEDITERRANEAN. — THE JOURNEY OVERLAND THROUGH GERMANY. — ARRIVAL IN ENGLAND. — SEPARATION FROM LADY NELSON. — HOISTS HIS FLAG IN THE CHANNEL FLEET, UNDER LORD ST. VINCENT.

JUNE, 1800–JANUARY, 1801. AGE, 42.

AT the time Nelson and the Hamiltons returned to Palermo, the Queen of Naples was wishing, for political reasons, to visit Vienna. To meet this wish Nelson took the "Foudroyant" and "Alexander" off the blockade of Malta, that they might carry herself and suite to Leghorn, together with the Hamiltons. He clung also to the hope that Keith would give him his powerful flagship to return to England, in which case the Hamiltons would go with him. "I go with our dear friends Sir William and Lady Hamilton," he wrote to Lord Minto; "but whether by water or land depends on the will of Lord Keith. May all orders be as punctually obeyed," alluding to the completion of the destruction of the Nile fleet by the capture of the "Guillaume Tell," "but never again an officer at the close of what I must, without being thought vain (for such I am represented by enemies), call a glorious career, be so treated!"

Keith's opinion of Nelson's obedience was probably somewhat different. The latter had written him on the 12th of May, that, being under an old promise to carry the Queen to the Continent, he proposed to take the two ships-of-the-line for that purpose, and Keith sent him a letter forbidding him to do so, and directing them to be sent back at once to Malta. Nelson, it is true, did not receive this; but it is impossible to reconcile with attention to orders the diversion of two ships of their force from the singularly important station appointed them by the commander-in-chief, without reference to him, and using them to carry about foreign sovereigns. On arriving in Leghorn, on the 14th of June, Nelson announced the fact to Keith, with apparent perfect unconsciousness that the latter could, be other than charmed. " I was obliged to bring the Alexander, or the party never could have been accommodated: I therefore trust you will approve of it." " I was so displeased by the withdrawing of the ships from before Malta," wrote Keith to Paget, "and with other proceedings, that her Majesty did not take any notice of me latterly." It would seem also that some harm had come of it. " What a clamour, too, letting in the ships to Malta will occasion. I assure you nothing has given me more real concern, it was so near exhausted." " Had not Nelson quitted the blockade," he wrote a week later, "and taken the ships off the station, it might have fallen about this time." [1]

Lord Keith had been engaged for six weeks past in the famous blockade and siege of Genoa, the garrison of which, spent with famine and disease, marched out on the 5th of June, 1800. On the 14th — the day Nelson reached Leghorn — was fought the Battle of Marengo, in which the Austrians were totally defeated, the French army under Bonaparte remaining victorious across their line of retreat to Mantua. The next day Mélas signed a convention, abandoning Northern Italy, as far as the Mincio, to the French, to whom were given up all the fortified places, Genoa included. At midnight of June 18, Nelson received an order from Keith to take all the ships at Leghorn to Spezia, for certain minor military purposes. Nelson sent the "Alexander" and a frigate, but remained himself in Leghorn with the "Foudroyant," ready, he wrote the admiral, "to receive the queen and royal family, should such an event be necessary." Keith rejoined with a peremptory order that no ships-of-the-line should be used for such purpose; the Queen, he said, had better get to Vienna as fast as she could, and not think of going back to Palermo. " If the French fleet gets the start of ours a day, Sicily cannot hold out even that one day." " Lord Keith," commented Nelson, " believes reports of the Brest fleet, which I give not the smallest credit to." " I own I do not believe the Brest fleet will return to sea," he told Keith; " and if they do the Lord have mercy on them,

[1] The Paget Papers, vol. i. pp. 253, 257.

for our fleet will not, I am sure." It was not the least of his conspicuous merits that he was blind to imaginative or exaggerated alarms. Keith saw too vividly all that might happen in consequence of recent reverses — much more than could happen.

On the 24th of June the latter reached Leghorn in person. "I must go to Leghorn," he complained, "to land the fugitives, and to be bored by Lord Nelson for permission to take the Queen to Palermo, and princes and princesses to all parts of the globe." The Queen was in a panic, and besought him with tears to give her the "Foudroyant," but Keith was obdurate. "Mr. Wyndham [1] arrived here yesterday from Florence," wrote Lady Minto on the 6th of July to her sister. "He left the Queen of Naples, Sir William and Lady Hamilton, and Nelson, at Leghorn. The Queen has given up all thoughts of coming here. She asked Lord Keith in her own proper person for the Foudroyant to take her back. He refused positively giving her such a ship. The Queen wept, concluding that royal tears were irresistible; but he remained unmoved, and would grant nothing but a frigate to convoy her own frigates [2] to Trieste. He told her Lady Hamilton had had command of the fleet long enough. The Queen is very ill with a sort of convulsive fit, and Nelson is staying there to nurse her; he does not intend going home till he has escorted her back to Palermo. His zeal for the public service seems entirely lost in his love and vanity, and they all sit and flatter each other all day long." It is only fair to say that there are indications, in the correspondence, of bad terms between the Hamiltons and Wyndham, who, therefore, was probably not a sympathetic observer. He had also before this written unpleasantly to Nelson, insinuating, apparently, a lack of attention to duty; for the latter in a letter to Troubridge says, "I send you an extract of Mr. Wyndham's unhandsome mode of expressing himself towards me." Towards Keith her Majesty manifested her displeasure by omitting him in the public leave she took of all the officials.

[1] British minister to Tuscany.

[2] There were some Neapolitan frigates in Leghorn, but the royal family were never willing to trust them.

The Queen finally resolved to continue her journey, but the victories of the French introduced into the political future an element of uncertainty, which caused her to delay a month in Leghorn, undecided whether to go by sea or land; and Nelson had vowed not to forsake her. Keith, after some days, relented so far as to authorize the "Alexander" taking the royal family to Trieste, but many of the party were averse to the sea voyage. There had been for some time living with the Hamiltons a Miss Knight, an English lady already in middle life, whose journal gives the chief particulars that have been preserved of this period. "The Queen," she wrote, "wishes, if possible, to prosecute her journey. Lady Hamilton cannot bear the thought of going by sea; and therefore nothing but impracticability will prevent our going to Vienna." When it was at last fixed, after many vacillations, that they should go to Ancona, and there take small Austrian vessels for Trieste, she exclaims, "to avoid the danger of being on board an English man-of-war, where everything is commodious, and equally well arranged for defence and comfort! But the die is cast, and go we must." She mentions that Lord Nelson was well, and kept up his spirits amazingly, but Sir William appeared broken, distressed, and harassed.

On the 11th the travellers started for Florence, passing within two miles of the French advanced posts. At Ancona they embarked on board some Russian frigates, and in them reached Trieste safely on the 2d of August. Nelson was received with acclamations in all the towns of the Pope's states. A party in which were not only the queen of a reigning sovereign, but an English minister and his wife, was sure of receiving attention wherever it passed or stopped ; but in the present case it was the naval officer who carried off the lion's share of homage, so widely had his fame spread throughout the Continent. At Trieste, says Miss Knight, "he is followed by thousands when he goes out, and for the illumination which is to take place this evening, there are many *Viva Nelson's* prepared."

The same enthusiasm was shown at Vienna, where they arrived on the 21st or 22d of August. "You can have no notion of the anxiety and curiosity to see him," wrote Lady

Minto.[1] "The door of his house is always crowded with people, and even the street when his carriage is at the door; and when he went to the play he was applauded, a thing which rarely happens here." "Whenever he appeared in public," records Miss Knight, "a crowd was collected, and his portrait was hung up as a sign over many shops — even the milliners giving his name to particular dresses, but it did not appear to me that the English nation was at all popular." At a dinner at Prince Esterhazy's, where he spent some days, his health was drunk with a flourish of trumpets and firing of cannon. "I don't think him altered in the least," continued Lady Minto, who remembered him from the old days in Corsica. "He has the same shock head and the same honest simple manners; but he is devoted to *Emma*, he thinks her quite an *angel*, and talks of her as such to her face and behind her back, and she leads him about like a keeper with a bear. She must sit by him at dinner to cut his meat, and he carries her pocket-handkerchief. He is a gig from ribands, orders and stars, but he is just the same with us as ever he was;" and she mentions his outspoken gratitude to Minto for the substantial service he had done him, and the guidance he had imparted to his political thought, — an acknowledgment he frequently renewed up to the last days of his life.

Lady Minto's nephew, Lord Fitzharris, the son of the Earl of Malmesbury, was then in Vienna, apparently as an attaché. He speaks in the same way of Nelson himself, but with less forbearance for Lady Hamilton; and he confirms the impression that Nelson at this time had lost interest in the service. Writing to his father, he says: "Nelson personally is not changed; open and honest, not the least vanity about him. He looks very well, but seems to be in no hurry to sail again. He told me he had no thoughts of serving again." "Lord Nelson and the Hamiltons dined here the other day; it is really disgusting to see her with him." A few days later there was a ball at Prince Esterhazy's, where Fitzharris was present. "Lady Hamilton is without exception the most coarse, ill-mannered, disagreeable woman I ever met with. The Princess had with great kindness got a number

of musicians, and the famous Haydn, who is in their service,
to play, knowing Lady Hamilton was fond of music. Instead
of attending to them she sat down to the Faro table, played
Nelson's cards for him, and won between £300 and £400.
In short, I could not disguise my feeling, and joined in the
general abuse of her." [1] The impression that Nelson would
decline further service had been conveyed to other friends.
Troubridge, who had meanwhile returned to England, wrote
two months later to a young lieutenant who wished to get on
board the admiral's next ship: " Lord Nelson is not yet
arrived in England, and between ourselves I do not think he
will serve again."

Both Lady Minto and Fitzharris have recorded an account
given them by Nelson, of his motives for action at the Battle
of the Nile. " He speaks in the highest terms of all the
captains he had with him off the coast of Egypt," writes the
former, " adding that without knowing the men he had to trust
to, he would not have hazarded the attack, that there was
little room, but he was sure each would find a hole to creep
in at." In place of this summary, her nephew gives words
evidently quite fresh from the speaker's lips. " He says,
'When I saw them, I could not help popping my head every
now and then out of the window, (although I had a d——d
toothache), and once as I was observing their position I
heard two seamen quartered at a gun near me, talking, and
one said to the other, ' D——n them, look at them, there they
are, Jack, if we don't beat them, they will beat us.' He says,
'I knew what stuff I had under me, so I went into the attack
with only a few ships, perfectly sure the others would follow
me, although it was nearly dark and they might have had
every excuse for not doing it, yet they all in the course of
two hours found a hole to poke in at. If,' he added, ' I had
taken a fleet of the same force from Spithead, I would sooner
have thought of flying than attacking the French in their
position, but I knew my captains, nor could I say which distinguished himself most.' " Yet to Lady Minto he revealed
the spirit he was of. " I told him I wished he had the command of the Emperor's army. He said, ' I'll tell you what.

[1] Malmesbury's Memoirs, vol. ii. p. 24.

If I had, I would only use one word — *advance*, and never say
retreat.' "

After a month's stop at Vienna, during which Sir William
Hamilton's health continued to cause anxiety, the party started
north for Prague, Dresden, and Hamburg, following the course
of the Elbe. On the 28th of September, Prague was reached,
and there Nelson was met by arrangement by the Archduke
Charles, the first in ability of the Austrian generals. The
next day, September 29th, was Nelson's birthday, and the
Archduke gave a grand entertainment in his honor. Continuing thence, the travellers on October 2d reached Dresden, to
which Court the British minister was Hugh Elliot, the brother
of Lord Minto. Here they came under the eye of Mrs. St.
George, a young Irish widow, who by a second marriage became
Mrs. Trench, and the mother of the late Archbishop of Dublin.
Her description and comments have been considered severe,
and even prejudiced; but they do not differ essentially from
those of the Mintos and Fitzharris, except in saying that on
one occasion, after dinner, Nelson took too much champagne,
and showed the effects. However much to be deplored, such
an occurrence is not so impossible as to invalidate the testimony
of an eye-witness, even in a man of Nelson's well-established
habitual abstemiousness, which indeed his health necessitated.
That the relater's impression, if unfavorable in some respects,
did not prejudice her in important matters, is shown by her
comment upon the admiral's letters to Lady Hamilton, when
published in 1814. " Though disgraceful to his principles of
morality on one subject, they do not appear to me, as they do
to most others, degrading to his understanding. They are
pretty much what every man, deeply entangled, will express,
when he supposes but one pair of fine eyes will read his letters;
and his sentiments on subjects unconnected with his fatal
attachment are elevated — looking to his hearth and his home
for future happiness ; liberal, charitable, candid, affectionate,
indifferent to the common objects of pursuit, and clear-sighted
in his general view of politics and life." [1]

Mrs. St. George's journal was not written for publication,
and did not see the light till thirty-odd years after her death.
" October 3d. Dined at Mr. Elliot's with only the Nelson

[1] Remains of Mrs. Trench, p. 293.

party. It is plain that Lord Nelson thinks of nothing but Lady Hamilton,[1] who is totally occupied by the same object. Lord Nelson is a little man, without any dignity; who, I suppose, must resemble what Suwarrow was in his youth, as he is like all the pictures I have seen of that General. Lady Hamilton takes possession of him, and he is a willing captive, the most submissive and devoted I have ever seen. Sir William is old, infirm, all admiration of his wife, and never spoke to-day but to applaud her. Miss Cornelia Knight seems the decided flatterer of the two, and never opens her mouth but to show forth their praise; and Mrs. Cadogan, Lady Hamilton's mother, is — what one might expect. After dinner we had several songs in honour of Lord Nelson, written by Miss Knight, and sung by Lady Hamilton.[2] She puffs the incense full in his face; but he receives it with pleasure, and snuffs it up very cordially." Lord Minto, whose friendship for Nelson was of proof, wrote eighteen months after this to his wife: "She goes on cramming Nelson with trowelfuls of flattery, which he goes on taking as quietly as a child does pap." [3]

"Lady Hamilton," wrote Mrs. St. George on succeeding days, "paid me those kinds of compliments which prove she thinks mere exterior alone of any consequence. . . . She loads me with all marks of friendship at first sight, which I always think more extraordinary than love of the same kind, pays me many compliments both when I am absent and present, and said many fine things about my accompanying her at sight. Still she does not gain upon me. . . . Mr. Elliot says, 'She will captivate the Prince of Wales, whose mind is as vulgar as her own, and play a great part in England,'" — a remark which showed shrewd judgment of character, as Nelson afterwards found to his intense disturbance. At Vienna the whole party had been presented at Court, but at Dresden the Electress refused to receive Lady Hamilton, on account of her former dissolute life. "She wished to go to Court," says Mrs. St. George, "on which a pretext was made to avoid receiving

[1] Mrs. St. George's description of Lady Hamilton has already been given, *ante*, p. 325.

[2] Miss Knight mentions the same ceremony occurring in Vienna.

[3] Life of Lord Minto, vol. iii. pp. 242–243.

company last Sunday, and I understand there will be no Court while she stays." Nelson felt resentment at this exclusion, though powerless, of course, to express it; but he declined an invitation to a private house which had not been extended to her. This incident naturally raised the question, what prospect there was of the lady being accepted at the Court of her own sovereign. "She talked to me a great deal of her doubts whether the Queen would receive her, adding, 'I care little about it. I had much rather she would settle half Sir William's pension on me,'" — a remark which showed more philosophy than self-esteem.

A week's visit in Dresden ended by the party taking boats for Hamburg, which they reached on the 21st of October, the journey being prolonged by stopping every night. They there remained ten days, of which no very noteworthy incidents have been recorded, although the general interest of all classes of people in the renowned warrior, of whom they had heard so much, continued to be manifested, sometimes in quaint and touching expression. On the 31st of October they embarked on board the mail-packet for England, and after a stormy passage landed at Yarmouth on the 6th of November, 1800. Two years and eight months had passed since Nelson sailed from Spithead, on a cruise destined to have so marked an influence on his professional reputation and private happiness. He was received on his landing with every evidence of popular enthusiasm, and of official respect from all authorities, civil and military. With the unvarying devout spirit which characterized him in all the greater events of his life, he asked that public service might be held, to enable him to give thanks in church for his safe return to his native country, and for the many blessings which he had experienced.

Until quite recently the fact of Lady Nelson not being at Yarmouth to meet her husband has been thought to indicate coldness, if not displeasure, on her part. When the first edition of this book was published, the present writer certainly shared that impression, which, whatever its origin, had a certain plausibility from the feelings of uneasiness in her, mentioned to Nelson by Davison,[1] writing in December, 1798. Although his language was veiled, the implication even then

[1] Nicolas, vol. iii. p. 138 (note).

was evident, and the scandalous reports afterwards current in
England, concerning the life at Palermo, scarcely tended to
soothe her anxieties. Nevertheless, however affected by the
rumors that reached her ears, Lady Nelson remained mistress
of herself and of her words, until the seeing of her eyes became more than she could bear. In 1898 were published for
the first time some long-missing letters of Nelson to her; parts
of a correspondence for which the indefatigable Sir Harris
Nicolas made "numerous inquiries without success." [1] From
these it appears that he had written her he would go at once
to London, when released from quarantine at Portsmouth,
where he then expected to arrive; "therefore I would not
have you come to Portsmouth on my account." As the same
reasons applied to any seaport, Lady Nelson observed her
husband's wishes by awaiting him in London. Not only so,
however, she carried complaisance so far as to ask Sir William
and Lady Hamilton to Nelson's country home, Round Wood,
near Ipswich. The letter conveying this invitation was among
those awaiting him at Yarmouth, and in his reply of November 6th he accepts in their name. [2] Meantime, however, Lady
Nelson and his father had gone to London, so that their first
meeting, after the famous Nile campaign, was there, at Nerot's
Hotel, on Saturday, November 8, 1800.

Thus, Lady Nelson's course, at the beginning of that brief
and critical period which ended in their permanent separation,
was, in forbearance and self-control, perfectly consistent with
the tone of her letters to him during his stay at the Neapolitan
Court. In these, the conditions at Palermo are ignored, and
the correspondence is confined to the talk of the day, mingled
with homely family news and simple unaffected expressions of
affection to himself. "I was so glad to see any one who could
give me such late accounts of my dear husband and my son,
that it had such an effect on me that I could not hear or see
and was obliged to call in our good father." One of her
latest extant letters to him, prior to his arrival in England,
dated March 29th, 1800, shows the same deference to his
wishes, the same affection, while withal quietly protesting her

[1] Nicolas, vol. i. preface, pp. xix, xx.
[2] The letters of Nelson here alluded to were published in "Literature,"
February–April, 1898.

own faithful striving to keep unimpaired the tie that united them.

"I have this instant received a note from Admiral Young, who tells me if I can send him a letter for you in an hour, he will send it, therefore, I have only time to say I have at last had the pleasure of receiving two letters from you, dated January 20th and 25th. I rejoice exceedingly I did not follow the advice of the physician and our good father to change the climate, and I hope my health will be established by hot sea-bathing and the warmth of the summer.

"I can with safety put my hand on my heart and say it has been my study to please and make you happy, and I still flatter myself we shall meet before very long. I feel most sensibly all your kindnesses to my dear son, and I hope he will add much to our comfort. Our good father has been in good spirits ever since we heard from you; indeed, my spirits were quite worn out, the time had been so long. I thank God for the preservation of my dear husband, and your recent success off Malta. The taking of the Généreux seems to give great spirits to all. God bless you, my dear husband, and grant us a happy meeting, and believe me," etc.[1]

The newly found letters prove that the length of time passing without news was not due to his failure to write. So far as published, however, they are wanting in the traces of tenderness which marked their former relations, as noted in previous passages of this work. "My dearest Fanny" has become "my dear Fanny;" "your most affectionate husband," "your affectionate." That such conjugal commonplaces as the earlier phrases no longer slip from his pen bears evidence, in the writer's opinion, to the stubborn integrity of the man scorning to deceive even himself by ordinary subterfuges.

It is possible that, like many men, though it would not be in the least characteristic of himself, Nelson, during his journey home, simply put aside all consideration of the evil day when the two women would be in the same city, and trusted to the chapter of accidents to settle the terms on which they might live; but he seems to have entertained an idea that he could maintain in London, with the acquiescence of his wife, the public relations towards Lady Hamilton tolerated by Neapoli-

[1] Alfred Morrison Collection of Autograph Letters (No. 473).

tan society. Miss Knight relates that, while at Leghorn, he
said he hoped Lady Nelson and himself would be much with
the Hamiltons, that they all would dine together very often,
and that when the latter went to their musical parties, he and
Lady Nelson would go to bed. In accordance with this pro-
gramme, he took his two friends to dine with his wife and
father, immediately upon his arrival in town. Miss Knight
went to another hotel with Lady Hamilton's mother, and was
that evening visited by Troubridge. He advised her to go
and stop with a friend; and, although no reason is given, it
is probable that he, who knew as much as any one of the past,
saw that the position of residence with the Hamiltons would
be socially untenable for a woman. Miss Knight accordingly
went to live with Mrs. Nepean, the wife of the Secretary to
the Admiralty.

A few days later there was again a dinner at the house
taken by the Hamiltons in Grosvenor Square. The Nelsons
were there, as was Miss Knight. The next day several of
the party attended the theatre, and Lady Nelson, it is said,
fainted in the box, overcome by feeling, many thought, at
her husband's marked attentions to Lady Hamilton. The
latter being in her way a character as well known as Nelson
himself, the affair became more than usually a matter of
comment, especially as the scene now provided for London
gossipers was a re-presentation of that so long enacted at
Palermo, and notorious throughout Europe; but it received
little toleration. "Most of my friends," wrote Miss Knight,
" were urgent with me to drop the acquaintance, but, circumstanced as I had been, I feared the charge of ingratitude,
though greatly embarrassed as to what to do, for things became
very unpleasant." Had it been a new development, it would
have presented little difficulty; but having quietly lived many
months in the minister's house under the same conditions,
only in the more congenial atmosphere of Palermo, it was not
easy now to join in the disapproval shown by much of London
society.

Lady Hamilton, of course, could not have any social acceptance, but even towards Nelson himself, in all his glory, a
marked coldness was shown in significant quarters. "The
Lady of the Admiralty," wrote he to his friend Davison,

" never had any just cause for being cool to me ; " an allusion probably to Lady Spencer, the wife of the First Lord. Coldness from her must have been the more marked, for after the Nile she had written him a wildly enthusiastic letter, recognizing with gratitude the distinction conferred upon her husband's administration by the lustre of that battle. " Either as a public or private man," he continued, " I wish nothing undone which I have done," — a remark entirely ambiguous and misleading as regards his actual relations to Lady Hamilton. He told Collingwood, at this same time, that he had not been well received by the King. " He gave me an account of his reception at Court," his old comrade writes, " which was not very flattering, after having been the adoration of that of Naples. His Majesty merely asked him if he had recovered his health; and then, without waiting for an answer, turned to General ——, and talked to him near half an hour in great good humour. It could not be about his successes." This slight was not a revival of the old prejudice entertained by the King before the war, which had been wholly removed by the distinguished services Nelson had rendered afterwards. Eighteen months before this Davison had written to him : " I waited upon the King early last Sunday morning, and was *alone* with him a full hour, when much of the conversation was about you. It is impossible to express how warmly he spoke of you, and asked me a thousand questions about you. . . . I have been again at the Queen's house, and have given the King a copy of your last letter to me, giving an account of your health, which he read twice over, with great attention, and with apparent emotion of concern. His Majesty speaks of you with the tenderness of a father." Samuel Rogers has an incidental mention of the effect produced upon Nelson by the treatment now experienced. " I heard him once during dinner utter many bitter complaints (which Lady Hamilton vainly attempted to check) of the way he had been treated at Court that forenoon : the Queen had not condescended to take the slightest notice of him. In truth, Nelson was hated at Court; they were jealous of his fame." [1] People, however, are rarely jealous of those who are not rivals.

The position which Nelson had proposed to himself to es-

[1] Table-Talk of Samuel Rogers.

tablish was of course impossible. The world was no more
disposed to worry about any private immoralities of his than
it did about those of other men, but it was not prepared to
have them brandished in its face, and it would have none
of Lady Hamilton, — nor would Lady Nelson. The general
public opinion at the time receives, probably, accurate expression from Sir William Hotham, a man then in London society.
"His vanity, excusable as such a foible is in such a man, led
him to unpardonable excesses, and blinded him to the advantages of being respected in society. . . . His conduct to Lady
Nelson was the very extreme of unjustifiable weakness, for he
should at least have attempted to conceal his infirmities, without publicly wounding the feelings of a woman whose own
conduct he well knew was irreproachable." [1]   On the other
hand, Nelson could not forget the kindnesses he had accepted
from Lady Hamilton, nor was he either able or willing to lessen an intimacy which, unless diminished, left the scandal
unabated. He was not able, for a man of his temperament
could not recede before opposition, or slight a woman now
compromised by his name; and he was not willing, for he was
madly in love. Being daily with her for seven months after
leaving Palermo, there occurs a break in their correspondence ;
but when it was resumed in the latter part of January, 1801,
every particle of the reticence which a possible struggle with
conscience had imposed disappears. He has accepted the new
situation, cast aside all restraints, and his language at times
falls little short of frenzy, while belying the respect for her
which he asserts continually and aggressively, as though against
his convictions.

The breach with Lady Nelson had in this short time become
final. We have not the means — happily — to trace through
its successive stages a rapid process of estrangement, of
which Nelson said a few months afterwards : "Sooner than
live the unhappy life I did when last I came to England, I
would stay abroad forever." A highly colored account is
given in Harrison's Life of Nelson, emanating apparently
from Lady Hamilton, of the wretchedness the hero experienced from the temper of his wife ; while in the "Memoirs

    [1] The author is indebted to Prof. J. Knox Laughton for some extracts from
Hotham's diary.

of Lady Hamilton," published shortly after her death, another side of the case is brought forward, and Lady Nelson appears as rebutting with quiet dignity the reproaches of her husband for heartlessness, displayed in her unsympathetic attitude towards her rival, when suffering from indisposition. Into these recriminations it is needless to enter; those who wish can read for themselves in the works mentioned. A marked symptom of growing alienation was afforded by his leaving her on the 19th of December, in company with the Hamiltons, to spend the Christmas holidays at Fonthill, the seat of William Beckford.

During this visit occurred a curious incident, which shows that the exultation unquestionably felt by Nelson in battle did not indicate insensibility to danger, or to its customary effects upon men, but resulted from the pleasurable predominance of other emotions, which accepted danger and the startling tokens of its presence as accompaniments, that only enhanced the majesty of the part he had to play. Beckford tells the story as follows: "I offered to show him what had been done by planting in the course of years. Nelson mounted by my side in a phaeton, drawn by four well-trained horses, which I drove. There was not the least danger, the horses being perfectly under my command, long driven by myself. Singular to say, we had not gone far before I observed a peculiar anxiety in his countenance, and presently he said: 'This is too much for me, you must set me down.' I assured him that the horses were continually driven by me, and that they were perfectly under command. All would not do. He would descend, and I walked the vehicle back again." [1] Nelson, of course, never claimed for himself the blind ignorance of fear which has been asserted of him; on the contrary, the son of his old friend Locker tells us, "The bravest man (so we have heard Lord Nelson himself declare) feels an anxiety 'circa præcordia' as he enters the battle; but he dreads disgrace yet more." [2] In battle, like a great actor in a great drama, he knew himself the master of an invisible concourse, whose homage he commanded, whose plaudits he craved, and whom, by the sight of deeds raised above the

[1] Beckford's Memoirs, London, 1859, vol. ii. p. 127.
[2] Locker's Greenwich Gallery, article "Torrington."

common ground of earth, he drew to sympathy with heroism
and self-devotion. There, too, he rejoiced in the noblest
exercise of power, in the sensation of energies and faculties
roused to full exertion, contending with mighty obstacles,
and acting amid surroundings worthy of their grandeur;
like Masséna, of whom it was said that he found his greatest
self only when the balls flew thick about him, and things
began to look their worst.

After his return from Fonthill Lady Nelson and himself
lived together again for a time in their London lodgings,
in Arlington Street, and there, according to the story told
forty-five years afterwards by Mr. William Haslewood, Nelson's solicitor, the crisis of their troubles was reached. "In
the winter of 1800, 1801, I was breakfasting with Lord and
Lady Nelson, at their lodgings in Arlington Street, and a
cheerful conversation was passing on indifferent subjects,
when Lord Nelson spoke of something which had been done
or said by 'dear Lady Hamilton;' upon which Lady Nelson rose from her chair, and exclaimed, with much vehemence, 'I am sick of hearing of dear Lady Hamilton, and
am resolved that you shall give up either her or me.' Lord
Nelson, with perfect calmness, said : 'Take care, Fanny,
what you say. I love you sincerely ; but I cannot forget
my obligations to Lady Hamilton, or speak of her otherwise than with affection and admiration.' Without one
soothing word or gesture, but muttering something about
her mind being made up, Lady Nelson left the room, and
shortly after drove from the house. They never lived together afterwards." Though committed to paper so many
years later, the incident is just one of those that sticks to
the memory, and probably occurred substantially as told.
Lady Nelson's outbreak will probably be differently regarded
by different persons; it shows at least that she was living
human flesh and blood. In later life, we are told by Hotham,
who was in the habit of frequently seeing her, up to her
death, in 1831, "she continually talked of him, and always
attempted to palliate his conduct towards her, was warm and
enthusiastic in her praises of his public achievements, and
bowed down with dignified submission to the errors of his
domestic life."

The same testimony is borne by a lady, of whom Nicolas speaks as "the personal and intimate friend both of Lord and Lady Nelson, and the widow of one of his most distinguished followers," but whose name he does not give.[1] "I am aware of your intention not to touch upon this delicate subject: I only allude to it in order to assure you, from my personal knowledge, in a long and intimate acquaintance, that Lady Nelson's conduct was not only affectionate, wise, and prudent, but admirable, throughout her married life, and that she had not a single reproach to make herself. I say not this to cast unnecessary blame upon *one* whose memory I delight to honour, but only in justice to that truly good and amiable woman. . . . If mildness, forbearance, and indulgence to the weaknesses of human nature could have availed, her fate would have been very different. No reproach ever passed her lips ; and when she parted from her Lord, on his hoisting his flag again, it was without the most distant suspicion that he meant it to be final, and that in this life they were never to meet again. I am desirous that you should know the worth of her who has so often been misrepresented, from the wish of many to cast the blame anywhere, but on him who was so deservedly dear to the Nation."

After their separation Lady Nelson wrote to her husband on three different occasions; the first, January 14, 1801, to thank him for the "generosity and tenderness" shown in the handsome allowance made to her; the second, in the following summer, to express her "thankfulness and happiness" that his life had been spared at Copenhagen; the third, December 18, 1801, begging, but in terms of dignified simplicity and affection, that the past might be forgotten and they live together again. The last was returned to her unread. The latter years of her life were passed partly in Paris, where she lived with her son and his family. Her eldest grandchild, a girl, was eight or ten years old at the time of her death. She remembers the great sweetness of her grandmother's temper, and tells that she often saw her take from a casket a miniature of Nelson, look at it affectionately, kiss it, and then replace it gently ; after which she would turn to her and say, " When you are older, little Fan, you too may know what it is

[1] Nicolas, vol. ii. p. 353.

to have a broken heart." This trifling incident, transpiring
as it now does for the first time, after nearly seventy years,
from the intimate privacies of family life, bears its own
mute evidence that Lady Nelson neither reproached her
husband, nor was towards him unforgiving.[1] Nelson's early
friend, the Duke of Clarence, who had given her away at
the wedding, maintained his kindly relations with her to
the end, and continued his interest to her descendants after
his accession to the throne.

Thus abruptly and sadly ended an attachment which, if
never ardent, had for many years run undisturbed its tender course, and apparently had satisfied Nelson's heart, until
the wave of a great passion swept him off his feet. "I remember," writes Miss Knight, "that, shortly after the Battle
of the Nile, when my mother said to him that no doubt he
considered the day of that victory as the happiest in his life,
he answered, 'No; the happiest was that on which I married
Lady Nelson.'" On the 13th of January, 1801, Nelson took
formal and final leave of her before hoisting his flag at Torbay.
"I call God to witness," he then said, "there is nothing in
you, or your conduct, that I wish otherwise." His alienation
from her was soon shared by most of his family, except his
father, who said to him frankly, that gratitude required he
should spend part of his time with Lady Nelson. Two years
before, he had written of her: "During the whole war [since
1793] I have been with Lady Nelson, a good woman, and attentive to an infirm old man," and they had continued to live
together. The old man persuaded himself that there was
nothing criminal in relations, the result of which, as regarded
his son and daughter-in-law, he could not but deplore; but his
letters to Lady Hamilton go little beyond the civility that was
necessary to avoid giving offence to Nelson. Nelson's two
married sisters, Mrs. Bolton and Mrs. Matcham, evidently
shared their father's belief. They and their children maintained with Lady Hamilton a friendly and even affectionate
correspondence, long after Trafalgar, and until the death of
the parties put an end to it.

Immediately upon landing at Yarmouth, Nelson had written

[1] The author is indebted for this anecdote to Mrs. F. H. B. Eccles, of
Sherwell House, Plymouth, the daughter of the "little Fan" who told it.

to the Admiralty that his health was perfectly restored, and that he wished to resume service immediately. He was soon designated to a command in the Channel fleet, under Earl St. Vincent, who had been commander-in-chief since the spring of 1800. The " San Josef," the three-decker boarded by him at Cape St. Vincent, was named to receive his flag, and on the 17th of January it was hoisted on board her, at Plymouth, — blue at the fore, he having been promoted Vice-Admiral of the Blue on New Year's Day. An arrangement, however, had already been made, that, if the impending difficulties with Denmark threatened hostilities, he should accompany the fleet sent to the Baltic, as second to Sir Hyde Parker, selected for the chief command. While he was reporting to St. Vincent, on the 16th, at Torbay, preparatory to hoisting his flag, a letter from Parker informed him that the armament was decided upon. This he showed at once to St. Vincent, who acquiesced of course in the disappointment, but expressed a hope that he would soon rejoin him.

By the first of February the " San Josef " had gone round to Torbay, the rendezvous of the Channel fleet under St. Vincent's command, and there it was that Nelson received the news of the birth, on the 29th or 30th of January, of the child Horatia, whose parentage for a long time gave rise to much discussion, and is even yet considered by some a matter of doubt. Fortunately, that question requires no investigation here; as regards the Life of Nelson, and his character as involved in this matter, the fact is beyond dispute that he believed himself the father, and Lady Hamilton the mother, of the girl, whose origin he sought to conceal by an elaborate though clumsy system of mystification. This might possibly have left the subject covered with clouds, though not greatly in doubt, had not Lady Hamilton, after wildly unnecessary lying on her own part, recklessly preserved her holdings of a correspondence which Nelson scrupulously destroyed, and enjoined her to destroy.

The sedulous care on his side to conceal the nature of their relations, and the reckless disregard of his wishes shown by her, is singularly illustrated by the method he took to bring the child into her charge, from that of the nurse to whom it had been intrusted. When it was somewhat over three years old, on the 13th of August, 1804, he wrote Lady Hamilton a letter, evidently to be used, where necessary, to account for its presence under his roof. "I am now going to state a thing to you and to request your kind assistance, which, from my dear Emma's goodness of heart, I am sure of her acquiescence in. Before we left Italy I told you of the extraordinary circumstance of a child being left to my care and protection. On your first coming to England I presented you the child, dear Horatia. You became, to my comfort, attached to it, so did Sir William, thinking her the finest child he had ever seen. She is become of that age when it is necessary to remove her from a mere nurse and to think of educating her. . . . I shall tell you, my dear Emma, more of this matter when I come to England, but I am now anxious for the child's being placed under your protecting wing." With this letter (or, possibly, with another written the same day) was found an enclosure, undated and unsigned, but in Nelson's handwriting. "My beloved, how I feel for your situation and that of our dear Horatia, our dear child . . ."[1]

The indifference to incidental consequences which was shown by Nelson, when once he had decided upon a course of action, was part of his natural, as well as of his more distinctively military character; but in this connection with Lady Hamilton he must have felt intuitively that not only her reputation was involved, but his own also. The hospitality, the attention, the friendship, extended to him at Naples and Palermo, were not from Lady Hamilton only but from her husband also, in whose house he lived, and who to the end, so far as the records show, professed for him unbounded esteem and confidence. This confidence had been betrayed, and the strongest line of argument formerly advanced, by those who disputed Lady Hamilton's being the mother of the child, has become now Nelson's severest condemnation.

"However great was Nelson's infatuation," says Sir Harris Nicolas, "his nice sense of honour, his feelings of propriety, and his love of truth, were unquestionable. Hence, though during a long separation from his wife on the public service in the Mediterranean, he so far yielded to temptation as to become the father of a child, it is nevertheless difficult to

[1] Morrison, The Hamilton and Nelson Papers, Nos. 777, 778, 779.

believe that he should for years have had a criminal intercourse with the wife of a man of his own rank, whom he
considered as his dearest friend, who placed the greatest
confidence in his honour and virtue, and in whose house he
was living. Still more difficult is it to believe, even if this
had been the case, that he should not only have permitted
every one of his relations, male and female, — his wife, his
father, his brothers, his brothers-in-law, his two sisters, and
all their daughters, — to visit and correspond with her, but
even have allowed three of his nieces to live for a considerable time with her; have ostentatiously and frequently written and spoken of her 'virtuous and religious' character, —
holding her up as an example to his family; have appointed
her the sole guardian of his child; have avowedly intended to
make her his wife; have acted upon every occasion as if the
purity of their intimacy was altogether free from suspicion;
and in the last written act of his life have solemnly called
upon his country to reward and support her. An honourable
and conscientious man rarely acts thus towards his mistress.
. . . Moreover, Nelson's most intimate friends, including the
Earl of St. Vincent, who called them 'a pair of sentimental
fools,' Dr. Scott, his Chaplain, and Mr. Haslewood, were of
the same opinion; and Southey says, 'there is no reason to
believe that this most unfortunate attachment was criminal.'"

This complicated and difficult path of deception had to be
trod, because the offence was not one of common error, readily
pardoned if discovered, but because the man betrayed, whatever his faults otherwise, had shown both the culprits unbounded confidence and kindness, and upon the woman, at
least, had been led by his love to confer a benefit which
neither should have forgotten.

CHAPTER XVI.

THE EXPEDITION TO THE BALTIC AND BATTLE OF COPENHAGEN. — NELSON
RETURNS TO ENGLAND.

FEBRUARY–JUNE, 1801.   AGE, 42.

THE trouble between Great Britain and Denmark, which now called Nelson again to the front, leading to the most difficult of his undertakings, and, consequently, to the most distinguished of his achievements, arose about the maritime rights of neutrals and belligerents. The contention was not new. In 1780 the Baltic States, Russia, Sweden, and Denmark, being neutrals in the war then raging, had combined to assert, by arms, if necessary, certain claims advanced by them to immunity from practices which international law had hitherto sanctioned, or concerning which it had spoken ambiguously. These claims Great Britain had rejected, as contrary to her rights and interests; but, being then greatly outnumbered, she temporized until the end of the war, which left her in possession of the principles at stake, although she had forborne to enforce them offensively. The coalition of the Baltic States, at that time, received the name of the Armed Neutrality.

From 1793 to 1800 Sweden and Denmark had again succeeded in maintaining their neutrality, and, as most other maritime states were at war, their freedom of navigation had thrown into their hands a large carrying trade. But, while their profit was thus great, it would be much greater, if their ships could be saved the interruptions to their voyages arising from the right of belligerents to stop, to search, and, if necessary, to send into port, a vessel on board which were found enemy's goods, or articles considered "contraband of war." The uncertainty hanging round the definitions of the latter phrase greatly increased the annoyance to neutrals; and serious disputes existed on certain points, as, for example, whether materials for ship-building, going to an enemy's port, were liable to capture. Great Britain maintained that they were, the neutrals that they were not; and, as the Baltic was one of the chief regions from which such supplies came, a principal line of trade for the Northern States was much curtailed.

Sweden and Denmark were too weak to support their contention against the sea-power of Great Britain. Where there is lack of force, there will always be found the tendency to resort to evasion to accomplish an end; and Denmark, in 1799, endeavored to secure for her merchant ships immunity from search by belligerent cruisers — which International Law has always conceded, and still concedes, to be within the rights of a belligerent — by sending them on their voyages in large convoys, protected by ships of war. It was claimed that the statement of the senior naval officer, that there were not in the convoy any articles subject to capture, was sufficient; and that the belligerent would in that case have no right to search. Great Britain replied that the right of search rested upon long-standing common consent, and precedent, and that it could not be taken from her against her will by any process instituted by another state. The Danish ships of war being instructed to use force against search, two hostile collisions followed, in one of which several men were killed and wounded, and the Danish frigate was taken into a British port — though afterwards released.

The latter of these conflicts occurred in July, 1800. Great Britain then sent an ambassador to Denmark, backing him with a fleet of nine ships of-the-line, with bomb-vessels; and at the end of August a convention was signed, by which the general subject was referred to future discussion, but Denmark agreed for the time to discontinue her convoys. The importance of the subject to Great Britain was twofold. First, by having the right to seize enemy's property in neutral ships, she suppressed a great part of the commerce which France could carry on, thus crippling her financially; and, second, by capturing articles of ship-building as contraband of war, she kept from the French materials essential to the maintenance of their navy, which their own country did not produce. British statesmen of all parties maintained that in these contentions there was at stake, not an empty and offensive privilege, but a right vital to self-defence, to the effective maintenance of which the power to search was fundamentally necessary.

In 1800 the Czar Paul I. had become bitterly hostile to Austria and Great Britain. This feeling had its origin in the disasters of the campaign of 1799, and was brought to a climax by the refusal of Great Britain to yield Malta to him, as Grand Master of the Order, after its capture from the French in September, 1800. It had been the full purpose of the British ministry to surrender it, and Nelson, much to his distaste, had received specific orders to that effect; but, besides the fact that the Russians had contributed nothing directly to the reduction of the island, the attitude of the Czar had become so doubtful, that common prudence forbade putting into the hands of a probable future enemy the prize so hardly won from a present foe. Paul had already announced his intention of reviving the Armed Neutrality of 1780 ; and when, in November, he learned the fall of Malta, he seized three hundred British vessels lying in Russian ports, marched their crews into the interior, and at the same time placed seals on all British warehoused property, — a measure intended to support his demand for the restitution of the island to him.

On the 16th of December a treaty was signed at St. Petersburg by Russia and Sweden, to which Denmark and Prussia promptly adhered, renewing the Armed Neutrality, for the support of their various claims. The consenting states bound themselves to maintain their demands by force, if necessary ; but no declaration of war was issued. Great Britain, in accepting the challenge, equally abstained from acts which would constitute a state of war ; but she armed at once to shatter the coalition, before it attained coherence in aught but words. From first to last, until the Armed Neutrality again dissolved, though there was hard fighting, there was not formal war.

The relation of these occurrences to the life of Nelson will not be fully understood, unless the general state of Europe be recalled, and the master hand of Bonaparte be recognized, underlying and controlling previous changes and present conditions. After the Battle of the Nile, and up to a year before this, Austria, Russia, and Great Britain had been united in arms against France; and, in addition to the undisputed control of the sea by the British Navy, they were pressing in overpowering numbers upon her eastern frontiers, from the North Sea to the Mediterranean. Blunders of their own had arrested the full tide of success, and the return of Bonaparte from Egypt reversed the current. Russia withdrew in anger, and Austria, beaten upon field after field, in Italy and Germany, by Bonaparte and Moreau, had finally consented to peace after the disastrous defeat of Hohenlinden, on the 3d of December, 1800. Great Britain was left without an ally; and Russia was added to the list of her active enemies by the skilful political manipulation of Bonaparte, who played upon the impulses and weaknesses of the half-mad Czar, releasing with distinguished marks of respect all Russian prisoners, and offering the vain gift of Malta, the French garrison of which was even then clutched by the throat in the iron grip of the British sea-power.

The renewal of the Armed Neutrality was thus, primarily, the work of Bonaparte. He alone had the keenness to see all the possibilities in favor of France that were to be found in the immense combination, and he alone possessed the skill and the power to touch the various chords, whose concert was necessary to its harmonious action. Although it was true, as Nelson said, that Paul was the trunk of the many-limbed tree, it was yet more true that Bonaparte's deft cajoling of the Czar, and the inducements astutely suggested by him to Prussia, were the vitalizing forces which animated the two principal parties in the coalition, in whose wake the weaker states were dragged. Through the former he hoped to effect a combination of the Baltic navies against the British; through the latter he looked to exclude Great Britain from her important commerce with the Continent, which was carried on mainly by the ports of Prussia, or by those of North Germany, which she could control. Thus, by the concerted and simultaneous action of direct weight of arms on the one hand, and of commercial embarrassment on the other, Bonaparte hoped to overbear the power of his chief enemy; and here, as on other occasions, both before and after, Nelson was at once the quickening spirit of the

enterprise, and the direct agent of the blow, which brought
down his plans, in ruins, about his ears.

Relaxing none of her efforts in other quarters of the world,
Great Britain drew together, to confront the new danger,
everything in the home waters that could float, till she had
gathered a fleet of twenty sail-of-the-line, with smaller cruisers
in due proportion. " Under the present impending storm
from the north of Europe," wrote St. Vincent, from his perch
above the waters of Torbay, "to enable us to meet such a
host of foes, no ship under my command must have anything
done to her at Plymouth or Portsmouth that can be done at
this anchorage." "We are now arrived at that period," wrote
Nelson, " what we have often heard of, but must now execute
— that of fighting for our dear Country; and I trust that, although we may not be able to subdue our host of enemies, yet
we may make them ashamed of themselves, and prove that they
cannot injure us." "I have only to say," he wrote to Earl
Spencer, who must have rejoiced to see the old spirit flaming
again in undiminished vigor, " what you, my dear Lord, are
fully satisfied of, that the service of my King and Country
is the object nearest my heart; and that a first-rate, or sloop
of war, is a matter of perfect indifference to your most faithful and obliged Nelson."

The " San Josef " being considered too heavy a ship for
the Baltic service, Nelson's flag was shifted on the 12th of
February to the " St. George," a three-decker of lighter draft.
Hardy accompanied him as captain, and on the 17th Nelson
received orders to place himself under the command of Sir
Hyde Parker. A few days afterwards, the " St. George "
went to Spithead, where she received on board six hundred
troops, under the command of Colonel William Stewart, to
whom we owe the fullest and most interesting account of the
expedition in general, and of the Battle of Copenhagen in
particular, that has been transmitted by an eye-witness. The
ship sailed again on the 2d of March for Yarmouth, where
she arrived on the 6th. The next day Nelson went to call
on the commander-in-chief, who was living on shore, his flag
flying on board a vessel in the roads. " I remember," says
Colonel Stewart, "that Lord Nelson regretted Sir Hyde being
on shore. We breakfasted that morning as usual, soon after

six o'clock, for we were always up before daylight. We went on shore, so as to be at Sir Hyde's door at eight o'clock, Lord Nelson choosing to be amusingly exact to that hour, which he considered as a very late one for business."

At this, his first official visit, the commander-in-chief, it is said, scarcely noticed him, and Nelson, as will be seen, complained freely of the treatment he at the beginning received. Parker was now verging on old age, but he had recently married a young wife, who was in Yarmouth with him, and the two had arranged to give a great ball on the 13th of March; altogether a bad combination for a military undertaking. Nelson, who was in haste to get away, — chiefly because of his sound martial instinct that this was peculiarly a case for celerity, but partly, also, because of anxiety to get the thing over and done, and to return to his home comforts, — appears to have represented matters unofficially to the Admiralty, a step for which his personal intimacy with St. Vincent and Troubridge afforded easy opportunity; and an express quickly arrived, ordering the fleet to sea at once.[1] "The signal is made to prepare to unmoor at twelve o'clock," wrote Nelson to Troubridge on the 11th. "Now we can have no desire for staying, for her ladyship is gone, and the *Ball* for Friday knocked up by yours and the Earl's unpoliteness, to send gentlemen to sea instead of dancing with white gloves. I will only say," he continues, "as yet I know not that we are even going to the Baltic, except from the newspapers, and at sea I cannot go out of my ship but with serious inconvenience," — owing to the loss of his arm. What was not told him before starting, therefore, could not be told by mouth till after arrival.

It will be remembered that Sir Hyde Parker had succeeded Hotham in the chief command of the Mediterranean, for a brief but critical month in 1795,[2] and that Nelson had then complained of his action as regards the general conduct of the campaign, and specifically for having reduced to the point of inefficiency the small squadron under Nelson's own direction, upon which the most important issues hinged. Possibly Parker had heard this, possibly the notorious disregard of

---

[1] Naval Chronicle, vol. xxxvii. p. 445.

[2] *Ante*, pp. 170–172.

Keith's orders a few months before influenced him to keep his
renowned, but independent, subordinate at a distance in official matters. It was not well advised; though probably the
great blunderers were the Admiralty, in sending as second
a man who had shown himself so exceptionally and uniquely
capable of supreme command, and so apt to make trouble for
mediocre superiors. If Lord St. Vincent's surmise was correct, Parker, who was a very respectable officer, had been
chosen for his present place because in possession of all the
information acquired during the last preparation for a Russian
war; while Nelson fancied that St. Vincent himself, as commander of the Channel fleet, had recommended him, in order
to get rid of a second in command who did not carry out satisfactorily the methods of his superior. If that were so, the
mistake recoiled upon his own head; for, while the appointment was made by Earl Spencer, St. Vincent succeeded him as
First Lord before the expedition sailed, and the old seaman
would much have preferred to see Nelson at the helm. He
was quite sure of the latter, he said, and should have been in
no apprehension if he had been of rank to take the chief command; but he could not feel so sure about Sir Hyde, as he had
never been tried. Whatever the truth, Lady Malmesbury's
comment after the event was indisputable: " I feel very sorry
for Sir Hyde; but no wise man would ever have gone with
Nelson, or over him, as he was sure to be in the background
in every case."

"I declare solemnly," wrote Nelson to Davison four days
after reporting, "that I do not know " — officially, of course —
"that I am going to the Baltic, and much worse than that I
could tell you. Sir Hyde is on board sulky. Stewart tells
me, his treatment of me is now noticed. Dickson came on
board to-day to say all were scandalized at his gross neglect.
Burn this letter; then it can never appear, and you can speak
as if your knowledge came from another quarter." That day
the orders came from the Admiralty to go to sea; and the
next, March 12, the ships then present sailed, — fifteen ships-
of-the-line and two fifties, besides frigates, sloops of war,
brigs, cutters, fire-ships, and seven bomb-vessels, — for, if the
Danes were obstinate, Copenhagen was to be bombarded. On
the 16th of March Nelson wrote both to Davison and Lady

Hamilton that he as yet knew nothing, except by common report. " Sir Hyde has not told me officially a thing. I am sorry enough to be sent on such an expedition, but nothing can, I trust, degrade, do what they will." His mind was in a condition to see the worst motives in what befell him. " I know, I see, that I am not to be supported in the way I ought, but the St. George is beginning to prepare this day for battle, and she shall be true to herself. . . . Captain Murray sees, as do every one, what is meant to disgrace me, but that is impossible. Even the Captain of the Fleet [Parker's Chief of Staff] sent me word that it was not his doing, for that Sir Hyde Parker had run his pen through all that could do me credit, or give me support; but never mind, Nelson will be first if he lives, and you shall partake of all his glory. So it shall be my study to distinguish myself, that your heart shall leap for joy when my name is mentioned." [1]

Enough reached his ears to draw forth unqualified expressions of dissent from the plans proposed, and equally clear statements as to what should be done, — all stamped unmistakably with the " Nelson touch," to use an apt phrase of his own. "Reports say," he tells Lady Hamilton, "we are to anchor before we get to Cronenburg Castle, that our minister at Copenhagen may negotiate. What nonsense ! How much better could we negotiate was our fleet off Copenhagen, and the Danish minister would seriously reflect how he brought the fire of England on his Master's fleet and capital ; but to keep us out of sight is to seduce Denmark into a war. . . . If they are the plans of Ministers, they are weak in the extreme, and very different to what I understood from Mr. Pitt.[2] If they originate with Sir Hyde, it makes him, in my mind, as — but never mind, your Nelson's plans are bold and decisive — all on the great scale. I hate your pen and ink men ; a fleet of British ships of war are the best negotiators in Europe." While the greatness and decision of his character remain unimpaired, perhaps even heightened, it will be noticed that self-reliance, never in any man more justified, has tended to degenerate into boastfulness, and restlessness under displeasing orders to become suspicion of the motives prompting them.

[1] Nelson to Lady Hamilton. Pettigrew, vol. i. pp. 442-444.
[2] Pitt had resigned from office since then.

"They all hate me and treat me ill," he says, speaking of Spencer's and St. Vincent's administrations. "I cannot, my dear friend, recall to mind any one real act of kindness, but all of unkindness." It must, of course, be remembered that, while such expressions portray faithfully the working of the inner spirit, and serve, by contrast, to measure the Nelson of 1801 against the Nelson of 1796, they were addressed to the most intimate of friends, and do not necessarily imply a corresponding bearing before the eyes of the world.

An amusing story is told of a shrewd stratagem resorted to by Nelson, on the passage to the Baltic, to thaw the barrier of frigidity in his superior, which not only was unpleasant to him personally, as well as injurious to the interests of the state, but threatened also to prevent his due share in the planning and execution of the enterprise in hand, thus diminishing the glory he ever coveted. The narrator, Lieutenant Layman, was serving on board the "St. George," and happened to mention, in Nelson's presence, that some years before he had seen caught a very fine turbot on the Dogger Bank, over which the fleet must pass on its way.

"This being a mere casual remark, nothing more would have been thought of it, had not Nelson, after showing great anxiety in his inquiries when they should be on the Dogger Bank, significantly said to Mr. Layman, 'Do you think we could catch a turbot?' After a try or two, a small turbot was caught. Lord Nelson appeared delighted, and called out, 'Send it to Sir Hyde.' Something being said about the risk of sending a boat, from the great sea, lowering weather, and its being dark, his Lordship said with much meaning, 'I know the Chief is fond of good living, and he shall have the turbot.' That his Lordship was right appeared by the result, as the boat returned with a note of compliment and thanks from Parker. The turbot having opened a communication, the effect was wonderful. At Merton Mr. Layman told Lord Nelson that a man eminent in the naval profession had said to him, 'Do tell me how Parker came to take the laurel from his own brow, and place it on Nelson's?' 'What did you say?' asked Nelson. 'That it was not a gift,' replied Layman, 'as your Lordship had gained the victory by a turbot.' 'A turbot!' 'Yes, my lord, I well recollect your great desire to catch a turbot, and

your astonishing many, by insisting upon its being immediately
sent to Sir Hyde, who condescended to return a civil note;
without which opening your Lordship would not have been
consulted in the Cattegat, and without such intercourse your
Lordship would not have got the detached squadron; without
which there would not have been any engagement, and consequently no victory.' Lord Nelson smilingly said, 'You are
right.'" [1]

On the 19th of March the fleet was collected off the northern
point of Denmark, known as the Skaw. From there the broad
channel, called the Kattegat, extends southward, between
Sweden and the northern part of the Danish peninsula, until
it reaches the large Island of Zealand, upon the eastern shore
of which Copenhagen lies. The two principal entrances into
the Baltic are on either side of Zealand. The eastern one,
separating it from Sweden, is called the Sound, that to the
west is known as the Great Belt; each, from the military
point of view, possessed its particular advantages and particular drawbacks. "We are slow in our motions as ever,"
wrote Nelson, whose impatient and decided character would
have used the fair wind that was blowing to enter the
Kattegat, and to proceed at once to Copenhagen, "but I
hope all for the best. I have not yet seen Sir Hyde, but I
purpose going this morning; for no attention shall be wanting on my part." The next day he reports the result of the
interview to his friend Davison: "I staid an hour, and
ground out something, but there was not that degree of
openness which I should have shown to my second in command." The fleet advanced deliberately, a frigate being
sent ahead to land the British envoy, Mr. Vansittart, whose
instructions were that only forty-eight hours were to be allowed the Danes to accept the demands of Great Britain,
and to withdraw from the coalition. The slowness here,
like every other delay, chafed Nelson, whose wish from the
beginning was to proceed at the utmost speed, not merely
from the Skaw, but from England, with whatever ships could
be collected; for he reasoned perfectly accurately upon the
safe general principle that delay favors the defence more
than the offence. "I only now long to be gone," he wrote

[1] Naval Chronicle, vol. xxxvii. p. 446.

before leaving Yarmouth: "time is precious, and every hour makes more resistance; strike quick, and home." It was particularly true in this case, for Denmark, long used to peace, had not thought war possible, and every day was precious to her in restoring and increasing the neglected protection of Copenhagen.

On the evening of March 20 the fleet anchored in the Kattegat, eighteen miles from Cronenburg Castle and the town of Elsinore, at which the Sound narrows to three miles. Both shores being hostile, Parker would not attempt to force the passage until he learned the result of the British mission to Copenhagen; meanwhile the Danes were working busily at the blockships and batteries of the city. On the 23d Mr. Vansittart returned with the terms rejected; and he brought, also, alarming reports of the state of the batteries at Elsinore and Copenhagen, which were much stronger than the previous information of the British Cabinet had shown, proving, as Nelson urged, that each day's delay increased the enemy's relative power. Sir Hyde called a council. "Now we are sure of fighting," wrote Nelson to Lady Hamilton. "I am sent for. When it was a joke I was kept in the background; to-morrow will I hope be a proud day for England — to have it so, no exertion shall be wanting from your most attached and affectionate friend."

He was accompanied to Parker's flagship by Lieutenant Layman, who went in the boat to steer for him. "On board the London," according to Layman, "the heads appeared very gloomy. Mr. Vansittart, who arrived at the same moment Nelson did, said that if the fleet proceeded to attack, it would be beaten, and the attempt was in danger of being relinquished. The Captain of the Fleet said to Layman that the Danes were too strong to attack, and a torpor verging to despondency prevailed in the councils. While others were dismayed, however, Lord Nelson questioned those just arrived from Copenhagen not only as to the force, but as to the position of the enemy. Such interrogatories he called 'bringing people to the post.' Having learned that the great strength of the enemy was at the head of the line, supported by the Crown Battery, his Lordship emphatically observed that to begin the attack there would be like taking a bull by the horns, and he therefore suggested the attempt by the tail." [1] In order to avoid the formidable works at Cronenburg, and yet come up in rear of Copenhagen, according to this proposition of Nelson's, it was proposed in the council to go by the Great Belt. That passage is more intricate, and therefore, from the pilot's point of view, more hazardous than the Sound. Nelson was not much deterred by the alarming reports. "Go by the Sound, or by the Belt, or anyhow," he said, "only lose not an hour."

The minutes of the council have not been transmitted, but it is evident from Nelson's own letter of the following day, soon to be quoted in full, and also from one written to him by Mr. Vansittart, after the latter reached London, that he urged upon Parker, and prevailed with him, to throw aside the instructions of the Government, under the changed conditions, and to adopt boldly the plan which, according to his present knowledge, should seem most certain to crush Denmark at once. After that, he would shatter the coalition by immediate steps against Russia. Only such a bold spirit, with the prestige of a Nelson, can dominate a council of war, or extort decisive action from a commander-in-chief who calls one. "The difficulty," wrote Nelson some time afterwards, "was to get our commander-in-chief to either go past Cronenburg or through the Belt [that is, by any passage], because, what Sir Hyde thought best, and what I believe was settled before I came on board the London, was to stay in the Cattegat, and there wait the time when the whole naval force of the Baltic might choose to come out and fight — a measure, in my opinion, disgraceful to our Country. I wanted to get at an enemy as soon as possible to strike a *home* stroke, and Paul was the enemy most vulnerable, and of the greatest consequence for us to humble." So pressing, daring, and outspoken were his counsels, so freely did he now, as at former times, advocate setting aside the orders of distant superiors, that he thought advisable to ask Vansittart, who was to sail immediately for England, to explain to the Admiralty all the conditions and reasons, which Vansittart did. St. Vincent, as First Lord, gave unhesitating approval to what his former lieutenant had advised.

[1] Naval Chronicle, vol. xxxvii., art. "Layman,"

Nelson's understanding of the situation was, in truth, acute, profound, and decisive. In the northern combination against Great Britain, Paul was the trunk, Denmark and Sweden the branches. Could he get at the trunk and hew it down, the branches fell with it; but should time and strength first be spent lopping off the branches, the trunk would remain, and "my power must be weaker when its greatest strength is required." As things then were, the Russian Navy was divided, part being in Cronstadt, and a large fraction, twelve ships-of-the-line, in Revel, an advanced and exposed port, where it was detained fettered by the winter's ice. Get at that and smite it, and the Russian Navy is disabled; all falls together. This would be his own course, if independent. As Parker, however, was obstinately resolved not to leave Denmark hostile in his rear, Nelson had to bend to the will of his superior. He did so, without forsaking his own purpose. As in the diverse objects of his care in the Mediterranean, where he could not compel, he sought diligently to compass his object by persuasion, by clear and full explanation of his lofty views, by stirring appeals to duty and opportunity, striving to impart to another his own insight, and to arouse in him his own single-minded and dauntless activity. Conceding, perforce, that Denmark was not to be left hostile in the rear, — although he indicates that this object might be attained by masking her power with a detachment, while the main effort was immediately directed against Revel, — his suggestions to Parker for reducing Denmark speedily are dominated by the same conception. Strategic and tactical considerations unite to dictate, that the fleet, whether it go by the Sound or the Belt, must quickly reach and hold a position beyond — and therefore in the rear of — Copenhagen. There it interposed between Denmark and Russia; from there it approached Copenhagen where its defences were weakest. This comprehensive exposition went, with Nelson's customary directness, straight to the root of the matter.

Next day, after returning to his own ship, Nelson drew up the following paper, which is at once so characteristic of his temperament and genius, and so lucid and masterly a review of the political and military conditions, that, contrary to the author's usual practice, it is given entire. Being devoted to a single subject, and inspired by the spirit of the writer when in a state of more than usual exaltation, it possesses a unity of purpose and demonstration, necessarily absent from most of his letters, in which many and diverse matters have to be treated.

24th March, 1801.

MY DEAR SIR HYDE, — The conversation we had yesterday has naturally, from its importance, been the subject of my thoughts ; and the more I have reflected, the more I am confirmed in opinion, that not a moment should be lost in attacking the enemy : they will every day and hour be stronger ; we never shall be so good a match for them as at this moment. The only consideration in my mind is, how to get at them with the least risk to our ships. By Mr. Vansittart's account, the Danes have taken every means in their power to prevent our getting to attack Copenhagen by the passage of the Sound. Cronenburg has been strengthened, the Crown Islands fortified, on the outermost of which are twenty guns, pointing mostly downwards, and only eight hundred yards from very formidable batteries placed under the Citadel, supported by five Sail of the Line, seven Floating batteries of fifty guns each, besides Small-craft, Gunboats, &c. &c. ; and that the Revel Squadron of twelve or fourteen Sail of the Line are soon expected, as also five Sail of Swedes. It would appear by what you have told me of your instructions, that Government took for granted you would find no difficulty in getting off Copenhagen, and in the event of a failure of negotiation, you might instantly attack; and that there would be scarcely a doubt but the Danish Fleet would be destroyed, and the Capital made so hot that Denmark would listen to reason and its true interest. By Mr. Vansittart's account, their state of preparation exceeds what he conceives our Government thought possible, and that the Danish Government is hostile to us in the greatest possible degree. Therefore here you are, with almost the safety, certainly with the honour of England more intrusted to you, than ever yet fell to the lot of any British Officer. On your decision depends, whether our Country shall be degraded in the eyes of Europe, or whether she shall rear her head higher than ever; again do I repeat, never did our Country depend so much on the success of any Fleet as on this. How best to honour our Country and abate the pride of her Enemies, by defeating their schemes, must be the subject of your deepest consideration as Commander-in-Chief; and if what I have to offer can be the least useful in forming your decision, you are most heartily welcome.

I shall begin with supposing you are determined to enter by the Passage of the Sound, as there are those who think, if you leave that passage open, that the Danish Fleet may sail from Copenhagen, and join the Dutch or French. I own I have no fears on that subject; for it is not likely that whilst their Capital is menaced with an attack, 9,000 of her best men should be sent out of the Kingdom. I suppose that some damage may arise amongst our masts and yards; yet perhaps there will not be one of them but could be made serviceable again. You are now about Cronenburg: if the wind be fair, and you determine to attack the Ships and Crown Islands, you must expect the natural issue of such a battle — Ships crippled, and perhaps one or two lost; for the wind which carries you in, will most probably not bring out a crippled Ship. This mode I call taking the bull by the horns. It, however, will not prevent the Revel Ships, or Swedes, from joining the Danes; and to prevent this from taking effect, is, in my humble opinion, a measure absolutely necessary — and still to attack Copenhagen. Two modes are in my view; one to pass Cronenburg, taking the risk of damage, and to pass up[1] the deepest and straightest Channel above the Middle Grounds; and coming down the Garbar or King's Channel, to attack their Floating batteries, &c. &c., as we find it convenient. It must have the effect of preventing a junction between the Russians, Swedes, and Danes, and may give us an opportunity of bombarding Copenhagen. I am also pretty certain that a passage could be found to the northward of Southolm for all our Ships; perhaps it might be necessary to warp a short distance in the very narrow part. Should this mode of attack be ineligible, the passage of the Belt, I have no doubt, would be accomplished in four or five days, and then the attack by Draco could be carried into effect, and the junction of the Russians prevented, with every probability of success against the Danish Floating batteries. What effect a bombardment might have, I am not called upon to give an opinion; but think the way would be cleared for the trial. Supposing us through the Belt with the wind first westerly, would it not be possible to either go with the Fleet, or detach ten Ships of three and two decks, with one Bomb and two Fireships, to Revel, to destroy the Russian Squadron at that place? I do not see the great risk of such a detachment, and with the remainder to attempt the business at Copenhagen. The measure may be thought bold, but I am of opinion the boldest measures are the safest; and our Country demands a most vigorous exertion of her force, directed with judgment. In supporting you, my dear Sir Hyde, through the arduous and important task you have undertaken, no exertion of head or heart shall be wanting from your most obedient and faithful servant,

NELSON AND BRONTE.

[1] That is, from north to south. It may be well to notice that to go from the Kattegat to the Baltic is *up*, although from north to south.

On the 25th the wind was too strong to allow the ships to lift their anchors. On the 26th the fleet weighed, and proceeded for a few hours in the direction of the Great Belt, which Parker had decided to follow. Captain Otway of the "London," Sir Hyde's flagship, chanced to have local knowledge of that passage, which had not come before the council, because he was not a member. When he ascertained the intention, he explained the difficulties and risks to the admiral, upon which the latter concluded that the batteries of Cronenburg and Elsinore presented fewer dangers. He accordingly directed the fleet to return toward the Sound, and sent Otway to tell Nelson he should take that route. "I don't care a d—n by which passage we go," replied the latter, "so that we fight them." "Sir Hyde Parker," he wrote the same day to Lady Hamilton, "has by this time found out the worth of your Nelson, and that he is a useful sort of man on a pinch; therefore, if he ever has thought unkindly of me, I freely forgive him. Nelson must stand among the first, or he must fall." Side by side with such expressions of dauntless resolve and unfailing self-confidence stand words of deepest tenderness, their union under one cover typifying aptly the twin emotions of heroic aspiration and passionate devotion, which at this time held within him alternate, yet not conflicting, sway. In the same letter he tells her fondly, "You know I am more bigoted to your picture — the faithful representation of you I have with me — than ever a Neapolitan was to St. Januarius, and look upon you as my guardian angel, and God, I trust, will make you so to me. His will be done." From the time of leaving he wrote to her practically every day. "Mr. S. is quite right," he says to her on one occasion, "that through the medium of your influence is the surest way to get my interest. It is true, and it will ever be, whilst you hold your present conduct, for you never ask anything that does not do honour to your feelings, as the best woman, as far as my knowledge goes, that ever lived, and it must do me honour the complying with them."

The fleet anchored again on the evening of the 26th of March, six miles from Cronenburg, and was there detained three days by head winds and calms. In this interval, Nelson's general plan of operations having been adopted, he shifted his flag to a lighter ship, the "Elephant," seventy-four, commanded by Captain Foley, the same who had led the fleet inside the French line in Aboukir Bay. On the 30th, the wind coming fair from northwest, the ships weighed and passed Cronenburg Castle. It had been expected that the Swedish batteries would open upon them, but, finding they remained silent, the column inclined to that side, thus going clear of the Danish guns. "More powder and shot, I believe, never were thrown away," wrote Nelson, "for not one shot struck a single ship of the British fleet. Some of our ships fired; but the Elephant did not return a single shot. I hope to reserve them for a better occasion."

That afternoon they anchored again, about five miles below Copenhagen. Parker and Nelson, accompanied by several senior officers, went at once in a schooner to view the defences of the town. "We soon perceived," wrote Stewart, "that our delay had been of important advantage to the enemy, who had lined the northern edge of the shoals near the Crown batteries, and the front of the harbour and arsenal, with a formidable flotilla. The Trekroner (Three Crowns) Battery" — a strong work established on piles, whose position will be given — "appeared, in particular, to have been strengthened, and all the buoys of the Northern, and of the King's Channels had been removed." Nelson, however, was, or feigned to be, less impressed. "I have just been reconnoitring the Danish line of defence," he wrote to Lady Hamilton. "It looks formidable to those who are children at war, but to my judgment, with ten sail-of-the-line I think I can annihilate them; at all events, I hope to be allowed to try." This is again the same spirit of the seaman " determined to attack " at Aboukir; the same resolution as before Bastia, where he kept shut in his own breast the knowledge of the odds, feeling that to do nothing was as bad as failure — and worse. A like eagerness does not seem to have prevailed on board the flagship. Parker had allowed himself to be stiffened to the fighting-point by the junior he had before disregarded, but that he looked to the issue with more than doubt may be inferred from the words of his private secretary, the Rev. Mr. Scott, who afterwards held the same relation to Nelson. "I fear," he wrote on the day of the council, " there is a great deal of Quixotism

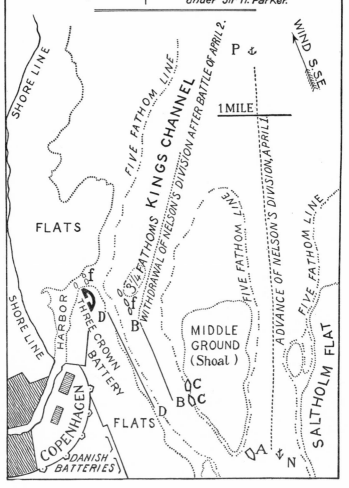

BATTLE OF COPENHAGEN
APRIL 2, 1801.

References:

A~ Agamemnon, at Anchor.
B.B~British Line of Battle.
C.C~British Ships Aground.
ff~British Frigates.

D.D~Danish Line of Hulks.
N~Anchorage of Nelson's Division,
    April 1–2.
P~Anchorage of British Main Fleet,
    under Sir H. Parker.

SHORE LINE

WIND S.SE

FIVE FATHOM LINE

KINGS CHANNEL

P ⚓

1 MILE

WITHDRAWAL OF NELSON'S DIVISION AFTER BATTLE OF APRIL 2.

3¾ FATHOMS

FLATS

FIVE FATHOM LINE

ADVANCE OF NELSON'S DIVISION, APRIL 1

FIVE FATHOM LINE

SHORE LINE

HARBOR

f

f

D

B

THREE CROWN BATTERY

MIDDLE GROUND (Shoal)

C

B C

SALTHOLM FLAT

COPENHAGEN

D

B

FLATS

DANISH BATTERIES

A ⚓ N

in this business; there is no getting any positive information of their strength."

Nelson's general plan of attack is set forth in main outlines in the letter already given, but it is desirable to give a somewhat more detailed description. It will be seen, by the annexed chart, that there are before Copenhagen two channels by which the city can be passed. Between the two lies a shoal, called the Middle Ground. The inner, known as the King's Channel, lay under the guns of the defences which had been hurriedly improvised for the present emergency. These consisted of a line of hulks, mostly mastless, ranged along the inner side of the King's Channel, close to the flats which bordered it, flanked at the northern end by the permanent work, called the Trekroner [1] Battery. Westward of the latter lay, across the mouth of the harbor proper, two more hulks, and a small squadron consisting of two ships-of-the-line and a frigate, masted, and in commission. This division was not seriously engaged, and, as a factor in the battle, may be disregarded.

The northern part of this defence was decisively the stronger. To attack there, Nelson called " taking the bull by the horns." The southern wing was much more exposed. Nor was this all. An advance from the north must be made with a northerly wind. If unsuccessful, or even, in case of success, if ships were badly crippled, they could not return to the north, where the fleet was. On the other hand, attack from the south presupposed a southerly wind, with which, after an action, the engaged ships could rejoin the fleet, if they threaded safely the difficult navigation. In any event there was risk, but none knew better than Nelson that without risks war is not made. To the considerations above given he added that, when south of the city, the British would be interposed between the other Baltic navies and Denmark. The latter, in that case, could not receive reinforcements, unless the English squadron were first defeated. He therefore proposed that ten ships-of-the-line, of the lighter draughts, which he offered himself to lead, should pass through the outer, or northern channel, gain the southern flank of the defence, and thence make the prin-

[1] Trekroner, which was then a favorite military name in Denmark, refers to the three Crowns of Denmark, Norway, and Sweden, once united.

cipal attack, while the rest of the fleet supported them by a demonstration against the northern end. The sagacity of this scheme is best attested from the enemy himself. " We have been deceived in the plan of attack," wrote the historian Niebuhr, then residing in the city; "and," now that the right wing of the defence is destroyed, "all is at stake." The nights of the 30th and 31st were employed in surveying the waters, laying down buoys to replace those removed by the Danes, and in further reconnoissance of the enemy's position. The artillery officers who were to supervise the bombardment satisfied themselves that, if the floating defences south of the Trekroner were destroyed, the bomb-vessels could be placed in such a position as to shell the city, without being themselves exposed to undue peril.

Parker gave Nelson twelve ships-of-the-line, two more than he had asked; a judicious addition, for the main part of the fighting was to fall to him, and the difficulties of pilotage might, and actually did, deprive him of several ships. Moreover, while it was proposed that the vessels remaining with Parker should approach and engage the northern defences, yet the time of attack depended upon a fair wind for Nelson; and as that would necessarily be foul for the other body, the diversion made by it might be, and proved to be, ineffective. Sound judgment dictated giving Nelson all that could be spared.

On the afternoon of the 31st another council was held, in which Nelson's plan was finally ratified; he again volunteered his services, which were accepted and his force detailed. As usual, the council was prolific in suggestions of danger. Stewart, who seems to have been present, writes: " During this Council of War, the energy of Lord Nelson's character was remarked: certain difficulties had been started by some of the members, relative to each of the three Powers we should either have to engage, in succession or united, in those seas. The number of the Russians was, in particular, represented as formidable. Lord Nelson kept pacing the cabin, mortified at everything that savoured either of alarm or irresolution. When the above remark was applied to the Swedes, he sharply observed, 'The more numerous the better;' and when to the Russians, he repeatedly said, 'So much the better, I wish they were twice as many, the easier the victory, depend on it.' He alluded, as he afterwards explained in private, to the total want of tactique among the Northern fleets; and to his intention, whenever he should bring either the Swedes or Russians to action, of attacking the head of their line, and confusing their movements as much as possible. He used to say, 'Close with a Frenchman, but out-manœuvre a Russian.'"

Nelson gave personal supervision to the general work of buoying the Northern Channel. On the morning of April 1st he made a final examination of the ground in the frigate "Amazon," commanded by Captain Riou, who fell in the next day's battle. Returning at about one in the afternoon, he signalled his division to weigh, and, the wind favoring, the whole passed without accident, the "Amazon" leading. By nightfall they were again anchored, south of the Middle Ground, not over two miles from that end of the Danish line. As the anchor dropped, Nelson called out emphatically, "I will fight them the moment I have a fair wind." As there were in all thirty-three ships of war, they were crowded together, and, being within shelling distance of the mortars on Amag Island, might have received much harm; but the Danes were too preoccupied with their yet incomplete defences to note that the few shells thrown dropped among their enemies.

"On board the Elephant," writes Stewart, who with his soldiers had followed Nelson from the "St. George," "the night of the 1st of April was an important one. As soon as the fleet was at anchor, the gallant Nelson sat down to table with a large party of his comrades in arms. He was in the highest spirits, and drank to a leading wind and to the success of the ensuing day. Captains Foley, Hardy, Fremantle, Riou, Inman, Admiral Graves, his Lordship's second in command, and a few others to whom he was particularly attached, were of this interesting party; from which every man separated with feelings of admiration for their great leader, and with anxious impatience to follow him to the approaching battle. The signal to prepare for action had been made early in the evening. All the captains retired to their respective ships, Riou excepted, who with Lord Nelson and Foley arranged the Order of Battle, and those instructions that were to be issued to each ship on the succeeding day. These three officers re-

tired between nine and ten to the after-cabin, and drew up
those Orders that have been generally published, and which
ought to be referred to as the best proof of the arduous nature
of the enterprise in which the fleet was about to be engaged.

" From the previous fatigue of this day, and of the two preceding, Lord Nelson was so much exhausted while dictating
his instructions, that it was recommended to him by us all,
and, indeed, insisted upon by his old servant, Allen, who
assumed much command on these occasions, that he should go
to his cot. It was placed on the floor, but from it he still
continued to dictate. Captain Hardy returned about eleven.
He had rowed as far as the leading ship of the enemy; sounding round her, and using a pole when he was apprehensive of
being heard. He reported the practicability of the Channel,
and the depth of water up to the ships of the enemy's line.
Had we abided by this report, in lieu of confiding in our
Masters and Pilots, we should have acted better. The Orders
were completed about one o'clock, when half a dozen clerks in
the foremost cabin proceeded to transcribe them. Lord Nelson's impatience again showed itself; for instead of sleeping
undisturbedly, as he might have done, he was every half hour
calling from his cot to these clerks to hasten their work, for
that the wind was becoming fair: he was constantly receiving
a report of this during the night." It was characteristic of
the fortune of the "heaven-born" admiral, that the wind
which had been fair the day before to take him south, changed
by the hour of battle to fair to take him north; but it is only
just to notice also that he himself never trifled with a fair
wind, nor with time.

The Orders for Battle, the process of framing which Stewart
narrates, have been preserved in full;[1] but they require a
little study and analysis to detect Nelson's thought, and their
tactical merit, which in matters of detail is unique among his
works. At the Nile and Trafalgar he contented himself with
general plans, to meet cases which he could only foresee in
broad outlines; the method of application he reserved to the
moment of battle, when again he signified the general direction
of the attack, and left the details to his subordinates. Here

[1] They are to be found in Nicolas's "Despatches and Letters of Lord
Nelson," vol. iv. p. 304.

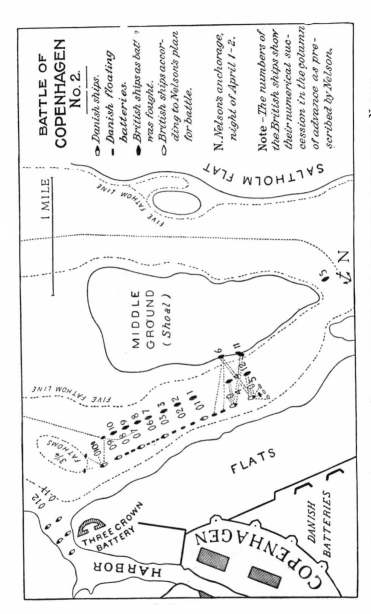

BATTLE OF
COPENHAGEN
No. 2.

⚓ *Danish ships.*
━ *Danish floating batteries.*
◆ *British ships as batt ?*
was fought.
◇ *British ships according to Nelson's plan for battle.*

N. *Nelson's anchorage, night of April 1-2.*

Note – *The numbers of the British ships show their numerical succession in the column of advance as prescribed by Nelson.*

1 MILE

FIVE FATHOM LINE

SALTHOLM FLAT

MIDDLE GROUND
(*Shoal*)

FIVE FATHOM LINE

3/4 FATHOMS

FLATS

THREE CROWN BATTERY

HARBOR

COPENHAGEN

DANISH BATTERIES

N

POSITIONS IN DETAIL, OF SHIPS AS ENGAGED, AND OF POSITIONS INTENDED BY NELSON.

at Copenhagen he had been able to study the hostile dispositions. Consequently, although he could not mark with precision the situations of the smaller floating batteries, those of
the principal blockships were known, and upon that knowledge
he based very particular instructions for the position each
ship-of-the-line was to occupy. The smaller British vessels
also had specific orders.

Taking the Trekroner as a point of reference for the Danish
order, there were north of it, on the Danish left flank, two
blockships. South of it were seven blockships, with a number
of miscellaneous floating batteries, which raised that wing of
the defence to eighteen — the grand total being therefore
twenty. This was also Nelson's count, except that he put one
small vessel on the north wing, reducing the southern to seventeen — an immaterial difference. South of the Trekroner,
the Danes had disposed their seven blockships — which were
mastless ships-of-the-line — as follows. Two were on the
right flank, supporting each other, two on the left, the three
others spaced between these extremes; the distance from the
Trekroner to the southernmost ship being about a mile and a
half. The intervals were filled with the floating batteries. It
will be recognized that the Danes treated this southern wing
as an entity by itself, of which they strengthened the flanks,
relying for the protection of the centre upon the nearness to
shoal water, which would prevent the line being pierced.

As thus described, the southern wing covered the front of
the city against bombardment. The two northern blockships
and the Trekroner did not conduce materially to that; they
protected chiefly the entrance of the harbor. It was therefore
only necessary to reduce the southern wing; but Nelson preferred to engage at once the whole line of vessels and the
Trekroner. It is difficult entirely to approve this refusal to
concentrate upon a part of the enemy's order, — an advantage
to which Nelson was fully alive, — but it was probably due to
underestimating the value of the Danish gunnery, knowing as
he did how long they had been at peace. He may, also, have
hoped something from Parker's division. Be this as it may,
he spread his ships-of-the-line, in the arrangement he prescribed, from one end to the other of the enemy's order.

Having done this, however, he adopted measures well calculated to crush the southern flank speedily, and then to accumulate superior numbers on the northern. The British were arranged in a column of attack, and the directions were that the three leading ships should pass along the hostile line, engaging as they went, until the headmost reached the fifth Dane, a blockship inferior to itself, abreast which it was to anchor by the stern, as all the British ships were to do. Numbers two and three were then to pass number one, and anchor successively ahead of her, supporting her there against the other enemy's batteries, while four and five were to anchor astern of her, engaging the two flank blockships, which would have received already the full broadsides of the three leading vessels. Nelson hoped that the two southern Danes, by this concentration of fire upon them, would be speedily silenced; and their immediate antagonists had orders, when that was done, to cut their cables and go north, to reinforce the fight in that quarter. The sooner to attain this end, a frigate and some smaller vessels were told off to take position across the bows of the two blockships, and to keep a raking fire upon them.

The dispositions for the other British vessels were more simple. They were to follow along the outer side of their own engaged ships, each one anchoring as it cleared the headmost ship already in action, — number six ahead of number five, number seven of number six, — so that the twelfth would be abreast the twentieth Dane. One ship-of-the-line was of course thought equivalent to two or three floating batteries, if opposed to them in an interval. By this arrangement, each of the British was covered in its advance, until it reached its prescribed antagonist as nearly fresh as possible, and the order of the British column was reversed from end to end.[1] A division of frigates and fireships, under Captain Riou, was held ready for any special service. The bomb-vessels were to anchor in the King's Channel, but well outside the line of battle, from which position they threw some bombs. Alongside each ship-of-the-line was towed a flat-boat, intended to carry soldiers in an attempt to storm the Trekroner, if circumstances favored; and other boats were sent for that purpose from Parker's division.

[1] Except numbers 4 and 5, whose stations, as has been said, were abreast the two southernmost Danes.

These orders were copied, and ready for distribution, by six in the morning. Nelson, who was already up and had breakfasted, signalled at seven for all captains, and by eight these had their instructions. The wind had become so fair that ships anchoring by the stern would lie perfectly well for using their broadsides at once. At this instant indecision appeared among the pilots, who were mostly men of only a little local experience, and that gained in vessels much smaller than those they were now to conduct. Nelson, reverting afterwards to these moments, said: "I experienced in the Sound the misery of having the honour of our Country intrusted to pilots, who have no other thought than to keep the ship clear of danger, and their own silly heads clear of shot. At eight in the morning of the 2d of April, not one pilot would take charge of a ship." There is in these words scarcely fair allowance for the men's ignorance. At length one of the Masters of the fleet, a Mr. Brierley, undertook to lead the column, and the signal to weigh in succession was made. The leading ship got off handsomely, but difficulties soon arose. Nelson's old "Agamemnon" was so anchored that she could not weather the Middle Ground; she consequently did not get into action at all. Two other ships, the "Bellona" and "Russell," seventy-fours, grounded on the west side of the Middle Ground, where they remained fast. Although they could use their guns, and did use them against those southern ships which Nelson particularly wanted crushed, the disadvantages of distance, of position, and of general helplessness, detracted exceedingly from their usefulness. The valid British force was thus reduced by one-fourth, — to nine vessels.

Nelson's ship, the "Elephant," was following the "Bellona" and "Russell," and he saw them ground. "His agitation during these moments was extreme," says an eye-witness. "I shall never forget the impression it made on me. It was not, however, the agitation of indecision, but of ardent, animated patriotism panting for glory, which had appeared within his reach, and was vanishing from his grasp." He doubtless well knew the thinly veiled reproaches of rashness, cast by timid counsels upon the daring, which even under these disadvantages was to cover with confusion their prophecies of disaster; but, as on many another day, and in that more famous incident, a few hours later, in this same battle, his tenacious purpose harbored no side-thought of retreat. " Before you receive this," he had written to Lady Hamilton, "all will be over with Denmark, — either your Nelson will be safe, and Sir Hyde Parker a victor, or he, your own Nelson, will be laid low." The signal to advance was kept flying, but new dispositions had to be made to meet the new and adverse conditions.[1] The remaining ships were made to close to the rear, as they anchored. The " Elephant" had been originally assigned as antagonist to the biggest Danish ship, the " Sjaelland," seventy-four; but, the " Bellona " having grounded, she now dropped into the latter's berth immediately ahead of the "Glatton; " and Nelson hailed the " Ganges," as she was passing, to place herself as close as possible ahead of the " Elephant." This movement was imitated by the " Monarch," which thus got the " Elephant's " position abreast the " Sjaelland." Here, according to Danish accounts, the contest stood for some time, until the " Defiance," Graves's flagship, arriving, anchored ahead of the " Monarch," completing the line of nine British ships. Captain Riou with his light division engaged the Trekroner, and the Danish blockship next south of it, which was by him terribly battered. From this moment, and for some time, to use subsequent words of Nelson, " Here was no manœuvring: it was downright fighting."

Meanwhile Parker's division, which had weighed as agreed, was some four miles off, beating up against Nelson's fair wind. It had not yet come into action, and the anxious chief, ever doubtful of the result of a step into which he had been persuaded, contrary, not, perhaps, to his will, but certainly to his bent, watched the indecisive progress of the strife with a mind unoccupied by any fighting of his own. Two

[1] The following is the order of the ships in the column of attack, as originally prescribed : —

1. Edgar, 74.		7. Elephant, 74.
2. Ardent, 64.		8. Ganges, 74.
3. Glatton, 54.		9. Monarch, 74.
4. Isis, 50.		10. Defiance, 74.
5. Agamemnon, 64.		11. Russell, 74.
6. Bellona, 74.		12. Polyphemus, 64.

VICE-ADMIRAL, SIR HYDE PARKER.

After the painting by G. Romney.

things were evident: that Nelson had met with some mishaps, and that the Danish resistance was more prolonged and sturdier than he had argued in the Council that it would be. Parker began to talk about making the signal to leave off action, and the matter was discussed between himself, his fleet-captain, and Otway, the captain of the ship. The latter opposed the idea strongly, and at last, as a stay, obtained the admiral's authority to go on board the "Elephant" and learn how things were. He shoved off accordingly, but before he reached Nelson the signal was made.

Nelson at the moment was walking the quarter-deck of the "Elephant," which was anchored on the bow of the Danish flagship "Dannebroge," engaging her and some floating batteries ahead of her. At this time, Stewart says, "Few, if any, of the enemy's heavy ships and praams had ceased to fire;" and, after mentioning various disappointments that had befallen the smaller British vessels, besides the failure of three heavy ships to reach their stations, he continues: "The contest, in general, although from the relaxed state of the enemy's fire, it might not have given much room for apprehension as to the result, had certainly not declared itself in favour of either side. Nelson was sometimes much animated, and at others heroically fine in his observations. A shot through the mainmast knocked a few splinters about us. He observed to me, with a smile, 'It is warm work, and this day may be the last to any of us at a moment;' and then, stopping short at the gangway, he used an expression never to be erased from my memory, and said with emotion, 'but mark you, I would not be elsewhere for thousands.'

"When the signal, No. 39, was made, the Signal Lieutenant reported it to him. He continued his walk, and did not appear to take notice of it. The lieutenant meeting his Lordship at the next turn asked, 'whether he should repeat it?' Lord Nelson answered, 'No, acknowledge it.'[1] On the officer returning to the poop, his Lordship called after him, 'Is No. 16 [For Close Action] still hoisted?' The lieutenant answering in the affirmative, Lord Nelson said, 'Mind you keep

---

[1] To acknowledge a signal is simply to hoist a flag, showing that it has been seen and understood. To repeat is to hoist the signal yourself, thus transmitting it as an order to those concerned.

it so.' He now walked the deck considerably agitated, which was always known by his moving the stump of his right arm. After a turn or two, he said to me, in a quick manner, ' Do you know what's shown on board the Commander-in-Chief, No. 39 ? ' On asking him what that meant, he answered, ' Why, to leave off action.' ' Leave off action ! ' he repeated, and then added, with a shrug, ' Now damn me if I do.' He also observed, I believe, to Captain Foley, ' You know, Foley, I have only one eye — I have a right to be blind sometimes ; ' and then with an archness peculiar to his character, putting the glass to his blind eye, he exclaimed, ' I really do not see the signal.' This remarkable signal was, therefore, only acknowledged on board the Elephant, not repeated. Admiral Graves did the latter, not being able to distinguish the Elephant's conduct: either by a fortunate accident, or intentionally, No. 16 was not displaced.

"The squadron of frigates obeyed the signal, and hauled off. That brave officer, Captain Riou, was killed by a raking shot, when the Amazon showed her stern to the Trekroner. He was sitting on a gun, was encouraging his men, and had been wounded in the head by a splinter. He had expressed himself grieved at being thus obliged to retreat, and nobly observed, ' What will Nelson think of us ? ' His clerk was killed by his side ; and by another shot, several of the marines, while hauling on the mainbrace, shared the same fate. Riou then exclaimed, ' Come then, my boys, let us all die together ! ' The words were scarcely uttered, when the fatal shot severed him in two. Thus, and in an instant, was the British service deprived of one of its greatest ornaments, and society of a character of singular worth, resembling the heroes of romance." Fortunately for the British, not a ship-of-the-line budged. Graves had indeed transmitted the order by repeating it, but as he kept that for close action also flying, and did not move himself, the line remained entire throughout a period when the departure of a single ship would have ruined all, and probably caused its own destruction.

This incident of refusing to see the signal has become as hackneyed as a popular ballad, and in its superficial aspect, showing Nelson as the mere fighting man, who, like a plucky dog, could not be dragged off his antagonist, might well now have been dismissed with the shortest and most summary mention. Of late years doubt has been cast over the reality of Nelson's disobedience, for the reason that Otway, whose mission has already been noted, carried a verbal message that the order was to be understood as permissive, leaving Nelson the liberty to obey or not. From Otway's biography, however, it appears that the signal was hoisted before he reached the "Elephant." Parker's Secretary, Mr. Scott, has also stated distinctly, that "it was arranged between the admirals, that, should it appear the ships which were engaged were suffering too severely, the signal for retreat would be made, to give Lord Nelson the option of retiring, if he thought fit." [1]

On the other hand, without affirming positively, it should be said that Nelson's own impressions do not seem to have agreed with Scott's. Not only did he say, some hours after the fight, "Well, I have fought contrary to orders, and I shall perhaps be hanged; never mind, let them," — which might pass as a continuation of the quarter-deck drama, if such it was, — but his account of the matter to Lord Minto is not consistent with any clear understanding, on his part, that he had such liberty of action. Nearly a year later, in March, 1802, Minto writes: "Lord Nelson explained to me a little, on Saturday last, the sort of blame which had been imputed to Sir Hyde Parker for Copenhagen; in the first place, for not commanding the attack in person, and in the next place for making signals to recall the fleet during the action; and everything would have been lost if these signals had been obeyed." If Nelson understood that the signal was to be construed as permissive only, it was extremely ungenerous, and most unlike Nelson, to have withheld an explanation which extenuated, if it did not excuse, one of the most dangerous and ill-judged orders that ever was conveyed by flags; nor is it probable that Parker, if the understanding had been explicit, would not have insisted with the Admiralty upon the fact, when he was smarting under the general censure, which had led to talk of an inquiry. It seems, also, unlikely that Nelson, having such a contingency in view, would have failed to give explicit instructions that his ships should not

[1] Life of Rev. Dr. A. J. Scott, p. 70.

withdraw (as Riou's frigates did) unless he repeated; nor is it easy to reconcile the agitation noted by Stewart with a previous arrangement of the kind asserted.

What Parker said was, probably, simply one of those by-remarks, with which an apprehensive man consoles himself that he reserves a chance to change his mind. Such provision rarely entered Nelson's head when embarking upon an enterprise in which "do or die" was the only order for success. The man who went into the Copenhagen fight with an eye upon withdrawing from action would have been beaten before he began. It is upon the clear perception of this truth, and his tenacious grip of it, that the vast merit of Nelson in this incident depends, and not upon the disobedience; though never was disobedience more justified, more imperative, more glorious. To retire, with crippled ships and mangled crews, through difficult channels, under the guns of the half-beaten foe, who would renew his strength when he saw the movement, would be to court destruction, — to convert probable victory into certain, and perhaps overwhelming, disaster. It was not, however, only in superiority of judgment or of fighting quality that Nelson in this one act towered like a giant above his superior; it was in that supreme moral characteristic which enabled him to shut his eyes to the perils and doubts surrounding the only path by which he could achieve success, and save his command from a defeat verging on annihilation. The pantomime of putting the glass to his blind eye was, however unintentionally, a profound allegory. There is a time to be blind as well as a time to see. And if in it there was a little bit of conscious drama, it was one of those touches that not only provoke the plaudits of the spectators, but stir and raise their hearts, giving them both an example of heroic steadfastness, and also the assurance that there is one standing by upon whom their confidence can repose to the bitter end, — no small thing in the hour of hard and doubtful battle. It had its counterpart in the rebuke addressed by him on this very occasion to a lieutenant, who uttered some desponding words on the same quarter-deck: "At such a moment, the delivery of a desponding opinion, unasked, was highly reprehensible, and deserved much more censure than Captain Foley gave you."

At two o'clock, an hour after the signal was made, the resistance of the Danes had perceptibly slackened; the greater part of their line, Stewart says, had ceased to reply. The flagship "Dannebroge" had been on fire as early as half-past eleven, and the commander-in-chief, Commodore Fischer, had felt necessary to shift his broad pendant to the "Holstein," the second ship from the north flank. The "Dannebroge" continued to fight bravely, losing two hundred and seventy killed and wounded out of a total of three hundred and thirty-six, but at length she was driven out of the line in flames, and grounded near the Trekroner, where she blew up after the action. The "Sjaelland," seventy-four, next north of her, was likewise carried out of the line by her cables being cut; while the "Holstein," and the northernmost ship of all, the "Indfödsretten," were so shattered, the latter mainly by Riou's frigates, that Fischer again shifted his flag, this time to the Trekroner. The two southern flank ships, upon whom the most concentrated attack was made, had also met with tremendous losses. Their flags were shot away many times, till at the last, by a Danish account, no one had time to raise them again, whence the impression arose amongst the British that these vessels, as well as some others, fought after having surrendered.

This incident, occurring in several cases, was the immediate cause of Nelson's taking a step which both then and since has been blamed as an unjustifiable stratagem. So much of the Danish fire south of the Trekroner had ceased, that that wing could be looked upon as subdued; some vessels were helpless, some had their flags down. Between himself and the Trekroner, Nelson alleged, there was a group of four Danes, unresisting and unmanageable, across and through which the battery was firing, and the British replying. Ships which had struck repelled boats sent to board them, and the batteries on Amag Island also fired upon those boats, and over the surrendered Danes. That there was some ground for the complaints made by him appears from the Danish admission just quoted, as well as from several British statements; Stewart's being explicit. Nelson accordingly sent a message ashore, under a flag of truce, to the Crown Prince, who was in general command, saying that if he were not allowed to

take possession of his prizes, he would have to burn them.
The message ran : —

Lord Nelson has directions to spare Denmark, when no longer
resisting; but if the firing is continued on the part of Denmark, Lord
Nelson will be obliged to set on fire all the floating batteries he has
taken, without having the power of saving the brave Danes who have
defended them.

NELSON AND BRONTE.

It was in the preparation and despatch of this note that
Nelson gave another illustration, often quoted, of his cool
consideration of all the circumstances surrounding him, and
of the politic regard to effect which he ever observed in his
official intercourse with men. It was written by his own hand,
a secretary copying as he wrote. When finished, the original
was put into an envelope, which the secretary was about to
seal with a wafer; but this Nelson would not permit, directing
that taper and wax should be brought. The man sent was
killed before he could return. When this was reported to the
admiral, his only reply was, " Send another messenger ; " and
he waited until the wax came, and then saw that particular
care was exercised to make a full and perfect impression of
the seal, which bore his own arms. Stewart said to him,
" May I take the liberty of asking why, under so hot a fire,
and after so lamentable an accident, you have attached so
much importance to a circumstance apparently so trifling ? "
Nelson replied, " Had I made use of the wafer, it would still
have been wet when presented to the Crown Prince; he would
have inferred that the letter was sent off in a hurry, and that
we had some very pressing reasons for being in a hurry. The
wax told no tales."
A flag of truce in a boat asks no cessation of hostilities,
except so far as the boat itself is concerned. As for the message sent, it simply insisted that the Danes should cease firing; failing which, Nelson would resort to the perfectly
regular, warlike measure of burning their ships. As the
ships were beaten, this might not be humane; but between it
and leaving them under the guns of both parties, the question

of humanity was only one of degree. If Nelson could extort from the Danes a cessation of hostilities by such a threat, he had a perfect right to do it, and his claim that what he demanded was required by humanity, is at least colorable. It must be observed, however, that he makes no suggestion of truce or armistice, — he demands that firing shall be discontinued, or he will resort to certain steps.

The Crown Prince at once sent back his principal aid-decamp, with a verbal message, which the latter reduced to writing, as follows: —

"His Royal Highness, the Prince Royal of Denmark, has sent me, General Adjutant Lindholm, on board to his Britannic Majesty's Vice-Admiral, the Right Honourable Lord Nelson, to ask the particular object of sending the flag of truce."

To this Nelson replied in writing: —

"Lord Nelson's object in sending on shore a flag of truce is humanity; he, therefore, consents that hostilities shall cease till Lord Nelson can take his prisoners out of the prizes, and he consents to land all the wounded Danes, and to burn or remove his prizes."

This message concluded with a complimentary expression of hope that good relations would be restored between the two nations, whom Nelson always carefully spoke of as natural friends. It will be observed that he again alludes only to the flag of truce sent by the boat, and, as at first he demanded, so now he consents to a cessation of hostilities, until he can secure his prisoners and remove his prizes. If he could rightly remove his prizes, which he avowed as part of his demand, then still more he could his own ships. This part of the negotiation he took upon himself to settle; for discussion of any further matters he referred Lindholm to Sir Hyde Parker, and the Danish officer started for the "London" at the same time that the English officer pushed off to carry Nelson's second message to the Crown Prince. The latter had already sent orders to the batteries to cease firing. The battle then ended, and both sides hoisted flags of truce.

Nelson at once began to remove his ships, which had suffered more than in any other battle he had ever fought. That he was fully aware of the imminent necessity for some of them to withdraw, and of the advantage the Danes had yielded him by accepting his terms, is indisputable, and his own opinion was confirmed by that of two of his leading captains, whom he consulted. This he never denied; but he did deny that he had used a *ruse de guerre*, or taken unfair advantage of a truce. On the score of humanity he had consented to a cessation of hostilities, conditional upon his freedom to take out of the surrendered ships the unwounded prisoners, and to remove the prizes. If the bargain was more to his advantage than to that of the Danes — which is a matter of opinion — it was none the less a bargain, of which he had full right to reap the benefit. The Danes did not then charge him with taking an unfair advantage. On the contrary, Lindholm, who was closely cognizant of all that passed in relation to these negotiations, wrote to him: " Your Lordship's motives for sending a flag of truce to our Government can never be misconstrued, and your subsequent conduct has sufficiently shown that humanity is always the companion of true valour." The truce that then began was prolonged from day to day till April 9th. During it both parties went on with their preparations for war. "These few days," wrote Niebuhr, on the 6th, "have certainly been employed in repairing the evil [of faulty preparation] as far as possible." It is clear that the Danes understood, what Nelson's message specified, a cessation of direct hostilities, not of other movements. The British during the same days were putting bomb-vessels in place, a perfectly overt act.

Nelson's success at Copenhagen was secured by address, as it had been won by force. But it had been thoroughly won. "We cannot deny it," wrote Niebuhr, "we are quite beaten. Our line of defence is destroyed. We cannot do much injury to the enemy, as long as he contents himself with bombarding the city, docks, and fleet. The worst is the Crown Batteries can be held no longer." Two or three days later he says again: "The truce has been prolonged. The remaining half of our defences are useless, now that the right wing is broken, — a defect over which I have meditated uselessly many a time since last summer." The result was due to Nelson's sagacious and emphatic advice as to the direction and manner of the attack, by which the strong points of the Danish positions were completely and unexpectedly turned. This plan, it is credibly stated, he had formed before leaving England, although he was not formally consulted by Parker until the 23d of March.

Having regard to the general political conditions, and especially to the great combination of the North at this time directed against Great Britain, the victory of Copenhagen was second in importance to none that Nelson ever gained; while in the severity of the resistance, and in the attendant difficulties to be overcome, the battle itself was the most critical of all in which he was engaged. So conspicuous were the energy and sagacity shown by him, that most seamen will agree in the opinion of Jurien de la Gravière : " They will always be in the eyes of seamen his fairest title to glory. He alone was capable of displaying such boldness and perseverance ; he alone could confront the immense difficulties of that enterprise and overcome them." Notwithstanding this and notwithstanding that the valor of the squadron, as manifested in its losses, was never excelled, medals were not issued for the battle, nor were any individual rewards bestowed, except upon Nelson himself, who was advanced in the peerage to be a Viscount, and upon his immediate second, Rear-Admiral Graves, who was made a Knight of the Bath. The reasons for this action are shown by the following extract from the diary of Mr. George Rose : " Wednesday, April 22d. Breakfasted with Lord St. Vincent by appointment. . . . His Lordship entered on the late glorious victory at Copenhagen, and told me the merit of the attack rested solely with Lord Nelson, as Sir Hyde Parker had been decidedly adverse to the attempt being made, and was overruled only by the perseverance and firmness of the former; and that in the middle of the action Sir Hyde had made the signal (No. 39) for discontinuing the engagement, which Lord Nelson said to the officer who communicated it to him, he was sure proceeded from some mistake. When it was mentioned to Admiral Graves, he asked if it was repeated by Lord Nelson ; and on being answered in the negative, he said, ' Then we have nothing to do with it.' Lord St. Vincent then added, ' For these and other causes,' probably alluding to the armistice, ' we have recalled Sir Hyde, and Lord Nelson is to remain with the command.' His Lordship proceeded to say that this measure of necessity put the Administration under some difficulty as to rewards of honour to the officers who had distinguished themselves ; and that he had thought it advisable to delay any distribution of medals or to recommend any stage in the peerage to Lord Nelson, conceiving that the whole might be done on the termination of the service with propriety, and without embarrassment respecting Sir Hyde Parker. . . . After I had left his Lordship, it occurred to me that as no measures can be kept with Sir Hyde Parker, it might be desirable to confer the intended step in the peerage on Lord Nelson now, and the medals on the other officers ; in which opinion Mr. Pitt concurring, I wrote to suggest that to his Lordship." [1]

" First secure the victory, then make the most of it," had been avowedly Nelson's motto before the Nile. In the Battle of Copenhagen he had followed much the same rule. After beating the force immediately opposed to him, he obtained the safe removal of his detachment from its critical position, by the shrewd use made of the advantage then in his hands. This achieved, and his ships having rejoined the main body, after various mishaps from grounding, under the enemy's guns, which emphasized over and over the adroit presence of mind he had displayed, it next fell to him to make the most of what the British had so far gained; having regard not merely to Denmark and Copenhagen, but to the whole question of British interests involved in the Coalition of the Baltic States. Parker intrusted to him the direct management of the negotiations, just as he had given him the immediate command of the fighting.

A circumstance, which completely changed the political complexion of affairs, was as yet unknown to him. On the night of March 24th the Czar Paul had been murdered, and with him fell the main motive force and support of the Armed Neutrality. Ignorant of this fact, Nelson's one object, the most to be made of the victory, was to get at the detachment of the Russian fleet — twelve ships — lying in the harbor of Revel, before the breaking up of the ice allowed it to join the main body at Cronstadt. The difficulty in the way lay not in his hesitation to act instantly, nor in the power of the British fleet to do so ; it lay in the conflicting views of other persons,

[1] Diaries, etc., of Rt. Hon. George Rose, vol. i. p. 347.

of the Crown Prince and of Parker, the representatives of Denmark and of Great Britain. Parker was resolved, so Nelson has told us, not to leave Denmark hostile in his rear, flanking his line of communications if he proceeded up the Baltic; and Nelson admits, although with his sagacious daring he would have disregarded, that the batteries commanding the shoal ground above Copenhagen might have seriously interrupted the passage. He was ready to run risks again for the very adequate object mentioned. On the other hand the Crown Prince, while recognizing the exposure of Copenhagen, feared to yield even to the menace of bombardment, lest he should incur the vengeance of the Czar. It was to find a middle term between these opposing motives that Nelson's diplomacy was exerted.

On the 3d of April he went ashore to visit the Crown Prince, by whom he was received with all possible attention. "The populace," says Stewart, "showed a mixture of admiration, curiosity, and displeasure. A strong guard secured his safety, and appeared necessary to keep off the mob, whose rage, although mixed with admiration at his thus trusting himself amongst them, was naturally to be expected. It perhaps savored of rashness in him thus early to risk himself among them; but with him his Country's cause was paramount to all personal considerations." Nelson himself did not note these threatening indications. Fond of observation, with vanity easily touched, and indifferent to danger, he heard only homage in the murmurs about him. "The people received me as they always have done; and even the stairs of the palace were crowded, huzzaing, and saying, 'God bless Lord Nelson.'"

His interview with the Crown Prince was private, only Lindholm being present. It ranged, according to his private letter to Addington, over the whole subject of the existing differences with Great Britain, and the respective interests of the two states. The most important points to be noticed in this personal discussion, which was preliminary to the actual negotiation, are, first, Nelson's statement of the cause for the presence of the British fleet, and, second, the basis of agreement he proposed. As regards the former, to a question of the Prince he replied categorically: The fleet is here "to crush a most formidable and unprovoked Coalition against

Great Britain." For the second, he said that the only foundation, upon which Sir Hyde Parker could rest his justification for not proceeding to bombardment, would be the total suspension of the treaties with Russia for a fixed time, and the free use of Danish ports and supplies by the British fleet. These two concessions, it will be observed, by neutralizing Denmark, would remove the threat to British communications, and convert Denmark into an advanced base of operations for the fleet. Nelson did not have great hope of success in negotiating, for he observed that fear of Russia, not desire for war, was controlling the Prince. Therefore, had he been commander-in-chief, he would at all risks have pushed on to Revel, and struck the coalition to the heart there. " I make no scruple," he wrote to St. Vincent after he had procured the armistice, "in saying that I would have been at Revel fourteen days ago. No man but those on the spot can tell what I have gone through, and do suffer. I wanted Sir Hyde to let me at least go and cruise off Carlscrona, [where the Swedish fleet was,] to prevent the Revel ships getting in. Think of me, my dear Lord, and if I have deserved well, let me retire; if ill, for heaven's sake supersede me, for I cannot exist in this state." Pegasus was indeed shackled.

The truce was continued from day to day, both sides preparing to renew hostilities, while the negotiators sat. Discussing thus, sword in hand, Nelson frankly told the other side that he wanted an armistice for sixteen weeks, to give him time to act against the Russian fleet, and then to return to Denmark. On the likely supposition that the latter would not greatly grieve over a Russian disaster, this openness was probably discreet. In the wrangling that preceded consent, one of the Danes hinted, in French, at a renewal of hostilities. " Renew hostilities!" said Nelson, who understood the language, but could not speak it, "tell him that we are ready at this moment; ready to bombard this very night." But, while he thus could use on occasion the haughty language of one at whose back stood a victorious fleet of twenty ships-of-the-line, "the best negotiators in Europe," to repeat his own words, his general bearing was eminently conciliatory, as became one who really longed for peace in the particular instance, and was alive to the mingled horror and inutility of the next move open to Great Britain, under Parker's policy, — the bombardment of Copenhagen. "Whoever may be the respective Ministers who shall sign the peace," wrote to him Count Waltersdorff, who with Lindholm conducted the Danish case and signed the armistice, "I shall always consider your lordship as the Pacificator of the North, and I am sure that your heart will be as much flattered by that title, as by any other which your grateful Country has bestowed upon you."

Had Paul lived, the issue might have been doubtful, and in that case England might well have rued the choice of a commander-in-chief whose chief function was to hamstring her greatest seaman; but the Danes received word of the murder, and on the 9th of April an agreement was reached. There was to be a cessation of hostilities for fourteen weeks, during which Denmark suspended her part in the Armed Neutrality, and would leave her ships of war in the same state of unpreparedness as they then were. The British fleet was at liberty to get supplies in all Danish ports. In return, it was merely stipulated that no attacks should be made on any part of the coast of Denmark proper. Norway [1] and the Danish colonies were not included, nor was Holstein. In a letter to Addington, Nelson pointed out that as a military measure, which it was, the result was that the hands of Denmark were tied, those of the fleet loosed, its communications secured, its base of supplies advanced, and last, but far from least, the timid counsels of its commander-in-chief disconcerted; no excuse for not advancing being left. Besides, as he said, to extort these concessions he had nothing in his hand but the threat of bombardment, which done, "we had done our worst, and not much nearer being friends." Sir Hyde would not have advanced.

As a military negotiation it is difficult to conceive one more adroitly managed, more perfectly conducive to the ends in view, or, it may be added, more clearly explained. The Government, with extraordinary dulness, replied in that patronizing official tone of superior wisdom, which is probably one of the most exasperating things that can be encountered by a man of such insight and action as Nelson had

[1] Norway was then attached to the Danish Crown, as now to that of Sweden.

displayed. " Upon a consideration of all the circumstances, His Majesty has thought fit to approve." "I am sorry," replied Nelson, "that the Armistice is only approved under *all* considerations. Now I own myself of opinion that every part of the *all* was to the advantage of our King and Country." As First Lord of the Admiralty, old St. Vincent had to transmit this qualified approval; but he wrote afterwards to Nelson : " Your Lordship's whole conduct, from your first appointment to this hour, is the subject of our constant admiration. It does not become me to make comparisons : all agree there is but one Nelson."

The armistice being signed and ratified, the fleet on the 12th of April entered the Baltic ; the heavy ships having to remove their guns, in order to cross the " Grounds," between the islands of Amager and Saltholm. Nelson was left behind in the " St. George," which, for some reason, was not ready. "My commander-in-chief has left me," he wrote to Lady Hamilton, " but if there is any work to do, I dare say they will wait for me. *Nelson will be first.* Who can stop him? " "We have reports," he says again, " that the Swedish fleet is above the Shallows, distant five or six leagues. All our fellows are longing to be at them, and so do I, as great a boy as any of them, for I consider this as being at school, and going to England as going home for the holidays, therefore I really long to finish my task." His confidence in himself and in his fortune was growing apace at this time, as was both natural and justifiable. " This day, twenty-two years," he writes soon after, on the 11th of June, " I was made a Post-Captain by Sir Peter Parker. If you meet him again, say that I shall drink his health in a bumper, for I do not forget that I owe my present exalted rank to his partiality, although I feel, if I had even been in an humbler sphere, that Nelson would have been Nelson still." Although always reverently thankful to the Almighty for a favorable issue to events, there does not seem to have been in him any keen consciousness of personal dependence, such as led Moltke to mark the text, " My strength is made perfect in weakness."

While thus lying, about twenty-four miles from the main body, a report came that the Swedish squadron had put to sea. Alarmed lest a battle might take place in his absence,

Nelson jumped into a boat alongside, and started for a six hours' pull against wind and current to join the fleet, in haste so great that he refused even to wait for a boat cloak. "His anxiety lest the fleet should have sailed before he got on board one of them," tells the officer who was with him, "is beyond all conception. I will quote some expressions in his own words. It was extremely cold, and I wished him to put on a great coat of mine which was in the boat: 'No, I am not cold; my anxiety for my Country will keep me warm. Do you not think the fleet has sailed?' 'I should suppose not, my Lord.' 'If they are, we shall follow them to Carlscrona in the boat, by G–d!' — I merely state this to show how his thoughts must have been employed. The idea of going in a small boat, rowing six oars, without a single morsel of anything to eat or drink, the distance of about fifty leagues, must convince the world that every other earthly consideration than that of serving his Country, was totally banished from his thoughts." Such preoccupation with one idea, and that idea so fine, brings back to us the old Nelson, who has found himself again amid the storm and stress of danger and of action, for which he was created.

About midnight he reached the "Elephant," where his flag was again hoisted; but he did not escape unharmed from the exposure he had too carelessly undergone. "Since April 15," he wrote several weeks afterwards to Lady Hamilton, "I have been rapidly in a decline, but am now, thank God, I firmly believe, past all danger. At that time I rowed five hours in a bitter cold night. A cold struck me to the heart. On the 27th I had one of my terrible spasms of heart-stroke, which had near carried me off, and the severe disappointment of being kept in a situation where there can be nothing to do before August, almost killed me. From that time to the end of May I brought up what every one thought was my lungs, and I was emaciated more than you can conceive."

The fleet proceeded in a leisurely manner toward Carlscrona, Nelson chafing and fretting, none the less for his illness, under the indecision and dilatoriness that continued to characterize Parker's movements. "My dear friend," he had written to Lady Hamilton, "we are very lazy. We Mediterranean people are not used to it." "Lord St. Vincent," he tells his

brother, " will either take this late business up with a very
high hand, or he will depress it; but how they will manage
about Sir Hyde I cannot guess. I am afraid much will be
said about him in the public papers ; but not a word shall be
drawn from me, for God knows they may make him Lord Copenhagen if they please, it will not offend me." But now that
Denmark has been quieted, he cannot understand nor tolerate
the delay in going to Revel, where the appearance of the fleet
would checkmate, not only Russia, but all the allied squadrons ;
for it would occupy an interior and commanding position
between the detachments at Revel, Cronstadt, and Carlscrona,
in force superior to any one of them. " On the 19th of April,"
he afterwards wrote bitterly to St. Vincent, " we had eighteen
ships of the line and a fair wind. Count Pahlen [the Russian
Cabinet Minister] came and resided at Revel, evidently to
endeavour to prevent any hostilities against the Russian fleet
there, which was, I decidedly say, at our mercy. Nothing, if
it had been right to make the attack, could have saved one ship
of them in two hours after our entering the bay ; and to prevent
their destruction, Sir Hyde Parker had a great latitude for
asking for various things for the suspension of his orders."
That is, Parker having the fleet at his mercy could have
exacted terms, just as Nelson himself had exacted them from
Denmark when Copenhagen was laid open ; the advantage,
indeed, was far greater, as the destruction of an organized
force is a greater military evil than that of an unarmed town.
This letter was written after Nelson had been to Revel, and
seen the conditions on which he based his opinion.

So far from taking this course, — which it may be said
would have conformed to instructions from his Government
then on their way, and issued after knowing Paul's death, —
Parker appeared off Carlscrona on April 20th. Two days
afterwards he received a letter from the Russian minister at
Copenhagen, saying that the Emperor had ordered his fleet to
abstain from all hostilities. Parker apparently forgot that he
was first a naval officer, and only incidentally a diplomatist;
for, instead of exacting guarantees which would have insured
the military situation remaining unchanged until definite
agreements had been reached, he returned to Kioge Bay, near
Copenhagen, but within the Shallows, leaving the Revel

squadron untrammelled, either by force or pledge, free to go out when the ice allowed, and to join either the Swedes or its own main body. Accordingly, it did come out a fortnight later, went to Cronstadt, and so escaped the British fleet.

While on this cruise towards Carlscrona, Nelson became involved in a pen-and-ink controversy about Commodore Fischer, who had commanded the Danish line at the Battle of Copenhagen, — one of two or three rare occasions which illustrate the vehemence and insolence that could be aroused in him when his vanity was touched, or when he conceived his reputation to be assailed. Fischer, in his official report of the action, had comforted himself and his nation, as most beaten men do, by dwelling upon — and unquestionably exaggerating — the significance of certain incidents, either actual, or imagined by the Danes; for instance, that towards the end of the battle, Nelson's own ship had fired only single guns, and that two British ships had struck, — the latter being an error, and the former readily accounted for by the fact that the " Elephant" then had no enemy within easy range. What particularly stung Nelson, however, seems to have been the assertion that the British force was superior, and that his sending a flag of truce indicated the injury done his squadron. Some of his friends had thought, erroneously in the opinion of the author, that the flag was an unjustifiable *ruse de guerre*, which made him specially sensitive on this point.

His retort, addressed to his Danish friend, Lindholm, was written and sent in such heat that it is somewhat incoherent in form, and more full of abuse than of argument, besides involving him in contradictions. That the British squadron was numerically superior in guns seems certain; it would have been even culpable, having ships enough, not to have employed them in any case, and especially when the attacking force had to come into action amid dangerous shoals, and against vessels already carefully placed and moored. In his official report he had stated that the " Bellona" and " Russell" had grounded; " but although not in the situation assigned them, yet so placed as to be of great service." In the present dispute he claimed that they should be left out of the reckoning, and he was at variance with the Danish accounts as to the effect of Riou's frigates. But such errors, he afterwards admitted to

32

Lindholm, may creep into any official report, and to measure
credit merely by counting guns is wholly illusory ; for, as he
confessed, with exaggerated humility, some months later, " if
any merit attaches itself to me, it was in combating the dangers
of the shallows in defiance of the pilots."

He chose, however, to consider that Fischer's letter had
thrown ridicule upon his character, and he resented it in
terms as violent as he afterwards used of the French admiral,
Latouche Tréville, who asserted that he had retired before a
superior force ; as though Nelson, by any flight of imagination, could have been suspected of over-caution.   Fischer
had twice shifted his broad pendant — that is, his own position — in the battle ; therefore he was a coward. " In his
letter he states that, after he quitted the Dannebrog, she long
contested the battle. If so, more shame for him to quit so
many brave fellows.   *Here* was no manœuvring : *it was* downright fighting, and it was his duty to have shown an example
of firmness becoming the high trust reposed in him."   This
was probably a just comment, but not a fair implication of
cowardice.   " He went in such a hurry, if he went before she
struck, which but for his own declaration I can hardly believe, that he forgot to take his broad pendant with him."
This Lindholm showed was a mistake. " He seems to exult
that I sent on shore a flag of truce. Men of his description,
if they ever are victorious, know not the feeling of humanity.
. . . Mr. Fischer's carcase was safe, and he regarded not the
sacred call of humanity."   This letter was sent to Lindholm,
to be communicated to the Crown Prince ; for, had not
Fischer addressed the latter as an eye-witness, Nelson " would
have treated his official letter with the contempt it deserved."
Lindholm kept it from Fischer, made a temperate reply defending the latter, and the subject there dropped.

On the 25th of April the fleet was at anchor in Kioge Bay,
and there remained until the 5th of May, when orders arrived
relieving Parker, and placing Nelson in chief command.
The latter was utterly dismayed. Side by side with the unquenchable zeal for glory and for his Country's service had
been running the equally unquenchable passion for Lady
Hamilton ; and, with the noble impulses that bore him up
in battle, sickness, and exposure, had mingled soft dreams of

flight from the world, of days spent upon the sunny slopes
of Sicily, on his estate of Bronté, amid scenes closely resembling those associated with his past delights, and with the
life of the woman whom he loved. To this he several times
alludes in the almost daily letters which he wrote her. But,
whether to be realized there or in England, he panted for the
charms of home which he had never known. " I am fixed,"
he tells her, " to live a country life, and to have many (I
hope) years of comfort, which God knows, I never yet had
— only moments of happiness," — a pathetic admission of the
price he had paid for the glory which could not satisfy him, yet
which, by the law of his being, he could not cease to crave. " I
wish for happiness to be my reward, and not titles or money ; "
and happiness means being with her whom he repeatedly calls
Santa Emma, and his " guardian angel," — a fond imagining,
the sincerity of which checks the ready smile, but elicits no
tenderness for a delusion too gross for sympathy.

Whatever sacrifices he might be ready to make for his
country's service, he was not willing to give up all he held
dear when the real occasion for his exceptional powers had
passed away ; and the assurances that the service absolutely
required his presence in the Baltic made no impression upon
him. He knew better. " Had the command been given me
in February," he said, " many lives would have been saved,
and we should have been in a very different situation ; but
the wiseheads at home know everything." Now it means
expense and suffering, and nothing to do beyond the powers
of an average officer. " Any other man can as well look about
him as Nelson." " Sir Thomas Troubridge," he complains,
after enumerating his grievances, " had the nonsense to say,
now I was a Commander-in-Chief I must be pleased. Does he
take me for a greater fool than I am ? " It was indeed shaving pretty close to insult to send out a man like Nelson as
second, when great work was in hand, and then, after he had
done all his superior had permitted, and there was nothing
left to do, to tell him that he was indispensable ; but to be congratulated upon the fact by a Lord of the Admiralty, which
Troubridge then was, was rather too much. He could not refuse
to accept the command, but he demanded his relief in terms
which could not be disregarded. His health, he said, made him

unequal to the service. For three weeks he could not leave his cabin. "The keen air of the North kills me." "I did not come to the Baltic with the design of dying a natural death."

Parker had no sooner departed than Nelson made the signal for the fleet to weigh, and started at once for Revel. He did not know whether or not the Russian ships were still there, and he felt that the change of sovereigns probably implied a radical change of policy; but he understood, also, that the part of a commander-in-chief was to see that the military situation was maintained, from day to day, as favorable as possible to his own country. He anticipated, therefore, by his personal judgment, the instructions of the Cabinet, not to enter upon hostilities if certain conditions could be obtained, but to exact of the Russian Government, pending its decision, that the Revel ships should remain where they were. "My object," he said, writing the same day he took command, "*was* to get at Revel before the frost broke up at Cronstadt, that the twelve sail of the line might be destroyed. I shall *now* go there as a friend, *but the two fleets shall not form a junction,* if not already accomplished, unless my orders permit it." For the same reason, he wrote to the Swedish admiral that he had no orders to abstain from hostilities if he met his fleet at sea. He hoped, therefore, that he would see the wisdom of remaining in port.

His visit to Revel, consequently, was to wear the external appearance of a compliment to a sovereign whose friendly intentions were assumed. To give it that color, he took with him only twelve ships-of-the-line, leaving the others, with the small vessels of distinctly hostile character, bombs, fireships, etc., anchored off Bornholm Island, a Danish possession. The resolution to prevent a junction was contingent and concealed. On the 12th the squadron arrived in the outer bay of Revel, and a complimentary letter, announcing the purpose of his coming, was sent to St. Petersburg. The next day he paid an official visit to the authorities, when his vanity and love of attention received fresh gratification. "Except to you, my own friend, I should not mention it, 'tis so much like vanity; but hundreds come to look at Nelson, '*that is him, that is him,*' in short 'tis the same as in Italy and Germany, and I now feel that a good name is better than riches, not amongst our great folks in England; but it has its fine feelings to an honest heart. All the Russians have taken it into their heads that I am like *Suwaroff, Le jeune Suwaroff;* " thus confirming the impression made upon Mrs. St. George at Dresden.

On the 16th of May a letter arrived from Count Pahlen, the Russian minister. The Czar declined to see a compliment in the appearance in Russian waters of so formidable a force, commanded by a seaman whose name stood foremost, not merely for professional ability, but for sudden, resolute, and aggressive action. "Nelson's presence," Niebuhr had written, "leads us to think, judging of him by his past conduct, that a furious attack will be made upon our harbor;" and he himself had recorded with complacency that a Danish officer, visiting the "London," upon learning that he was with the fleet in the Kattegat, had said, "Is he here? Then I suppose it is no joke, if he is come." "The Baltic folks will never fight me, if it is to be avoided." "The Emperor, my Master," wrote Pahlen, "does not consider this step compatible with the lively desire manifested by His Britannic Majesty, to reestablish the good intelligence so long existing between the two Monarchies. The only guarantee of the loyalty of your intentions that His Majesty can accept, is the prompt withdrawal of the fleet under your command, and no negotiation with your Court can take place, so long as a naval force is in sight of his ports."

Nelson had of course recognized that the game was lost, as soon as he saw that the Russian fleet was gone. The conditions which had mainly prompted his visit were changed, and the Russian Government was in a position to take a high tone, without fear of consequences. "After such an answer," he wrote indignantly to St. Vincent, "I had no business here. Time will show; but I do not believe he would have written such a letter, if the Russian fleet had been in Revel." "Lord Nelson received the letter a few minutes before dinner-time," wrote Stewart. "He appeared to be a good deal agitated by it, but said little, and did not return an immediate reply. During dinner, however, he left the table, and in less than a quarter of an hour sent for his secretary to peruse a letter which, in that short absence, he had composed. The signal for preparing to weigh was immediately made; the answer above-mentioned was sent on shore; and his Lordship caused the fleet to weigh, and to stand as far to sea as was safe for that evening."

Nelson took hold of Pahlen's expression, that he had come "with his whole fleet" to Revel. Confining himself to that, he pointed out the mistake the minister had made, for he had brought "not one-seventh of his fleet in point of numbers." He mentioned also the deference that he had paid to the Revel authorities. "My conduct, I feel, is so entirely different to what your Excellency has expressed in your letter, that I have only to regret, that my desire to pay a marked attention to His Imperial Majesty has been so entirely misunderstood. That being the case, I shall sail immediately into the Baltic." Retiring thus in good order, if defeated, he had the satisfaction of knowing that it was not his own blunder, but the wretched dilatoriness of his predecessor, that had made the Czar, instead of the British admiral, master of the situation.

Stopping for twenty-four hours at Bornholm on the way down, Nelson on the 24th anchored in Rostock Bay, on the German coast of the Baltic, and there awaited the relief he confidently expected. He had scarcely arrived when a second letter from Pahlen overtook him. The minister expressed his regret for any misunderstanding that had arisen as to the purpose of his first visit, and continued, "I cannot give your excellency a more striking proof of the confidence which the Emperor my Master reposes in you, than by announcing the effect produced by your letter of the 16th of this month. His Imperial Majesty has ordered the immediate raising of the embargo placed upon the English merchant ships." Nelson plumed himself greatly upon this result of his diplomacy. "Our diplomatic men are so slow. Lord St. Helens told me that he hoped in a month he should be able to tell me something decisive. Now, what can take two hours I cannot even guess, but Ministers must do something for their diamond boxes. I gained the unconditional release of our ships, which neither Ministers nor Sir Hyde Parker could accomplish, by showing my fleet. Then they became alarmed, begged I would go away, or it would be considered as warlike. On my complying, it pleased the Emperor and his ministers so much, that the whole of the British shipping were given up." There is nothing like the point of view; but it must be admitted that Nelson extricated himself from an unpleasant position with great good temper and sound judgment.

He remained in his flagship between Rostock and Kioge Bay, until relieved by Vice-Admiral Pole on the 19th of June. Nothing of official importance occurred during these three weeks; for the naval part of the Baltic entanglement was ended, as he had foreseen. A pleasant picture of his daily life on board the "St. George" at this time has been preserved for us by Colonel Stewart: "His hour of rising was four or five o'clock, and of going to rest about ten; breakfast was never later than six, and generally nearer to five o'clock. A midshipman or two were always of the party; and I have known him send during the middle watch [1] to invite the little fellows to breakfast with him, when relieved. At table with them, he would enter into their boyish jokes, and be the most youthful of the party. At dinner he invariably had every officer of the ship in their turn, and was both a polite and hospitable host. The whole ordinary business of the fleet was invariably despatched, as it had been by Earl St. Vincent, before eight o'clock. The great command of time which Lord Nelson thus gave himself, and the alertness which this example imparted throughout the fleet, can only be understood by those who witnessed it, or who know the value of early hours. . . . He did not again land whilst in the Baltic; his health was not good, and his mind was not at ease; with him, mind and health invariably sympathized."

While thus generally pleasant on board ship, he resolutely refused intercourse with the outside world when not compelled by duty. In this there appears to have been something self-imposed, in deference to Lady Hamilton. There are indications that she felt, or feigned, some jealousy of his relations with others, especially with women, corresponding to the frenzied agitation he manifested at the association of her name with that of any other man, and especially with that of the then Prince of Wales. Whatever her real depth of attachment to him, her best hope for the future was in his constancy, and that he would eventually marry her; for Sir William's death could not be far distant, and matters might otherwise favor the hope that both he and she cherished. Her approaching widowhood would in fact leave her, unless her husband's will was exceptionally generous, in a condition as precarious, her

---

[1] Midnight to four A. M.

acquired tastes considered, as that from which her marriage
had rescued her; and her uneasiness would naturally arouse
an uncertain and exacting temper as, in the old days at Naples,
when Hamilton could not make up his mind. The condition
of Nelson's health furnished him an excuse for declining all
civilities or calls, even from a reigning prince, on the ground
that he was not well enough to go ashore and return them.
Soon after this, however, he was able to write Lady Hamilton
that he was perfectly recovered. " As far as relates to health,
I don't think I ever was stronger or in better health. It is
odd, but after severe illness I feel much better." Thus he
was, when definitely informed that his relief was on the way.
"To find a proper successor," said Lord St. Vincent, when
announcing the fact to him, " your lordship knows is no easy
task; for I never saw the man in our profession, excepting
yourself and Troubridge, who possessed the magic art of in-
fusing the same spirit into others, which inspired their own
actions ; exclusive of other talents and habits of business, not
common to naval characters." "I was so overcome yesterday,"
wrote Nelson to Lady Hamilton, " with the good and happy
news that came about my going home, that I believe I was in
truth scarcely myself. The thoughts of going do me good,
yet all night I was so restless that I could not sleep. It is
nearly calm, therefore Admiral Pole cannot get on. If he was
not to come, I believe it would kill me. I am ready to start
the moment I have talked with him one hour."

On the 19th of June Nelson left the Baltic in the brig "Kite,"
and on the 1st of July landed at Yarmouth.

NOTE. — Since this work was first published, the author has learned
that in the year 1847 her present Majesty authorized the grant of a
naval medal to the survivors of naval engagements that had taken
place between the years 1793 and 1840. Under this ordering, medals
were issued for the Battle of Copenhagen. Although a gracious act
in the government of the day, such a tardy recognition, when the
most conspicuous actors were dead, scarcely invalidates, in the author's opinion, the statement on page 489 that medals were not issued.
This note is added, however, as necessary to a complete account of
the matter.

CHAPTER XVII.

Nelson commands the "Squadron on a Particular Service," for the Defence of the Coast of England against Invasion. — Signature of Preliminaries of Peace with France.

July–October, 1801. Age, 43.

BEFORE sailing for the Baltic, and throughout his service in that sea, the longing for repose and for a lover's paradise had disputed with the love of glory for the empire in Nelson's heart, and signs were not wanting that the latter was making a doubtful, if not a losing, fight. Shortly before his departure for the North, he wrote to St. Vincent, "Although, I own, I have met with much more honours and rewards than ever my most sanguine ideas led me to expect, yet I am so circumstanced that probably this Expedition will be the last service ever performed by your obliged and affectionate friend." His old commander was naturally perturbed at the thought that the illustrious career, which he had done so much to foster, was to have the ignoble termination to be inferred from these words and the notorious facts. "Be assured, my dear Lord," he replied, "that every *public*[1] act of your life has been the subject of my admiration, which I should have sooner declared, but that I was appalled by the last sentence of your letter: for God's sake, do not suffer yourself to be carried away by any sudden impulse."

During his absence, the uncertain deferment of his desires had worked together with the perverse indolence of Sir Hyde Parker, the fretting sight of opportunities wasted, the constant chafing against the curb, to keep both body and mind in perpetual unrest, to which the severe climate contributed by undermining his health. This unceasing discomfort had given enhanced charm to his caressing dreams of

[1] These suggestive italics are in the letter as printed by Clark and M'Arthur, and reproduced by Nicolas.

reposeful happiness, soothed and stimulated by the companionship which he so far had found to fulfil all his power of admiration, and all his demands for sympathy. Released at last, he landed in England confidently expecting to realize his hopes, only to find that they must again be postponed. Reputation such as his bears its own penalty. There was no other man in whose name England could find the calm certainty of safety, which popular apprehension demanded in the new emergency, that had arisen while he was upholding her cause in the northern seas. Nelson repined, but he submitted. Within four weeks his flag was flying again, and himself immersed in professional anxieties.

War on the continent of Europe had ceased definitively with the treaty of Lunéville, between France and Austria, signed February 9, 1801. Over four years were to elapse before it should recommence. But, as Great Britain was to be the first to take up arms again to resist the encroachments of Bonaparte, so now she was the last to consent to peace, eager as her people were to have it. Malta had fallen, the Armed Neutrality of the North had dissolved, the French occupation of Egypt was at its last gasp. Foiled in these three directions by the sea-power of Great Britain, unable, with all his manipulation of the prostrate continent, to inflict a deadly wound, Bonaparte now resorted to the threat of invasion, well aware that, under existing conditions, it could be but a threat, yet hoping that its influence upon a people accustomed to sleep securely might further his designs. But, though the enchanter wove his spells to rouse the demon of fear, their one effect was to bring up once more, over against him, the defiant form of his arch-subverter. Both the Prime Minister, Addington, and the First Lord of the Admiralty assured Nelson that his presence in charge of the dispositions for defence, and that only, could quiet the public mind. "I have seen Lord St. Vincent," he wrote the former, "and submit to your and his partiality. Whilst my health will allow, I can only say, that every exertion of mine shall be used to merit the continuance of your esteem." St. Vincent, writing to him a fortnight later, avowed frankly the weight attached to his very name by both friend and foe. "Our negotiation is drawing near its close, and must terminate one way or another in a few days, and, I need not add, how very important it is that the enemy should know that *you* are constantly opposed to him."

The purpose of Bonaparte in 1801 is not to be gauged by the same measure as that of 1803–1805. In 1798 he had told the then government of France that to make a descent upon England, without being master of the sea, would be the boldest and most difficult operation ever attempted. Conditions had not changed since then, nor had he now the time or the money to embark in the extensive preparations, which afterwards gave assurance that he was in earnest in his threats. An adept in making false demonstrations, perfectly appreciative of the power of a great name, he counted upon his own renown, and his amazing achievement of the apparently impossible in the past, to overawe the imagination of a nation, whose will, rather than whose strength, he hoped to subdue. Boulogne and the small neighboring ports, whose nearness clearly indicated them as the only suitable base from which an invasion could start, were in that year in no state to receive the boats necessary to carry an army. This the British could see with their own eyes ; but who could be sure that the paper flotilla at Boulogne, like the paper Army of Reserve at Dijon a year before, had not elsewhere a substantial counterpart, whose sudden appearance might yet work a catastrophe as unexpected and total as that of Marengo ? And who more apt than Bonaparte to spread the impression that some such surprise was brewing ? " I can venture to assure you that no embarkation of troops can take place at Boulogne," wrote Nelson, immediately after his first reconnoissance ; but he says at the same time, " I have now more than ever reason to believe that the ports of Flushing and Flanders are much more likely places to embark men from, than Calais, Boulogne, or Dieppe ; for in Flanders we cannot tell by our eyes what means they have collected for carrying an army." "Great preparations at Ostend," he notes a week later ; "Augereau commands that part of the Army. I hope to let him feel the bottom of the Goodwin Sand." It was just this sort of apprehension, specific in direction, yet vague and elusive in details, that Bonaparte was skilled in disseminating.

St. Vincent, and the Government generally, agreed with

Nelson's opinion. "We are to look to Flanders for the great effort," wrote the Earl to him. Neither of them had, nor was it possible for clear-headed naval officers to have, any substantial, rational, fear of a descent in force; yet the vague possibility did, for the moment, impress even them, and the liability of the populace, and of the commercial interests, to panic, was a consideration not to be overlooked. Besides, in a certain way, there was no adequate preparation for resistance. The British Navy, indeed, was an overwhelming force as compared to the French; but its hands were fully occupied, and the fleet Nelson had just left in the Baltic could not yet be recalled. It was, however, in purely defensive measures, in the possession of a force similar to that by which the proposed attack was to be made, and in dispositions analogous to coast defences, that the means were singularly defective, both in material and men. "Everything, my dear Lord," wrote Nelson, the day after he hoisted his flag at Sheerness, "must have a beginning, and we are literally at the foundation of our fabric of defence; " but, he continues, reverting to his own and St. Vincent's clear and accurate military intuitions, "I agree perfectly with you, that we must keep the enemy as far from our own coasts as possible, and be able to attack them the moment they come out of their ports."

"Our first defence," he writes a fortnight later, showing the gradual maturing of the views which he, in common with St. Vincent, held with such illustrious firmness in the succeeding years, "is close to the enemy's ports. When that is broke, others will come forth on our own coasts." It was in the latter that the unexpected anxieties of 1801 found the Government deficient, and these it was to be Nelson's first care to organize and dispose. By the time his duties were completed, and the problems connected with them had been two months under his consideration, he had reached the conclusion which Napoleon also held, and upon which he acted. "This boat business may be a part of a great plan of Invasion, but can never be the only one." From the first he had contemplated the possibility of the French fleets in Brest and elsewhere attempting diversions, such as Napoleon planned in support of his later great projects. "Although I feel confident that the fleets of the enemy will meet the same fate which has

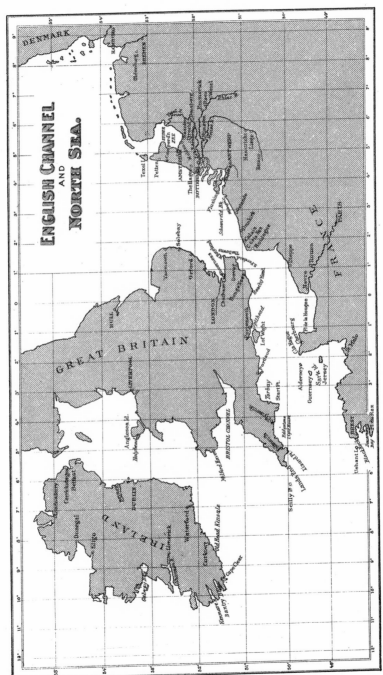

ENGLISH CHANNEL
AND
NORTH SEA.

DENMARK

GREAT BRITAIN

IRELAND

FRANCE

(For Life of Nelson.)

always attended them, yet their sailing will facilitate the coming over of their flotilla, as they will naturally suppose our attention will be called only to the fleets."

What was feared in 1801 was not a grand military operation, in the nature of an attempt at conquest, or, at the least, at injury so serious as to be disabling, but rather something in the nature of a great raid, of which the most probable object was the city of London, the chief commercial centre. It was upon this supposition that the instructions of the Admiralty to Nelson were framed, and upon this also the memorandum as to methods, submitted by him to it, on the 25th of July, 1801. " It is certainly proper to believe the French are coming to attack London." " I will suppose that 40,000 men are destined for this attack, or rather surprise." His plan is given first in his own words, as due to a matter of so much importance; and to them the writer appends a summary of the principal features, as understood by him. These are not always easily to be seen on the face of the paper, owing to the small time for its preparation, and the consequent haste — off-hand almost — with which it was drawn up, as is further indicated from the copy in the Admiralty being in his own writing.

MEMORANDA BY LORD NELSON, ON THE DEFENCE OF THE THAMES, ETC.

25th July, 1801.

Besides the stationed Ships at the different posts between the North Foreland and Orfordness, as many Gun-vessels as can be spared from the very necessary protection of the Coast of Sussex and of Kent to the westward of Dover, should be collected, for this part of the Coast must be seriously attended to; for supposing London the object of surprise, I am of opinion that the Enemy's object *ought* to be the getting on shore as speedily as possible, for the dangers of a navigation of forty-eight hours, appear to me to be an insurmountable objection to the rowing from Boulogne to the Coast of Essex. It is therefore most probable (for it is certainly proper to believe the French are coming to attack London, and therefore to be prepared) that from Boulogne, Calais, and even Havre, that the enemy will try and land in Sussex, or the lower part of Kent, and from Dunkirk, Ostend, and the other Ports of Flanders, to land on the Coast of Essex or Suffolk; for I own myself of opinion that, the object being to get on shore somewhere within 100 miles of London, as speedily as possible, that the Flats in the mouth of the Thames will not be the only place necessary to attend to; added to this, the Enemy will create a powerful diversion by the sailing of the Combined Fleet, and the either sailing, or creating such an appearance of sailing, of the Dutch Fleet, as will prevent Admiral Dickson from sending anything from off the great Dutch Ports, whilst the smaller Ports will spew forth its Flotilla, — viz., Flushing, &c. &c. It must be pretty well ascertained what number of small Vessels are in each Port.

I will suppose that 40,000 men are destined for this attack, or rather surprise, of London; 20,000 will land on the west side of Dover, sixty or seventy miles from London, and the same number on the east side: they are too knowing to let us have but one point of alarm for London. Supposing 200 craft, or 250, collected at Boulogne &c., they are supposed equal to carry 20,000 men. In very calm weather, they might row over, supposing no impediment, in twelve hours; at the same instant, by telegraph, the same number of troops would be rowed out of Dunkirk, Ostend, &c. &c. These are the two great objects to attend to from Dover and the Downs, and perhaps one of the small Ports to the westward. Boulogne (which I call the central point of the Western attack) must be attended to. If it is calm when the Enemy row out, all our Vessels and Boats appointed to watch them, must get into the Channel, and meet them as soon as possible: if not strong enough for the attack, they must watch, and keep them company till a favourable opportunity offers. If a breeze springs up, our Ships are to deal *destruction;* no delicacy can be observed on this great occasion. But should it remain calm, and our Flotilla not fancy itself strong enough to attack the Enemy on their passage, the moment that they begin to touch our shore, strong or weak, our Flotilla of Boats must attack as much of the Enemy's Flotilla as they are able — say only one-half or two-thirds; it will create a most powerful diversion, for the bows of our Flotilla will be opposed to their unarmed sterns, and the courage of Britons will never, I believe, allow one Frenchman to leave the beach. A great number of Deal and Dover Boats to be on board our vessels off the Port of Boulogne, to give notice of the direction taken by the Enemy. If it is calm, Vessels in the Channel can make signals of intelligence to our shores, from the North Foreland to Orfordness, and even as far as Solebay, not an improbable place, about seventy or eighty miles from London.

A Flotilla to be kept near Margate and Ramsgate, to consist of Gun-boats and Flat-boats; another Squadron to be stationed near the centre, between Orfordness and North Foreland, and the third in

Hoseley Bay.[1] The Floating Batteries are stationed in all proper positions for defending the different Channels, and the smaller Vessels will always have a resort in the support of the stationed ships. The moment of the Enemy's movement from Boulogne, is to be considered as the movement of the Enemy from Dunkirk. Supposing it calm, the Flotillas are to be rowed, and the heavy ones towed, (except the stationed Ships), those near Margate, three or four leagues to the north of the North Foreland; those from Hoseley Bay, a little approaching the Centre Division, but always keeping an eye towards Solebay; the Centre Division to advance half-way between the two. The more fast Rowing boats, called Thames Galleys, which can be procured the better, to carry orders, information, &c. &c.

Whenever the Enemy's Flotilla can be seen, our Divisions are to unite, but not intermix, and to be ready to execute such orders as may be deemed necessary, or as the indispensable circumstances may require. For this purpose, men of such confidence in each other should be looked for, that (as far as human foresight can go,) no little jealousy may creep into any man's mind, but to be all animated with the same desire of preventing the descent of the Enemy on our Coasts. Stationary Floating Batteries are not, from any apparent advantage, to be moved, for the tide may prevent their resuming the very important stations assigned them; they are on no account to be supposed neglected, even should the Enemy surround them, for they may rely on support, and reflect that perhaps their gallant conduct may prevent the mischievous designs of the Enemy. Whatever plans may be adopted, the moment the Enemy touch our Coast, be it where it may, they are to be attacked by every man afloat and on shore: this must be perfectly understood. *Never fear the event.* The Flat Boats can probably be manned (partly, at least,) with the Sea Fencibles, (the numbers or fixed places of whom I am entirely ignorant of,) but the Flat Boats they may man to be in grand and subdivisions, commanded by their own Captains and Lieutenants, as far as is possible. The number of Flat Boats is unknown to me, as also the other means of defence in Small Craft; but I am clearly of opinion that a proportion of the small force should be kept to watch the Flat-Boats from Boulogne, and the others in the way I have presumed to suggest. These are offered as merely the rude ideas of the moment, and are only meant as a Sea plan of defence for the City of London; but I believe other parts may likewise be menaced, if the Brest fleet, and those from Rochfort and Holland put to sea; although I feel confident that the Fleets of the Enemy will meet the same fate which has always attended them, yet their sailing will facilitate the coming over of their Flotilla, as they will naturally suppose our attention will be called only to the Fleets.

[1] Hollesley Bay.

Coming by water, the expectation seems to have been that the enemy might proceed up the river, or to a landing on some of the flats at the mouth of the Thames. Nelson says expressly that he does not think those alone are the points to be guarded; but he characterizes his paper as being " only meant as a sea plan of defence for the city of London," and the suggestion already noticed, that the enemy's fleet will support the attack by diversions, is merely mentioned casually. London being the supposed object, and the Thames the highway, the purely defensive force is to be concentrated there; the Channel coasts, though not excluded, are secondary. "As many gun-vessels as can be spared from the very necessary protection of the coast of Sussex, and of Kent to the westward of Dover, should be collected between the North Foreland and Orfordness, for this part of the coast must be seriously attended to."

The attack is expected in this quarter, because from Flanders and Flushing it is the most accessible. The object, Nelson thinks, will be to get on shore as speedily as possible, and therefore somewhere within one hundred miles of London. Anywhere from the westward of Dover round to Solebay — " not an improbable place " — must be looked upon as a possible landing. If there are forty thousand men coming, he regards it as certain that they will come in two principal bodies, of twenty thousand each — " they are too knowing to let us have but one point of alarm for London." " From Boulogne, Calais, and even Havre, the enemy will try and land in Sussex, or the lower part of Kent; and from Dunkirk, Ostend, and the other ports of Flanders, to land on the coast of Essex or Suffolk." "In very calm weather, they might row over [from Boulogne], supposing no impediment, in twelve hours; at the same instant, by telegraph, the same number of troops would be rowed out of Dunkirk, Ostend, &c. &c." " Added to this, the enemy will create a powerful diversion by the sailing of the combined fleet, and the either sailing, or creating such an appearance of sailing, of the Dutch fleet, as will prevent Admiral Dickson [commander-in-chief in the North Sea] from sending anything from off the great Dutch ports, whilst the smaller ports will spew forth its flotilla — viz, Flushing &c. &c."

To frustrate that part of this combined effort which is supposed to be directed against the Channel coast, Nelson proposes that, " if it is calm when the enemy row out, all our vessels and boats appointed to watch them, must get into the Channel, and meet them as soon as possible; if not strong enough for the attack, they must watch, and keep them company till a favourable opportunity offers. . . . Should it remain calm," so that the cruising ships cannot assist, " the moment that they begin to touch our shore, strong or weak, our flotilla of boats must attack as much of the enemy's flotilla as they are able — say only one-half or two-thirds — it will create a most powerful diversion, for the bows of our flotilla will be opposed to their unarmed sterns."

The dispositions to defend the entrance of the Thames, being considered the more important, are the more minute. Blockships are stationed in the principal channels, as floating fortifications, commanding absolutely the water around them, and forming strong points of support for the flotilla. It is sagaciously ordered that these " are not, from any apparent advantage, to be moved, for the tide may prevent their resuming the very important stations assigned them." Nelson was evidently alive to that advantage in permanent works, which puts it out of the power of panic to stampede them; tide is not the only factor that prevents retrieving a false step. The eastern flotilla is organized into three bodies, the right wing being near Margate, the left in Hollesley Bay near Harwich, the centre, vaguely, between Orfordness and the North Foreland. When the alarm is given, they are to draw together towards the centre, but not to emphasize their movement sufficiently to uncover either flank, until the enemy's flotilla can be seen ; then they are " to unite, but not intermix."

To both divisions — that in the Channel and that on the East Coast — the commander-in-chief, in concluding, renews his charge, with one of those "Nelson touches" which electrified his followers: "Whatever plans may be adopted, the moment the enemy touch our coast, be it where it may, they are to be attacked by every man afloat and on shore: this must be perfectly understood. *Never fear the event.*"

This plan for the defence of London against an attack by surprise, drawn up by Nelson on the spur of the moment, was based simply upon his general ideas, and without specific information yet as to either the character or extent of the enemy's preparations, or of the means of resistance available on his own side. It has, therefore, something of an abstract character, embodying broad views unmodified by special circumstances, and possessing, consequently, a somewhat peculiar value in indicating the tendency of Nelson's military conceptions. He assumes, implicitly, a certain freedom of movement on the part of the two opponents, unrestricted by the friction and uncertainty which in practice fetter action; and the use which, under these conditions, he imagines either will make of his powers, may not unfairly be assumed to show what he thought the correct course in such a general case.

Prominent among his ideas, and continuous in all his speculations as to the movements of an enemy, from 1795 onward, is the certainty that, for the sake of diversion, Bonaparte will divide his force into two great equal fragments, which may land at points so far apart, and separated by such serious obstacles, as were Solebay and Dover. Those who will be at the trouble to recall his guesses as to the future movements of the French in the Riviera, Piedmont, and Tuscany, in 1795 and 1796, as well as his own propositions to the Austrians at the same period, will recognize here the recurrence, unchastened by experience or thought, of a theory of warfare it is almost impossible to approve. That Bonaparte, — supposed to be master of his first movements, — if he meant to land in person at Dover, would put half his army ashore at Solebay, is as incredible as that he would have landed one half at Leghorn, meaning to act with the other from the Riviera. If this criticism be sound, it would show that Nelson, genius as he was, suffered from the lack of that study which reinforces its own conclusions by the experience of others; and that his experience, resting upon service in a navy so superior in quality to its enemies, that great inferiority in number or position could be accepted, had not supplied the necessary corrective to an ill-conceived readiness to sub-divide.

The resultant error is clearly traceable, in the author's opinion, in his dispositions at Copenhagen, and in a general tendency to allow himself too narrow a margin, based upon an under-valuation of the enemy not far removed from contempt.

It was most fortunate for him, in the Baltic, that Parker increased to twelve the detachment he himself had fixed at ten. The last utterances of his life, however, show a distinct advance and ripening of the judgment, without the slightest decrease of the heroic resolution that so characterized him. " I have twenty-three sail with me," he wrote a fortnight before Trafalgar, " and should they come out I will immediately bring them to battle; . . . but I am *very, very, very* anxious for the arrival of the force which is intended. It is, as Mr. Pitt knows, annihilation that the country wants, and not merely a splendid victory of twenty-three to thirty-six. Numbers only can annihilate."

The assumption that Bonaparte's plan would be such as he mentioned, naturally controlled Nelson in the dispositions he sketched for the local defence of the shore lines. The invasion being in two bodies, the defence was to be in two bodies also; nor is there any suggestion of a possibility that these two might be united against one of the enemy's. The whole scheme is dual; yet, although the chance of either division of the British being largely inferior to the enemy opposed to it is recognized, the adoption of a central position, or concentration upon either of the enemy's flotillas, apparently is not contemplated. Such uncertainty of touch, when not corrected by training, is the natural characteristic of a defence essentially passive; that is, of a defence which proposes to await the approach of the enemy to its own frontier, be that land or water. Yet it scarcely could have failed soon to occur to men of Nelson's and St. Vincent's martial capacities, that a different disposition, which would clearly enable them to unite and intercept either one of the enemy's divisions, must wreck the entire project; for the other twenty thousand men alone could not do serious or lasting injury. The mere taking a position favorable to such concentration would be an adequate check. The trouble for them undoubtedly was that which overloads, and so nullifies, all schemes for coast defence resting upon popular outcry, which demands outward and visible protection for every point, and assurance that people at war shall be guarded, not only against broken bones, but against even scratches of the skin.

This uneducated and weak idea, that protection is only

adequate when co-extensive with the frontier line threatened,
finds its natural outcome in a system of defence by very small
vessels, in great numbers, capable of minute subdivision and
wide dispersal, to which an equal tonnage locked up in larger
ships cannot be subjected. Although St. Vincent was at the
head of the Admiralty which in 1801 ordered that Nelson
should first organize such a flotilla, and only after that proceed to offensive measures, the results of his experience now
were to form — or at the least to confirm in him — the conclusion which he enunciated, and to which he persistently
held, during the later truly formidable preparations of Napoleon. " Our great reliance is on the vigilance and activity
of our cruisers at sea, any reduction in the number of which,
by applying them to guard our ports, inlets, and beaches,
would in my judgment tend to our destruction." Very
strangely, so far as the author's opinion goes, Nelson afterwards expressed an apparently contrary view, and sustained
Mr. Pitt in his attack upon St. Vincent's administration on
this very point; an attack, in its tendency and in the moment
chosen, among the most dangerous to his country ever attempted by a great and sagacious statesman. Nelson, however, writing in May, 1804, says: "I had wrote a memoir,
many months ago, upon the propriety of a flotilla. I had that
command at the end of the last war, and I know the necessity
of it, even had you, and which you ought to have, thirty or
forty sail of the line in the Downs and North Sea, besides
frigates &c.; but having failed so entirely in submitting my
mind upon three points I was disheartened." This Memoir
has not been preserved, but it will be noticed that, in expressing his difference from St. Vincent in the words quoted, he
assumes, what did not at any time exist, thirty or forty sail-
of-the-line for the North Sea and the Downs. St. Vincent's
stand was taken on the position that the flotilla could not be
manned without diminishing the cruisers in commission, which
were far short of the ideal number named by Nelson. It may
be believed, or at least hoped, that if forced to choose between
the two, as St. Vincent was, his choice would have been that
of the great Earl. It seems clear, however, that in 1804 he
believed it possible that the Army of Invasion *might* get as
far as the shores of England — a question which has been

much argued. "I am very uneasy," he then wrote to Lady Hamilton, "at your and Horatia being on the coast: for you cannot move, if the French make the attempt."

Whatever weight may be attributed to this criticism on Nelson's hastily sketched scheme, there can scarcely be any discord in the note of admiration for the fire that begins to glow, the instant he in thought draws near the enemy. There, assuredly, is no uncertain sound. They must be met as soon as possible; if not strong enough to attack, they must be watched, and company kept, till a favorable opportunity offers. If none occur till they draw near the beach, then, "Whatever plans may be adopted, the moment they touch our coast, be it where it may, they are to be attacked by every man afloat and on shore : this must be perfectly understood. Never fear the event." The resolution shown by such words is not born of carelessness ; and the man who approaches his work in their spirit will wring success out of many mistakes of calculation — unless indeed he stumble on an enemy of equal determination. The insistence upon keeping the enemy under observation, "keeping company" with them, however superior in numbers, may also be profitably noted. This inspired his whole purpose, four years later, in the pursuit of the French to the West Indies — if the odds are too great for immediate attack, "We won't part without a battle." It was the failure to hold the same principle of action, applicable to such diverse cases, that ruined Calder in the same campaign.

With the general views that have been outlined, Nelson hastened to his task. His commission for the new service was dated July 24, three weeks after his return from the Baltic. On the 25th he presented the memorandum of operations which has been discussed, on the 26th the Admiralty issued their instructions, and on the 27th he hoisted his flag upon the "Unité" frigate at Sheerness. "I shall go on board this day," he said, "in order to show we must all get to our posts as speedily as possible." His orders, after mentioning the general reason for creating the "Squadron on a Particular Service," as his command was officially styled, designated the limits of his charge, coastwise, as from Orfordness, on the Suffolk shore, round to Beachy Head, on the Channel. On the enemy's side of the water, it extended from

end to end of the line of ports from which the especial danger
of an invasion by troops might be supposed to issue — from
Dieppe to Ostend; but the mouth of the Scheldt was implicitly included.

The district thus assigned to him was taken out of the
commands hitherto held by some very reputable admirals,
senior to himself, who otherwise retained their previous
charges, surrounding and touching his own; while at the
Scheldt he trenched closely upon the province of the commander-in-chief in the North Sea. Such circumstances are
extremely liable to cause friction and bad blood, and St. Vincent, who with all his despotism was keenly alive to the just
susceptibilities of meritorious officers, was very careful to
explain to them that he had with the greatest reluctance
yielded to the necessity of combining the preparations for
defence under a single flag-officer, who should have no other
care. The innate tact, courtesy, and thoughtful consideration
which distinguished Nelson, when in normal conditions, removed all other misunderstandings. "The delicacy you have
always shown to senior officers," wrote St. Vincent to him,
" is a sure presage of your avoiding by every means in your
power to give umbrage to Admiral Dickson, who seems disposed to judge favourably of the intentions of us all: it is, in
truth, the most difficult card we have to play." " Happy
should I be," he said at another time, " to place the whole
of our offensive and defensive war under your auspices, but
you are well aware of the difficulties on that head." From
first to last there is no trace of a serious jar, and Nelson's
instructions to his subordinates were such as to obviate the
probability of any. " I feel myself, my dear Lord," he wrote
St. Vincent, relative to a projected undertaking on the Dutch
coast, " as anxious to get a medal, or a step in the peerage
as if I had never got either. If I succeeded, and burnt the
Dutch fleet, probably medals and an earldom. I must have
had every desire to try the matter, regardless of the feelings
of others; but I should not have been your Nelson, that
wants not to take honours or rewards from any man; and if
ever I feel great, it is, my dear Lord, in never having, in
thought, word, or deed, robbed any man of his fair fame."

He was accompanied from London by a young commander,

Edward Parker, who seems first to have become known to him in the Baltic, and who now acted as an additional aide. The latter was filled with the admiration, felt by most of those thrown into contact with Nelson, for the rapidity with which he transacted business, and set all about him in movement. "He is the cleverest and quickest man, and the most zealous in the world. In the short time we were in Sheerness, he regulated and gave orders for thirty of the ships under his command, made every one pleased, filled them with emulation, and set them all on the *qui vive*." In forty-eight hours he was off again for the Downs, by land, having to make some inquiries on the way as to the organization, and readiness to serve, of the Sea Fencibles, a large body of naval reserves, who were exempt from impressment upon the understanding that they would come forward for coast defence, in case of threatened invasion. Concerning their dispositions he received fairly flattering assurances, which in the event were not realized. If the men were certified that they would not be detained after the danger was over, it was said, they certainly would go on board. "This service, my dear Lord," he wrote to St. Vincent, "above all others, would be terrible for me: to get up and harangue like a recruiting sergeant; but as I am come forth, I feel that I ought to do this disagreeable service as well as any other, if judged necessary."

Three days more, and he was off Boulogne in a frigate with some bomb-vessels. The French admiral, Latouche Tréville, had moored in front of the pier a line of gun-vessels, twenty-four in number, fastened together from end to end. At these, and at the shipping in the small port, some bombs were thrown. Not much injury was done on either side. Prevented by an easterly wind from going on to Flushing, as he had intended, Nelson returned to Margate on the 6th of August, issued a proclamation to the Fencibles, assuring them that the French undoubtedly intended an invasion, that their services were absolutely required at once on board the defence-ships, and that they could rely upon being returned to their homes as soon as the danger was over. Out of twenty-six hundred, only three hundred and eighty-five volunteered to this urgent call. "They are no more willing to give up their occupations than their superiors," wrote Nelson, with charac-

teristically shrewd insight into a frame of mind wholly alien
to his own self-sacrificing love of Country and of glory.

Hurrying from station to station, on the shores, and in the
channels of the Thames, he was on the 12th of August back at
Margate, evidently disappointed in the prospects for coast-
defence, and more and more inclining to the deep-sea cruising,
and to action on the enemy's coast, recommended by the Admiralty, and consonant to his own temper, always disdainful
of mere defensive measures. "Our active force is perfect,"
he wrote to St. Vincent, "and possesses so much zeal that I
only want to catch that Buonaparte on the water." He has
satisfied himself that the French preparations were greatly
exaggerated ; Boulogne in fact could not harbor the needed
vessels, unless enlarged, as afterwards by Napoleon. "Where
is our invasion to come from ? The *time* is gone." Nevertheless, he favors an attack of some sort, suggests an expedition against Flushing, with five thousand troops, and proposes
a consultation. St. Vincent replied that he did not believe in
consultations, and had always avoided them. "I disapprove
of unnecessary consultations as much as any man," retorted
Nelson, "yet being close to the Admiralty, I should not feel
myself justified in risking our ships through the channels of
Flushing without buoys and pilots, without a consultation
with such men as your Lordship, and also I believe you would
think an order absolutely necessary." "Lord St. Vincent tells
me he hates councils," he writes rather sorely to Addington.
"So do I between military men ; for if a man consults
whether he is to fight, when he has the power in his own hands,
it is certain that his opinion is against fighting; but that is not
the case at present, and I own I do want good council.
Lord St. Vincent is for keeping the enemy closely blockaded ;
but I see they get alongshore inside their sand banks, and
under their guns, which line the coast of France. Lord Hood
is for keeping our squadrons of defence stationary on our own
shore (except light cutters to give information of every movement of the enemy). . . . When men of such good sense, such
great sea-officers, differ so widely, is it not natural that I
should wish the mode of defence to be well arranged by the
mature consideration of men of judgment ?"

Meanwhile he had again gone off Boulogne, and directed

an attack in boats upon the line of vessels moored outside. He took great care in the arrangements for this hazardous expedition, giving personal supervision to all details. " As you may believe, my dear Emma," he wrote to her who had his closest confidence, " my mind feels at what is going forward this night; it is one thing to order and arrange an attack, and another to execute it; but I assure you I have taken much more precaution for others, than if I was to go myself — then my mind would be perfectly at ease." He professed, and probably felt, entire confidence in the result. Fifty-seven boats were detailed for the attack. They were in four divisions, each under a commander; Edward Parker having one. Each division was to advance in two columns, the boats of which were secured one to another by tow-ropes; a precaution invaluable to keep them together, though rendering progress slower. The points in the enemy's line which each division was to make for were clearly specified, and special boats told off and fitted to tow out any vessels that were captured. Simultaneous with this onslaught, a division of howitzer flat-boats was to throw shot into the port.

At half-past eleven on the night of August 15th, the boats, which had assembled alongside the flag-frigate "Medusa," shoved off together; but the distance which they had to pull, with the strong, uncertain currents, separated them; and, as so often happens in concerted movements, attacks intended to be simultaneous were made disconnectedly, while the French were fully prepared. The first division of the British arrived at half-past twelve, and after a desperate struggle was beaten off, Commander Parker being mortally wounded. Two other divisions came up later, while the fourth lost its way altogether. The affair was an entire failure, except so far as to show that the enemy would be met on their own shores, rather than on those of Great Britain. The British loss was forty-four killed, and one hundred and twenty-eight wounded.

Nelson returned to the Downs, bitterly grieved, but not greatly discouraged. The mishap, he said, was due to the boats not arriving at the same moment; and that, he knew, was caused by conditions of currents, which would ever prevent the dull flat-boats of the enemy moving in a concert that the cutters of ships of war had not attained. " The craft which I have seen," he wrote, " I do not think it possible to *row* to England; and sail they cannot." As yet, however, he had not visited Flushing, and he felt it necessary to satisfy himself on that point. On the 24th of August, taking some pilots with him, he went across and inspected the ground, where the officer in charge of the British observing squadron was confident something might be effected. Nelson, however, decided otherwise. "I cannot but admire Captain Owen's zeal in his anxious desire to get at the enemy, but I am afraid it has made him overleap sand-banks and tides, and laid him aboard the enemy. I could join most heartily in his desire; but we cannot do impossibilities, and I am as little used to find out the impossibles as most folks; and I think I can discriminate between the impracticable and the fair prospect of success." By the 27th of August he had returned to the Downs, where, with a brief and unimportant intermission, he remained until the cessation of hostilities with France in October.

Satisfied that invasion was, for that year at least, an empty menace, Nelson fell again into the tone of angry and fretful complaint which was so conspicuous in the last weeks of his stay in the Baltic. To borrow the words of a French admirer, " He filled the Admiralty with his caprices and Europe with his fame." Almost from his first contact with this duty, it had been distasteful to him. " There is nothing to be done on the great scale," he said. " I own, my dear Lord," he told St. Vincent, " that this boat warfare is not exactly congenial to my feelings, and I find I get laughed at for my puny mode of attack." As usual, he threw himself with all his might into what he had to do, but the inward friction remained. " Whilst I serve, I will do it actively, and to the very best of my abilities. I have all night had a fever, which is very little abated this morning; my mind carries me beyond my strength, and will do me up; but such is my nature. I require nursing like a child."

That he was far from well is as unquestionable as that his distemper proceeded largely from his mind, if it did not originate there. " Our separation is terrible," he writes to Lady Hamilton; " my heart is ready to flow out of my eyes. I am not unwell, but I am very low. I can only account for it by my absence from all I hold dear in this world." From the first he had told St. Vincent that he could not stay longer than September 14th, that it was beyond his strength to stand the equinoctial weather. The veteran seaman showed towards him the same delicate consideration that he always had, using the flattering urgency which Nelson himself knew so well how to employ, in eliciting the hearty co-operation of others. "The public mind is so much tranquillised by your being at your post, it is extremely desirable that you should continue there : in this opinion all His Majesty's servants, with Sir Thomas Troubridge, agree. Let me entreat your Lordship to persevere in the measures you are so advantageously employed in, and give up, at least for the present, your intention of returning to town, which would have the worst possible effect at this critical juncture. The dispositions you have made, and are making, appear to us all as the most judicious possible." " I hope you will not relinquish your situation at a moment when the services of every man are called for by the circumstances the Country is placed in, so imperiously that, upon reflection, I persuade myself you will think as I, and every friend you have, do on this subject." Nelson admitted, in a calmer moment, that "although my whole soul is devoted to get rid of this command, yet I do not blame the Earl for wishing to keep me here a little longer." " Pray take care of your health," the latter says again, " than which nothing is of so much consequence to the Country at large, more particularly so to your very affectionate St. Vincent." " Your health is so precious at all times, more particularly so at this crisis."

St. Vincent tried in vain to conjure with the once beloved name of Troubridge, whom Nelson used to style the "Non-pareil," whose merits he had been never weary of extolling, and whose cause he had pleaded so vehemently, when the accident of his ship's grounding deprived him of his share in the Battle of the Nile. From the moment that he was chosen by St. Vincent, who called him the ablest adviser and best executive officer in the British Navy, to assist in the administration of the Admiralty, Nelson began to view him jealously. " Our friend Troubridge is to be a Lord of the Admiralty, and I have a sharp eye, and almost think I see it. No, poor

fellow, I hope I do him injustice; he cannot surely forget my
kindness to him." But when the single eye has become
double, suspicion thrives, and when tortured by his desire to
return to Lady Hamilton, Nelson saw in every obstacle and
every delay the secret hand of Troubridge. "I believe it is
all the plan of Troubridge," he wrote in one such instance,
"but I have wrote both him and the Earl my mind." To
St. Vincent, habit and professional admiration enabled him
to submit, if grudgingly, and with constant complaints to
his *confidante;* but Troubridge, though now one of the Board
that issued his orders, was his inferior in grade, and he resented the imagined condition of being baffled in his wishes
by a junior. The latter, quick-tempered and rough of speech,
but true as his sword, to use St. Vincent's simile, must have
found himself put to it to uphold the respect due to his
present position, without wronging the affection and reverence which he undoubtedly felt for his old comrade, and
which in the past he had shown by the moral courage that
even ventured to utter a remonstrance, against the infatuation
that threatened to stain his professional honor.

Such straining of personal relations constantly accompanies
accession to office; many are the friendships, if they can be
called such, which cannot endure the experience that official
action may not always be controlled by them. If such is to be
noted in Nelson, it is because he was no exception to the common rule, and it is sad that a man so great should not in this
have been greater than he was. St. Vincent felt it necessary
to tell him, with reference to the difficulty of granting some
requests for promotion, "Encompassed as I am by applications
and presumptuous claims, I have nothing for it but to act upon
the defensive, as your Lordship will be compelled to do, whenever you are placed in the situation I at present fill." This
Nelson contents himself with quoting; but of Troubridge he
says: "Troubridge has so completely prevented my mentioning any body's service, that I am become a cypher, and he has
gained a victory over Nelson's spirit. Captain Somerville has
been begging me to intercede with the Admiralty again; but
I have been so *rebuffed,* that my spirits are gone, and the
great Troubridge has what we call *cowed* the spirits of Nelson; but I shall never forget it. He told me if I asked any-

thing more that I should get nothing. No wonder I am not well."

The refusal of the Admiralty to give him leave to come to London, though founded on alleged motives of state, he thinks absurd. "They are beasts for their pains," he says; "it was only depriving me of one day's comfort and happiness, for which they have my hearty prayers." His spleen breaks out in oddly comical ways. "I have a letter from Troubridge, recommending me to wear flannel shirts. Does he care for me? *No;* but never mind." "Troubridge writes me, that as the weather is set in fine again, he hopes I shall get walks on shore. He is, I suppose, laughing at me; but, never mind." Petulant words, such as quoted, and others much more harsh, used to an intimate friend, are of course to be allowed for as indicating mental exasperation and the excitement of baffled longings, rather than expressing permanent feeling; but still they illustrate mental conditions more faithfully than do the guarded utterances of formal correspondence. Friendship rarely regains the ground lost in them. The situation did undoubtedly become exasperating towards the end, for no one pretended that any active service could be expected, or that his function was other than that of a signal displayed, indicating that Great Britain, though negotiating for peace, was yet on her guard. Lying in an open roadstead, with a heavy surf pouring in on the beach many days of the week, a man with one arm and one eye could not easily or safely get back and forth; and, being in a small frigate pitching and tugging at her anchors, he was constantly seasick, so much so "that I cannot hold up my head," afflicted with cold and toothache, — "but none of them cares a d—n for me and my sufferings."

In September the Hamiltons came to Deal, off which the ship was lying, and remained for a fortnight, during which he was happy; but the reaction was all the more severe when they returned to town on the 20th. "I came on board, but no Emma. No, no, my heart will break. I am in silent distraction. . . . My dearest wife, how can I bear our separation? Good God, what a change! I am so low that I cannot hold up my head." His depression was increased by the condition of Parker, the young commander, who had been wounded

off Boulogne, and had since then hovered between life and
death. The thigh had been shattered too far up for amputation, and the only faint hope had been that the bones might
reunite. The day that the Hamiltons left, the great artery
burst, and, after a brief deceitful rally, he died on the 27th of
September. Nelson, who was tenderly attached to him, followed him to the grave with emotion so deep as to be noticeable
to the bystanders. "Thank God," he wrote that afternoon,
"the dreadful scene is past. I scarcely know how I got over
it. I could not suffer much more and be alive." "I own," he
had written to St. Vincent immediately after the repulse, "I
shall never bring myself again to allow any attack to go forward, where I am not personally concerned; my mind suffers
much more than if I had a leg shot off in this late business."

The Admiralty refusing any allowances, much of the
expense of Parker's illness and of his funeral fell upon Nelson, who assumed all his debts. It was but one instance
among many of a liberality in money matters, which kept him
constantly embarrassed. To the surgeon who had attended
the wounded, and to the captain of the "Medusa," a much
richer man than he was, but who had shown him kindness, he
gave handsome remembrances of the favors which he was
pleased to consider done to himself personally. In a like
spirit he wrote some months afterwards, concerning a proposed
monument to Captain Ralph Willett Miller, who had fought
under his flag. "I much doubt if all the admirals and captains will subscribe to poor dear Miller's monument; but I
have told Davison, that whatever is wanted to make up the
sum, I shall pay. I thought of Lord St. Vincent and myself
paying £50 each; some other admirals may give something,
and I thought about £12 each for the captains who had served
with him in the actions off Cape St. Vincent and the Nile.
The spirit of liberality seems declining; but when I forget
an old and dear friend, may I cease to be your affectionate
Nelson and Bronté." Yet at this period he felt it advisable
to sell the diamonds from the presents given him by foreign
sovereigns. He was during these weeks particularly pressed,
because in treaty for a house which he bought at Merton in
Surrey, and for which he had difficulty in raising funds. In
this his friend Davison helped him by a generous and un-

limited offer of a loan. "The Baltic expedition," wrote Nelson in his letter of thanks, "cost me full £2,000. Since I left London it has cost me, for Nelson cannot be like others, near £1,000 in six weeks. If I am continued here, ruin to my finances must be the consequence."

On the 1st of October the Preliminaries of Peace with France were signed, and on the 9th news of their ratification reached Nelson on board his ship. "Thank God! it is peace," he exclaimed. Yet, while delighted beyond measure at the prospect of release from his present duties, and in general for the repose he now expected, he was most impatient at the exuberant demonstrations of the London populace, and of some military and naval men. "Let the rejoicings be proper to our several stations — the manufacturer, because he will have more markets for his goods, — but seamen and soldiers ought to say, 'Well, as it is peace, we lay down our arms; and are ready again to take them up, if the French are insolent.' There is no person in the world rejoices more in the peace than I do, but I would burst sooner than let a d——d Frenchman know it. We have made peace with the French despotism, and we will, I hope, adhere to it whilst the French continue in due bounds; but whenever they overstep that, and usurp a power which would degrade Europe, then I trust we shall join Europe in crushing her ambition; then I would with pleasure go forth and risk my life for to pull down the overgrown detestable power of France." When the mob in London dragged the carriage of the French ambassador, his wrath quite boiled over. "Can you cure madness?" he wrote to his physician; "for I am mad to read that our d——d scoundrels dragged a Frenchman's carriage. I am ashamed for our Country." "I hope never more to be dragged by such a degenerate set of people," he tells Lady Hamilton. "Would our ancestors have done it? So, the villains would have drawn Buonaparte if he had been able to get to London to cut off the King's head, and yet all our Royal Family will employ Frenchmen. Thanks to the navy, they could not." Nelson's soul was disturbed without cause. Under the ephemeral effervescence of a crowd lay a purpose as set as his own, and of which his present emotions were a dim and unconscious prophecy.

On the 15th of October he received official notification for
the cessation of hostilities with the French Republic, the precise date at which they were to be considered formally at an
end having been fixed at the 22d of the month. The Admiralty declined to allow him to leave his station until that day
arrived. Then he had their permission to take leave of
absence, but not to haul down his flag. " I heartily hope a
little rest will soon set you up," wrote St. Vincent, " but until
the definitive treaty is signed, your Lordship must continue in
pay, although we may not have occasion to require your personal services at the head of the squadron under your orders."
In accordance with this decision, Nelson's flag continued to
fly as Commander-in-Chief of a Squadron of ships " on a particular service," throughout the anxious period of doubt and
suspicion which preceded the signing of the treaty of Amiens,
on the 25th of March, 1802. It was not till the 10th of the
following April that he received the formal orders, to strike
his flag and come on shore.

On the 22d of October, 1801, he left the flagship and set off
for his new home in Surrey.

CHAPTER XVIII.

RELEASE FROM ACTIVE SERVICE DURING THE PEACE OF AMIENS. — HOME LIFE AT MERTON. — PUBLIC INCIDENTS.

OCTOBER, 1801–MAY, 1803. AGE, 43–44.

DURING the brief interval between his return from the Baltic, July 1, 1801, and his taking command of the Squadron on a Particular Service, on the 27th of the same month, Nelson had made his home in England with the Hamiltons, to whose house in Piccadilly he went immediately upon his arrival in London. Whatever doubt may have remained in his wife's mind, as to the finality of their parting in the previous January, or whatever trace of hesitation may then have existed in his own, had been definitively removed by letters during his absence. To her he wrote on the 4th of March, immediately before the expedition sailed from Yarmouth: "Josiah [1] is to have another ship and to go abroad, if the Thalia cannot soon be got ready. I have done *all* for him, and he may again, as he has often done before, wish me to break my neck, and be abetted in it by his friends, who are likewise my enemies; but I have done my duty as an honest, generous man, and I neither want or wish for anybody to care what becomes of me, whether I return, or am left in the Baltic. Living, I have done all in my power for you, and if dead, you will find I have done the same; therefore my only wish is, to be left to myself: and wishing you every happiness, believe that I am, your affectionate Nelson and Bronté." Upon this letter Lady Nelson endorsed: "This is My Lord Nelson's Letter of dismissal, which so astonished me that I immediately sent it to Mr. Maurice Nelson,[2] who was sincerely

[1] Josiah Nisbet, her son.

[2] Nelson's eldest brother. There appear to have been two copies of this letter in Nelson's hand. One, of which the latter half only remains, is in the British Museum. It bears the endorsement of Lady Nelson, as given. The other copy, entire, is in the Alfred Morrison collection — Number 536. Nelson probably sent a copy to Lady Hamilton to satisfy her exigencies that the

34

attached to me, for his advice. He desired me not to take the
least notice of it, as his brother seemed to have forgot himself."

A separation preceded and caused by such circumstances as
this was, could not fail to be attended with bitterness on both
sides; yet one could have wished to see in a letter which is
believed, and probably was intended, to be the last ever addressed by him to her, some recollection, not only of what he
himself had done for his step-son, but that once, to use his own
expression, " the boy " had " saved his life;" and that, after
all, if he was under obligations to Nelson, he would have been
more than youth, had no intemperance of expression mingled
with the resentment he felt for the slights offered his mother
in the face of the world. With Nelson's natural temperament
and previous habits of thought, however, it was imperative,
for his peace of mind, to justify his course of action to himself; and this he could do only by dwelling upon the wrong
done him by those who, in the eyes of men generally, seemed,
and must still seem, the wronged. Of what passed between
himself and Lady Nelson, we know too little to apportion the
blame of a transaction in which she appears chiefly as the sufferer. Nisbet, except in the gallantry and coolness shown by
him at Teneriffe, has not the same claim to consideration, and
his career had undoubtedly occasioned great and legitimate
anxiety to Nelson, whose urgency with St. Vincent was
primarily the cause of a premature promotion, which spoiled
the future of an officer, otherwise fairly promising.[1] If the

breach was final. The two correspond, word for word, — as far, that is, as
the former remains. Maurice Nelson died in April, 1801.

[1] Nelson several times spoke of Nisbet's early promise. The author is
indebted to Mrs. F. H. B. Eccles, Nisbet's granddaughter, for a copy of the
following letter from St. Vincent to his sister Mrs. Ricketts: —

LONDON, January 22, 1807.

MY DEAR SISTER, — Upon reflexion it appears best to send you the only
letters I can find relative to Captain Nisbet, and to authorize you to assert in
my name that Lord Nelson assured me that he owed his life to the resolution
and admirable conduct of his stepson, when wounded at Teneriffe, and that
he had witnessed many instances of his courage and enterprise.

Yours most affectionately,

ST. VINCENT.

This letter explains how St. Vincent, feeling the value of Nelson's life to
the country, granted, in the still warm memories of Teneriffe, a promotion
which must have been sorely against his judgment.

relations between the two had not been so soon strained by
Nelson's attentions to Lady Hamilton, things might have
turned out better, through the influence of one who rarely
failed to make the most of those under his command.

The annual allowance made to Lady Nelson by her husband,
after their separation, was £1,800; which, by a statement he
gave to the Prime Minister, two years later, when asking an
increase of pension, appears to have been about half of his
total income. On the 23d of April, 1801, when daily expecting
to leave the Baltic for England, he sent her a message through
their mutual friend Davison: "You will, at a proper time, and
before my arrival in England, signify to Lady N. that I expect,
and for which I have made such a very liberal allowance to
her, to be left to myself, and without any inquiries from her;
for sooner than live the unhappy life I did when last I came
to England, I would stay abroad for ever. My mind is fixed
as fate: therefore you will send my determination in any way
you may judge proper." [1] To Lady Hamilton he wrote about
the same time, assuring her, under the assumption of mystery
with which he sought to guard their relations against discovery
through the postal uncertainties of the day, that he had no
communication with his wife: "Thomson [2] desires me to say
he has never wrote his aunt [3] since he sailed, and all the
parade about a house is nonsense. He has wrote to his father,
but not a word or message to her. He does not, nor cannot,
care about her; he believes she has a most unfeeling heart." [4]

His stay with the Hamiltons in Piccadilly, though broken
by several trips to the country, convinced Nelson that if they
were to live together, as he wished to do, it must be, for his
own satisfaction, in a house belonging to him. It is clear
that the matter was talked over between Lady Hamilton and
himself; for, immediately upon joining his command in the
Downs, he began writing about the search for a house, as a
matter already decided, in which she was to act for him.

[1] Nicolas, vol. vii. Addenda, p. ccix. In a letter to Lady Hamilton of
the same date, Nelson says: "Read the enclosed, and send it if you approve.
Who should I consult but my friends?" (Morrison, vol. ii. p. 142.) Whether
the enclosed was this letter to Davison cannot be said; but it is likely,
Compare foot-note, page 529.

[2] Nelson. [3] Lady Nelson.
[4] Morrison, vol. ii. p. 137.

"Have you heard of any house ? I am very anxious to have
a home where my friends might be made welcome." As usual,
in undertakings of every kind, he chafed under delays, and he
was ready to take the first that seemed suitable. " I really
wish you would buy the house at Turnham Green," he writes
her within a week. The raising of the money, it is true, presents some difficulty, for he has in hand but £3,000. " It is, my
dear friend," he moralizes, " extraordinary, but true, that the
man who is pushed forward to defend his country, has not
from that country a place to lay his head in; but never mind,
happy, truly happy, in the estimation of such friends as you,
I care for nothing."

Lady Hamilton, however, was a better business-man than
himself, and went about his purchase with the deliberation of
a woman shopping. At the end of three weeks he was still
regretting that he could not " find a house and a little piece of
ground, for if I go on much longer with my present command,
I must be ruined. I think your perseverance and management will at last get me a home." By the 20th of August
she was suited, for on that date he writes to her, " I
approve of the house at Merton ;" and, as the Admiralty
would not consent to his leaving his station even for a few
days, all the details of the bargain were left in her hands. " I
entreat, my good friend, manage the affair of the house for
me." He stipulates only that everything in it shall be his,
" to a book or a cook," or even "to a pair of sheets, towels,
&c." "I entreat I may never hear about the expenses again.
If you live in Piccadilly or Merton it makes no difference, and
if I was to live at Merton I must keep a table, and nothing
can cost me one-sixth part which it does at present." "You
are to be, recollect, Lady Paramount of all the territories and
waters of Merton, and we are all to be your guests, and to
obey all lawful commands."

In this way were conducted the purchase and preparation of
the only home of his own on English ground that Nelson ever
possessed, where he passed his happiest hours, and from which
he set out to fight his last battle. The negotiation was concluded three days before the rumors of the peace got abroad,
therefore about the 27th of September, 1801; and in consequence, so Sir William Hamilton thought, the property was

acquired a thousand pounds cheaper than it otherwise might have been — a piece of financial good luck rare in Nelson's experience. "We have now inhabited your Lordship's premises some days," continued the old knight, "and I can now speak with some certainty. I have lived with our dear Emma several years. I know her merit, have a great opinion of the head and heart that God Almighty has been pleased to give her; but a seaman alone could have given a fine woman full power to chuse and fit up a residence for him without seeing it himself. You are in luck, for in my conscience I verily believe that a place so suitable to your views could not have been found, and at so cheap a rate. The proximity to the capital,"—Nelson found it an hour's drive from Hyde Park —"and the perfect retirement of this place, are, for your Lordship, two points beyond estimation; but the house is so comfortable, the furniture clean and good, and I never saw so many conveniences united in so small a compass. You have nothing but to come and enjoy immediately; you have a good mile of pleasant dry walk around your own farm. It would make you laugh to see Emma and her mother fitting up pig-sties and hen-coops, and already the Canal is enlivened with ducks, and the cock is strutting with his hens about the walks."

As time passed, Sir William did not realize the comfort he had anticipated from surroundings so pleasant as those he described. He was troubled in money matters, fearing lest he might be distressed to meet the current expenses of the house. "If we had given up the house in Piccadilly," he lamented to Greville, "the living here would indeed be a great saving; but, as it is, we spend neither more nor less than we did." Why he did not give it up does not appear. As Lady Paramount over the owner of the place, Lady Hamilton insisted upon entertaining to a degree consonant to the taste neither of Lord Nelson, who was only too pleased to humor her whims, nor of her husband, who had an old man's longing for quiet, and, besides, was not pleased to find himself relegated to a place in her consideration quite secondary to that of his host. "It is but reasonable," he wrote to Greville, in January, 1802, "after having fagged all my life, that my last days should pass off comfortably and quietly.

Nothing at present disturbs me but my debt, and the nonsense I am obliged to submit to here to avoid coming to an explosion, which would be attended with many disagreeable effects, and would totally destroy the comfort of the best man and the best friend I have in the world. However, I am determined that my quiet shall not be disturbed, let the nonsensical world go on as it will."

Neither the phlegm on which he prided himself, nor his resolutions, were sufficient, however, to keep the peace, or to avoid undignified contentions with his wife. Some months later he addressed her a letter, which, although bearing no date, was evidently written after a prolonged experience of the conditions entailed upon himself by this odd partnership; for partnership it was, in form at least, the living expenses being divided between the two.[1] In their quiet reasonableness, his words are not without a certain dignified pathos, and they have the additional interest of proving, as far as words can prove, that, battered man of the world though he was, he had no suspicion, within a year of his death, that the relations between his host and his wife were guilty towards himself.

"I have passed the last 40 years of my life in the hurry & bustle that must necessarily be attendant on a publick character. I am arrived at the age when some repose is really necessary, & I promised myself a quiet home, & altho' I was sensible, & said so when I married, that I shou'd be superannuated when my wife wou'd be in her full beauty and vigour of youth. That time is arrived, and we must make the best of it for the comfort of both parties. Unfortunately our tastes as to the manner of living are very different. I by no means wish to live in solitary retreat, but to have seldom less than 12 or 14 at table, and those varying continually, is coming back to what was become so irksome to me in Italy during the latter years of my residence in that country. I have no connections out of my own family. I have no complaint to make, but I feel that the whole attention of my wife is given to Ld. N. and his interest at Merton. I well know the purity of Ld. N.'s friendship for Emma and me, and I know how very uncomfortable it wou'd make his Lp, our best friend, if a separation shou'd take place, & am therefore determined to do all in my power to prevent such an extremity, which wou'd be

[1] On the 21st of September, 1802, six months before Hamilton's death, he was still £1,200 in Nelson's debt. (Morrison, vol. ii. p. 404.)

essentially detrimental to all parties, but wou'd be more sensibly felt by our dear friend than by us. Provided that our expences in house-keeping do not encrease beyond measure (of which I must own I see some danger), I am willing to go on upon our present footing; but as I cannot expect to live many years, every moment to me is precious, & I hope I may be allow'd sometimes to be my own master, & pass my time according to my own inclination, either by going my fishing parties on the Thames or by going to London to attend the Museum, R. Society, the Tuesday Club, & Auctions of pictures. I mean to have a light chariot or post chaise by the month, that I may make use of it in London and run backwards and forwards to Merton or to Shepperton, &c. This is my plan, and we might go on very well, but I am fully determined not to have more of the very silly altercations that happen but too often between us and embitter the present moments exceedingly. If realy one cannot live comfortably together, a *wise* and well *concerted separation* is preferable; but I think, considering the probability of my not troubling any party long in this world, the best for us all wou'd be to bear those ills we have rather than flie to those we know not of. I have fairly stated what I have on my mind. There is no time for nonsense or trifling. I know and admire your talents & many excellent qualities, but I am not blind to your defects, and confess having many myself ; therefore let us bear and forbear for God's sake." [1]

There are other accounts by eye-witnesses of the home life at Merton, in which participated, from time to time, not only the many outside guests, of whose burden Hamilton complained, but also most of the members of the Nelson family. Lord Minto, who had returned to England from Vienna, and whose personal friendship to Nelson never slackened, wrote to his wife, in March, 1802 : "I went to Lord Nelson's on Saturday to dinner, and returned to-day in the forenoon. The whole establishment and way of life are such as to make me angry, as well as melancholy; but I cannot alter it, and I do not think myself obliged, or at liberty, to quarrel with him for his weakness, though nothing shall ever induce me to give the smallest countenance to Lady Hamilton. She looks ultimately to the chance of marriage, as Sir William will not be long in her way, and she probably indulges a hope that she may survive Lady Nelson; in the meanwhile she and Sir William, and the whole set of them, are living with

[1] Morrison, No. 684.

him at his expense. She is in high looks, but more immense than ever. The love she makes to Nelson is not only ridiculous, but disgusting : not only the rooms, but the whole house, staircase and all, are covered with nothing but pictures of her and him, of all sizes and sorts, and representations of his naval actions, coats-of-arms, pieces of plate in his honour, the flag-staff of L'Orient, &c. — an excess of vanity which counteracts its own purpose. If it was Lady Hamilton's house there might be a pretence for it; to make his own house a mere looking-glass to view himself all day is bad taste. Braham, the celebrated Jew singer, performed with Lady Hamilton. She is horrid, but he entertained me in spite of her." Of this same period, but a year later, at the time of Hamilton's death, Minto wrote : " Lady Hamilton talked very freely [to me] of her situation with Nelson, and the construction the world may have put upon it, but protested that their attachment had been perfectly pure, which I declare I can believe, though I am sure it is of no consequence whether it be so or not. The shocking injury done to Lady Nelson is not made less or greater, by anything that may or may not have occurred between him and Lady Hamilton."

On the 6th of November, 1861, Mr. Matcham, a nephew of Lord Nelson, wrote for the " Times " some reminiscences of the great admiral, as he had known him in private life, both at this period, and three years later, just before Trafalgar. His letter was elicited by the publication of the " Remains of Mrs. Trench." In this had appeared extracts from her journal, when Mrs. St. George, containing statements derogatory to Nelson's conduct in Dresden, when on the journey from Trieste to Hamburg in the year 1800; some of which have been quoted already in this work.[1] Mr. Matcham's words, so far as they relate to Nelson himself, are here given in full: [2]

I too Sir, as well as " the Lady," had some knowledge of that person, so much honoured and so much maligned; and although I do not defend his one great error (though in that, with some palliation, there were united elements of a generous and noble nature), I venture to say that whoever forms a notion of his manners and deportment

[1] *Ante*, p. 441.

[2] From Mr. G. Lathom Browne's " Nelson : His Public and Private Life," London, 1891, p. 412.

in private life from this account of him, will labour under a very great delusion.

I visited my uncle twice during the short periods in which he was on shore — once in 1802, during his journey to Wales, when he was received at Oxford and other places; and the second time at his house at Merton, in 1805, for three weeks preceding the 15th of September, when he left to embark at Portsmouth to return no more; and I can assert with truth that a more complete contrast between this lady's portrait and my thorough recollection of him could not be forced on my mind. Lord Nelson in private life was remarkable for a demeanour quiet, sedate, and unobtrusive, anxious to give pleasure to every one about him, distinguishing each in turn by some act of kindness, and chiefly those who seemed to require it most.

During his few intervals of leisure, in a little knot of relations and friends, he delighted in quiet conversation, through which occasionally ran an undercurrent of pleasantry, not unmixed with caustic wit. At his table he was the least heard among the company, and so far from being the hero of his own tale, I never heard him voluntarily refer to any of the great actions of his life.

I have known him lauded by the great and wise; but he seemed to me to waive the homage with as little attention as was consistent with civility. Nevertheless, a mind like his was necessarily won by attention from those who could best estimate his value.

On his return from his last interview with Mr. Pitt, being asked in what manner he had been received, he replied that he had reason to be gratified with his reception, and concluded with animation, " Mr. Pitt, when I rose to go, left the room with me, and attended me to the carriage " — a spontaneous mark of respect and admiration from the great statesman, of which, indeed, he might well be proud.

It would have formed an amusement to the circle at Merton, if intemperance were set down to the master of the house, who always so prematurely cut short the *sederunt* of the gentlemen after dinner.

A man of more temperate habits could not, I am persuaded, have been found. It appears that the person of Lord Nelson (although he was not as described, a little man, but of the middle height and of a frame adapted to activity and exertion) did not find favour with the lady ; and I presume not to dispute her taste, but in his plain suit of black, in which he alone recurs to my memory, he always looked what he was — a gentleman. Whatever expletives of an objectionable kind may be ascribed to him, I feel persuaded that such rarely entered into his conversation. He was, it is true, a sailor, and one of a warm and generous disposition ; yet I can safely affirm that I never heard a coarse expression issue from his lips, nor do I recollect one word or action of his to which even a disciple of Chesterfield could reasonably object. If such did arise, it would be drawn forth when a friend was attacked, or even an enemy unjustly accused; for his disposition was so truly noble, that it revolted against all wrong and oppression. His heart, indeed, was as tender as it was courageous. Nor do I think, Sir, that it is a necessary concession to truth that . you or others should lower your conception of this popular personage, on account of the exaggerated colours in which he is here drawn. Those who best knew the man the most estimated his value, and many who like myself could not appreciate his professional superiority, would yet bear witness to his gentleness, kindness, good-breeding, and courtesy.

He was not " a rude and boisterous captain of the sea." From his early years, by the introduction of his uncle, the Comptroller of the Navy, he was associated with the *élite* of his own profession; and the influences of his own paternal home, and his acquaintance with the first families of his native county, to many of whom he was related, would not allow a man of his intelligence and proper pride to foster coarseness beyond the habits of his age.

It appears to me that, however flattering or consolatory the recital of the follies or foibles of great men may be to that mediocrity which forms the mass of mankind, the person who undertakes to cater for mere amusement withdraws something from the common stock of his country. The glory of Great Britain depends as much on the heroes she has produced, as on her wealth, her influence, and her possessions; and the true patriot and honourable man, if he cannot add to their lustre, will at least refrain from any premeditated act which may dim their fame, and diminish that high estimation of them which expedience, nationality, and gratitude should alike contribute to sustain.

A NEPHEW OF ADMIRAL LORD NELSON.

A glimpse of the family life at Merton, and of the society which gathered there, has been casually preserved for us. It presents not only an interesting group of the admiral's associates, but also the record of a conversation concerning him, under his own roof, transmitted by one of the parties to it; particularly instructive, because showing the contradictory traits which illustrated his character, and the impression made by him upon his contemporaries and intimates, — men who had seen him upon all kinds of occasions, both great and small. It corroborates, too, the report of these superficial inconsistencies made by the Duke of Wellington on a later occasion. The narrator, Lieutenant Layman, was the same who had recently been with Nelson in the Baltic, and who has before been quoted in connection with that expedition. Sir Alexander Ball will be remembered as one of his chief supports during the long chase that preceded the Battle of the Nile, as well as in the action, and afterwards during the protracted operations around Malta. Hood was also a Nile captain.

"During the temporary peace, Mr. Layman spent some days at Merton, with Sir Alexander Ball and Sir Samuel Hood. One day, after tea in the drawing-room, Lord Nelson was earnestly engaged in conversation with Sir Samuel. Mr. Layman observed to Sir Alexander, that Lord Nelson was at work by his countenance and mouth, that he was a most extraordinary man, possessing opposite points of character; little in little things, but by far the greatest man in great things he ever saw: that he had seen him petulant in trifles, and as cool and collected as a philosopher when surrounded by dangers, in which men of common minds, with clouded countenance, would say, 'Ah! what is to be done?' It was a treat to see his animated and collected countenance in the heat of action. Sir Alexander remarked this seeming inconsistency, and mentioned that, after the Battle of the Nile, the captains of the squadron were desirous to have a good likeness of their heroic chief taken, and for that purpose employed one of the most eminent painters in Italy. The plan was to ask the painter to breakfast, and get him to begin immediately after. Breakfast being over, and no preparation being made by the painter, Sir Alexander was selected by the other captains to ask him when he intended to begin; to which the answer was, 'Never.' Sir Alexander said, he stared, and they all stared, but the artist continued: 'There is such a mixture of humility with ambition in Lord Nelson's countenance, that I dare not risk the attempt.'" [1]

There is yet another casual mention of the Merton home life, illustrative of more than one feature of Nelson's native character. Many years later the daughter of the Vicar of the parish, when transmitting a letter to Sir Harris Nicolas, added: "In revered affection for the memory of that dear man, I cannot refrain from informing you of his unlimited charity and good-

[1] Naval Chronicle, vol. xxxvii. p. 445.

ness during his residence at Merton. His frequently expressed desire was, that none in that place should want or suffer affliction that he could alleviate ; and this I know he did with a most liberal hand, always desiring that it should not be known from whence it came. His residence at Merton was a continued course of charity and goodness, setting such an example of propriety and regularity that there are few who would not be benefited by following it." His thoughtfulness and generosity to those about him was equally shown in his charges to his agents at Bronté, for the welfare of the Sicilian peasantry upon his estate. In the regularity and propriety of observance which impressed the clergyman's daughter, he carried out the ideal he had proposed to Lady Hamilton. "Have we a nice church at Merton ? We will set an example of good-ness to the under parishioners."

Whatever of censure or of allowance may be pronounced upon the life he was living, there was in the intention just quoted no effort to conciliate the opinion of society, which he was resolute in braving ; nor was it inconsistent with the general tenor of his thoughts. In the sense of profound recognition of the dependence of events upon God, and of the obligation to manifest gratitude in outward act, Nelson was from first to last a strongly religious man. To his sin he had contrived to reconcile his conscience by fallacies, analogies to which will be supplied by the inward experience of many, if they will be honest with themselves. The outcome upon character of such dealings with one's self is, in the individual case, a matter to which man's judgment is not competent. During the last two years and a half of Nelson's life, the chaplain of the " Victory " was associated with him in close intimacy as confidential secretary, with whom he talked freely on many matters. " He was," said this gentleman, "a thorough clergyman's son — I should think he never went to bed or got up without kneeling down to say his prayers." He often expressed his attachment to the church in which he had been brought up, and showed the sincerity of his words by the regularity and respect with which he always had divine service performed on board the " Victory," whenever the weather permitted. After the service he had generally a few words with the chaplain on the subject of the sermon, either thanking him for its being a good one, or remarking that it was not so well adapted as usual to the crew. More than once, on such occasions, he took down a volume of sermons in his own cabin, with the page already marked at some discourse which he thought well suited to such a congregation, and requested Dr. Scott to preach it on the following Sunday.[1]

On the 29th of October, 1801, just one week after he left the Downs, Nelson took his seat in the House of Lords as a Viscount, his former commander-in-chief, Hood, who was of the same rank in the peerage, being one of those to present him. While in England he spoke from time to time on professional subjects, or those connected with the external policy of the country, on which he held clear and decided opinions, based, naturally, upon naval exigencies. His first speech was a warm and generous eulogy of Sir James Saumarez, once second to himself at the Battle of the Nile, an officer with whom it is not too much to say he was not in close personal sympathy, as he had been with Troubridge, but who had just fought two desperate squadron actions under conditions of singular difficulty, out of which he had wrenched a success that was both signal and, in the then state of the war and negotiations, most opportune. "Sir James Saumarez's action," said Lord St. Vincent, "has put us upon velvet."

Nelson's own thirst for glory made him keenly appreciative of the necessity to be just and liberal, in distributing to those who had achieved great deeds the outward tokens of distinguished service, which often are the sole recompense for dangers run and hardships borne. Scarcely had he retired from his active command in the Channel when he felt impelled to enter upon a painful and humiliating controversy, on behalf of those who had shared with him all the perils of the desperate Battle of Copenhagen; for which, unlike himself, they had received no reward, but from whom he refused to be dissociated in the national esteem and gratitude.

On the 19th of November, 1801, the City of London voted its thanks to the divisions of the Army and the Navy, whose joint operations during the previous summer had brought to an end the French occupation of Egypt, begun by Bonaparte in 1798. Nelson had for some time been uneasy that no such

[1] Life of Rev. A. J. Scott, D.D., p. 191.

notice had been taken of the Battle of Copenhagen, for the custom of the Corporation of the chief city of the Empire, thus to honor the great achievements of their armed forces, was, he asserted, invariable in his experience; consequently, the omission in the case of Copenhagen was a deliberate slight, the implication of which, he thought, could not be disregarded. Delay, up to the time then present, might be attributed to other causes, not necessarily offensive, although, from a letter to his friend Davison, he seems to have feared neglect; but the vote of thanks to the two Services for their successes in Egypt left no room to doubt, that the failure to take similar action in the case of Copenhagen was intentional.

This Nelson regarded, and justly, as an imputation upon the transactions there. Where a practice is invariable, omission is as significant as commission can be. Either the victory was doubtful, or of small consequence, or, for some other reason, not creditable to the victors. He wrote at once to the Lord Mayor. After recalling the facts, he said: "If I were only personally concerned, I should bear the stigma, now first attempted to be placed upon my brow, with humility. But, my Lord, I am the natural guardian of the characters of the Officers of the Navy, Army, and Marines, who fought, and so profusely bled, under my command on that day. . . . When I am called upon to speak of the merits of the Captains of his Majesty's ships, and of the officers and men, whether seamen, marines, or soldiers, I that day had the happiness to command, *I say*, that never was the glory of this country upheld with more determined bravery than upon that occasion, and more important service was never rendered to our King and Country. It is my duty to prove to the brave fellows, my companions in dangers, that *I* have not failed, at every proper place, to represent, as well as I am able, their bravery and meritorious services."

This matter was the occasion of bringing him into collision with the Admiralty and the Government on the same subject. Although his private representations, soon after his return to England, had obtained from Lord St. Vincent, as he thought, a promise that medals should be issued for the battle, no steps thereto had been taken. He now enclosed to the Prime Minister and to the First Lord a copy of his letter to the

Lord Mayor; and to both he alluded to the assurance he believed had been made him. "I have," he said, "been expecting the medals daily since the King's return from Weymouth." St. Vincent's reply was prompt as himself. With reference to the former matter, he confined himself to drily thanking Nelson, without comment, "for communicating the letter you have judged fit to write to the Lord Mayor;" but as to the medals, he wrote a separate note, telling him that he had "given no encouragement, but on the contrary had explained to your Lordship, and to Mr. Addington, the impropriety of such a measure being recommended to the King."

Nelson, to use his own word, was "thunder-struck" by this statement. "I own," he said, "I considered the words your Lordship used as conveying an assurance. It was an apology for their not being given before, which, I understood you, they would have been, but for the difficulty of fixing who was to have them. . . . I have never failed assuring the Captains, that I have seen and communicated with, that they might depend on receiving them. . . . I could not, my dear Lord, have had any interest in misunderstanding you, and representing that as an intended Honour from the King which you considered as so improper to be recommended to the King: therefore I must beg that your Lordship will reconsider our conversation — to me of the very highest concern, and think that I could not but believe that we would have medals. I am truly made ill by your letter." St. Vincent replied briefly, "That you have perfectly mistaken all that passed between us in the conversation you allude to, is most certain. At the same time I am extremely concerned that it should have had so material an effect upon your health," etc. "Either Lord St. Vincent or myself are liars," wrote Nelson to Davison. The conclusion is not inevitable to those who have had experience of human misunderstandings; but, recalling Mr. Rose's interview with St. Vincent in April,[1] it seems likely that in July the mind of the latter was still undecided, and that consequently Nelson's recollection of what he then said was correct.

The Prime Minister took a week to reply. When he did, he deprecated the sending of any letter to the Mayor, for

[1] *Ante*, p. 489.

reasons, he said, "not merely of a public nature, but connected
with the interest I shall ever take in your well-earned fame."
These reasons, he added, he would be ready to give him in a
private interview. Nelson had asked his opinion upon the
terms of the letter; but, impatient after waiting three days,
had already sent it in when this answer came. Probably, with
his usual promptness, he called at once; for on the same day,
November 28, that he received Addington's letter he withdrew
that to the Mayor.[1] "By the advice of a friend, I have now
to request that your Lordship will consider my letter as withdrawn, *as the discussion of the question may bring forward
characters which had better rest quiet.*"[2] In short, honors,
due to those who fought, were withheld out of consideration
to those who had not fought. Nelson himself recognized the
difficulty. "They are not Sir Hyde Parker's real friends who
wish for an inquiry," he had written to Davison before leaving the Baltic. "His friends in the fleet wish everything of
this fleet to be forgot, for we all respect and love Sir Hyde;
but the dearer his friends, the more uneasy they have been
at his *idleness*, for that is the truth — no criminality." But,
as he characteristically said of another matter occurring about
this time, "I was told the difficulties were insurmountable.
My answer was, 'As the thing is necessary to be done, the
more difficulties, the more necessary to try to remove them.'"

As regards the soundness of Nelson's grounds, and the propriety of his action in this matter, it must, first, be kept in
mind, that, before the City voted its thanks to the Navy
engaged in Egypt, he had spoken in the House of Lords in
favor of the thanks of the Government to the same force,
although, as a whole, it had there played a subordinate part;
and also, that, although deprived of the medal which he hoped
to get in common with others, he had himself been rewarded
for Copenhagen by promotion in the peerage.[3] This separation between himself and the mass of those who fought under
him, necessarily intensified the feeling of one always profusely
generous, in praise as in money; but his point otherwise was
well taken. The task was ungracious and unpleasant, it
may almost be called dirty work to have thus to solicit

[1] Nicolas, vol. iv. p. 533.
[2] Ibid., vol. vii. p. ccx. (Author's italics.)   [3] Ibid., vol. v. p. 60.

honors and distinction for deeds in which one has borne the principal part; but dirty work must at times be done, with hands or words, and the humiliation then rests, not with him who does it, but with them who make it necessary. Had the victors at Copenhagen fought a desperate fight, and were they neglected? If so, and the outside world looked indifferently on, who from among them should first come forth to defend their glory from implication of some undefined stain, if not their Commander-in-Chief, one whose great renown could well spare the additional ray of lustre which he demanded for them. Whether underneath lay some spot of self-seeking, of the secondary motive from which so few of us are free, matters little or nothing. The thing was right to be done, and he did it. If the Government and the City of London, by calculated omission, proclaimed, as they did, that these men had not deserved well of their country, it became him to say, as he did, openly to the City, subordinately to his superiors, that they had done men's work and deserved men's reward.

"If Lord Nelson could forget the services of those who have fought under his command, he would ill deserve to be so supported as he always has been." Thus he closed his last letter to the Lord Mayor on this subject, a year after the correspondence began. It was such noble sympathy with all beneath him, the lack of which has been charged against the great Commander of the British Army of this period, that won for Nelson the enthusiastic affection which, in all parts of his command, however remote from his own eyes, aroused the ardent desire to please him. No good service done him escaped his hearty acknowledgment, and he was unwearied in upholding the just claims of others to consideration. In the matter of Copenhagen, up to the time he left the country, eighteen months later, he refused any compromise. He recognized, of course, that he was powerless in the face of St. Vincent's opposition; but, he wrote to one of the captains engaged, "I am fixed never to abandon the fair fame of my companions in dangers. I have had a meeting with Mr. Addington on the subject; I don't expect we shall get much by it, except having had a full opportunity of speaking my mind." The Premier's arguments had been to him wholly inconclusive. Oddly enough, as things were, the Sultan sent him a decoration for Copenhagen. Coming from a foreign sovereign, there was, in accepting it, no inconsistency with his general attitude; but in referring the question to the Government, as was necessary, he told the Prime Minister, "If I can judge the feelings of others by myself, there can be no honours bestowed upon me by foreigners that do not reflect ten times on our Sovereign and Country." [1]

In conformity with this general stand, when it was proposed in June, 1802, to give him the thanks of the City, for taking command of the force destined to defend it against invasion, he wrote to request that the motion might be withdrawn, on the express ground that no thanks had been given those engaged at Copenhagen. "I should feel much mortified, when I reflected on the noble support I that day received, at any honour which could separate me from them." He alleged the same reason, in the following September, for refusing to dine with the Corporation. "Never, till the City of London think justly of the merits of my brave companions of the 2d of April, can I, their commander, receive any attention from the City of London." A like refusal was sent to his invitation for Lord Mayor's day.

After the interview with Mr. Addington, the question of medals was dropped. He had explained his position fully, and felt that it was hopeless to attempt more, so long as the Admiralty was against him; but when the Administration changed, in May, 1804, he wrote to Lord Melville, the new First Lord, enclosing a statement of facts, including his correspondence with St. Vincent, and requesting a reconsideration of the matter. "The medal," he said, is withheld, "for what reason Lord St. Vincent best knows. I hope," he concluded, "for your recommendation to his Majesty, that he may be pleased to bestow that mark of honour on the battle of Copenhagen, which his goodness has

[1] It is possible that Nelson here used the word "reflect" in the primary sense of reflecting honor; but in the secondary sense of being a reflection upon those who had denied a just claim, the phrase, ambiguous as it stands, represented accurately his feelings. "I own, my dear Sir," he said again to the Premier, with reference to this decoration, "great as this honour will be, it will have its alloy, if I cannot at the same time wear the medal for the Battle of Copenhagen, the greatest and most honourable reward in the power of our Sovereign to bestow, as it marks my personal services."

given to the Battle of St. Vincent, the First of June, of Camperdown, and the Nile." Melville, in a very sympathetic and courteous letter, declined, for a reason whose weight must be admitted: "When badges of triumph are bestowed in the heat and conflict of war, they do not rankle in the minds even of the enemy, at whose expense they are bestowed; but the feeling, I suspect, would be very different in Denmark, if the present moment was to be chosen for opening afresh wounds which are, I trust, now healed, or in the daily progress of being so." So it resulted that no mark of public recognition was conferred, during Nelson's life, upon the most difficult, the most hazardous, and, at the moment, perhaps the most critically important of his victories, which he himself considered the greatest of his achievements.

This unfortunate and embittering controversy was the most marked and characteristic incident of his residence at Merton, between October, 1801, when he first went there, and May, 1803, when he departed for the Mediterranean, upon the renewal of war with France. Living always with the Hamiltons, the most copious stream of private correspondence was cut off; and being unemployed after April, 1802, his official letters are confined to subjects connected rather with the past than with the then present time. Upon general naval questions he had, however, something to say. A trip to Wales suggests a memorandum to the Prime Minister concerning the cultivation and preservation of oak timber in the Forest of Dean. He submits to him also his views as to the disposition of Malta, in case the provision of the Treaty of Amiens, which re-established there the Order of the Knights under the guarantee of the six great Powers, should fail, owing to the refusal of Russia to join in the proposed guarantee. At the time he wrote, — December, 1802, — the question was become burning, threatening the rupture of the existing peace between France and Great Britain; a result which, in fact, soon followed, and turned mainly upon this point. The essential aim in the provision, he observed, was that neither of the two countries should have the island. If the Order could not be restored, then it ought to go to Naples, again under the guarantee of the Powers. It was useless to England, for operations against France; and in the hands of the latter

was a direct menace to Sicily. This arrangement would accord
with the spirit of the treaty; but if it also was impracticable,
Great Britain had no choice but to keep Malta herself. It
would cost £300,000 annually, but anything was better than
to chance its falling again into the hands of France.

In like manner he submitted to the Admiralty plans for the
more certain manning of the Navy, and for the prevention of
desertion. The material conditions of seamen while in the
service, the pay and provisions, were, he considered, all that
could be desired; but still there was great indisposition to
enlist, and the desertions in the last war, 1793–1801, rose to
the enormous figure of forty-two thousand. The remedy he
outlined was a Registration of seamen, and of certificates to
be given them, bearing a personal description by which they
could be identified, and on which their character and services
would appear. For lack of such papers, seamen by hundreds
were in London in distress, although large amounts of money
were due them at prize agencies, where the agent feared to
pay for want of identification. A certificate showing five
years' faithful service should entitle the holder to an annual
bounty of two guineas, to be increased by further periods.
Such provisions were well calculated to appeal to men accustomed to entertain prudential considerations, and to create
gradually a class with whom they would weigh, and who would
by them be retained in permanent employment. In meeting
the case of desertions, caused by the heedlessness and weakness of seamen, Nelson became more vague. The nature of the
trouble he recognized clearly enough, but there is a lack of
definiteness in the remedy he proposed to meet an evil which
still exists. "The mainspring of all my plan is, that of
Certificates fully descriptive of the persons; the very greatest
good must result from it. Something should be attempted at
these times to make our seamen, at the din of war, fly to
our Navy, instead of flying from it." His plan is substantially that now adopted.

Closely connected with the discontent of seamen was the
subject of prize-money, in the receipt and distribution of
which great irregularities and abuses existed among the
agents, to remove which also he made particular and detailed
suggestions; and he strongly supported, though with dis-

criminating criticism, the Bill for an Inquiry into Naval
Abuses, which embodied the most prominent of St. Vincent's
administrative measures while at the head of the Admiralty.
But, though thus supporting the Earl in his policy of investigation, and retaining his respect for him as a sea-officer, he
was utterly dissatisfied with the general conduct of the Admiralty and with its attitude towards himself in particular.
" I attribute none of the tyrannical conduct of the late Board
to Lord St. Vincent," he wrote two years later. " For the
Earl I have a sincere regard, but he was dreadfully ill-advised,
and I fear the Service has suffered much from their conduct."
It would seem as if he did not, after the first moments of
annoyance, forget the irritation he felt against Troubridge at
being retained in the Downs against his will, and, as he
thought, without necessity. " I thank you," he wrote to
Captain Murray, " for taking the trouble of driving seven
miles to make me a visit; for, could you believe it, there are
those who I thought were my firm friends, some of near
thirty years' standing — who have never taken that trouble ! "
This may not refer to Troubridge, but the description an-
swers to him, and it appears that in the Nelson-Hamilton
circle his name now stood as a type of ingratitude.[1]

Writing to Davison in September, 1802, after a trip of six
weeks made to Wales, in company with the Hamiltons, he
says: " Our tour has been very fine and interesting, and
the way in which I have been everywhere received most
flattering to my feelings ; and although some of the higher
powers may wish to keep me down, yet the reward of the
general approbation and gratitude for my services is an ample
reward for all I have done ; but it makes a *comparison* fly up to
my mind, not much to the credit of some in the higher Offices
of the State." He seems to have felt that neither in his
influence with the Admiralty, nor in reference to his opinions
on foreign topics, did he receive the recognition that his distinguished services, abilities, and experience claimed. " Having failed entirely in submitting my thoughts on three points "
— those just cited, manning, desertion, and prize-money —
" I was disheartened ; " and to this he attributes his not send-

---

[1] See Pettigrew, vol. ii. p. 225 ; Morrison, vol. ii. p. 176.

ing in a memoir which he had prepared upon the subject of
the Flotilla for Coast Defence.

But, while he resented this neglect, it did not greatly interfere with his happiness, which was at this time wellnigh
complete. He complains of ill health, it is true, from time
to time, and his means were insufficient duly to keep up the
two establishments — Lady Nelson's and Merton — for which
he was pecuniarily responsible. Under this embarrassment
he chafed, and with a sense of injustice which was not unfounded ; for, if reward be proportioned to merit and to the
importance of services rendered, Nelson had been most inadequately repaid. For the single victories of St. Vincent
and Camperdown, each commander-in-chief had received a
pension of £3,000. The Nile and Copenhagen together had
brought him no more than £2,000 ; indeed, as he had already
been granted £1,000 a year for St. Vincent, another thousand
may be said to have been all he got for two of the greatest
victories of the war. In submitting a request for an increase,
he asked pertinently, " Was it, or not, the intention of his
Majesty's Government to place my rewards for services
lower than Lord St. Vincent or Lord Duncan ? " There was,
of course, the damaging circumstance that the conditions
under which he chose to live made him poorer than he
needed to be ; but with this the Government had no concern.
Its only care should have been that its recompense was commensurate with his deserts, and it is revolting to see a man
like Nelson, naturally high-toned and always liberal, forced
to the undignified position of urging — and in vain — for the
equal remuneration that should have been granted spontaneously long before.

In his criticisms of the Admiralty's general course, it does
not appear whether Nelson, who was hereafter to be the
greatest sufferer from St. Vincent's excessive economies, realized
as yet the particular injury being done by them to the material
of the Navy. In his passion for reform, the veteran seaman
obstinately shut his eyes to the threatening condition of the
political atmosphere, and refused to recognize the imminent
danger of a renewal of the war, because it necessarily would
postpone his projected innovations. Assuming the continuance of peace with all the violence of a prejudice, he

permitted the strength and resources of the Navy to deteriorate rapidly, both by direct action and by omission to act. "Lord St. Vincent," wrote Minto in November, 1802, "is more violent than anybody against the war, and has declared that he will resign if ministers dare go to war. His principal reason is, I believe, that the ships are so much out of repair as to be unfit for service." "Lord Nelson," he says at the same period, "has been with me a long time to-day. He seems much of my mind on material points, but especially on the necessity of being better prepared than we now are." The admiral's own letters at this time make little allusion to the measures, or the neglects, which were rapidly undermining the efficiency of the fleet; but a year after leaving England he wrote, "With all my personal regard for Lord St. Vincent, I am sorry to see that he has been led astray by the opinion of ignorant people. There is scarcely a thing he has done since he has been at the Admiralty that I have not heard him reprobate before he came to the Board."

Much as he enjoyed his home and desired peace, Nelson had never felt assured of its continuance. Like Great Britain herself during this repose, he rested with his arms at his side, ready for a call. The Prime Minister, Addington, has transmitted a curious story of the manner in which he exemplified his ideas of the proper mode of negotiating with Bonaparte. "It matters not at all," he said, taking up a poker, "in what way I lay this poker on the floor. But if Bonaparte should say it *must* be placed in this direction," suiting the action to the word, "we must instantly insist upon its being laid in some other one." At the same time Bonaparte, across the Channel, was illustrating in almost identical phrase the indomitable energy that was common to these two men, the exponents of the two opposing and irreconcilable tendencies of their age. "If the British ministry should intimate that there was anything the First Consul had not done, because he was prevented from doing it, that instant he would do it." "You have proved yourself too true a prophet," wrote an occasional correspondent to Nelson, "for you have said ever since the peace that it could not be of long duration." Jar after jar, as Bonaparte drove his triumphal chariot over the prostrate continent, announced the instability of existing

conditions; and the speech from the throne on the 16th of
November, 1802, was distinctly ominous, if vague. Nelson
then seconded the address in the House of Peers, in words
so characteristic of his own temper, and of that then prevailing in the nation, that they serve to explain the strong accord between him and it, and to show why he was so readily
and affectionately distinguished as its representative hero.
They are thus reported : —

" I, my Lords, have in different countries, seen much of the miser-
ies of war. I am, therefore, in my inmost soul, a man of peace. Yet
I would not, for the sake of any peace, however fortunate, consent to
sacrifice one jot of England's honour. Our honour is inseparably
combined with our genuine interest. Hitherto there has been nothing
greater known on the Continent than the faith, the untainted honour,
the generous public sympathies, the high diplomatic influence, the
commerce, the grandeur, the resistless power, the unconquerable
valour of the British nation. Wherever I have served in foreign
countries, I have witnessed these to be sentiments with which Britons
were regarded. The advantages of such a reputation are not to be
lightly brought into hazard. I, for one, rejoice that his Majesty has
signified his intention to pay due regard to the connection between
the interests of this country and the preservation of the liberties of
Europe. It is satisfactory to know, that the preparations to maintain our dignity in peace, are not to be neglected. Those supplies
which his Majesty shall for such purposes demand, his people will
most earnestly grant. The nation is satisfied that the Government
seeks in peace or war no interest separate from that of the people at
large; and as the nation was pleased with that sincere spirit of peace
with which the late treaty was negotiated, so, now that a restless and
unjust ambition in those with whom we desired sincere amity has
given a new alarm, the country will rather prompt the Government
to assert its honour, than need to be roused to such measures of vigorous defence as the exigency of the times may require."

During the winter, Bonaparte, resentful of Great Britain's
claim to a voice in the politics of the Continent, became more
and more distinctly menacing in deed and word. On the 20th
of February, 1803, in a message to the legislature, he made
the imprudent, because useless, vaunt, "This government
says with just pride, England, alone, cannot to-day contend
against France." Two days later Minto, who was in opposition, was told by Nelson, "in strict confidence," that for some

time back there had been great doubts between peace and war in the ministry. "One measure in contemplation has been to send him to the Mediterranean, by way of watching the armament and being ready if wanted. He says that he is thought the fitter for that delicate service, as on the one hand he wishes the continuance of peace, and therefore is not likely to precipitate matters, and on the other hand Bonaparte knows that if he hoists his flag it will not be in joke." It had for some time been arranged that, if war came, he was to have the Mediterranean command.

On the 8th of March, 1803, the King sent a message to Parliament, that, in consequence of military preparations going on in the ports of France and Holland, he judged expedient to adopt additional measures of precaution for the security of his dominions. While this was under discussion in the Upper House, Nelson, impressed with the idea that war must come, left his seat, and wrote to the Prime Minister the following line: "Whenever it is necessary, I am *your* Admiral." Yet he felt the tug at his heart-strings as he never had before. "War or Peace?" he writes to his old flag-captain, Berry. "Every person has a different opinion. I fear perhaps the former, as I hope so much the latter." Only with large reservations would he now have repeated the rule Codrington tells us he inculcated, — "that every man became a bachelor after passing the Rock of Gibraltar, and he was not very tardy in showing that he practised what he preached. Honour, glory and distinction were the whole object of his life, and that dear domestic happiness never abstracted his attention." He did, indeed, rail at marriage [1] during his last cruise, now fast approaching; but his passionate devotion to Lady Hamilton, and his yearning for home, knew no abatement. Yet, through all and over all, the love of glory and the sense of honor continued to the last to reign supreme. "Government cannot be more anxious for my departure," he tells St. Vincent, "than I am, if a war, to go."

Meantime the necessary preparations were quietly progressing, while the diplomatic discussions with France became more and more bitter and hopeless, turning mainly on the

[1] This habit is mentioned by Captain James Hillyar, for extracts from whose journals the author is indebted to Admiral Sir W. R. Mends, G. C. B.

question of Malta, though the root of the trouble lay far deeper. The "Victory," of a hundred guns, was named for Nelson's flag, her officers appointed, and the ship commissioned. On the 6th of May he received orders to prepare for departure. On the 12th the British ambassador left Paris, having handed in the Government's ultimatum and demanded his passports. On the 16th Great Britain declared war against France, and the same day Nelson at the Admiralty received his commission as commander-in-chief in the Mediterranean. Within forty-eight hours he joined the "Victory" at Portsmouth, and on the 20th sailed for his station.

Thus ended the longest period of retirement enjoyed by Nelson, from the opening of the war with France, in 1793, until his death in 1805. During it, besides the separation from Lady Nelson, two great breaks occurred in his personal ties and surroundings. One was the death of his father, on the 26th of April, 1802, at the age of seventy-nine. There had been no breach in the love between the two, but it seems to the author impossible to overlook, in the guarded letters of the old man to his famous son, a tinge of regret and disapproval for the singular circumstances under which he saw fit to live. That he gladly accepted the opinion professed by many friends, naval and others, and carefully fostered by the admiral, that his relations with Lady Hamilton were perfectly innocent, is wholly probable; but, despite the usual silence concerning his own views, observed by himself and Nelson, two clues to his thought and action appear in his letters. One is the remark, already quoted, that gratitude required him to spend some of his time with Lady Nelson. The other, singular and suggestive, is the casual mention to Nelson, on October 8, 1801, that he had received an anonymous letter, containing "severe reproaches for my conduct to you, which is such, it seems, as will totally separate us." [1] In whose interest would such a letter most likely be penned? On the 17th of October he wrote Lady Nelson that he ought to be able to stay with her without offending his children; but she, with great magnanimity, for his countenance meant much to her, advised a separation, because the deprivation of seeing his own family was cruel. In the event, he visited Merton in November, and

[1] Morrison Collection, No. 632, October 8, 1801.

it has been said, upon the authority of Lady Hamilton, that he intended to make it his home; but going to Bath for the winter, he there died. Nelson mourned him sincerely, but was prevented by illness from being present at the funeral. He is a man known to us only by his letters, which are marked by none of the originality that distinguishes the professional utterances of the admiral, and cannot be said to rise much above the commonplace; but they show a strong and unaffected piety, and a cheerful, resolute acceptance of the infirmities of protracted old age, which possess charm and inspire respect. There is also a clear indication of the firmness that characterized Nelson himself, in the determination, amid all the feebleness of age, and notwithstanding his pride and love for his famous son, upon whom, too, he was partially dependent, that he would not abandon the wife, to whom he continued to write. His attitude in this regard, as far as can be inferred from his letters, commands sympathy and admiration.

A year later, on the 6th of April, 1803, Sir William Hamilton also died, "in Lady Hamilton's and my arms," wrote Nelson, "without a sigh or a struggle. The world never lost a more upright and accomplished gentleman." Lady Hamilton, with ready tears, recorded : "Unhappy day for the forlorn Emma. Ten minutes past ten dear blessed Sir William left me." The grouping of figures and emotions at that deathbed was odd almost beyond comprehension; one of the most singular studies which human nature has presented to itself of its powers of self-cajolement. A man systematically deceived, yet apparently sincerely regarded, and affectionately tended to the last by his betrayers, one of whom at least prided himself, and for the most part not unjustly, upon his fidelity to his friends. Hamilton, alone among the three, seems to have been single-minded — to have viewed their mutual relations to the end, not with cynical indifference, but with a simplicity of confidence hard to be understood in a man of his antecedents. It may have been, however, that he recognized the inevitable in the disparity of years and in his wife's early training, and that he chose to cover her failings with a self-abnegation which was not without nobility. Upon such a tacit affirmation he set a final seal in a codicil to his will, well calculated to silence those who saw scandal in the association between his wife and his friend. "The copy of Madam Le Brunn's picture of Emma, in enamel, by Bone, I give to my dearest friend Lord Nelson, Duke of Bronté, a very small token of the great regard I have for his Lordship, the most virtuous, loyal, and truly brave character I ever met with. God bless him, and shame fall on those who do not say amen."

Sir William's death, by withdrawing the husband's countenance to Nelson's remaining under the same roof, might have complicated matters for the two lovers, but the outbreak of war necessitated the admiral's departure a month later. When he returned to England for the last time, in August, 1805, he was, deservedly, the object of such wide-spread popular devotion, and his stay was so short, that the voice of censure was hushed amid the general murmur of affectionate admiration. The noble qualities of the man, the exalted spirit of self-sacrifice and heroic aspiration that breathed in his utterances, and was embodied, not only in his brilliant deeds, but in the obscure, patient endurance of the last two years, evoked a sentiment which spread over him and her a haze of tender sympathy that still survives. In the glory of Trafalgar, in his last touching commendation of her and his child to the British Government, in the general grief of the nation, there was justly no room to remember their fault; both acquaintance and strangers saw in her only the woman whom he loved to the end. The sisters of Nelson, women of mature years and irreproachable character, maintained a correspondence with Lady Hamilton during their lives; long after his death, and the departure of his influence, removed any interested motive for courting her friendship. Between them and Lady Nelson, on the other hand, the breach was final. Their occasional mention of her is unfriendly, and upon the whole contemptuous; while she, as far as can be judged from their letters, returned to them an equal measure of disdain.

CHAPTER XIX.

COMMANDER-IN-CHIEF IN THE MEDITERRANEAN. — THE LONG WATCH
OFF TOULON. — OCCUPATIONS OF A COMMANDER-IN-CHIEF.

MAY, 1803–JANUARY, 1805. AGE, 45–46.

WHEN Nelson, after a three years' absence, returned to
the Mediterranean in 1803, he found the conditions,
upon which the military balance of power there depended,
greatly altered from those he had known during the period of
his previous service. He had been present, indeed, almost
an eye-witness, at the tremendous reverse associated with the
name of Marengo, for that battle, it will be remembered, was
fought while he was at Leghorn on his return to England;
but Marengo, and the conventions following it, were at the
moment only the beginning of an end which then could not
be foreseen.

The most significant token of the entire change of conditions — of the predominant, far-reaching, and firmly fastened
grip of France on the land — was the presence of an army
corps of fifteen thousand men in the extreme southeast of
Italy, occupying the Kingdom of Naples from the river
Ofanto, on the Adriatic coast, round to the Bradano on the
Gulf of Taranto, and including the useful ports of Brindisi
and Taranto. This distant and ex-centric extension of the
arms of the Republic bespoke Bonaparte's confidence in the
solidity of his situation in the South of Europe; for under
previous circumstances, even after his victorious campaign of
1796, he had always deprecated an occupation of Naples, and
relied upon threats and a display of force to insure the quies-
cence of that state. That one of his first steps, upon the
renewal of war with Great Britain, should have been to place
a large body of troops in a position he once considered so exposed, shows the fulness of his conviction that upon the Continent he had, for the moment, nothing to fear from the other

Great Powers. Strongly stirred as they had been by his high-handed aggressions, none as yet ventured to call him directly to account. Great Britain, the least immediately affected, had stepped into the lists, and demanded not only that aggression should cease, but that the state of the Continent should be restored as it existed when she signed the treaty of Amiens. With this requirement she maintained the war, single-handed, from May, 1803, to the autumn of 1805.

It was not without reason that Bonaparte reckoned upon the inaction of the Continent. Austria, although profoundly discontented by much he had done since the peace of Lunéville, in 1801, was too thoroughly disheartened and exhausted by the unsuccessful and protracted struggle which preceded it, to be ready to renew the strife. Limited as she now was, by the treaty, to the eastern bank of the Adige, there was in Northern Italy no force to threaten the French communications, between their divisions in the valley of the Po and the one at the heel of the peninsula. Prussia, playing a double part for years back, seeking from day to day the favor of the most powerful, was wholly committed for the time to the First Consul; while Russia, although her youthful sovereign had abandoned the anti-British policy of his predecessor, remained undecided as to the general course she should pursue amid the ever-shifting perplexities of the day. Less fantastic in imagination than his insane father, Alexander I. inherited a visionary tendency, which hindered practical action, and showed itself in plans too vast and complicated for realization, even when two rulers of the overwhelming power of himself and Napoleon, at a later date, set their hands to the task. Swayed, alternately, by sympathy with the ancient order of things, which Great Britain for the moment represented, and by prospects of Russian aggrandizement, which Bonaparte dangled before his eyes, the Czar halted between two opinions, pleasing himself, meanwhile, in weaving, with associates of his own age, schemes for a general reorganization of Europe. In these the interests of Russia naturally, and quite properly, had a leading part, and not least in those seas and regions that fell within the limits of Nelson's command.

The power of the great states which lay to the northward and eastward of him being thus neutralized, Bonaparte found

H. M. Ships "Agamemnon," "Captain," "Vanguard," "Elephant," and "Victory."

From an engraving by Fittler, after the painting by N. Pocock.

upon the land nothing to oppose his will, or to contest his influence, in the smaller and weaker nations to the southward and westward, close to his own doors, but isolated from the rest of Europe, except by sea — a weighty exception. Spain, reduced to virtual vassalage in the previous war, no longer even pretended to dispute his orders. She was not engaged in the present hostilities, simply because it suited him better to take a money tribute from her, and to enjoy for French ships the benevolent neutrality of Spanish ports, more necessary to them than to the British. Moreover, if Spain joined in the war, Minorca, restored to her at the peace, would be at the mercy of Great Britain, and Port Mahon, the fine haven of that island, was always a menace to Toulon. The harbors of remote Portugal, where Lisbon formerly had given powerful support to the British fleet, were now closed to it for offensive operations; and Nelson, within whose command its seaboard lay, was strictly enjoined to refrain from any such use of them, even from sending in prizes, except under stress of weather. In Italy, Piedmont had been incorporated with France, while the Italian and Ligurian (Genoa) Republics in the North were so identified with her in action, and so submissive to her, that the capture of the latter's ships was at once ordered by Nelson; and he recommended to his Government that a formal blockade should be proclaimed of her ports, as well as of Leghorn, where the French flag was flown on the same staff as the Tuscan. The States of the Pope, intermediate between these tributaries of Bonaparte in the North and his garrisoned province in Naples, enjoyed only such precarious independence as he from day to day allowed. But, mighty as was the growth of French ascendency, as shown by these changes, the very advantages accruing to France from her advanced maritime positions laid her further open to the Sea Power of Great Britain. The neutrality of Genoa and Tuscany could no longer embarrass the British admiral, as it had Nelson in 1795 and 1796. Offensive operations against them were now merely a question of adequate force, and the South of France depended greatly upon free access to their ports. Taking Piedmont from the King of Sardinia, too, relieved any scruples the British might have concerning their use of the island of Sardinia injuring a

friendly monarch, a consideration which kept them away
from Sicily.

Nelson, instructed by the experience and observation of the
recent past, and by a certain prescient sagacity which was at
once native and cultivated in him, recognized that the Mediterranean, with its immense indented coast line, its positions
of critical importance, — such as the Straits of Gibraltar and
the Bosphorus, Egypt and Malta, — and its comparatively
short water distances, was the field of operations to which the
maritime ambitions of Bonaparte, debarred a wider flight by
the sea-power of Great Britain, must inevitably incline.   To
this contributed also its remoteness from England, as well as
its nearness to France and to the ports subject to her influence
in Italy and Spain; while the traditional ambitions of French
rulers, for three centuries back, had aspired to control in the
Levant, and had regarded Turkey for that reason as a natural
ally.   It was, therefore, not merely as magnifying his own
office, nor yet as the outcome of natural bias, resulting from
long service in its waters, that Nelson saw in the Mediterranean the region at once for defence and offence against
Bonaparte ; where he might be most fatally checked, and
where also he might be induced most surely to steps exhaus-
tive to his strength.   This conviction was, indeed, rather an
instance of accurate intuition than of formulated reasoning.
Clear, ample, and repeated, as are his demonstrations of the
importance of the various positions at stake, and of the measures necessary to be taken, they rather apply to the necessities
of the moment than indicate a wide scheme of policy, which
should divert the energies of the enemy to the South of
Europe, and so provide the best of defences against his projected invasion of England.   Yet even of such broader view
tokens are not wanting.   "To say the truth," he writes to
the Queen of Naples, "I do not believe we had in the last
war, and, according to all appearance, we shall not have in
the present one either, plans of a sufficiently grand scale to
force France to keep within her proper limits.   Small measures produce only small results.   The intelligent mind of your
Majesty will readily comprehend the great things which might
be effected in the Mediterranean.   On this side Buonaparte is
the most vulnerable.   It is from here that it would be the

most easy to mortify his pride, and so far humble him, as to make him accept reasonable conditions of peace."

It cannot be claimed, however, that there entered into Nelson's thoughts, for Italy, any such diversion as that by which the Spanish Peninsular War some years later drained the life blood of France. The time, indeed, was not yet ripe, nor would the scene have been in any way as favorable to Great Britain; and, moreover, so far from being ready to threaten, her energies were effectually constrained to her own defence, by the superior audacity and direct threats of Bonaparte. Even the limited suggestions for the employment of troops in the Mediterranean, made by Nelson from time to time, failed to receive attention, and he himself was left to struggle on as best he might, with inadequate means and upon a bare defensive, even in naval matters. Great Britain, in short, had stripped herself, incautiously, so bare, and was so alarmed by the French demonstrations of invasion, that she for the moment could think only of the safety of her territory and of her home waters, and her offensive operations were confined to the sea.

Bonaparte understood as fully as Nelson the importance of the Mediterranean to him. His mind was set upon the extension of France's dominion therein, — in its islands, upon its northern and southern shores, and in the East; nor was he troubled with scruples as to the means by which that object might be attained. During the short peace of Amiens, Lord Keith had felt it necessary to take precautions against the reoccupation of Corfu by the French troops; and again at a later date had stationed a ship for the same purpose at the Madalena Islands, belonging to Sardinia, which Nelson afterwards made a rendezvous for his fleet. Algiers, too, had attracted the First Consul's attention. "Algiers will be French in one year after a peace," wrote Nelson in August, 1804. "You see it, and a man may run and read; that is the plan of Buonaparte." "The Ministers of the Dey must know, that an armament at Toulon, and a large army, after the peace with Great Britain, was intended to land and plunder Algiers, which they doubtless would have effected, had not a British fleet been placed in Oristan Bay [Sardinia] to watch their motions." These and similar reasons had led the British Gov-

36

ernment to maintain the Mediterranean Squadron nearly upon
a war footing during the peace.   But, if Bonaparte's purpose
was fixed to control the Mediterranean some day, it now was
set also upon the invasion of England; and although he
looked and plotted in many directions, taking long views, and
neglecting no opportunity to secure advanced footholds for
future uses, he had not yet reached the stage in his development when he would divide his energies between two gigantic
undertakings.   One at a time, and with an accumulation of
force abundantly adequate to the end in view, was his policy
all the days of Nelson.   The Mediterranean with its varied
interests was to him at this time one of several means, by
which he hoped to distract British counsels and to dissever
British strength; but it was no part of his design to provoke
Great Britain to measures which would convert her alarm for
the Mediterranean peninsulas into open war with them, or in
them, compelling France either to recede from thence, or to
divert thither a force that might weaken his main effort.   His
aim was to keep anxiety keenly alive, and to cut short the
resources of his enemy, by diplomatic pressure upon neutral
states, up to the last extreme that could be borne without war
against them being declared, as the lesser evil; and the nearer
he could approach this delicate boundary line, without crossing it, the greater his success.   " I do not think a Spanish
war [that is, a declaration by Spain] so near," wrote Nelson
in November, 1803.   " We are more likely to go to war with
Spain for her complaisance to the French; but the French can
gain nothing, but be great losers, by forcing Spain to go to
war with us; therefore, I never expect that the Spaniards
will begin, unless Buonaparte is absolutely mad, as many say
he is.   I never can believe that he or his counsellors are such
fools as to force Spain to begin."

The course instinctively advocated by Nelson, transpiring
through occasional utterances, was directly contrary to Bonaparte's aims and would have marred his game.   " We never
wanted ten thousand troops more than at this moment," Nelson wrote shortly after he had reached the station and become
acquainted with the state of affairs.   " They might save
Naples, Sicily, the Morea and Egypt, by assisting and giving
confidence to the inhabitants."   " It has been my plan to

have 10,000 disposable troops in the Mediterranean," he wrote
to Acton ; and he regretted to the Ministry that they should
have withdrawn all the fine army which had regained Egypt
in 1801. "The sending them home," he remarked to an occasional correspondent, "was a very inconsiderate measure, to
say nothing further of it." His idea was to garrison Gaeta
and Naples on the coast of the mainland, and Messina in
Sicily ; and to throw a force into the mountains of Calabria,
which should sustain and give cohesion to the insurrection
that he confidently expected would follow. With the British
fleet covering the approaches by water, and sustaining and
reinforcing garrisons in the ports, there would be imposed
upon the enemy, unless he chose to abandon Southern Italy, a
scene of operations in a distant, difficult country, with a long
and narrow line of communications, flanked throughout by the
sea, and particularly by the two fortified harbors which he
proposed to occupy. "The peasantry would, I believe, defend
their mountains, and at least it would give a check to the
movements of the French, and give us time to get a fleet into
the Mediterranean." That the attempt would have been
ultimately successful, against such power as Napoleon then
wielded, cannot be affirmed ; but, until put down, it necessarily would have engaged a force very disproportionate to its
own numbers, drawing off in great part the army destined
against England, as it was diverted two years later by Austria,
and giving opportunity for changes in the political conditions,
even to the formation of a new Coalition.

Nelson, therefore, was not far from right in reasoning that
the Mediterranean should, and therefore would, be the chief
scene of operations. In Bonaparte's eyes, to invade Britain
was, justly, the greatest of all ends, the compassing of which
would cause all the rest to fall. Nelson, weighing the difficulties of that enterprise more accurately than could be done
by one unaccustomed to the sea, doubted the reality of the
intention, and thought it more consonant to the true policy of
France to seize control of the Mediterranean, by a sudden concentration of her fleets, and then to transport her troops by
water to the heel of Italy, to the Ionian Islands, to the Morea,
to Egypt. So stationed, with fortified stepping-stones rising
at short intervals from the deep, future movements of troops

and supplies from point to point would be but an affair of
coasters, slipping from battery to battery, such as he had
experienced to his cost in the Riviera. In this project he
thought it likely that France could secure the co-operation of
Russia, by allowing the latter her share of the spoils of Turkey, especially in Constantinople. He saw, indeed, that the
partition would involve some difficulty between the two part-
ners, and in his correspondence he attributes the Morea and
the islands, now to one, now to the other; but the prediction,
elicited piece-meal from his letters, received a close fulfilment
four years later in the general tenor of the agreements of
Tilsit, nor was it less accurate in its dim prophecy of a
disagreement.

Such, in broad outline, were the prepossessions and views
Nelson took with him from England in 1803, as modified by
the information he received upon reaching the station; and
such the counter-projects of Bonaparte, to whom belonged,
as the privilege of the offensive, the choice of direction for
his attack. The essential difference between the two was,
that one believed the invasion of England, however difficult,
to be possible, and therefore to be the true and first object of
his efforts; while the other, without pronouncing that attempt
impossible, saw its difficulties so clearly, that he conceived his
enemy must be aiming for the Mediterranean from the beginning. It is permissible to remark that Bonaparte, after the
failure of the invasion, first busied himself in reducing Austria, Prussia, and Russia, successively, to the state of inaction
in which they were in 1803; next came to an understanding
with the latter, such as Nelson had foreseen; and then turned
to the Mediterranean, where he established his own rule in
Naples, in the Ionian Islands, on the eastern shore of the
Adriatic, and finally in the Spanish peninsula. Beyond that
his advance was stayed by the Sea Power of Great Britain,
which at last wrought his ruin. Thus in the event the
predictions of the British admiral were postponed, but not
falsified.

Nelson's characteristic impatience and energy hurried him
on from the moment he took up his command. "I cannot
sail before to-morrow," he said repeatedly in Portsmouth,
"and that's an age." "If the Devil stands at the door," he

tells St. Vincent, "we shall sail to-morrow forenoon." The Admiralty, in its primary anxiety about Brest, imposed upon him a delay under which he chafed angrily. He was directed to meet off that port the squadron of Admiral Cornwallis, in order that, if the latter wanted the "Victory," she might be left there, and an intimation was even given that he was "on no account to pass Admiral Cornwallis, so as to run any chance of his being deprived of the services of the Victory, if he should judge it necessary to detain her." Nelson resented the implication that he was capable of evading an order, like a frigate-captain parting company to better his chance of prize-money. "I beg to assure you that I hold it impossible for any officer, under such orders as their Lordships' to me, to designedly miss Admiral Cornwallis off Brest."

On the 22d of May he was off Ushant, between which and Cornwallis's rendezvous he passed twenty-four hours, fuming and fretting over a delay that was losing him a fresh, fair, northerly wind; the more so, that he was satisfied Cornwallis neither needed nor wanted the ship. "From his conduct," — not being on his rendezvous, — "I am clear there can be nothing in Brest to demand his attention." On the 23d, however, he could stand it no longer. "What a wind we are losing!" "If the wisdom of my superiors had not prevented me," he growled, "at this moment I should have been off the coast of Portugal. I am aware of the importance of my getting to the Mediterranean, and think I might safely have been allowed to proceed in the Victory." At 6 P.M. of that day, Cornwallis not turning up, he tumbled himself and his suite on board the frigate "Amphion," which was in company, and continued his voyage, going out in all the discomfort of "a convict," to use St. Vincent's expression; "seven or eight sleeping in one cabin," as Nelson himself described it. "It is against my own judgment but in obedience to orders," he told the Earl; while to the Prime Minister, with whom he was in personal correspondence, he lamented the loss, "for I well know the weight of the Victory in the Mediterranean." As he anticipated, Cornwallis did not want the ship, and she joined Nelson two months afterwards off Toulon.

Late in the evening of June 3d, the "Amphion" anchored at Gibraltar, whither she brought the first certain news of the war, though it had been declared nearly three weeks before. The next day was actively employed in giving necessary instructions to the yard officials, and detailing cruisers to guard the entrance to the Straits, and to maintain the communications with the Barbary coast, upon which the Rock depended for supplies of fresh provisions. At 4 p. m. the ship again sailed for Malta, accompanied by the frigate "Maidstone," to which, on the 11th of June, was transferred, for direct passage to Naples by the north of Sicily, the new British minister to the Two Sicilies, Mr. Elliot, who had embarked with Nelson on board the "Victory," and afterwards gone with him to the "Amphion." Throughout the following two years an active correspondence, personal and diplomatic, was maintained with this gentleman, who, like his brother, Lord Minto, placed the utmost dependence upon the political sagacity and tact of the admiral. When the latter, a year later, spoke of leaving the station on account of his health, Elliot wrote to him: "Where such great interests are concerned, I shall not presume to dwell upon my own feelings, although I cannot but recall to your Lordship that I only consented to depart as abruptly as I did from England, to undertake this arduous and ruinous mission, from the expectation that my efforts to direct the councils of this Kingdom would have been seconded by your pre-eminent talents and judgment." After the two frigates parted, the "Amphion" kept on to Malta, where she arrived on the 15th of June.

With the separation of the "Maidstone" Nelson began the extensive diplomatic correspondence, which employed so much of his time during this command, and through which we are made familiar with the workings of his mind on the general political conditions of the Mediterranean. She carried from him letters to the King and Queen of the Sicilies, to their Prime Minister, Acton, and to the British minister to the Court of Sardinia. To these succeeded, upon his arrival in Malta, — as a better point of departure for the farther East, now that the French held the west coast of the Adriatic, — despatches to the British minister to the Porte, to the Grand Vizier and the Capitan Pacha, to the Republic of the Seven Islands, as the group of Corfu and its sisters was now styled, and to the British representative to their government.

All these communications were, of course, tentative, based upon a yet imperfect knowledge of conditions. For the most part they conveyed, besides the notification of his having taken the command, chiefly general assurances of the good-will of the writer's government, and an undefined intimation that all had best be on their guard against French scheming and aggressions. To Naples he spoke more definitely, and indicated at once the considerations that would dictate his course, and, he intimated, should control theirs also. He had been instructed, he said, to consider the welfare of the Two Sicilies as one of the first of British objects, and his Government was convinced of the advantages that would accrue both to Sicily and Naples, if their neutrality could be maintained. They had to do, however, with an enemy that was not only powerful, but wily and unscrupulous; one whose action would be governed wholly by considerations of interest and expediency, not by those of right. Great Britain could not, probably, keep the French out of Naples, but she could out of Sicily, provided, and only provided, Messina was adequately garrisoned and held. If, however, there was any hasty overt action taken, looking to the security of Sicily, it might merely precipitate the seizure of Naples and the entire conquest of the King's continental dominions ; or, " ten times more humiliating," leave him " an odious commissary to raise contributions from his unhappy subjects for the French." On the other hand, if, to avert suspicion, there was too much slackness in the measures to guard Sicily, Messina might be suddenly seized, the gates of the island thus thrown open, and, Sicily once lost, " *Naples falls of course.*" " It is a most important point," he wrote to Elliot soon after, " to decide when Sicily ought to be placed in a state of security. For the present, I am content to say that Messina need not be taken possession of; but the strictest watch must be kept by Sir John Acton that we are not lulled into a fatal security, and thus lose both Kingdoms. To save for the moment Naples, we risk the two Kingdoms, and General Acton must join me in this heavy responsibility." " My whole opinion rests in these few words — *that we must not risk Sicily too far in trying to save Naples ; therefore, General Acton, yourself and myself must keep a good lookout.*"

This summed up the conditions for Naples during the long two years of watching and waiting, while Bonaparte, concentrating his purposes upon his invasion scheme, was content to leave things quiet in the South. To check, as far as might be, the designs of the French towards Morea or towards Sicily, on either side of the central position they held at the heel of Italy, Nelson employed a proportionately large number of cruisers — five — between Messina and the mouth of the Adriatic; while, to provide for the safety of the royal family, he kept always a ship-of-the-line in the Bay of Naples, the British minister holding orders for her captain to embark them at a moment's notice, and take them to Sicily. " I have kept everything here to save Italy, if in my power," he wrote Elliot two months later, " and you know I was ordered to send a squadron outside the Straits. Fourteen days ago, a French seventy-four got into Cadiz from Santo Domingo, and two French frigates, with some merchant ships. What will they say at home ? However, I feel I have done right, and care not." "I must place a squadron between Elba and Genoa," he says again, " to prevent that expedition from moving, and also send some ships to the Straits' mouth, and keep enough to watch the ships in Toulon. These are all important objects, but nothing when compared to the security of the Sicilies."

Nelson's anxiety for Sicily threw him again into contact with an instance of that rigid and blind conformity to orders which always exasperated him. He had brought out directions to the general commanding in Malta, to hold a detachment of two thousand British troops in readiness to go at once to Messina, on the appearance of danger, and to garrison the works there, if he thought they could be spared from the defence of Malta. Nelson told the Prime Minister that discretion, as to such a step, was a responsibility greater than the average officer could bear, and would certainly defeat the object in view ; for he would never feel his charge secure enough to permit such a diminution. There was at this time in Malta a body of Neapolitan soldiers, which had been sent there during the peace of Amiens, in accordance with a stipulation of the treaty. The general received an order to send them to Messina. Nelson had pointed out to him that if he did so, in the divided state of feeling in the Neapolitan dominions, and with the general character of Neapolitan officers, for both efficiency and fidelity, the citadel would not be safe from betrayal at their hands. " I have requested him to keep the orders secret, and not to send them; for if they got into Messina, they would certainly not keep the French out one moment, and it would give a good excuse for not asking us to secure Messina." " If General Acton sends for them we must submit ; but at present we need not find means of sending them away." The British general, however, sent them over, and then the Neapolitan governor, as Nelson foretold, said it was quite unnecessary for any British to come. "I must apprise you," wrote Nelson to Addington, "that General Villettes, although a most excellent officer, will do nothing but what he receives, ' You are hereby required and directed;' for to obey, is with him the very acme of discipline. With respect to Sicily, I have no doubt but that the French will have it. My former reasons for inducing General Villettes to keep the Neapolitan troops in Malta, was to prevent what has happened ; but, in a month after my back was turned, Villettes obeyed his orders, and now the Governor of Messina says, 'We can defend it, and want no assistance.' His whole conduct, I am bold to say, is either that of a traitor or a fool." [1]

Upon his own subordinates Nelson laid a distinct charge, that he should expect them to use their judgment and act upon it with independence, sure of his generous construction and support of their action. " We must all in our several stations," he tells one of them, " exert ourselves to the utmost, and not be nonsensical in saying, ' I have an order for this, that, and the other,' if the King's service clearly marks what ought to be done. I am well convinced of your zeal." In accordance with this, he was emphatic in his expressions of commendation for action rightly taken ; a bare, cold approval was not adequate reward for deeds which he expected to reproduce his own spirit and temper, vivifying the whole of his command, and making his presence virtually co-extensive with its utmost limits. No severer condemnation, perhaps, was ever implied by him, than when he wrote to Sidney Smith, unqualifiedly, " I strictly charge and command you never to

---

[1] This sentence refers to the governor ; not to Villettes, as the construction might indicate.

give any French ship or man leave to quit Egypt." To deny
an officer discretion was as scathing an expression of dissatisfaction as Nelson could utter; and as he sowed, so he reaped,
in a devotion and vigor of service few have elicited equally.

In Malta Nelson remained but thirty-six hours. Arriving
at 4 P. M. on the evening of June 15th, he sailed again at
4 A. M. of the 17th. He had expected partly to find the fleet
there; but by an odd coincidence, on the same day that he
hoisted his flag in Portsmouth, it had sailed, although in
ignorance of the war, to cruise between Sicily and Naples;
whence, on the day he left Gibraltar, the commanding officer,
Sir Richard Bickerton, had started for Toulon, — "very judiciously," said Nelson, — the instant he heard of the renewal
of hostilities.

The "Amphion" passed through the Straits of Messina,
and within sight of Naples, carrying Nelson once more over
well-known seas, and in sight of fondly remembered places.
"I am looking at *dear* Naples, if it is what it was," he wrote
to Elliot from off Capri. "Close to Capri," he tells Lady
Hamilton, "the view of Vesuvius calls so many circumstances
to my mind, that it almost overpowers my feelings." "I
am using force upon myself to keep away," he had already
said to Acton; "for I think it likely, was I to fly to Naples,
which I am much inclined to do, that the French might turn
it to some plea against those good sovereigns." In his anxiety
to join the fleet, and get in touch of the French, the length of
the passage, three weeks, caused him great vexation, and
deepened his convictions of the uselessness of the island to
his squadron off Toulon. "My opinion of Malta, as a naval
station for watching the French in Toulon, is well known; and
my present experience of what will be a three weeks' passage,
most fully confirms me in it. The fleet can never go there, if
I can find any other corner to put them in; but having said this,
I now declare, that I consider Malta as a most important outwork to India, that it will ever give us great influence in the
Levant, and indeed all the southern parts of Italy. In this
view, I hope we shall never give it up." "Malta and Toulon
are entirely different services. It takes upon an average seven
weeks to get an answer to a letter. When I am forced to send
a ship there, I never see her under two months."

With Gibraltar, however, Malta gave the British two impregnable and secure bases of operations, within reasonable distance of one another, and each in close proximity to points most essential to control. During Nelson's entire command, the three chief centres of interest and of danger were the Straits of Gibraltar, the heel of Italy, and Toulon. The narrowing of the trade routes near the two former rendered them points of particular exposure for merchant shipping. Around them, therefore, and in dependence upon them, gathered the largest bodies of the cruisers which kept down privateering, and convoyed the merchant ships, whose protection was not the least exacting of the many cares that fell upon Nelson. Upon the Malta division depended also the watch over the mouth of the Adriatic and the Straits of Messina, by which Nelson hoped to prevent the passage of the French, in small bodies, to either Sicily, the Morea, or the Ionian islands. Malta in truth, even in Nelson's time, was the base for operations only less important than the destruction of the Toulon fleet. The latter he rightly considered his principal mission, success in which would solve most other maritime difficulties. " My first object must ever be to keep the French fleet in check; and, if they put to sea, to have force enough with me to *annihilate* them. That would keep the Two Sicilies free from any attack from sea."

On the 8th of July the " Amphion " joined the fleet off Toulon. It numbered then nine ships-of-the-line, with three smaller cruisers. " As far as outside show goes," he reported to St. Vincent, " the ships look very well; but they complain of their bottoms, and are very short of men." The fact was, as he afterwards explained, that before the war came they had been expecting every day to go to England, and consequently had been allowed to run down gradually, a result which doubtless had been hastened by St. Vincent's stringent economies. Gibraltar and Malta were both bare, Nelson wrote six months later, and it was not the fault of the naval storekeepers. The ships, everywhere, were " distressed for almost every article. They have entirely eat up their stores, and their real wants not half complied with. I have applications from the different line-of-battle-ships for surveys on most of their sails and running rigging, which cannot be complied with, as there is neither cordage nor sails to replace the unserviceable stores, and, therefore, the evil must be combated in the best manner possible." As the whole Navy had suffered from the same cause, there was no reserve of ships at home to replace those in the Mediterranean, which, besides lacking everything, were between eight and nine hundred men short of their complement, or about one hundred for each ship-of-the-line. "We can send you neither ships nor men," wrote St. Vincent as winter drew on; and even a year later, the administration which followed his found it impossible to replace the "crazy" vessels, of which Nelson said only four were fit for winter cruising. "It is not a storeship a week," he declared, "that would keep them in repair." The trouble was greater because, when leaving Malta, they had anticipated only a cruise of three weeks, which for many of them became two years.

Despite the difficulties, he determined that the fleet as a body should not go into port; nor should the individual ships-of-the-line, except when absolutely necessary, and then to Gibraltar, not Malta. "I have made up my mind never to go into port till after the battle, if they make me wait a year, provided the Admiralty change the ships who cannot keep the sea in winter;" nor did the failure of the Admiralty to meet this proviso alter his resolution. It was the carrying out of this decision, with ships in such condition, in a region where winds and seas were of exceptional violence, and supplies of food and water most difficult to be obtained, because surrounded in all directions by countries either directly hostile, or under the overmastering influence of Bonaparte, that made the exercise of Nelson's command during this period a triumph of naval administration and prevision. It does not necessarily follow that an officer of distinguished ability for handling a force in the face of an enemy, will possess also the faculty which foresees and provides for the many contingencies, upon which depend the constant efficiency and readiness of a great organized body; though both qualities are doubtless essential to constitute a great general officer. For twenty-two months Nelson's fleet never went into a port, other than an open roadstead on a neutral coast, destitute of supplies; at the end of that time, when the need arose to pursue an enemy for four thousand miles, it was found massed, and in all respects perfectly prepared for so distant and sudden a call. To quote his own words, written a year before this summons in reply to an intimation from the Admiralty to be on his guard against Spain, "I have the pleasure to acquaint you that the squadron under my command is all collected, except the Gibraltar,[1] complete in their provisions and stores to near five months, and in a perfect state of readiness to act as the exigency of the moment may determine." "With the resources of your mind," wrote St. Vincent, when unable to reinforce him, "you will do very well;" and Nelson, when he put off his harness, might have boasted himself that the prediction was more than fulfilled.

Provisions, water, and supplies of all sorts were brought to the ships on their station, either at sea, or in unfrequented roadsteads within the limits of the cruising ground. "I never could have spared the ships to go to Gibraltar for them," he wrote to St. Vincent, to whom he expressed his satisfaction with the way the plan worked. He soon abandoned, in fact, the method of sending individual ships for water, because of the long absence thus entailed. When water could not be brought in transports, or rather could not easily be transhipped owing to the badness of the season, he thought it better to take the whole fleet to the nearest watering-place than to divide its strength. Fresh provisions, absolutely indispensable to the health of the ships' companies, constituted the greatest of difficulties. Opposition to furnishing them must be expected wherever French influence could be felt. "The great distance from Malta or Gibraltar renders the getting such refreshments from those places, in a regular manner, absolutely impossible;" and from the Spanish ports, Barcelona or Rosas, which were near his cruising ground, they could be had only "clandestinely." Government Bills would not be taken there, nor in Barbary or Sardinia, where bullocks might be got. Hard money must be paid, and about this there was some routine bureau difficulty. "I certainly hate to have anything to do with the management of money," he wrote, "but I submit the propriety of lodging public money on board the fleet, for the purpose of paying for fresh beef and vegetables, provided, but on *no account otherwise*, that the simple

[1] Unfit for sea, and kept at Naples for political reasons.

receipt from the captain of the ship may be a sufficient voucher for the disbursement of such money." Absolutely disposed as he was to assume political or military responsibilities, he was not willing, even for the health of the fleet, to incur the risk of pecuniary imputations for himself or his captains.

Great dexterity of management was required to obtain these supplies, without drawing, upon those who gave them, such tokens of displeasure from Bonaparte as might result in their discontinuance. Towards Spain, although he felt for her perplexities, Nelson took a firm tone. She was nominally neutral, and enjoyed privileges as such; he insisted therefore that she should deal equal measure to both belligerents. "I am ready to make large allowances for the miserable situation Spain has placed herself in; but there is a certain line beyond which I cannot submit to be treated with disrespect." That line of forbearance was dictated, of course, less by indulgence towards Spain than by the necessities of Great Britain, which Nelson, however indignant, was too good a diplomatist to drop out of sight; but he kept up a pressure which secured very substantial assistance, though grudgingly given. "Refreshments we have a right to as long as we remain at peace, and if this goes on " — the refusal, that is, to allow provisions to be bought in quantities — "you may acquaint them that I will anchor in Rosas with the squadron, and receive our daily supplies, which will offend the French much more than our staying at sea."

Towards Naples, as secretly friendly to Great Britain, he was of course far more tender ; and, while he rejected no suggestion without consideration, he regarded the distance as too great to render such a means of subsistence certain. The numerous privateers that haunted every port would intercept the transports and render convoys necessary; it was not worth while, for so small an advantage, to involve Naples, in its already critical state, in a dispute with France. An occasional purchase, however, seems to have been made there; and even France herself was at times brought to contribute, indirectly, to the support of the squadron which was watching one of her principal ports. "Latterly our cattle and onions have been procured from France," wrote Nelson ; "but from the apparent incivilities of the Spaniards, I suppose we are on the eve of being shut out." To escape the notice of the French agents, it was obviously desirable to distribute as widely as possible the sources of supply, so as not to concentrate observation upon any one, or upon the general fact.

It was, however, upon Sardinia that Nelson in the end chiefly depended. The importance of this island, both in fact and in his estimation, was so great, that it may be said to have constituted the chief object of his thought and anxiety, after his own squadron and the French, which also he at times prophetically spoke of as his own. " I do not mean to use the shells you have sent me at sea," he writes to General Villettes, " for that I hope to consider burning *our own* ships; but in case they run ashore, then a few put into their sides will do their business." In addition to its extremely favorable central position, Sardinia, as compared to Sicily, did not entail the perplexity that its use by the British might cause a friendly sovereign the loss of his continental dominions. Those of the King of Sardinia had passed already nearly, if not wholly, out of his hands. The island itself was so wild, poor, and neglected, that, even if seized by the enemy, the King would lose little. The net revenue derived from it was only £5,000.

During the previous war Nelson's attention had not been called much to Sardinia. Up to the withdrawal from the Mediterranean in 1796, Corsica had been a sufficient, and more suitable, base for the operations of the fleet, which until then had been upon the Riviera and the northern coast of Italy. When he returned in 1798, even after the Battle of the Nile and the disasters of the French in 1799, the unsettled condition of Naples, the blockade of Malta, and the affairs of Egypt, had combined to keep him in the South; while the tenure of the allies in Northern Italy, up to the Battle of Marengo, was apparently so secure as to require no great support from the fleet. Irrespective of any personal influences that may have swayed him, Sicily was better suited then to be the centre from which to superintend the varied duties of his wide command.

When he returned in 1803, the old prepossessions naturally remained. In a survey of the political conditions written for the Prime Minister when on the passage to Toulon, much is

said of Malta, Sicily, and Naples, but Sardinia is dismissed
with a passing hope that the French would not seize it. After
joining the fleet off Toulon, however, he had to realize that,
if it was to remain at sea, as he purposed and effected, and yet
be kept fully provisioned and watered, it must at times make
an anchorage, which should be so far convenient as to keep it,
practically, as much on its station as when under way. In
this dilemma his attention was called to the Madalena Islands,
a group off the northeast end of Sardinia, where wood and
water could be obtained. Between them and the main island
there was a good harbor, having the decisive advantage of
two entrances, by one or other of which it could be left in
winds from any quarter. A survey had been made a year
before, during the peace, by a Captain Ryves, now commanding a ship in the fleet. As winter approached, Nelson decided
to examine the spot himself, which he did in the last days of
October, taking advantage of a moonlight week when the
enemy would be less likely to leave port. He found it admirably adapted for his purposes, and that fresh provisions,
though not of the best quality, could be had. "It is certainly
one of the best anchorages I have met with for a fleet," he
wrote, "but I suppose the French will take it now we have
used it." This they did not attempt, and the British fleet
continued to resort to it from time to time, obtaining water
and bullocks.

Such a roadstead as an occasional rendezvous, where transports could discharge their stores to the vessels, and ships be
refitted and supplied, would make the fleet as secure of holding its position as were the cruisers that depended upon Malta
and Gibraltar. Its being two hundred miles from Toulon was
not a serious drawback, for it was no part of Nelson's plan to
keep the fleet close to Toulon. When he took command, he
found it so stationed, but he soon removed to a position thirty
to forty miles west of the harbor's mouth, which seems to
have been his general summer rendezvous. "Lord Nelson,"
wrote a young officer of the fleet,[1] "pursues a very different
plan from Sir Richard Bickerton. The latter kept close to
the harbour, but Lord Nelson is scarce ever in sight of the
land, and there is but one frigate inshore." "I chose this

[1] The Honourable Mr. Waldegrave, afterwards Admiral Lord Radstock.

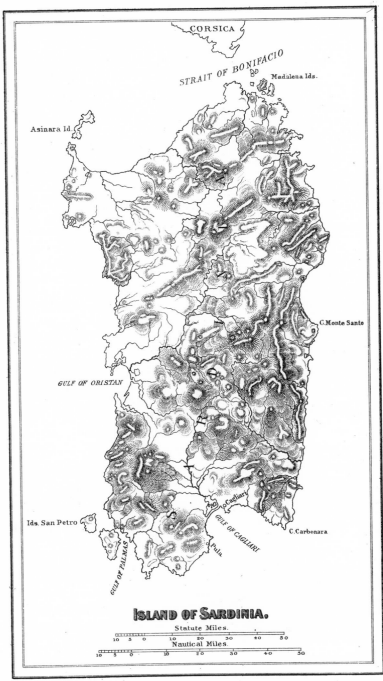

CORSICA

STRAIT OF BONIFACIO

Madalena Ids.

Asinara Id.

C. Monte Santo

GULF OF ORISTAN

Ids. San Petro

o Cagliari

GULF OF CAGLIARI

GULF OF PALMAS

C. Carbonara

o Pula

ISLAND OF SARDINIA.

Statute Miles.
10 5 0 10 20 30 40 50

Nautical Miles.
10 5 0 10 20 30 40 50

position," Nelson said, " to answer two important purposes : one to prevent the junction of a Spanish fleet from the westward; and the other, to be to windward, so as to enable me, if the northerly gale came on to the N. N. W., to take shelter in a few hours under the Hières Islands, or if N. N. E., under Cape San Sebastian." "It is not my intention to close-watch Toulon, even with frigates," he wrote, and his dispositions were taken rather with a view to encourage the enemy to come out; although, of course, he took every precaution that they should not get far without being observed, and assured himself by frequent reconnoitring that they had not left port. "My system is the very contrary of blockading," he told Admiral Pole. "Every opportunity has been offered the enemy to put to sea," he says again, "for it is there we hope to realize the hopes and expectations of our Country." There was also the obvious advantage that, if habitually out of sight, the enemy could not know his movements, nor profit by his occasional absences in any direction.

From Madalena he extended his observations over the whole island of Sardinia, upon the holding of which he thenceforth laid the greatest stress, and entertained most anxious fears lest the French should snatch it out of his hands. "If we could possess Sardinia, we should want neither Malta nor any other. It is the most important island, as a naval and military station, in the Mediterranean. It possesses at the northern end the finest harbour in the world [Madalena]. It is twenty-four hours' sail from Toulon ; it covers Italy ; it is a position that the wind which carries the French to the westward is fair for you to follow. In passing to the southward they go close to you. In short, it covers Egypt, Italy, and Turkey." He was anxious that the British Government should buy it. "If we, from delicacy, or commiseration of the unfortunate king of Sardinia, do not get possession of that island, the French will. If I lose Sardinia, I lose the French fleet."

His apprehensions were not verified ; as also they were not during his command, either in the Morea, in Naples, or in Sicily. Napoleon took no active steps against Sardinia, although the proceedings there did not escape the sharp eyes of the French agents, but elicited from them vivacious remonstrances. "The government of the Republic," wrote one, "has a right to complain of this excessive complaisance. To give regular support to a squadron blockading a port, to revictual it, in one word, periodically, is to tread under foot the neutrality which is professed. I shall notify my government of a fact which demands all its attention, and in which it is painful to me to see a cause of misunderstanding between France and his Sardinian Majesty." It is singularly confirmatory of the reality of Bonaparte's intention to attempt the invasion of England, that he confined his efforts in the South — in the Mediterranean — to feints and demonstrations. What he did there looked to the future, not to the present; although, doubtless, he stood always so ready that no opportunity offering advantage would have passed neglected. The active mind of Nelson, condemned to the uncertainties of the defensive and to military idleness, however it may have been burdened with administrative routine and official correspondence, found ample time to speculate on the designs of Bonaparte, and the latter took care that he should have matter enough to occupy him — and if possible mislead him — in rumor and in movements. " At Marseilles they are fitting, as reports say, eighty or ninety gunboats, and intend sending them, by the canal of Languedoc to Bordeaux; but I am sure this is not true. They are to go alongshore to the Heel of Italy, and to embark and protect their army either to Sicily or the Morea, or to both; and the Navy of Europe can hardly prevent these alongshore voyages." In this will be noticed the recurrence of ideas familiar to him in the Riviera eight years before; the expectation of ex-centric operations into which Bonaparte was rarely betrayed.

Frequent stories also reach him of projects to invade and seize Sardinia. Vessels are fitting for that purpose, now at Marseilles, now at Villefranche; now the expedition is to come from Corsica only. " A light linen jacket, trowsers, red cap, and a pair of shoes, is the whole expense of Government; the plunder of the Sardinian Anglo-Sardes is held out as the reward." To prevent it he seeks the authority of his Government and of the King of Sardinia to garrison Madalena. The straits of Bonifacio are but ten miles wide; it is impossible therefore for a cruiser to prevent boats passing. If the attempt is made, no scruples about the neutrality of Sardinia shall tie his hands. "I have directed the frigates to pursue them, even should they chase into Sardinia, and to take or destroy them, and also the Corsican troops; for if I wait till the island is taken I should feel deserving of reprobation. Of course, they will say we have broken the neutrality, if we attack them in the ports of Sardinia before their conquest, and if we do not I shall be laughed at for a fool. *Prevention is better than cure.*" With his usual long-headed circumspection, however, even when most bent on an extreme step, he warns the Prime Minister, to whom he is writing, to mention his purpose to the Russian ambassador — that the latter may understand the apparent breach of neutrality; for Russia has constituted herself a champion of the Sardinian monarch. "I mention my intention that idle reports may not be attended to."

As the winter of 1803–4 approached, and it became evident that Spain was to persevere in her neutrality, Nelson removed his fleet to a rendezvous about thirty miles south of Cape San Sebastian, on the Spanish coast — the Number 97 continually mentioned in his official letters to captains. There the highlands of Spain afford some shelter from the furious northerly gales, which, sweeping over France from the Atlantic, are compressed as in a funnel between the Pyrenees and the Alps, to fall with redoubled violence on the Gulf of Lyons. Only the utmost care and the most skilful seamanship could preserve the rickety ships, upon whose efficiency so much depended, and which, if damaged, there was none to replace. I "bear up for every gale," wrote Nelson. "I must not in our present state quarrel with the northwesters — with crazy masts and no port or spars near us." Even in September, he writes, there are "three days' gale of severe blowing weather out of the seven, which frequently comes on suddenly, and thereby exposes the topmasts, topsail yards and sails, to great hazard, under every care and attention; and there are no topmasts or topsail yards in store, either at Gibraltar or Malta." "The French fleet keep us waiting; and such a place as all the Gulf of Lyons, for gales of wind from the N. W. to N. E., I never saw; but by always going away large, we generally lose much of their force and the heavy sea.

By the great care and attention of every captain, we have suffered much less than could have been expected. I do not believe Lord St. Vincent would have kept the sea with such ships. However, with nursing our ships, we have roughed it out better than could have been expected. We either run to the southward, or furl all the sails and make the ships as easy as possible." Under such circumstances, it was no small nor unworthy boast he made near the close of the cruise, when the first ineffectual attempt of the French to leave Toulon ended in numerous accidents. "These gentlemen are not accustomed to a Gulf of Lyons gale, which we have buffeted for twenty-one months, and not carried away a spar." Nelson himself, though reckless to desperation when an adequate object was at stake, in the moments of repose husbanded his means, and looked to the efficiency of his instruments, with the diligence of a miser. With his own hand he noted the weather indications, including the barometer, at least three times every twenty-four hours, and occasionally even more often.

A rendezvous, however advantageous, was not permitted by Nelson to become a permanent station, or a long-continued resting-place for the fleet. In the inevitable monotony of a watch protracted so far beyond his original expectations, his sleepless solicitude for the health and contentment of the ships' companies warned him that lack of mental interest saps the spirit, and wears away the strength, beyond the power of mere bodily comfort to prevent. On Number 97 was kept always a ship — frigate or smaller cruiser — with word where the admiral was to be found at any time; and thither resorted the vessels returning from their missions to all parts of the station, or coming out from England. "Rejoin me at Number 97," their instructions ran, "where you will find me, or orders for your further proceedings." Other rendezvous there were, of course, each with its own number, and with a cruiser if at sea; but in the anchorages occasionally resorted to, as Madalena, or the Gulf of Palmas in the south of Sardinia, communications were left on shore. With the threads thus reaching from these centres to the different parts of his command, Nelson's habit was to keep his fleet in motion from point to point, in the stretch of sea bounded on the one side by the coast of Spain, as far south as the Balearics, and on the east by the islands of Sardinia and Corsica. Through this hunting-ground, from end to end of which he roamed in unceasing restlessness, like a lion roaring for his prey, the Toulon fleet must pass, wherever bound, and by the judicious distribution of the cruisers — all too few — allowed him by St. Vincent's economies, he hoped to get timely and sufficient information of its leaving port.

" The great thing in all military service is health," he wrote to his old friend, Dr. Moseley, who had been with him in the far-back Central American expedition in 1780; " and you will agree with me, that it is easier for an officer to keep men healthy, than for a physician to cure them. Situated as this fleet has been, without a friendly port, where we could get all the things so necessary for us, yet I have, by changing the cruizing ground, not allowed the sameness of prospect to satiate the mind — sometimes by looking at Toulon, Ville Franche, Barcelona, and Rosas; then running around Minorca, Majorca, Sardinia and Corsica; and two or three times anchoring for a few days, and sending a ship to the last place for *onions*, which I find the best thing that can be given to seamen; having always good mutton for the sick, cattle when we can get them, and plenty of fresh water. In the winter it is the best plan to give half the allowance of grog, instead of all wine. These things are for the commander-in-chief to look to; but shut very nearly out from Spain, and only getting refreshments by stealth from other places, my command has been an arduous one." " Our men's minds," he added, " are always kept up with the daily hopes of meeting the enemy." An order indicating one of the squadron movements, of which he here speaks, may be worth quoting. " Whereas it is my intention," he writes at Number 97 to the captain there stationed, " to proceed with the squadron, the first westerly wind, off Toulon, for the purpose of reconnoitring the enemy at that port, and from thence pass through Rendezvous No. 102, to secure any information the ships there may have obtained of them, you are hereby required and directed to keep on your station and inform any of his Majesty's ships arriving on said rendezvous," etc.

The health of the crews, thus carefully watched, remained

excellent throughout, and is mentioned by him continually with evident pride as well as satisfaction. Occasional slight outbursts of scurvy are noted, despite his efforts for fresh food, and he mentions hectic complaints — " of the few men we have lost, nine in ten are dead of consumption " — but upon the whole, the general condition is unparalleled in his experience. "We are healthy beyond example, and in great good humour with ourselves," he writes in October, 1803, " and so sharp-set, that I would not be a French Admiral in the way of any of our ships for something." It would be tedious to quote the numerous assertions to the same effect scattered up and down his correspondence at this time; but in December, 1804, when near the end of this long period of suspense, and after eighteen months at sea, he writes to the Admiralty : " The Fleet is in perfect good health and good humour, unequalled by anything which has ever come within my knowledge, and equal to the most active service which the times may call for." Dr. Gillespie, who joined the " Victory " as physician to the fleet in January, 1805, wrote immediately afterwards that out of her eight hundred and forty men, but one was confined to his bed by sickness, and that the other ships, though upwards of twenty months off Toulon, were in a like condition of health.

The same could not then, nor for long before, be said of Nelson himself. The first flush of excitement in leaving Eng- land and taking command, the expectation and change of scene in going out, affected him favorably. " As to my health," he says, immediately after joining the fleet, " thank God, I have not had a finger ache since I left England ; " but this, unfortunately, did not endure. It was his first experience of the weightier anxieties of a commander-in-chief ; for when he had succeeded to that position, temporarily, in the Mediter- ranean and the Baltic, he had found either a squadron in good running order, or at the least no serious hitch about necessary maintenance. Now all this was different. The difficulties about supplies and the condition of his ships have been men- tioned, as have also his fears for Naples, Sicily, and the Morea, — all of which, in his belief, might possibly be conquered, even without the interposition of the Toulon fleet. The latter, however, kept him most uneasy ; for he could get no certain knowledge as to its destination, or the probable time of its moving; and the wide field for injury open to it, if his vigilance were eluded, kept his eager, unquiet mind continually on the strain of speculation and anticipation. " I hope they will come out and let us settle the matter. You know I hate being kept in suspense." The nervous excitability — irritability — that often overlay the usually cordial kindliness and gracious bearing of the man, was an easy prey to such harassment. It breaks out at times in his letters, but was only occasionally visible to those around him. By the first of December he already foresees that he cannot last long. "Next Christmas, please God, I shall be at Merton; for, by that time, with all the anxiety attendant on such a command as this, I shall be done up. The mind and body both wear out."

As autumn drew towards winter, the bitter cold went through his feeble frame, and in the wild weather he was "always tossed about, and always sea-sick." "We have had a most terrible winter," he writes, even before the New Year. " It has almost knocked me up. I have been very ill, and am now far from recovered; but I hope to hold out till the battle is over, when I must recruit." " My heart, my Lord, is warm," he tells Lord Hobart, the Secretary of State for War, " my head is firm, but my body is unequal to my wishes. I am visibly shook; but as long as I can hold out, I shall never abandon my truly honourable post." He feared also blindness. " My eyesight fails me most dreadfully," he writes to his old friend Davison. " I firmly believe that, in a very few years, I shall be stone-blind. It is this only, of all my maladies, that makes me unhappy ; but God's will be done." The first winter was unusually severe, and during it was added, to his official cares and personal suffering, an extreme anxiety about Lady Hamilton, for he was expecting the birth of a second child in January. This child, a girl, lived but a short time; he never saw her. The effect of these various causes upon his health was so great, that the physicians, as early as January, 1804, were advising his return. " The medical gentlemen are wanting to survey me, and to send me to Bristol for the re-establishment of my health," he tells Minto ; but he adds, "do not mention it (it is my concern) I beg of you." Reports were then unusually persistent that the enemy was about to put to sea. "*I* must not be sick until after the French fleet is taken."

To the last moment the destination of the French and the purposes of Bonaparte remained unknown to him, a fruitful source of guessing and worry. "It is at best but a guess," he wrote to Ball, after a year's pondering, "and the world attaches wisdom to him that guesses right." Yet his conclusions, however reached, though subject to temporary variations, were in the main correct. Strongly impressed though he was with the importance and exposure of Egypt, he inclined upon the whole to the belief that the French were bound to the westward, out of the Straits and into the Atlantic. This confirmed him in taking his general summer rendezvous to the westward, where he was to windward of such a movement, as well as interposed between Toulon and any Spanish fleet attempting to go there. "My station to the westward of Toulon, an unusual one," he writes to Addington in August, 1803, "has been taken upon an idea that the French fleet is bound out of the Straits and probably to Ireland. I shall follow them to the Antipodes." Two months later he says: "Plausible reasons may certainly be given for every one of the plans" suggested by his various correspondents; but he thinks that either Alexandria or outside the Mediterranean is the most probable. "To those two points my whole attention is turned." "Their destination, is it Ireland or the Levant? That is what I want to know;" but in December he still holds to his first impression: "My opinion is, certainly, out of the Mediterranean."

In this perplexity Elliot suggested to him to receive on board the fleet some good Frenchmen, who could land from time to time and get information in Toulon, — a proposition which drew from Nelson a characteristic and amusing explosion. "Mr. Elliot wanted to send me some *good* Frenchmen, to go ashore and get me information. My answer to all these offers is 'No.' I can be told nothing of any consequence to me; but a copy of the French admiral's orders, when he is to put to sea, and where he is destined to, is the only useful information I can care about. I can see the number and force at Toulon any day I please, and as for the names of the Captains or Admirals I care not what they are called; there-

fore, as you may suppose, I have none of these 'good Frenchmen' about me." "I put no confidence in them," he tells
Elliot. "You think yours good : the Queen thinks hers the
same : I believe they are all alike. Whatever information
you can get me, I shall be very thankful for; but not a
Frenchman comes here. Forgive me, but my mother hated
the French." "I never trust a Corsican or a Frenchman. I
would give the devil ALL the good ones to take the remainder."

As winter advanced, his perplexities increased, for each
correspondent, by long dwelling on his particular concern,
saw its danger and importance growing in his own eyes, and
dwelt upon them with greater emphasis in his letters. "Ball
is sure they are going to Egypt; the Turks are sure they are
going to the Morea; Mr. Elliot at Naples, to Sicily ; and the
King of Sardinia, to his only spot. Every power thinks they
are destined against them; but whatever the French may intend to do," he concludes, with a quaint humor occasional
with him, "I trust, and with confidence, they are destined for
Spithead." He recognized, too, that Bonaparte himself was
not wholly master of his own projects when contending with
such uncertain elements; and the great master of War, in this
instance as in many others, had placed his force so centrally,
in the heel of Italy, that he threatened with equal facility in
two opposite directions, to his own advantage and his enemies'
perplexity. "Circumstances may even make it necessary to
alter its destination by Buonaparte; Egypt or Ireland, and I
rather lean to the latter destination." Anything, indeed, is
possible; for, as winter approaches, "we can be sure of nothing
in so short a run," — as to Sardinia or Sicily.

For a little while during February, 1804, he was further
stirred up by reports that the French were about to concentrate their naval forces, from Brest and Ferrol, in the Mediterranean; and this he was inclined to believe, unfavorable
as the season would be for maritime operations in that stormy
sea, with the inexperienced crews of the enemy. In the summer his conviction of the importance of the Mediterranean
had fully prepared him for such an attempt. "Naples, the
Morea, and ultimately Egypt, are in Buonaparte's view," he
had then written. "With this idea, I fully expect that the
French fleet from Brest will assuredly come into the Medi-

terranean, to protect this army across the water. I shall try and fight one party or the other, before they form a junction." "Much may be done before British reinforcements arrive," he reminded St. Vincent. "Your Lordship knows what Admiral Bruix might have done, had he done his duty, and they may buy their experience." Now he says to Ball, "The Admiralty tells me nothing, they know nothing; but my private letters say, that the Brest squadron, as well as Ferrol,[1] is bound here — if so, we shall have work enough upon our hands." Thirty thousand troops, also, were ready to embark in Marseilles and Nice. The conclusion, in view of so great a force assembling, was natural: "Egypt, I have no doubt, is the favourite and ultimate object of the Corsican tyrant." Nelson's spirit rises with the occasion. "I shall try to intercept them, but I cannot go so far to the westward as is necessary; for I will not lose sight of the Toulon fleet. What a most zealous man can do to meet all points of difficulty, shall be done. My squadron is the finest for its numbers in the world, and much may be expected of it. Should superior numbers join, we must look it in the face. *Nil desperandum!* God is good, and our cause is just."

This alarm passed away like others. Bonaparte had no idea of pushing ships into the Mediterranean, or embarking his naval forces on any doubtful experiments, until he had first tested the possibility of that supreme adventure, the invasion of England. When that mighty imagination passed away like a dream that leaves no trace, he ordered his fleets into the Mediterranean, as Nelson had expected, and the result was Trafalgar.

As the spring of 1804 opened, the French admiral at Toulon began to exercise his ships outside the harbor, singly or in small groups, like half-fledged birds learning to fly; or, to use Nelson's expression, "My friend Monsieur La Touche sometimes plays bo-peep in and out of Toulon, like a mouse at the edge of her hole." The only drill-ground for fleets, the open sea, being closed to him, he could do no better than these furtive excursions, to prepare for the eagle's flight Napoleon had prescribed to him. "Last week, at different times, two sail

[1] Five French ships-of-the-line, returning from the West Indies, had taken refuge in Ferrol.

of the line put their heads out of Toulon, and on Thursday, the 5th [April], in the afternoon, they all came out." "Yesterday [the 9th] a rear-admiral and seven sail, including frigates, put their nose outside the harbour. If they go on playing this game, some day we shall lay salt upon their tails, and so end the campaign."

These outings — "capers," Nelson called them — naturally became more venturesome by little and little, as the British suffered them to proceed without serious attempt at molestation, or near approach on their part. Nelson veiled the keenness of his watch, as he crouched for a spring, with a drowsy appearance of caution and indifference. The French admiral, Latouche Tréville, was he who had commanded at Boulogne when Nelson's boats were repelled with slaughter; and it was also he who in 1792 had sent a grenadier to the King of Naples, with a peremptory summons to diplomatic apology in one hand, and a threat of bombardment in the other. For both these affairs Nelson considered he had a personal score to settle. "I rather believe my antagonist at Toulon begins to be angry with me: at least, I am trying to make him so; and then, he may come out, and beat me, as he says he did off Boulogne. He is the Admiral that went to Naples in December, 1792, who landed the grenadier. I owe him something for that."

The French having eight sail-of-the-line certainly ready for sea, and two or three more nearly so — how nearly Nelson was not sure — he now endeavored to lure them out. "I have taken a method of making Mr. La Touche Tréville angry. I have left Sir Richard Bickerton, with part of the fleet, twenty leagues from hence, and, with five of the line, am preventing his cutting capers, which he has done for some time past, off Cape Sicie." "He seems inclined to try his hand with us," he writes a week later, "and by my keeping so great an inferiority close to him, perhaps he may some day be tempted." Nelson had near Toulon at the time nine ships-of-the-line. Had he succeeded in bringing Latouche Tréville to attack his five, he would have hoped, even with such odds, for a decisive victory; but, failing that, he was assured that the Toulon fleet would be out of the game for that summer. It was important to bring matters to an issue, for, as he wrote

Elliot, his force was diminishing daily through the deterioration of ships never from the first fit for their work. Measured by the standard of the ships in the Channel, " I have but four sail fit to keep the sea. I absolutely keep them out by management." Except the four, all needed docking, and there was not a dock open to the British west of Constantinople.

But, while thus keenly anxious to force an action, he was wary to obtain tactical conditions that should insure a success, adequate both to the risk he ran, and to the object at which he aimed. " I think their fleet will be ordered out to fight close to Toulon, that they may get their crippled ships in again, and that we must then quit the coast to repair our damages, and thus leave the coast clear ; but my mind is fixed not to fight them, unless with a westerly wind, outside the Hières, and with an easterly wind, to the westward of Sicie." Crippled there, to leeward of their port, the other British division coming up fresh, as a reserve, from the southward, where it lay concealed, would both cut them off, and rescue any of their own fleet that might have been overpowered. Bickerton's orders were to remain due south from Port Cros, one of the Hyères, at a distance such that, with the upper canvas furled, his ships could not be seen from the islands, but could keep the main division in sight from their mastheads. In all cases of anticipated battle, Nelson not only took his measures thus thoughtfully, but was careful to put his subordinates in possession both of his general plans, and, as far as possible, of the underlying ideas. Thus, in a memorandum issued about this time to the captains, he says : " As it is my determination to attack the French fleet in any place where there is a reasonable prospect of getting fairly alongside of them, I recommend that every captain will make himself, by inquiries, as fully acquainted as possible with the following places, viz., Hières Bay [with its three entrances], Gourjean Bay, (of which I send a chart from the latest surveys made,) Port Especia, and, in particular the northern Passage into Leghorn Roads, from which side it is only, in my opinion, possible to attack an enemy's fleet to advantage ; and with the Gulf of Ajaccio." To these instructions he adds some details of practical preparation for anchoring under fire, and the reasons therefor. In the same spirit, when expecting the Brest fleet in the Mediterranean, he says: "I am perfectly prepared how to act with either a superior or an inferior force. My mind is firm as a rock, and my plans for every event fixed in my mind." No man ever was served better than Nelson by the inspiration of the moment; no man ever counted on it less.

In communicating his ideas to his subordinates Nelson did not confine himself to official intercourse; on the contrary, his natural disposition impelled him rather to familar conversation with them on service subjects. "Even for debating the most important naval business," we learn through his confidential secretary at this period, "he preferred a turn on the quarter-deck with his captains, whom he led by his own frankness to express themselves freely, to all the stiffness and formality of a council of war."[1] An interesting instance of these occasional counsels has been transmitted to us by one of his captains, then little more than a youth, but the last to survive of those who commanded ships under him. "Throughout the month of October, 1804, Toulon was frequently reconnoitred, and the Phœbe and Amazon were ordered to cruize together. Previous to their going away Lord Nelson gave to Captains Capel and Parker several injunctions, in case they should get an opportunity of attacking two of the French frigates, which now got under weigh more frequently. The principal one was, that they should not each single out and attack an opponent, but 'that both should endeavour together to take *one frigate;* if successful, chase the other; but if you do not take the second, still you have won a victory, and your country will gain a frigate.' Then, half laughing, and half snappishly, said kindly to them as he wished them good-bye, 'I daresay you consider yourselves a couple of fine fellows, and when you get away from me you will do nothing of the sort, but think yourselves wiser than I am!'"[2]

The game of cat and mouse, off Toulon, occasioned one incident which greatly upset Nelson's composure, and led to a somewhat amusing display of ire, excited by a statement of

[1] Life of Rev. A. J. Scott, p. 124.

[2] Phillimore's Last of Nelson's Captains, p. 122. A portion of this incident has before been quoted, in another connection (page 303, note). It is repeated, because again applicable, to illustrate a different trait of Nelson's character.

the French admiral, published throughout Europe, that his renowned antagonist had run away from him. On the 13th of June, two French frigates and a brig were seen under the Hyères Islands, where they had been seen by Latouche Tréville, upon the report that some enemy's cruisers were in the neighborhood. Nelson despatched two frigates after them, which, owing to light winds, did not get near until the next day. The French vessels being then seen from the "Victory" to be close in with the batteries, the "Excellent," 74, was sent to support the frigates, and some time afterwards the other four ships also bore up for the main entrance to the islands. Upon this, Latouche Tréville got under way, and at about 5 P. M. came out of the harbor with his eight sail-of-the-line. Nelson's division reduced their canvas, hauling to the wind in line of battle, on the starboard tack, which, with the then wind, was with their heads off shore, and the "Excellent" was recalled, although she could not rejoin till midnight. In this order they hove-to (stopped), with two reefs in the topsails and the main yards square, at 7.30 P. M., which at that time of the year was broad daylight, and in this general position remained till next morning.

As the distance between the hostile bodies was apparently from twelve to fifteen miles, the French admiral's observations may have failed to recognize that the enemy, by backing his topsails, had offered a fair challenge; else, in his report of this very commonplace occurrence, he could scarcely have used, concerning the movement of heading south, the expression, *prit chasse*, which, whether rendered "retired," or "retreated," or, as Nelson did, "ran away," was a misrepresentation of the facts, and heightened by the assertion that he pursued till night-fall, and next morning could not see the enemy. Writing to Elliot four days after the affair happened, Nelson mentioned casually his view of the matter. "Monsieur La Touche came out with eight sail of the line and six frigates, cut a caper off Sepet, and went in again. I brought-to for his attack, although I did not believe anything was meant serious, but merely a gasconade." "On the morning of the 15th," he tells Acton on the same day, "I believe I may call it, we chased him into Toulon." His purpose evidently was, as has been shown, to fight, if the enemy meant business, to leeward of the port, and far enough off to give Bickerton a chance to come up. Great was his wrath, two months later, when Latouche's statement reached him, and he found that not only no mention was made of the relative numbers, but that the offensive expression quoted had been used. "I do assure you," he wrote to the Admiralty, enclosing a copy of the day's log, "I know not what to say, except by a flat contradiction; for if my character is not established by this time for not being apt to run away, it is not worth my time to attempt to put the world right." He might well have rested there, — an imputation that might have injured an untried man could provoke only a smile when levelled at his impregnable renown; but his ruffled mind would not let him keep quiet, and in private correspondence he vented his rage in terms similar to those used of the Danish commodore after Copenhagen. "You will have seen Monsieur La Touche's letter of how he chased me and how I *ran*. I keep it; and, by G—d, if I take him, he shall *eat* it." He is a "poltroon," a "liar," and a "miscreant." It may be added that no admiral, whether a Nelson or not, could have abandoned the "Excellent" under the conditions.

Immediately after this abortive affair, Nelson, convinced by it that something more than a taunt was needed to bring his enemy under his guns, stationed frigates at the Hyères, and to cruise thence to the eastward as far as Cape Taillat, to intercept the commerce between Italy and Toulon and Marseilles. For this purpose he had recommended, and the Government had ordered, a blockade of all Genoese ports including Spezia; Genoa, now the Ligurian Republic, being considered as much France as Toulon. Nothing, he said, could distress France more. This blockade had been but feebly enforced, owing to the lack of small cruisers; but he hoped to attain the same end by the frigates off the Hyères. "I really am of opinion," he told their commander, "that it will force La Touche out." In the latter, however, he had to do with an opponent of skill as well as of resolution. Firmly imbued with the French tradition, and with Bonaparte's instructions, which subordinated his local action entirely to the great scheme in which the Toulon fleet had its appointed part, Latouche Tréville was. neither to be provoked nor betrayed into an action, by which, however tempting the promise, his fleet might be made unfit for their intended service. Nelson did him no more than justice, when he said, " I am confident, when he is ordered for any service, that he will risk falling in with us, and the event of a battle, to try and accomplish his orders;" but, short of the appointed time, nothing else could entice him. In vain did the British admiral bait his trap by exposing frigates, without visible support, to draw him to leeward, while the hostile fleet hovered out of sight to windward. The shrewd Frenchman doubtless felt the temptation, but he distrusted the gifts too plausibly tendered.

Besides the interest of the public service, Nelson had the strongest personal motives for bringing matters to an issue. The prolonged suspense and the anxiety were exhausting him, the steady tension even of the normal conditions fretted him beyond endurance; but when a crisis became accentuated by an appearance that the enemy had eluded him, his feelings of distress, acting upon an enfeebled organization, and a nervous temperament so sensitive that he started at the mere dropping of a rope beside him, drove him almost to distraction. On such an occasion he wrote: " I am absolutely beginning this letter in a fever of the mind. It is thick as butter-milk, and blowing a Levanter; and the Narcissus has just spoke me to say, 'she boarded a vessel, and they understood that the men had seen, a few days before, twelve sail of ships of war off Minorca. It was in the dusk, and he did not know which way they were steering.' This is the whole story, and a lame one. You will imagine my feelings, although I cannot bring my mind to believe. To miss them, God forbid. . . . If I should miss these fellows, my heart will break: I am actually only now recovering the shock of missing them in 1798. God knows I only serve to fight those scoundrels; and if I cannot do that, I should be better on shore." When the weather cleared, and a reconnoissance showed the news was false, his intense relief found expression in the words: " I believe this is the only time in my life, that I was glad to hear the French were in port." " The French ships," he says at another time, " have either altered their anchorage, or some of them have got to sea in the late gales: the idea has given me half a fever. If that admiral were to cheat me out of my hopes of meeting him, it would kill me much easier than one of his balls.   Since we sat down to dinner Captain Moubray has made the signal, but I am very far from being easy."

On the 12th of May, 1804, there was a change of administration in England.   Earl St. Vincent left the Admiralty, as First Lord, and was succeeded by Lord Melville.   A few days before this Nelson, by a general promotion, had become Vice-Admiral of the White, the rank in which he died eighteen months later.

The return of summer had improved his health from the low condition into which it had fallen during the winter, but he did not flatter himself as to the future.   The combination of colorless monotony with constant racking anxiety slackened the springs of moral energy, which, and which alone, responding joyously to a call to action, afforded the stimulus capable of triumphing over his bodily weakness, and causing it for the moment to disappear.   "This is an odd war," he said, "not a battle!"   Tying himself to the ship, in profound sympathy with the crews, he never went ashore from the time he left Malta in June, 1803, until he reached Gibraltar in July, 1805; nor was he ever outside of the "Victory" from July 30, 1803, the day he went on board her from the "Amphion."   "Always shut up in the Victory's cabin," as he himself wrote, "cannot be very good for the constitution.   I think you will find me grown thin, but never mind."   Other officers, especially of the frigates, got their occasional runs ashore; but his slight figure was continually in view, walking the front of the poop, to the unconscious contentment of the men, thus reminded ever that their admiral shared their deprivations.   This profound seclusion to the narrow circle of the flagship, although often broken by the presence of officers from the other vessels, who, whether cruising in company with the fleet, or arriving with tidings from different ports, were daily partakers of the admiral's hospitable table, could not but depress him; and there was with him the constant sense of loss, by absence from those he held most dear.   "I have not a thought except on you and the French fleet," he tells Lady Hamilton; "all my thoughts, plans, and toils tend to those two objects.   Don't laugh at my putting you and the French fleet together, but you cannot be separated."

Yet even towards her his mind is fixed as of old, that she

38

must take a place second to duty. She had, it appears, insisted upon her wish to come out to the station to be near him. Malta and Italy were both, he said, out of the question. His place was off Toulon, as long as the French fleet was there; therefore he could not go into harbor; nay, "I might absolutely miss you, by leaving the Mediterranean without warning. The ·other day we had a report the French were out, and seen steering to the westward. We were as far as Minorca when the alarm proved false." As for coming on board the "Victory" to live, which she seems to have suggested, "Imagine what a cruize off Toulon is; even in summer time we have a hard gale every week, and two days' heavy swell. It would kill you; and myself to see you. Much less possible to have Charlotte, Horatia, &c., on board ship! And I, that have given orders to carry no women to sea in the Victory, to be the first to break them! I know, my own dear Emma, if she will let her reason have fair play, will say I am right; but she is like Horatia, very angry if she cannot have her own way." "Horatia is like her mother; will have her own way, or kick up a devil of a dust," — an observation both Greville and Hamilton had had to make. "Your Nelson," he concludes, "is called upon, in the most honourable manner, to defend his country. Absence to us is equally painful: but, if I had either stayed at home, or neglected my duty abroad, would not my Emma have blushed for me? She could never have heard my praises, and how the country looks up." "The call of our country," he says again, "makes it indispensable for both our honours — the country looks up to the services of the poorest individual, much more to me, and are you not a sharer of my glory?"

Of his daily life on board, and intercourse with others, we have intimations, fragmentary yet sufficient. "Our days," he himself says, "pass so much alike that, having described one, you have them all. We now [October] breakfast by candle light; and all retire, at eight o'clock, to bed." "We cruise, cruise, and one day so like another that they are hardly distinguishable, but *hopes*, blessed *hopes*, keeps us up, that some happy day the French may come out, then I shall consider my duty to my country fulfilled." Of one of these monotonous days we have received a description from an

officer,[1] a member of the admiral's mess, who had then too
lately entered upon them to feel the full weight of their
deadly sameness.

"At 6 o'clock my servant brings a light and informs me
of the hour, wind, weather, and course of the ship, when I
immediately dress and generally repair to the deck, the dawn
of day at this season and latitude being apparent at about
half or three-quarters of an hour past six. Breakfast is announced in the Admiral's cabin, where Lord Nelson, Rear
Admiral Murray, (the Captain of the Fleet,) Captain Hardy,
commander of the Victory, the chaplain, secretary, one or
two officers of the ship, and your humble servant assemble
and breakfast on tea, hot rolls, toast, cold tongue, &c., which
when finished we repair upon deck to enjoy the majestic
sight of the rising sun (scarcely ever obscured by clouds in
this fine climate) surmounting the smooth and placid waves
of the Mediterranean, which supports the lofty and tremendous bulwarks of Britain, following in regular train their
admiral in the Victory. Between the hours of 7 and 2 there
is plenty of time for business, study, writing, and exercise,
which different occupations I endeavour to vary in such a
manner as to afford me sufficient employment. At 2 o'clock
a band of music plays till within a quarter of 3, when the
drum beats the tune called, 'The Roast Beef of Old England'
to announce the Admiral's dinner, which is served up exactly
at 3 o'clock, and which generally consists of three courses and
a dessert of the choicest fruit [a fact which bespeaks the
frequency of communications with the land], together with
three or four of the best wines, champagne and claret not
excepted. If a person does not feel himself perfectly at his
ease it must be his own fault, such is the urbanity and hospitality which reign here, notwithstanding the numerous titles,
the four orders of Knighthood, worn by Lord Nelson,[2] and
the well earned laurels which he has acquired. Coffee and
liqueurs close the dinner about half-past 4 or 5 o'clock, after
which the company generally walk the deck, where the band

[1] The letter of this gentleman, Dr. Gillespie, from which a quotation has
already been made, was published in the London "Times" of October 6, 1886.

[2] This incidental remark may be noted, as bearing upon the statement,
now rejected, that his orders were put on especially for battle.

of music plays for nearly an hour.[1] A 6 o'clock tea is announced, when the company again assemble in the Admiral's cabin, where tea is served up before 7 o'clock, and, as we are inclined, the party continue to converse with his lordship, who at this time generally unbends himself, though he is at all times as free from stiffness and pomp as a regard to proper dignity will admit, and is very communicative. At 8 o'clock a rummer of punch with cake or biscuit is served up, soon after which we wish the Admiral a good night (who is generally in bed before 9 o'clock). Such is the journal of a day at sea in fine or at least moderate weather, in which this floating castle goes through the water with the greatest imaginable steadiness."

Another medical officer, who served on board the " Victory " soon after the writer of the lines just quoted, has transmitted some other interesting particulars of Nelson's personal habits and health, which relate to the general period now under narration.

"An opinion has been very generally entertained, that Lord Nelson's state of health, and supposed infirmities arising from his former wounds and hard services, precluded the probability of his long surviving the battle of Trafalgar, had he fortunately escaped the Enemy's shot: but the writer of this can assert that his Lordship's health was uniformly good, with the exception of some slight attacks of indisposition arising from accidental causes; and which never continued above two or three days, nor confined him in any degree with respect to either exercise or regimen: and during the last twelve months of his life, he complained only three times in this way. It is true, that his Lordship, about the meridian of life, had been subject to frequent fits of the gout; which disease, however, as well as his constitutional tendency to it, he totally overcame by abstaining for the space of nearly two years from animal food, and wine, and all other fermented drink ; confining his diet to vegetables, and commonly milk and water. And it is also a fact, that early in life, when he first went to sea, he left off the use of salt, which he then believed to be the sole cause of scurvy, and never took it afterwards with his food.

[1] There is here no mention of smoking; nor has any allusion to it, or to tobacco, caught the author's eye in Nelson's letters.

"His Lordship used a great deal of exercise, generally walking on deck six or seven hours in the day. He always rose early, for the most part shortly after daybreak. He breakfasted in summer about six, and at seven in winter: and if not occupied in reading or writing despatches, or examining into the details of the Fleet, he walked on the quarter-deck the greater part of the forenoon; going down to his cabin occasionally to commit to paper such incidents or reflections as occurred to him during that time, and as might be hereafter useful to the service of his country. He dined generally about half-past two o'clock. At his table there were seldom less than eight or nine persons, consisting of the different Officers of the Ship: and when the weather and the service permitted, he very often had several of the Admirals and Captains in the Fleet to dine with him; who were mostly invited by signal, the rotation of seniority being commonly observed by his Lordship in these invitations. At dinner he was alike affable and attentive to every one: he ate very sparingly himself; the liver and wing of a fowl, and a small plate of macaroni, in general composing his meal, during which he occasionally took a glass of champagne. He never exceeded four glasses of wine after dinner, and seldom drank three; and even those were diluted with either Bristol or common water.

"Few men subject to the vicissitudes of a Naval life, equalled his Lordship in an habitual systematic mode of living. He possessed such a wonderful activity of mind, as even prevented him from taking ordinary repose, seldom enjoying two hours of uninterrupted sleep; and on several occasions he did not quit the deck during the whole night. At these times he took no pains to protect himself from the effects of wet, or the night air; wearing only a thin great coat: and he has frequently, after having his clothes wet through with rain, refused to have them changed, saying that the leather waistcoat which he wore over his flannel one would secure him from complaint. He seldom wore boots, and was consequently very liable to have his feet wet. When this occurred he has often been known to go down to his cabin, throw off his shoes, and walk on the carpet in his stockings for the purpose of drying the feet of them. He chose rather to adopt this uncomfortable expedient, than to give his servants the trouble of assisting him to put on fresh stockings; which, from his having only one hand, he could not himself conveniently effect.

" From these circumstances it may be inferred, that though Lord Nelson's constitution was not of that kind which is generally denominated strong, yet it was not very susceptible of complaint from the common occasional causes of disease necessarily attending a Naval life. The only bodily pain which his Lordship felt in consequence of his many wounds, was a slight rheumatic affection of the stump of his amputated arm on any sudden variation in the state of the weather; which is generally experienced by those who have the misfortune to lose a limb after the middle age. His Lordship usually predicted an alteration in the weather with as much certainty from feeling transient pains in his stump, as he could by his marine barometer; from the indications of which latter he kept a diary of the atmospheric changes, which was written with his own hand.

" His Lordship had lost his right eye by a contusion which he received at the siege of Calvi, in the island of Corsica. The vision of the other was likewise considerably impaired: he always therefore wore a green shade over his forehead, to defend this eye from the effect of strong light; but as he was in the habit of looking much through a glass while on deck, there is little doubt that had he lived a few years longer, and continued at sea, he would have lost his sight totally." [1]

The business hours of the day from seven to two were spent by Nelson largely with his secretaries. We know from Colonel Stewart that in the Baltic, where his command was more numerous than in the Mediterranean, his habit was to get through the ordinary business of the squadron before eight o'clock; for the rest, the greater part of the detail work would fall upon the Captain of the Fleet, then Rear-Admiral George Murray, who would require only general instructions and little interference for carrying on the laborious internal administration of the fleet. The Admiral's energies were sufficiently taxed in considering and meeting, so far as his resources

[1] Dr. Beatty's Narrative of the Death of Lord Nelson. Nicolas, vol. vii. p. 259.

would permit, the numerous and complicated demands for external services in the different quarters of his wide command — the ingenious effort to induce two and two to make five, in which so much of the puzzle of life consists. His position necessarily involved extensive diplomatic relations. Each British Minister around the shores of the Mediterranean had his own particular care; the British admiral was in confidential communication with all, and in every movement had to consider the consequences, both of what he did and of what he left undone. It was a day when force ruled, and all the nations of Europe, whether they wished or not, had to put their chief trust in the sword, and in those who bore it. Not the least of Nelson's qualifications for his post was that he possessed intimate knowledge and experience of political conditions in the Mediterranean, knew the peoples and the rulers well, and to great sagacity and sound judgment added a temper at once firm and conciliatory. "He had in a great degree," said a contemporary who knew him well,[1] "the valuable but rare quality of conciliating the most opposite tempers, and forwarding the public service with unanimity amongst men not of themselves disposed to accord;" and although the remark referred primarily to his conduct in the naval service, it will readily be seen that this aptitude is nowhere more useful than in the tangled maze of conflicting national interests. " My line of conduct," he wrote to Hobart, a year after taking his command, "in obedience to the spirit of his Majesty's instructions communicated through your Lordship, has been simply this, — to conciliate all, to protect all from French rapacity. I have been honoured with your letter of January 7th, and it has given me most sincere pleasure that my whole conduct in my command here has been such as to meet his Majesty's approbation." The new Ministry, upon assuming office, requested him in the most flattering terms to continue his direct correspondence on political subjects with them, as with their predecessors.

Yet, while conciliatory, he could at times be curt and arbitrary enough. Fault was found with the blockade of Genoa on the ground that it did not comply with the requirements of international law; the complaint resting, apparently, on the

[1] Sir William Hotham.

statement that the blockaders could not be seen from Genoa.
Nelson replied that the proof of evident danger to vessels
seeking to enter or leave, rested on the fact that captures were
made; and it is, on the face of it, absurd to say that there can
be no danger to a vessel seeking to enter a blockaded port,
because the blockading vessels are not visible from the latter.
Much more depends upon their number, disposition, and speed.
"From my knowledge of Genoa and its Gulf," said Nelson,
" I assert without fear of contradiction, that the nearer ships
cruise to Genoa, the more certain is the escape of vessels from
that port, or their entrance into it insured.   I am blockading
Genoa, according to the orders of the Admiralty, and in the
way I think most proper.   Whether modern law or ancient
law makes my mode right, I cannot judge; and surely of the
mode of disposing of a fleet, I must, if I am fit for my post,
be a better judge than any landsman, however learned he may
appear.   It would be the act of a fool to tell Europe where I
intend to place the ships, for the purpose of effectually obeying my orders; not a captain can know it, and their positions
will vary, according to the information I may receive. . . . I
endeavour, as well as I am able, to obey my orders, without
entering into the nice distinctions of lawyers.   I will not
further take up your time on a subject which, without being a
lawyer, merely as a man, could have admitted of no dispute."
Along with much truth, there was in this a certain amount of
special pleading, as appeared when he took the further position that, to intercept ships from Genoa, bound to the Atlantic,
there was no better place than the Gut of Gibraltar.   When a
definition of international law is stretched as far as that, it
will have little elastic force left.

A petty, yet harassing, diplomatic difficulty, curiously illustrative of maritime conditions at that day, ran unsettled
through almost the whole of his command.   Malta, under the
Knights, had been always at war with the Barbary Powers;
and there was trouble in impressing upon the rulers of the
latter that, when it passed into British hands, its people and
ships were under British protection.   Several Maltese vessels
had been taken by Algerine cruisers, and their crews enslaved.
When Nelson came out in 1803, he found pending these cases,
and also the question of compelling, or inducing, the Dey to

receive back the British consul, whom he had expelled with insult. In the absence of a British representative, the negotiations were intrusted wholly to the admiral.

Nelson's feelings were strongly excited. He was tenacious of everything he conceived to touch his country's honor, and long service in the Mediterranean had made him familiar with the outrages on its defenceless coasts practised by these barbarians, under the pretence of war with the weaker states. Even in the remote and impoverished north of Sardinia, the shepherds near the beaches watched their flocks with arms beside them, day and night, to repel the attacks of marauders from the sea. Not only were trading-vessels seized, but descents were made upon the shore, and the inhabitants swept off into slavery. Speaking of one such case in 1799, he had said: "My blood boils that I cannot chastise these pirates. They could not show themselves in the Mediterranean did not our Country permit. Never let us talk of the cruelty of the African slave trade, while we permit such a horrid war." But he knew, both then and afterwards, that Great Britain, with the great contest on her hands, could not spare the ships which might be crippled in knocking the barbarians' strongholds about their ears, and that no British admiral would be sustained in a course that provoked these pirates to cast aside the fears that restrained them, and to declare war on British commerce, which, as it was, he had difficulty to protect. He estimated ten ships-of-the-line as the force necessary, in case the batteries at Algiers were to be attacked. Exmouth, twelve years later, with fuller information, thought and found five to be sufficient.

Nelson's conduct and self-control was sorely tested by the necessity of temporizing with this petty foe, who reckoned securely on the embarrassments of Great Britain. He acted with great judgment, however, holding a high tone, and implying much in the way of menace, without at any time involving himself in a definite threat, from which he could not recede without humiliation; careful and precise in his demands, but never receding from them, or allowing them to be evaded, when once made; sensible of the difficulties in his way, as well those raised by his own Government as those dependent upon his opponent, but equally aware that he held in his hands, if authorized to use it, the power to suppress the career of depredation, upon which the Dey relied to support his revenue, and to content his officers. Personally, he favored a short and summary proceeding, accordant to his own decided character. The Dey proving immovable when first summoned, he proposed to the British Government "that on the 28th of April next, when, if he means to send his cruisers to sea, they will be out, that, on that day, every ship under my command should have strict orders (to open on that day) to take, sink, burn, and destroy every Algerine, and that on that day the port of Algiers should be declared in a state of blockade. Thus the Dey could get neither commerce, presents, or plunder; and, although the other Powers may rejoice at the war with us, yet I am firmly persuaded that it will be most advantageous to us for the next hundred years." At the same time, with his usual circumspection, he issued a general direction to all commanders of convoys to carry their charges well clear of the Algerine coast, until matters were settled. In the end, the British Ministry yielded much more than Nelson approved, but, however sorely against the grain, he carried out all his instructions with scrupulous subordination. It was only three days before the active campaign began with the sortie of the French fleet, that he was rejoined by the ship to whose captain were intrusted the final arrangements with Algiers.

For his diplomatic and naval correspondence, Nelson had two principal secretaries, public and private, both, awkwardly enough, named Scott; but the latter, being a clergyman and chaplain of the ship, was colloquially brevetted Doctor, a distinction which, for convenience, will be observed when it is necessary to mention him. He had become known to Nelson while serving in the same capacity with Sir Hyde Parker, and had been found very useful in the negotiations at Copenhagen. An accomplished linguist and an omnivorous reader, Dr. Scott was doubly useful. Upon him devolved the translating of all despatches and letters, not only from, but to, foreign courts and officials; for Nelson made a point of sending with all such papers a copy in the language of the person addressed, and an apology for failing to do so sometimes appears, on account of his secretary's absence. The latter was also a man of wide information, acquired, not as his superior's chiefly was, by mingling among men and dealing with affairs, but from books ; and the admiral, while rightly valuing the teachings of experience above all, was duly sensible that one's own experience is susceptible of further extension through that of others, imparted either by word or pen. Nelson entertained a persuasion, so Scott has told us, that no man ever put his hand to paper without having some information or theory to deliver, which he fancied was not generally known, and that this was worth looking after through all the encumbering rubbish. For the same reason, besides being naturally sociable, he liked to draw others into conversation, and to start subjects for discussion, from which, when fairly under way, he would withdraw himself into silence and allow the company to do the talking, both in order to gather ideas that might be useful to himself, and also to observe character transpiring in conversation. Bourrienne has told us that Bonaparte took pleasure in provoking similar debates. Scott himself, a man essentially unpractical, afforded Nelson amusement as well as interest. and was the object of a good deal of innocent chaffing. He would, in those after-dinner gatherings which Gillespie mentions, lead the doctor into arguments on literature, politics, Spanish and even naval affairs, and would occasionally provoke from him a lecture on navigation itself, to the great entertainment of Murray, Hardy, and the other officers present.[1] "Ah, my dear Doctor!" he would say chaffingly, "give me knowledge practically acquired — experience! experience! experience! and practical men!"

Nelson, however, was too big and too broad a man not to know that, while by doing the same thing, or bearing the same thing, many times, — by experience, that is, — one acquires a facility not otherwise communicable, in a novel situation a man is abler to act, the more he has availed himself of the knowledge and the suggestions of others. Absorbed with the duties of his station, it was of the first importance that he should possess every information, and ponder every idea, small and great, bearing upon its conditions, as well as upon the general political state of Europe in that period of

[1] Many of these details are taken with little alteration from the "Life of Rev. A. J. Scott."

ominous waiting, wherein great events were evidently coming to birth. Day after day, Dr. Scott's biographer tells us, was passed by the two together, sitting in two black leathern arm-chairs with roomy pockets, stuffed with papers, written and printed, journals and pamphlets, gathered from every source — from prizes, from passing neutral vessels, from cruisers returning from neutral or friendly ports, or picked up by the doctor himself in the not infrequent trips on which he was sent, ostensibly for pleasure, but with a keen eye also to the collection of intelligence. Marked externally by the abstraction of a book-worm, entirely unpractical and heedless in the common affairs of life, and subject to an occasional flightiness of action, the result in part of an injury to his head while in the service, Scott gave those who saw him going about an impression of guilelessness, which covered him from the suspicion of having a mission. He had, says his biographer, " in union with a capacity for very difficult services, a simplicity that often put him at disadvantage in worldly matters, and it became a common joke with the Admiral, that ' the doctor would always want somebody to take care of him.' "

Nelson had everything read to him; first of all, newspapers, which were sent regularly to the fleet by British agents in various quarters. Upon them chiefly, and not upon England, he depended for knowledge of what was happening; in Great Britain itself, as well as on the Continent. From ten to twelve weeks was no uncommon length of time for him to be without word from home. " I never hear from England," he wrote to Elliot in the summer of 1804, " but as we manage to get the Paris papers regularly through Spain. From ten days to a fortnight we get them from their date at Paris : therefore we know the very great events which are passing in Europe — at least as much as the French people; " a shrewd limitation. These, therefore, together with Spanish, Italian, and other sheets, it was Scott's daily task to read aloud to his chief, who found therein not only information but amusement. He insisted also upon hearing the numerous ephemeral pamphlets, of which the age was prolific, and which found their way to him. His quickness in detecting the drift of an author was marvellous. Two or three pages of a pamphlet were generally sufficient to put him in complete possession of the writer's object, while nothing was too trivial for his attention where there existed a possibility of its contributing a clue to the problems of his command. Not the least onerous of the doctor's duties was the deciphering of private letters found in prizes, a channel by which important public interests are often betrayed. Nelson's quickness to see the bearing and value of an apparently trifling mention, dropped by the way by a careless pen, rendered such an exercise of his ingenuity at once a pleasure and a profit. The public secretary, Mr. Scott, was equally struck with the alertness and sagacity of his employer's mind. " I have heard much of Lord Nelson's abilities as an officer and statesman, but the account of the latter is infinitely short. In my travels through the service I have met with no character in any degree equal to his Lordship; his penetration is quick, judgment clear, wisdom great, and his decisions correct and decided : nor does he in company appear to bear any weight on his mind." It was with difficulty, after a prolonged session, that the doctor could at times beg off, and leave, stuffed in the arm-chair pockets, for another day's work, a dozen or two of such letters, sealed to Nelson by his imperfect eyesight and inadequate mastery of other tongues. The arm-chairs, lashed together, formed at times a couch upon which the admiral " slept those brief slumbers for which he was remarkable;" in those moments, doubtless, when anxiety about the enemy's movements did not permit him to go regularly to bed.

In common with all those closely associated with Nelson, Dr. Scott was particularly struck with the kindliness and cordiality of his bearing and actions ; which is the more to be noted, because no one, probably, had more occasion to see the movements of irritability, of impatience, which lay very near the surface, than did his secretaries, through whom his most vexatious work must be done. That he was vehement to express annoyance has appeared frequently in these pages. The first Lord Radstock, who was senior to him in the service, and knew him well, writing to his son, then a midshipman in the " Victory," is constant and extreme in his admiration of Nelson; but he gives the caution to be careful of impressions made upon a chief upon whom advancement depends. Quick in all his ways, a moment's heedlessness, possibly misunderstood or misrepresented, may produce lasting injury. "Lord Nelson is of so hasty a temper, that in spite of all his natural goodness, I should fear that he would too readily give ear to those in whom he had placed his confidence. He is a man of strong passions, and his prejudices are proportionate." "On many occasions," says another writer, "Lord Nelson evinced an impatience that has been considered as irreconcileable with magnanimity; but the secret workings of his soul have not been received into the account or analysis of character, for we find the same individual, while employed in watching the French fleet off Toulon, display the most unexampled patience and forbearance, and never betray the smallest symptom of inquietude or disappointment." [1] Murray, the Captain of the Fleet, when first offered his appointment, had hesitated to accept. Upon Nelson urging him, he gave as his reason that the nature of the duties often led to disagreements between the admiral and his chief of staff, and that he was unwilling to risk any diminution of the regard existing between him and his Lordship; a remark true enough in the general, but clearly of somewhat special application. Nelson assured him that, should anything go contrary to his wishes, he would waive his rank and explain or expostulate with him as his friend, and when, after two years' service, Murray had to leave the ship, he refused to replace him, — he would have Murray or none. In truth, such readiness to flare up must needs be the defect of that quality of promptness, that instant succession of deed to thought, which was a distinguishing feature of Nelson's genius and actions. Captain Hillyar more than once alludes to this trait as characteristic of the fleet, to which its chief had transmitted his own spirit. "I have had to-day to lament," he says, speaking of some trifling disappointment, "the extreme promptitude with which we all move when near his lordship."

But, while traces of this failing may be detected here and there by the watchful reader, as Nelson himself gleaned useful indications amid the rubbishy mass of captured correspondence, there survives, among the remains left by those in daily contact with him, only the record of a frank, open bear-

[1] Memoir of Sir Thomas Hardy, in Clarke and M'Arthur's Life of Nelson, vol. iii. p. 234.

ing, and unfailing active kindness. "Setting aside his heroism," wrote Dr. Scott after Trafalgar, "when I think what an affectionate, fascinating little fellow he was, how dignified and pure his mind, how kind and condescending his manners, I become stupid with grief for what I have lost." "He is so cheerful and pleasant," wrote the public secretary, Mr. Scott, "that it is a happiness to be about his hand." Dr. Gillespie notes "his noble frankness of manners, freedom from vain formality and pomp (so necessary to the decoration of empty little great men), which can only be equalled by the unexampled glory of his naval career, and the watchful and persevering diligence with which he commands this fleet." "Nelson was the man to *love*," said Captain Pulteney Malcolm, who knew intimately both him and Wellington. "I received Captain Leake," Nelson himself says, speaking of an army officer on a special mission to the Mediterranean, "with that openness which was necessary to make myself as well acquainted with him in three days, as others might do in as many years. I have given him all the knowledge of the men, their views, &c. &c., as far as I have been able to form a judgment." The remark is valuable, for it shows that frankness and cordiality were recognized by him as the wisest and most politic method of dealing with men. "Our friend, Sir Alexander," he says testily, "is a very great diplomatic character, and even an admiral must not know what he is negotiating about. You shall judge, viz., 'The Tunisian envoy is still here, negotiating. He is a moderate man; and, apparently, the best disposed of any I ever did business with.' Could even the oldest diplomatic character be drier? I hate such parade and nonsense."

Captain Hillyar, who commanded one of the frigates that were ever coming and going, writes in his journal: "If extreme kindness and attention could render me happy, I have this day experienced both from our revered and good commander-in-chief. How can I repay his kindness? By obeying his injunctions 'not to be in a hurry to get married,'[1] or by a continued perseverance in discharging those duties with alacrity and honour, which he is more immediately concerned in?" "Lord Nelson talked a great deal against matrimony

---

[1] Hillyar was then engaged to a lady in Malta.

yesterday, and I feel will not trust me at Malta, while we are
capable of remaining at sea. It was all, however, in a good
natured way. He is going to charge me with two of his boys
[midshipmen]. I am pleased that an opportunity is offered
for showing my gratitude in a small degree for his almost
fatherly kindness. I wish you knew him ; if he has failings,
reflections on his virtues cause them to be forgotten, and the
mind dwells with pleasure on a character where bravery, generosity, and good nature, are joined to a heart that can feel for
the woes of others, and delights in endeavouring to alleviate
them." Hillyar was experiencing what Radstock had remarked : "Gain his esteem, and there is nothing he will not
dash through to put you forward." "Gain his esteem, and
you will have nothing to fear, for I know not a more honourable man existing, or one who would more readily do you
justice in all respects." "I am well aware," wrote another
young captain to Nelson himself, " of the good construction
which your Lordship has ever been in the habit of putting on
circumstances, although wearing the most unfavourable appearances. . . . Your Lordship's good opinion constitutes the
summit of my ambition, and the most effective spur to my
endeavours."

Nelson loved to bestow promotion, when deserved, on the
spot, to give a man his spurs, if it might be, on the field of
battle; but vacancies would not always offer at the happy
moment. A brother of Hillyar's was a midshipman in one
of two boats, sent to visit a suspicious vessel. A sudden and
staggering fire killed the lieutenant in command, besides disabling a number of the boats' crews. The men hesitated;
but the lad, left in charge, cheered them on and carried the
vessel by boarding. Although he was but a couple of months
over fifteen, Nelson gave him at once his commission into the
vacancy made by the lieutenant. One very dark night, the
" Victory " being under way, a midshipman, at the imminent
risk of his life, leaped into the sea to save a seaman who had
fallen overboard, and otherwise would have been drowned.
Nelson gave him, too, his commission the following morning ;
but, seeing the jubilation among the young man's messmates,
and thinking the act might be a dangerous precedent, he
leaned over the poop and said, smiling good-naturedly, " Stop,

young gentlemen! Mr. Flin has done a gallant thing to-day, and he has done many gallant things before, for which he has now got his reward. But mind, I'll have no more making lieutenants for men falling overboard."

The power thus to reward at discretion, and speedily, though liable to abuse, was, he claimed, essential to the due influence of a commander-in-chief; his subordinates must feel that it was in his power to make their future, to distinguish them, and that they were in so far dependent upon him. Nevertheless, with him as with others, personal interest had a weight which qualified his argument. The premature [1] and disastrous promotion of his stepson, at his request, by St. Vincent, was a practical abuse which in most minds would outweigh theoretical advantages. Writing to Sir Peter Parker about this time, he said, "You may be assured I will lose no time in making your grandson a post-captain. It is the only opportunity ever offered me, of showing that my feelings of gratitude to you are as warm and alive as when you first took me by the hand: I owe all my honours to you, and I am proud to acknowledge it to all the world." Such enduring gratitude is charming to see, and tends to show that Nelson recognized some other reason for Parker's favor to himself than deference to Suckling's position; but it is scarcely a good working principle for the distribution of official patronage, although the younger Parker was a good and gallant officer.

Among the military duties that weighed upon Nelson, not the least was the protection of British trade. The narrow waters of the Mediterranean favored the operations of privateers, which did not have to go far from their ports, and found shelter everywhere; for the littoral states, in their weakness and insecurity, could but feebly enforce neutrality either in their continental or insular territories. In fact, both parties to the war, Great Britain and France, derived from the infringement of neutrality advantages which checked their remonstrances, and gave the feebler nations an apt retort, when taken to task in their painful efforts to preserve an attitude that was rather double-faced than neutral. If France, on

[1] As Lady Nelson's first marriage was in 1779, Josiah Nisbet could not have been eighteen when made a commander, in 1797.

39

the one hand, was deriving a considerable revenue from Spanish subsidies, and subsisting an army corps upon Neapolitan territory, Great Britain, on the other, could scarcely have maintained her fleet in the Gulf of Lyons, if unable to get fresh provisions and water from neutral ports; for, save Gibraltar and Malta, she had none that was her own or allied. Under these conditions, small privateers, often mere rowboats, but under the colors of France or the Italian Republic, swarmed in every port and inlet; in the Adriatic, — a deep, secluded pocket, particularly favorable to marauding, — in the Ionian Islands, along the Barbary coast, upon the shores of Spain, and especially in Sicily, whose central position and extensive seaboard commanded every trade-route east of the Balearics.

Nelson's correspondence is full of remonstrances addressed to the various neutral states — including even Austria, whose shore-line on the Adriatic was extensive — for their toleration of these abuses, which rested ultimately upon the fear of Bonaparte. He has, also, constant explanations to make to his own Government, or to British ministers at the different Courts, of the acts of his cruisers in destroying the depredators within neutral limits, when found red-handed. He makes no apologies, but stands firmly by his officers, who, when right, could always count upon his support in trouble. He never left a man in the lurch, or damned him with faint approval. " The protection afforded the enemy's privateers and rowboats in the different neutral ports of these seas, so contrary to every known law of neutrality, is extremely destructive of our commerce. . . . Although their conduct is infamous, yet their doing wrong is no rule why we should. There is a general principle which I have laid down for the regulation of the officers' conduct under my command — which is never to break the neutrality of any port or place; but never to consider as neutral any place from whence an attack is allowed to be made. It is certainly justifiable to attack any vessel in a place from whence she makes an attack." " I very fully approve every part of Captain ——'s conduct on the above occasion," he writes to the Admiralty in such a case.

The supplying of convoys, therefore, was ceaseless, for the depredations of the marauders were unending. "I am pulled to pieces by the demands of merchants for convoys," Nelson said; and he recognized that it must be so, for he entirely disapproved of even a fast-sailing vessel attempting to make a passage unprotected. "I wrote to the Admiralty for more cruisers until I was tired," he told Ball, "and they left off answering those parts of my letters. The late Admiralty thought I kept too many to the eastward of Sicily; the Smyrna folks complain of me, so do the Adriatic, so they do between Cape de Gatte and Gibraltar. If I had the vessels, I do assure you not one of them should go prize-hunting: that I never have done, I am a poorer man than the day I was ordered to the Mediterranean command, by upwards of £1,000; but money I despise except as it is useful, and I expect my prize money is embarked in the Toulon fleet." "I am distressed for frigates," was his continual cry. "From Cape St. Vincent to the head of the Adriatic I have only eight; which, with the service of watching Toulon, and the necessary frigates with the fleet, are absolutely not one half enough." For military duties, "frigates are the eyes of a fleet. I want ten more than I have in order to watch that the French should not escape me, and ten sloops besides, to do all duties." For nine stations which ought to be filled, "I have but two frigates; therefore, my dear Ball, have a little mercy, and do not think I have neglected the protection of the trade of Malta." This was written soon after joining the station, and he represents the number as diminishing as time passed. "It is shameful!" he cries in a moment of intense anxiety.

In this fewness of cruisers he was forced to keep his vessels constantly on the go, — to the Levant, to the Adriatic, to Sicily, to Italy, — scouring the coasts for privateers, gathering merchant ships by driblets, picking up information, and at the end of the round returning to Malta with their fractions of the large convoy. When this was assembled, a frigate or a ship-of-the-line, with one or two smaller ships of war, sailed with it for Gibraltar at a date fixed, approximately, months before. Meanwhile, at the latter place a similar process of collection had been going on from the ports of the western Mediterranean, and, after the Malta convoy arrived, the whole started together in charge of a division, composed usually of vessels of war that had to return to England for repairs.

To arrange and maintain this complicated process, and to
dovetail it with the other necessary cruising duties, having in
consideration which ships should first go home, required careful study and long foresight — infinite management, in fact.
" The going on in the routine of a station," he tells Ball, who
seems to have trod on his toes, " if interrupted, is like stopping
a watch — the whole machine gets wrong. If the Maidstone
takes the convoy, and, when Agincourt arrives, there is none
for her or Thisbe, it puzzles me to know what orders to give
them. If they chace the convoy to Gibraltar, the Maidstone
may have gone on with it to England, and in that case, two
ships, unless I begin to give a new arrangement, will either go
home without convoy, or they must return [to Malta] in contradiction to the Admiralty's orders to send them home; I am
sure you see it in its true point of view." "I dare not send a
frigate home without a convoy," he says later. "Not an officer ·
in the service bows with more respect to the orders of the
Admiralty than myself," he writes.St. Vincent; " but I am sure
you will agree with me, that if I form plans for the sending
home our convoys, and the clearing the different parts of the
station from privateers, and the other services requisite, and
that the Admiralty in some respects makes their arrangements,
we must clash." Then he points out how the Admiralty
diverting a ship, unknown to him, has tumbled over a whole
train of services, like a child's row of blocks.

An extremely critical point in the homeward voyage was
the first hundred miles west of Gibraltar; and it was a greater
thorn in Nelson's side, because of a French seventy-four, the
" Aigle," which had succeeded in entering Cadiz just after he
got off Toulon. For the ordinary policing of that locality he
assigned a division of three frigates, under a Captain Gore,
who possessed his confidence. "The enemy's privateers and
cruisers," he tells him, " are particularly destructive to our
trade passing the skirts of the station." Privateering was
thus reduced; but when a convoy sailed, he tried always to
have it accompanied through that stage by a ship of size sufficient to grapple with the " Aigle." For a while, indeed, he
placed there an eighty-gun ship, but the gradual deterioration
of his squadron and the increase of Latouche Tréville's obliged
him to recall her, and at times his anxiety was great; not the

less because Gore, like other frigate captains, entertained the fancy that his three frigates might contend with a ship-of-the-line. "Your intentions of attacking that ship with the small squadron under your command are certainly very laudable; but I do not consider your force by any means equal to it." The question of two or three small ships against one large involves more considerations than number and weight of guns. Unity of direction and thickness of sides — defensive strength, that is — enter into the problem. As Hawke said, "Big ships take a good deal of drubbing." Howe's opinion was the same as Nelson's; and Hardy, Nelson's captain, said, "After what I have seen at Trafalgar, I am satisfied it would be mere folly, and ought never to succeed." [1] What Hardy saw at Trafalgar, however, was not frigates against ships-of-the-line, but vessels of the latter class opposed, smaller against greater.

It seems singular, with such a weak link in the chain of communication from the Mediterranean to England, that the Admiralty, on the outbreak of the war with Spain, in the latter part of 1804, should have divided Nelson's command at this very point, leaving as a somewhat debatable ground, for mutual jealousy, that through which valuable interests must pass, and where they must be transferred. The reason and manner of this division, impolitic and inopportune as it was, and bitterly as Nelson resented it, seem to have been misunderstood. Convinced that he could not endure another winter such as the last, he made a formal application, about the middle of August, 1804, for permission to go home for a while. "I consider the state of my health to be such as to make it absolutely necessary that I should return to England to re-establish it. Another winter such as the last, I feel myself unable to stand against. A few months of quiet may enable me to serve again next spring; and I believe that no officer is more anxious to serve than myself." In accordance with this last intimation, which speaks his whole heart, he wrote privately to the First Lord that he would like to come back in the spring, if his health were restored, as he believed it would be; and he assured him that his second, Bickerton, whose rank did not entitle him to the chief command under ordinary con-

[1] Phillimore's "The Last of Nelson's Captains," p. 146.

ditions, was perfectly fitted to hold it during his absence — in short, to keep the place warm for his return.

Nelson knew that the Admiralty was besieged with admirals, many senior to himself, seeking for employment, and that it would be very difficult for it to resist the pressure for the vacancy in " my favourite command," to resume which he was impelled by both his sense of duty and his love of glory. He wrote therefore to Elliot, and to the King of the Two Sicilies, in the same sense as he had to Melville, recalling his well-tried devotion to the interests of that Court, which a successor might not equally show, and suggesting that his cause would be strengthened by an application for his return on the part of the King. The latter consequently intimated to the British Government that he hoped Lord Nelson would be sent back. He was, in truth, so much agitated over the prospect of his going, that he offered him a house in either Palermo or Naples, if he wished to remain in the South to recruit; an offer which Elliot, equally uneasy, urged him to accept.

The Government did exactly what was asked. Nelson received permission to go to England, when he felt it necessary, leaving the command in the hands of Bickerton; but at the same time the Admiralty had to meet the rush of claimants for the vacancy, all the more pressing because rumors were afloat of a Spanish war, which would make the Mediterranean not only the most important, but, in prize-money, the most lucrative command. Among the applicants was Sir John Orde, who had been nursing a technical grievance ever since he had been passed over, in Nelson's favor, for the command of the detachment with which the Battle of the Nile was fought. Nelson's leave was issued on the 6th of October, and on the 26th Orde was given a small squadron — five ships-of-the-line — to blockade Cadiz. Being senior to Nelson, and of course to Bickerton, he could only have this position by reducing the latter's station, which had extended to Cape Finisterre. The line between the two commands was drawn at the Straits' mouth, a rather vague phrase, but Gibraltar was left with Nelson. Orde thus got the station for prize-money, and Nelson that for honor, which from youth until now he most valued. " The arrangement," wrote his friend, Lord Radstock, " will be a death-stroke to his hopes of the galleons: but as your chief has ever showed himself to be as great a despiser of riches as he is a lover of glory, I am fully convinced in my own mind that he would sooner defeat the French fleet than capture fifty galleons."

Nevertheless, Nelson was sorely aggrieved, and complained bitterly to his correspondents. " I have learnt not to be surprised at anything; but the sending an officer to such a point, to take, if it is a Spanish war, the whole harvest, after all my trials (God knows unprofitable enough ! for I am a much poorer man than when we started in the Amphion,) seems a little hard; but *patienza.*" " He is sent off Cadiz to reap the golden harvest, as Campbell was to reap my sugar harvest. It's very odd, two Admiralties to treat me so : surely I have dreamt that I have ' done the State some service.' But never mind; I am superior to those who could treat me so." His contempt for money, however acquired, except as a secondary consideration, remained unchanged. " I believe I attend more to the French fleet than making captures; but what I have, I can say as old Haddock said, 'it never cost a sailor a tear, nor the nation a farthing.' This thought is far better than prize-money ; — not that I despise money — quite the contrary, I wish I had one hundred thousand pounds this moment." " I am keeping as many frigates as possible round me," he wrote to his friend Ball, "for I know the value of them on the day of battle : and compared with that day, what signifies any prizes they might take ? " [1] Nor did such utterances stand alone. " I hope war with Spain may be avoided," he wrote. " I want not riches at such a dreadful price. Peace for our Country is all I wish to fight for, — I mean, of course, an honourable one, without which it cannot be a secure one." But his outlays were very heavy. Besides the £1,800 annually paid to Lady Nelson, he gave Lady Hamilton £1,200 a year, exclusive of what was spent on the house and grounds at Merton ; and it may be inferred from Dr. Gillespie that the cost of the cabin mess, beyond the table money allowed by the Government, was assumed by him. He himself said, early in the cruise, " Unless we have a Spanish war, I shall live here at a great expense, although Mr. Chevalier [his steward] takes every care."

---

[1] Flag-officers had a share in all prizes taken by vessels of their squadrons.

"God knows, in my own person, I spend as little money as any man; but you[1] know I love to give away."

That he was thus sore was most natural; but it was also natural that the Government should expect, in view of his strong representations about his health, that the three weeks between the issuing his leave and Orde's orders would have insured his being on his way home, before the latter reached his station. Had things fallen out so, it would not have been Nelson, the exceptional hero of exceptional services, but Bickerton, a man with no peculiar claims as yet, who would have lost the prize-money; for Nelson himself had just won a suit against St. Vincent, which established that the moment a commander-in-chief left his station, his right lapsed and that of the next flag-officer commenced. Nor was the division of the station an unprecedented measure. It had been extended from the Straits to Cape Finisterre at the time St. Vincent withdrew from the Mediterranean, in 1796; and in 1802, when Lord Keith asked for additional aids, on account of the enormous administrative work, the Admiralty made of the request a pretext for restricting his field to the Mediterranean, a step which Keith successfully resisted.

Before Nelson received his leave he had begun to change his mind about going home. This was due, partly, to a slight betterment in his health, which he at this time mentions; chiefly, it would seem, to the prospects of a Spanish war. This, by doubling the number of his enemies and the quarters whence they might come, contributed to the pleasurable excitement that was always a tonic to his physical frame, and roused the eager desire for conspicuous action, which was his most prominent passion. Indications also assured him that the expectation of the French coming out, in which appearances had so often deceived him, was now on the point of being realized; that Bonaparte's projects, whatever they were, were approaching maturity. His "guess," founded on the reports before him, was wonderfully penetrative. He did not see all the way through the French mill-stone, but he saw very deep into it; his inference, indeed, was one in which intuition and sagacity bore equal shares. "If the Russians continue increasing their naval force in this country [that is,

[1] Davison.

in the eastern Mediterranean], I do not think the French
will venture to the eastward;—therefore, I rather expect they
will, as the year advances, try to get out of the straits; and
should they accomplish it with 7,000 troops on board, I am
sure we should lose half our West India Islands, for I think
they would go there, and not to Ireland. Whatever may be
their destination, I shall certainly follow, be it even to the
East Indies." The last allusion is interesting, for it shows
the wide flight of his speculations, which had found utterance
before in the casual remark that his ships were provisioned
for a voyage to Madras; and, even as a guess, it struck
perilously near one of Bonaparte's purposes. The splendid
decision, formulated so long before the case arose, to follow
wherever they went, held in its womb the germ of the great
campaign of Trafalgar; while in the surmise that the Toulon
fleet was bound to the West Indies, the arrow of conjecture
had gone straight to the bull's-eye.

In this same letter, addressed to General Villettes, at
Malta, formerly his coadjutor at the siege of Bastia, Nelson,
in the intimacy of friendship, reveals what was to him at
once the secret of health and the fulfilment of desire; the
congenial atmosphere in which his being throve, and expanded
to fulfil the limits of his genius. " Such a pursuit would do
more, perhaps, towards restoring me to health than all the
doctors; but I fear" (his application for leave having gone in)
" this is reserved for some happier man. Not that I complain; I have had a good race of glory, but we are never
satisfied, although I hope I am duly thankful for the past;
but one cannot help, being at sea, longing for a little more."
" I hope," he had written a few months earlier to Lord Minto,
" some day, very soon, to fulfil the warmest wishes of my
Country and expectations of my friends. I hope you may be
able, at some debate, to say, as your partiality has said before, 'Nelson has done more than he has done before;' I can
assure you it shall be a stimulus to my exertion on the day of
battle. . . . Whatever happens, I have run a glorious race."

On the 12th of October Nelson received a piece of news
which elicited instantaneously a flash of action, illustrative
at once of the promptness of his decisions and of the brisk-
ness of temper that has been noted already. A letter arrived

from Captain Gore, commanding the detachment outside of the Straits, that two frigates, sent from the Brest squadron by Admiral Cornwallis, had arrived, with a captain senior to himself, who had taken him under his orders, and carried two of Nelson's frigates off Cadiz to intercept the Spanish treasure-fleet expected there from America. Cornwallis's action had been taken by orders from England, but no communication to that effect, either from him or from the Admiralty, reached Nelson at this moment. Astounded by a measure which could scarcely fail to cause war, and convinced, as he said, that Spain had no wish to go to war with Great Britain, he gave himself a night to pause; but early next day he wrote to the Admiralty, intimating pretty plainly that, if done by its direction, this was not the way the commander of the Mediterranean fleet should receive word of so momentous a step taken in his district, while to Gore he sent emphatic orders to disobey Cornwallis, although the latter was Nelson's senior. Summing up with admirable lucidity the facts before him, and thereby proving that the impression under which Cornwallis's action probably was taken was erroneous, he said: "Unless you have much weightier reasons than the order of Admiral Cornwallis, or that you receive orders from the Admiralty, it is my most positive directions that neither you, or any ship under your orders, do molest or interrupt in any manner the lawful commerce of Spain, with whom we are at perfect peace and amity."

It is permissible, because instructive, to note that in this order, while Nelson amply provides for discretion on the part of his subordinate, he throws the full weight of his authority on the difficult horn of a possible dilemma, the act — so momentous to an officer — of disobedience to a present superior; in this case the captain sent by Cornwallis. Contrast this with the Government's orders to the commander of the troops at Malta, when it wished him to send a garrison to Messina.[1] Instead of saying, "You will send so many men, *unless* you think you *cannot* spare them," its orders ran: "You will send, *if* you think you *can* spare them." Of course, as Nelson invariably experienced, an officer addressed in the latter style found always a lion in his path. So his orders to Gore

[1] *Ante*, p. 568.

were not " Obey, *if,*" but " Disobey, *unless ;* " and Gore knew, as every man in the Mediterranean knew by long trial, that, if he disobeyed, he would have at his back, through thick and thin, the first sea-officer in Great Britain. But Nelson's orders were always stamped with the positive, daring, lucid character of his genius and its conceptions ; and so, except in unworthy hands, they were fulfilled in spirit as well as in letter.

An interesting illustration of this trenchant clearness is to be found in instructions given to the captain of the " Donegal," an eighty-gun ship, sent under very critical circumstances to cruise off Cadiz, in September, 1803. It appears to the author not only characteristic of Nelson, but a perfect example of the kind of directions a junior would wish to have in a difficult case, when desirous to carry out the spirit of his superior's orders. It explains itself.

26th September, 1803.

To CAPTAIN SIR RICHARD JOHN STRACHAN, BART.,
H. M. SHIP DONEGAL.

The occurrences which pass every day in Spain forbode, I fancy, a speedy War with England ; therefore it becomes proper for me to put you on your guard, and advise you how to act under particular circumstances. By looking at the former line of conduct on the part of Spain, which she followed just before the commencement of the last War, we may naturally expect the same events to happen. The French Admiral Richery was in Cadiz, blocked up by Admiral Man ; on August the 22nd, they came to sea, attended by the Spanish Fleet, which saw the French safe beyond St. Vincent, and returned into Cadiz. Admiral Man very properly did not choose to attack Admiral Richery under such an escort. This is a prelude to what I must request your strict attention to; at the same time, I am fully aware that you must be guided, in some measure, by actual circumstances.

I think it very probable, even before Spain breaks with us, that they may send a Ship or two of the Line to see L'Aigle round Cape St. Vincent ; and that if you attack her in their presence, they may attack you; and giving them possession of the Donegal, would be more than either you or I should wish, therefore I am certain it must be very comfortable for you to know my sentiments. From what you hear in Cadiz, you will judge how far you may venture yourself in company with a Spanish Squadron ; but if you are of opinion that you may trust yourself near them, keeping certainly out of gun-shot, send your Boat with a letter to the Spanish Commodore, and desire to know whether he means to defend the French Ships; and get his answer in writing, and have it as plain as possible. If it be 'yes, that he will fire at you if you attack the French under his protection,' then, if you have force enough, make your attack on the whole body, and take them all if you can; for I should consider such an answer as a perfect Declaration of War. If you are too weak for such an attack, you must desist; but you certainly are fully authorized to take the Ships of Spain whenever you meet them. Should the answer be ambiguous, you must then act as your judgment may direct you, and I am sure that will be very proper. Only recollect, that it would be much better to let the French Ships escape, than to run too great a risk of losing the Donegal, yourself, and the Ship's company.

I am, &c.

NELSON AND BRONTE.

This letter fulfils his own request to the Admiralty : " All I wish and submit to their Lordships is, that if the business is left to me, my orders may be decisive."

Later in the same day that Nelson received Gore's letter, the Admiralty's orders arrived, sent, as despatches too often were, by a vessel so small and slow that it would seem they counted upon her insignificance to elude an enemy's notice. The delay served, as has been said, to give proof of the rapidity of Nelson's action; the receipt of the orders enabled him also to show how much clearer were his conceptions of adequacy than those of ordinary men. To stop treasure-ships, or to embargo merchant-ships, when difficulty was threatening, was no new idea to the British Government. The latter had been done with Baltic merchantmen at the time of the Armed Neutrality. In the case of Spain, it was a measure particularly efficacious, for the financial solvency and belligerent capacity of that country depended upon the galleons, which brought to her the tribute of her colonies ; and her relations and dealings with France at this time were so partial and suspicious as to justify precautions. Evidently, however, such a step, being avowedly preventive and not offensive, should be taken in such a way as to avert all chance of possible disaster. Several Spanish frigates being expected, the British Government charged four vessels of the same rate with the task of arresting them. Nelson, the instant he got his orders, detached to the spot an eighty-gun ship, to which he added four other cruisers, thinking, as he said in his orders to the captain selected, that "this is a service of the highest importance, and that an officer of your rank and experience should be employed therein." With such odds against him, the Spanish commander would need no military justification for submission. As it was, he resisted, necessitating a fight, which under the circumstances was barbarous and brutal, and ended in one of the Spanish vessels blowing up with several women on board; a result due wholly to the blundering lack of foresight which sent a corporal's guard to do the work of a sheriff's posse.

This incident, of the order to arrest the treasure-ships, which was made general for all vessels of that class, was probably the determining occasion of Nelson's decision to remain in the Mediterranean. War with Spain, with consequent increased activity on the part of France, though not certain, became probable. There was at that time on board the "Victory" a Dr. Lambton Este, who had gone to the Mediterranean in a civil capacity, and was on his way home. Nelson, hoping to return soon himself, asked Este to remain until he started, and to accompany him in a worn-out seventy-four, the "Superb," which he was holding for that purpose. It seems that, in looking forward to the resumption of his command, he expected it would be the scene of a more widespread political activity, especially in the far East where Este had been employed, and that, for this purpose, he wished to attach the latter to his person. "There may be more occupation there for us all, hereafter, than we just now foresee, or may expect."

In confirmation of this general forecast, we are told by Dr. Scott that, when the admiral left England before Trafalgar, arrangements had been made with the Foreign Office for Este with six clerks to be attached to the flagship, to conduct the diplomatic correspondence. The fact is doubly interesting. It shows, on the one hand, the accuracy of Nelson's foresight as to the vast importance the Mediterranean was about to assume, to meet which he thus was making provision in a general way; although neither he nor any other man could have anticipated the extraordinary, complicated snarl of the political threads in Napoleon's later years. The cares from these, it may be said in passing, were by Nelson's death devolved upon Collingwood; who, though a strong man, was killed by them, through general debility resulting from confinement, and through organic injury produced by bending over his desk. On the other hand, it cannot but be grateful to those who admire the hero, to see that Nelson looked forward to no inglorious ease, but to a life of strenuous work, as well as, if it might be so, of military honor. Had he lived, we may hope, the days after Trafalgar would not have been the grave of his renown.

On the first of November his decision was taken. He sent for Este and said, "Oh, my good fellow! I have abandoned the idea of going to England, at present. I shall not go yet, and when I may go is quite uncertain — must depend upon events, and upon my own precarious health; at the same time, I am doing you an evident injustice, by detaining you here so long in uncertainty." Este of course expressed his willingness to remain while needed, but Nelson interrupted him, saying, "No, *my* wish is that you should go, — I am anxious that you should go, and go without further delay. To tell you the truth, I am not entirely disinterested. Go home; get confirmed in your appointment, according to my desire, and return to me as soon afterwards as you can. Should I retain my command in the Mediterranean, with the powers already conceded to me, I shall require your assistance." It seems probable that he was anxious to get some one home as rapidly as possible, to forestall, if time permitted, a final recall, which the appointment of a successor would be. " Long before this time," he had written Lady Hamilton, "I expect, another admiral is far on his way to supersede me. I should for your sake, and for many of our friends, have liked an odd hundred thousand pounds [by a Spanish war]; but, never mind. If they give me the choice of staying a few months longer, it will be very handsome; and, for the sake of others, we would give up very much of our own felicity."

The despatches and routine papers were got ready rapidly, and placed in charge of Este, who sailed for Lisbon, in a sloop-of-war, on the 6th of November, furnished with orders to all officials to expedite him on his way, and particularly to captains not to communicate with the ship, because the plague, then raging in Gibraltar, would involve her, if visited, in the delays of quarantine. On the 18th of November, off Cape St. Vincent, Este met the "Swiftsure," seventy-four, bringing Orde out. It has been charged that the latter discourteously delayed to notify Nelson of his taking over part of the station.[1] It appears, however, from this encounter, that his letter to that effect, dated the 17th,[2] though headed "off Cadiz," was actually prepared before he reached his position there. It was forwarded to Nelson by the "Anson," whose captain was senior officer of the division till then blockading the port, whom Orde relieved and sent on with his despatch. The "Anson" joined Nelson on the 15th of December. The "Swiftsure," which was also destined to his squadron, did not reach him until the 25th. It seems, therefore, fair to acquit Orde of a discourtesy as aimless as it would be reprehensible.

Just before Este's departure Nelson had reconnoitred Toulon. A new vice-admiral had hoisted his flag in place of Latouche Tréville, who had died on the 20th of August. "He has given me the slip," wrote Nelson, who felt himself balked of his vengeance. "The French papers say he died of walking so often up to the signal-post, upon Sepet, to watch us: I always pronounced that would be his death." His successor was Villeneuve, the predestined victim of Trafalgar. "They now amuse themselves with night-signals," Nelson informed the First Lord; "and by the quantity of rockets and blue lights they show with every signal, they plainly mark their position. These gentlemen must soon be so perfect in theory, that they will come to sea to put their knowledge into practice. Could I see that day, it would make me happy." The time was now not far distant. The weariness of waiting was soon to give way to the anxious fever of doubtful and protracted pursuit, of prolonged uncertainty and steadfast endurance, through which he advanced to his final triumph, just as he had to those of the past.

The seizure of the Spanish treasure-ships, with its lamentable catastrophe, took place on the 5th of October. Nelson had the news on the 8th of November, which, extraordinary as it may appear, was before the fact was known in Madrid. On the 10th of November, when the British minister received his passports upon his own demand, no word had reached there.

[1] Pettigrew, vol. ii. p. 444.   [2] Nicolas, vol. vi. p. 288.

On the 15th, Nelson was informed that a British vessel had been fired upon by the batteries of Barcelona, which was an error; but receiving at the same time a letter from the minister, probably to the effect that he would break off relations on the 10th, he inferred that war existed, and issued orders for a general seizure of Spanish vessels of war and commerce throughout the station. This was done on his own responsibility, but he guarded himself by stringent provisions against any injury beyond detention being inflicted; and he alleged, very reasonably, that a commander-in-chief who never got letters from home less than two months old must act upon his own motion. "I am completely in the dark. It is now more than two months since the John Bull [the last despatch boat] sailed." "I have set the whole Mediterranean to work," he tells Lady Hamilton on the 23d; "and if I had had the spare troops at Malta at my disposal, Minorca would at this moment have had English colours flying." A Swedish ship, carrying a Spanish regiment from Barcelona to the latter island, was among the first captures.

"With respect to my making war upon Spain, and Sir John Orde not having done it," so he wrote to Elliot, "I believe you will think I have acted not precipitately, but consistent with the firmness of John Bull. I can't tell what schemes ministers may have; but when I am without orders, and unexpected occurrences arise, I shall always act as I think the honour and glory of my King and Country demand. Upon the most mature and serious consideration I can give the subject, the present lays within the compass of a nutshell. Our Ministers demand certain points to be conceded to them; they, to give a spur, detain the Spanish treasure. Spain, the moment she hears of it, kicks your minister out of Madrid; a plain proof they had not acceded to our propositions. Indeed, Mr. Frere,[1] you will see by his letter, did not believe it would have a favourable termination, even had not the frigates been detained. I send your Excellency his letters. I feel I have done perfectly right. No desire of wealth could influence my conduct; for I had nothing to take worth two-pence to me. Sir John Orde was sent, if it was a Spanish war, to take the money; but until he saw my orders, he did not act. I sup-

[1] Late British minister to Spain.

pose he was fearful of that responsibility which I am ever ready to take upon me; and now he is to wallow in wealth, whilst I am left a beggar. But such things are. I receive the kindest letters from Lord Melville and the Secretary of State, but they think the French fleet is prize enough for me." No wonder Nelson found that diplomatists were slow, measured by himself as a standard; but what a wonderful instinct it shows in him, that, with action ever prompt to the verge of precipitancy, he made so few blunders in deed. There are several errors of fact in his summary of reasons, but his action was absolutely well-timed — to the very hour.

Meanwhile, and up to the 15th of December, when Orde's letter was received, no reply had come to his application for leave, and no intimation of a successor. A fresh complication here arose by the entire break-down of one of his two junior admirals — Rear-Admiral Campbell — whose health became so affected that it was necessary to send him immediately home. He quitted the fleet on the 4th of December. Nelson rightly felt that he himself could not go, leaving Bickerton without any assistant. He went further; for, when a rumor came that Orde was to relieve him, he determined that he would offer his services to him, as second, until a successor to Campbell should arrive. As there was friction between himself and Orde, who had, besides, a not very pleasant official reputation, this intention, to take a lower place where he had been chief, was not only self-sacrificing, but extremely magnanimous; it was, however, disfigured by too much self-consciousness. " I have wrote to Lord Melville that I should make such an offer, and that I entreated him to send out a flag-officer as soon as possible, but I dare say Sir John Orde is too great a man to want my poor services, and that he will reject them; be that as it may, you will, I am sure, agree with me, that I shall show my superiority to him by such an offer, and the world will see what a sacrifice I am ready to make for the service of my King and Country, for what greater sacrifice could I make, than serving for a moment under Sir John Orde, and giving up for that moment the society of all I hold most dear in this world ? "

Orde's letter reached Nelson in Pula Roads, in the Gulf of Cagliari, at the southern extremity of Sardinia; an out-of-the-way position which probably accounts for much of its delay. He remained there, or in the Gulf of Palmas, a little to the westward, for about a week, and on the 19th of December left for his station off Cape San Sebastian. At the latter place, on Christmas Day, he was joined by the "Swiftsure," which brought him a great batch of official mail that had come out with Orde. He thus received at one and the same time his leave to go home and the Admiralty's order reducing his station. Unluckily, the latter step, though taken much later than the issuing of his leave, had become known to him first, through Orde; and the impression upon his mind remained with that firmness of prejudice which Radstock had noted in him. He does not appear at any time to have made allowance for the fact that his command was cut down under a reasonable impression that he was about to quit it.

Immediately after the "Swiftsure" joined at Rendezvous 97, he took the fleet off Toulon. The enemy was found to be still in port, but the rumors of an approaching movement, and of the embarkation of troops, were becoming more specific. He remained off the harbor for at least a week, and thence went to Madalena, where he anchored on the 11th of January, 1805. This was, though he knew it not, the end of the long watch off Toulon.

Short as the time was, Nelson had already experienced the inconvenience of a senior admiral, lying, like an enemy, on the flank of his communications with Great Britain, and dealing as he pleased with his vessels. One frigate at least had been sent already to England, without his knowledge and consent. "I have in a former letter," he tells the First Lord, "stated my opinion freely upon the stations of Gibraltar and Cadiz being given to the same officer; for without that is done, our convoys can never be considered safe. There is also another consideration, why the Officer at Gibraltar should be under the orders of the Admiral commanding the Mediterranean fleet — which is, that any admiral independent of that station, takes all the stores he chooses, or fancies he wants, for the service of his fleet; thereby placing the fleet in the Gulf of Lyons in great distress for many articles."

Off Toulon, having a large official mail to make up in reply to that brought by the "Swiftsure," he thought it both quicker and safer, under all the conditions of the time, to send it to Lisbon. He therefore called on board the "Victory" a smart young frigate-captain, William Parker, a nephew of Lord St. Vincent, gave him orders to take the despatches to Lisbon, and added, "Sir John Orde takes my frigates from me, and sends them away in some other direction from what I wish. I cannot even get my despatches home. You must contrive to get to the westward and go into Lisbon, and avoid his ships. I have not signed your orders," alluding to memorandum instructions separate from the formal orders, "because Sir John Orde is my senior officer; but, if it should come to a Court Martial, Hardy can swear to my handwriting, and you shall not be broke. Take your orders, and good bye; and remember, Parker, if you cannot weather *that fellow*, I shall think you have not a drop of your old uncle's blood in your veins." The memorandum directed him to pass Cape Spartel in the night, steering to the southward and westward to avoid Orde, and ended thus: "Bring-to [stop] for nothing, if you can help it. Hoist the signal for quarantine, and that you are charged with despatches. If you are forced to speak by a superior officer, show him only my order for not interfering with you; and unless he is an admiral, superior to me, you will obey my orders instead of any pretended ones from him, from my superior officer."

Parker executed his commission successfully, but in doing so met with a curious adventure. Leaving Gibraltar with a north wind, favorable for his purpose, he passed Spartel as directed, and, the night being moonlight, saw in the distance Orde's squadron cruising under easy sail. Unluckily, one of the outlying lookout frigates discovered him, gave chase, and overtook him. Her captain himself came on board, and was about to give Parker orders not to proceed to the westward, Orde jealously objecting to any apparent intrusion upon his domain. Parker stopped him hastily from speaking on the quarter-deck, within earshot of others, and took him into the cabin. The stranger had been one of Nelson's old midshipmen and a favorite; had started with him in the "Agamemnon," and by him had been made a commander after the Nile. "Captain Hoste," said Parker, "I believe you owe all your advancement in the service to my uncle, Lord St. Vincent, and to Lord Nelson. I am avoiding Sir John Orde's squadron by desire of Lord Nelson; you know his handwriting; *I must go on.*" [1] (Parker being senior to Hoste, the latter could not detain him by his own authority; and he understood from this avowal that Orde's orders, if produced, would become a matter of record, would be disobeyed, and a court-martial must follow.) "The question of a court-martial would be very mischievous. Do you not think it would be better if you were not to meet the 'Amazon' this night?" Captain Hoste, after a little reflection, left the ship without giving his admiral's orders to Parker. [2]

Having determined not to leave Bickerton alone, Nelson decided to keep secret his own leave to return to England. "I am much obliged by their Lordships' kind compliance with my request, which is absolutely necessary from the present state of my health," he writes on the 30th of December; "and I shall avail myself of their Lordships' permission, the moment another admiral, in the room of Admiral Campbell, joins the fleet, unless the enemy's fleet should be at sea, when I should not think of quitting my command until after the battle." "I shall never quit my post," he tells a friend, "when the French fleet is at sea, as a commander-in-chief of great celebrity once did," — a not very generous fling at St. Vincent. "I would sooner die at my post, than have such a stigma upon my memory." "Nothing has kept me here," he writes Elliot, "but the fear for the escape of the French fleet, and that they should get to either Naples or Sicily in the short days. Nothing but gratitude to those good Sovereigns could have induced me to stay one moment after Sir John Orde's extraordinary command, for his general conduct towards me is not such as I had a right to expect."

During this last month of monotonous routine, while off Toulon and at Madalena, he had occasion to express opinions on current general topics, which found little room in his mind after the French fleet began to move. There was then a report of a large expedition for foreign service forming in

---

[1] Author's italics.

[2] The whole of this account is taken from the Life of Sir William Parker. Phillimore's Last of Nelson's Captains, pp. 125–129.

England, and rumor, as usual, had a thousand tongues as to its destination. "A blow struck in Europe," Nelson wrote to Lord Moira, "would do more towards making us respected, and of course facilitate a peace, than the possession of Mexico or Peru," — a direction towards which the commercial ambitions of Great Britain had a traditional inclination, fostered by some military men and statesmen, who foresaw the break-up of the Spanish colonial system. "Above all, I hope we shall have no buccaneering expeditions. Such services fritter away our troops and ships, when they are so much wanted for more important occasions, and are of no use beyond enriching a few individuals. I know not, if these sentiments coincide with yours; but as glory, and not money, has through life been your pursuit, I should rather think that you will agree with me, that in Europe, and not abroad, is the place for us to strike a blow." "I like the idea of English troops getting into the Kingdom of Naples," he tells Elliot at this same time ; whence it may be inferred that that was the quarter he would now, as upon his first arrival, choose for British effort. "If they are well commanded, I am sure they will do well. They will have more wants than us sailors." The expedition, which sailed the following spring, was destined for the Mediterranean, and reinforced the garrisons of Gibraltar and Malta to an extent that made the latter a factor to be considered in the strategy of the inland sea; but when it arrived, Nelson had left the Mediterranean, not to return.

As regards general politics, Nelson, writing to the Queen of Naples, took a gloomy view of the future. The Prime Minister of the Two Sicilies, Sir John Acton, had some time before been forced out of office and had retired to Palermo, an event produced by the pressure of French influence, which Nelson regarded now as absolutely dominant in that kingdom, and menacing to Europe at large. "Never, perhaps, was Europe more critically situated than at this moment, and never was the probability of universal Monarchy more nearly being realized, than in the person of the Corsican. I can see but little difference between the name of Emperor, King, or Prefect, if they perfectly obey his despotic orders. Prussia is trying to be destroyed last — Spain is little better than a province of France — Russia does nothing on the grand scale.

Would to God these great Powers reflected, that the boldest measures are the safest! They allow small states to fall, and to serve the enormous power of France, without appearing to reflect that every kingdom which is annexed to France, makes their own existence, as independent states, more precarious." How shrewd a prophecy this was as regards Prussia and Spain, those two countries were to learn by bitter experience; and remote Russia herself, though she escaped the last humiliation, saw in the gigantic hosts whose onset a few years later shook her to her centre, the armed subjects of the many smaller states, in whose subjugation she had acquiesced during the period of the Czar's moral subservience to Napoleon.

Nelson's essentially military genius had in political matters a keenly sensitive intuition of the probable action of his fellow-warrior, Bonaparte. "Russia's going to war in the way I am sure she will, will cause the loss of Naples and Sardinia; for that Court will not send 100,000 men into Italy, and less are useless for any grand purpose." "Your Excellency's summary account of the situation of Naples since the negotiations with Russia," he wrote to Elliot in October, "are perfectly clear; but the times are such that kingdoms must not be played with. So far from Russia assisting Naples, it may involve her, without the greatest care and circumspection, in total ruin. Naples must not be hastily involved in war with France. Sicily must be saved. The Calabrians must be kept from the entrance of French troops. If we are consulted, we must assist Naples in keeping off the blow as long as possible." That Napoleon's action would have been as here surmised, had his purposes then tended towards the Mediterranean instead of the English Channel, we have his own assertion. "At the solicitation of your ambassador at St. Petersburg," wrote he to the Queen of Naples, three months later, referring to the same subject, "ten thousand Russians have been sent to Corfu. . . . If it had entered into my plans to make war upon the King of Naples, I should have done it on the entrance of the first Russian in Corfu, but I wish for peace with Naples, with Europe entire, with England even." Napoleon's wishes for peace, except on the condition of having his own way, are scarcely to be taken seriously; but his care to keep things quiet in the South corroborates the other indications of his firm purpose to invade England. He was too astute to precipitate troubles elsewhere while that was pending. The appearance of the Russians in Corfu, although unwise in Nelson's view, relieved his fears for the islands and the Morea, and enabled him to reduce a little his detachment about the heel of Italy.

Towards the middle of December Nelson had received information, which was substantially correct, "from various places, and amongst others, from the King of Sardinia [then in Gaeta], that the French were assembling troops near Toulon, and had taken some of the best troops and a corps of cavalry from the Riviera of Genoa. Every seaman was pressed and sent to Toulon. On the 16th the Active spoke a vessel from Marseilles, who reported that seven thousand troops had embarked on board the French fleet."

It was in Madalena Roads that the long-expected summons came at last. In the afternoon of January 19, 1805, blowing a heavy gale of wind from the northwest, the two lookout frigates from off Toulon came in sight, with the signal flying that the French fleet was at sea. At 3 P. M. they anchored near the "Victory." Three hours later Nelson had left Madalena forever.

CHAPTER XX.

JANUARY–AUGUST, 1805. AGE, 46.

TO understand rightly the movements of Nelson during the
first months of 1805, up to his return to England in
August, and to appreciate fully the influence of this closing
period of his career upon the plans and fortunes of Napoleon,
it is necessary to state briefly the projects of the latter, as
formulated in his correspondence.

The great object of the Emperor was to invade England,
crossing the Channel with the army, 150,000 strong, which
for two years past he had been assembling and drilling in
the neighborhood of Boulogne. To this end all his plans
were subsidiary — to it all movements at this moment were
intended to conduce. He had no illusions as to the difficulties
of the enterprise; he recognized fully that the odds were
against success, but he had too often achieved the apparently
impossible to permit the word to stop him in an attempt,
which, if accomplished, would cause all other obstacles to
disappear from his path of conquest. There were chances
in his favor. Warily and steadfastly he advanced, step by
step, determined to take no risk that could by the utmost
care be changed into security, but equally resolved to dare
the hazard, if by the military movements set in action by
his unsurpassed genius, he could for a moment obtain the
particular combination which would, to use his own phrase,
make him master of the world. What if the soldiers of the
Grand Army never returned from England ? There were
still in France men enough, as good as they were before his
energizing spirit wrought them into the force which in its
might trod the Continent under foot. Like Nelson dying at
Trafalgar, it too would have laid down its life, leaving its

work finished. Neither man nor army could have a prouder memorial.

The particular combination upon which Napoleon was willing to stake everything was a naval control of the Straits of Dover for a very few days, coincident with the presence there of an army ready and equipped to cross at once. The latter condition was merely a question of preparation — long, tedious, and expensive, but perfectly feasible. In the early months of 1805 it was realized. The army, a substantial, absolute fact, was there, awaiting only the throwing of the bridge. The naval part of the problem was far more difficult. In the face of the naval supremacy of Great Britain, the sought-for control could only be casual and transient — a fleeting opportunity to be seized, utilized, and so to disappear. Its realization must be effected by stratagem, by successful deception and evasion. The coveted superiority would be not actual, but local, — the French fleet in force there, the British fleet, though the greater in force, elsewhere; the weight of the former concentrated at one point by simultaneous movements of its different detachments, which movements had been so calculated and directed that they had misled the British divisions, and, of themselves, diverted them from the decisive centre. Subsidiary to this main effort, Napoleon also contemplated a simultaneous landing of some twenty thousand men in Ireland, which, like the naval movements, would distract and tend to divide the unity of the British resistance. The British admirals considered this project to be easier than the invasion of Great Britain, and it engaged their much more serious attention.

There were three principal French detachments to be united, — in Brest twenty ships, in Toulon ten, in Rochefort five. To these the outbreak of the war between Great Britain and Spain added the forces of the latter kingdom, in Ferrol and Cadiz, aggregating fifteen serviceable ships ; but this was not until March, 1805. Of the three French contingents, the one from Rochefort was small ; and, as a factor, although important, it was not essential. Its failure might weaken or impede the progress of the general movement, without entirely destroying it ; but it was of necessity that the Toulon and Brest divisions both should fulfil their missions, accurately and on time, if the great combination, of which they were parts, was to advance to a triumphant conclusion. This emphasized to the British the importance, which Nelson always so keenly felt, of meeting the enemy immediately after they left port. Once away, and their destination in doubt, the chances in favor of any scheme were multiplied. In their greatest and final effort, Cornwallis, off Brest, was fortunate, in that the plans of the Emperor first, and afterwards unusual weather conditions, retained the French fleet there in harbor; a result to which the material efficiency of his own ships, and their nearness to their base, much contributed.

Upon Nelson, with his crazy ships, on the other hand, fell the burden of counteracting a successful evasion of the Toulon fleet, of foiling, by sagacious and untiring pursuit through immense and protracted discouragements, the efforts of the one division which had been committed to his watch. Although it became much superior to his own force, he drove it out of the position in the West Indies first appointed for the meeting, followed it back to Europe, arrived before it, and then, finding it had gone to Ferrol, carried his squadron, without orders, counselled simply by his own genius, to the aid of Cornwallis; by which act the British navy, to the number of thirty-five ships-of-the-line, was massed in a central position, separating the two enemy's bodies, and able to act decisively against a foe approaching from either direction. Thus a second time he prevented the enemy from forming a junction, unless they fought for it — an alternative Napoleon wished to avoid. To him fell all the strain of uncertainty, all the doubtful and complicated mental effort, all the active strategic movement, of the campaign, and to him consequently has been attributed justly the greater meed of glory; though care must be taken not to ignore or undervalue the well-played parts of other admirals, which were essential to the success of the great defensive campaign comprehended under the name Trafalgar.

The point selected by the Emperor for the meeting of his naval divisions, in both the unsuccessful attempts made in 1805, was the West Indies. There was the most powerful foreign arsenal, Martinique, left in the hands of France, and there the greatest single interest of the widespread commerce upon which depended the life of Great Britain. The latter, therefore, was specially sensitive to anything threatening the safety of the West India Islands. "I should think the West Indies the more likely place for the French to succeed in," wrote Nelson to Ball, on the 6th of September, 1804. " Suppose the Toulon fleet escapes, and gets out of the Straits, I rather think I should bend my course to the westward; for if they carry 7,000 men — with what they have at Martinico and Guadaloupe — St. Lucia, Grenada, St. Vincent, Antigua, and St. Kitts would fall, and, in that case, England would be so clamorous for peace that we should humble ourselves." This is a noteworthy passage, for it shows great sagacity of prediction, and, in announcing beforehand his resolve, — of which this is not the sole previous mention, — it dispels entirely the idea that he was decoyed to the West Indies. It explains, also, the remarkable outburst of gratitude that hailed him on his return from a chase which had been wholly unsuccessful as regards his own chief object — the annihilation of the French fleet. He had failed to find it, but he had driven the enemy out of the West Indies before they could do any serious injury to the vital interests of the country. A man cannot be said to be decoyed, because, in pursuance of a judgment deliberately formed beforehand, he does the thing which the moment demands; unless it can be shown that he has thereby uncovered greater interests. This Nelson did not do. He saved the West Indies, and returned in time to protect Great Britain and Ireland from invasion.

It is through the perplexities of this momentous period that we have now to follow him, and we shall do so to most advantage by taking as our clue his own avowed primary motive of action, the finding and destroying of the French fleet. A man dealing with Napoleon was bound to meet perplexities innumerable, to thread a winding and devious track, branching out often into false trails that led nowhere, and confused by cross-lights which glittered only to mislead. In such a case, as in the doubtful paths of common life, the only sure guide to a man's feet is principle; and Nelson's principle was the destruction of the French fleet. No other interest, his own least of all, could divert him from it. For it he was willing not only to sacrifice fortune, but to risk renown; and so, amid troubles manifold, he walked steadfastly in the light of the single eye.

While Napoleon's object remained the same throughout, his methods received various modifications, as all plans must do when circumstances change. In his original intention the execution of the main effort was intrusted to Latouche Tréville, by far and away the best admiral he had. Upon his death, the Toulon fleet was committed to Villeneuve. Its sailing was to take place as nearly as possible at the same time as that of the Rochefort division. They were to go to the West Indies, proceed at once, independently, to offensive operations, then to unite and return together to Rochefort. Napoleon's calculation was that the British, impressed by this simultaneous departure, and uncertain about the enemy's purpose, must send at once thirty ships-of-the-line in pursuit, in order to secure all the different quarters they would think endangered. This diversion, if realized, would facilitate the operations of the Brest fleet, which was to land an army corps in Ireland, and then to cover the crossing of the main body at Boulogne into England; the precise character of its movements depending necessarily upon conditions of wind at the moment of execution.

The Rochefort ships sailed on the 11th of January. For a week before and a week after that date the winds at Toulon hung between northeast and southeast, favorable, therefore, for a voyage to the Straits of Gibraltar; but Villeneuve argued, judiciously, that a fleet intent on evasion only, and to avoid fighting, should move with great speed until lost to sight — that is, should start with a very fresh breeze, the direction of which was of secondary moment. This view of the matter escaped Nelson's attention, and therefore contributed seriously to mislead him in his reasoning as to the enemy's probable object.

On the 17th of January the wind at Toulon shifted to north-northwest, with signs of an approaching gale, such as the Gulf of Lyons is noted for. The next morning Villeneuve sent a division to drive away Nelson's lookouts. This duty was imperfectly performed. It should have been done by a frigate squadron strong enough to force them out of sight of the main body, and having orders to rejoin the latter at a distant rendezvous. As it was, the British frigates did not lose touch of the hostile fleet, which sailed that evening. They dogged it late into the night, going at times thirteen knots before the blast of the storm, in order to keep clear of the enemy; and at two in the morning of January 19th, being then in the latitude of Ajaccio, satisfied that the French were steering steadily south-southwest, and under a press of sail, which indicated a mission of importance, they parted company and hastened to Nelson, whom they joined twelve hours later, as already stated.

Nelson needed no time to deliberate. His mind was long before fixed to follow, and there was but one way to do so. The enemy's course, as reported, led to the southern end of Sardinia, after reaching which the wind was fair for Naples, Sicily, and the East. The British ships were moored — two anchors down. At half-past four they were under way, standing in single column for the narrow passage between Biche and Sardinia, the "Victory" leading, each vessel steering by the stern lights of the one ahead of her. At seven P. M. all were clear, and the fleet hauled up along the east coast of Sardinia, which made a lee for them. "At midnight," Nelson notes in his journal, "moderate breezes and clear." During the same hours the untrained squadron of Villeneuve was losing topmasts in the fury of the gale.

The following afternoon,[1] as the British drew out from under the lee of Sardinia, they found the wind blowing a hard gale from south-southwest, which lasted all that night. The fleet could make no way against it, but neither could the French utilize it, unless, which was unlikely, they had got much farther to the southward than Nelson had. When he left Madalena, he had sent a frigate ahead, with orders to round Sardinia by the south and try to get sight or word of the enemy. On the morning of the 22d she rejoined, the fleet having then drifted to fifty miles east of Cape Carbonara, the southeastern point of Sardinia. At 11 A. M. her captain informed Nelson that the afternoon before he had seen a French frigate standing into the Gulf of Cagliari, but, the weather

---

[1] At noon, January 20, "Mount Santo bore N. W., distant six leagues." — "Victory's" Log. Cape Monte Santo is sixty miles north of the southern extremity of Sardinia.

being thick, giving an horizon of only three miles, nothing more had been discovered. The admiral had sent word of the French sailing to Acton at Palermo, and through him to Naples and Malta, Ball being requested to seek for information in every practicable direction. Naples was for the moment safe, as the British squadron stood across any possible road by which the French could approach it.

The gale, hauling gradually to the westward, lasted in its force until the morning of January 25th. During these three days Nelson received no news, but he did much thinking and had made up his mind. The French might be intending to land in Cagliari, to windward of which they had been during these four days that he had been to leeward. With Cagliari, therefore, he must communicate; the Viceroy of Sardinia would know if any landing had been attempted or threatened. If Sardinia was safe, he would next go or send to Palermo for news, and thence push for the Faro of Messina, where he would cover both that important fortress and the approaches to Naples from either side of Sicily. "You will believe my anxiety," he wrote to Acton in Palermo, on the 25th. "I have neither ate, drank, or slept with any comfort since last Sunday" (the 20th). "I am naturally very anxious," he tells Ball, "therefore you must forgive my short letter. We have a dead foul wind and heavy sea. I cannot, for want of frigates, send off this letter." The lack of small cruisers, so often lamented in quieter days, now embarrassed him cruelly. The few he had were dispersed in all directions in search of news, and to communicate with Acton he had to detach one of his fastest ships-of-the-line, the "Leviathan," intending himself to follow her with the fleet to Palermo. At the latter point he could obtain all the intelligence of the common enemy which might have reached any Sicilian port, before he carried out his already formed purpose of chasing to leeward, to the Morea and Egypt. With firm grip, though in agony of mind, he held himself in hand, determined, burning as he was to pursue somewhere, not to yield the advantage of the wind till he had reached a reasonable certainty — as in 1798 — that the circumstances justified it. "I hope," he says to Acton, "that the governor of Augusta [1] will not give up the post to

---

[1] On the east coast of Sicily.

the French fleet; but if he does, I shall go in and attack them; for I consider the destruction of the enemy's fleet of so much consequence, that I would gladly have half of mine burnt to effect their destruction. I am in a fever. God send I may find them!" Throughout the long chase which followed, all, so to say, slept on their arms. On the 11th of March he wrote: "Ever since January 21st we have been prepared for battle: not a bulkhead [1] up in the fleet. Night or day, it is my determination not to lose one moment in attacking them."

On the 26th Nelson communicated with Cagliari, and learned that no landing had been attempted in Sardinia. The same day the frigate "Phœbe" rejoined, with information that a French eighty-gun ship had anchored in Ajaccio on the evening of the 19th, dismasted and crippled. Putting these facts together, and in connection with his own movements, he inferred conclusively that either the French had gone back to Toulon in consequence of injuries, or that they had given him the slip, had got round Sicily, and proceeded to the eastward. The latter was improbable, because the westerly gales, as he had noted, could scarcely have allowed them to weather Maritimo; [2] it was not, however, impossible. A return to Toulon was, antecedently, equally improbable, although it proved to be the alternative adopted by Villeneuve. "Although I knew one of the French ships was crippled, yet I considered the character of Bonaparte; and that the orders given by him, on the banks of the Seine, would not take into consideration winds or weather; nor indeed could the accident of three or four ships alter, *in my opinion*, [3] a destination of importance: therefore such an accident did not weigh in my mind and I went first to the Morea and then to Egypt." This quotation is especially interesting, as it proves how closely Nelson scanned every known element in a problem, even to the temperament of his opponent; and it also shows the substantial agreement in judgment between him and Napoleon. The latter, Thiers writes, "was sensibly displeased

[1] Bulkheads are the light partitions which divide cabins, offices, etc. from the rest of the decks. For battle they are removed to allow freer communication, and to lessen the risk of fire and splinters.

[2] An island twenty miles west of Sicily.

[3] Author's italics.

on hearing of this resultless sortie. ' What is to be done,' he
said, ' with admirals who allow their spirits to sink, and determine to hasten home at the first damage they receive ?   All
the captains ought to have had sealed orders to meet off the
Canary Islands.   The damages should have been repaired *en
route.*   A few topmasts carried away, some casualties in a gale
of wind, were every-day occurrences.   But the great evil of our
Navy is, that the men who command it are unused to all the
risks of command.' "

Still without definite tidings, compelled to act upon his own
inferences — for merely doing nothing was action under such
circumstances — Nelson reasoned that, if the French had
returned, he could not overtake them, and if they had gone
east, he had no time to lose before following.   He fell back
therefore from his windward position to the Straits of Messina,
through which the whole squadron beat on the 31st of January — " a thing unprecedented in nautical history," he wrote
to the Admiralty, " but although the danger from the rapidity
of the current was great, yet so was the object of my pursuit;
and I relied with confidence on the zeal and ability of the fleet
under my command."   The same day, knowing now that
Sicily and Naples were not threatened, he despatched six
cruisers for intelligence, " in all directions from Tunis to
Toulon ; " three of them being frigates, which were to rendezvous off the latter port and resume the watch of the French, if
found there.   A seventh vessel was sent ahead of the squadron
to Koron, off which he appeared on the 2d of February, and,
still getting no news, went on to Alexandria, where he communicated with the British consul on the 7th.   " I beg the
boat may not be detained, nor must any communication be
had with the officer, so as to put the ship in quarantine.   The
officer is ordered not to wait more than thirty minutes ; for
you will readily believe my anxiety to find out the enemy's
fleet."   No news was to be had ; but it was ascertained that
Egypt was practically defenceless against any renewed
attempts of the French.

Nelson at once started back to the westward.   On the 19th
of February, twelve days after leaving Alexandria, he was off
Malta, and there for the first time received information that
the enemy had returned to Toulon in a very crippled state.

It was now necessary to regain his station as speedily as possible, and also to resume the operation of victualling the squadron, which had been interrupted at Madalena by the news of the enemy's sailing. The captain left there in charge of the transports had taken them for safety to Malta, in pursuance of the orders left with him, and they would have to be convoyed again to the Gulf of Palmas, which was appointed for their joining. The incident shows at once the forehandedness of Nelson, in that he was able immediately to go on so long a chase, and also the difficulties attendant upon the administration of the fleet. Against the prevailing winds the convoy did not reach Palmas until the 14th of March. The fleet had preceded it there by a week. After a tedious beat, in which eight days were consumed to make the three hundred and fifty miles to windward, Nelson anchored on the 27th of February in Pula Roads, Gulf of Cagliari, just to hold on. " What weather ! " wrote he to Bickerton, when the anchor dropped. " Did you ever see such in almost any country? It has forced me to anchor here, in order to prevent being drove to leeward, but I shall go to sea the moment it moderates." Palmas is only forty miles to windward of Pula, but it was not till the 8th of March, after three or four ineffectual efforts, that the squadron got there. "From the 19th of February to this day," wrote Nelson to Ball, " have we been beating, and only now going to anchor here as it blows a gale of wind at northwest. It has been without exception, the very worst weather I have ever seen." Bad as it was, it was but a sample of that he was to meet a month later, in the most wearing episode of his anxious life.

Besides the weary struggle with foul winds and weather, other great disappointments and vexations met Nelson at Palmas. During his absence to the eastward, one despatch vessel had been wrecked off Cadiz and fallen into the hands of the Spaniards, another had been intercepted by the battered French fleet as it approached Toulon, and a convoy, homeward-bound from Malta, had been waylaid, the two small ships of war which formed the escort had been taken, and the merchant ships dispersed. This last misfortune he ascribed unhesitatingly to the division of the command. "It would not have happened, could I have ordered the officer off Cadiz to

41

send ships to protect them." The incident was not without
its compensations to one who valued honor above loss, for his
two petty cruisers had honored themselves and him by such a
desperate resistance, before surrendering to superior force, that
the convoy had time to scatter, and most of it escaped.   There
was reason to fear that the despatch vessel taken off Toulon
had mistaken the French fleet for the British, which it had
expected to find outside, and that her commander might have
had to haul down his flag before getting opportunity to throw
the mail-bags overboard.   In that case, both public and private
letters had gone into the enemy's possession.   "I do assure
you, my dearest Emma," he wrote Lady Hamilton, "that
nothing can be more miserable, or unhappy, than your poor
Nelson."   Besides the failure to find the French, "You will
conceive my disappointment !   It is now [1] from November 2nd
that I have had a line from England."

A characteristic letter was elicited from Nelson by the loss
of the despatch-vessel off Cadiz, the brig "Raven," whose
commander, Captain Layman, had gained his cordial professional esteem in the Copenhagen expedition, in connection
with which he has already been mentioned.   As usual in the
case of a wreck, a court-martial was held.   This censured the
captain, much to Nelson's vexation; the more so because, at
his request, Layman had not produced before the court certain
orders for the night given by him, the proved neglect of which
would have brought a very heavy punishment upon the officer of
the watch.   In weighing the admiral's words, therefore, allowance may be made for a sense of personal responsibility for the
finding of the court; but the letter, which was addressed to
the First Lord, contains expressions that are most worthy of
attention, not only because illustrative of Nelson's temperament
and mode of thought, but also for a point of view too rarely
taken in the modern practice, which has grown up in peace.

MY DEAR LORD, — Give me leave to recommend Captain Layman
to your kind protection; for, notwithstanding the Court Martial has
thought him deserving of censure for his running in with the land,
yet, my Lord, allow me to say, that Captain Layman's misfortune
was, perhaps, conceiving other people's abilities were equal to his
own, which, indeed, very few people's are.

[1] March 9th.

I own myself one of those who do not fear the shore, for hardly any great things are done in a small ship by a man that is; therefore, I make very great allowances for him. Indeed, his station was intended never to be from the shore in the straits: and if he did not every day risk his sloop, he would be useless upon that station. Captain Layman has served with me in three ships, and I am well acquainted with his bravery, zeal, judgment, and activity; *nor do I regret the loss of the Raven compared to the value of Captain Layman's services, which are a national loss.*[1]

You must, my dear Lord, forgive the warmth which I express for Captain Layman; but he is in adversity, and, therefore, has the more claim to my attention and regard. If I had been censured every time I have run my ship, or fleets under my command, into great danger, I should long ago have been *out* of the Service, and never *in* the House of Peers.

I am, my dear Lord, most faithfully, your obedient servant,

NELSON AND BRONTE.

It is something to meet with the clear recognition that a man may be of more value than a ship. As Clarendon said, it is not all of an officer's duty to bring his ship safe home again.

On the voyage back from Alexandria he had busied himself with vindications of his course in going there, manifesting again that over-sensitiveness to the judgment of others, which contrasts so singularly with his high resolve and self-dependence when assuming the greatest responsibilities. To Ball, to the Admiralty, and to the First Lord privately, he sent explanations of his action, accompanied by a summary of his reasons. As the latter have been given, one by one, as each step was taken, it is not necessary here to say more than that, in the author's judgment, each successive movement was made upon good grounds, and rightly timed. This is true, although Nelson was entirely misled as to Bonaparte's object. The ruse of the latter, as put into effect by Villeneuve, not only deceived the British admiral, but, in its issue, confounded the French. The critical moment of decision, for the whole fruitless campaign, was when Nelson determined to go first off Messina, then to the Morea, and finally to Egypt upon the inference that by this time one of three things must have happened. Either (1) he must have met the French fleet, person-

[1] Author's italics.

ally or by his lookouts, or (2) it had returned to Toulon, or
(3) it had gone on to Egypt. The first being eliminated, the
choice he made between the others, wide as was the flight for
which it called, was perfectly accurate. It is difficult to know
which most to admire, — the sagacity which divined the actual,
though not the intended, movements of the enemy, the fiery
eagerness which gave assurance of a fierce and decisive battle,
or the great self-restraint which, in all his fever of impatience,
withheld him from precipitating action before every means of
information was exhausted. There will be occasion to note
again the same traits in the yet sharper trial he was soon to
undergo.

His conclusion upon the whole matter, therefore, though
erroneous as to the fact, may be accepted as entirely justified
by all the indications; and it must be added that, with the
dispositions he took, nothing could have saved the French fleet
but its prompt retreat to Toulon. " Had they not been crippled," he wrote Davison, "nothing could have hindered our
meeting them on January 21st, off the south end of Sardinia."
" I have not the smallest doubt," he concluded his letter to the
Admiralty, " but that the destination of the French armament
which left the coast of France on the 18th of January, was
Alexandria; and, under all the circumstances which I have
stated, I trust their Lordships will approve my having gone to
Egypt in search of the French fleet." There was, however,
no occasion for him to be forward in suggesting the sacrifice
of himself, as he did to Melville. " At this moment of sorrow
I still feel that I have acted right. The result of my inquiries
at Coron and Alexandria confirm me in my former opinion;
and therefore, my Lord, if my obstinacy or ignorance is so
gross, I should be the first to recommend your superseding me."
It may be noted here that Nelson never realized — he did not
live long enough to realize — how thoroughly Bonaparte had
learned from Egypt his lesson as to the control of the sea by
sea-power, and what it meant to a maritime expedition which
left it out of the account. To the end of his reign, and in the
height of his sway, he made no serious attempt to occupy Sardinia or even Sicily, narrow as was the water separating the
latter from Naples, become practically a French state, over
which his brother and brother-in-law reigned for six years.

Nelson to the last made light of the difficulties of which Bonaparte had had bitter experience. " France," he wrote to the Secretary for War, " will have both Sardinia and Sicily very soon, if we do not prevent it, and Egypt besides." " We know," he said in a letter to Ball, " there would be no difficulty for single polaccas to sail from the shores of Italy with 300 or 400 men in each, (single ships ;) and that, in the northerly winds, they would have a fair chance of not being seen, and even if seen, not to be overtaken by the Russian ships. Thus, 20,000 men would be fixed again in Egypt, with the whole people in their favour. Who would turn them out ? "

Nelson left the Gulf of Palmas as soon as the wind served, which was on the 9th of March. It was necessary to revictual ; but, as the time of the storeships' arrival was uncertain, he thought best to make a round off Toulon and Barcelona, to renew the impression of the French that his fleet was to the westward. This intention he carried out, " showing myself," to use his own words, " off Barcelona and the coast of Spain, and the islands of Majorca and Minorca, until the 21st of March." " I shall, if possible," he wrote to a captain on detached service, " make my appearance off Barcelona, in order to induce the enemy to believe that I am fixed upon the coast of Spain, when I have every reason to believe they will put to sea, as I am told the troops are still embarked. From Barcelona I shall proceed direct to Rendezvous 98." [1] Accordingly, on the 26th of March he anchored at Palmas, and began at once to clear the transports. " By the report of the Fleet Captain, I trust [it will be evident that] it could not with propriety be longer deferred." Still satisfied that the French were bound to Egypt, he would here be close to their necessary route, and with a look-out ship thirty miles to the westward felt assured they would not escape him. Four days after he anchored, Villeneuve started on his second venture, and thinking, as Nelson had plotted, that the British fleet was off Cape San Sebastian, he again shaped his course to pass east of the Balearics, between them and Sardinia. The news of his sailing reached Nelson five days later, on April 4th, at 10 A. M. He had left Palmas the morning before, and was then twenty miles west of it, beating against a head wind. The weary

[1] Apparently Gulf of Palmas.

work of doubt, inference, and speculation was about to begin
once more, and to be protracted for over three months.

In the present gigantic combination of Napoleon, the Brest
squadron, as well as those of Rochefort and Toulon, was to go
to the West Indies, whence the three should return in mass to
the English Channel, to the number of thirty-five French
ships-of-the-line. To these it was hoped to add a number of
Spanish ships, from Cartagena and Cadiz. If the movements
were successful, this great force would overpower, or hold in
check, the British Channel Fleet, and secure control of the
Straits of Dover long enough for the army to cross. It is with
the Toulon squadron that we are immediately concerned, as
it alone for the present touches the fortunes of Nelson.
Villeneuve's orders were to make the best of his way to the
Straits of Gibraltar, evading the British fleet, but calling off
Cartagena, to pick up any Spanish ships there that might be
perfectly ready to join him. He was not, however, to delay
for them on any account, but to push on at once to Cadiz.
This port he was not to enter, but to anchor outside, and there
be joined by the "Aigle," the ship that had so long worried
Nelson, and also by six or eight Spanish ships believed to be
ready. As soon as these came out, he was to sail with all
speed for Martinique, and there wait forty days for the Brest
squadron, if the latter, whose admiral was to be commander-
in-chief of the allied fleets, did not appear sooner. Villeneuve
had other contingent instructions, which became inoperative
through the persistent pursuit of Nelson.

The French fleet sailed during the night of March 30, with
a light northeast wind, and steered a course approaching due
south, in accordance with Villeneuve's plan of going east of
Minorca. The British lookout frigates, "Active" and "Phœbe,"
saw it at eight o'clock the next morning, and kept company
with its slow progress till eight P. M., when, being then sixty
miles south by west, true, from Toulon, the "Phœbe" was
sent off to Nelson. During the day the wind shifted for a
time to the northwest. The French then hauled up to southwest, and were heading so when darkness concealed them from
the British frigates, which were not near enough for night observations. After the "Phœbe's" departure, the "Active"
continued to steer as the enemy had been doing when last

seen, but at daybreak they were no longer in sight. Just
what Villeneuve did that night does not appear; but no vessel
of Nelson's knew anything more about him till April 18th,
when information was received from a chance passer that he
had been seen on the 7th off Cape de Gata, on the coast of
Spain, with a fresh easterly wind steering to the westward.

Villeneuve doubtless had used the night's breeze, which
was fresh, to fetch a long circuit, throw off the "Active," and
resume his course to the southward. It was not till next day,
April 1st, that he spoke a neutral, which had seen Nelson near
Palmas. Undeceived thus as to the British being off Cape
San Sebastian, and the wind having then come again easterly,
the French admiral kept away at once to the westward, passed
north of the Balearic Islands, and on the 6th appeared off
Cartagena. The Spanish ships there refusing to join him, he
pressed on, went by Gibraltar on the 8th, and on the 9th anchored off Cadiz, whence he drove away Orde's squadron.
The "Aigle," with six Spanish ships, joined at once, and that
night the combined force, eighteen ships-of-the-line, sailed
for Martinique, where it arrived on the 14th of May. By
Villeneuve's instructions it was to remain in the West Indies
till the 23d of June.

When the captain of the "Active" found he had lost sight
of the French, he kept away for Nelson's rendezvous, and
joined him at 2 P. M of April 4th, five or six hours after the
"Phœbe." Prepossessed with the opinion that Naples, Sicily,
or Egypt was the enemy's aim, an opinion which the frigate's
news tended to confirm, Nelson at once took the fleet midway
between Sardinia and the Barbary coast, spreading lookouts
on either side. Thus, without yielding ground to leeward, he
covered all avenues leading to the eastward. He summed up
his purpose in words which showed an entire grasp of the
essentials of his perplexing situation. "I shall neither go to
the eastward of Sicily, or to the westward of Sardinia, until
I know something positive." Amid the diverse objects demanding his care, this choice of the strategic position was
perfectly correct; but as day followed day without tidings,
the distress of uncertainty, and the strain of adhering to his
resolve not to move without information to guide him, became almost unbearable — a condition not hard to be realized

by those who have known, in suspense, the overpowering impulse to do something, little matter what. It is an interesting illustration of the administrative difficulties of the fleet, that three supply-ships joined him on the 5th of April, and their stores were transferred at sea while momentarily expecting the enemy's appearance; one at least being completely discharged by the night of the 6th

On this date, Nelson, having waited forty-eight hours to windward of Sicily, decided to fall back on Palermo; reckoning that if any attempt had been made upon Naples or Sicily, he should there hear of it. The lookouts which were scattered in all directions were ordered to join him there, and a frigate was sent to Naples. On the 9th and 10th he was off Palermo, and, though he got no word of the French, received two pieces of news from which his quick perceptions jumped to the conclusion that he had been deceived, and that the enemy had gone west. "April 10, 7 A.M. Hallowell is just arrived from Palermo. He brings accounts that the great Expedition is sailed,[1] and that seven Russian sail-of-the-line are expected in the Mediterranean; therefore I may suppose the French fleet are bound to the westward. I must do my best. God bless you. I am very, very miserable, but ever, my dear Ball," etc.

A week more was to elapse before this dreadfully harassing surmise was converted into a certainty. On the 9th he started back from Palermo, intending to go towards Toulon, to make sure that the French had not returned again. Meeting a constant strong head wind, he was nine days getting again to the south of Sardinia, a distance of less than two hundred miles. There, on the 18th, the vessel was spoken which informed him that she had seen the French off Cape de Gata, three hundred miles to the westward, ten days before. "If this account is true," he wrote to Elliot, "much mischief may be apprehended. It kills me, the very thought." Yet, now that the call for decision sounds, he knows no faltering, nor does he, as in hours of reaction, fret himself about the opinions of others. "I am going out of the Mediterranean," he says in farewell. "It may be thought that I have protected too well Sardinia, Naples, Sicily, the Morea, and Egypt; but I feel I

[1] From England,

have done right, and am, therefore, easy about any fate which may await me for having missed the French fleet."

The following day a vessel joined from Gibraltar, with certain information that the enemy had passed the Straits. Nelson had no need to ponder the next step. His resolve had been taken long before to follow to the Antipodes. He comforted himself, mistakenly, that his watchfulness was the cause that the French had abandoned the attempt against Egypt in force. "Under the severe affliction which I feel at the escape of the French fleet out of the Mediterranean," he wrote the Admiralty, "I hope that their Lordships will not impute it to any want of due attention on my part; but, on the contrary, that by my vigilance the enemy found it was impossible to undertake any expedition in the Mediterranean." Mindful, also, that Bonaparte's great attempt of 1798 had depended upon the absence of the British fleet, he left a squadron of five frigates to cruise together to the windward of Sicily, lest the French even now might try to send transports with troops to the eastward, under the protection of small armed vessels.

The number of letters written on the 18th and 19th of April show how thoroughly his mind was prepared for contingencies. Despatched in all directions, they outline his own intended course, for the information of those who might have to co-operate, as well as that which he wished to be pursued by the officers under his orders. They are issued neat and complete, at one cast, and no other follows for a week. He surmises, from the fact of the Spanish ships accompanying the movement, that it is directed, not against the West Indies, but for either Ireland or Brest; not a bad "guess," which is all he would have claimed for it, for the West Indies were actually only a rallying-point on the roundabout road to the Channel prescribed by Napoleon. "Therefore," he wrote to the Admiralty, "if I receive no intelligence to do away my present belief, I shall proceed from Cape St. Vincent, and take my position fifty leagues west from Scilly, approaching that island slowly, that I may not miss any vessels sent in search of the squadron with orders. My reason for this position is, that it is equally easy to get to either the fleet off Brest, or to go to Ireland, should the fleet be wanted at either station." The suitableness of this position to any emergency arising about the British Islands can be realized at a glance, bearing in mind that westerly winds prevail there. A copy of the letter was sent to Ireland, and another to the commander of the Channel fleet off Brest. "I have the pleasure to say," he concludes, "that I shall bring with me eleven as fine ships of war, as ably commanded, and in as perfect order, and in health, as ever went to sea."

It will be interesting to support even Nelson's opinion of his own squadron by that of an unbiassed and competent witness. Sir Edward Codrington was associated with it, still nearly entire, some three months later, after the return from the West Indies; the "Orion," which he commanded, being one of a detachment of eighteen ships-of-the-line sent off from Brest by Admiral Cornwallis. "Lord Nelson's squadron (of which we have now eight with us) seems to be in very high order indeed; and although their ships do not look so handsome as objects, they look so very warlike and show such high condition, that when once I can think Orion fit to manœuvre with them, I shall probably paint her in the same manner." There was, it would seem, a Nelson pattern for painting ships, as well as a "Nelson touch" in Orders for Battle. "I have been employed this week past," wrote Captain Duff of the "Mars," "to paint the ship à la Nelson, which most of the fleet are doing." This, according to the admiral's biographers, was with two yellow streaks, but the portholes black, which gave the sides an appearance of being chequered.

The frigate "Amazon," sent ahead with the letters, was ordered to go on to Lisbon, get all the news she could, and rejoin at Cape St. Vincent. She passed Gibraltar on the 29th, and, getting decisive information just outside the Straits, held on there. It was not till the 6th that Nelson reached Gibraltar, where he anchored for only four hours. This gain of a week by a frigate, in traversing ground for which the fleet took seventeen days, may well be borne in mind by those unfamiliar with the delays attending concerted movements, that have to be timed with reference to the slowest units taking part in the combination.

The days of chase, over which we have hurried in a few lines, passed for Nelson not only wearily, but in agony of soul. Justified as his action was to his own mind, and as it must be by the dispassionate review of military criticism, he could not but be tormented by the thought of what might have been, and by his temper, which lacked equanimity and fretted uncontrollably to get alongside the enemy — to do the duty and to reap the glory that he rightly conceived to be his own. "I am entirely adrift," he complained, "by my frigates losing sight of the French fleet so soon after their coming out of port." His purpose never faltered, nor did the light that led him grow dim. His action left nothing to be desired, but the chafing of his spirit approached fury. Lord Radstock, writing from London to his son, says: "I met a person yesterday, who told me that he had seen a letter from Lord Nelson, concluding in these words: 'O French fleet, French fleet, if I can but once get up with you, I'll make you pay dearly for all that you have made me suffer!' Another told me that he had seen a letter from an officer on board the Victory, describing his chief 'as almost raving with anger and vexation.' This," continues Radstock, who knew him very well, "I can readily credit, so much so, indeed, that I much fear that he will either undertake some desperate measure to retrieve his ground, or, should not such an opportunity offer, that he will never suffer us to behold him more."

Being in London, the writer just quoted was in close touch with the popular feeling of anxiety, a suspicion of which he could well imagine Nelson also had, and which added to his burden. "It is believed here," he says on the 21st of May, "that the combined fleet from Cadiz is bound to the West Indies. This is by no means improbable. . . . The City people are crying out against Sir J. O.,[1] and, as usual, are equally absurd and unjust. Some are so ridiculous as to say that he ought to have captured some of the Toulon squadron, whilst others, more moderate, think that he might at all events, have so crippled the enemy as to have checked the expedition.[2] You may readily guess that your chief is not

[1] Sir John Orde.

[2] Orde's squadron never exceeded six ships-of-the-line, while Villeneuve's numbered eleven without the Spaniards. It will be seen further on that Nelson blamed Orde for not keeping track of the enemy's movements, and sending word to him at Gibraltar, and elsewhere, of the direction taken. As

out of our thoughts at this critical moment. Should Providence once more favour him, he will be considered our guardian angel; but, on the other hand, should he unfortunately
take a wrong scent, and the Toulon fleet attain their object,
the hero of the 14th of February and of Aboukir will be —
I will not say what, but the ingratitude of the world is but
too well known on these occasions."

A week before, on the 13th of May, the same officer had
written : " Where are you all this time ? [1] for that is a point
justly agitating the whole country more than I can describe.
I fear that your gallant and worthy chief will have much
injustice done him on this occasion, for the cry is stirring
up fast against him, and the loss of Jamaica would at once
sink all his past services into oblivion. All I know for certain
is that we ought never to judge rashly on these occasions, and
never merely by the result. Lord Barham [2] told me this morning that the Board had no tidings of your squadron. This is
truly melancholy, for certainly no man's zeal and activity
ever surpassed those of your chief. . . . The world is at once
anxious for news and dreading its arrival." The Admiralty
itself, perplexed and harassed by the hazards of the situation,
were dissatisfied because they received no word from him,
being ignorant of the weather conditions which had retarded
even his frigates so far beyond the time of Villeneuve's arrival
at Cadiz. Radstock, whose rank enabled him to see much of
the members of the Board, drew shrewd inferences as to their
feelings, though mistaken as to Nelson's action. " I fear
that he has been so much soured by the appointment of Sir
John Orde, that he has had the imprudence to vent his spleen
on the Admiralty by a long, and, to the Board, painful silence.
I am sure that they are out of humour with him, and I have

far as the author's information goes, he agrees with this censure. To fight
eleven ships with six could only be justified by extreme circumstances ; but
to lose sight of them in spring weather infers even worse judgment than fighting would. It was of the first importance to learn the destination of so large
a body, considering that the interests of Great Britain were threatened in
directions so diverse as the Channel, the East Indies, and the West Indies.

[1] Lord Radstock's son had been transferred before this from the " Victory " to the " Hydra ; " but his father did not yet know the fact, and supposed him with Nelson.

[2] First Lord of the Admiralty, who had very lately succeeded Melville.

my doubts whether they would risk much for him, were he to meet with any serious misfortune."

Through such difficulties in front, and such clamor in the rear, Nelson pursued his steadfast way, in anguish of spirit, but constant still in mind. "I am not made to despair," he said to Melville, "what man can do shall be done. I have marked out for myself a decided line of conduct, and I shall follow it well up; although I have now before me a letter from the physician of the fleet, enforcing my return to England before the hot months." "Broken-hearted as I am, at the escape of the Toulon fleet," he tells the governor of Gibraltar, "yet it cannot prevent my thinking of all the points intrusted to my care, amongst which Gibraltar stands prominent." "My good fortune seems flown away," he cries out to Ball. "I cannot get a fair wind, or even a side wind. Dead foul! — dead foul! But my mind is fully made up what to do when I leave the Straits, supposing there is no certain information of the enemy's destination. I believe this ill-luck will go near to kill me; but as these are times for exertions, I must not be cast down, whatever I feel." A week later, on the 26th of April, he complains: "From the 9th I have been using every effort to get down the Mediterranean, but to this day we are very little advanced. From March 26th, we have had nothing like a Levanter,[1] except for the French fleet. I have never been one week without one, until this very important moment. It has half killed me; but fretting is of no use." On the 1st of May he wrote to the Admiralty, "I have as yet heard nothing of the enemy;" beyond, of course, the fact of their having passed the Straits.

On the 4th of May the squadron was off Tetuan, on the African coast, a little east of Gibraltar, and, as the wind was too foul for progress, Nelson, ever watchful over supplies, determined to stop for water and fresh beef, which the place afforded. There he was joined by the frigate "Decade" from Gibraltar, and for the first time, apparently, received a rumor that the allied fleets had gone to the West Indies. He complains, certainly not unreasonably, and apparently not unjustly, that Sir John Orde, who had seen the French arrive off Cadiz, had not dogged their track and ascertained their

[1] An east wind.

route ; a feat certainly not beyond British seamanship and
daring, under the management of a dozen men that could be
named off-hand. " I believe my ill luck is to go on for a
longer time, and I now much fear that Sir John Orde has not
sent his small ships to watch the enemy's fleet, and ordered
them to return to the Straits mouth, to give me information,
that I might know how to direct my proceedings : for I cannot very properly run to the West Indies, without something
beyond mere surmise; and if I defer my departure, Jamaica
may be lost. Indeed, as they have a month's start of me, I
see no prospect of getting out time enough to prevent much
mischief from being done. However, I shall take all matters
into my most serious consideration, and shall do that which
seemeth best under all circumstances." " I am like to have
a West India trip," he wrote to Keats, one of his favorite
captains ; "but that I don't mind, if I can but get at them."

The wind hauling somewhat to the southward on the 5th,
allowed the fleet to lay a course for Gibraltar. The operation
of getting bullocks was stopped at once, and the ships weighed.
In this brief stay, the water of the fleet had been completed
and another transport cleared. Next day Gibraltar was
reached. The wind, westerly still, though fair for this stretch,
remained foul for beating out of the Straits against a current
which ever sets to the eastward ; and many of the officers,
presuming on a continuance of the weather that had so long
baffled them, hurried their washing ashore. Nelson, however,
keenly vigilant and with long experience, saw indications of a
change. " Off went a gun from the Victory, and up went the
Blue Peter,[1] whilst the Admiral paced the deck in a hurry,
with anxious steps, and impatient of a moment's delay. The
officers said, ' Here is one of Nelson's mad pranks.' But he
was right." [2] The wind came fair, a condition with which the
great admiral never trifled. Five hours after the anchors
dropped they were again at the bows, and the fleet at last
standing out of the Mediterranean; the transports in tow of
the ships of war. Nelson's resolve was fast forming to go to
the West Indies. In fact, at Tetuan, acting upon this possibility, he had given conditional orders to Bickerton to remain

[1] The signal flag for a vessel about to sail.
[2] Life of the Rev. A. J. Scott, p. 171.

in command of the Mediterranean squadron, assigning to that
service half a dozen frigates and double that number of smaller
cruisers, and had transferred to him all station papers necessary for his guidance, — a promptness of decision which sufficiently shows one of the chief secrets of his greatness. "If I
fail," said he to Dr. Scott, "if they are not gone to the West
Indies, I shall be blamed: to be burnt in effigy or West-
minster Abbey is my alternative." Evidently he was not
unmindful of the fickle breath of popular favor, whose fluctuations Radstock was noting. Dr. Scott, who witnessed his
chief's bearing at this time, always considered that he never
exhibited greater magnanimity than in this resolution, which
Jurien de la Gravière also has called one of his finest inspirations.

Great, indeed, was his promptitude, alike in decision and in
act; but he was no less great in his delays, in the curb he
placed on his natural impetuosity. "God only knows, my
dear friend," he wrote at this moment to Davison, "what I
have suffered by not getting at the enemy's fleet;" but, in all
his impatience, he would not start on that long voyage until
he had exhausted every possibility of further enlightenment.
"Perseverance and patience," he said, "may do much;" but
he did not separate the one from the other, in deed or in word.
Circumspection was in him as marked a trait as ardor. "I
was in great hopes," he wrote the Admiralty, "that some of
Sir John Orde's frigates would have arrived at Gibraltar, from
watching the destination of the enemy, from whom I should
have derived information of the route the enemy had taken,
but none had arrived." Up to April 27th nothing had been
heard of them at Lisbon. "I am now pushing off Cape St.
Vincent, and hope that is the station to which Sir John Orde
may have directed his frigates to return from watching the
route of the enemy. If nothing is heard there, I shall probably think the rumours which are spread are true, that their
destination is the West Indies, and in that case think it my
duty to follow them." "I am as much in the dark as ever,"
he wrote on the same date, May 7th, to Nepean, one of the
puisne lords. "If I hear nothing, I shall proceed to the
West Indies."

The wind continued fair for nearly forty-eight hours, when

it again became westerly; but the fleet was now in the
Atlantic. On the 9th of May the "Amazon" rejoined, bringing a letter from another ship of war, which enclosed a report
gathered from an American brig that had left Cadiz on the
2d. According to this, while there were in Cadiz diverse
rumors as to the destination of the allied fleets, the one most
generally accepted was that they were bound to the West
Indies. That night the fleet anchored in Lagos Bay, to the
eastward of Cape St. Vincent, and the unending work of discharging transports was again resumed. Nelson, shortly
before leaving Gibraltar, had received official notification that
a convoy carrying five thousand troops was on its way to the
Mediterranean, and would depend upon him for protection.
He felt it necessary to await this in his present position, and
he utilized the time by preparing for a very long chase.

At Lagos, Rear-Admiral Campbell of the Portuguese Navy,
who had served with the British in the Mediterranean six
years before, visited the "Victory," and certain intelligence
that Villeneuve was gone to the West Indies was by him
given to Nelson. The latter had now all the confirmation
needed, by such an one as he, to decide upon his line of
action. " My lot is cast, my dear Ball, and I am going to the
West Indies, where, although I am late, yet chance may have
given them a bad passage, and me a good one: I must hope
the best." "Disappointment has worn me to a skeleton,"
he writes to his late junior in the Mediterranean, Campbell,
"and I am in good truth, very, very far from well." " If I
had not been in pursuit of the enemy's fleet, I should have
been at this moment in England, but my health, or even my
life, must not come into consideration at this important crisis;
for, however I may be called unfortunate, it never shall be
said that I have been neglectful of my duty, or spared myself."
"It will not be supposed I am on a party of pleasure," he
wrote to the Secretary of the Admiralty, "running after
eighteen sail of the line with ten, and that to the West Indies;" but, he summed up his feelings to Davison, " Salt
beef and the French fleet, is far preferable to roast beef and
champagne without them."

On the 10th of May only was his purpose finally and absolutely formed, for on that day he sent a sloop to Barbadoes,

his intended point of arrival, to announce his coming; requesting that an embargo might be laid at once on all vessels in port, to prevent the news reaching the enemy at Martinique or elsewhere. In the morning of the 11th the fleet weighed, and at 4 P. M. the expedition from England arrived. It was accompanied by two ships-of-the-line, to which Nelson joined a third, the "Royal Sovereign," which sailed so badly, from the state of her bottom, that she would retard a movement already too long delayed. At seven that evening the fleet was under full sail for the West Indies.

The voyage across was uneventful; the ships, as customary for this passage, stood to the southward and westward into the trade winds, under whose steady impulse they advanced at a daily average speed of one hundred and thirty-five miles, or between five and six miles an hour. This rate, however, was a mean between considerable extremes, — a rate of nine miles being at times attained. The slackest winds, which brought down the average, are found before reaching the trades, and Nelson utilized this period to transmit to the fleet his general plan for action, in case he found the allies at sea. The manner in which this was conveyed to the individual ships is an interesting incident. The speed of the fleet is necessarily that of its slowest member; the faster ships, therefore, have continually a reserve, which they may at any moment bring into play. The orders being prepared, a frigate captain was called on board the "Victory" and received them. Returning to his own vessel, he made all sail until on the bow [1] of one of the ships-of-the-line. Deadening the way of the frigate, a boat was dropped in the water and had only to pull alongside the other vessel as it came up. The frigate remained slowed until passed, and the boat, having delivered its letter, came easily alongside again, — the whole operation being thus conducted with the least expenditure of time and exertion.[2]

There was in the fleet one ship that had been steadily in commission since 1801, and was now in very shaky condition. This was the "Superb," seventy-four. She had only been kept out by the extreme exertions of her commander, Keats, one of the most distinguished captains of the day, and he had

---

[1] Ahead, but a little to one side.
[2] Phillimore's Last of Nelson's Captains.

entreated that he should not be sent away now, when the
moment of battle seemed near. By a singular irony of fate,
this zealous insistence caused him to miss Trafalgar, at which
the "Royal Sovereign," that parted at Lagos, was present,
repaired and recoppered, — a new ship. Keats, whose energy
and readiness made him a great favorite with Nelson, obtained
permission not to stop when other ships did, but always to
carry a press of sail; and he lashed his studdingsail booms to
the yards, as the constant direction of the trade-winds allows
them to be carried steadily. Notwithstanding all that could
be done, the "Superb" seems to have set the pace, and slower
than could have been wished; which drew from Nelson's customary kindly thoughtfulness a few lines too characteristic to
be omitted.

MY DEAR KEATS, — I am fearful that you may think that the
Superb does not go so fast as I could wish. However that may be,
(for if we all went ten knots, I should not think it fast enough,) yet
I would have you be assured that I know and feel that the Superb
does all which is possible for a ship to accomplish; and I desire that
you will not fret upon the occasion. . . . Whatever may happen,
believe me ever, my dear Keats, your most obliged and sincere friend,
                                           NELSON AND BRONTE.

A week seems to have elapsed before he could get a suitable
opportunity for sending this, and he then, on the 27th of May,
added: "Our passage, although not very quick, has been far
from a bad one;" and he thought that they would gain fourteen days upon the allies. The actual gain was ten, the
latter being thirty-four days from Cadiz to Martinique, the British
twenty-four to Barbadoes. The enemy were therefore three
weeks in the West Indies before Nelson arrived; but in that
time they neither accomplished nor undertook anything but
the recapture of Diamond Rock, a precipitous islet off the
south end of Martinique, which the British had held for some
time, to the great annoyance of the main island.

Reaching Barbadoes on the afternoon of June 4th, Nelson
found that the day before information had been received from
General Brereton, commanding the troops at Santa Lucia, that
the allied fleets had passed there, going south, during the
night of May 28–29. The intelligence was so circumstantial

that it compelled respect, coming from the quarter it did. "There is not a doubt in any of the Admirals' or Generals' minds," wrote Nelson to the Admiralty, in the despatch announcing his arrival, "but that Tobago and Trinidada are the enemy's objects." Nelson himself was sceptical, — the improbability seemed great to his sound military perceptions; but, confident as he was in his own conclusions in dilemmas, his mind was too sane and well balanced to refuse direct and credible evidence. Summing up the situation with lamentations, six weeks later, he said to Davison: "When I follow my own head, I am, in general, much more correct in my judgment, than following the opinion of others. I resisted the opinion of General Brereton's information till it would have been the height of presumption to have carried my disbelief further. I could not, in the face of generals and admirals, go N. W., when it was *apparently* clear that the enemy had gone south." His purpose had been not to anchor, but to pick up such ships-of-the-line as he found there, — two seventy-fours,[1] as it turned out, — and to proceed with them to Martinique, which he naturally assumed to be the enemy's headquarters. As it was, receiving a pressing request from the commanding general at Barbadoes to let him accompany the fleet with two thousand troops, he anchored in Carlisle Bay at 5 P. M. At half-past nine the next morning he was again under way for Trinidad. Some curious misunderstandings maintained this mistaken impression as to the enemy's actions, until communication with Trinidad was had on the evening of June 7th. It was found then that no hostile force had appeared, although the British fleet for a moment had been believed to be such.

Nelson at once started north again. A report reached him that a second squadron, of fourteen French and Spanish ships from Ferrol, had arrived at Martinique. He said frankly that he thought this very doubtful, but added proudly: "Powerful as their force may be, they shall not with impunity make any great attacks. Mine is compact, theirs must be unwieldy, and although a very pretty fiddle, I don't believe that either Gravina or Villeneuve know how to play upon it." On the 9th he for the first time got accurate information. An official

[1] The "Northumberland" and the "Spartiate."

letter from Dominica [1] announced that eighteen ships-of-the-line, with smaller vessels, had passed there on the 6th of June. But for the false tidings which on the 4th had led him, first to pause, and then to take a wrong direction, Nelson argued, and not unjustly, that he would have overtaken them at this point, a bare hundred miles from Barbadoes. "But for wrong information, I should have fought the battle on June 6th where Rodney fought his." The famous victory of the latter was immediately north of Dominica, by which name it is known in French naval history. "There would have been no occasion for opinions," wrote Nelson wrathfully, as he thought of his long anxieties, and the narrow margin by which he failed, "had not General Brereton sent his damned intelligence from St. Lucia; nor would I have received it to have acted by it, but that I was assured that his information was very correct. It has almost broke my heart, but I must not despair." It was hard to have borne so much, and then to miss success from such a cause. "Brereton's wrong information could not be doubted," he told his intimates, "and by following it, I lost the opportunity of fighting the enemy." "What a race I have run after these fellows; but God is just, and I may be repaid for all my moments of anxiety."

When Villeneuve, with his ill-trained and sickly [2] fleet, left Martinique on the 4th of June, he had, of course, no knowledge of Nelson's approach. Nearly up to that date it was not known, even in London, where the latter had gone. A frigate had reached the French admiral on the 29th of May, with orders from Napoleon to make some attempts against the British islands during the time he was awaiting the Brest squadron. For this reason he sailed, and just outside the harbor was joined by two ships from France, raising his force to twenty of the line. He steered north, intending to gain to windward, and thence return upon Barbadoes, his first proposed conquest. On the 8th of June, off Antigua, were captured fourteen British merchant-ships, which had imprudently put to sea from that island. From these Villeneuve got a report that Nelson had arrived with fourteen ships-of-the-line,

[1] The island immediately north of Martinique.
[2] "The French and Spaniards landed 1,000 sick when they arrived at Martinico, and buried full that number during their stay." Nicolas, vol. vi. p. 480.

to which his imagination added five he believed to be at Barbadoes. He decided at once to return to Europe, abandoning all his projects against the British possessions. Transferring hastily a number of troops to frigates, as garrisons for the French islands, he sailed the next day for the northward to gain the westerly winds which prevail in the higher latitudes. Of the forty days he was to remain in the West Indies — reduced to thirty-five by subsequent instructions — only twenty-six had passed. Whatever else might result in the future, Nelson was justified in claiming that his pursuit, effected under such discouragements, had driven the enemy out of the West Indies, saved the islands, and, as he added, two hundred sail of sugar ships. Only extreme imprudence, he fairly maintained, was responsible for the loss of the fourteen from Antigua.

Nelson himself was off Antigua on the 12th of June, exactly one week after he left Barbadoes. There he received all the information that has just been mentioned as to the enemy's movements. A rapid decision was necessary, if he might hope yet to overtake his fortune, and to baffle finally the objects of the allies, whatever they might be. "I must be satisfied they have bent their course for Europe before I push after them, which will be to the Straits' mouth;" but later in the same day he has learned that they were standing to the northward when last seen, and had sent back their troops to Guadaloupe, therefore, "I hope to sail in the morning after them for the Straits' mouth." That night the troops were landed, and a brig of war, the "Curieux," was despatched to England with word of his intentions. At the same time, while believing the allies were bound back to the Mediterranean, he recognized that it was possible they might be going farther north, to one of the Biscay ports, and consequently took measures to notify the commanding officer off Ferrol to be on his guard. The frigate charged with this communication was kept with the fleet until the 19th, by which time he had obtained at sea additional and more precise knowledge of Villeneuve's direction. This important warning was duly received, and in advance of the enemy's appearance, by the admiral for whom it was intended.

In taking this second decision, to abandon the West Indies once more to themselves, as a month before he had abandoned the Mediterranean, Nelson had to rely only upon his own natural sagacity and practised judgment. "I hear all, and even feel obliged, for all is meant as kindness to me, that I should get at them. In this diversity of opinions I may as well follow my own, which is, that the Spaniards are gone to the Havannah, and that the French will either stand for Cadiz or Toulon — I feel most inclined to the latter place ; and then they may fancy that they will get to Egypt without any interruption." "So far from being infallible, like the Pope, I believe my opinions to be very fallible, and therefore I may be mistaken that the enemy's fleet has gone to Europe ; but I cannot bring myself to think otherwise, notwithstanding the variety of opinions which different people of good judgment form."

Still, as before, his judgments, if rapid, are not precipitate. Though characterized by even more of insight than of reasoning, no conditions are left out of sight, nor, as he declared, was a deaf ear turned to any suggestion. Upon the whole, one is more struck by the accuracy of the inferences than by the antecedent processes as summarized by himself ; yet the weight of evidence will be found on the side he espouses. Erroneous in particulars, the general conclusions upon which he bases his future course are justified, not only by the results now known to us, but to impartial review of their probability at the moment. Most impressive of all, however, is the strength of conviction, which lifts him from the plane of doubt, where unaided reason alone would leave him, to that of unhesitating action, incapable of looking backward. In the most complete presentation of all his views, the one he wished brought before the Prime Minister, if his conduct on this momentous occasion were called in question, he ends thus : " My opinion is firm as a rock, that some cause, *orders*, or *inability* to perform any service in these seas, has made them resolve to proceed direct for Europe, sending the Spanish ships to the Havannah." It is such conviction, in which opinion rather possesses a man than is possessed by him, that exalts genius above talent, and imbues faith with a power which reason has not in her gift.

There were among his conclusions certain ones which placed Nelson's mind, however fretted by disappointment, at ease concerning any future harm the enemy might be able to do.

Another wreath of laurel, which seemed almost within his grasp, had indeed evaded him, and no man felt more keenly such a loss; but he was reasonably sure that, if Villeneuve were gone to Europe, he could not outstrip pursuit by long enough to do much harm. The harassing fear, which he had borne through the long beat down the Mediterranean and the retarded voyage to Martinique, had now disappeared. Going out he had gained ten days upon the allies; they had only five days' start of him in the return. He recognized, moreover, the great significance of their inactivity during the three weeks they had the Windward Islands, if not all the West Indies, defenceless before them. "If they were not able to make an attack for three weeks after their arrival, they could not hope for greater success after our means of resistance increased, and their means of offence were diminished." If this consideration, on the one hand, showed the improbability of their proceeding against Jamaica, after Nelson's coming, when they had not ventured before, it gave also an inkling of their probable efficiency for immediate action in Europe. "They will not give me credit for quitting the West Indies for a month to come;" therefore it was unlikely that they would think it necessary to proceed at once upon their next enterprise, after reaching port. "I must not despair of getting up with them before they enter the Straits," he writes Elliot. "At least, they will have no time to carry any of their future plans into execution, and do harm to any of the countries under my charge." If his thirst for glory was unslaked, his fears of disaster had disappeared.

Villeneuve, guided by instructions recently received from Napoleon, to meet the case of the Brest squadron not getting away, had gone actually for Ferrol, where he was to join a squadron of five French and nine Spanish ships, which would raise his own force to thirty-four of the line; but Nelson, unable to know this, argued correctly that, in the uncertainty, he must leave this chance to the Biscay ships, and that for himself the Mediterranean possessed the first claim. At noon of June 13th, nine days after reaching Barbadoes, he got away from Antigua. The necessity for gaining the westerly winds made his course for some time the same as that of Villeneuve, and left him not without hopes that he might yet

fall in with the allies, especially if, as he thought; they were
destined to the Straits. On the 17th an American schooner
was spoken, which had seen the combined squadron two days before, steering also to the northward. This report, wrote Nelson
to the Admiralty, " can leave me no room to doubt but that I am
hard upon the heels of the enemy's fleet. I think we cannot
be more than eighty leagues from them at this moment, and
by carrying every sail, and using my utmost efforts, I shall
hope to close with them before they get to either Cadiz or
Toulon." The news was sent ahead by two vessels, which
parted from the fleet on the 19th of June, — one for Gibraltar,
with despatches and letters for the admiral and ministers in
the Mediterranean ; one for Lisbon, whence this important
intelligence would be forwarded to England and to the commanding officer off Ferrol. Still believing them bound for
the Straits, Nelson expressed in the fleet the opinion that they
would keep well to the southward of the Azores, so as not to
be seen by British cruisers centred there. In this he was
mistaken, as he was in their final destination; both fleets
sighted the islands, — the French on the 30th of June to the
northward of the group, while the British passed through it on
the 8th of July. He admitted, however, that he was doubtful in the matter. " It is very uncertain whether they will go
to Ferrol or Cadiz ; " and nothing can indicate more clearly his
perplexity, and his sense of the urgency of the case, than his
parting on the same day with two of the four small cruisers
he had with him, in order to insure that Ferrol as well as
Gibraltar should have prompt warning.

It was at about this time that Nelson expressed, to one or
more of his captains, his views as to what he had so far
effected, what he had proposed to do if he had met the hostile
fleets, and what his future course would be if they were yet
found. " I am thankful that the enemy have been driven
from the West India Islands with so little loss to our Country.
I had made up my mind to great sacrifices; for I had determined, notwithstanding his vast superiority, to stop his career,
and to put it out of his power to do any further mischief. Yet
do not imagine I am one of those hot brained people, who
fight at an immense disadvantage, *without an adequate object.*[1]

[1] Author's italics.

My object is partly gained," that is, the allies had been forced out of the West Indies. "If we meet them, we shall find them not less than eighteen, I rather think twenty sail of the line, and therefore do not be surprised if I should not fall on them immediately : *we won't part without a battle.*[1] I think they will be glad to leave me alone, if I will let them alone; which I will do, either till we approach the shores of Europe, or they give me an advantage too tempting to be resisted."

It is rare to find so much sagacious appreciation of con‑ ditions, combined with so much exalted resolution and sound discretion, as in this compact utterance. Among the external interests of Great Britain, the West Indies were the greatest. They were critically threatened by the force he was pursuing; therefore at all costs that force should be so disabled, that it could do nothing effective against the defences with which the scattered islands were provided. For this end he was prepared to risk the destruction of his squadron. The West Indies were now delivered ; but the enemy's force remained, and other British interests. Three months before, he had said, "I had rather see half my squadron burnt than risk what the French fleet may do in the Mediterranean." In the same spirit he now repeats : "Though we are but eleven to eigh‑ teen or twenty, we won't part without a battle." Why fight such odds ? He himself has told us a little later. "By the time the enemy has beat our fleet soundly, they will do us no harm this year." Granting this conclusion, — the reason‑ ableness of which was substantiated at Trafalgar, — it cannot be denied that the sacrifice would be justified, the enemy's combinations being disconcerted. Yet there shall be no head‑ long, reckless attack. "I will leave them alone till they offer me an opportunity too tempting to be resisted," — that speaks for itself, — or, "until we approach the shores of Europe," when the matter can no longer be deferred, and the twenty ships must be taken out of Napoleon's hosts, even though eleven be destroyed to effect this. The preparedness of mind is to be noted, and yet more the firmness of the conviction, in the strength of which alone such deeds are done. It is the man of faith who is ever the man of works.

Singularly enough, his plans were quickly to receive the

[1] Author's italics.

best of illustrations by the failure of contrary methods. Scarcely a month later fifteen British ships, under another admiral, met these twenty, which Nelson with eleven now sought in vain. They did not part without a battle, but they did part without a decisive battle; they were not kept in sight afterwards; they joined and were incorporated with Napoleon's great armada; they had further wide opportunities of mischief; and there followed for the people of Great Britain a period of bitter suspense and wide-spread panic. " What a game had Villeneuve to play ! " said Napoleon of those moments. " Does not the thought of the possibilities remaining to Villeneuve," wrote Lord Radstock of Calder's fruitless battle, " make your blood boil when you reflect on the never to be forgotten 22d of July ? Notwithstanding the inferiority of Lord Nelson's numbers," he says at the same time, with keen appreciation of the man he knew so well, " should he be so lucky as to fall in with the enemy, I have no doubt that *he would never quit them* [1] until he should have destroyed or taken some of the French ships; and that he himself would seek the French admiral's ship, if possible, I would pledge my life on it." " There is such an universal bustle and cry about invasion, that no other subject will be listened to at present by those in power. I found London almost a desert, and no good news stirring to animate it ; on the contrary, the few faces I saw at the Admiralty at once confirmed the truth of the report of the combined squadron having safely arrived at Ferrol." This was after Calder had met and fought them, and let them get out of his sight.

Lord Minto, speaking of the same crisis, says: " There has been the greatest alarm ever known in the city of London, since the combined fleet [Villeneuve's] sailed from Ferrol. If they had captured our homeward-bound convoys, it is said the India Company and half the city must have been bankrupt." These gleams of the feelings of the times, reflected by two men in close contact with the popular apprehensions, show what Nelson was among British admirals to the men of his day, and why he was so. " Great and important as the victory is," wrote Minto, three months later, after the news of Trafalgar, " it is bought too dearly, even for our interest,

[1] Author's italics,

by the death of Nelson. We shall want more victories yet, and to whom can we look for them? The navy is certainly full of the bravest men, but they are mostly below the rank of admiral; and brave as they almost all are, there was a sort of heroic cast about Nelson that I never saw in any other man, and which seems wanting to the achievement of *impossible things* which became easy to him, and on which the maintenance of our superiority at sea seems to depend against the growing navy of the enemy." "The clamour against poor Sir Robert Calder is gaining ground daily," wrote Radstock, condemnatory yet pitiful towards the admiral who had failed duly to utilize the opportunity Nelson then was seeking in vain, "and there is a general cry against him from all quarters. Thus much one may venture to say, that had your old chief commanded our squadron, the enemy would have had but little room for lying or vapouring, as I have not a shadow of a doubt but that he would either have taken or destroyed the French admiral."

But there was but one Nelson, and he meantime, faint yet pursuing, toiled fruitlessly on, bearing still the sickness of hope deferred and suspense protracted. "Midnight," he notes in his private diary of June 21st. "Nearly calm, saw three planks which I think came from the French fleet. Very miserable, which is very foolish." "We crawled thirty-three miles the last twenty-four hours," he enters on the 8th of July. "My only hope is, that the enemy's fleet are near us, and in the same situation. All night light breezes, standing to the eastward, to go to the northward of St. Michael's.[1] At times squally with rain." Amid these unavoidable delays, he was forecasting and preparing that no time should be lost when he reached the Straits and once more came within the range of intelligence. The light winds, when boats could pass without retarding the ships, were utilized in preparing letters to the officials at Gibraltar and Tangiers, to have ready the stores necessary for the fleet upon arrival. These papers were already on board the two frigates remaining with him, with the necessary instructions for their captains, so that they might part at any moment judged fitting, irrespective of weather conditions. Again he cautions the authorities to

[1] One of the easternmost of the Azores.

keep his approach a profound secret. No private letters for
Gibraltar were permitted in the mail-bags, lest they should
unwittingly betray counsel. The vessels were directed to
rejoin him forty miles west of Cape Spartel, giving him thus
time to decide upon his course before he reached Gibraltar;
for it was quite on the cards that he might find it imperative
to hurry north without anchoring. On the 13th of July, five
hundred miles from Cape St. Vincent, one of these ships left
him, probably the last to go.

On the 18th of July, Cape Spartel was sighted. " No French
fleet," wrote the admiral in his diary, " nor any information
about them: how sorrowful this makes me, but I cannot help
myself!" "I am, my dear Mr. Marsden," he wrote to the
Secretary of the Admiralty, "as completely miserable as my
greatest enemy could wish me ; but I blame neither fortune or
my own judgment. Oh, General Brereton! General Brereton!"
To his friend Davison he revealed yet more frankly the bitterness of his spirit, now that the last hope was dashed, and it was
even possible that the mis-step of going to Trinidad had caused
him to incur a further mistake, by leaving the allies in the
West Indies. " But for General Brereton's damned information,
Nelson," he said, half prophetically, "would have been, living
or dead, the greatest man in his profession that England ever
saw. Now alas! I am nothing — perhaps shall incur censure
for misfortunes which may happen, and have happened."

But if he himself were disappointed, and foreboded the discontent of others, the greatness of what he had done was
quickly apparent, and received due recognition from thoughtful men. " Either the distances between the different quarters of the globe are diminished," wrote Mr. Elliot from Naples,
" or you have extended the powers of human action. After
an unremitting cruise of two long years in the stormy Gulf of
Lyons, to have proceeded without going into port to Alexandria, from Alexandria to the West Indies, from the West Indies back again to Gibraltar; to have kept your ships afloat,
your rigging standing, and your crews in health and spirits —
is an effort such as never was realized in former times, nor, I
doubt, will ever again be repeated by any other admiral. You
have protected us for two long years, and you saved the West
Indies by only a few days." Thus truly summarized, such

achievements are seen to possess claims to admiration, not to
be exceeded even by the glory of Trafalgar.

Although no French fleet was visible, as Nelson approached
the Straits, there were a half-dozen British ships-of-the-line,
under the command of his old friend Collingwood, blockading Cadiz. When Orde was driven off that station by Villeneuve on the 9th of April, and retired upon Brest, he had already
sent in an application to be relieved from a duty which he
himself had sought, and had held for so short a time; alleging
a bundle of grievances which show clearly enough the impracticable touchiness of the man. His request was at once
granted. Early in May, Collingwood was sent from England
with eight sail-of-the-line for the West Indies; but learning
on the way that Nelson had gone thither, he detached to him
two of his swiftest seventy-fours, and, with great good judgment, himself took position off Cadiz, where he covered the
entrance of the Mediterranean, and effectually prevented any
ships from either Cartagena or Ferrol concentrating in the
neighborhood of the Straits.

Nelson received word from some of his lookouts appointed
to meet him here, that nothing had been heard of the allied
squadrons. The anxiety which had never ceased to attend
him was increased by this prolonged silence. He had no
certainty that the enemy might not have doubled back, and
gone to Jamaica. He would not stop now to exchange with
Collingwood speculations about the enemy's course. "My
dear Collingwood, I am, as you may suppose, miserable at not
having fallen in with the enemy's fleet; and I am almost
increased in sorrow by not finding them [here]. The name
of General Brereton will not soon be forgot. I must now
only hope that the enemy have not tricked me, and gone to
Jamaica; but if the account,[1] of which I send you a copy, is
correct, it is more than probable that they are either gone to
the northward, or, if bound to the Mediterranean, not yet
arrived." His surmise remains accurate. He then continues,
with that delicate and respectful recognition of the position
and ability of others, which won him so much love: "The
moment the fleet is watered, and got some refreshments, of

[1] The report of the American schooner, which saw the allied fleet, June
15th.

which we are in great want, I shall come out and make you a visit; not, my dear friend, to take your command from you, (for I may probably add mine to you,) but to consult how we can best serve our Country, by detaching a part of this large force." Circumstances prevented his neighborly intention from taking effect. A week later Nelson returned north with his squadron, and the friends did not meet until shortly before Trafalgar.

In reply to Nelson's letter, Collingwood summed up his view of the situation as so far developed. "I have always had an idea that Ireland alone was the object they had in view, and still believe that to be their ultimate destination — that they will now liberate the Ferrol squadron from Calder, make the round of the Bay,[1] and, taking the Rochefort people with them, appear off Ushant — perhaps with thirty-four sail, there to be joined by twenty more. Admiral Cornwallis collecting his out squadrons may have thirty and upwards. This appears to be a probable plan; for unless it is to bring their great fleets and armies to some point of service — some rash attempt at conquest — they have been only subjecting them to chance of loss, which I do not believe the Corsican would do, without the hope of an adequate reward."

It is upon this letter, the sagacious and well-ordered inferences of which must be candidly admitted, that a claim for superiority of discernment over Nelson has been made for its writer. It must be remembered, however, not as a matter of invidious detraction from one man, but in simple justice to the other, whose insight and belief had taken form in such wonderful work, that Nelson also had fully believed that the enemy, if they left the Mediterranean, would proceed to Ireland; and further, and yet more particularly, Collingwood's views had been confirmed to him by the fact, as yet unknown to Nelson, that the Rochefort squadron, which sailed at the time Villeneuve first escaped in January, had since returned to Europe on the 26th of May. "The flight to the West Indies," Collingwood said, in a letter dated the day after the one just quoted, "was to take off our naval force, which is the great impediment to their undertaking. The Roche-

1 Of Biscay.

ADMIRAL COLLINGWOOD.

From the painting by Henry Howard, at Greenwich Hospital.

fort Squadron's return confirmed me." "I well know what your lordship's disappointment is," he wrote, with generous sympathy; "and I share the mortification of it. It would have been a happy day for England, could you have met them; small as your force was, I trust it would have been found enough. This summer is big with events. Sincerely I wish your Lordship strength of body to go through — *and to all others, your strength of mind.*" Testy even to petulance as these two great seamen were at times in small matters, when overwrought with their manifold anxieties, they nowhere betray any egotistic concern as to the value attached by others to their respective speculations, the uncertainties of which none knew better than they, who had to act upon their conclusions.

Meantime, at the very moment they were exchanging letters, pregnant movements were taking place, unknown to either. The brig "Curieux," despatched to England by Nelson the night before he left Antigua, had fallen in with the allied squadrons, nine hundred miles north-northeast from Antigua, on the 19th of June — just a week after she sailed. Keeping company with them long enough to ascertain their course and approximate numbers, the captain then hastened on, anchoring in Plymouth on the 7th of July. "I am sorry," wrote Nelson when he heard of this meeting, "that Captain Bettesworth did not stand back and try to find us out;" but grateful as the word would have been to him, the captain was better advised to make for a fixed and certain destination. At daylight of the 9th the news was in the hands of the First Lord, who issued instant orders for the blockading squadrons off Rochefort and Ferrol to unite, and to take post one hundred miles west of Cape Finisterre. On the 19th of July Admiral Calder was in this position, with fifteen ships-of-the-line, and received through Lisbon the information of the French movements, which Nelson had forwarded thither an exact month before. On the 20th Nelson's fleet anchored at Gibraltar, and he went ashore, "for the first time since the 16th of June, 1803." On the 22d Calder and Villeneuve met and fought. Two Spanish ships-of-the-line were captured, but the battle was otherwise indecisive. Calder hesitated to attack again, and on the 26th lost sight of the enemy, who, on the

28th, put into Vigo Bay; whence, by a lucky slant of wind, they reached Ferrol on the first of August with fifteen ships, having left three in Vigo. Calder sent five of his fleet to resume the blockade of Rochefort, and himself with nine joined Cornwallis off Brest, raising the force there to twenty-six. This junction was made August 14th. The next day appeared there the indefatigable Nelson, with his unwearied and ever ready squadron of eleven ships — veterans in the highest sense of the word, in organization, practice, and endurance; alert, and solid as men of iron.

This important and most opportune arrival came about as follows. Anchoring on the 19th of July at Gibraltar, Nelson found everything ready for the re-equipment of his ships, owing to his foresight in directing it. All set to work at once to prepare for immediate departure. When I have "completed the fleet to four months' provisions, and with stores for Channel service," he wrote to the Admiralty, "I shall get outside the Mediterranean, leaving a sufficient force to watch Carthagena, and proceed as upon a due consideration, (on reading Vice-Admiral Collingwood's orders, and those which Rear-Admiral Sir Richard Bickerton may have received during my absence,) may suggest to be most proper. Should I hear that the enemy are gone to some of the ports in the Bay, I shall join the squadron off Ferrol, or off Ushant, as I think the case requires." There will be observed here the same striking combination of rapidity, circumspection, and purpose prepared by reflection for instant action in emergencies, that characterized him usually, and especially in these four months of chase. "The squadron is in the most perfect health," he continues, "except some symptoms of scurvy, which I hope to eradicate by bullocks and refreshments from Tetuan, to which I will proceed to-morrow." The getting fresh beef at Tetuan, it will be remembered, had been stopped by a fair wind on the 5th of May. Since then, and in fact since a month earlier, no opportunity of obtaining fresh provisions had offered during his rapid movements. "The fleet received not the smallest refreshment, not even a cup of water in the West Indies," he told the Queen of Naples. The admiral himself got only a few sheep, in the nine days' round.

Even now, the intention to go to Tetuan, advisable as the

step was, was contingent upon the opportunity offering of reaching a position whence he could move with facility. Nelson did not mean to be back-strapped again within the Mediterranean, with a west wind, and a current setting to leeward, if the enemy turned up in the Atlantic. "If the wind is westerly," he wrote on the early morning of the 22d, "I shall go to Tetuan: if easterly, out of the straits." At half-past nine that day the fleet weighed, and at half-past seven in the evening anchored at Tetuan, whither orders had already gone to prepare bullocks and fresh vegetables for delivery. At noon of the 23d the ships again lifted their anchors, and started. "The fleet is complete," he wrote the First Lord that day, "and the first easterly wind, I shall pass the Straits." Fortune apparently had made up her mind now to balk him no more. Thirty-six hours later, at 3.30 A. M. of July 25th, being then off Tarifa, a little west of Gibraltar, the sloop-of-war "Termagant," one of his own Mediterranean cruisers, came alongside, and brought him a newspaper, received from Lisbon, containing an account of the report carried to England by the "Curieux." "I know it's true," he wrote to the Admiralty, "from my words being repeated, therefore I shall not lose a moment, after I have communicated with Admiral Collingwood, in getting to the northward to either Ferrol, Ireland, or Ushant; as information or circumstances may point out to be proper." In his haste to proceed, and wishing to summon the "Amazon" frigate to rejoin him, he sent the "Termagant" at once to Gibraltar, without understanding that she was just from there and had on board his clothes left for washing; in consequence of which precipitancy she "carried all my things, even to my last shirt, back again." "As I fancied he came from Lisbon," he explained, "I would not allow him to stop." "My dear Parker," he wrote the frigate-captain, "make haste and join me. If all places fail you will find me at Spithead." Parker, who was a favorite of the admiral's, followed out the careful detailed instructions which accompanied this note, but could not overtake the fleet, and from incidents of the service never met Nelson again.

With a fresh easterly gale the squadron pressed again into the Atlantic. As it went on for Cape St. Vincent, Colling-

wood's division was seen some distance to leeward, but, as
not infrequently happens in and near the Mediterranean, the
wind with it came from the opposite quarter to that which
Nelson had. The latter, therefore, would not stop, nor lose
a mile of the ground over which his fair breeze was carrying
him. "My dear Collingwood," he wrote, " We are in a fresh
Levanter. You have a westerly wind, therefore I must forego
the pleasure of taking you by the hand until October next,
when, if I am well enough, I shall (if the Admiralty please)
resume the command. I am very far from well; but I am
anxious that not a moment of the services of this fleet should
be lost." Matters therefore were left standing much as they
were when he passed in a week before. He had taken upon
himself, however, with a discretion he could now assume
freely, to change the Admiralty's orders, issued during his
absence, withdrawing most of the small cruisers from about
Malta, to reinforce Collingwood's division. When he first
learned of this step, he said it was a mistake, for double the
number he had left there were needed; " but the orders of
the Admiralty must be obeyed. I only hope officers will not
be blamed for the events which it is not difficult to foresee
will happen." With the crowd of enemy's privateers in those
waters, Malta, he was assured, would be cut off from all communication. He soon made up his mind that he would use
his own discretion and modify the dispositions taken. " Malta
cannot more than exist, and our troops would be placed in a
position of great distress," he told the Admiralty. " I transmit a statement of the force I think necessary to the eastward
of Carthagena for performing the services intrusted to my
care, and when I get the lists I shall apportion them as far
as their number will allow, and my judgment will admit."
" I hope the Board will consider this as not wishing to alter
any arrangement of theirs, but as a measure absolutely necessary." Within his own field Nelson was now, by proved professional genius, above the restraint of Boards; and when he
reached England the new First Lord had the wisdom to admit
it, in this supreme crisis, by giving him full control, within
the resources of the country, over the constitution of the
fleet with which he fought Trafalgar.

Letters left for Bickerton and Collingwood placed them in

possession of his ideas, including the revocation of the Admiralty's order; and, in an official letter, he earnestly recommended the latter officer to adhere to his arrangements. Word was also sent forward to Cornwallis, and to the commander-in-chief at Cork, as well as to the Admiralty, to notify them of his approach. To the northward of Cape St. Vincent he met the northerly winds that prevail on the Portuguese coast. Delayed by these, he was three full weeks making the passage from Gibraltar to the Channel Fleet, which he joined at 3 P. M. of August 15th, twenty-five miles west of Ushant. To this point his movements were finally determined by a frigate, which was spoken on the 12th of August, and informed him that up to three days before no intelligence had been received of the enemy's arrival in the Bay of Biscay, or on the Irish coast. Cornwallis excused him from the customary personal visit, and authorized him to proceed at once to Portsmouth with the "Victory," in pursuance of the Admiralty's leave which he so long had had in his hands. On the morning of August 18th, the long and fruitless chase of the allied fleet was brought to an end by the dropping of the "Victory's" anchor at Spithead. To Davison Nelson summed up his disappointment in the exasperated expression, "D—n General Brereton."[1]

From newspapers received off Ushant he first learned of Calder's battle, and the public dissatisfaction with the results. He had undergone too much frustration and anxiety himself not to feel for an officer who had made a mistake, although it may safely be said that Calder's mistake was not only one Nelson could not have made, but was the exact opposite of the course which Nelson by anticipation had said he would

[1] The extent of Brereton's fault (if at fault) depended, probably, upon the character and responsibility of the man he had on lookout at so critical a moment, and the care with which he tested the report made to him. Brereton did not know of Nelson's arrival, possibly not of his approach. At the same time men must take the blame of carelessness, when harm comes of it. Ball, commenting to Nelson upon the incident, said : "I think orders should be given, that when a fleet is discovered, an officer should be sent for to witness it, and that one should be at the signal hill at the rising and setting of the sun. I have often reflected on these circumstances, and on the little attention generally paid them." As it stands, the whole affair is a warning to officers, of what results may flow from errors small in themselves.

adopt. He expressed himself in words of generous sympathy. "I was bewildered by the account of Sir Robert Calder's victory, and the joy of the event; together with the hearing that *John Bull* was not content, which I am sorry for. Who can, my dear Fremantle, command all the success which our Country may wish? We have fought together, and therefore well know what it is. I have had the best disposed fleet of friends, but who can say what will be the event of a battle? and it most sincerely grieves me, that in any of the papers it should be insinuated, that Lord Nelson could have done better. I should have fought the enemy, so did my friend Calder; but who can say that he will be more successful than another? I only wish to stand upon my own merits, and not by comparison, one way or the other, upon the conduct of a brother officer. You will forgive this dissertation, but I feel upon the occasion." These words, which spoke the whole of his honest heart, were the more generous, because he believed Calder to be one of the few professional enemies that he had.

From the place where Villeneuve was met, Nelson reasoned, again, that the primary intention of the allies, returning from the West Indies, had been to enter the Straits. "By all accounts I am satisfied their original destination was the Mediterranean, but they heard frequently of our track." This persistence in his first view was partly due to the confidence with which he held to his own convictions, — the defect of a strong quality, — partly, doubtless, to the fact that Villeneuve had blundered in his homeward course, and fetched unnecessarily to leeward of his port, with reference to winds perfectly understood by seamen of that day. In fact he had no business to be where he brought up, except on the supposition that he was making for the Straits.

CHAPTER XXI.

AUGUST 19–SEPTEMBER 15, 1805. AGE, 46.

THE "Victory" was delayed in quarantine twenty-four hours, when orders from London directed her release. At 9 P. M. of the 19th of August, Nelson's flag was hauled down, and he left the ship for Merton, thus ending an absence of two years and three months. His home being but an hour's drive from the heart of London, the anxieties of the time, and his own eagerness to communicate his views and experience, carried him necessarily and at once to the public offices — to the Admiralty first, but also to the Secretaries for Foreign Affairs and for War, both of whom had occasion for the knowledge and suggestions of so competent and practised an observer. The present head of the Admiralty, Lord Barham, had succeeded to the office, unexpectedly, upon the sudden retirement of Melville the previous May. He was a naval officer, eighty years of age, who since middle life had exchanged the active sea-going of the profession, for civil duties connected with it. He had thus been out of touch with it on the military side; and although Nelson was of course well known to him by reputation and achievement, he had not that intimate personal experience of his character and habit of thought, upon which was based the absolute confidence felt by St. Vincent, and by all others who had seen the great warrior in active service. "Lord Barham is an almost entire stranger to me," wrote Nelson; but after their interview he left with him the journals in which were embodied the information obtained during his recent command, with his comments upon the affairs of the Mediterranean in particular, and, as incidental thereto, of Europe in general. Barham, who gave proof of great military capacity during his short term of office, was so much impressed by the sagacity and power of Nelson's remarks, that he assured the Cabinet he ought by all means to go back to the Mediterranean; and it may be assumed that the latter's wish so to do would have been gratified, at the time of his own choosing, had not other events interposed to carry him away earlier, and to end his career.

It was upon one of these visits to Ministers that Nelson and Wellington met for the only time in their lives. The latter had just returned from a long service in India, reaching England in September, 1805. His account of the interview, transmitted to us by Croker, is as follows: —

WALMER, October 1st, 1834.

We were talking of Lord Nelson, and some instances were mentioned of the egotism and vanity that derogated from his character. "Why," said the Duke, "I am not surprised at such instances, for Lord Nelson was, in different circumstances, two quite different men, as I myself can vouch, though I only saw him once in my life, and for, perhaps, an hour. It was soon after I returned from India. I went to the Colonial Office [1] in Downing Street, and there I was shown into the little waiting-room on the right hand, where I found, also waiting to see the Secretary of State, a gentleman, whom, from his likeness to his pictures and the loss of an arm, I immediately recognized as Lord Nelson. He could not know who I was, but he entered at once into conversation with me, if I can call it conversation, for it was almost all on his side and all about himself, and in, really, a style so vain and so silly as to surprise and almost disgust me. I suppose something that I happened to say may have made him guess that I was *somebody*, and he went out of the room for a moment, I have no doubt to ask the office-keeper who I was, for when he came back he was altogether a different man, both in manner and matter. All that I had thought a charlatan style had vanished, and he talked of the state of this country and of the aspect and probabilities of affairs on the Continent with a good sense, and a knowledge of subjects both at home and abroad, that surprised me equally and more agreeably than the first part of our interview had done; in fact, he talked like an officer and a statesman. The Secretary of State kept us long waiting, and certainly, for the last half or three quarters of an hour, I don't know

---

[1] In a letter to the Earl of Mornington, dated December 21st, 1805, Wellington, then Wellesley, said, "I arrived in England about September 10th." The margin of time for meeting Nelson, who left Merton on the 13th, was therefore small, and fixes very closely the date of this interesting interview. The Colonial and War Offices seem then to have been under one head.

that I ever had a conversation that interested me more. Now, if the Secretary of State had been punctual, and admitted Lord Nelson in the first quarter of an hour, I should have had the same impression of a light and trivial character that other people have had; but luckily I saw enough to be satisfied that he was really a very superior man ; but certainly a more sudden and complete metamorphosis I never saw."[1]

This is not the only record that remains to us of those interesting interviews with Cabinet Ministers, although the most have passed away unnoted. It was in one of them that he uttered a military opinion, for whose preservation we are indebted to his own mention of it in a private letter; an opinion so characteristic of his habits of thought, his reasoned motives of action, that, although it has before been quoted, it is fitting to repeat it in his own words and in full.

When he reached England, the naval situation, as far as then known, was that Napoleon had twenty-one French ships-of-the-line in Brest, and twenty-eight or nine, French and Spanish, in Ferrol ; while Cornwallis had thirty-five British off Brest. This was the condition on the 15th of August, when Nelson parted from the fleet off Ushant. Very soon after his arrival in town, news was received that Villeneuve had gone to sea from Ferrol, and that Cornwallis, when informed of the fact, had divided his fleet, with great lack of judgment, keeping himself seventeen ships to confront the Brest squadron, while eighteen were sent to look for Villeneuve under the command of Admiral Calder. In the public discontent with the latter, it was not reassuring to know that, at a moment when every one's nerves were on the rack, he was again intrusted with the always difficult task of coping with a much superior force. While this state of excitement prevailed, Nelson called upon the Secretary of State, Lord Castlereagh, on the 23d of August. " Yesterday," he wrote to Captain Keats, "the Secretary of State, which is a man who has only sat one solitary day in his office, and of course knows but little of what is passed, and indeed the Minister,[2] were all full of the enemy's fleet, and as I am now set up for a *Conjuror*, and God knows they will very soon find out I am far from

[1] Correspondence and Diaries of John Wilson Croker, vol. ii. p. 233.
[2] The Prime Minister Pitt.

being one, I was asked my opinion, against my inclination, for if I make one wrong guess the charm will be broken; but this I ventured without any fear, that if Calder got close alongside their twenty-seven or twenty-eight sail, that by the time the enemy had beat our fleet soundly, they would do us no harm this year."

This acute perception of the reason why it was at times desirable and proper to hurl a smaller though more efficient force against superior numbers, content that the latter, as a factor, were for the campaign annihilated, — this realization of the possible fruitfulness of a defeat, or rather, of a battle wisely lost, as contrasted with what Jomini calls the sterile glory of fighting battles merely to win them, — is one of the most marked and decisive features of Nelson's genius as a general officer. It recurs over and over again, and at all periods, in his correspondence, this clear and full appreciation of the relation of the parts to the whole.[1] It underlay his sustained purpose during the long pursuit of the preceding months, that, if he found the allied squadron, "they would not part without a battle." Whatever else the result, that particular division would do no harm that year, and with it necessarily fell the great combination, whatever that might be, of which it was an essential factor. "The event would have been in the hands of Providence," he wrote to Barham; "but we may without, I hope, vanity, believe that the enemy would have been fit for no active service after such a battle." There is wanting to the completeness of this admirable impulse only the steadying resolve that he would bide his time, so as, to use Napoleon's phrase, to have the most of the chances on his side when he attacked. This also we know he meant to do. "I will *wait*, till they give me an opportunity too tempting to be resisted, or till they draw near the shores of Europe." In such qualification is to be seen the equipoise of the highest order of ability. This union of desperate energy with calculating wariness was in him not so much a matter of reasoning, though reason fully endorses it, as it was the gift of nature, — genius, in short. Reasoning of a very high order illuminates Nelson's mental processes and justifies his conclusions, but it is not in the power of reason,

[1] Compare, for example, *ante*, p. 361.

when face to face with emergency, to bridge the chasm that separates perception, however clear, from the inward conviction which alone sustains the loftiest action. "Responsibility," said St. Vincent, "is the test of a man's courage." Emergency, it may be said, is the test of his faith in his beliefs.

While those at the head of the State thus hung upon his counsels, and drew encouragement from his indomitable confidence, the people in the streets looked up to him with that wistful and reverent dependence which does not wholly understand, but centres all its trust upon a tried name. They knew what he had done in the now distant past, and they had heard lately that he had been to the West Indies, and had returned, having saved the chief jewel among the colonies of the empire. They knew, also, that their rulers were fearful about invasion, and that in some undefined way Nelson had stood, and would yet stand, between them and harm. The rapidity of his movements left little interval between the news of his being back at Gibraltar and the announcement of his arrival at Portsmouth, which was not generally expected. On the 19th of August, a day after the "Victory" anchored at Spithead, Lord Radstock wrote: "'T is extraordinary no official accounts have been received from Lord Nelson since the 27th of July. He then hinted that he might perhaps go to Ireland; nevertheless, we have had no tidings of him on that coast. I confess I begin to be fearful that he has worried his mind up to that pitch, that he cannot bear the idea of showing himself again to the world, until he shall have struck some blow, and that it is this hope that is now making him run about, half-frantic, in quest of adventures. That such unparalleled perseverance and true valor should thus evaporate in air is truly melancholy."

If any doubt of the approval of his countrymen mingled with the distress Nelson unquestionably felt at having missed the enemy, he was touchingly undeceived. As soon as the "Victory" and his flag were made out, the people flocked to Portsmouth, collecting on the ramparts of the town and other points of view, in inaudible testimony of welcome. As the barge pulled to the shore, and upon landing, he was greeted with loud and long-continued cheering. In London the same demonstrations continued whenever he was recognized in public. " Lord Nelson arrived a few days ago," wrote Radstock. " He was received in town almost as a conqueror, and was followed round by the people with huzzas. So much for a great and good name most nobly and deservedly acquired." " I met Nelson in a mob in Piccadilly," wrote Minto at the same time, "and got hold of his arm, so that I was mobbed too. It is really quite affecting to see the wonder and admiration, and love and respect of the whole world; and the genuine expression of all these sentiments at once, from gentle and simple, the moment he is seen. It is beyond anything represented in a play or in a poem of fame." In these few days was concentrated the outward reward of a life spent in the service of his country. During them, Nelson was conspicuously the first man in England, — first alike in the love of the people and in importance to the State.

On the private side, also, his life for this brief respite was eminently happy, marred only by the prospect of a speedy departure, the signal for which sounded even sooner than was expected. By his own account, he was only four times in London, and all the moments that could be spared from external calls he spent at Merton, where there gathered a large family party, including all his surviving brothers and sisters, with several of their children. "I cannot move at present," he writes on the 31st of August, in declining an invitation, " as all my family are with me, and my stay is very uncertain; and, besides, I have refused for the present all invitations." " I went to Merton on Saturday " (August 24th), wrote Minto, " and found Nelson just sitting down to dinner, surrounded by a family party, of his brother the Dean, Mrs. Nelson, their children, and the children of a sister. Lady Hamilton at the head of the table, and Mother Cadogan [1] at the bottom. I had a hearty welcome. He looks remarkably well and full of spirits. His conversation is a cordial in these low times. Lady Hamilton has improved and added to the house and the place extremely well, without his knowing she was about it. He found it already done. She is a clever being, after all: the passion is as hot as ever."

Over all hung, unseen, the sword of Damocles. Nelson

[1] Lady Hamilton's mother.

himself seems to have been possessed already by vague pre-monitions of the coming end, which deepened and darkened around him as he went forward to his fate. The story told of his saying to the upholsterer, who had in charge the coffin made from the mast of the "Orient," that a certificate of its identity should be engraved on the lid, because he thought it highly probable that he might want it on his return, is, indeed, but a commonplace, light-hearted remark, which derives what significance it has purely from the event; but it is easy to recognize in his writings the recurrent, though intermittent, strain of unusual foreboding. Life then held much for him; and it is when richest that the possibility of approaching loss possesses the consciousness with the sense of probability. Upon a soul of his heroic temper, however, such presentiments, though they might solemnize and consecrate the passing moments, had no power to appall, nor to convert cheerfulness into gloom. The light that led him never burned more brightly, nor did he ever follow with more unfaltering step.

Fixed in his mind to return to his command in October, he soon felt that, in the uncertainties of the French movements, a call might come at any moment. Although he nowhere says so, his mind was doubtless made up that, if Villeneuve's twenty-nine sail went to, or near, the Mediterranean, he would go out at once. "Every ship," he writes on the 31st of August, "even the Victory, is ordered out, for there is an entire ignorance whether the Ferrol fleet is coming to the northward, gone to the Mediterranean, or cruizing for our valuable homeward-bound fleet." "Mr. Pitt," he tells a friend as early as the 29th, "is pleased to think that my services may be wanted. I hope Calder's victory (which I am most anxiously expecting) will render my going forth unnecessary." "I hold myself ready," he writes again on the 3d of September, "to go forth whenever I am desired, although God knows I want rest; but self is entirely out of the question." [1]

It was not, therefore, to a mind or will unprepared that the sudden intimation came on the 2d of September — just a fort-night after he left the "Victory." That morning there arrived in town Captain Blackwood of the frigate "Euryalus," which

[1] Nelson to Right Hon. George Rose, August 29 and September 3, 1805: Nicolas, vol. vii. pp. 18, 19, 29.

had been despatched by Collingwood to notify the Admiralty
that the missing Villeneuve had turned up with his squadron
at Cadiz, on the 20th of August. Blackwood was an old
friend and follower. It was he who had commanded the
" Penelope " in March, 1800, and more than any one present
had insured the capture of the " Guillaume Tell," when she
ran out from Malta,[1] — the greatest service, probably, rendered to Nelson's reputation by any man who ever sailed
under his orders. He stopped first at Merton at five o'clock
in the morning, and found Nelson already up and dressed.
The latter said at once, " I am sure you bring me news of the
French and Spanish fleets, and I think I shall yet have to
beat them." Later in the day he called at the Admiralty,
and there saw Blackwood again. In the course of conversation, which turned chiefly upon future operations in the Mediterranean, he frequently repeated, " Depend on it, Blackwood,
I shall yet give Mr. Villeneuve a drubbing," an expression
whose wording evinces animation and resolve,— far removed
from the troubled indecision from which, by her own account,
Lady Hamilton freed him.

It was speedily determined by the Government that the combined fleets in Cadiz should be held there, or forced to fight if
they left; the country had passed through a fortnight of too
great anxiety, to risk any chance of its repetition by a renewed evasion. Ignorant of the reasons which dictated Villeneuve's course, and that it was not accordant but contrary
to his orders, it was natural to suppose that there was some
further object indicated by the position now taken, and that
that object was the Mediterranean. Moreover, so large a
body of commissioned ships — nearly forty — as were now
assembled, could not fail to tax severely the resources of a
port like Cadiz, and distress would tend to drive them out
soon. Thirty thousand able-bodied men are a heavy additional load on the markets of a small city, blockaded by sea,
and with primitive communications by land. Upon this rested
Nelson's principal hope of obliging them to come forth, if
Napoleon himself did not compel them. Their position, he
wrote the Secretary for War soon after he joined the fleet,

[1] *Ante*, p. 431.

seemed to favor an attack by rockets; "but I think we have a better chance of forcing them out by want of provisions : it is said hunger will break through stone walls, — ours is only a wall of wood." "'It is said that there is a great scarcity of provisions in Cadiz." He then mentioned that the allies were endeavoring to meet this difficulty by sending neutral vessels, loaded with food-stuffs, from French ports to all the small harbors on either side of Cadiz, whence the stores carried by them could be transferred by coasting-boats, — a process which ships were powerless to stop. Collingwood, therefore, had seized the neutrals, and sent them into Gibraltar, a step which Nelson had approved and continued. For it he then demanded the authority of his government. "Should it be thought proper to allow the enemy's fleet to be victualled, I request that I may be informed as soon as possible."

In connection with this subject Nelson made an allusion to a policy with which Castlereagh, the minister he was addressing, was afterwards identified, — that of the celebrated Orders in Council of 1807, and the license system connected with it. This is one of the few intimations we have of the wide range of subjects upon which he conversed with members of the Cabinet while in England; and it is interesting, not only as showing how far back those measures originated, but also as illustrating his own prophetic intuition of the construction which would be placed upon such proceedings. " I can have nothing, as an Admiral, to say upon the propriety of granting licences; but from what your Lordship told me of the intention of Ministers respecting the neutral trade, it strikes me, some day it may be urged that it was not for the sake of blockade, but for the purpose of taking all the trade into her own hands, that Great Britain excluded the Neutrals. Your Lordship's wisdom will readily conceive all that Neutral Courts may urge at this apparent injustice, and of might overcoming right." [1] This shrewdly accurate forecast of a contention which was not to arise till after his death is but one instance

[1] This is the earliest intimation that has come under the author's eye of the formulation (as distinguished from the development) of the groups of Orders in Council of 1807, bearing upon the Neutral Trade, which were issued and carried out by a Ministry other than the one which Nelson knew. The measure was clearly under consideration before Trafalgar.

among many of Nelson's clearness of judgment, in political as
well as in military matters.

Nelson's services, upon this, his final departure from England, were rather requested by the Government than by him
volunteered — in the ordinary sense of the word. He went
willingly enough, doubtless, but in obedience, proud and glad,
to the summons, not only of the popular cry, but of the Cabinet's wish. "I own I want much more rest," he wrote to
Elliot, immediately after joining the fleet off Cadiz; "but it
was thought right to desire me to come forth, and I obeyed."
"I expected to lay my weary bones quiet for the winter," he
told another friend in Naples, "but I ought, perhaps, to be
proud of the general call which has made me to go forth."
The popularly received account, therefore, derived from Lady
Hamilton, of her controlling influence in the matter, may be
dismissed as being — if not apocryphal — merely one side of
the dealing by which he had to reconcile the claims of patri-
otic duty with the appeals of the affections. As told by
Southey, her part in his decision was as follows: "When
Blackwood had left him, he wanted resolution to declare his
wishes to Lady Hamilton and his sisters, and endeavoured to
drive away the thought. He had done enough, he said: 'Let
the man trudge it who has lost his budget!' His countenance
belied his lips; and as he was pacing one of the walks in the
garden, which he used to call the quarter-deck, Lady Hamilton came up to him, and said she saw he was uneasy. He
smiled, and said: 'No, he was as happy as possible; he was
surrounded by his family, his health was better since he had
been on shore, and he would not give sixpence to call the
king his uncle.' She replied, that she did not believe him,
that she knew he was longing to get at the combined fleets,
that he considered them as his own property, that he would
be miserable if any man but himself did the business, and
that he ought to have them, as the price and reward of his two
years' long watching, and his hard chase. 'Nelson,' said she,
'however we may lament your absence, offer your services;
they will be accepted, and you will gain a quiet heart by it;
you will have a glorious victory, and then you may return
here, and be happy.' He looked at her with tears in his
eyes: 'Brave Emma! Good Emma! If there were more

Emmas, there would be more Nelsons.' His services were as willingly accepted as they were offered."

The fidelity with which Nelson destroyed Lady Hamilton's letters prevents our knowing just what was her attitude towards his aspirations for glory, and her acquiescence in his perils, in view of the entire dependence of her future upon his life; a dependence such as an honored wife could by no means feel, for the widow of Nelson could rely safely upon the love of the nation. Certain it is that his letters to her contain enough appeals to the sense she should have of his honor, to show that he stood in need of no strengthening at her hands; and it seems legible enough, between the lines, that he had rather to resist the pull of her weakness, or her interest, than to look for encouragement in the path of hardship and self-denial. It is certain, too, that some days before Blackwood arrived, Nelson understood that he might be wanted soon, and avowed his entire willingness to go, while not affecting to conceal his hope that circumstances might permit him to remain until October, the time he had fixed to Collingwood for his return. Whatever the inside history, the matter was quickly settled. On September 3d, the day after Blackwood's arrival, he writes to Rose: " I shall rejoice to see you on board the Victory, if only for a moment; but I shall certainly not be an advocate for being at Portsmouth till one of the Victory's anchors are at the bows." [1] The next day, the 4th, Lord Minto writes: "Lord Nelson has been here to-day. He is going to resume the command of the Mediterranean as soon as the Victory is ready, which will be within a week." On the 5th he himself tells a friend, " *All my things* are this day going off for Portsmouth."

The ten days that followed were for him, necessarily, very busy; but mental preoccupation — definiteness of object — was always beneficial to him. Even the harassing run to and from the West Indies had done him good. " I am but so-so," he had written to his brother upon arrival; " yet, what is very odd, the better for going to the West Indies, even with the anxiety." To this had succeeded the delightful fortnight at home, and now the animation and stir of expected active

[1] That is, the ship ready to sail in half an hour, one of the two anchors which moor a ship being lifted.

service. Minto had already noted his exhilaration amid the general public gloom, and after his death, speaking of these last days, said, "He was remarkably well and fresh, and full of hope and spirit." The care of providing him with adequate force he threw off upon the Admiralty. There was, of course, a consultation between him and it as to the numbers and kind of vessels he thought necessary, but his estimate was accepted without question, and the ships were promised, as far as the resources went. When Lord Barham asked him to select his own officers, he is said to have replied, "Choose yourself, my lord, the same spirit actuates the whole profession; you cannot choose wrong." He did, nevertheless, indicate his wishes in individual cases; and the expression, though characteristic enough of his proud confidence in the officers of the navy, must be taken rather as a resolve not to be burdened with invidious distinctions, than as an unqualified assertion of fact.

Nelson, however, gave one general admonition to the Cabinet which is worthy to be borne in mind, as a broad principle of unvarying application, more valuable than much labored detail. What is wanted, he said, is the annihilation of the enemy — "Only numbers can annihilate."[1] It is brilliant and inspiring, indeed, to see skill and heroism bearing up against enormous odds, and even wrenching victory therefrom; but it is the business of governments to insure that such skill and heroism be more profitably employed, in utterly destroying, with superior forces, the power of the foe, and so compelling peace. No general has won more striking successes over

[1] The author wishes to guard himself from seeming to share the perversion, as he thinks it, of this saying, into an argument against heavy ships, because the heavier the ships, the smaller the number. Without here expressing any opinion upon this controverted subject, he would simply quote on the other side the view attributed to Nelson during the chase to the West Indies. "He knew that the French had no three-decked ships in their fleet, and he reckoned on the great superiority in close action of three batteries of guns over two." (Last of Nelson's Captains, p. 137.) With this may be joined a quotation from himself involving implicitly the same idea: "Two [two-deckers] alongside an enemy are better than three-deckers *a great way off*." This evidently suggests the idea that one three-decker was better than two seventy-fours, conditions being similar. In truth, numbers should be read "numbers of guns" — or, better still, "numbers, other things being equal."

superior numbers than did Napoleon ; no ruler has been more careful to see that adequate superiority for his own forces was provided from the beginning. Nelson believed that he had fully impressed the Prime Minister that what was needed now, after two and a half years of colorless war, was not a brilliant victory for the British Navy, but a crushing defeat for the foe. " I hope my absence will not be long," he wrote to Davison, " and that I shall soon meet the combined fleets with a force sufficient to do the job well : for half a victory would but half content me. But I do not believe the Admiralty can give me a force within fifteen or sixteen sail-of-the-line of the enemy ; and therefore, if every ship took her opponent, we should have to contend with a fresh fleet of fifteen or sixteen sail-of-the-line. But I will do my best; and I hope God Almighty will go with me. I have much to lose, but little to gain; and I go because it 's right, and I will serve the Country faithfully." He doubtless did not know then that Calder, finding Villeneuve had gone to Cadiz, had taken thither the eighteen ships detached with him from the Brest blockade, and that Bickerton had also joined from within the Mediterranean, so that Collingwood, at the moment he was writing, had with him twenty-six of the line. His anticipation, however, was substantially correct. Despite every effort, the Admiralty up to a fortnight before Trafalgar had not given him the number of ships he thought necessary, to insure certain watching, and crushing defeat. He was particularly short of the smaller cruisers wanted.

On the 12th of September Minto took his leave of him. " I went yesterday to Merton," he wrote on the 13th, " in a great hurry, as Lord Nelson said he was to be at home all day, and he dines at half-past three. But I found he had been sent for to Carleton House, and he and Lady Hamilton did not return till half-past five." The Prince of Wales had sent an urgent command that he particularly wished to see him before he left England. " I stayed till ten at night," continues Minto, "and I took a final leave of him. He goes to Portsmouth to-night. Lady Hamilton was in tears all day yesterday, could not eat, and hardly drink, and near swooning, and all at table. It is a strange picture. She tells me nothing can be more pure and ardent than this flame." Lady Hamilton may have had the

44

self-control of an actress, but clearly not the reticence of a well-bred woman.

On the following night Nelson left home finally. His last act before leaving the house, it is said, was to visit the bed where his child, then between four and five, was sleeping, and pray over her. The solemn anticipation of death, which from this time forward deepened more and more over his fearless spirit, as the hour of battle approached, is apparent in the record of his departure made in his private diary : —

> Friday Night, September 13th.
>
> At half-past ten drove from dear dear Merton, where I left all which I hold dear in this world, to go to serve my King and Country. May the great God whom I adore enable me to fulfil the expectations of my Country ; and if it is His good pleasure that I should return, my thanks will never cease being offered up to the Throne of His Mercy. If it is His good Providence to cut short my days upon earth, I bow with the greatest submission, relying that He will protect those so dear to me, that I may leave behind. His will be done : Amen, Amen, Amen.

At six o'clock on the morning of the 14th Nelson arrived at Portsmouth. At half-past eleven his flag was again hoisted on board the "Victory," and at 2 P. M. he embarked. His youngest and favorite sister, Mrs. Matcham, with her husband, had gone to Portsmouth to see him off. As they were parting, he said to her : "Oh, Katty! that gypsy;" referring to his fortune told by a gypsy in the West Indies many years before, that he should arrive at the head of his profession by the time he was forty. "What then ? " he had asked at the moment; but she replied, "I can tell you no more ; the book is closed." [1] The Battle of the Nile, preceding closely the completion of his fortieth year, not unnaturally recalled the prediction to mind, where the singularity of the coincidence left it impressed ; and now, standing as he did on the brink of great events, with half-acknowledged foreboding weighing on his heart, he well may have yearned to know what lay beyond that silence, within the closed covers of the book of fate.

---

[1] The author has to thank the present Earl Nelson for this anecdote.

CHAPTER XXII.

THE ANTECEDENTS OF TRAFALGAR.

SEPTEMBER 15–OCTOBER 19, 1805.   AGE, 47.

THE crowds that had assembled to greet Nelson's arrival at Portsmouth, four weeks before, now clustered again around his footsteps to bid him a loving farewell. Although, to avoid such demonstrations, he had chosen for his embarkation another than the usual landing-place, the multitude collected and followed him to the boat. "They pressed forward to obtain sight of his face," says Southey; "Many were in tears, and many knelt down before him, and blessed him as he passed. England has had many heroes, but never one," he justly adds, "who so entirely possessed the love of his fellow countrymen as Nelson." There attached to him not only the memory of many brilliant deeds, nor yet only the knowledge that more than any other he stood between them and harm, — his very name a tower of strength over against their enemies. The deep human sympathy which won its way to the affections of those under his command, in immediate contact with his person, seamen as well as officers, had spread from them with quick contagion throughout all ranks of men; and heart answered to heart in profound trust, among those who never had seen his face. "I had their huzzas before," he said to Captain Hardy, who sat beside him in the boat. "Now I have their hearts."

He was accompanied to the ship by Mr. Canning and Mr. Rose, intimate associates of Mr. Pitt, and they remained on board to dine. Nelson noted that just twenty-five days had been passed ashore, "from dinner to dinner." The next morning, Sunday, September 15th, at 8 A. M., the "Victory" got under way and left St. Helen's, where she had been lying at single anchor, waiting to start. Three other line-of-battle ships belonging to his fleet, and which followed him in time for Trafalgar, were then at Spithead, but not yet ready. The "Victory" therefore sailed without them, accompanied only by Blackwood's frigate, the "Euryalus." The wind outside, being west-southwest, was dead foul, and it was not till the 17th that the ship was off Plymouth. There it fell nearly calm, and she was joined by two seventy-fours from the harbor. The little squadron continued its course, the wind still ahead, until the 20th of the month, when it had not yet gained a hundred miles southwest from Scilly. Here Nelson met his former long-tried second in the Mediterranean, Sir Richard Bickerton, going home ill; having endured the protracted drudgery off Toulon only to lose, by a hair's breadth, his share in the approaching triumph.

On the 25th the "Victory" was off Lisbon. "We have had only one day's real fair wind," wrote Nelson to Lady Hamilton, "but by perseverance we have done much." The admiral sent in letters to the British consul and naval officers, urging them to secure as many men as possible for the fleet, but enjoining profound secrecy about his coming, conscious that his presence would be a deterrent to the enemy and might prevent the attempt to leave Cadiz, upon which he based his hopes of a speedy issue, and a speedy return home for needed repose. His departure from England, indeed, could not remain long unknown in Paris; but communications by land were slow in those times, and a few days' ignorance of his arrival, and of the reinforcement he brought, might induce Villeneuve to dare the hazard which he otherwise might fear. "Day by day," he wrote to Davison, "I am expecting the allied fleet to put to sea — every day, hour, and moment." "I am convinced," he tells Blackwood, who took charge of the inshore lookout, "that you estimate, as I do, the importance of not letting these rogues escape us without a fair fight, which I pant for by day, and dream of by night." For the same reasons of secrecy he sent a frigate ahead to Collingwood, with orders that, when the "Victory" appeared, not only should no salutes be fired, but no colors should be shown, if in sight of the port. The like precautions were continued when any new ship joined. Every care was taken to lull the enemy into confidence, and to lure him out of port.

At 6 P. M. of Saturday, September 28th, the "Victory" reached the fleet, then numbering twenty-nine of the line; the main body being fifteen to twenty miles west of Cadiz, with six ships close in with the port. The next day was Nelson's birthday — forty-seven years old. The junior admirals and the captains visited the commander-in-chief, as customary, but with demonstrations of gladness and confidence that few leaders have elicited in equal measure from their followers. "The reception I met with on joining the fleet caused the sweetest sensation of my life. The officers who came on board to welcome my return, forgot my rank as commander-in-chief in the enthusiasm with which they greeted me. As soon as these emotions were past, I laid before them the plan I had previously arranged for attacking the enemy; and it was not only my pleasure to find it generally approved, but clearly perceived and understood." To Lady Hamilton he gave an account of this scene which differs little from the above, except in its greater vividness. "I believe my arrival was most welcome, not only to the Commander of the fleet, but also to every individual in it; and, when I came to explain to them the '*Nelson touch*,' it was like an electric shock. Some shed tears, all approved — 'It was new — it was singular — it was simple!' and, from admirals downwards, it was repeated — 'It must succeed, if ever they will allow us to get at them! You are, my Lord, surrounded by friends whom you inspire with confidence.' Some may be Judas's; but the majority are certainly much pleased with my commanding them." No more joyful birthday levee was ever held than that of this little naval court. Besides the adoration for Nelson personally, which they shared with their countrymen in general, there mingled with the delight of the captains the sentiment of professional appreciation and confidence, and a certain relief, noticed by Codrington, from the dry, unsympathetic rule of Collingwood, a man just, conscientious, highly trained, and efficient, but self-centred, rigid, uncommunicative; one who fostered, if he did not impose, restrictions upon the intercourse between the ships, against which he had inveighed bitterly when himself one of St. Vincent's captains. Nelson, on the contrary, at once invited cordial social relations with the commanding officers. Half of the thirty-odd were summoned to dine on board the flagship the first day, and half the second. Not till the third did he permit himself the luxury of a quiet dinner chat with his old chum, the second in command, whose sterling merits, under a crusty exterior, he knew and appreciated. Codrington mentions also an incident, trivial in itself, but illustrative of that outward graciousness of manner, which, in a man of Nelson's temperament and position, is rarely the result of careful cultivation, but bespeaks rather the inner graciousness of the heart that he abundantly possessed. They had never met before, and the admiral, greeting him with his usual easy courtesy, handed him a letter from his wife, saying that being intrusted with it by a lady, he made a point of delivering it himself, instead of sending it by another.

The "Nelson touch," or Plan of Attack, expounded to his captains at the first meeting, was afterwards formulated in an Order, copies of which were issued to the fleet on the 9th of October. In this " Memorandum," which was doubtless sufficient for those who had listened to the vivid oral explanation of its framer, the writer finds the simplicity, but not the absolute clearness, that they recognized. It embodies, however, the essential ideas, though not the precise method of execution, actually followed at Trafalgar, under conditions considerably different from those which Nelson probably anticipated; and it is not the least of its merits as a military conception that it could thus, with few signals and without confusion, adapt itself at a moment's notice to diverse circumstances. This great order not only reflects the ripened experience of its author, but contains also the proof of constant mental activity and development in his thought; for it differs materially in detail from the one issued a few months before to the fleet, when in pursuit of Villeneuve to the West Indies. As the final, and in the main consecutive, illustrations of his military views, the two are presented here together.

PLAN OF ATTACK.[1]

The business of an English Commander-in-Chief being first to bring an Enemy's Fleet to Battle, on the most advantageous terms to

[1] May, 1805.

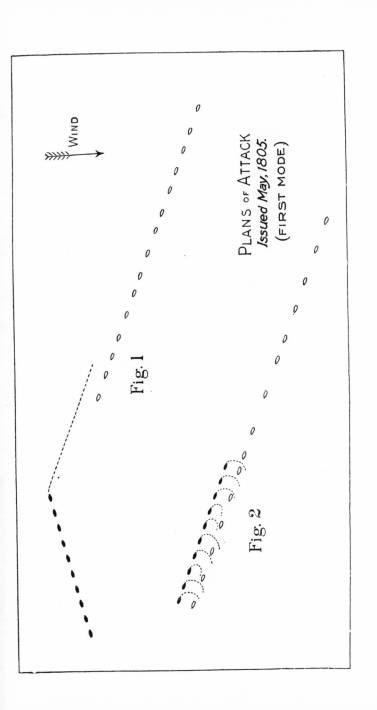

WIND

Fig. 1

PLANS OF ATTACK
Issued May, 1805.
(FIRST MODE)

Fig. 2

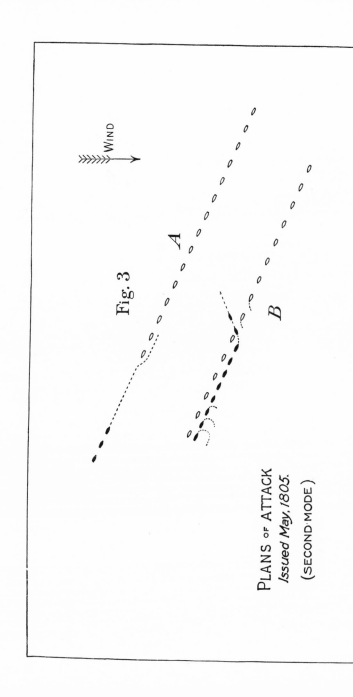

Fig. 3

Wind

A

B

PLANS OF ATTACK
Issued May, 1805.
(SECOND MODE)

himself, (I mean that of laying his Ships close on board the Enemy, as expeditiously as possible;) and secondly, to continue them there, without separating, until the business is decided; I am sensible beyond this object it is not necessary that I should say a word, being fully assured that the Admirals and Captains of the Fleet I have the honour to command, will, knowing my precise object, that of a close and decisive Battle, supply any deficiency in my not making signals; which may, if extended beyond these objects, either be misunderstood, or, if waited for, very probably, from various causes, be impossible for the Commander-in-Chief to make: therefore, it will only be requisite for me to state, in as few words as possible, the various modes in which it may be necessary for me to obtain my object, on which depends, not only the honour and glory of our Country, but possibly its safety, and with it that of all Europe, from French tyranny and oppression.

If the two Fleets are both willing to fight, but little manœuvring is necessary; the less the better; — a day is soon lost in that business: therefore I will only suppose that the Enemy's Fleet being to leeward, standing close upon a wind on the starboard tack, and that I am nearly ahead of them, standing on the larboard tack, of course I should weather them. The weather must be supposed to be moderate; for if it be a gale of wind, the manœuvring of both Fleets is but of little avail, and probably no decisive Action would take place with the whole Fleet. Two modes present themselves: one to stand on, just out of gunshot, until the Van-Ship of my Line would be about the centre Ship of the Enemy, then make the signal to wear together, then bear up, engage with all our force the six or five Van-Ships of the Enemy, passing, certainly, if opportunity offered, through their Line. This would prevent their bearing up, and the Action, from the known bravery and conduct of the Admirals and Captains, would certainly be decisive: the second or third Rear-Ships of the Enemy would act as they please, and our Ships would give a good account of them, should they persist in mixing with our Ships. The other mode would be, to stand under an easy but commanding sail, directly for their headmost Ship, so as to prevent the Enemy from knowing whether I should pass to leeward or windward of him. In that situation, I would make the signal to engage the Enemy to leeward, and to cut through their Fleet about the sixth Ship from the Van, passing very close; they being on a wind, and you going large, could cut their Line when you please. The Van-Ships of the Enemy would, by the time our Rear came abreast of the Van-Ship, be severely cut up, and our Van could not expect to escape damage. I would then have our *Rear* Ship, and every Ship in succession, wear, continue the Action with either the Van-Ship, or second Ship, as it might appear most eligible from her crippled state; and this mode pursued, I see nothing to prevent the capture of the five or six Ships of the Enemy's Van. The two or three Ships of the Enemy's Rear [1] must either bear up, or wear; and, in either case, although they would be in a better plight probably than our two Van-Ships (now in the Rear) yet they would be separated, and at a distance to lee-ward, so as to give our Ships time to refit; and by that time, I believe, the Battle would, from the judgment of the Admiral and Captains, be over with the rest of them. Signals from these moments are useless, when every man is disposed to do his duty. The great object is for us to support each other, and to keep close to the Enemy, and to leeward of him.

If the Enemy are running away, then the only signals necessary will be, to engage the Enemy as arriving up with them; and the other ships to pass on for the second, third, &c., giving, if possible, a close fire into the Enemy in passing, taking care to give our Ships engaged notice of your intention.

MEMORANDUM.

(Secret)

Victory, off Cadiz, 9th October, 1805.

Thinking it almost impossible to bring a Fleet of forty Sail of the Line into a Line of Battle in variable winds, thick weather, and other circumstances which must occur, without such a loss of time that the opportunity would probably be lost of bringing the Enemy to Battle in such a manner as to make the business decisive, I have therefore made up my mind to keep the Fleet in that position of sailing (with the exception of the First and Second in Command) that the Order of Sailing is to be the Order of Battle, placing the Fleet in two Lines

[1] The author does not here understand the speaking of "two or three" rear ships, when the van is supposed to be five or six — making a total of not over nine or ten enemies. If this order of attack was issued, as expressly stated by Clarke and M'Arthur, on the chase to the West Indies, Nelson then was fully aware that he with ten ships was in pursuit of eighteen. (See *ante*, p. 656.) It appears to the author more probable that it was issued to the fleet when off Toulon, in anticipation of a possible meeting with the French squadron there, when the disparity of force was less — say, eight to ten. This impression is confirmed by the "Plan of Attack" speaking of the junior "Admirals" — in the plural. There was but one such in the pur-suit to the West Indies. It is quite possible, however, that the same order was re-issued upon the later occasion, re-copied without change of words. In any event, it confirms other statements and actions of Nelson's, that an enemy should not be fought ship to ship, but by a concentration on part of his order.

of sixteen Ships each, with an Advanced Squadron of eight of the fastest sailing Two-decked Ships, which will always make, if wanted, a Line of twenty-four Sail, on whichever Line the Commander-in-Chief may direct.

The Second in Command will, after my intentions are made known to him, have the entire direction of his Line to make the attack upon the Enemy, and to follow up the blow until they are captured or destroyed.

If the Enemy's Fleet should be seen to windward in Line of Battle, and that the two Lines and the Advanced Squadron can fetch them, they will probably be so extended that their Van could not succour their Rear.

I should therefore probably make the Second in Command's signal to lead through, about their twelfth Ship from their Rear, (or wherever he could fetch, if not able to get so far advanced) ; my Line would lead through about their Centre, and the Advanced Squadron to cut two or three or four Ships a-head of their Centre, so as to ensure getting at their Commander-in-Chief, on whom every effort must be made to capture.

The whole impression of the British Fleet must be to overpower from two or three Ships a-head of their Commander-in-Chief, supposed to be in the Centre, to the Rear of their Fleet. I will suppose twenty Sail of the Enemy's Line to be untouched, it must be some time before they could perform a manœuvre to bring their force compact to attack any part of the British Fleet engaged, or to succour their own Ships, which indeed would be impossible without mixing with the Ships engaged.

Something must be left to chance ; nothing is sure in a Sea Fight beyond all others. Shot will carry away the masts and yards of friends as well as foes ; but I look with confidence to a Victory before the Van of the Enemy could succour their Rear, and then that the British Fleet would most of them be ready to receive their twenty Sail of the Line, or to pursue them, should they endeavour to make off.

If the Van of the Enemy tacks, the Captured Ships must run to leeward of the British Fleet ; if the Enemy wears, the British must place themselves between the Enemy and the Captured, and disabled British Ships ; and should the Enemy close, I have no fears as to the result.

The Second in Command will in all possible things direct the movements of his Line, by keeping them as compact as the nature of the circumstances will admit. Captains are to look to their particular Line as their rallying point. But, in case Signals can neither be seen or perfectly understood, no Captain can do very wrong if he places his Ship alongside that of an Enemy.

Of the intended attack from to windward, the Enemy in Line of
Battle ready to receive an attack,

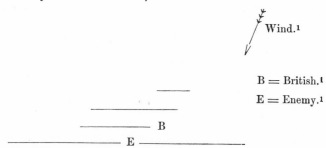

Wind.[1]

B = British.[1]
E = Enemy.[1]

B

E

The divisions of the British Fleet will be brought nearly within
gun shot of the Enemy's Centre.   The signal will most probably then
be made for the Lee Line to bear up together, to set all their sails,
even steering sails, in order to get as quickly as possible to the Enemy's
Line, and to cut through, beginning from the 12 Ship from the
Enemy's Rear.   Some Ships may not get through their exact place,
but they will always be at hand to assist their friends ; and if any
are thrown round the Rear of the Enemy, they will effectually complete the business of twelve Sail of the Enemy.

Should the Enemy wear together, or bear up and sail large, still
the twelve Ships composing, in the first position, the Enemy's Rear,
are to be the object of attack of the Lee Line, unless otherwise directed from the Commander-in-Chief, which is scarcely to be expected,
as the entire management of the Lee Line, after the intentions of the
Commander-in-Chief, is signified, is intended to be left to the judgment of the Admiral commanding that Line.

The remainder of the Enemy's Fleet, 34 Sail, are to be left to the
management of the Commander-in-Chief, who will endeavour to take
care that the movements of the Second in Command are as little
interrupted as is possible.

NELSON AND BRONTE.

It will be borne in mind that the first of these instructions
was issued for the handling of a small body of ships — ten —
expecting to meet fifteen to eighteen enemies; whereas the
second contemplated the wielding of a great mass of vessels,
as many as forty British, directed against a possible combination of forty-six French and Spanish.   In the former case,
however, although the aggregate numbers were smaller, the

[1] Inserted by author.

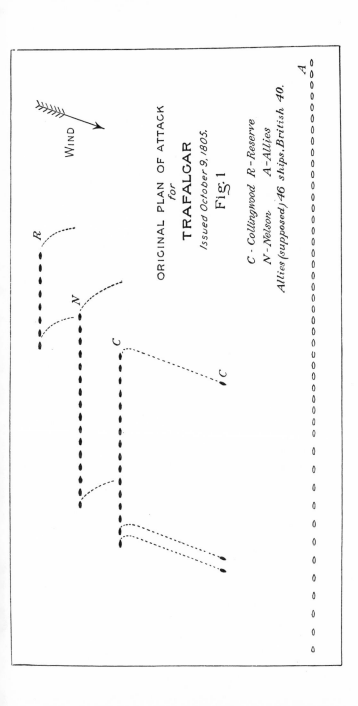

ORIGINAL PLAN OF ATTACK
for
TRAFALGAR
Issued October 9, 1805.

Fig. 1

C - Collingwood   R - Reserve
N - Nelson   A - Allies
Allies (supposed) 46 ships. British 40.

Wind

disproportion of force was much greater, even after allowance made for the British three-deckers; and we know, from other contemporary remarks of Nelson, that his object here was not so much a crushing defeat of the enemy — "only numbers can annihilate" — as the disorganization and neutralization of a particular detachment, as the result of which the greater combination of the enemy would fall to pieces. "After they have beaten our fleet soundly, they will do us no more harm this summer." [1] Consequently, he relies much upon the confusion introduced into the enemy's movements by an attack, which, though of much inferior force, should be sudden in character, developing only at the last moment, into which the enemy should be precipitated unawares, while the British should encounter it, or rather should enter it, with minds fully prepared, — not only for the immediate manœuvre, but for all probable consequences.

In accordance with the same general object — confusion — he directs his assault upon the van, instead of, as at Trafalgar, upon the rear; according to his saying in the Baltic, recorded by Stewart,[2] "Close with a Frenchman, but out-manœuvre a Russian," for which purpose he would throw his own force, preferably, upon the van of the latter. The reason is obvious, upon reflection; for in attacking and cutting off the head — van and centre — of a column of ships, the rear, coming up under full way, has *immediate* action forced upon it. There is no time for deliberation. The van is already engaged, and access to it more or less impeded, by the hostile dispositions. The decision must be instant — to the right hand, or to the left, to windward, or to leeward — and there is at least an even chance that the wrong thing will be done, as well as a probability, falling little short of certainty, that all the ships of the rear will *not* do the same thing; that is, they will be thrown into confusion with all its dire train of evils, doubt, hesitancy, faltering, and inconsequent action. It is hard work to knit again a shattered line under the unremittent assault of hardened veterans, such as Nelson's Mediterranean ships.

The method employed in the second of these instructions, the celebrated Memorandum, differs essentially from that of

---

[1] *Ante,* pp. 665, 680.   [2] *Ante,* p. 475.

the Plan of Attack, though both are simply developments of the one idea of concentration. It is unfortunate for us that Nelson, like most men of action, reveals his reasoning processes, not in ordered discussion, but by stray gleams of expression, too often unrecorded, from which we can infer only the general tenor of his thought. It is in the chance phrase, transmitted by Stewart, coupled with the change of object, so definitely announced in the second instance, — the crushing, namely, of the enemy's great fleet, and not the mere crippling of a detachment such as went to the West Indies, — that the author thinks to find the clew to the difference of dispositions, in the first case, from those prescribed and followed for Trafalgar — the "Nelson touch" that thrilled the captains. There is again, indeed, in the latter, the distinct reliance upon confusion, for the line of the foe is to be broken in two places; but now the confusion introduced is in the part of the enemy that is assailed, not, as before, in that which is left out of action. Confusion, in short, is now imposed by external force, rather than induced by internal perplexity, — a condition surer, and therefore more liable to result in a crushing victory, for it depends upon the vigor of the offensive, and not on the weakness of the defensive, which may prove a deceitful reliance. Moreover, effectual crushing requires time, even when, as in the final memorandum, a great concentration of superiority is intended on part of an enemy's order. Now, when the van and centre are attacked, the rear is pointed fair, and, if it does not lose its head, comes quickly up to the rescue; but when, in the contrary case, the centre and rear receive the assault, the van, being left out of action, not only has to turn round, but naturally stands away, for an interval dependent upon the initiative of its immediate commander, as occurred to an extreme degree at Trafalgar. Thus time, the invaluable five minutes or half hour, is gained for the offensive to bring its first concentration to a successful issue, as well as to prepare to repel the van of the defensive, if it countermarches, as it should. "I look with confidence to a victory before the van of the enemy could succour their rear, and then that the British fleet would most of them be ready to receive their twenty sail of the line, or to pursue them, should they endeavour to make off."

The organization of a distinct body of eight fast-sailing ships-of-the-line, to be carried to such part of the field as might appear necessary to the commander-in-chief in a particular emergency, resulted inevitably, perhaps, from the considerations presented by Nelson in the opening sentences of the Memorandum, and from the great number of ships he then hoped to have. There were precedents for such a formation, in the practice of the day ; but, as far as recalled by the author, they were the advanced guards, the skirmish line, of the fleet, not, as in this case, essentially a reserve. In Nelson's present thought, the employment of this force would be, not antecedent to, but consequent upon, the particular indications of the day. Probably they would not be held back as long — for as distinct indications — as in the case of an army's reserve ; but nevertheless, the chief object of their separate organization was to redress, at the moment, the unforeseen developments of a battle, whether at the instant of engagement or during its subsequent progress. The unfortunate Villeneuve, who commanded the allies, an accomplished though irresolute seaman, had adopted a similar arrangement, placing twelve detached ships under his colleague Gravina ; but, with sailing vessels, the effective use of such a force depended largely upon the windward position, which the allies did not have. If placed to leeward of a lee line, it was in the power of the assailant to throw them out of action altogether ; if to windward, to attack them separately ; therefore at Trafalgar Villeneuve ordered them back into the line. Nelson likewise then embodied his reserve in the two columns of attack, because he had fewer vessels than he expected, and because the light wind forbade the wasting of time in evolutionary refinements. The incident of the simultaneous adoption of the same provision by the two opposing admirals, however, is interesting as indicative of the progress of naval thought, though still hampered by the uncertainties of the motive power.

The second of these Orders, that of October 9, is memorable, not only for the sagacity and comprehensiveness of its general dispositions, but even more for the magnanimous confidence with which the details of execution were freely intrusted to those upon whom they had to fall. It was evidently drawn up in the first instance for Collingwood only; the word "your" in the original draught having been struck out, and "second in command," substituted. The comparison already made between it and its predecessor of May, may not uninstructively be followed by a study of the difference in details between itself and the execution it actually received at the Battle of Trafalgar. To aid this purpose the author has traced, in marginal notes, the succession of the leading ideas.

After a statement of General Considerations, and a frank attribution of full powers to the second in command for carrying out his part, Nelson lays down the manner of Attack from to Leeward. This condition not obtaining at Trafalgar, the plan cannot be contrasted with the performance of that day. Upon this follows a luminous enunciation of the general idea, namely, Collingwood's engaging the twelve rear ships, which underlies the method prescribed for each attack — from to leeward and to windward. Of the latter Nelson fortunately gives an outline diagram, which illustrates the picture before his own mind, facilitating our comprehension of his probable expectations and allowing a comparison between them and the event as it actually occurred. It is not to the discredit, but greatly to the credit, of his conception, that it was susceptible of large modification in practice while retaining its characteristic idea.

Looking at his diagram,[1] and following his words, it will be seen that the British lines are not formed perpendicularly to that of the enemy (as they were at Trafalgar), but parallel to it. Starting from this disposition, near the enemy and abreast his centre, the lee line of sixteen ships was to bear up *together*, and advance in line, not in column (as happened at Trafalgar); their object being the twelve rear ships of the enemy. This first move stands by itself; the action of the weather line, and of the reserve squadron still farther to windward, are held in suspense under the eye of the commander-in-chief, to take the direction which the latter shall prescribe as the struggle develops. The mere menace of such a force, just out of gunshot to windward, would be sufficient

[1] The author has introduced an arrow to show the direction of the wind as viewed by Nelson; the arrow flying *with* the wind.

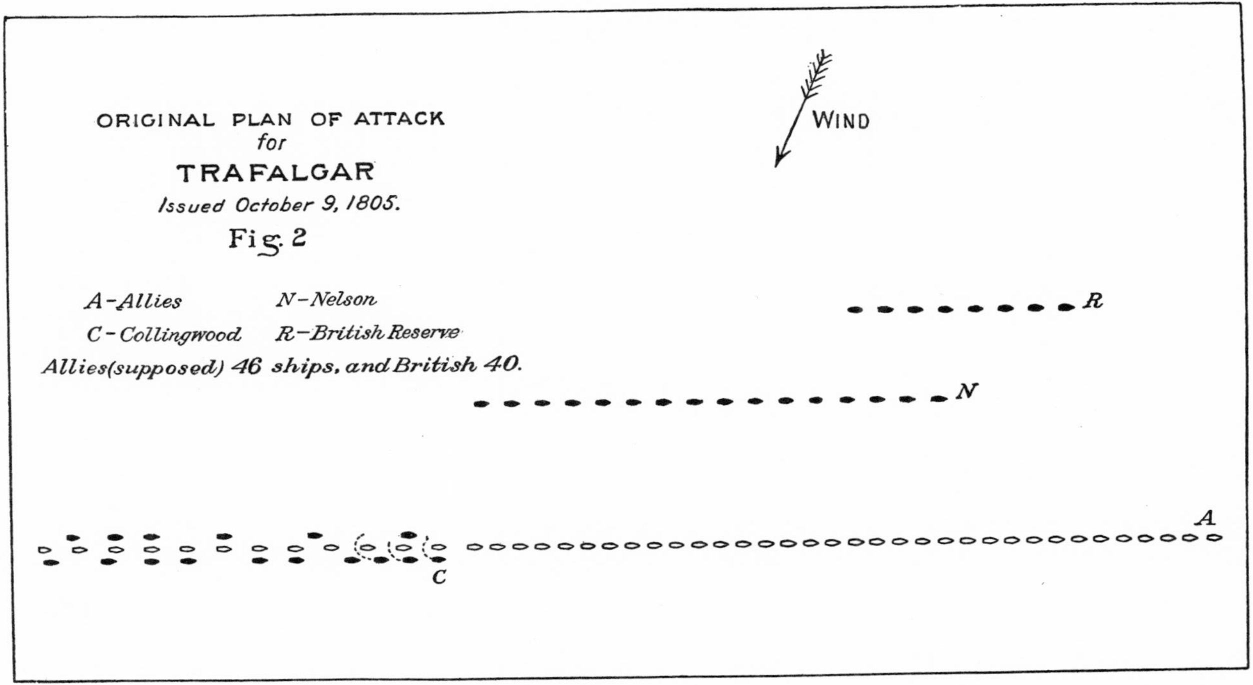

ORIGINAL PLAN OF ATTACK
for
TRAFALGAR
Issued October 9, 1805.
Fig. 2

A—*Allies*   N—*Nelson*
C—*Collingwood*   R—*British Reserve*
Allies(supposed) 46 ships, and British 40.

WIND

R

N

A

C

to prevent any extensive manœuvre of the unengaged enemies. Nelson doubtless had in mind the dispositions, more than a century old, of Tourville and De Ruyter, by which a few ships, spaced to windward of an enemy's van, could check its tacking, because of the raking fire to which they would subject it. Unquestionably, he would not have kept long in idle expectancy twenty-four ships, the number he had in mind; but clearly also he proposed to hold them until he saw how things went with Collingwood. Thus much time would allow, granting the position he assumed and a reasonable breeze. His twenty-four to windward held an absolute check over the supposed thirty-four unengaged, of the enemy.

The attack as planned, therefore, differed from that executed (1) in that the lee line was not to advance in column, but in line, thereby dispersing the enemy's fire, and avoiding the terrific concentration which crushed the leaders at Trafalgar; and (2) in that the weather squadrons were not to attack simultaneously with the lee, but after it had engaged, in order to permit the remedying of any mishap that might arise in delivering the crucial blow. In both these matters of detail the plan was better than the modification; but the latter was forced upon Nelson by conditions beyond his control.

It will be observed that, when considering attacking from to leeward, he orders a simultaneous movement of the three British divisions, — lee, weather, and reserve; for the obvious reason that if he held his own divisions in reserve to leeward he could not at all count upon bringing them into action at will; and, moreover, such an attack would probably have to be in columns, and, if simultaneous, would be less liable to disaster than in succession, mutual support diverting the enemies' fire. In fact, the highest order of offensive combination was only possible when having the advantage of the wind — fair, and enough of it.

The plan upon which Trafalgar was to be fought, as above described and analyzed, was formed some time before leaving England, and it is not unreasonable to suppose that it was in fact a modification of the earlier idea, laid down during the chase to the West Indies. On the 10th of September, three days only before quitting Merton, Nelson called upon his old friend, Lord Sidmouth,[1] who until recently had been Prime Minister. In the course of the interview he explained his intentions as regards the attack. "Rodney," he said, "broke the enemy's line in one place,[2] I will break it in two;" and with his finger he indicated upon a table the general character of the assault, to be made in two lines, led by himself and Collingwood. He felt confident, according to Sidmouth's narration, that he should capture either their van and centre or their centre and rear. It was of course out of his power to prevent the enemy inverting their order, by the simultaneous turning round of every ship, at the time of engagement, so that the attack intended for the rear should fall upon it become the van. Against this contingency he provided by the words, "should the enemy wear together, still the twelve ships composing, *in the first position*, the enemy's rear, are to be the object of attack of the lee line." Sidmouth did not commit his recollection of this incident to writing until many years later, and, not being a seaman, very likely failed to comprehend some of the details — there seems to the author to be in the story a confusion of what Nelson planned with what Nelson did; but a great conception is largely independent of details, and the essential features of Trafalgar are in Sidmouth's account. The idea was doubtless imparted also to the family circle at Merton, where probably the expression, "Nelson touch," originated. It occurs chiefly, if not wholly, in his letters to Lady Hamilton, to whom, some days before reaching the fleet, he wrote, "I am anxious to join, for it would add to my grief if any other man was to give them the Nelson touch, which WE say is warranted never to fail;" but there may be a quaint allusion to it in the motto he told Rose he had adopted: "Touch and Take."

When Nelson left England, he was intrusted by the First Lord with the delicate and unpleasant mission of communicating to Sir Robert Calder the dissatisfaction of the Government with his conduct, in the encounter with the allied fleets the previous July; especially for failing to keep touch with

[1] Formerly Mr. Addington, who was at the head of the Government during the Copenhagen expedition.

[2] This was a mistake on Nelson's part. Rodney's fleet actually, though accidentally, broke through De Grasse's order in two (if not three) places.

them and bring them again to action. The national outcry was too strong to be disregarded, nor is it probable that the Admiralty took a more lenient view of the matter. At all events, an inquiry was inevitable, and the authorities seem to have felt that it was a favor to Calder to permit him to ask for the Court which in any case must be ordered. "I did not fail," wrote Nelson to Barham, "immediately on my arrival, to deliver your message to Sir Robert Calder ; and it will give your Lordship pleasure to find, as it has me, that an inquiry is what the Vice-Admiral wishes, and that he had written to you by the Nautilus, which I detained, to say so. Sir Robert thinks that he can clearly prove, that it was not in his power to bring the combined squadrons again to battle."

Nelson felt a profound sympathy for the unfortunate officer, pursued by the undiscriminating and ignorant fury of popular clamor, the extent and intensity of which he had had opportunity to realize when in England. While he probably did not look for so tragic an issue, the execution of Byng under a similar odium and a similar charge, although expressly cleared of cowardice and disaffection, was still fresh in the naval mind. "Sir Robert has an ordeal to pass through," he wrote Collingwood, "which he little expects." His own opinion upon the case seems to have undergone some modification, since the generous outburst with which he at first deprecated the prejudgment of a disappointed and frightened people ; nor could it well fail, as details became known to him, that he should pass a silent censure upon proceedings, which contravened alike his inward professional convictions, and his expressed purposes of action for a similar contingency. " I have had, as you will believe, a very distressing scene with poor Sir Robert Calder," he told Lady Hamilton. "He has wrote home to beg an inquiry, feeling confident that he can fully justify himself. I sincerely hope he may, but — I have given him the advice as to my dearest friend. He is in adversity, and if he ever has been my enemy, he now feels the pang of it, and finds me one of his best friends." " Sir Robert Calder," he wrote to another correspondent, "has just left us to stand his trial, which I think of a very serious nature." Nelson was obliged to detain him until reinforcements arrived from England, because Calder was unwilling to undergo the

45

apparent humiliation of leaving his flagship under charges, and she could not yet be spared. It was not the least of this unlucky man's misfortunes that he left the fleet just a week before the battle, where his conduct would undoubtedly have redeemed whatever of errors he may have committed. One of the last remarks Nelson made before the action began, was, "Hardy, what would poor Sir Robert Calder give to be with us now!"

Calder's reluctance to quit his flagship, and the keen sensitiveness with which he expressed his feelings, drew from Nelson a concession he knew to be wrong, but which is too characteristic, both in the act itself and in his own account of it, to be omitted. "Sir Robert felt so much," he wrote to the First Lord, "even at the idea of being removed from his own ship which he commanded, in the face of the fleet, that I much fear I shall incur the censure of the Board of Admiralty, without your Lordship's influence with the members of it. I may be thought wrong, as an officer, to disobey the orders of the Admiralty, by not insisting on Sir Robert Calder's quitting the Prince of Wales for the Dreadnought, and for parting with a 90-gun ship, before the force arrives which their Lordships have judged necessary; but I trust that I shall be considered to have done right as a man, and to a brother officer in affliction — my heart could not stand it, and so the thing must rest. I shall submit to the wisdom of the Board to censure me or not, as to them may seem best for the Service; I shall bow with all due respect to their decision."

From the military point of view this step was indefensible, but it is in singular keeping with Nelson's kindness of heart, his generosity of temper, and with a certain recklessness of consequences, — when supported by inward conviction of right, or swayed by natural impulses, — which formed no small part of his greatness as a warrior. "Numbers only can annihilate;" yet to spare the feelings of an unhappy man, whom he believed to have been his enemy, he parted with one of the best units from his numbers, although, even with her present, he was inferior to the allies. He felt keenly, however, the responsibility he assumed, not only towards the Admiralty, but towards his own success and reputation. At one time he seems, with unusual vacillation, even to have returned upon his decision, and to have notified Calder that the ship could not be spared; for on the 12th of October the latter wrote him: "The contents of your Lordship's letter have cut me to the soul. If I am to be turned out of my ship, after all that has passed, I have only to request I may be allowed to take my Captain, and such officers as I find necessary for the justification of my conduct as an officer, and that I may be permitted to go without a moment's further loss of time. My heart is broken." This appeal broke down all Nelson's power of resistance. He deprived himself on the eve of battle of a first-rate ship, taking only the precaution of sending his entire correspondence with Calder, public and private, to explain his course, though scarcely to justify it. The significance of this act is enhanced by the known importance which he himself attached to the presence or absence of even a third-rate ship-of-the-line. When the expedition to the Baltic was on the eve of starting, a seventy-four went aground, in leaving the Downs. Lieutenant Layman having been conspicuously instrumental in getting her off, Nelson told him that he had in consequence written in his favor to the Admiralty; and upon Layman's remarking that what he had done scarcely deserved so much, the admiral replied, "I think differently, the loss of one line-of-battle ship might be the loss of a victory."

When Nelson joined the fleet, he found it stationed some fifteen to twenty miles from Cadiz. He soon moved the main body to fifty miles west of the port. "It is desirable," he admitted, "to be well up in easterly winds, but I must guard against being caught with a westerly wind near Cadiz, as a fleet of ships with so many three-deckers would inevitably be forced into the Straits, and then Cadiz would be perfectly free for the enemy to come out with a westerly wind, as they served Lord Keith in the late war." The memory of his weary beat out of the Mediterranean the previous April, against wind and current, remained vividly in his mind; and he feared also that the willingness of the enemy to come out, which was his great object, would be much cooled by the certainty that his fleet could not be avoided, and by seeing such additions as it might receive. "I think we are near enough," he wrote Collingwood, "for the weather if it is fine, the wind serves, and we are in sight, they will never move." "I rely on you," he tells Blackwood, "that we can't miss getting hold of them, and I will give them such a shaking as they never yet experienced; at least I will lay down my life in the attempt." An advanced squadron of fast-sailing seventy-fours was thrown out ten or twelve miles east of the fleet, through which daily signals could be exchanged with Blackwood's squadron of frigates, that cruised day and night close to the harbor's mouth. This disposition received a farther development after the 10th of October, when the combined fleets shifted from the inner harbor to the Bay of Cadiz, and gave other tokens of a speedy start. On the 14th of the month he made the following entry in his diary : "Enemy at the harbour's mouth. Placed Defence and Agamemnon from seven to ten leagues west of Cadiz, and Mars and Colossus five leagues east of fleet [that is, under way between the fleet and the former group], whose station is from fifteen to twenty leagues west of Cadiz ; and by this chain I hope to have constant communication with the frigates off Cadiz." To the captain of the "Defence" he wrote that it was possible the enemy might try to drive off the frigate squadron, in order to facilitate their own evasion ; in which case the inner ships-of-the-line would be at hand to resist the attempt.

Despite these careful dispositions, his mind was still ill at ease lest the enemy might escape undetected. He never had frigates enough to make the result as sure as it ought to be, where such vast issues were at stake. While eight at least were needed to be always with the fleet before Cadiz, he had but five; and to maintain even so many it was necessary to cut short other services and essential stations. This deficiency he urged upon the Government still more than he did the inadequacy of the line-of-battle force; for his fear of the enemy eluding him was greater than that of a conflict with superior numbers. As regards the latter contingency, he wrote to Lord Barham that, if the enemy came out, he would immediately bring them to battle ; "but, although I should not doubt of spoiling any voyage they might attempt, yet I hope for the arrival of the ships from England, that as an enemy's fleet they may be annihilated." On the other hand, "the last fleet was lost to me for want of frigates." Besides his own direct representations, he pressed Rose to obtain an intimation to the Admiralty from the Prime Minister, that the latter was personally solicitous that more small cruisers should be supplied. Both Collingwood and Nelson believed the allies bound to the Mediterranean; but in this they might be mistaken, and as the real object might be again the West Indies, lookouts should be placed off Cape Blanco on the coast of Africa, and off the Salvages,[1] both which he knew had been sighted by Villeneuve, in the outward voyage of the previous spring.

To his concern about the immediate situation before Cadiz were added the universal cares of the Mediterranean, with all parts of which he renewed his correspondence, occupying his active mind with provisions for forwarding the cause of Great Britain and her allies. Under his many anxieties, however, he preserved his buoyant, resolute temper, not worrying over possible happenings against which he was unable to provide. "The force is at present not so large as might be wished," he writes to Ball, "but I will do my best with it; they will give me more when they can, and I am not come forth to find difficulties, but to remove them." "Your Lordship may depend upon my exertions," he tells Barham. The possibility that he himself might fall was, as always, present to his thoughts, and never did life mean more to him than it now did; yet, as the twilight deepened, and the realization of danger passed gradually into a presentiment of death, he faced the prospect without gloom — steadfast still in mind. "Let the battle be when it may, it will never have been surpassed. My shattered frame, if I survive that day, will require rest, and that is all I shall ask for. If I fall on such a glorious occasion, it shall be my pride to take care that my friends shall not blush for me. These things are in the hands of a wise and just Providence, and His will be done! I have got some trifle, thank God, to leave those I hold most dear, and I have taken care not to neglect it. Do not think I am low-spirited on this account, or fancy anything is to happen to me; quite the contrary — my mind is calm, and I have only to think of destroying our inveterate foe."

Of these days of preoccupation, while in hourly expectation

[1] A desert group of small islands between Madeira and the Canaries.

of the issue, overcharged with official anxieties, and facing, however fearlessly, a growing impression that he himself would not survive the conflict for which he longed, an anecdote has been transmitted that shows again how to the end, and whatever his personal cares, his quick sympathy went out to men of all classes. Word had been passed through the fleet that a mail was about to start for England, which would not improbably be the last opportunity of writing home before the enemy came forth. The letters had been collected as usual, the bags were all on board the departing vessel, and she herself, under full sail, had got already some distance away, when Nelson saw a midshipman come up and speak to Lieutenant Pasco, the signal officer, who, upon hearing what was said, stamped his foot in evident vexation, and uttered an exclamation. The admiral, of whose nearness Pasco was not aware, called him, and asked what was the matter. "Nothing that need trouble your Lordship," was the reply. "You are not the man to lose your temper for nothing," rejoined Nelson. "What was it?" "Well, if you must know, my Lord, I will tell you. You see that cockswain," pointing to one of the most active of the petty officers; "we have not a better man on board the Victory and the message which put me out was this. I was told that he was so busy receiving and getting off the mail-bags, that he forgot to drop his own letter to his wife into one of them, and he has just discovered it in his pocket." "Hoist a signal to bring her back," was Nelson's instant command; "who knows that he may not fall in action to-morrow. His letter shall go with the rest," — and the despatch vessel was brought back for that alone.[1] In telling the story, Pasco used to say it was no wonder that the common sailors idolized Nelson, since he was always thinking about them, and won their hearts by showing his own.

In addition to the combined fleets in Cadiz, which numbered thirty-six of the line, besides frigates, the enemy had a half-dozen of the line in Cartagena, which showed signs of moving, and whose junction must be prevented, if possible. Partly for this reason, partly because it was necessary to renew the water of the ships, Nelson sent a detachment of six of the

[1] The author is indebted for this reminiscence to Mr. Stuart J. Reid, who received it from Pasco's son, also an officer in the Navy.

line to Gibraltar and Tetuan, immediately after he took charge. To the junior admiral who commanded it, and who lamented that they might lose their share in the expected battle, he replied : " I have no other means of keeping my fleet complete in provisions and water. The enemy *will* come out, and we shall fight them ; but there will be time for you to get back first." They did not, however, return as thus expected, a misadventure which was chiefly due to their having to guard a convoy past Cartagena, — a potent illustration of the influence exerted by a powerful squadron, judiciously placed on the flank of an important trade route, or line of communication ; but even had they rejoined, six others were told off to leave at once in turn. Nelson did not dare to take the fleet in mass to Tetuan, as he used to Madalena ; for he could never be sure of getting out of the Straits when he wished, or when the enemy moved. Thus his fleet was reduced, by both administrative and strategic exigencies, to twenty-three ships-of-the-line. Fortunately, four more joined before the battle, raising the numbers actually engaged to twenty-seven. It will be recognized that Calder's ninety-gun ship was no small loss.

Such were the general dispositions in which the sailing of the enemy was awaited. A main body of eighteen to twenty, fifty miles west of Cadiz, a frigate squadron close in to the harbor, and two groups of ships-of-the-line extended between these extremes. With a westerly wind, approach to the port would be easy for all ; with an easterly, Nelson wrote to Blackwood, he would habitually beat up for Cadiz, never going north of the port. His whereabouts in case of thick weather was thus always known. He notified Collingwood and his other subordinates, that if the enemy came out, he should stand for Cape Spartel, the African outpost of the Straits, to bar the entrance of the allies to the Mediterranean. Signals were arranged, precise, yet not so elaborate as to tend to confusion, by which the departure and general direction of the enemy could be continually transmitted, from the furthest lookouts to the main body, by night as by day.

On the 13th of October his old ship, the " Agamemnon," joined the fleet. She was commanded by Sir Edward Berry, who had been first lieutenant in her with Nelson, had accompanied him in boarding the " San Nicolas " and " San Josef "

at St. Vincent, and was afterwards his flag-captain at the Nile.
When her approach was reported to the admiral, he exclaimed
gleefully, "Here comes Berry! Now we shall have a battle;"
for Berry, having been in more fleet actions than any captain
in the British Navy,[1] had a proverbial reputation for such
luck. The event did not belie the prediction. Five days
later, on the 18th of the month, Nelson noted in his diary:
"Fine weather, wind easterly; the combined fleets cannot
have finer weather to put to sea;" and the following morning,
at half-past nine, the signal, repeated from masthead to masthead, from the inshore frigates to their commander-in-chief
fifty miles at sea, announced that the long-expected battle
was at hand — for "The Enemy are coming out of port."

---

[1] Besides three of the battles associated with Nelson's name — St. Vincent,
the Nile, and Trafalgar — Berry as a midshipman had been in the five fleet
actions between Suffren and Hughes, in the East Indies, in 1782 and 1783.
("The Nelson Memorial," by John Knox Laughton, pp. 83, 284.)

CHAPTER XXIII.

Trafalgar. — The Death of Nelson.

October 19–21, 1805.   Age, 47.

CONTRARY to the general policy that for many years had governed the naval undertakings of France and Spain, the combined fleets put to sea on the 19th of October, 1805, with the fixed purpose of daring the hazard of battle, which they could scarcely expect to avoid. They numbered thirty-three ships-of-the-line, eighteen French and fifteen Spanish, and were accompanied by five frigates and two brigs, all of which were French. This great force in its aggregate was one. There were not two separate entities, a French fleet and a Spanish fleet, acting in concert, as is often the case in alliances. Whatever the administrative arrangements, for cruising and for battle the vessels of the two nations were blended in a single mass, at the head of which was the French admiral, just as the general direction of the naval campaign was in the hands of the French Emperor alone. The commander-in-chief was Vice-Admiral Villeneuve, the same that Nelson recently had pursued to the West Indies and back to Europe. The commander of the Spanish contingent, Vice-Admiral Gravina, was less his colleague than his subordinate. There were also flying in the combined fleet the flags of four junior admirals, two French and two Spanish, and the broad pendants of several commodores.

In the allied force there were four three-decked ships, of from one hundred to one hundred and thirty guns, all Spanish, of which one, the "Santísima Trinidad," was the largest vessel then afloat. Among Nelson's twenty-seven there were seven three-deckers, of ninety-eight to one hundred guns; but in the lower rates the British were at a disadvantage, having but one eighty-gun ship and three sixty-fours, whereas the allies had six of the former and only one of the latter. All the other vessels of the line-of-battle were seventy-fours, the normal medium type, upon which the experience of most navies of that day had fixed, as best fitted for the general purposes of fleet warfare. Where more tonnage and heavier batteries were put into single ships, it was simply for the purpose of reinforcing the critical points of an order of battle; an aim that could not be as effectively attained by the combination of two ships, under two captains.

As Nelson said in his celebrated order, so large a body as thirty-three heavy vessels is not easily handled, even at sea; and leaving port with them is an operation yet more difficult. Consequently, the movement which began soon after daylight on the 19th was not completed that day. Owing to the falling of the wind, only twelve ships got fairly clear of the bay, outside of which they lay becalmed. The following morning the attempt was resumed, and by two or three o'clock in the afternoon of the 20th the whole combined fleet was united, and standing with a fresh southwest wind to the northward and westward, to gain room to windward for entering the Straits.

As has been said, the movement that Blackwood recognized at 7 A. M. of the 19th was communicated to the admiral at half-past nine. According to his announced plan, to cut the enemy off from the Mediterranean, he at once made signal for a General Chase to the southeast, — towards Cape Spartel, — and the fleet moved off in that direction with a light southerly wind. At noon Nelson sat down in his cabin to begin his last letter to Lady Hamilton. The words then written he signed, as though conscious that no opportunity to continue might offer; nor is it difficult to trace that some such thought was then uppermost in his mind, and sought expression in the tenderness of farewell. The following day, however, he added a few lines, in which the dominant note was fear that the enemy might again elude him, by returning into port; an apprehension that expelled the previous haunting sense of finality. There he laid down the pen, never again to address her directly. The letter, thus abruptly closed by death, was found open and unsigned upon his desk after the battle.

Victory, October 19th, 1805, Noon.
CADIZ, E. S. E., 16 Leagues.

MY DEAREST BELOVED EMMA, the dear friend of my bosom. The signal has been made that the Enemy's Combined Fleet are coming out of Port. We have very little wind, so that I have no hopes of seeing them before to-morrow. May the God of Battles crown my endeavours with success; at all events, I will take care that my name shall ever be most dear to you and Horatia, both of whom I love as much as my own life. And as my last writing before the Battle will be to you, so I hope in God that I shall live to finish my letter after the Battle. May Heaven bless you prays your

NELSON AND BRONTE.

October 20th.

In the morning, we were close to the Mouth of the Straits, but the wind had not come far enough to the Westward to allow the Combined Fleets to weather the Shoals off Trafalgar; but they were counted as far as forty Sail of Ships of War, which I suppose to be thirty-four of the Line, and six Frigates. A group of them was seen off the Lighthouse of Cadiz this morning, but it blows so very fresh and thick weather, that I rather believe they will go into the Harbour before night. May God Almighty give us success over these fellows, and enable us to get a Peace.

He wrote the same day to his daughter, addressing the letter to Miss Horatia Nelson Thompson,[1] by which name she had hitherto been known. In the Codicil to his Will, signed on the morning of the 21st, a few hours before the battle, he called her his adopted daughter, and desired that she would in future use the name of Nelson only.

Victory, October 19th, 1805.

My dearest Angel, — I was made happy by the pleasure of receiving your letter of September 19th, and I rejoice to hear that you are so very good a girl, and love my dear Lady Hamilton, who most dearly loves you. Give her a kiss for me. The Combined Fleets of the Enemy are now reported to be coming out of Cadiz; and therefore I answer your letter, my dearest Horatia, to mark to you that you are ever uppermost in my thoughts. I shall be sure of your prayers for my safety, conquest, and speedy return to dear Merton, and our dearest good Lady Hamilton. Be a good girl, mind what Miss Connor says to you. Receive, my dearest Horatia, the affectionate parental blessing of your Father,

NELSON AND BRONTE.

[1] The name Thompson was spelled by Nelson indifferently with or without the " p," which, as Nicolas observes, confirms the belief that it was fictitious. The fact is singular; for, from a chance remark of his, it appears that he meant it to be Thomson. (Morrison, Letter No. 569.)

The 20th of October opened with fresh breezes from south-southwest and heavy rains. At daybreak the British fleet was near the Straits' mouth, between Capes Trafalgar and Spartel, unable to see anything, but certain that, with the existing winds, the enemy could not have anticipated it there. Blackwood's frigates, out of sight to the northward, were dogging the path of the allies, of whose general position they were certain, although the thick weather hid them from observation. At 7 A. M. the frigate "Phœbe" signalled to Nelson that the enemy bore north. With the wind as it was, and considering the position of the land, they must be standing to the northwest, so that the British fleet wore and steered the same course, keeping parallel to the enemy and spreading lookouts in their direction. Soon after noon, the weather clearing, Blackwood saw the combined fleets where he believed them to be, under low sail, and so close that the "Euryalus" went about immediately. At 1 P. M. he left the squadron in temporary charge of a junior captain, and with his own ship kept away south to speak the admiral. At two he sighted the main body, and at 3.20 was near enough to send the telegraphic message, "The enemy appears determined to push to the westward." "That," wrote Nelson in his diary, "they shall *not* do, if in the power of Nelson and Bronté to prevent them," and he telegraphed back, "I rely upon your keeping sight of the enemy." The frigates and lookout ships, he noted in his journal, had so far discharged their duties most admirably, informing him promptly of all the hostile movements; he was justified therefore in the confidence that they would do as well in the night now approaching.

While Blackwood was communicating, Nelson himself was much of the time on the "Victory's" poop. Seeing there a number of midshipmen assembled, he observed to them, "This day or to-morrow will be a fortunate one for you, young gentlemen," alluding to their prospect of promotion after a successful battle. The same day at dinner, he said to some of the company, "To-morrow I will do that which will give you younger gentlemen something to talk and think about for the rest of your lives, but I shall not live to know about it myself;" and he added that he expected to capture

twenty to twenty-two of the hostile fleet.[1]   It may be inferred
from this remark that by the dinner hour, between three and
five, he had become satisfied that the enemy either would not,
or could not, return into port, according to the fear he had
expressed to Lady Hamilton, and that a battle therefore was
certain.   The letter to her, from its mention of the weather
as thick, must have been written in the forenoon.   His
expectation that the morrow would prove the decisive day
was reinforced by one of those prepossessions for coincidences,
half jesting, half serious, which are natural to men, but fall
too far short of conviction to be called superstitious.   On the
21st of October, 1757, his uncle Maurice Suckling had commanded one of three ships-of-the-line which had beaten off a
superior force.   Nelson had several times said to Captain
Hardy and Dr. Scott, "The 21st will be our day;" and on the
morning of the battle, when the prediction was approaching.
fulfilment, he again remarked that the 21st of October was
the happiest day in the year for his family; but he mentioned
no reason other than that just given.

The main bodies of the contending navies did not come in
sight of each other during the 20th; the British lookout
frigates, between the two, and three or four miles from the
allied line, could see their own fleet only from the masthead.
At about 2 p. m., soon after the weather cleared, the wind
shifted to west-northwest, taking the ships aback.   After
filling their sails again to the new wind, as this was now fair
for their approach to the Straits' mouth, the combined fleets
wore, and headed to the southward.   The British remaining
on the same tack as before, — the port, — stood to the northward until 8 p. m., when they also wore to the southwest;
but this interval of steering in nearly opposite directions
changed the relative bearings.   At midnight, by the log of
Blackwood's frigates, the enemy stretched along the eastern
horizon, while the British bore southwest; the space between
the two being ten miles.   The "Euryalus," three miles from
the allies, saw the loom of the lights of her own fleet.   Still
fearful lest the view of his ships should shake the enemy's

[1] The author is indebted for this anecdote to Mr. Edgar Goble, of Fareham,
Hants, whose father, Thomas Goble, then secretary to Captain Hardy, was
present at the table.

purpose, Nelson was careful not to lessen this distance; the more so because the British, having the wind, could attack when they pleased, provided the enemy by continuing to the southward deprived themselves of the power to regain Cadiz. Two British frigates were directed to keep them in sight during the night, reporting their movements to two others who were stationed a little farther from them, whence a chain of line-of-battle ships communicated with the "Victory." Thus, throughout the dark hours, signal lights and guns flashed across the waters to Nelson instantaneous information of every noteworthy occurrence in the hostile order.

Since the morning of the 19th, the weather, fine for some days previous, had become unsettled, working up for the southwest gale which wrought so much damage among the victims of the fight. As the night of the 20th advanced, the wind fell, and at midnight there were only light westerly breezes, inclining to calm. The same conditions continued at dawn, and throughout the day of the 21st until after the battle; but there was also a great swell from the westward, the precursor of a storm. At 4 A. M. the British fleet again wore, and was standing northeast when the day broke.

After leaving Cadiz, in order to avoid separations during the night, or in thick weather, the combined fleets had been disposed in five columns, a formation whose compactness, though not suited to an engagement, was less liable to straggling than a single long line, and brought all parts more directly under the control of the commander-in-chief at the centre. Of the five, the two to windward, of six ships each, constituted a reserve, similar to Nelson's proposed detachment of eight. It was commanded by Admiral Gravina, and was intended to reinforce such part of the battle as should appear to require it; an object for which the windward position was of the utmost moment, as it was for all naval initiative in that day. This advantage the allies did not have on the morning of Trafalgar. When Villeneuve, therefore, formed the line of battle, these twelve ships were at once incorporated with it, taking the lead of their order as it stood to the southward, with the wind at west-northwest, — a long column stretching over five miles of sea from end to end.

In a general sense, then, it may be said that, when daylight showed the enemies to each other, the British fleet was heading to the northward, and that of the allies to the southward; the latter being ten or twelve miles east of their opponents. In the far distance, Cape Trafalgar, from which the battle takes its name, was just visible against the eastern sky. At twenty minutes before seven Nelson made in quick succession the signals, "To form the order of sailing," — which by his previous instructions was to be the order of battle, — and "To prepare for battle." Ten minutes later followed the command to "Bear up," the "Victory" setting the example by at once altering her course for the enemy. Collingwood did the same, and the ships of the two divisions fell into the wake of their leaders as best they could, for the light wind afforded neither the means nor the time for refinements in manœuvring. Fourteen ships followed the "Royal Sovereign," which bore Collingwood's flag, while the remaining twelve gathered in Nelson's division behind the "Victory."[1] The two columns steered east, about a mile apart, that of Nelson being to the northward; from which circumstance, the wind being west-northwest, it has been called commonly the weather line.

Thus, as Ivanhoe, at the instant of encounter in the lists, shifted his lance from the shield to the casque of the Templar, Nelson, at the moment of engaging, changed the details of his plan, and substituted an attack in two columns, simultaneously made, for the charge of Collingwood's division, in line and in superior numbers, upon the enemy's flank; to be followed, more or less quickly, according to indications, by such movement of his own division as might seem advisable. It will be observed, however, that the order of sailing remained the order of battle, — probably, although it is not so stated, the fleet was already thus disposed when the signal was made, needing only rectification after the derangements incident to darkness, — and further, that the general direction of attack continued the same, Collingwood guiding his column upon the enemy's southern flank, while Nelson pointed a few ships

[1] One sixty-four, the "Africa," had separated to the northward during the night, and joined in the battle by passing alone along the enemy's line, much of the time under fire. She belonged, therefore, to Nelson's column, and co-operated with it during the day.

north of their centre. In this way was preserved the comprehensive aim which underlay the particular dispositions of
his famous order: "The whole impression of the British fleet
must be to overpower from two or three ships ahead of their
commander-in-chief, supposed to be in the Centre, to the Rear
of their fleet." The northern flank of the allies — ten or a
dozen ships — was consequently left unengaged, unless by
their own initiative they came promptly into action; which,
it may be added, they did not do until after the battle was
decided.

When the development of the British movement was recognized by Villeneuve, he saw that fighting was inevitable; and,
wishing to keep Cadiz, then twenty miles to the northward
and eastward, under his lee, he ordered the combined fleets
to wear together.[1] The scanty wind which embarrassed the
British impeded this manœuvre also, so that it was not completed till near ten o'clock. Nelson, however, noted its beginning at seven, and with grave concern; for not only would it
put the allies nearer their port, as it was intended to do, but
it would cause vessels crippled in the action to find to leeward
of them, during the gale which he foresaw, the dangerous
shoals off Trafalgar instead of the open refuge of the Straits.
The appreciation of the peril thus entailed led him to make
a signal for all the ships to be prepared to anchor after the
battle, for it was not to be hoped that the spars of many of
them would be in a condition to bear sail. The result of the
allied movement was to invert their order. Their ships, which
had been steering south, now all headed north; the van
became the rear; Gravina, who had been leading the column,
was in the rear ship; and it was upon this rear, but still the
southern flank of the hostile array, that the weight of Collingwood's attack was to fall.

Soon after daylight Nelson, who, according to his custom,
was already up and dressed, had gone on deck. He wore as

---

[1] Nelson in his journal wrote: "The enemy wearing *in succession.*" As
the allies' order was reversed, however, it is evident that he meant merely
that the ships wore one after the other, from rear to van, but in their respective stations, each waiting till the one astern had, to use the old phrase,
"marked her manœuvre," — a precaution intended to prevent collisions,
though it necessarily extended the line.

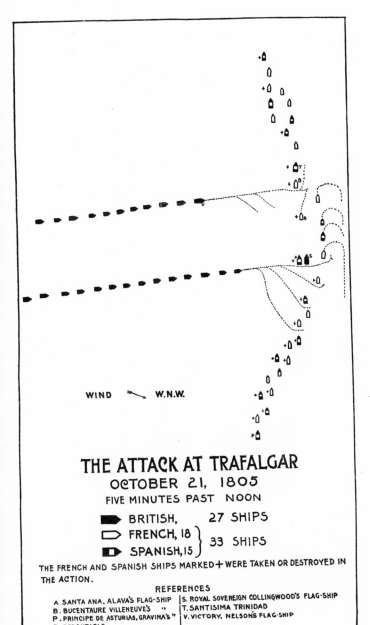

THE ATTACK AT TRAFALGAR

OCTOBER 21, 1805

FIVE MINUTES PAST NOON

WIND — W.N.W.

BRITISH, 27 SHIPS

FRENCH, 18 ⎫
SPANISH, 15 ⎭ 33 SHIPS

THE FRENCH AND SPANISH SHIPS MARKED + WERE TAKEN OR DESTROYED IN THE ACTION.

REFERENCES

A. SANTA ANA, ALAVA'S FLAG-SHIP
B. BUCENTAURE VILLENEUVE'S "
P. PRINCIPE DE ASTURIAS, GRAVINA'S "
R. REDOUTABLE

S. ROYAL SOVEREIGN COLLINGWOOD'S FLAG-SHIP
T. SANTISIMA TRINIDAD
V. VICTORY, NELSON'S FLAG-SHIP

usual his admiral's frock coat, on the left breast of which were stitched the stars of four different Orders that he always bore. It was noticed that he did not wear his sword at Trafalgar, although it lay ready for him on the cabin table; and it is supposed he forgot to call for it, as this was the only instance in which he was known not to carry it when engaged. At about six o'clock he summoned Captain Blackwood on board the " Victory." This officer had had a hard fag during the past forty-eight hours, dogging the enemy's movements through darkness and mist; but that task was over, and his ambition now was to get command of one of two seventy-fours, whose captains had gone home with Calder to give evidence at his trial. " My signal just made on board the Victory," he wrote to his wife. " I hope to order me to a vacant line-of-battle ship." Nelson's purpose, however, as far as stated by Blackwood, was simply to thank him for the successful efforts of the past two days, and to have him by his side till the flag-ship came under fire, in order to receive final and precise instructions, as the situation developed, for the conduct of the frigates during and after the battle. To Blackwood's congratulations upon the approach of the moment that he had, to use his own word, panted for, he replied: " I mean to-day to bleed the captains of the frigates, as I shall keep you on board to the very last moment."

Blackwood found him in good but very calm spirits, preoccupied with the movements of the allies, and the probable results of his own plan of attack. He frequently asked, " What would you consider a victory ? " Blackwood answered: " Considering the handsome way in which the battle is offered by the enemy, their apparent determination for a fair trial of strength, and the proximity of the land, I think if fourteen ships are captured, it will be a glorious result." Nelson's constant reply was that he would not be satisfied with anything short of twenty. He admitted, however, that the nearness of the land might make it difficult to preserve the prizes, and he was emphatic in directing that, if the shattered enemies had any chance of returning to Cadiz, the frigates were to be actively employed in destroying them, and were not to be diverted from that single aim in order to save either ships or men. Annihilation, he repeated, was his aim, and nothing

46

short of it; and he must have regretted the absence of the six of the line in the Mediterranean, imperative as that had been. Word had been sent for them to Gibraltar by Blackwood the moment the enemy moved, but they were still away with the convoy.

Blackwood, being a great personal friend of the admiral, took the liberty, after exchanging greetings, of submitting to him the expediency of shifting his flag to the "Euryalus,". and conducting the battle from her. Nelson made no reply, but immediately ordered more sail to be made upon the "Victory." Finding himself foiled in this, Blackwood then made a direct request for the command of one of the two vacant seventy-fours. This would give him a chance to share in the fight, which in a frigate he probably would not have, but it would also displace the first lieutenant of the ship from the position to which he had succeeded temporarily. Nelson replied instantly, "No, Blackwood, it is those men's birthright, and they shall have it." [1] The incident shows vividly the lively sympathy and sense of justice which ever distinguished Nelson; for it must have pained him to deny a request so consonant to his own temper, coming from one whom he had long known and valued, both as a friend and as an officer, and of whose recent service such orders would have been a graceful and appropriate acknowledgment. It may be desirable to explain to unprofessional readers what was the claim of the lieutenants which Nelson refused to ignore. The efficiency of the ships for the coming day's work was due to them scarcely less than to the absent captains, and if they survived the battle, having been in command through it, they would reap not only the honor but also their confirmation in the rank of post-captain, through having exercised it in actual battle. This succession the admiral aptly called their birthright.

Nelson availed himself of Blackwood's presence to have him, together with Hardy, witness his signature to a paper, in which he bequeathed Lady Hamilton and the child Horatia to the care of the nation, and which consequently has been styled a Codicil to his Will. Unless Blackwood's memory a

---

[1] The author is indebted for these incidents to Admiral Sir W. R. Mends, G. C. B., who received them from the second baronet, Sir Henry M. Blackwood, when serving with him as first lieutenant.

few years later was at fault, in stating that his signal was
made at six o'clock,[1] it is likely enough that this early summons was for the special purpose of giving formal completeness, by the attestation of two of his closest friends, to a
private duty which was the last to engage Nelson's attention
and affections; for, in addition to the date, the place and hour
of his writing are fixed by the words, "In sight of the Combined Fleets of France and Spain, distant about ten miles."
This was the common estimate of the relative positions, made
by the British fleet at large at daybreak, and coincides fairly
well with the inferences to be drawn, from the slow rate of
speed at which the wind permitted the British to advance,
and from the hour the conflict began. Nor was there time,
nor convenient room, for further delay. A freshening breeze
might readily have brought the fleet into action in a couple
of hours, and it is the custom in preparing for battle — the
signal for which was made at 6.40 — to remove most of the
conveniences, and arrangements for privacy, from the living
spaces of the officers; partly to provide against their destruction, chiefly to clear away all impediments to fighting the
guns, and to moving about the ship. In the case of the
admiral, of course, much might be postponed to the last moment, but in fact his cabin was cleared of fixtures immediately
after he went on the poop in the early morning; for it is
distinctly mentioned that while there he gave particular directions in the matter, and enjoined great care in handling the
portrait of Lady Hamilton, saying, "Take care of my guardian
angel."

It seems, therefore, probable that this so-called Codicil was
written in the quiet minutes of the morning, while the fleet
was forming its order of sailing and bearing up for the enemy,
but before the admiral's cabin was cleared for battle. In it

---

[1] The "Euryalus's" log gives eight o'clock as the hour of the captain's
going on board the "Victory;" but Blackwood not only says six, but also
mentions that his stay on board lasted five and a half hours, which gives
about the same time for going on board. The other frigate captains did not
go till eight. Blackwood, as the senior, might need a fuller and longer continued interview, because the general direction of the frigate squadron would
be in his hands; or Nelson might particularly desire the presence of a close
professional friend, the captains of the ships-of-the-line having their hands
now full of preparations.

Nelson first recounted, briefly but specifically, "the eminent services of Emma Hamilton" to the state, on two occasions, as believed by himself to have been rendered. Into the actuality of these services it is not necessary here to inquire;[1] it is sufficient to say that Nelson's knowledge of them could not have been at first hand, and that the credence he unquestionably gave to them must have depended upon the evidence of others, — probably of Lady Hamilton herself, in whom he felt, and always expressed, the most unbounded confidence. "Could I have rewarded these services," the paper concludes, "I would not now call upon my Country; but as that has not been in my power, I leave Emma Lady Hamilton, therefore, a legacy to my King and Country, that they will give her an ample provision to maintain her rank in life. I also leave to the beneficence of my Country my adopted daughter, Horatia Nelson Thompson;, and I desire she will use in future the name of Nelson only. These are the only favours I ask of my King and Country at this moment when I am going to fight their battle. May God bless my King and Country, and all those who I hold dear. My relations it is needless to mention: they will of course be amply provided for."

At seven o'clock Nelson had returned from the poop to the cabin, for at that hour was made in his private journal the last entry of occurrences, — "At seven the combined fleets wearing in succession." Here it seems likely that he laid down the pen, for, when he was found writing again, some hours later, it was to complete the long record of experiences and of duties, with words that summed up, in fit and most touching expression, the self-devotion of a life already entering the shadow of death.

Between eight and nine o'clock the other frigate commanders came on board the "Victory;" aides-de-camp, as it were, waiting to the last moment to receive such orders as might require more extensive wording, or precise explanation, than is supplied by the sententious phrases of the signal-book. Blackwood himself, a captain of long standing and of tried

---

[1] The question of Lady Hamilton's services on the occasions mentioned by Nelson, vigorously asserted by herself, has been exhaustively discussed by Professor John Knox Laughton, in the "United Service Magazine" for April and May, 1889. His conclusions are decisively adverse to her claims.

ability, was in fact intrusted contingently with no small share of the power and discretion of the commander-in-chief. " He not only gave me command of all the frigates, but he also gave me a latitude, seldom or ever given, that of making any use I pleased of his name, in ordering any of the sternmost line-of-battle ships to do what struck me as best." While thus waiting, the captains accompanied the admiral in an inspection which he made of the decks and batteries of the flagship. He addressed the crew at their several quarters, cautioned them against firing a single shot without being sure of their object, and to the officers he expressed himself as highly satisfied with the arrangements made.

Meanwhile the two fleets were forming, as best they could with the scanty breeze, the order in which each meant to meet the shock of battle. The British could not range themselves in regular columns without loss of time that was not to be thrown away. They advanced rather in two elongated groups, all under full sail, even to studding-sails on both sides, the place of each ship being determined chiefly by her speed, or, perhaps, by some fortuitous advantage of position when the movement began. The great point was to get the heads of the columns into action as soon as possible, to break up the enemy's order. That done, those which followed could be trusted to complete the business on the general lines prescribed by Nelson. Collingwood's ship, the " Royal Sovereign," being but a few days out from home, and freshly coppered, easily took the lead in her own division. After her came the " Belleisle," also a recent arrival off Cadiz, but an old Mediterranean cruiser which had accompanied Nelson in the recent chase to the West Indies. Upon these two ships, as upon the heads of all columns, fell the weight of destruction from the enemy's resistance.

The " Victory," always a fast ship, had likewise little difficulty in keeping her place at the front. Blackwood, having failed to get Nelson on board his own frigate, and realizing the exposure inseparable from the position of leader, ventured, at about half-past nine, when still six miles from the enemy, to urge that one or two ships should be permitted to precede the " Victory." Nelson gave a conditional assent — " Let them go," if they can. The " Téméraire," a three-decker,

being close behind, was hailed to go ahead, and endeavored to
do so; but at the same moment the admiral gave an indication of how little disposed he was to yield either time or position. The lee lower studding-sail happening to be badly set,
the lieutenant of the forecastle had it taken in, meaning to
reset it; which Nelson observing, ran forward and rated him
severely for delaying the ship's progress. Anything much less
useful than a lee lower studding-sail is hard to imagine, but
by this time the admiral was getting very restive. "About
ten o'clock," says Blackwood, "Lord Nelson's anxiety to close
with the enemy became very apparent: he frequently remarked that they put a good face upon it; but always
quickly added: 'I'll give them such a dressing as they never
had before.'"

Seeing that the "Téméraire" could not pass the "Victory"
in time to lead into the hostile order, unless the flagship gave
way, Blackwood, feeling perhaps that he might wear out his
own privilege, told Hardy he ought to say to the admiral that,
unless the "Victory" shortened sail, the other ships could not
get into place; but Hardy naturally demurred. In any event,
it was not just the sort of proposition that the captain of the
ship would wish to make, and it was very doubtful how Nelson
might take it. This the latter soon showed, however; for, as
the "Téméraire" painfully crawled up, and her bows doubled
on the "Victory's" quarter, he hailed her, and speaking as he
always did with a slight nasal intonation, said: "I'll thank
you, Captain Harvey, to keep in your proper station, which is
astern of the Victory." The same concern for the admiral's
personal safety led the assembled officers to comment anxiously
upon the conspicuous mark offered by his blaze of decorations,
knowing as they did that the enemy's ships swarmed with
soldiers, that among them were many sharpshooters, and that
the action would be close. None, however, liked to approach
him with the suggestion that he should take any precaution. At length the surgeon, whose painful duty it was
a few hours later to watch over the sad fulfilment of his
apprehensions, said that he would run the risk of his Lordship's displeasure; but before he could find a fitting opportunity to speak, a shot flew over the "Victory," and the
admiral directed all not stationed on deck to go to their

quarters. No remark therefore was made; but it is more likely that Nelson would have resented the warning than that he would have heeded it.

The French and Spanish fleets, being neither a homogeneous nor a well-exercised mass, experienced even greater difficulty than the British in forming their array; and the matter was to them of more consequence, for, as the defensive has an advantage in the careful preparations he may make, so, if he fail to accomplish them, he has little to compensate for the loss of the initiative, which he has yielded his opponent. The formation at which they aimed, the customary order of battle in that day, was a long, straight, single column, presenting from end to end an unbroken succession of batteries, close to one another and clear towards the foe, so that all the ships should sweep with their guns the sea over which, nearly at right angles, the hostile columns were advancing. Instead of this, embarrassed by both lack of wind and lack of skill, their manœuvres resulted in a curved line, concave to the enemy's approach; the horns of the crescent thus formed being nearer to the latter. Collingwood noted that this disposition facilitated a convergent fire upon the assailants, the heads of whose columns were bearing down on the allied centre; it does not seem to have been remarked that the two horns, or wings, being to windward of the centre, also had it more in their power to support the latter — a consideration of very great importance. Neither of these advantages, however, was due to contrivance. The order of the combined fleets was the result merely of an unsuccessful effort to assume the usual line of battle. The ships distributed along the crescent lay irregularly, sometimes two and three abreast, masking each other's fire. On the other hand, even this irregularity had some compensations, for a British vessel, attempting to pass through at such a place, fell at once into a swarm of enemies. From horn to horn was about five miles. Owing to the lightness of the breeze, the allies carried a good deal of sail, a departure from the usual battle practice. This was necessary in order to enable them to keep their places at all, but it also had the effect of bringing them continually, though very gradually, nearer to Cadiz. Seeing this, Nelson signalled to Collingwood, "I intend to pass through the van of the enemy's line, to prevent him from getting into Cadiz," and the course of the "Victory," for this purpose, was changed a little to the northward.

After this, towards eleven o'clock, Nelson went below to the cabin. It was his habit, when an engagement was expected, to have all the bulkheads[1] upon the fighting decks taken down, and those of his own apartments doubtless had been removed at least as soon as the enemy's sailing was signalled; but it was possible to obtain some degree of privacy by hanging screens, which could be hurried out of the way at the last moment. The "Victory" did not come under fire till 12.30, so that at eleven she would yet be three miles or more distant from the enemy,[2] and screens could still remain. Shortly after he entered, the signal-lieutenant, who had been by his side all the morning, followed him, partly to make an official report, partly to prefer a personal request. He was the ranking lieutenant on board, but had not been permitted to exercise the duties of first lieutenant, because Nelson some time before, to avoid constant changes in that important station, had ordered that the person then occupying it should so continue, notwithstanding the seniority of any who might afterwards join. Now that battle was at hand, the oldest in rank wished to claim the position, and to gain the reward that it insured after a victory, — a request natural and not improper, but more suited for the retirement of the cabin than for the publicity of the deck.

Whatever the original injustice, — or rather hardship, — it is scarcely likely, remembering the refusal encountered by Blackwood, that Nelson would have consented now to deprive of his "birthright" the man who so far had been doing the work; but the petition was never preferred. Entering the cabin, the officer paused at the threshold, for Nelson was on his knees writing. The words, the last that he ever penned, were written in the private diary he habitually kept, in which were noted observations and reflections upon passing occurrences, mingled with occasional self-communings. They followed now, without break of space, or paragraph, upon the last incident recorded — " At seven the enemy wearing in succession " — and they ran thus : —

"May the Great God, whom I worship, grant to my

1 See *ante*, p. 639.   2 That is, with a one and a half knot breeze.

Country, and for the benefit of Europe in general, a great and glorious victory; and may no misconduct in any one tarnish it; and may humanity after victory be the predominant feature in the British fleet. For myself, individually, I commit my life to Him who made me, and may His blessing light upon my endeavours for serving my Country faithfully. To Him I resign myself and the just cause which is entrusted to me to defend. Amen. Amen. Amen."

The officer, Lieutenant Pasco, waited quietly till Nelson rose from his knees, and then made his necessary report; but, although his future prospects hung upon the wish he had to express, he refrained with singular delicacy from intruding it upon the preoccupation of mind evidenced by the attitude in which he had found his commander. The latter soon afterwards followed him to the poop, where Blackwood was still awaiting his final instructions. To him Nelson said, "I will now amuse the fleet with a signal;" and he asked if he did not think there was one yet wanting. Blackwood replied that the whole fleet seemed very clearly to understand what they were about, and were vying with each other to get as near as possible to the leaders of the columns. Upon this succeeded the celebrated signal, the development of which to its final wording is a little uncertain. Comparing the various accounts of witnesses, it seems probably to have been as follows. Nelson mused for a little while, as one who phrases a thought in his own mind before uttering it, and then said, "Suppose we telegraph 'Nelson confides that every man will do his duty.'" In this form it was the call of the leader to the followers, the personal appeal of one who trusts to those in whom he trusts, a feeling particularly characteristic of the speaker, whose strong hold over others lay above all in the transparent and unswerving faith he showed in their loyal support; and to arouse it now in full force he used the watchword "duty," sure that the chord it struck in him would find its quick response in every man of the same blood. The officer to whom the remark was made, suggested "England" instead of "Nelson." To the fleet it could have made no difference, — to them the two names meant the same thing; but Nelson accepted the change with delight. "Mr. Pasco," he called to the signal officer,

"I wish to say to the fleet, 'England confides that every man will do his duty;'" and he added, "You must be quick, for I have one more to make, which is for close action." This remark shows that the columns, and particularly Collingwood's ship, were already nearing the enemy. Pasco answered, "If your Lordship will permit me to substitute 'expects' for 'confides,' it will be sooner completed, because 'expects' is in the vocabulary,[1] and 'confides' must be spelt." Nelson replied hastily, but apparently satisfied, "That will do, Pasco, make it directly;" but the slightly mandatory "expects" is less representative of the author of this renowned sentence than the cordial and sympathetic "confides." It is "Allez," rather than "Allons;" yet even so, become now the voice of the distant motherland, it carries with it the shade of reverence, as well as of affection, which patriotism exacts.

It is said that Collingwood, frequently testy, and at the moment preoccupied with the approaching collision with the Spanish three-decker he had marked for his opponent, exclaimed impatiently when the first number went aloft, "I wish Nelson would stop signalling, as we know well enough what we have to do." But the two life-long friends, who were not again to look each other in the face, soon passed to other thoughts, such as men gladly recall when death has parted them. When the whole signal was reported to him, and cheers resounded along the lines, Collingwood cordially expressed his own satisfaction. A few moments later, just at noon, the French ship "Fougueux," the second astern of the "Santa Ana," for which the "Royal Sovereign" was steering, fired at the latter the first gun of the battle. As by a common impulse the ships of all the nations engaged hoisted their colors, and the admirals their flags, — a courteous and chivalrous salute preceding the mortal encounter. For ten minutes the "Royal Sovereign" advanced in silence, the one centre of the hostile fire, upon which were fixed all eyes, as yet without danger of their own to distract. As she

[1] The vocabulary of the telegraphic signal book provides certain words which can be signalled by a single number. Words not in this vocabulary must be spelled letter by letter, — each letter of the alphabet having its own number.

drew near the two ships between which she intended to pass, Nelson exclaimed admiringly, "See how that noble fellow Collingwood carries his ship into action." At about the same instant Collingwood was saying to his flag-captain, "Rotherham, what would Nelson give to be here!"

These things being done, Nelson said to Blackwood, "Now I can do no more. We must trust to the great Disposer of all events, and to the justice of our cause. I thank God for this great opportunity of doing my duty." When his last signal had been acknowledged by a few ships in the van, the admiral directed Pasco to make that for close action, and to keep it up. This was accordingly hoisted on board the flagship, where it was flying still as she disappeared into the smoke of the battle, and so remained till shot away. The "Victory" was about two miles from the "Royal Sovereign" when the latter, at ten minutes past twelve, broke through the allied order, and she had still a mile and a half to go before she herself could reach it. At twenty minutes past twelve Villeneuve's flagship, the "Bucentaure," of eighty guns, fired a shot at her, to try the range. It fell short. A few minutes later a second was fired, which dropped alongside. The distance then was a mile and a quarter. Two or three followed in rapid succession and passed over the "Victory." Nelson then turned to Blackwood, and directed him and Captain Prowse of the "Sirius" to return to their ships, but in so doing to pass along the column and tell the captains he depended upon their exertions to get into action as quickly as possible. He them bade them again to go away. Blackwood, who was standing by him at the forward end of the poop, took his hand, and said, "I trust, my Lord, that on my return to the Victory, which will be as soon as possible, I shall find your Lordship well and in possession of twenty prizes." Nelson replied, "God bless you, Blackwood, I shall never speak to you again."

The "Victory" was all the time advancing, the feeble breeze urging her progress, which was helped also by her lurching through the heavy following swell that prevailed. Before Blackwood could leave her, a shot passed through the maintopgallantsail, and the rent proclaimed to the eager eyes of the foes that the ship was fairly under their guns. Thereupon

everything about the "Bucentaure," some seven or eight ships,
at least, opened upon this single enemy, as the allied rear and
centre had upon the "Royal Sovereign;" for it was imperative
to stop her way, if possible, or at least to deaden it, and so to
delay as long as might be the moment when she could bring
her broadside to bear effectively. During the forty minutes
that followed, the "Victory" was an unresisting target to her
enemies, and her speed, slow enough at the first, decreased
continually as the hail of shot riddled the sails, or stripped
them from the yards. Every studding-sail boom was shot
away close to the yard arms, and this light canvas, invaluable
in so faint a wind, fell helplessly into the water. During
these trying moments, Mr. Scott, the admiral's public secretary, was struck by a round shot while talking with Captain
Hardy, and instantly killed. Those standing by sought to
remove the body without drawing Nelson's attention to the
loss of one so closely associated with him; but the admiral
had noticed the fall. "Is that poor Scott," he said, "who is
gone?" The clerk who took the dead man's place was killed
a few moments later by the wind of a ball, though his person
was untouched.

The "Victory" continuing to forge slowly ahead, despite
her injuries, and pointing evidently for the flagship of the
hostile commander-in-chief, the ships round the latter, to use
James's striking phrase, now "closed like a forest." The
nearer the British vessel drew, the better necessarily became
the enemies' aim. Just as she got within about five hundred
yards — quarter of a mile — from the "Bucentaure's" beam,
the mizzen topmast was shot away. At the same time the
wheel was hit and shattered, so that the ship had to be steered
from below, a matter that soon became of little importance.
A couple of minutes more, eight marines were carried off by a
single projectile, while standing drawn up on the poop, whereupon Nelson ordered the survivors to be dispersed about the
deck. Presently a shot coming in through the ship's side
ranged aft on the quarter-deck towards the admiral and
Captain Hardy, between whom it passed. On its way it
struck the fore-brace bitts — a heavy block of timber — carrying thence a shower of splinters, one of which bruised Hardy's
foot. The two officers, who were walking together, stopped,

and looked inquiringly at each other. Seeing that no harm was done, Nelson smiled, but said, "This is too warm work, Hardy, to last long." He then praised the cool resolution of the seamen around him, compelled to endure this murderous fire without present reply. He had never, he said, seen better conduct. Twenty men had so far been killed and thirty wounded, with not a shot fired from their own guns.

Still the ship closed the "Bucentaure." It had been Nelson's purpose and desire to make her his special antagonist, because of Villeneuve's flag; but to do so required room for the "Victory" to turn under the French vessel's stern, and to come up alongside. As she drew near, Hardy, scanning the hostile array, saw three ships crowded together behind and beyond the "Bucentaure." He reported to Nelson that he could go close under her stern, but could not round-to alongside, nor pass through the line, without running on board one of these. The admiral replied, "I cannot help it, it does not signify which we run on board of. Go on board which you please: take your choice." At one o'clock the bows of the "Victory" crossed the wake of the "Bucentaure," by whose stern she passed within thirty feet, the projecting yard arms grazing the enemy's rigging. One after another, as they bore, the double-shotted guns tore through the woodwork of the French ship, the smoke, driven back, filling the lower decks of the "Victory," while persons on the upper deck, including Nelson himself, were covered with the dust which rose in clouds from the wreck. From the relative positions of the two vessels, the shot ranged from end to end of the "Bucentaure," and the injury was tremendous. Twenty guns were at once dismounted, and the loss by that single discharge was estimated, by the French, at four hundred men. Leaving the further care of the enemy's flagship to her followers, secure that they would give due heed to the admiral's order, that "every effort must be made to capture the hostile commander-in-chief," the "Victory" put her helm up, inclining to the right, and ran on board a French seventy-four, the "Redoutable," whose guns, as well as those of the French "Neptune," had been busily playing upon her hitherto. At 1.10 she lay along the port side of the "Redoutable," the two ships falling off with their heads to the eastward, and moving slowly before the wind to the east-southeast.

In the duel which ensued between these two, in which Nelson fell, the disparity, so far as weight of battery was concerned, was all against the French ship; but the latter, while greatly overmatched at the guns, much the greater part of which were below deck, was markedly superior to her antagonist in small-arm fire on the upper deck, and especially aloft, where she had many musketeers stationed. Nelson himself was averse to the employment of men in that position, thinking the danger of fire greater than the gain, but the result on this day was fatal to very many of the " Victory's " men as well as to himself. As the ship's place in the battle was fixed for the moment, nothing now remained to be done, except for the crews to ply their weapons till the end was reached. The admiral and the captain, their parts of direction and guidance being finished, walked back and forth together on the quarter-deck, on the side farthest from the " Redoutable," where there was a clear space of a little over twenty feet in length, fore and aft, from the wheel to the hatch ladder leading down to the cabin. The mizzen top of the " Redoutable," garnished with sharpshooters, was about fifty feet above them. Fifteen minutes after the vessels came together, as the two officers were walking forward, and had nearly reached the usual place of turning, Nelson, who was on Hardy's left, suddenly faced left about. Hardy, after taking a step farther, turned also, and saw the admiral in the act of falling — on his knees, with his left hand touching the deck ; then, the arm giving way, he fell on his left side. It was in the exact spot where Scott, the secretary, had been killed an hour before. To Hardy's natural exclamation that he hoped he was not badly hurt, he replied, " They have done for me at last ; " and when the expression of hope was repeated, he said again, " Yes, my back-bone is shot through." " I felt it break my back," he told the surgeon, a few minutes later. The ball had struck him on the left shoulder, on the forward part of the epaulette, piercing the lung, where it severed a large artery, and then passed through the spine from left to right, lodging finally in the muscles of the back. Although there was more than one mortal injury, the immediate and merciful cause of his speedy death was the internal bleeding from the artery. Within a few moments of his wounding some forty officers and men were cut down by the same murderous fire from the tops of the enemy. Indeed so stripped of men was the upper deck of the "Victory" that the French made a movement to board, which was repulsed, though with heavy loss.

The stricken hero was at once carried below, himself covering his face and the decorations of his coat with his handkerchief, that the sight of their loss might not affect the ship's company at this critical instant. The cockpit was already cumbered with the wounded and dying, but the handkerchief falling from his face, the surgeon recognized him, and came at once to him. "You can do nothing for me, Beatty," he said; "I have but a short time to live." The surgeon also uttered the involuntary exclamation of encouragement, which rises inevitably to the lips at such a moment; but a short examination, and the sufferer's statement of his sensations, especially the gushing of blood within the breast, which was vividly felt, convinced him that there was indeed no hope. "Doctor, I am gone," he said to the Rev. Mr. Scott, the chaplain, who knelt beside him; and then added in a low voice, "I have to leave Lady Hamilton, and my adopted daughter Horatia, as a legacy to my Country."

After the necessary examination had been made, nothing further could be done, nor was attempted, than to obtain the utmost possible relief from suffering. Dr. Scott and the purser of the "Victory" sustained the bed under his shoulders, raising him into a semi-recumbent posture, the only one that was supportable to him, and fanned him; while others gave him the cooling drink — lemonade — which he continually demanded. Those about did not speak to him, except when addressed; but the chaplain, to whom Nelson frequently said, "Pray for me, Doctor," ejaculated with him short prayers from time to time. The agony of mortal pain wrung from him repeated utterance, though no unmanly complaint; and his thoughts dwelt more upon home and the battle than upon his own suffering and approaching death. His mind remained clear until he became speechless, about fifteen minutes before he passed away, and he took frequent notice of what occurred near him, as well as of sounds on deck.

The hour that succeeded his wounding was the decisive

one of the fight; not that the issue admitted of much doubt, after once Nelson's plans had received fulfilment, and the battle joined, — unless the delinquent van of the allies had acted promptly, — but in those moments the work was done which was thenceforth, for the enemy, beyond repair. Overhead, therefore, the strife went on incessantly, the seamen toiling steadily at their guns, and cheering repeatedly. Near the admiral lay Lieutenant Pasco, severely but not fatally wounded. At one burst of hurrahs, Nelson asked eagerly what it was about; and Pasco replying that another ship had struck, he expressed his satisfaction. Soon he became very anxious for further and more exact information of the course of the battle, and about the safety of Captain Hardy, upon whom now was devolved such guidance as the fleet, until the action was over, must continue to receive from the flagship of the commander-in-chief. In accordance with his wishes many messages were sent to Hardy to come to him, but for some time it was not possible for that officer to leave the deck. During this period, up to between half-past two and three, the ships of the two British divisions, that followed the leaders, were breaking successively into the enemy's order, and carrying out with intelligent precision the broad outlines of Nelson's instructions. The heads of the columns had dashed themselves to pieces, like a forlorn hope, against the overpowering number of foes which opposed their passage — an analysis of the returns shows that upon the four ships which led, the "Victory" and "Téméraire," the "Royal Sovereign" and "Belleisle," fell one-third of the entire loss in a fleet of twenty-seven sail. But they had forced their way through, and by the sacrifice of themselves had shattered and pulverized the local resistance, destroyed the coherence of the hostile line, and opened the road for the successful action of their followers. With the appearance of the latter upon the scene, succeeded shortly by the approach of the allied van, though too late and in disorder, began what may be called the second and final phase of the battle.

While such things were happening the deck could not be left by Hardy, who, for the time being, was commander-in-chief as well as captain. Shortly after Nelson fell, the "Téméraire" had run on board the "Redoutable" on the other side,

CAPTAIN THOMAS MASTERMAN HARDY.

From the painting by Robert Evans, at Greenwich Hospital.

and the French " Fougueux " upon the " Téméraire," so that
for a few minutes the four ships were fast together, in the
heat of the fight. About quarter past two, the " Victory "
was shoved clear, and lay with her head to the northward,
though scarcely with steerage way. The three others remained in contact with their heads to the southward. While
this *mêlée* was in progress, the French flagship " Bucentaure "
surrendered, at five minutes past two; but, before hauling
down the flag, Villeneuve made a signal to his recreant van, —
" The ships that are not engaged, take positions which will
bring them most rapidly under fire." Thus summoned, the
ten vessels which constituted the van began to go about, as
they should have done before ; and, although retarded by the
slack wind, they had got their heads to the southward by half-
past two. Five stood to leeward of the line of battle, but
five to windward. The latter would pass not far to the westward of the " Victory," and to meet this fresh attack demanded
the captain's further care, and postponed his going to the
death-bed of his chief. The latter had become very agitated
at the delay, thinking that Hardy might be dead and the news
kept from him. " Will nobody bring Hardy to me ? " he
frequently exclaimed. " He must be killed; he is surely
destroyed." At last a midshipman came down with the message that " circumstances respecting the fleet required the
captain's presence on deck, but that he would take the first
favourable moment to visit his Lordship." Nelson, hearing
the voice, asked who it was that spoke. The lad, Bulkeley,
who later in the day was wounded also, was the son of a
former shipmate in the far back days of the San Juan expedition, and the dying admiral charged the lad with a
remembrance to his father.

Two ships of Nelson's column, as yet not engaged, — the
" Spartiate " and the " Minotaur," — were then just reaching
the scene. Being in the extreme rear, the lightness of the
breeze had so far delayed them. Arriving thus opportunely,
they hauled to the wind so as to interpose between the " Victory " and the approaching van of the allies. Covered now
by two wholly fresh ships, the captain felt at liberty to quit
the deck, in accordance with Nelson's desire. The two tried
friends — Hardy had been everywhere with him since the day

47

of St. Vincent, and was faithful enough to speak to Lady Hamilton more freely than she liked — shook hands affectionately. "Well, Hardy," said Nelson, "how goes the battle? How goes the day with us?" "Very well, my Lord," replied Hardy. "We have got twelve or fourteen of the enemy's ships in our possession, but five of their van have tacked, and show an intention of bearing down upon the Victory. I have therefore called two or three of our fresh ships round us, and have no doubt of giving them a drubbing." "I hope none of *our* ships have struck, Hardy." "No, my Lord," was the answer, "there is no fear of that." Nelson then said, "I am a dead man, Hardy. I am going fast: it will be all over with me soon. Come nearer to me. Pray let my dear Lady Hamilton have my hair, and all other things belonging to me." Hardy observed that he hoped Mr. Beatty could yet hold out some prospect of life. "Oh no!" replied Nelson; "it is impossible. My back is shot through. Beatty will tell you so." Hardy then returned to the deck, shaking hands again before parting.

Nelson now desired the surgeons to leave him to the attendants, as one for whom nothing could be done, and to give their professional care where it would be of some avail. In a few moments he recalled the chief surgeon, and said, "I forgot to tell you that all power of motion and feeling below my breast are gone; and *you* very well *know* I can live but a short time." From the emphasis he placed on his words, the surgeon saw he was thinking of a case of spinal injury to a seaman some months before, which had proved mortal after many days' suffering; yet it would seem that, despite the conviction that rested on his mind, the love of life, and of all it meant to him, yet clung to the hope that possibly there might be a reprieve. "One would like to live a little longer," he murmured; and added, "What would become of poor Lady Hamilton if she knew my situation!" "Beatty," he said again, "*you know* I am gone." "My Lord," replied the surgeon, with a noble and courteous simplicity, "unhappily for our country, nothing can be done for you;" and he turned away to conceal the emotion which he could not at once control. "I know it," said Nelson. "I feel something rising in my breast," putting his hand on his left side, "which tells me

HORATIA, AT 22 YEARS OF AGE.

*From a miniature by Sir William Charles Ross, in the possession
of Mr. Nelson Ward.*

Fifteen minutes after Hardy left him for the second time, the admiral became speechless; and when this had continued five minutes, the surgeon, who was busied among the other wounded, was summoned again. He found him upon the verge of dissolution, the hands cold and the pulse gone; but upon laying his hand upon his forehead, Nelson opened his eyes, looked up, and then closed them forever. Five minutes later he was dead. The passing was so quiet that Dr. Scott, still rubbing his breast, did not perceive it, until the surgeon announced that all was over. It was half-past four o'clock, just three hours after the fatal wound was received. Not till an hour later did the last of the eighteen prizes strike, and firing cease altogether; but the substantial results were known to Nelson before consciousness left him. To quote the rugged words of the "Victory's" log, "Partial firing continued until 4.30, when a victory having been reported to the Right Honourable Lord Viscount Nelson, K. B., he died of his wound."

Of the five ships of the allied van which passed to windward of the "Victory," one was cut off and captured by the "Minotaur" and "Spartiate." The other four continued on the wind to the southwest, and escaped to sea. By the surrender of Villeneuve the chief command of the combined fleets remained with the Spanish admiral Gravina. The latter, at quarter before five, fifteen minutes after Nelson breathed his last, retreated upon Cadiz, making signal for the vessels which had not struck to rally round his flag. Ten other ships, five French and five Spanish, — in all eleven sail-of-the-line, — made good their escape into the port.

"Before sunset," wrote an eye-witness on board the "Belleisle," "all firing had ceased. The view of the fleet at this period was highly interesting, and would have formed a beautiful subject for a painter. Just under the setting rays were five or six dismantled prizes; on one hand lay the Victory with part of our fleet and prizes, and on the left hand the Royal Sovereign and a similar cluster of ships. To the northward, the remnant of the combined fleets was making for Cadiz. The Achille, with the tricoloured ensign still displayed, had burnt to the water's edge about a mile from us, and our tenders and boats were using every effort to save the brave fellows who had so gloriously defended her; but only two hundred and fifty were rescued, and she blew up with a tremendous explosion."

There, surrounded by the companions of his triumph, and by the trophies of his prowess, we leave our hero with his glory. Sharer of our mortal weakness, he has bequeathed to us a type of single-minded self-devotion that can never perish. As his funeral anthem proclaimed, while a nation mourned, " His body is buried in peace, but his Name liveth for evermore." Wars may cease, but the need for heroism shall not depart from the earth, while man remains man and evil exists to be redressed. Wherever danger has to be faced or duty to be done, at cost to self, men will draw inspiration from the name and deeds of Nelson.

Happy he who lives to finish all his task. The words " I have done my duty," sealed the closed book of Nelson's story with a truth broader and deeper than he himself could suspect. His duty was done, and its fruit perfected. Other men have died in the hour of victory, but for no other has victory so singular and so signal graced the fulfilment and ending of a great life's work. " Finis coronat opus " has of no man been more true than of Nelson. There were, indeed, consequences momentous and stupendous yet to flow from the decisive supremacy of Great Britain's sea-power, the establishment of which, beyond all question or competition, was Nelson's great achievement ; but his part was done when Trafalgar was fought. The coincidence of his death with the moment of completed success has impressed upon that superb battle a stamp of finality, an immortality of fame, which even its own grandeur scarcely could have insured. He needed, and he left, no successor. To use again St. Vincent's words, " There is but one Nelson."

INDEX

INDEX

ure of, dependent on support of the natives, 200 ; abandonment of, by the British, 210, 214–217 ; threatened invasion of Sardinia from, 578.

"Curieux," British brig of war, sent by Nelson to England from West Indies with news of his movements, 661 ; falls in with combined fleets, 671 ; Nelson's comment on hearing the fact, 671, 673.

Davison, Alexander, intimate friend of Nelson, Nelson expresses despondency to, 353 ; the "Lady of the Admiralty's" coolness, 446 ; account given by, of George III. speaking of Nelson, 447 ; Nelson's mention of Sir Hyde Parker to, 462, 463, 465, 544 ; aids Nelson pecuniarily, 526 ; charged by Nelson with a final message to Lady Nelson, 531 ; Nelson's expressions to, about St. Vincent, 543 ; about treatment of himself by the government, 549 ; "Salt beef and the French fleet," 656 ; about General Brereton, 675.

De Vins, Austrian general, commands on the Riviera in 1795, 159 ; Nelson's association with, 159, 165–168, and opinion of, 168.

Dresden, Nelson's visit to, in 1800, 441–443.

Drinkwater, Colonel, returns from Elba in frigate with Nelson, 1797, 223 ; incidents narrated of the voyage, 227–229 ; witnesses the Battle of St. Vincent, 240 ; interview with Nelson after the battle, 242 ; characteristic anecdote of Nelson, 264.

Duckworth, Sir J. T., British admiral, association with Nelson during operations in the Mediterranean, 1799, 358, 360, 362, 394, 409.

Dundas, British general, commanding troops in Corsica, 104 ; controversy with Lord Hood, 104 ; Nelson's opinion, 104.

Egypt, Bonaparte's expedition to, in 1798, 276–290 ; Nelson's pursuit, 280–282, 283–289 ; Nelson's constant attention to, 316, 346, 348, 560, 562, 575, 577, 584, 585, 586,

621, 639, 640, 643–645, 648, 662 ; his urgency that the French army be not permitted to leave, 420–422.

El Arish, Convention of, signed, 421.

Elba, island of, Nelson's opinion of importance of, 202 ; his seizure of, 202 ; evacuation of, 221–225, 245.

"Elephant," British ship-of-the-line, Nelson's flagship at Copenhagen, 472, 475, 479–487.

Elgin, Earl of, British ambassador to Turkey, opinion upon the state of things at Palermo during Nelson's residence there, 340 ; Nelson's divergence of opinion from, concerning the French quitting Egypt, 420–422.

Elliot, Sir Gilbert, afterwards Lord Minto, British representative in Corsica, 1794, 102 ; Viceroy of Corsica, 131 ; friendship between him and Nelson, 131, 235, 240, 242, 535, 617, 682 ; Nelson's correspondence with, 147, 173, 202, 204, 235, 240, 304, 407, 427, 435, 583, 617 ; directs the seizure of Elba by Nelson, 202 ; present at the evacuation of Corsica, 215, and of Elba, 223 ; passage with Nelson to Gibraltar, 223–229 ; witnesses the Battle of St. Vincent, 235, 240 ; advocacy of Nelson's claims to distinction, 242, 346 ; incidental mention of Nelson by, 263, 433, 442, 483, 536, 551, 552, 666, 682, 687, 689 ; mention of Lady Hamilton by, 325–327, 442, 536, 682, 689 ; ambassador to Vienna, 339, note.

Elliot, Hugh, British minister at Dresden during Nelson's visit in 1800, 441–442 ; minister to the two Sicilies during Nelson's Mediterranean command, 1803–1805, 566, 668 ; takes passage out with Nelson, 566 ; correspondence between Nelson and, quoted, 567, 568, 570, 584, 585, 588, 590, 604, 614, 624, 628, 629, 648, 663, 668, 686.

Este, Lambton, association with Nelson mentioned, 621–623.

Fischer, Commodore, commander-in-chief of Danish fleet at the Battle of Copenhagen, 485 ; Nelson's controversy with, on account of his

as his representative in Naples, 386, 387; goes himself to Bay of Naples, but remains on board Nelson's flagship, 395; alienation of, from the queen, 395, 409; returns to Palermo, 405; confers upon Nelson the dukedom of Bronté, 405; Nelson renews correspondence with, in 1803, 566; Nelson's apprehensions for, 567, 571; Nelson keeps a ship-of-the-line always in the Bay of Naples to receive royal family, 568; application of, to the British government, to send Nelson back to the Mediterranean, after sick-leave, 614; agitation of, at the prospect of Nelson's departure, 614; offers him a house at Naples or at Palermo, 614.

Naples, Queen of, agitation at hearing of the Battle of the Nile, 318; friendship with Lady Hamilton, 324, 328, 364, 395; characteristics of, 332, 409; association with Nelson, 332–333; Nelson's devotion to, 335; distrust of her subjects, 337, 357, 409; flight to Palermo, 338; apprehensions of, 359; alienation of the King from, 395, 409; wishes to visit Vienna, and is carried to Leghorn by Nelson, with two ships-of-the-line, 435; refused further assistance of the same kind by Lord Keith, 437; her distress of mind, and anger with Keith, 437; proceeds to Vienna by way of Ancona, 438; Nelson renews correspondence with, in 1803–1805, 560, 566, 629.

Nelson, Rev. Edmund, father of Lord Nelson, 4; Nelson and his wife live with, 1788–1793; 78; Mrs. Nelson continues to live with, after Nelson goes to the Mediterranean, 177, 219, 263, 444–446, 452; his testimony to Lady Nelson's character, 452; attitude towards Lady Hamilton, 452, 554; persuaded of the absence of criminality in her relations with Nelson, 452, 554; refuses to be separated from Lady Nelson, 452, 554, 555; death of, 554; character of, 554, 555.

NELSON, HORATIO, LORD.

Historical Sequence of Career:

Parentage and birth, 4; first going to sea, 5; service in merchantman, 8; cruise to the Arctic Seas, 10; to the East Indies, 12; acting lieutenant, 13; lieutenant, 14; cruise to West Indies, 14; commander and post-captain, 18; Nicaraguan expedition, 22; invalided home, 26; command of "Albemarle," 1781, 27; paid off and visits France, 35; cruise of the "Boreas," 1784, 38; refuses to obey orders of commander-in-chief, first, to recognize broad pendant of a captain "not in commission," 42, and, second, when directed not to enforce the Navigation Act, 46–54; engagement to Mrs. Nisbet, 59; marriage, 64; return to England, and "Boreas" paid off, 1787, 65–69; exposure of frauds in the West Indies, 68, 70–74; half-pay, 1788–1792, 77–80; commissions the "Agamemnon," February, 1793, 84; joins the Mediterranean fleet under Lord Hood, 88; constant detached service, 92–96; blockade of Corsica, 99; siege of Bastia, 103–113; siege of Calvi, 116–125; loss of right eye, 119; refitting in Leghorn, 128–136; action of "Agamemnon" with "Ça Ira," 139; partial fleet action of March 14, 1795, 141; partial fleet action of July 13, 1795, 152; command of a detached squadron on the Riviera of Genoa, under Hotham, 1795, 157–174, and under Jervis, 1796, 183–195; hoists broad pendant as commodore, 188; leaves "Agamemnon" for "Captain," 196; the blockade of Leghorn, 199; seizure of Elba, 202, and of Capraia, 209; evacuation of Corsica, 210–216; British fleet retires to Gibraltar, 216; mission to evacuate Elba, 221; action with Spanish frigates, 221; rejoins Jervis off Cape St. Vincent, 229; Battle of Cape St. Vincent, 1797, 229; made a Knight of the Bath, 243; promoted rear-admiral, 244; mission into the Mediterranean, 246; blockade and bombardment of Cadiz, 247–250; the Teneriffe expedition, 253; loses his right arm, 259; invalided home, 262; rejoins Mediterranean fleet in the "Vanguard," 1798, 265; sent to watch the Toulon armament, 270; Campaign of the Nile, 276–313; Battle of the Nile, 294–306; severely wounded in the head, 300; advanced to the peerage as Baron Nelson of the Nile, 309; arrives at Naples, 317; meeting with Lady Hamilton, 318; urges Naples to declare war against France, 333; war between Naples and France, 336; Neapolitan court carried to Palermo by, 338; residence at Palermo and contemporary events, 1799,— Sidney Smith and the Levant, 343; Ionian Islands, 347; Malta, 348; Barbary States, 350; about Naples, 354; incursion of French fleet under Admiral Bruix, 357–366; serious imputations against character of, 367–368; proceeds to Naples, 367; incident of the surrender of the Neapolitan insurgents, 368; the Caracciolo incident, 389; refuses to obey an order of Lord Keith, 396: reiterated refusal, 398; left temporarily commander-in-chief by Keith's departure, 405–423; created Duke of Bronté by King of Naples, 405; dissatisfaction at not being continued as commander-in-chief, 407; Keith's return, 1800, 423; superseded by Keith's return, 423; capture of " Le Généreux," 424; capture of " Le Guillaume Tell," in Nelson's absence, 430; returns to England through Germany, 1800, 438–443; breach with Lady Nelson, 443–453; promoted vice-admiral, 453; hoists flag on board " San Josef," in the Channel Fleet, under Lord St. Vincent, 1801, 453; birth of the child Horatia, 453; the Baltic expedition, 456–504; Battle of Copenhagen, 473–487; incident of disobeying the signal to leave off action, 481; incident of the flag of truce, 485; created a viscount, 489; negotiations, 490; return to England, 504; charged with defence of the coast of England against invasion, 505–528; retirement from active service during the Peace of Amiens, 529–554; interest in public questions, 547–553; commissioned commander-in-chief in the Mediterranean, 1803, 554; death of his father, 554; arrival in the Mediterranean, 565; the long watch off Toulon, 571–625; last promotion, Vice-Admiral of the White, 1804, 593; escape and pur-

suit of the French Toulon fleet, 1805, 636–656; follows it and its Spanish auxiliaries to the West Indies, 657; returns to Gibraltar, 668; carries his squadron to Cornwallis off Brest, 653–675; returns himself to England, August, 1805, 675; last stay in England, 677–690; resumes command in the Mediterranean, 693; the Battle of Trafalgar, 713; mortally wounded, 734; death of, 741.

Personal Characteristics :

Appearance, in boyhood, 12; at twenty-one, 19; at twenty-four, 33; at twenty-seven, 57; at thirty-six, 33; at forty-two, 439, 442; at forty-three, 501; later years, 536–538, 598, 607, 678, 688; expression, 539.

Health, inherited delicacy of constitution, 4; invalided from East Indies, 12; from West Indies, 25, 26, 27; in Baltic, 28; in Canada, 31; mentioned, 38, 64, 67, 79, 102, 125, 126, 127, 176, 201, 251, 264, 315, 344, 354, 403, 404, 428–432, 434, 453, 495, 500, 503, 506, 522, 525 (sea-sickness), 582, 583, 593, 596–598, 613, 653, 682, 688; influence of active employment upon, 66, 67, 102, 111, 176, 201, 248, 251, 688.

Charm of manner and considerateness of action, 15, 21, 28, 40, 41, 44, 64, 80, 92, 141, 248, 307, 408, 412, 413, 439, 464, 465, 493, 503, 539, 544, 597, 599, 605–607, 658, 669, 676, 691, 693, 694, 704–707, 710, 722.

Vanity, and occasional petulance, 118, 130, 131, 218–219, 237–240, 252, 269, 330, 332–333, 402–403, 407, 424, 427–428, 429, 432, 433, 437, 442, 448, 463, 471, 494, 500–501, 522–525, 527, 605, 606, 660, 679.

Courage, illustrated, 7, 11, 16, 125, 233, 249, 258–260, 262, 481, 486, 491, 683, 709, 726.

Love of glory and honor, 7, 17, 19, 21, 25, 32, 34, 55, 65, 102, 106, 108, 114, 118, 129, 130, 147, 148, 184, 205, 212, 218, 239, 242, 244, 250, 258, 264, 307, 359, 424, 450, 460, 481, 494, 495, 500, 518, 553, 617, 693.

Strength and tenacity of convictions, 15, 32, 45, 49, 53, 54, 63, 107, 108, 116, 117, 192, 205, 208, 267, 268, 286, 291, 294, 360, 365, 401, 420, 422, 465, 467, 468, 471, 475, 484, 521,

762 INDEX

Nelson's flagship in the Baltic expedition, 460; Nelson quits, for the "Elephant," for the Battle of Copenhagen, 472.

St. Vincent, Battle of Cape, 229–237.

St. Vincent, Earl. *See* Jervis.

Stewart, Lieutenant-Colonel, accompanies the Baltic expedition on board Nelson's flagship, 460; narrative of the expedition, and anecdotes of Nelson by, quoted, 460, 472, 474–476, 481–483, 485–486, 491, 501, 503.

Stuart, General, in command of the British troops at the siege of Calvi, 114, 116–124; apparent friction between Lord Hood and, 121–124; Nelson's high opinion of, 119, 122.

Suckling, Catherine, maiden name of Nelson's mother, 4.

Suckling, Captain Maurice, Nelson's maternal uncle, 5; receives Nelson on board his ship, the "Raisonnable," on entering the navy, 5; care for Nelson during his early years, 8–14; made Comptroller of the Navy, 14; procures Nelson's promotion to lieutenant, 14; death of, 18; Nelson's care, when wounded at Teneriffe, to save the sword of, 259; successful naval engagement of, on the date of Trafalgar, and expectation formed therefrom by Nelson, 717.

Suckling, William, Nelson's maternal uncle, Nelson appeals to, for aid to marry, 36, 60; makes an allowance to Nelson, 60; letters of Nelson to, 36, 60, 114.

Suwarrow, Russian marshal, commands the combined Russian and Austrian campaign in Italian campaign of 1799, 356, 405, 409, 417; personal resemblance of Nelson to, 442, 501.

Sweden, joins Russia, Denmark, and Prussia in the Armed Neutrality of 1800, 456–459.

Syracuse, Nelson refreshes his squadron in, before the Battle of the Nile, 291–293; Nelson's opinion of, as a base for his operations after the battle, 315, 316; insecurity of, with headquarters at Palermo, 354; Nelson ordered by Keith to make his headquarters at, 430.

'Téméraire," British ship-of-the-line, Nelson's supporter at Trafalgar, 725, 736.

Teneriffe, Nelson's expedition against, 253–261.

Tetuan, Nelson's visits to, for water and fresh provisions, 653–655, 672; sends a detachment to, before Trafalgar, 711.

"Theseus," British ship-of-the-line, Nelson's flagship before Cadiz and at Teneriffe, 247–248, 256, 259.

Thomson, name under which Nelson speaks of himself in his correspondence with Lady Hamilton, 531; and borne by his daughter prior to his own death, 715.

Toulon, delivered by its inhabitants to Lord Hood, 91, 92; retaken by the French, 100; Nelson reconnoitres, 169, 185; Jervis's efficient blockade of, 196, 206; Nelson's method of watching, 572–574, 576, 584, 589.

Trafalgar, Battle of, general plan of action, as originally conceived, 696–698; discussed, 698–701; contrasted with the tactics of the battle as fought, 702–704; anecdote concerning its conception, 704; narrative of, 713–742.

Trench, Mrs. *See* St. George.

Tripoli, maintains formal war with Naples and Portugal, for the purposes of piracy, 350, 410; Nelson's diplomatic difficulties with, 350, 351.

Troubridge, Sir Thomas, nobly supports Nelson in his initiative at the Battle of St. Vincent, 231–233, 237–241; advises and accompanies Nelson in the Teneriffe expedition, 253–261; limitations of, 256, 257, and admirable qualities, 260–261, 524; sent with a detachment of ten ships-of-the-line to join Nelson in the Nile campaign, 276, 278, 279; mentioned, 281, 285, 291, 293; his ship, the "Culloden," unfortunately grounds before getting into action at the Nile, 301; Nelson's praise of, 311, 413; incidental services in the waters of Italy and Malta, 336, 347, 355–356, 358, 359, 389, 396, 408, 415, 429; remonstrates with Nelson on his life at Palermo, 340; sent by Nelson on a special mission to Alexandria, 344; singular anecdote of, 352;

The Naval Institute Press is the book-publishing arm of the U.S. Naval Institute, a private, nonprofit, membership society for sea service professionals and others who share an interest in naval and maritime affairs. Established in 1873 at the U.S. Naval Academy in Annapolis, Maryland, where its offices remain today, the Naval Institute has members worldwide.

Members of the Naval Institute support the education programs of the society and receive the influential monthly magazine *Proceedings* and discounts on fine nautical prints and on ship and aircraft photos. They also have access to the transcripts of the Institute's Oral History Program and get discounted admission to any of the Institute-sponsored seminars offered around the country.

The Naval Institute also publishes *Naval History* magazine. This colorful bimonthly is filled with entertaining and thought-provoking articles, first-person reminiscences, and dramatic art and photography. Members receive a discount on *Naval History* subscriptions.

The Naval Institute's book-publishing program, begun in 1898 with basic guides to naval practices, has broadened its scope to include books of more general interest. Now the Naval Institute Press publishes about one hundred titles each year, ranging from how-to books on boating and navigation to battle histories, biographies, ship and aircraft guides, and novels. Institute members receive significant discounts on the Press's more than eight hundred books in print.

Full-time students are eligible for special half-price membership rates. Life memberships are also available.

For a free catalog describing Naval Institute Press books currently available, and for further information about subscribing to *Naval History* magazine or about joining the U.S. Naval Institute, please write to:

Membership Department
U.S. Naval Institute
291 Wood Road
Annapolis, MD 21402-5034
Telephone: (800) 233-8764
Fax: (410) 269-7940
Web address: www.usni.org